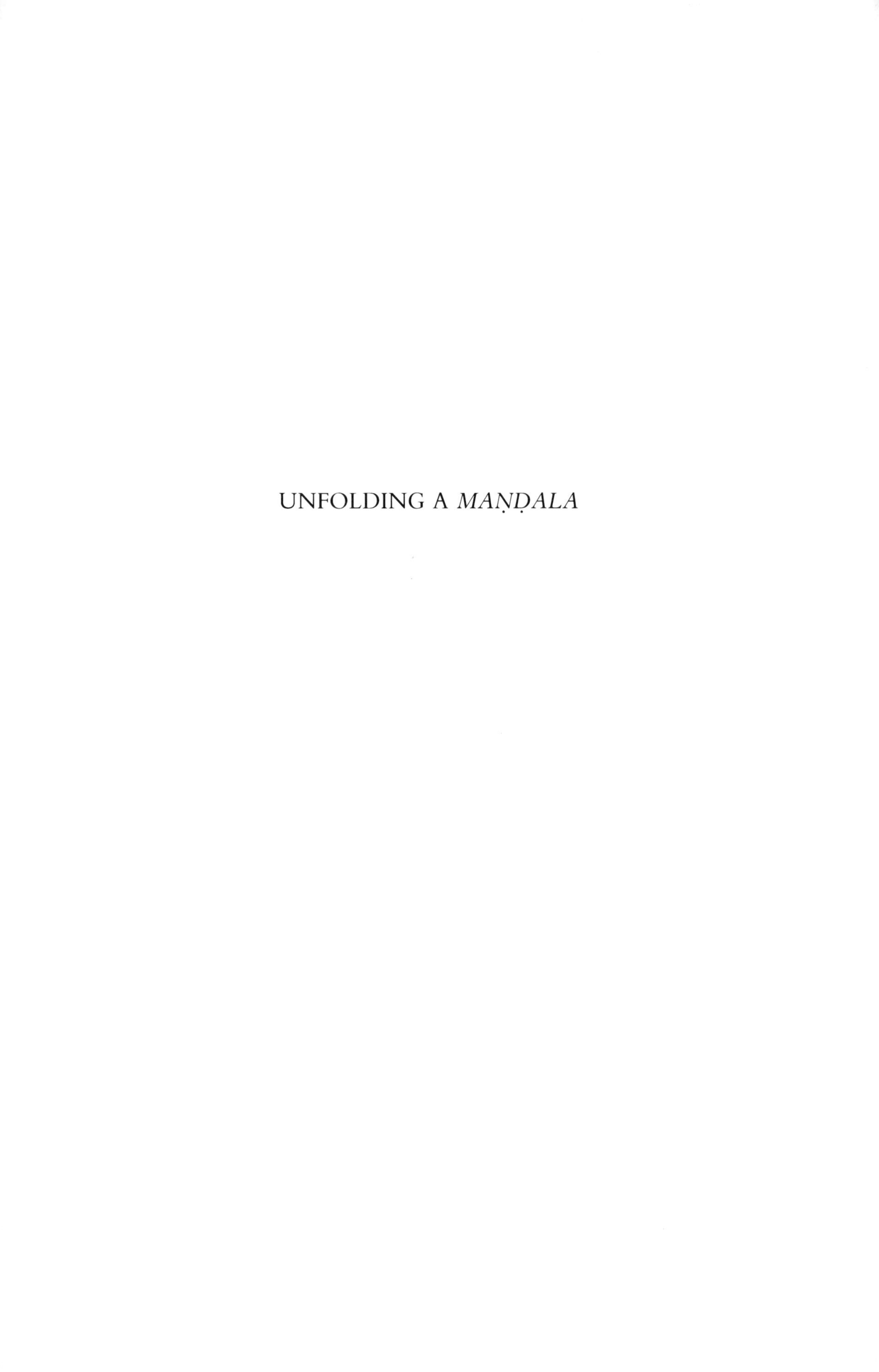

UNFOLDING A *MAṆḌALA*

SUNY Series in Buddhist Studies
Kenneth Inada, Editor

Unfolding a *Maṇḍala*

The Buddhist Cave
Temples at Ellora

Geri H. Malandra

STATE UNIVERSITY OF NEW YORK PRESS

Published by
State University of New York Press, Albany

For information, address State University of New York
Press, State University Plaza, Albany, N.Y., 12246
Production by Diane Ganeles
Marketing by Fran Keneston

Library of Congress Cataloging-in-Publication Data

Malandra, Geri Hockfield.
    Unfolding a mandala : the Buddhist cave temples at Ellora / Geri
H. Malandra.
        p.   cm. — (SUNY series in Buddhist studies)
    Includes bibliographical references and index.
    ISBN 0-7914-1355-1 (CH : acid-free). — ISBN 0-7914-1356-X (PB :
acid-free)
    1. Art, Tantric-Buddhist—India—Ellora.   2. Mandala (Buddhism)—
India—Ellora.   3. Ellora Caves (India)   I. Title.   II. Series.
N8193.3.T36I46   1993
726′.143′0954792—dc20   92-8142
                                                              CIP

CONTENTS

LIST OF FIGURES AND ILLUSTRATIONS

All photographs are by the author unless otherwise credited, and are reproduced with permission of the Archaeological Survey of India unless otherwise indicated. The American Institute of Indian Studies is abbreviated as AIIS. The Asian Art Archives of the University of Michigan are abbreviated as AAAUM.

Text Figures: Iconographic Plans

These are located in the text where each cave is discussed. Please note that iconographic plans are adapted from cave plans in original site reports, and are not to scale. To facilitate reading, some images have been rotated on these plans from their actual orientation.

ACKNOWLEDGMENTS

A study such as this would have been impossible without assistance and encouragement from numerous people. The American Institute of Indian Studies supported my first year's field season at Ellora, and a later, short-term research trip to study sites elsewhere in India. Beyond the financial support of AIIS, I am most grateful to the staff of the Art and Archaeology Center in Ramnagar, Varanasi for help with research in the photo archives and in providing photographs. I am also pleased to acknowledge grants from the University of Minnesota College of Liberal Arts and Office of International Education, and a three-month leave to complete this work, as well as the less tangible but equally important support of colleagues for time devoted to this project. Dr. Donald Johnson, director of the Ames Library of South Asia, deserves special thanks for his timely assistance in securing important publications.

For assistance in using the resources of the Deccan College library and for general support, I thank Professor M. K. Dhavalikar, Department of Archaeology. In Pune, Dr. S. G. Tulpule became both friend and mentor; he deserves thanks for his interest and help with my work. A special note of thanks is due to Carmel Berkson who helped me see Ellora's images in a new way. For help in examining material at other sites, I would like to acknowledge Dr. K. K. Chakravarti, Director, Madhya Pradesh Department of Archaeology and Museums; Dr. G. K. Chendrol, Deputy Directory of Archaeology and Shri V. P. Nagaich, Archaeologist, M.G.M. Museum, Raipur; Dr. Chandrashekhar Gupta, Nagpur University; Dr. A. P. Jamkhedkar, Director, Maharashtra State Archaeology and Museums; Dr. G. C. Chauley, Superintending Archaeologist, Archeological Survey of India/ Bhubaneswar Circle; Dr. M. C. Joshi, Archaeological Survey of India, New Delhi; and Dr. B. N. Tandon, Director (Science), A.S.I., Dehra Dun.

Through the years of this study, Dr. Walter Spink has offered generous and enthusiastic support, including use of the Archives of Asian Art at the University of Michigan and advance copies of many manuscripts, as well as the inspiration of his enthusiasm, interest in alternative explanations, and devotion to "his" caves at Ajanta. Dr. Eleanor Zelliot's support has been even longer-lived; her interest and insights into Maharashtrian culture and history are deeply appreciated. Dr. Janice Leoshko offered exciting insights from her work on Bodhgaya and encouraged me to think about Ellora in a broader perspective. In both large and small ways, Drs. Frederick and Catherine Asher have offered generous help, which I am pleased to acknowledge here.

Last, but certainly not least, are the many ways my husband, Dr. William Malandra, and daughter, Emily, supported this project. For the invaluable critical eye of a scholar, for patience and moral support, for sharing precious time with Ellora, I dedicate this book to them.

Ellora is a kaleidoscopic expression of religious architecture on a monumental scale, its mile long basaltic scarp punctuated by thirty-four major rock-cut temples. Within these sanctuaries carved into the hills northwest of Aurangabad, we encounter hundreds of larger than life size images of gods of three major religions—Śaivism, Buddhism, and Jainism. After one visit, or even after years of study, this is too much to absorb at once. Each visit reveals new dimensions, just as each visitor will have a unique experience of the temples. And even now, as new caves are being discovered and paintings revealed, our understanding of Ellora continues to grow and change.[1]

How can we create a structure for these experiences in order to reveal Ellora's manifold meanings? Various studies have described the context, layout, and iconography of its Brahmanical temples, but less attention has been paid to explicating the place of its twelve Buddhist caves in the wider spheres of artistic and religious movements of the early medieval period.[2] The present work will explore the historical, artistic, and doctrinal dimensions of its Buddhist period, focusing on the *maṇḍalas* that provided integrative schemes for the temples.

Last of the great rock-cut sites of the Western Deccan, Ellora's Buddhist cave temples were excavated during the seventh and early eighth centuries when there was a surge of activity at Buddhist centers throughout India and beyond to Asia. These twelve temples are like a museum preserving *in situ* a visual record of the early development of tantric Buddhist art, from the relatively simple form seen in Cave 6 (ca. 600 C.E.) to the splendid and complex perfection of the latest, Cave 12 (ca. 730). The artisans and monks who created Ellora's caves worked within the centuries-old tradition of Buddhist rock-cut architecture, but at every stage new ideas—in particular, innovations in iconography—illustrate the creative integration of old and new.

Its importance resides in three related features. First, its Buddhist sculpture includes many images new or unique in the seventh and early eighth centuries. Second, because it is a rock-cut site, its *in situ* images are preserved in a programmatic context lost at built sites, which were more easily disturbed or even plundered. Third, *maṇḍalas* carved both in relief and expanded into the large-scale, three-dimensional shrine programs of the earliest and latest caves present us with surprisingly early, but still clear-cut evidence for organizational schemes of the images. The *maṇḍala*, whose basic meaning can refer to anything round or circular, has in religious contexts an extended meaning as an arrangement—condensed or quite complex—of patterns or pictures of deities used in rituals to guide worship or meditation. As chapter 1 will explain in greater detail, *maṇḍalas* were a diagnostic and important component of the teachings encompassed in the general development of tantric Buddhism; they were carried for example, by tantric teachers from India to Ladakh, and by early Shingon teachers from China to Japan, and were displayed in temple sanctums. This use of *maṇḍalas* has long been recognized in later tantric iconographical texts and at Buddhist sites of later periods, but is encountered at Ellora at a relatively early time. The iconography of the sculptures is in some cases comparable to that of images found at contemporary or later sites in eastern and central India. However, the absence of systematic iconographic or stylistic relationships between Ellora and sites in the traditional centers of Buddhism has deterred scholars from discussing Ellora in the broader context of Buddhist art in India.

This, essentially an art historical study, is complicated by a common methodological problem: many of its images have no clear relationship to texts that might explain their meaning or record iconographical details. While it may be assumed that no object can be made to speak as eloquently of itself as a dialogue between object and text can, it is also true that ideal pairings are seldom encountered in the history of Indian art, or more generally, in the histories of early art. This problem has been explored in greater methodological detail outside of Indian art history. For example, in the study of early Byzantine mosaic art of the fifth and sixth centuries, texts may seldom appear to be the direct inspiration for a given image. Yet, at the same time, it can be shown that they both embody common "thought patterns." If examples are chosen randomly, this assumption may not appear to be legitimate. However, when text and image come from the same milieu, even one (like the early Byzantine period) in which text and image rarely come from precisely the same time and place, the assumption has some validity. Moreover, the more complicated the pattern of motifs repeated in image and text, the greater the likelihood that a similar pattern of meanings underlies them.[3]

For Ellora, less precision is possible for correspondences than might be made, compared with Byzantine studies where rather precise correlations can be drawn between, for example, rhetorical style and narrative art. Despite the steadily increasing number of iconographic texts being discovered, edited, and published, there is so far no known text that conforms in a systematic way to the overall iconography of Ellora's Buddhist caves. Yet, we know from the dissemination of teachings, texts, and Buddhist art in the seventh through ninth centuries, that new ideas were rapidly circulating as the Buddhist world expanded, and it is from this more dispersed material that analogies must be drawn. Moreover, given the dearth of precisely correlated written and visual material, in a study like this one, the monument itself must be examined with particular care. I would argue further that Ellora's visual "texts" can help push back the horizon for the development of a kind of Buddhism which we know from later written texts and monuments, was expounded throughout most of Asia.

Art historians may be more comfortable than historians of religion with the proposition that we should suspend our expectation of finding a textual standard that would confirm and validate the art historical evidence. Yet, even among South Asian art historians, a tendency persists to seek a formal literary text to "prove" the meaining of what we observe in sculpture or architecture. Consider, for example, a recent study, which offers a new interpretation of the concept of Buddhist relics, based on a close reading of inscriptions from third-century Nagarjunakonda. The author notes that previous studies of this site have been hampered by art historians' adherence to formal literary sources, a "perfunctory preference . . . which is quite common in historical works on Indian Buddhism [that] can have only little relationship to what practicing Buddhists actually did. At the very least it rather effectively impedes an adequate appraisal of other kinds of sources."[4] Although this refers primarily to the use of various kinds of written sources, the argument might be taken to have equal relevance for even more varied sources, including sculpture and architecture. This is of particular importance for places like Ellora, where no literary sources—formal or otherwise—are available to "explain" the structure and, by inference, Buddhist practices of the site.

Another way to frame the problem is to propose that what makes a place like Ellora so fascinating and important is that is does *not* conform in every detail to what we know from religious texts. Instead, it offers something different, a new "text" that must be reconstructed from visual sources. If we are to understand Ellora, its study *requires* an art historical approach to sort out its order from an overwhelming number of architectural and sculptural details. The reconstruction and explication offered here become, then, a kind of secondary written text that can help scholars in making comparisons with other sites and texts. For this reason, much of the presentation here is descriptive, analyzing images in stylistic contexts to establish a developmental framework and in iconographical contexts to demonstrate "doctrinal" evolution. Where appropriate, comparisons are made to available texts and to material from other Buddhist sites. However, given the uneven relationships these comparisons reveal, it is Ellora's internal unifying principle—the *maṇḍala*—that is most helpful in explaining its development. In this way, the site becomes its own text, its iconography taking on an importance that depends upon but also transcends the details of specific identifications. This is, then, a work of art history directed to a broader goal, revealing through "visual exegesis" Ellora's importance for the study of Buddhist art, history, and ideas.

This investigation begins with Ellora's position in religious geography and history. Formally recognized as a *tīrtha*—a center of worship and ritual—in royal inscriptions since the early 700s C.E., the site attracted support and activity of key political and religious leaders. As a *tīrtha* it was the appropriate place to locate extraordinary monuments, like the Śaiva Kailāsa temple, unprecedented and unrivaled in scope and detail, but it also attracted patrons and worshipers of other faiths, including Buddhists who responded in similar fashion to the growing power of this religious center. The site preserves a record of these movements, as teachers, worshipers, rulers, and artists converged and collaborated in a burst of creativity that accelerated in the late seventh century and peaked under the Rāṣṭrakūṭas in the second half of the eighth century.

To explicate the "archeology" of Ellora's *maṇḍala*, chapters 2, 3, and 4 organized in three chronological parts, trace its application through the development of the caves. This narrative, necessarily descriptive, should enable the reader to visualize the layout of each temple, and to understand both the rationale for the arrangement of sculptures, determined by cave location and timing of excavation as well as by iconographical requirements, and also, the relationships of architectural and sculptural style among the caves. These relationships are not only important aesthetically but also, given the absence of historical records for Ellora, they provide the basis for establishing the relative chronology upon which this reconstruction is based. The primary focus here is to illustrate the development of individual images in their programmatic, or *maṇḍalic*, context. Thus, many subsidiary or intrusive images and most architectural material are not discussed. Detailed iconographic discussion is limited to subjects, such as the *maṇḍala* itself and groups of Bodhisattvas, necessary to this illustration. There are many cases, however, where comparison among various caves, and to other sites, is important but these discussions are reserved for chapter 5. Material on the relative chronology that forms the basis for the development proposed here is reserved for an appendix. For a ready summary of the sometimes lengthy descriptive passages, the reader is referred to the iconographical reconstructions that are summarized on the "iconographical plans" in each chapter.

Because Ellora is unique, previous studies have slighted its relationships to other Buddhist monuments. Yet, as chapter 5 will show, it is related in significant ways to other Buddhist sites on the "periphery" of the Buddhist world in the seventh and eighth centuries. These sites preserve iconographical information either specific to teachings disseminated beyond the Buddhist heartland, or long since lost from those central places so much disturbed by the events of later history. Studies of certain iconographic problems and comparative studies of specific sites will explore these relationships which, taken together, create a picture of early tantric Buddhism as a dynamic international movement whose teachings spread rapidly throughout the Buddhist world, affecting sites on the "periphery" perhaps without mediation through the heartland. In this way, we can imagine—taking two traditional definitions of *maṇḍala*—its unfolding to include both the diagrams, which govern its sculptural programs, and less literally, in broader perspective, the association of a loose circle of places like it, related by iconography and, we may infer, tantric teachings.

To facilitate understanding of this sometimes complicated material, "iconographic plans" are included for each of the ten caves that contains important sculpture, in addition to the larger scale illustrations provided. Images are illustrated in their approximate location in the cave, but rotated so that all are legible from the same (reader's) direction. All photographs are by the author unless otherwise indicated. Sanskrit words are transliterated according to the standard orthographic system, and are defined where necessary the first time they appear. Place names follow spellings in J. Schwartzberg, *A Historical Atlas of South Asia* (1978).

1 . TĪRTHA AND MAṆḌALA: THE PLACE, THE PEOPLE, THE GODS

The Place

In September 1683, the Moghul emperor Aurangzeb and his court at Aurangabad were embroiled in a series of campaigns against the native Marāṭhā rulers of the Deccan. Aurangzeb's chronicler recorded the progress of these campaigns in sober detail, pausing in his account of military and political maneuvers only to mention important tombs of the Muslim faithful. When the account turns to the region around Aurangabad and nearby Daulatabad, however, the narrative takes a remarkable direction. At this point, the court historian felt compelled to describe something extraordinary:

> A short distance from [Daulatabad] is a place named Ellora where in ages past, sappers possessed of magical skill excavated in the defiles of the mountain spacious houses for a length of one *kos* [mile]. On all their ceilings and walls many kinds of images with lifelike forms have been carved. The top of the hill looks level, so much so that no sign of the buildings within it is apparent (from outside). In ancient times when the sinful infidels had dominion over this country, certainly they and not demons (*jinn*) were the builders of these caves, although tradition differs on the point; it was a place of worship of the tribe of false believers. At present it is a desolation in spite of its strong foundations; it rouses the sense of warning (of doom) to those who contemplate the future (end of things). In all seasons, and particularly in the monsoons, when this hill and the plain below resemble a garden in the luxuriance of its vegetation and the abundance of water, people come to see the place. A waterfall a hundred yards in width tumbles down from the hill. It is a marvelous place for strolling, charming to the eye. Unless one sees it, no written description can correctly picture it. How then can my pen adorn the page of my narrative?[1]

In this account, the chronicler surpassed his usual attention to detail, leaving us with an outstanding early view of Ellora's power and fascination. The account of neither a passive observer nor an unthinking repetition of local legend, this remarkably dense eyewitness portrait is suffused with key elements of Ellora's physical and spiritual presence that made it a prominent religious and political center for centuries before Aurangzeb took over the region.

At first, the reference to "sinful infidels" might incline a modern reader to doubt the objectivity of our writer but the formulaic reference to non-Muslims actually reinforces the positive impression Ellora made on him. If he understood that this site once belonged to the "infidels," if he knew that it was a place where "false believers" worshiped, if he could easily see the many images with "lifelike forms" on the ceilings and walls, why, then, did he bother with it at all? And why was he careful to point out, contrary to local tradition, that it must have been those *people*, not demons, who built the caves? What he noticed might have horrified or disgusted his fellow believers; many similar temple sites were devastated by faithful Muslims who were offended by the graphic, anthropomorphic imagery of Hindu and Buddhist shrines.

But he was not disgusted. Instead, despite barriers of religious difference, this Muslim court historian seems to have apprehended Ellora's special power. First, he notices a most magical and essential quality: that from a distance, the site appears to be simply a hill in which, it turns out, entire "buildings" are excavated. Then, there is his surprise that, despite its strong foundations, it is a "desolation." Next, there is its effect: it "rouses the sense of warning to those who contemplate the future." Perhaps this is simply a fatalistic observation based on the desertion of Ellora by its past worshipers, that nothing can remain alive forever. However, for such thoughts to arise, the observer must have been engaged in an activity essential to the ancient purpose of the site: contemplation. Only in this framework does the conclusion of the passage make sense. Here, we are told that Ellora is a marvelous place for strolling, "charming to the eye." Luxuriant foliage and the hundred-yard long waterfall, precious displays of the ghats' post-monsoon glory, emphasize its physical attractiveness, a charm chosen for and designed to promote reflection.

Through a "nonbeliever's" eyes we are given a rare view of Ellora's spiritual power. If it could make such a strong impression on a disinterested observer, how much stronger must its impact have been on those devotees who came piously to worship in the more than thirty Hindu, Buddhist, and Jain shrines! Perhaps without knowing the reason, Aurangzeb's chronicler sensed Ellora's vitality as

one of the special religious centers of India, a *tīrtha*, a sanctified space perceived to be particularly conducive to crossing from the mundane to the spiritual world, to communicating with the gods. This chapter will explore the elements of physical location, political context, and religious ideas that contributed to Ellora's development as a *tīrtha*, a religious center with special spiritual overtones that for the past fourteen hundred years has exerted a powerful impact on visitors of many faiths, and that has attracted patrons and worshipers of three major religions, including the Buddhism that will be the focus of this book.

Geography and Travelers' Accounts

A basic factor in Ellora's evolution as a sacred site is its location on an ancient route that even today connects Paithan (ancient Pratiṣṭhāna, a major center of trade) on the Godavari River with Aurangabad, and then continues north to Maheshwar (Māhiṣmatī) on the Narmada and Ujjain in Madhya Pradesh (both regional political and religious centers). This well-traveled route is marked by hill passes and river fords, large commercial towns and ancient sites, that skirted the steep scarps of the hilly plateau region of the northwest Deccan.[2]

Numerous inscriptions in Buddhist cave sites throughout the Western Deccan of the second and third centuries specifically attest to the travel by Buddhist monks and nuns, and lay devotees, from site to site throughout the region. At the same time, dedicatory inscriptions from the secular community demonstrate the close connection between religious and commercial activity. Monasteries depended on donations from the laity and, although sacred sites would not have been located at the center of towns or cities, they were close enough to trade routes to permit relatively easy access both by itinerant monks and local patrons.[3] Although we have no comparable inscriptions that record Buddhist patronage at Ellora, given its ease of access it seems likely that the centuries-old practice of lay-monastic circulation and cooperation applied there, too.

Located within sight of a route traversed

2

by worshipers, traders, and travelers, from which the caves can easily be seen, Ellora was never entirely forgotten. In the tenth century, it was well enough known to attract the interest of al-Masudi, a resident of Baghdad, who visited India in 915–16. In his travelogue, *Les Prairies d'Or*, al-Masudi describes

> . . . the great temple named Aladra [Ellora], where Indians come on pilgrimage from the farthest regions. The temple has an entire city dedicated to its support and it is surrounded by thousands of cells where devotees consecrated to the worship of the idol dwell.[4]

From this we can see that at the beginning of the tenth century Ellora was still a vibrant community drawing visitors from many faiths and, according to this account, from all over India. We now know there were not "thousands" of cells around the caves, but otherwise this description corroborates historical records and the evidence at the site itself that show it was in active use at least as a Jain religious center, patronized by the later Rāṣtrakūṭa kings, who controlled the Deccan from the eighth to tenth centuries when al-Masudi made his visit. His account affirms its familiarity among national and international travelers who, responding to its appeal as a *tīrtha*, were able to visit in times conducive to trans-regional journeys. As will be discussed below, Rāṣṭrakūṭa control of the Deccan seems to have encouraged regional interaction that, from the late seventh century onward, would have a profound effect on the development of Buddhism at Ellora.

Although we do know that the caves continued to attract visitors, by the thirteenth century Ellora seems to have lost an organized religious community and political support. The *Līḷācaritra*, an Old Marathi work compiled in 1278, describes the visit to the caves by the famous Maharashtrian saint, Cakradhāra, who visited the caves not for worship, but to seek a place of refuge.[5] In these anecdotes, Cakradhāra and his disciples witness strange sounds and frightening visions. A disciple asks the saint how such a structure came to be. He answers, the whole mountain is hollow; no one knows its entrances and exits. This description hints at the

arrangement of the caves, connected to their wings by "internal passages." Yet, the implication that the site was a maze of underground passages shows that three hundred years after al-Masudi described it as a thriving pilgrimage center, Ellora could be associated with fantastic stories that suggest the end of active use—and understanding—of the site.

Meanwhile, the strategic importance of the area did not diminish. In the late thirteenth century, Yādava kings built a fort along this route, so desirable for military purposes that Muslim invaders from the north subsequently struggled to conquer it. The fort, Devagiri, was taken over by Sultan Qutb ud-dīn Mubārak in 1317. In 1327 Muhammad bin Tughluq moved from Delhi to establish a dual capital of his Sultanate at Devagiri, which he renamed Daulatabad and expanded in order to control movement along the road. Even today, on the way from Aurangabad to Ellora and points north, travelers must pass through the gates built into the perimeter of the imposing fortification.

Another "outsider," the Muslim historian, Firishtah, confirms Ellora's continued strategic position in the early seventeenth century. During a dispute over the betrothal of a Gujarati princess, he wrote, she and her entourage took flight from Gujarat to the Deccan. Halting near Daulatabad (an easily defensible location), 300 hundred of the troops defending her "went without leave to see the caves of Ellora."[6] Although this account sheds little light on the use or condition of the site, it does reflect its fame and the ease with which travelers could visit.

Later in that century, the road was still in use. The seventeenth-century traveler Jean de Thévenot, the first European to journey there (1666), described the difficulty of travel on the road up to the plateau near Daulatabad. He wrote, "I chose rather to run some little risk than to miss an opportunity of seeing those pagodas, which are so renowned all over the Indies,"[7] but he also commented on how smoothly the road had been worn into the rock from which it was cut. In addition, he described a retaining wall three feet thick and four feet high, designed to prevent travelers and their conveyances from falling over the cliff. Such features suggest a heavily used road; it may have been difficult to reach from the coast, but inland the way was apparently well known and well used.

Ellora was easier to reach, than to understand. Thévenot duly noted the numerous "pagods," the mile long extent of the site, and the prominence of "heathen" saints. He was even guided through the caves by a "brahman" who pointed out figures and told stories about them. Unfortunately, Thévenot did not understand the stories, confessing: "seeing he understood nothing of the Persian tongue, nor I the Indian, I could make nothing at all of it."[8]

In the next century, Ellora's attraction to travelers did not diminish; neither did understanding increase. The Venetian Niccolao Manucci, whose history of the Moghuls reached Paris in 1701 or 1702, attributed the excavations to the Chinese:

> Signs of the presence of the Chinese are not wanting in Hindustan. These are found chiefly in the country of the Dacan (Dakhin), where there is a hill called Alura (Ellora), twenty-four leagues distant from Aurangabad, towards the west. At that place there are several caves dug out by pickaxes, forming lovely open courts, halls, rooms, cells having corner-stones ornamented with various Chinese figures, and some reservoirs of natural water provided with many steps. In one of these halls there are thirteen statues, sculpted out of the live rock. Each one has its own special form. . . . As they are so cleverly done, and their appearance somewhat Chinese, many say that they were executed by the ancient Chinese.[9]

By the early nineteenth century, Ellora had become an important stop for travelers out to experience picturesque and romantic adventures in India. The route was difficult enough to be exciting but, well-worn by years of administrative and commercial travel, it was actually easier to travel than routes that led to other major ancient sites. J. B. Seeley's *The Wonders of Ellora or the Narrative of a Journey to the Temples or Dwellings Excavated out of a Mountain of Granite at Ellora in the East Indies* (1825) exemplifies the detailed and imaginative accounts that emerged from such visits.[10] This genre of travel writing is important less for the information it provides than for the

attitude toward the site it conveys. Seeley approached the caves with the combination of curiosity, awe, and holiday spirit still experienced today by the thousands of tourists who visit Ellora each year, drawn as were their predecessors for the past thousand years, by its ease of access, extraordinary scale, and a spirit that touches believers and nonbelievers alike.

The People

As the development of Ellora's Buddhist *maṇḍala* is explored, questions of patronage, or at least political context, and chronology will emerge. Unfortunately, Ellora's Buddhist patrons remain anonymous. Given evidence from other cave temple sites in this part of India, noted above, the obvious attraction of Ellora to later rulers, and what we know about the development of other key religious centers such as Banaras for Hindus, or Bodhgaya for Buddhists,[11] it is unlikely that a *tīrtha* of such complexity as Ellora could have developed without support from wealthy and powerful patrons. Such patronage was essential to maintain and protect the religious community and to guarantee an allocation of resources to support it; this was in fact one of the duties of a traditional ruler in ancient India, and continued to be an activity favored by the powerful into modern times. For Ellora, where there are no written records of any patronage before work began on the mid-eighth-century Rāṣṭrakūṭa caves, this context must be established by analogy to similar sites, and by using material that pertains, if indirectly, to the probable circumstances of patronage during its early phases. The summary, below, of political conditions surrounding Ellora is critical to establish both a chronological framework and a picture of the context in which its Buddhist caves developed.

Many other cave temple sites from the first century B.C.E. onward in the Deccan are associated with inscriptions that provide considerable information about the political context of support for these establishments. In most

4

cases, major donative inscriptions were incised, even where, as at Ajanta, a nearby Buddhist cave site of the late 400s, contemporary painted inscriptions were added as well. So the absence of significant carved inscriptions from Ellora's earlier phases seems to reflect a genuine absence of major donative records. Even if there were painted inscriptions, it is doubtful that these would have been used to record the most important donations. This suggests that Ellora's artisans and residents relied on a different kind of support, less directly connected to proclamations of royal beneficence than at comparable sites in the Deccan or beyond where, for instance in eastern India, the Pāla dynasty was well known for its sponsorship of major Buddhist centers. Support for Ellora's Buddhist caves, at least, seems to have been somehow "looser" than for their predecessors, not tied, for instance, to the prestige of a local ruler. This point is important because such a situation may have been conducive to the influx of ideas from outside the region. Thus, Ellora, usually regarded simply as the end of a local tradition, in fact reflects developments seen in a much wider range of Buddhist centers across central and eastern India even as it represents the culmination of the political and religious collaborations required to produce works on such a massive scale.

The site developed in three major phases, an early Hindu phase (ca. 550 to 600), a Buddhist phase (ca. 600 to 730), and a last phase (ca. 730 to 950), which comprised both Hindu and Jain excavations sponsored by the Rāṣṭrakūṭa dynasty, the only known ancient patrons of Ellora.

Politics and Chronology: Vākāṭakas, Kalacuris, Cālukyas, Rāṣṭrakūṭas

The conditions that made possible the development of a complex cave temple site had evolved many years before Ellora was begun. Its most significant predecessor is Ajanta, as innovative in its day as Ellora was to be 150 years later. At Ajanta, in the latter part of the fifth century, more than twenty Buddhist cave temples were excavated, clearly the result of support of politically powerful patrons, local ministers of the ruling Vākāṭaka dynasty, a Hindu empire whose activities stretched northward to Gupta territory and southeast toward the earlier Buddhist centers at Amaravati and Nagarjunakonda (in what is now Andhra Pradesh). Major dedicatory inscriptions place work on Ajanta in the period between 465 and 485;[12] they show that these Buddhist vassals could sponsor work semi-autonomously at Ajanta, in the center of the Vākāṭaka Empire. This situation provides an important model for a hypothetical reconstruction of patronage at Ellora a century and half later.

Ajanta presents another important point of comparison for Ellora's development. Much of the Ajanta style can be explained in terms of more or less local or regional developments, combined with considerable influence from Buddhist iconography at northern sites such as Sarnath. However, there are also clear sources of influence from major Buddhist centers to the southeast, Amaravati and Nagarjunakonda, demonstrating continued travel and exchange of ideas throughout the Deccan plateau in the Vākāṭaka period.[13] Such exchanges cannot be traced to specific political events, yet the physical evidence preserved in the caves illustrates the persistence of cultural interchange that took place in the midst of political struggles of various dynasties and their feudatories. Ellora probably developed under similar circumstances, its environs controlled by a local dynasty loosely allied to a major ruling empire, enjoying interchange with religious and commercial communities throughout the Deccan.

Ellora's first phase, from ca. 550 to 600, was Hindu, perhaps the result of patronage by the Kalacuri dynasty, which emerged after a period of dynastic struggle that followed the decline of Vākāṭaka power around 500. Since the Kalacuris may have sponsored Ellora's first cave temples, which share significant features with the Buddhist caves, the background for their activities is important to establish.

At the turn of the fifth century, a Hindu dynasty known as the Traikūṭakas apparently controlled the coast near modern Bombay. This is indicated by several records, including a 494/5 inscription from the Buddhist caves at

Kanheri, which refers to the "augmenting kingdom of the Traikūṭakas."[14] But an inscription, dated to 533, refers to the Traikūṭaka capital as "Anuriddhapura of the Katachchuris," suggesting that the Kalacuris had established themselves by this time.[15] Like the Vākāṭakas and Traikūṭakas, the Kalacuris were Hindus, devotees of Śiva in his form of Lakulīśa, to whom the main excavation of the great Śiva temple at Elephanta, off the coast at Bombay, was dedicated. Silver coins of Kṛṣṇarāja, the most important Kalacuri king, have been found in Nasik District and on the islands of Bombay and Salsette; more important, large numbers of copper coins of Kṛṣṇarāja have been found on Elephanta island.[16] These finds, together with the Śaiva affiliation of the Kalacuris mentioned in inscriptions, strongly suggest an association between the Kalacuri king, Kṛṣṇarāja, and Elephanta's Śaiva excavations and, moreover, that the Kalacuris controlled the region along the coast near Bombay. It is more difficult to determine how far east that control extended. They may have actually controlled the Ellora region as well, and sponsored Ellora's earliest Brahmanical caves,[17] as suggested by sectarian evidence from the caves themselves. For example, Cave 29, an early Hindu cave temple, is dedicated to Lakulīśa and is most comparable architecturally and iconographically to the Elephanta Śiva temple. Since Kṛṣṇarāja ruled in the period ca. 535 to 575, and, assuming he patronized major religious edifices of his time, both caves should be ascribed to the mid-sixth century. Kalacuri power continued through the end of the sixth century, declining only with the defeat of Kṛṣṇarāja's grandson, Buddharāja, by the Cālukya king, Maṅgaleśa, in 601.

This conquest marks one of the most significant changes in political and cultural activity in the Deccan for the entire classical and early medieval period. From 601 onward, the period during which Ellora's Buddhist caves developed, political influence from the southern Deccan began to extend northward, through Maharashtra, reaching at its greatest extent into the Gangetic plain. Yet material traces of this shift from a northern to a southern focus of power are visible only in isolated stylistic similarities between Ellora's earliest

caves and contemporary monuments of the Cālukyas.

The beginning of the end of Kalacuri power is marked by a 601 inscription of the Cālukya king, Maṅgaleśa, which reports that he set out to conquer northern territories and defeated king Buddha, who is identified as the Kalacuri ruler Buddharāja, grandson of Kṛṣṇarāja, and son of Śaṅkaragaṇa.[18] However, since two inscriptions of Buddharāja, dated 609 and 610, follow the 601 record of Maṅgaleśa, it is clear that by this time Cālukya power was not well established in the northwest Deccan.[19] It was not until 634, with the accession of the Cālukya king, Pulakeśin II, who made numerous conquests in the north, that Cālukya control was truly established over Maharashtra.[20]

Cālukya activities were not limited to wars and conquest. At home in their late sixth century capital of Badami (Karnataka), the Cālukyas sponsored major excavations of cave temples. Maṅgaleśa dedicated the excavation of Badami Cave 3, in an inscription dated 578; the other caves of this group can also be placed in the period between 560 and 580, and thus, were contemporary with excavations being carried out under Kalacuri patronage (or at least political control) further north at Ellora.[21] By the early seventh century, the Cālukyas had expanded their temple building activities to structural sanctuaries. The inscription of Pulakeśin II of 634 is associated with one such temple, the Meguti temple at Aihole.

Returning to the situation at Ellora, it seems likely that it was in the period around the initial Cālukya conquest of the Kalacuris in 601 that the first Hindu phase of work ceased. Although direct dynastic patronage may not have been necessary to develop the site, probably a stable political environment was. Thus, in the turmoil of the years from 600 onward, Hindu patronage ended with the excavation of Cave 14, the cave iconographically most similar to the Badami Hindu caves. During the next century, work began and continued on the Buddhist caves, perhaps as a result of monastic movement inland from the coast following the Cālukya disruption of Kalacuri activities.

During the period from ca. 600 to 730,

when Ellora's Buddhist caves were being excavated, political events in the Deccan focused around the growth of Cālukya power, their struggles with the Pallavas to the southeast, and the emergence of the Rāṣṭrakūṭas who, under Dantidurga, conquered the Cālukyas around 750.[22] The Rāṣṭrakūṭas became the major political force of the mid-eighth to ninth centuries in the Deccan and, at Ellora, drew upon the skill and experience of artisans, who knew both Maharashtrian and southern architectural techniques, to produce the Kailāsa temple, the culmination of ten centuries of cave temple architecture.

Looking at the situation in the mid-600s, it is important for developments at Ellora to describe as specifically as possible what Cālukya sovereignty meant. By 634, Cālukya power was firmly established in former Kalacuri territory along the coast. The inscription praising Pulakeśin's accomplishments also states explicitly that he "acquired the sovereignty over the three Mahārāṣṭrakas with their nine and ninety thousand villages"; these probably included Maharashtra, Konkan, and Karnataka. He is also said to have subdued a Rāṣṭrakūṭa Govinda, a figure whose family was to be important in this area later in the century (see below).[23] However, there is little direct evidence that the Cālukyas closely supervised all of Maharashtra. Epigraphical evidence suggests instead that while they were often concerned with coastal Maharashtra, they generally ignored the inland regions, including the area around Ellora. For instance, even in the early 700s, local coinage was still called "Kṛṣṇarāja-rūpakas," illustrating the persistence of a regional, pre-Cālukya medium of exchange.[24]

What was the impact of the Cālukyas on Maharashtra in the seventh century? The Satara copper plate of 617 records a grant by Viṣṇuvardhana I, son of Pulakeśin II, of a village to a group of brahmans.[25] This village has been located in modern Satara District, where the plate was found. Cālukya donations were also made further north in Nasik District. For example, the Lohaner plates of Pulakeśin II, dated in 630, record a grant by Satyāśraya (Pulakeśin) of a village to a brahman who lived in Lohanagara, or modern Lohaner.[26] This evidence suggests that the Cālukyas patronized Brahmanical activities in the western part of Maharashtra in the period up to 630.

From around 630 to 680, when Ellora's Buddhist caves reveal increasing connections to iconography outside Maharashtra, it appears that this region was left largely to local governance. We have no records of Cālukya activity here for the following fifty years while the attention of the Cālukyas was turned toward their adversaries in the south, the Pallavas.[27] However, the records of the Chinese pilgrim Hsüan-tsang, who travelled in South India in 641 and 642, shed some light on the political geography of the mid-seventh century Deccan. According to Hsüan-tsang, the king of Maharashtra was Pulakeśin and his capital (not named in this account), "borders on the west on a great river." It was 1,000 *li* (about 167 miles) from Bharukaccha (Broach). This capital has not been conclusively identified, although it should probably be identified with modern Nasik, northwest of Ellora.[28]

Late in the seventh century, when Ellora's latest Buddhist caves with a new iconographical scheme were initiated, the Cālukyas reasserted their interest in Maharashtra. Members of the royal family and their feudatories continued to control the region from Gujarat south to modern Thana District and east to the ghats, as donations for the support of Hindu activity attest. The Nasik plates of Dharaśraya Jayasiṁhavarman, dated 685, record his grant of a village, Dhoṇḍaka (modern Dhondegaon, northwest of Nasik), in the Nasik region, to a brahman.[29] A grant of Vijayāditya, dated in 696–97, records the gift of a village called Jamalagrāma in the western region of the Cālukya country (near modern Morkhande in Nasik District), to three brahmans.[30] And, perhaps closest of all to Ellora, Vijayāditya may have issued a grant on copper plates, from Elāpura in 705–06, giving a village called Bahmanavata (Brahmansvata) to Keśavasvāmin of Kollagar.[31]

Taken together, the epigraphical evidence and Hsüan-tsang's account indicate that Cālukya control of Maharashtra in the mid-seventh century centered on Nasik, but the extent of this control remains unclear. The Elāpura grant of Vijayāditya could suggest that it extended to Ellora, but the more numerous Cālukya grants in the Nasik region seem to reflect sporadic activity by the ruling dynasty, in support of a Brahmanical population, calculated to reaffirm its power in a largely independent region. At Nasik itself, for example, there is no material sign of Cālukya influence on or additions to the Buddhist cave temples that had been used up to the last decade of the sixth century. The Cālukyas or their feudatories may have been Ellora's nearest neighbors to the west during the seventh century, but their impact seems to have been more political than cultural.[32] If Cālukya records were all the evidence available for this period, it would appear that there was no Buddhist activity at Ellora in the seventh century.

If the Cālukyas and their coastal feudatories were not directly involved in the Ellora region, could there have been another dynasty that was responsible for its remarkable continuity for well over a century? Looking east (the direction from which its new Buddhist ideas seem to have arrived), records most relevant to this development come from inscriptions of an early branch of the Rāṣṭrakūṭa dynasty that, in the next century, would conquer the Cālukyas, take over the Deccan, and make Ellora its capital. These early Rāṣṭrakūṭa records have been found in northeast Maharashtra, an area hitherto ignored in the search for information about Ellora's history. During the second half of the seventh century, this family seems to have been located in the region around modern Akola and Amraoti Districts, as attested by three copper plate inscriptions of a king, Nannarāja, dated in 693, 709, and 731.[33] The inscriptions record grants of village lands and give Nannarāja's Rāṣṭrakūṭa genealogy, tracing it back to a grandfather, Govindarāja, who probably lived in the period 630 to 655.

These dates are crucial, since they make it possible to identify this Govindarāja with the Rāṣṭrakūṭa Govinda mentioned in the 634 Cālukya inscription of Pulakeśin II. It has been inferred that Pulakeśin first subdued Govinda, then made members of Govinda's Rāṣṭrakūṭa family his feudatories. However, since neither Nannarāja nor his ancestors possessed royal titles or titles typical of Cālukya feudatories elsewhere in the Deccan,[34] it is

possible that these Rāṣṭrakūṭas were Cālukya feudatories only until the death of Pulakeśin, after which time they ruled independently.[35] This would fit the evidence from Maharashtra where Cālukya inscriptions are not found after 630, and where cultural activity such as cave temple excavation proceeded without obvious Cālukyan influence or support. Moreover, a connection has been shown between the language of Nannarāja's records and that of earlier grants of the Kalacuri kings Śaṅkaragaṇa and Buddharāja.[36] This suggests that these early Rāṣṭrakūṭas looked more to local or regional precedents than to more distant Cālukya examples as they sought means to establish their power.

There is some evidence that Nannarāja's family extended its activity into the Ellora region. This is suggested first by a controversial inscription incised on the rear wall of a cell connecting Caves 26 and 27 at Ajanta.[37] Although its decipherment is difficult, there is no dispute over the reading of Nanarāja of the Rāṣṭrakūṭa family in the second line.[38] Furthermore, the third line of the inscription mentions a Vajraṭadeva, who can be identified with Vajraṭa, known from other inscriptions of the late seventh century and later as an enemy of the Cālukyas.[39] When paleographic analysis is combined with historical evidence from the inscription, it seems most likely that the inscription should be assigned to the late seventh century,[40] placing the early Rāṣṭrakūṭas at least as far west a Ajanta in the middle of Ellora's Buddhist phase in the mid-600s.

Adding further strength to the argument that an early branch of the Rāṣṭrakūṭa dynasty was present in the Ellora region in the seventh century is the discovery in a field near Aurangabad of a set of copper plates mentioning a hitherto unknown Rāṣṭrakūṭa king, Karkarāja. Ascribable on paleographic grounds to the seventh century, the plates mention several individuals with typical Rāṣṭrakūṭa names: Svāmirāja, Durgarāja, Karkarāja, Govindarāja, and a Mahārāṣṭrakūṭa.[41] These plates suggest, then, that a branch of this dynasty was indeed in the Ellora region during the period when the Buddhist caves were being excavated. Yet even in this case, there was no direct connection between politics and patronage at the caves as the last phase of Buddhist activity commenced in the late 600s.

It was in the early eighth century, after nearly two centuries of religious development, that Ellora itself became a center of political power, when around 735 the Rāṣṭrakūṭa king Dantidurga succeeded in taking over the Cālukya Empire, moving north from a base in the Canarese-speaking region called Laṭṭalura in their inscriptions, modern Latur in Osmanabad District, about 125 miles southeast of Ellora.[42] Dantidurga ruled from 735 to 757, so his ancestors probably occupied Latur during the seventh century while the family of Nannarāja controlled the area further north, from Aurangabad to Akola Districts. Further west, Cālukya power still extended to Nasik District.[43] For example, the 685 Nasik plates of Jayasiṃha, son of Vikramāditya, record the prince's total defeat of the army of Vajjaḍa (possibly the same Vajraṭa mentioned in the Ajanta Cave 27 inscription) in the country between the Mahi and Narmada rivers. And, as noted earlier, Ellora may have been mentioned in an inscription of the Cālukya king Vijayāditya, who recorded at "Elāpura" in 705–06 a donation of land. If Elāpura is the same as Ellora, not entirely certain from the context of the plates, the record would suggest that the Cālukyas had become concerned about their control over the area.[44] The concern was justified; it was during this period that Dantidurga consolidated his power as a feudatory of the Cālukyas and began active patronage of Hindu excavations at Ellora as he moved to establish his own empire.

Its strategic position on a major thoroughfare and its attraction as a *tīrtha* must have contributed to Dantidurga's move to Ellora. This apparently occurred while he was still a Cālukya feudatory, since his titles listed in a grant issued from Elāpura (Ellora) in 741–42 are those borne by important Cālukya feudatories but not by independent rulers. Dantidurga's involvement as an emperor with Ellora is confirmed by an important inscription carved on the front wall of a detached shrine in front of Cave 15, a Śaiva temple. Written around 750, this inscription reports that Dantidurga had defeated the Cālukya king, Kīrtivarman II, and conquered Kāñcī,

Kaliṅga, Kośala, Śriśala, Mālvā, Lāṭa, and Taṅka. The formulaic nature of the list disguises its importance. The consolidation of control over these areas to the east included places with which Buddhist Ellora was already interacting. Maharashtra is conspicuous by its absence from this list, otherwise a formal repetition of similar Cālukya lists that had included Maharashtra in rosters of conquered territories. In this case negative evidence, that is, the absence of Maharashtra from the list of conquests of Dantidurga, may be helpful in understanding the political situation at the beginning of the eighth century. Since Dantidurga's records do not refer to his conquest of Maharashtra, it seems likely that Rāṣṭrakūṭa control, first held by Nannarāja's family, and then by Dantidurga, was never a matter of dispute.[45]

With Dantidurga's consolidation of Rāṣṭrakūṭa power, Ellora for the first time was associated directly with a ruling dynasty. Three inscriptions record this association, offering scant historical evidence compared with the massive scale of the caves themselves. In his Ellora plates of 741–42, Dantidurga records the gift of a village to certain brahmans from Gujarat. Most important, Dantidurga made this gift at Elāpura, after bathing in the Guheśvaratīrtha.[46] This provides the first direct evidence that the *tīrtha* was used for ritual purposes by the royal family. Although he still did not bear the full titles of a king, and does not yet mention conquering the Cālukyas, Dantidurga was already making gifts of territory to private citizens, the traditional prerogative of a ruler, further signifying well established Rāṣṭrakūṭa regional authority.

Because of its location on the west wall of the exterior hall ("Nandimaṇḍapa") of Cave 15 at Ellora, the Daśāvatāra inscription (named after the cave's popular name) is the most reliable piece of historical evidence about the site, and the only one connected physically to the caves.[47] Incised near the end of work on Cave 15, the inscription mentions a visit by Dantidurga to the caves. Since he was active in the period 735–757, this provides an important, if not absolutely firm, date for excavation of Cave 15, and a *terminus ante quem* for work on the Buddhist caves 9 which on stylistic grounds are clearly earlier than Cave 15.

The inscription records in formulaic, laudatory detail Dantidurga's genealogy. Dantidurga, the last named Rāṣṭrakūṭa in the record, is described as having made Vallabharāja (that is, the Cālukya king, Kīrtivarman II) his tributary. According to the inscription, Dantidurga went to the caves with his army. Thus, as do the slightly earlier Ellora plates of the same king, the Daśāvatāra inscription suggests that early in his reign, Dantidurga took refuge there not only for ritual purposes, but also to rest his troops and, we may only infer, to oversee work on the new excavations he was sponsoring. Also implied in this description is a social and economic system sufficient to support his activities, for example, artisans to carve the stone, villagers to provide food and services for the royal retinue, troops, and brahmans he chose to favor.

Direct Rāṣṭrakūṭa patronage of excavations at Ellora is documented only in a later, oblique reference to Dantidurga's uncle and successor, Kṛṣṇarāja, who ruled ca. 757–772. In a genealogical sequence recorded in the 812 plates of another Rāṣṭrakūṭa ruler, Karkarāja II, issued from Baroda,[48] Kṛṣṇarāja is described as one who possessed a certain friendliness towards brahmans; he was the one by whom:

> . . . was caused to be constructed a temple on the hill at Elāpura, of wonderful structure,—on seeing which the best of immortals who move in celestial cars, struck with astonishment, . . . [say] . . . 'This temple of Śiva is self-existent; in a thing made by art such beauty is not seen,'—a temple, the architect-builder of which, in consequence of the failure of his energy as regards [the construction of] another such work, was himself suddenly struck with astonishment, saying, 'Oh, how was it that I built it!'[49]

Here, finally, is a clear association of a major political patron and a magnificent Śiva temple, identified as Cave 16, popularly known as the Kailāsa temple. Of course, Kṛṣṇarāja received the credit for causing a temple to be built but we cannot be certain that he initiated the excavation or that it was completed during his reign. It has even been suggested that the temple area had been blocked out long before the Rāṣṭrakūṭas arrived at Ellora, and while most work may have been completed during Kṛṣṇarāja's reign, some additions were made into the ninth century.[50] In any case, this is the most direct evidence extant for patronage, politics, and chronology at Ellora. Moreover, although it pertains to a mid-eighth-century Śaiva excavation, it is also important for understanding Ellora's latest Buddhist caves which, as will be discussed in the next chapter, share certain stylistic elements with the Kailāsa temple.

The Baroda inscription is also valuable because it refers to the artisan responsible for creating the great temple at Elāpura. Such recognition is unprecedented in records from Maharashtra, but is paralleled in an inscription on the Virupaksha temple at Pattadakal, a Cālukya dedication, which describes the architect, Sūtradhāri Gunda, as the greatest artisan of South India.[51] It is noteworthy that medieval legend also preserves a record of an architect who built a great temple at Ellora.[52] According to this legend, a Manikeśwar cave temple was built by Queen Maṇikāvatī, wife of a king of Alajapur, to commemorate the miraculous cure her husband achieved by bathing in a tank at Mhaisamala (near Ellora). She took a vow for the god Ghṛṣṇeśvara that if the king were cured, she would build a temple in honor of Śiva, and would fast until the temple was completed. Although it seemed impossible that a temple could be finished quickly enough for her to survive the fast, the king found an artisan, Kokasa, a resident of Paithan near Aurangabad, who was able to completely carve the *śikhara* (multistoried roof) of the temple in a week. The queen's vow was thus fulfilled, and the temple was named in her honor. Adding historical veracity to this legend, inscriptions of the eleventh to thirteenth centuries mention sculptors who were members of the family of a Kokasa, suggesting a possible link between the Manikeśwar legend and a historical family of artists who may actually have worked on excavations at Ellora, possibly even descendants of those who created the earlier Buddhist caves without the benefit of direct royal patronage.[53]

Sacred Geography: Ellora as a Tīrtha

As noted above, Ellora functioned as a *tīrtha*, a place of special sanctity where communion with the gods and passage from the secular to sacred sphere occurs most easily. History shows that as a *tīrtha* it attracted visitors from distant lands, religious communities of several faiths including Buddhists, and a major dynasty that made Ellora its capital in the mid-700s. To explain this attraction for kings and artists, and to establish the context in which its Buddhist caves could develop in circumstances more "cosmopolitan" than at other Buddhist sites, requires an examination of its location not in geographical or political space, but in the sacred space delineated by India's extensive system of sacred sites or *tīrthas* and the tradition of pilgrimage, *tīrtha-yātra*, to them.

Better known for its thirty-four Hindu, Buddhist, and Jain excavations, Ellora is also recognized as the site of Ghṛṣṇeśvara *tīrtha*, one of the twelve pan-Indian *jyotirliṅgas* (*liṅgas* of light) of Śaivism.[54] A temple for the worship of Ghṛṣṇeśvara is located in the village, about a mile west of the caves.[55] Although it does not rank at the top of important pilgrimage sites,[56] the presence of the *tīrtha* together with cave shrines of three major religions, make the site and the area around it particularly rich and complex. Yet, Ellora has not often been the focus of discussions of pilgrimage in India that tend to emphasize major religious centers. These centers hold claim to unique events or activities that have granted them special sanctity: according to the epics, Krishna's home *is* Brindavan, the Buddha's enlightenment came *at* Bodhgaya, *śrāddha* (offerings to ancestors) is performed most propitiously at Gaya. Pilgrimage to these places is often the model or ideal behind pilgrimage to places further down the scale of "*yātric*" importance.

There are, of course, natural limitations on the number of original or central pilgrimage sites (there is only one Bodhgaya), and pilgrims may face a variety of impediments in traveling to them. It should not be surprising that regional, subregional, and local sites have developed, and in India in fact, outnumber those "original" ones of national or international importance. Travel to these regional sites "can be regarded as a complex surrogate for the journey to the source and heartland of the faith,"[57] where "reduplicative shrines," may imitate major pilgrimage centers. This phenomenon of spatial transposition or regional substitution has often been noted in the context of Indian pilgrimage to sacred sites. The substitution can work in both directions. Thus, it has been said, "all the *tīrthas* on earth are . . . in Kāshī";[58] worship at Kāshī (Banaras) is equivalent to worshipping at all sacred sites on earth. Or, in the opposite direction, a devotee of a Maharashtrian saint would argue that one should "stay in Maharashtra because every place worth going to is there";[59] in other words, one can find sites in Maharashtra equivalent in holiness to those elsewhere in India. In this way, regional sites can substitute for national ones.[60]

Ellora exemplifies such transformations, effected by the interaction of geography, politics, and religion, that create an important regional *tīrtha*. It must then be viewed within the context of the universal sacred systems to which its architecture, sculpture, and religious practice refer. Its sacred location and existence were determined, first by the presence of a constant source of water. The caves were developed to integrate the presence of seasonally active streams into the arrangement of its temples. Cisterns were also cut outside certain caves (3, 7, 12, and 23) to trap water for refreshment and ritual use. From this perspective, it is no accident that both the earliest Hindu and Buddhist caves were the ones excavated closest to the most active streams, that have worn horseshoe-shaped gullies into the scarp. Water was essential for sustenance, for ritual, and for properly placing the site in spiritual geography; it links Ellora to key religious sites throughout India.[61] As we know from Aurangzeb's chronicle, the waterfalls would have been visible to earlier travelers, as they were to later ones, and, it may be inferred, to those searching for a propitious temple site. (See Fig. 12) And an undated masonry tank with well carved stone steps has been found above the surrounding hills, underscoring and repeating at this particular site the pan-Indian concern for water.[62]

The earliest reference to Ellora as a *tīrtha* comes from epigraphical records of the Rāṣṭrakūṭas, who conquered the Cālukyas and took control of the Deccan in the mid-eighth century. In the 742 C.E. copper plate inscription of Dantidurga, that king is associated with Elāpura and with *guheśvaratīrtha*, although no temple is mentioned.[63] Later, in the 812 C.E. Baroda inscription of Karkarāja II, a miraculous Śiva temple at Elāpura (most probably the Kailāsa temple, Cave 16) is ascribed to the reign of Dantidurga's successor, Kṛṣṇarāja I.[64] These records reveal key information about Ellora's development as a *tīrtha*. Patronage of the caves had been taken up by the most important dynasty of the Deccan, one that chose to support Śaiva excavations at a place already in the mid-700s explicitly referred to as a sacred site: *guheśvaratīrtha*, the *tīrtha* of the "Lord of the Cave." It is possible furthermore to infer that Elāpura had been known as a *tīrtha* for some time before the Rāṣṭrakūṭas moved there, since the name appears in the 742 inscription that precedes by several years most of the Rāṣṭrakūṭa work at the site. Kṛṣṇarāja's Kailāsa temple, explicitly referring to Śiva's abode in the Himalayas, expresses clearly the view of Ellora as a *tīrtha* for his worship, a Mount Kailāsa in Maharashtra, where Śiva could descend in response to prayers offered at the temple.

The sacred nature of the site eventually came to extend beyond the caves themselves. The shrine of Ghṛṣṇeśvara in Ellora village probably preserves a later form of the name Guheśvaratīrtha mentioned in the 742 Rāṣṭrakūṭa inscription. The modern temple marking the *tīrtha*, erected near the stream that flows from the falls above Cave 29, is even visible from Cave 21, itself a Śaiva temple.[65] (See Fig. 13) Purāṇic and other textual references show that long after the Rāṣṭrakūṭas left Ellora, its recognition as a *tīrtha* continued. Despite the absence of a formal religious community in the medieval period, the site achieved continued recognition as a *tīrtha* in Hindu religious texts as it was absorbed into a broader system of sacred sites. Elāpura is mentioned in chapter 22 of the *Matsya Purāṇa*, which places great emphasis on the Narmada region;[66] it is included in a list added to the *Purāṇa* of holy places where

śrāddha (rites for the ancestors) should be performed.[67] Moreover, Elāpura is mentioned as one of the fifty Śākta *pīṭhas* (centers) listed in the sixteenth- or seventeenth-century *Jñānārṇava Tantra*.[68] Ellora—the site and the village—never became as complex as southern temple towns. Yet, it is possible to infer from the growth of the *tīrtha* itself that this development depended on and then reinforced the concentration of resources across an entire region and a division of labor that depended on those resources, analogous to the triangular system of sacred kings, religious systems and local productive relations that transformed places like Tanjavur or Puri into a thriving urban, religious centers.[69]

As noted earlier, Ellora was in fact a Śaiva site more than a century before the Rāṣṭrakūṭas moved there. Its earliest excavations, of the late sixth century, were also dedicated to Śiva. Cave 29, located next to the most active waterfall, is clearly based on the architectural plan and iconographical program of the Śiva temple on Elephanta island.[70] It emerges from the surrounding ocean as Mt. Kailāsa rises from the Himalayas. Unnamed in ancient records, these early Hindu caves mark the first steps in the recognition of a major *tīrtha* there.

For a century the situation changed when, around 600, Buddhists took over the southern end of the site. Forced inland by political disturbances on the coast, Buddhist patrons must have been attracted by a reliable water supply, and by resources and protection visible both in the active patronage of the Hindu caves and at the Buddhist community in the nearby caves at Aurangabad. In establishing their community at Ellora, its later Buddhist patrons and artisans may also have considered its similarity to Bodhgaya, one of the most important Buddhist sites, where Buddhist and Hindu interaction was well known. While the Hindu analogy between Ellora's Kailāsa temple and the mythological Mt. Kailāsa is clear, the significance of the antecedents of the Buddhist temples requires more elaboration.

Among many others, probably the best known example of coexisting Śaiva and Buddhist use of a sacred area is Bodhgaya in eastern India. There, the legend of the founding of the Mahābodhi temple attributes its reconstruction to a worshiper of Maheśvara (Śiva), who rebuilt a *vihāra* (a Buddhist monastic residency) near the *Bodhi* temple (which marks the site of the Buddha's enlightenment) on the instructions of Śiva himself. Later, King Śaśāṅka cut down the tree and meant to replace the statute of Buddha in the *vihāra* with one of Maheśvara.[71] Near the Mahābodhi temple, a relief with images of the Hindu gods Surya, Lakulīśa, and Viṣṇu was found, inscribed in the twenty-sixth year of Dharmapāla (809–10) with a dedication of an image of Mahādeva.[72] When the Tibetan Buddhist monk Dharmasvāmin visited Bodhgaya in 1234–36, he claimed to have seen an image of Maheśvara drawn on the door, which had been erected to protect the Mahābodhi image from the depredations of Turushka invaders.[73]

No similar legends explain the situation at Ellora; literary accounts refer only to Hindu activities there. Yet the juxtaposition of Buddhist and Śaiva (and later Jain) shrines, of generally separate periods, is another instance where adherents of different religions competed for or shared space that may have been viewed as a reduplication of more sacred places: Mount Kailāsa for Hindus, Bodhgaya for Buddhists. We may conclude that recognition of the sanctity of certain places could be more important than the distinction among various sects or even major religious traditions. Ellora's position in the Śaiva systems of *jyotirliṅgas* and *śrāddha* centers did not prevent the development of Buddhist temples. On the contrary, its Hindu prestige and strength as a *tīrtha* may have encouraged use by other, non-Hindu communities.[74]

Just as the Kailāsa temple refers explicitly to another sacred place, Ellora's Buddhist images also suggest a direct analogy to an equally important place, Bodhgaya. The main shrine images in the later Buddhist caves depict the Buddha holding his right hand in *bhūmisparśamudrā*, the gesture of touching the earth (see chapter 4 for detailed discussion of these images). This *mudrā* symbolizes the event of his enlightenment, which took place at Bodhgaya. The meaning of these images was emphasized by the addition of small images of Bhūdevī (the earth goddess) and Aparājitā at the base of the Buddhas' thrones. In the Bodhgaya enlightenment story, Bhū-

devī rises to attest to the Buddha's integrity as he faces Māra's attack.[75] The image of Aparājitā, trampling on the back of Gaṇapati, and thus surmounting the surmounter of all obstacles, condenses the lesson to be learned about the power of enlightenment and of the Buddha himself.[76] It is most important to note that such images are unique to Ellora as a "southern" site, but have been found at several places in eastern India, including Bodhgaya itself.[77] (See Fig. 170–173) The precision of the Ellora compositions strongly suggests that worship in the shrines would have been viewed as a substitution for or transposition of worship at Bodhgaya.

At the end of Ellora's history, in a Jain context, Ellora's nature continued to be acknowledged as a *tīrtha* sacred enough to transpose to the caves one even more sacred. The Jain excavations, following the major Rāṣṭrakūṭa Hindu work, are attributable to political as well as religious causes. Amoghavarṣa I (814–878) was a convert to Jainism and, following his predecessors, he used the site to express his own faith, sponsoring several impressive Jain excavations at the northernmost end of the scarp.[78] There, at a later period, a large image of the *tīrthaṅkara* (Jain saint) Pārśvanātha was carved; an inscription on the image dated in 1234–35 records the donation of the image by a Cakreśvara. According to this record, he made " . . . many huge images of the lordly Jinas . . . and converted the Charaṇādri thereby into a holy *tīrtha*, just as Bharata [made] Mount Kailāsa [a *tīrtha*]."[79] Again, the regional substitution of a local *tīrtha*, Ellora, for the heavenly one, Cāraṇādri or Kailāsa, is explicit.

Ellora as *tīrtha* was powerful enough to embody key places in the greater spiritual systems of Hinduism, Buddhism, and Jainism. And while work ceased with the Jain caves, recognition of the *tīrtha* did not end. As we know, in the seventeenth century Ahalyabai Holkar sponsored a rebuilding of the Ghṛṣṇeśvara temple which replaced one used even earlier. Contemporary practice continues to affirm Ellora's place in living systems of Śaiva and Buddhist pilgrimage, as tourists and pilgrims alike travel to the Ghṛṣṇeśvara temple and to the caves. Today, ocher-robed monks from Southeast Asia worship Buddha images while devout Hindus make offerings to images of Śiva in the caves and at the temple in the nearby village, continuing a tradition that goes back to the sixth century.

Ellora as a Tantric Buddhist Center

With a centuries-old tradition of Buddhist rock-cut architecture behind it, under political conditions that both offered protection from direct conflict and opened the region up to influence from other parts of India, and with a growing stature as a *tīrtha*, the stage was set for Ellora to "take off" as a Buddhist center. Its Buddhist caves have usually been explained in terms of the tradition of the fifth- and sixth-century Mahāyāna Buddhist monuments at Ajanta, Kanheri, and Aurangabad.[80] But here, this regionally distinct tradition was opened up to a broader range of developments that characterized the growth of Buddhist centers throughout India during the seventh and eighth centuries.

Following the decline of patronage at Ajanta in the last quarter of the fifth century, Mahāyāna Buddhism continued to receive sporadic support, reflected both in traditional and innovative iconographic additions to caves at Kanheri and Nasik, and in the inception of new sanctuaries at Aurangabad. Coincident with Cālukya conquests along the west coast around 600, Buddhism at inland sites in Maharashtra seems to have received a surge of support, perhaps the result of a migration of Buddhist monks, artisans, and patrons from the coast under pressure from Cālukya disturbances there. But it was at Ellora, already beginning its history as a *tīrtha* under its earlier Hindu patrons, that this increased investment in Buddhist monuments resulted in the culmination of the traditions of western Deccani Buddhist rock-cut architecture.

Through the sixth century, this tradition focused on worship of the Buddha in anthropomorphic form, the focal point of nearly every shrine at Mahāyāna sites throughout Maharashta. However, during this time, new Buddhist concepts were evolving, as tradi-

tional Mahāyāna worship was transformed into the beliefs, rituals, and images characteristic of tantric Buddhism.[81] The Buddha was still the center of worship, but could be visualized in a number of varying emanations, with new hosts of attendant deities added to his retinue. A new body of texts called *tantras* developed to record the esoteric and functional (as opposed to philosophical) details of religious practice, describing for example, the laying out of sacred diagrams (*maṇḍalas*) and the performance of initiation rituals within them.[82] Common to all were rituals—designed to result in "quick" enlightenment—that also made use of such physical guides to worship and visualization as *mantras* (verbal formulae) and *mudrās* (symbolic hand positions). Although intended to guide preparations for ritual initiations, the texts describing *maṇḍalas* also provide an invaluable record of iconography, showing how images appeared and where they were to be located in a sacred enclosure. Their importance in the transmission of tantric teachings is reflected by the traditional account of the introduction of esoteric Buddhism into Japan by Kobo-daishi (Kukai). Upon his return from extensive study in China in 806, he brought with him hundreds of Sanskrit texts, statues of Buddhas and Bodhisattvas, and *mahāmaṇḍalas*, *dharma-maṇḍalas*, and *samayamaṇḍalas*, painted on orders of Kukai's teacher, Hui-kuo.[83] The production and display of *maṇḍalas* became a key element in the ritual apparatus of Shingon temples, flanking the altar in the inner sanctum.[84] The significance of this use of the *maṇḍala* will become apparent when, in chapter 2, Ellora's first *maṇḍala*, flanking the central shrine image of its earliest Buddhist temple, is considered.

In the later Tibetan canon, the tantras were divided into four general classes each headed by a different emanation of the Buddha: *kriyā* (action) *tantras*, with Amitāyus presiding; *caryā* (performance) *tantras*, with Vairocanābhisambodhi presiding; *yoga* (yoga) *tantras*, with Sarvavid Vairocana presiding; and *anuttarayoga* (supreme yoga) *tantras*, with Guhyasamāja Akṣobhya presiding.[85] The first two, often called *Mantrayāna* Buddhism, exemplified by teachings recorded in the *Mañjuśrīmūlakalpa* and the *Mahāvairocanasūtra*, fo-

14

cused on correct recitation of magical formulae, worship of relics, buildings, and numerous deities, repair of *stūpas*, and similar themes that extended relatively easily from the older, Mahāyāna tradition. The difference was how the incantations and rituals were used. Now, the *primary* purpose was the rapid achievement of enlightenment (Buddhahood), not the benefits that were hoped to accrue to others when special prayers were recited in Mahāyāna tradition. In both the *kriyā* and *caryā tantras*, the Buddha is the historical Śākyamuni, still visualized in various "historical" roles, such as preaching the first sermon or defeating Māra and achieving enlightenment at Bodhgaya. It was this form of esoteric Buddhism that blossomed in Japan in the ninth century. By contrast, the latter two, often called *Vajrayāna* Buddhism after the *vajra* that symbolizes the adamantine state that these practices will engender, taught that Buddhahood was attainable through highly ritualized series of consecrations described, for instance, in the *yoga tantra* text, the *Sarvatathāgatatattvasaṁgraha*, which is said to be promulgated by Śākyamuni as Vairocana. In this text, the Buddhas of ten directions escort Śākyamuni to the highest heaven. After he achieves five stages of enlightenment, he becomes Vairocana, and only then descends to defeat Māra, when he preaches the doctrine in a place of gods or a heavenly park or heaven. In the *anuttarayoga* texts, such as the *Guhyasamājatantra*, consecrations are ritualized performances of intercourse, introducing new erotic and horrific aspects of the Buddhist pantheon. It is important, however, to note that these teachings were not entirely independent. Thus for example, *maṇḍalas* of the *yoga* and *anuttarayoga* classes retain elements of *maṇḍalas* described in the *Mañjuśrīmūlakalpa*, a tantra of the *kriyā* class.

How could such new ideas find expression in the "old" style of the rock-cut monasteries? During the seventh and eighth centuries, the teachings of tantric Buddhism were spreading rapidly both throughout India and beyond to Nepal, Tibet, China, Japan, and Southeast Asia. The popularity of *tantras* and worship of the deities they embody varied from region to region. The *kriyā*, *caryā*, and *yoga tantras* were spread through Southeast and East Asia,

while the popularity of the fourth, the *anuttarayoga tantras*, was restricted largely to Tibet.[86] In this context, the significance of Ellora's Buddhist caves emerges, including some of the earliest known sculptural representations of tantric deities whose images were to proliferate in later centuries in the international world of Buddhism.[87] Compared with the art of later Buddhism, Ellora's tantric images often appear to be unrefined or even experimental. In some cases, the unpolished quality of the sculptures seems to suggest that they are "sketches" of forms the artisans were unaccustomed to rendering in stone. This is not so surprising when Ellora's chronological and geographical positions are considered. Its seventh-century tantric imagery is extremely early; images with like iconographic features appear with frequency only in the art of the eighth, ninth, and tenth centuries elsewhere in India.

The struggle to express this new vision of Buddhism is illustrated at Ellora where early tantric deities are portrayed with increasingly complex iconography as its Buddhist phase approaches its end. Even the earliest of its Buddhist caves differ significantly from those at earlier sites, although certain key elements (a *stūpa* in the apsidal *caitya* hall, Buddha images, and attendants in the shrine areas, pillared halls, etc.,) remained. However, as the next chapters will explain, important iconographic and programmatic differences between the earlier and later caves imply a development of tantric ideology and practice. A new array of Bodhisattvas, female figures, and others multiply in the later Buddhist residence and worship halls. This pantheon, always celibate, but including prominent female deities, is similar to those described in *kriyā* and *yoga* tantric texts, although no text known to us today completely explains the layout of the caves. Neither do other monuments thus far studied match its iconography and programs detail for detail. Ellora is a unique and valuable exhibit of tantric Buddhist art in its earliest stages.

The presence alone of an extended list of Bodhisattva and female images would suggest that Ellora was influenced by nascent tantric teachings. By analogy to the spread of esoteric teachings from China to Japan, we   15 might well expect evidence of *maṇḍalas* somewhere at the site.[88] As John Huntington has shown for nearby, and nearly contemporary Aurangabad Caves 6 and 7, the layout of these late sixth-century caves may well have been determined by *maṇḍalas* similar to the *garbhadhātu-* and *vajradhātu-maṇḍalas* of Japanese esoteric Shingon Buddhism. However, there is no direct evidence at Aurangabad that such *maṇḍalas* existed at the site—not surprising when the historical records show so clearly that most were transmitted in drawn or painted form on perishable paper or cloth. In this context, Ellora is particularly exciting because no inference is needed to determine whether *maṇḍalas* were used at the site—rock-cut *maṇḍalas* are preserved *in situ* to confirm the assumption that should be made based on the new iconography, that a complex of tantric teachings operated to determine the layout of the caves. Like a diagram in a museum, the relief *maṇḍalas* point out what we should expect to find in full-scale sculptures within the temples.

Apart from its sculptures, evidence for sectarian affiliation at Ellora is extremely sparse.[89] The only Buddhist inscription at the site is located in the balcony of the Cave 10 *caitya*: it merely records the widely distributed credal formula that begins "*ye dharma hetu . . .*" Its letter style places it in the late seventh or early eighth century, but beyond this it does not help to determine the dates or beliefs of the people responsible for the Buddhist excavations there.[90] We might also expect an obvious source of information on mid-seventh century Buddhism to be the description of Maharashtra found in the travelogue of Hsüan-tsang. Unfortunately, he did not describe Ellora, although he did discuss religion in Maharashtra generally. According to him, there were one hundred monasteries and five thousand priests who practiced both Mahā-yāna and Hīnayāna Buddhism; there were also one hundred Deva temples that housed many "heretics" of different beliefs.[91]

The key to this puzzle may lie outside Maharashtra. While Ellora continued the local cave temple tradition, its Buddhist iconography, especially in the later Buddhist caves, is linked to developments seen further east at roughly contemporary sites such as Sirpur, roughly contemporary sites such as Sirpur, Bodhgaya, and Ratnagiri. While the diffusion of iconography and style within Maharashtra has been accepted without question, little attention has been paid to the mechanism(s) that brought tantric ideas—being developed in eastern and central India—to Ellora. Legends about the lives of famous tantric teachers hint at a possible answer to this question.

In medieval Tibetan texts, our best source on the history of tantric Buddhism, we find strands of a story that link a famous tantric teacher with Vidarbha (eastern Maharashtra) and Orissa, bringing close to Ellora our picture of the growth of Tantrism. In these stories, a teacher named Saraha (also known as Rāhulabhadra) either belonged to Uḍḍiyāna, or was born in Vidarbha (eastern Maharashtra), or, according to Taranātha, was associated with Candanapāla of Oḍviśa.[92] Taranātha, the premier Tibetan historian of Buddhism, wrote that in this Candanapāla's time, while Saraha was still a brahman, Viṣ-ṇukalpa, king of Oḍviśa (Orissa) built one hundred and eight Buddhist temples and made them centers for Mahāyāna teachers of the time. In Taranātha's version of the story, Saraha, alias Rāhula, went to Nalanda, a major international Buddhist university, where he was ordained. However, another Tibetan source says that he was converted to Man-trayāna by King Chove Sukalpa of Orissa, and that he performed the *mahāmudrā* ritual (a tantric ritual) in Maharashtra. According to the account that placed Saraha's birth in Vid-arbha, he converted the people of Vidarbha (to tantric Buddhism, we may assume).[93] Finally, Rāhula/Saraha may be more firmly linked to Orissa by the appearance of the name Rāhularuci, described as a *mahāmaṇ-ḍalācarya* and *paramaguru* (teacher of the great *maṇḍala* and chief guru), in an inscription on a seventh- or eighth-century image found at Khadipada, Balasore District, Orissa.[94] Here, Rāhularuci's title *mahāmaṇḍalācarya* underscores the importance of the *maṇḍala*'s teaching in Buddhist identity of this period. Moreover, the inscription demonstrates a case where a teacher is clearly known as an instructor in the worship of *maṇḍalas*, from a place (Orissa), which we know shared significant iconographic systems with Ellora, at a similar time.

The "Maharashtra connection" continued into the next generations of tantric teachers. Saraha's disciple was Nāgārjuna who, according to one medieval Tibetan source, is said to have been born a brahman in Vidarbha in Maharashtra. He went north for his Buddhist education, where he was instructed in *Kālacakra* (one of the most esoteric tantric rituals) by Saraha at Nalanda. Nāgārjuna then moved to the southeast, living sometimes at Ghaṇṭaśaila and sometimes as Śrīparvata (Nagarjunakonda) in Andhra Pradesh. It was from this region that he later brought the *Mahākālaratna* (a tantra of the *anuttarayoga* class) and other *tantras* from Dhanyakaṭaka *vihāra*.[95] In the next generation, Nāgārjuna's most famous student, Nāgabodhi, was also from Śrīparvata.[96] And Nāgabodhi's disciple, Vajrabodhi, is supposed to have been born in Central India around 670; he studied at Nalanda, but turned to Tantrism when he traveled in west and south India. It was Vajrabodhi who brought tantric teachings to China, where he died in 741.[97]

Although few points in this patchwork history can be substantiated, and there are few facts to help create order from the disparate strands of legend, certain aspects of the legends seem to be consistent. First, if Vajrabodhi lived around 700, then two "student-generations" earlier, Saraha would have been teaching in the mid-seventh century. This seems to fit together with the general date of the Khadipada inscription. Second, the tradition makes a very clear connection between early tantric teachers and Orissa, as well as a less certain connection between them and eastern Maharashtra (Vidarbha). Although these associations do not carry the strength of historical data, they should not be ignored or discounted entirely. At the very least, they may be the vestiges of poorly documented behavior that supply a tantalizing hint of an explanation for the religious development at Ellora, during a time when tantric teachers could circulate from the center to the peripheries of the Buddhist world, spreading their teachings within the space of a generation to establishments across India and beyond.[98]

If such legends as these offer only fragmentary glimpses of the diffusion of tantric ideas, its concrete manifestation can be seen in the Buddhist caves themselves, whose tantric iconography might be viewed as an artifact from the time when several key figures were first systematizing and disseminating their teachings, and perhaps even seeing them rendered permanently into stone monuments. Ellora's spirit as a *tīrtha*, already recognized by the early 700s when its latest, most elaborate Buddhist caves were being created, may have helped attract one of these men, who saw the potential to create an unprecedented Buddhist monument, as Rāṣṭrakūṭa kings were to do for Brahmanical worship at nearly the same time. Was it Saraha, known to have converted the people of Vidarbha, who arrived supplied with an array of *sūtras* and *maṇḍalas*, as Kukai did in Japan in 806? Ellora itself remains the only "text" that might provide an answer.

The Maṇḍala *at Ellora*

In the next chapters, it will be demonstrated that a *maṇḍala*, a schematic diagram portraying deities in a set order, provides a guide to the organizational scheme of Ellora's Buddhist caves from earliest to latest. As noted above, use of *maṇḍalas* to guide meditation was a primary characteristic of tantric Buddhism. The rock-cut *maṇḍalas* found both in the earliest Buddhist excavation, Cave 6 (Fig. 29), and in the latest, Cave 12 (Fig. 199, 212, 213) offer compelling evidence of the tantric affiliation of the site.

Their presence has profound significance as the external, permanent manifestation of a complex of practices used by tantric Buddhists to achieve rapid enlightenment. As cosmological diagrams that could also be drawn on cloth, paper, or stone, and, recorded in tantric texts, they preserve the outline of cosmological beliefs that shaped rituals and meditations long since vanished. They are much more than the diagrams we see and, in fact, may be defined in a number of ways. Thus, the *Mahāvairocanasūtra* (a major text of tantric Buddhism), defines the *maṇḍala*, in the words of the Buddha speaking to the Bodhisattva Vajrapāṇi, "A *maṇḍala* is what gives birth to   17 all Buddhas and has incomparable and most excellent flavor." A commentator, Śubhakara-siṁha, adds that *maṇḍala* means "circle," it is that which gives birth to Buddhas, the seed of Bodhicitta, and also it is *ghee*, that is, an essence, that which is most refined and clarified.[99] At the same time, it is a sacred ground, which an initiate approaches in carefully orchestrated steps, and into which the gods are invited to descend. It is "the whole universe in its essential plan, in its process of emanation and reabsorption."[100]

The conception of the *maṇḍala* as a diagram is extended into a visualization of concrete architectural space, and was transformed into actual temple architecture and sculpture. The universe-in-the-*maṇḍala* is thus described and represented as a palace and, at the same time, the *maṇḍala* as a whole is conceived as being located in a *kūṭāgāra*, a three-storied eaved palace resting on top of mount Sumeru. In the Tibetan tradition, one of the first steps in using the *maṇḍala* is the ritual of "Generation of the Residence," containing the *kūṭāgāra* with seats for deities. The *Niṣpannayogāvalī* (another important tantric text) specifically says that *maṇḍalas* were situated in the *kūṭāgāra* on Sumeru, with the main deity in the center.[101] Such *maṇḍalas* as these include layers, or galleries in which reside numerous manifestations of Buddhas, Bodhisattvas, and other deities, whose arrangement varies from *maṇḍala* to *maṇḍala*.

The textual analogy between architectural and *maṇḍalic* arrangements which, it is argued here, is reflected at Ellora, is further strengthened by an emphasis on triads. According to the *Mahāvairocanasūtra*, the "layers" may also be viewed as a triad: the Matrix *Maṇḍala* is arrayed in three layers (or spheres around the center) that correspond to the three mysteries and the three *dharma*-bodies, the *nirmāṇakāya, sambhogakāya,* and *dharmakāya,* where the latter is the central mansion of the *maṇḍala*.[102] A biography of the great Tibetan translator Rin-chen-bzang-po recounts that, when visited by Atīśa, a famous Indian tantric Buddhist teacher, they retired for the night into a three-storey temple. The first floor was circled by deities of the *Guhyasamājatantra,* the second by divinities of the *Hevajratantra,* and the third by the *maṇḍala* of the *Cakrasamvara*

gods. At twilight, Rin-chen-bzang-po meditated on the first floor, at midnight on the second, and at dawn on the top floor.

The sense of architectural "threeness" connects, if only distantly, the Tibetan tradition to the vertical structure of the three-storied Ellora Caves 11 and 12. Three-storey structures were an innovation in Indian Buddhist temples of the seventh and early eighth centuries, suggesting another element in the advent of new teaching at Ellora. Ellora's *maṇḍala* was certainly simpler than those worshiped in the Tibetan legend; a single scheme, or perhaps a group of three closely related *maṇḍalas,* were applied to the three floors of Cave 12. Still, this tale suggests that the use of a three-storied temple was indeed a part of tantric ritual, so that we might imagine a sequential use of the ascending floors in Cave 12, perhaps progessing upward from dusk to dawn as in the Tibetan story.[103] Extending this idea further, in chapter 2, it will be shown that the idea of a three-storied architectural space determined by the *maṇḍala* was even earlier expressed at Ellora in *horizontal* space where, in Caves 2, 3, and 4, iconographic and programmatic details show relationships among those caves similar to those found later in the vertical arrangements of sculptures in the three floors of Cave 12. In both the horizontal and vertical cases, the shrines are circled by images of Buddhist deities, much as the floors of the Tibetan temple were encircled by deities of the *Guhyasamājatantra, Hevajratantra,* and *Cakrasamvara*.

We have no evidence for the rituals actually performed in Ellora's cave temples, but the extensive records of early Japanese esoteric sects provide suggestive analogies, which may be connected to certain iconographic details in the caves. Thus, the ritual use of the *maṇḍala* which, for example, takes seven days in the Japanese Shingon initiation, begins with rites to drive away demons (Māra) and to awaken the earth gods.[104] In doing so, the acolyte mirrors the key stage in Śākyamuni's enlightenment at Bodhgaya when, challenged by Māra, he called upon the earth goddess, Bhūdevī, to witness the enlightenment he achieved and thus, repel the demon and his hosts. In the Shingon tradition, the worshiper himself kneels with knees

18

and toes touching the earth, torso upright (it will be interesting to note the images of worshipers in this position in Ellora's Buddhist caves), then touches the earth with a *vajra*, a transformation of the *bhūmisparśamudrā* found on Buddha images representing the enlightenment. The analogy can be carried further, positing the *maṇḍala* as "an ideal Bodhgaya, an 'adamantine plane,' that is, an incorruptible surface, the representation of the very instant in which is accomplished the revulsion to the other plane, in which one becomes Buddha."[105] As noted above, and as will become clear in the next chapter, the iconography of the shrines in Caves 11 and 12 make this analogy quite explicit. From the doorways themselves to the central Buddha images seated on thrones supported by Māra's dwarfs, to the images of the earth goddess, Bhūdevī, and Aparājitā (emphasizing the defeat of obstacles), these shrines clearly focus on recreating the essence of Bodhgaya-as-seat-of-enlightenment.

Beyond its general cosmological functions, each *maṇḍala* focuses on a particular deity, or set of deities central to the teaching of particular forms of tantric Buddhism. From descriptions in such texts as the *Mañjuśrīmūlakalpa, Sādhanamālā, Niṣpannayogāvalī,* and *Kriyāsaṃgraha,* lists have been compiled describing thirty-seven different *maṇḍalas,* including *mahāmaṇḍalas* that contain smaller *maṇḍalas*[106] (the nine-*maṇḍala* Diamond World *Maṇḍala* of the Shingon sect exemplifies this macrocosmic structure centered on Vairocana);[107] a Tibetan compilation lists 132 *maṇḍalas.*[108] Specific *maṇḍalas* were associated with individual teachers. Thus, Amoghavajra, a famed Chinese monk, is known to have translated the *Aṣṭamaṇḍalakasūtra* (*maṇḍala* of eight Bodhisattvas, centered on Śākyamuni) into Chinese in the mid-700s.[109]

As noted earlier, Shingon tradition says that its founder, Kobo-daishi (Kukai), brought the layout of the Matrix and Diamond World *Maṇḍalas* from China to Japan in the early 800s.[110] These he had displayed in temple shrines, ultimately leading to adjustments in entire temple complexes (analogous to the adjustments proposed here at Ellora), which in the Shingon tradition stood for the *dharmadhātu* and *garbhadhātu.* The arrangement

of the *maṇḍalas* is reflected in temple and monastery layouts, interior plans of main halls, in the movements of rituals, as well as in sculpture and painting. Thus, at the Kongobu-ji temple on Mount Koya, the head temple of the Shingon sect, the traditional lecture hall became the scene of esoteric rites, divided into inner and outer precincts, with images of the two *maṇḍalas* painted on its walls. At the Daigo-ji temple in Kyoto, of the tenth century, its five-storied pagoda is a representation of the *maṇḍala* in two worlds. Within these temples, sculptures were intended to make the worshiper feel that deities stand before him, "exactly as if they had sprung full-fledged from the *maṇḍala* on the altar top."[111]

Somewhat later, but closer to home, the great Tibetan teacher, Rin-chen-bzang-po, translator of the *Tattvasaṃgraha,* brought the new *maṇḍalas* included in this system to the Ladakh/Himachal Pradesh region in the late 900s. In the era of international tantric Buddhism, it appears that dissemination and translation of *tantras* could be almost immediately followed by representation of their *maṇḍalas* in built forms.[112] At Ta-pho, thirty-two stucco images are arranged within the main assembly hall, so that the worshiper is placed at the center of the *Vajradhātu maṇḍala.* Four larger Buddha images, attended by four Bodhisattvas each, represent the Buddhas of the four directions, accompanied by the eight goddesses of offering. This is, then, a life-size sculptural reproduction of a completely integrated *maṇḍala.*[113] A rare occurrence, this temple confirms the argument made here, that the earlier temples at Ellora also recreate a *maṇḍala.* The demand for and receptivity to new teachings and the *maṇḍalas* that represented them is further illustrated by the iconography of temples at Alchi, where sanctuaries based on the teaching of the *Sarvadurgatipariśodhanatantra* (a *yoga* tantra) were erected in the early 1000s. The group of five temples is called the Chos-'khor, *dharma maṇḍala* in Sanskrit; this demonstrates explicitly that a group of temples could be viewed as a *maṇḍala,* and provides an analogy for the arrangement of Ellora's first *maṇḍala* which, as will be explained in chapter 2, was extended horizontally in Caves 2, 3, and 4. Alchi is most noteworthy for its extraordinarily well-preserved wall paintings, where the assembly hall alone includes six *maṇḍalas* of Vairocana, his manifestations and entourage. The walls of the Sum-Tsek, a three-tier temple, are similarly replete with painted *maṇḍalas*.[114] As the only existing painted *maṇḍalas* on the Indian subcontinent, they are of considerable importance, but their complexity precludes direct connection to the less elaborate *maṇḍalas* from Ellora, created three centuries earlier.

Ellora's rock-cut *maṇḍalas*, much simpler than these later forms, are essentially two-dimensional diagrams, carved on walls in very shallow relief. In location, if not complexity, they are comparable to the more complex, numerous painted *maṇḍalas* of tenth- and eleventh-century Himalayan Buddhist temples. As was the case at Ta-pho, at Ellora the *maṇḍalas* were also transformed into the three-dimensional programs of the cave shrines where life-size sculptures were carved in relief so deep as to create the impression that they are free-standing, creating an impression—as in Japanese esoteric temples, that the images had sprung full-fledged from a *maṇḍala*. This three-dimensionality is enhanced by the physical arrangement of the sculptures: worshipers had to move through caves and shrine areas in order to view all images. Thus, instead of proceeding mentally through a two-dimensional *maṇḍala* that might have been painted on a wall or on cloth suspended from the shrine ceiling in the sanctum, the worshiper could literally walk through a set of three-dimensional, horizontal *maṇḍalas*—the shrines themselves. And, in Cave 12, this extension into space is intensified as the worshiper moves vertically through the three floors of the cave, perhaps representations of the *kūṭāgāra*, within which are the *maṇḍalas* to be worshipped by the initiates. The similarity between Ellora's *maṇḍalas* and groups of Bodhisattvas in its later shrines has been recognized for over a century,[115] but the relationship has never been explored in detail. The connection between the simpler, nine-Buddha *maṇḍalas* in Cave 6 and the sculptures of Cave 2 has received even less attention. Although the links between relief *maṇḍalas* and sculptural Bodhisattva iconography should be sufficient proof that a teaching encompassing a *maṇḍala* operated at Ellora, the earlier evidence from Caves 6 and 2 extends this assumption back in time and suggests that such a teaching or teachings might have had a comprehensive effect on the development of the site as a whole. In the following chapters, the logic of this effect will be demonstrated by an explication of the iconography and programs of the caves. Recently, John Huntington has argued that Cave 6 and 7 at Aurangabad, near Ellora, represent the application to the iconography of rock-cut caves of a pair of *maṇḍalas* that are extremely important in Japanese Shingon Buddhism.[116] But only at Ellora, for the first time, were *maṇḍalas* carved on the walls, permanent proof of the use of such diagrams that is only implied at sites such as Aurangabad. The relationship between *maṇḍala* as a diagram and as shrine program provides the key to understanding the iconographic and spatial aspects of the development of Ellora's century-long Buddhist phase.

Among examples analogous to Ellora, where a *maṇḍala* was systematically applied to the layout of a Buddhist monument, Barabudur, in Java, is perhaps the best known case.[117] This connection is more than superficial, in view of its structure, composed of five terraces, three circular platforms supporting seventy-two small *stūpas*, surrounding a large, central *stūpa* on the topmost terrace, with symmetrically arranged Buddha images displaying the varying *mudrās* of the *pañcatathāgata* system. Since Paul Mus's monumental work published in the 1930s,[118] considerable efforts have been made to interpret its significance as a three-dimensional *maṇḍala*, as a *stūpa*, and as a reflection of tantric Buddhism that passed from South India to Java on its way to China and Japan.[119] Recent studies have demonstrated connections between Barabudur and specific tantric texts—the *Mahāvairocanasūtra* tradition of Shingon Buddhism, or the *Gaṇḍavyūhasūtra*, or the teachings of Vajravarman as reflected in the Tibetan tradition of the *Sarvadurgatipariśodhanatantra*.[120] Barabudur's structure and content differ from Ellora's Buddhist caves sufficiently so that we should not assume that they reflect a common literary tradition, but Barabudur studies suggest both promise and prudence in seeking a textual basis for Ellora's

20

maṇḍala. These studies demonstrate that it is possible to go beyond the general statement that "Barabudur is like a *maṇḍala*," but at the same time, consensus has not yet been reached on *the* text or teaching that inspired creation of the monument, confirming the earlier point that strict adherence to links between formal literary texts and material remains will be frustrating, and ultimately, unproductive when other sorts of evidence are available.

Closer to home, a cluster of sites in eastern Orissa—Lalitagiri, Udayagiri, and Ratnagiri—provide a different sort of evidence for the use of *maṇḍalas* and specific texts in the construction of Buddhist monuments. As will be explained in chapters 4 and 5, at all three sites, steles and individual images represent an eight-Bodhisattva *maṇḍala* nearly identical to Ellora's.[121] Equally important, images of *bhūmisparśamudrā* Buddhas, attended by Avalokiteśvara and Vajrapāṇi, are found at all three, again analogous to the central shrine images of Ellora's latest caves. Nancy Hock has recently shown that the first of two tantric Buddhist stages at Ratnagiri depended on a *kriyātantra* text like the *Mañjuśrīmūlakalpa*, which emphasizes the three Buddha families headed by Avalokiteśvara, Vajrapāṇi, and Śākyamuni,[122] but excludes horrific or erotic representations of deities. By contrast, Ratnagiri's later stage was inspired by the *Guhyasamāja*, an *anuttarayoga* text that included worship of Hevajra and Heruka, horrific deities not found at Ellora. The similarities between the earlier phase at Ratnagiri and the later Buddhist phase at Ellora suggest that both were in the *kriyātantra* tradition, while differences make it clear that the two sites did not share all the details of a single teaching.

As the following section will make clear, the case for connecting a written text with Ellora requires even more caution. The relief *maṇḍalas* assure us that we should seek support from the tantric textual tradition on *maṇḍalas* in explicating the caves, even if they do not promise that precise correlation will be made. As is the case with Ratnagiri and Barabudur, there are several lines that can be pursued. For instance, with eight Bodhisattvas in the *maṇḍala* and in the shrines, Ellora may have been inspired by a teaching like the *Aṣṭamahābodhisattvamaṇḍalasūtra* of the *yogatantra* tradition prevalent in China and Japan.[123] This *maṇḍala*, centered on an image of Vairocana with hands held in *dhyānamudrā* (meditation gesture) does not, however, correspond to the central *bhūmisparśamudrā* shrine images in the latest caves. Some features of the *Sarvadurgatipariśodhanatantra*, another text of the *yogatantra* school, known in two Tibetan versions, centered on Mahāvairocana/Śākyasiṁha,[124] suggest yet another possible identification of the central Buddha images in Ellora's later caves, but this *tantra* makes use of the more complex five-Buddha system, clearly absent from Ellora. However, with Avalokiteśvara and Vajrapāṇi as shrine attendants, and with no significant sign that the five-Buddha system was in use at Ellora, it may be that, like Ratnagiri's first phase, it reflects a simpler form of *kriyātantric* Buddhism, or a teaching that—earlier than the canonization of either *kriyā* or *yoga* tantra, preserves vestiges of both.

Like Ratnagiri and Barabudur, which remain uniquely complex expressions of esoteric Buddhist teaching, Ellora is also unique and may remain the most satisfactory "text" about itself, preserving on the periphery of the tantric world a relatively early expression of a teaching not completely transmitted into written form. In the following pages, this text—the monument—as *maṇḍala* will be explored in detail.

2. BUDDHIST CAVES OF THE FIRST PERIOD: THE BEGINNING OF THE MAṆḌALA

The development and use of Ellora as a religious site can be divided into discrete periods: early Hindu, Buddhist, later Hindu, and Jain. However, Ellora is notable for smooth, apparently peaceful artistic transitions from period to period. So, while we see a distinct shift around 600 C.E. from Hindu (Śaiva) to Buddhist activity, the similar style of the late-sixth-century Hindu and early-seventh-century Buddhist cave temples suggests that the same artisans shifted from one end of the site to the other, and were kept at work by a new set of patrons. This physical continuity illustrates the power of the *tīrtha* to attract patrons, resources, and artisans, creating a cultural and economic momentum that carried over into a Buddhist phase not connected in any doctrinal way to the Hindu basis of the *tīrtha*, but very likely a factor in influencing a new *maṇḍala* teacher to make Ellora his base.

Cave 6, the earliest Buddhist temple, is particularly interesting and important, displaying even at this early stage not long after 600 C.E., the kernel of the *maṇḍala* that evolved over the next century. From an art historical point of view, it provides many examples of stylistic continuity and iconographical and programmatic innovation, illustrating the smooth shift of artisans from Hindu to Buddhist work. Caves 5 and 2, also early caves, reveal other important stylistic connections to the first Hindu phase. At the same time, Caves 2, 3, and 4, taken as a group, may be an early, horizontal version of the three-tiered *maṇḍala* later excavated vertically in Caves 11 and 12. (Caves 1 and 7, never completed and with no significant sculpture, are of archaeological interest only.)

Cave Location and Chronology

A comparison of cave location and features—Buddha images, thrones, attendant Bodhisattva images, female figures, cherubs, pillars and other architectural details, and plans—provides the most reliable means to develop a relative chronology that can form the basis for understanding the development of Ellora's *maṇḍala* over time. Within a period of more than a century, from 600 to 730 C.E. there were groups of early, middle or transitional, and late caves, with connecting links among the groups. Over these years, the style changed from the rather heavy figural sculpture of its late sixth-century Hindu caves to a slimmer, mid-seventh-century style to the energetic, finely carved figures of its mid-eighth-century Rāṣṭrakūṭa monuments.

Early discussions of Ellora's chronology suggested a period of less than one hundred years between Caves 1 and 12. Usually Caves 1 through 5 were grouped in the early stage from 450 to 600 C.E. Cave 10 was often seen as a midway point, with a date around 650. And the later phase, composed of Caves 6 through 12, was ascribed to the mid-seventh and early eighth centuries. "Problem caves," like Caves 2 and 8, were sometimes ascribed dates in the late seventh or early eighth centuries.[1] These earlier reconstructions of Ellora's chronology did not diverge greatly from the numbered order of the caves, which proceeds from Cave 1 at the south end of the site to Cave 12, the last of the Buddhist series (plan, Fig. 2). More recent studies have altered this view to show that the Buddhist phase was preceded by a Brahmanical period during the late sixth century, encompassing the creation of Caves 27, 29, 21, 28, 19, 26, 20, 17, and 14.[2]

Moreover, even a superficial look at Ellora shows how much greater the difference is between its earliest and latest Buddhist caves, compared with Ajanta. For this reason, studying changes in conventional features, like pillars or Buddha images, is productive at Ellora. This contrasts with assessments of the situation generally found in other western caves, where changes in such conventionalized elements provide confusing evidence for chronology.[3]

Comparisons of sculpture and architecture of other regions in India show that general trends in art of the period are reflected at Ellora, confirming the proposed seventh to early eighth century dates. Such a framework makes it possible to establish, for example, what characterizes an early seventh-century Buddha image, how this type changed into a mid-seventh-century image, and how, by the early eighth century, new elements replaced the old patterns.

The reconstruction here is based first on the relative position of the caves along the scarp. Unlike some earlier studies, my work suggests that the chronological order of the caves does not follow their physical order. Instead the order was predicated on the position of the earliest Buddhist excavations, Caves 6 and 5. Stylistic relationships between the earlier Brahmanical caves and the first Buddhist ones amplify this relative chronology. A finer

analysis, based on an examination of changes in treatment of shrine images and secondary figures, helps explain the three-period grouping proposed here. Additional evidence for the length of time, and speed, of work on each cave comes from examining intrusive sculpture and patterns of unfinished features.

Each cave is a self-sufficient entity, with an internal programmatic order designed to guide the worshiper through the *maṇḍala*, past a series of attendant figures to the central Buddha image in each shrine. This order was the crucial one from a functional point of view, and one that changed during the Buddhist phase. The chronological framework to be presented here, and in more detail in appendix A, is the necessary first step toward analysis of changes in iconographical meaning and function.

Integrating the partial sequences, based on relative locations of the caves, provides a general chronological framework for the development of Ellora's *maṇḍala*. Cave 6 was the Buddhist cave started earliest, followed closely in time by Caves 5, 2, and 3. Because of their locations in peripheral or lower areas, work on Caves 5RW, 4, 7, and 8 began later than those of the first group. Caves 10 and 9, excavated in the same outcrop of stone, follow, with Caves 11 and 12 forming the logical end of the sequence. As I will discuss in the following pages, groupings of caves according to a *maṇḍalic* scheme begin in this framework, but do not follow it point for point. Instead, we must imagine a conceptual plan for the Buddhist caves that was implemented over a long period, by different artisans, so that some stylistic differences may occur within iconographically related groups.

Comparisons detailed in appendix A show how Cave 6 is connected to the late sixth-century Brahmanical caves. Most influential among these excavations was Cave 21, whose shrine doorway (Fig. 18), female figures (Fig. 22, 23) and pillars (Fig. 24, 55) were the sources of similar features in Cave 14, such as its square fluted cushion capital pilasters and the *makara*-arch frames over its sculptural panels. And Cave 21 was also at least partially the source for elements found in Caves 5 and 2. Yet, Cave 6, the earliest Buddhist excavation, is the only one to reflect the jewel-like refinement of Cave 21. By contrast the sculpture of Cave 14 is comparatively stiff. This difference suggests that work may have begun on Cave 6 soon after Cave 21 was completed, during which time a different group of artisans worked on Cave 14, the last of the early Hindu caves. Since Cave 6 does share some elements with Cave 14 as well as Cave 21, it is possible that Cave 6 was begun in a period during which different workshops were active at Ellora at the same time, partially influencing one another.

Their close relationship belies the traditional assumption that there was a serial development at Ellora, with one religious group replacing the other without any overlapping of activity. Spink was the first to question this assumption, suggesting instead that Caves 14 and 6 were contemporary. He further connected the shift from Śaiva Caves 21 and 17 to Vaiṣṇava iconography of Cave 14 with the

decline in Kalacuri power and the rise of the Cālukyas around 610,[4] and placed the date of Cave 6 ca. 610. The relationship between Caves 21 and 6 suggests that there was a smooth transition from Brahmanical to Buddhist activity, hardly evidence for a major disruption at the site even if politics and patronage had changed hands. Hindu and Buddhist work probably overlapped around 600, as it most probably did again in the early eighth century. Most important is the shift of artisans who worked on the Śaiva Cave 21, directly transferring many elements of sculptural style and architectural detail to Buddhist Cave 6, which became the point of genesis for Ellora's *maṇḍala*, whose development we can now trace.

The relative chronology proposed here, indicating approximate dates of completion or end of work on cave temples, may be summarized as follows:

Years	Ellora	Other Sites
475		Ajanta
550		Elephanta
575	Early Hindu Caves	Aurangabad Mahāyāna Caves
	Cave 29	
	Cave 21	Kanheri Mahāyāna Caves
	Cave 17	Badami Cave 3 (578)
	Cave 14	Nasik Mahāyāna Caves
600	Early Buddhist Caves	
	Cave 6	
	Cave 5	
	Cave 2	
	Cave 3	
630	Cave 5 Right Wing	
	Cave 4	
650	Middle Period Caves	
	Cave 8	
	Cave 9	
	Cave 10	
680	Additions to Cave 10	
700	Late Buddhist Caves	
	Cave 11	
	Cave 12	
730	Cave 12 completed	
	Rāṣṭrakūṭa-Period Hindu Caves Begin	
	Cave 15	
	Cave 16	
	Cave 25	
	Cave 22	
745	Dantidurga takes over control of Deccan	

The Beginning of the Maṇḍala *in Caves 6 and 5*

Even a casual glance at any of the Buddhist caves reveals the seated figure of the Buddha as the focal point of worship. But, the Buddha image is always embedded in spheres of figures, some serving conventionalized functions as attendants, and others, occupying more significant positions in Ellora's nascent *maṇḍala*. These spheres vary from cave to cave, while the Buddha image remains more stable, providing a check on the chronology of development of the *maṇḍala* blocked out by archaeological and architectural features.

In Cave 6, the *maṇḍala* is expressed in two ways. Most literally, the earliest *maṇḍalas* appear carved in shallow relief on the left and right walls of the shrine (Fig. 29). Here, the *maṇḍala* is a large, nine-part, square diagram. Each section holds a Buddha seated in *vajraparyaṅkāsana* pose, making the *dharmacakramudrā* gesture. Under the left shrine wall diagram is a group of worshipers; under the right diagram is a triad, probably representing Avalokiteśvara, Jambhala, and Mañjuśrī (Fig. 30).[5] The Buddhas' gesture (*mudrā*), repeated nine times in each *maṇḍala*, corresponds to that of the central shrine image in Cave 6. In location, if not subject matter and complexity, these *maṇḍalas* are strongly reminiscent of the hanging, painted *maṇḍalas* that flank the main images of Japanese esoteric Buddhist shrines.[6]

The Cave 6 *maṇḍalas* may be interpreted in several ways. First, and most obvious, they provide multiple images for worship in the shrine, functioning as any carved or painted images would have done. Second, they may be taken as representing an iconographical concept, expressed in an essentially two-dimensional form in the Cave 6 shrine, but expanded elsewhere at Ellora into three dimensions. Thus, in Cave 2 (see below), another early Buddhist excavation, ten nearly life-size Buddha images were carved in galleries along the left and right walls of the main hall. A later, but parallel unfolding of a *maṇḍala* is demonstrated at the To-ji temple in Kyoto (based on the original teachings and directions of the great Shingon teacher, Kukai), where

images of the deities of the Diamond World *maṇḍala* are placed in the temple in accord with the ritual use of this *maṇḍala*.[7] The location of the Cave 6 *maṇḍala* may also anticipate the carved *maṇḍalas* on the walls of a subshrine between the first and second floors of Cave 12, as well as part of the program of the third floor of Cave 12, the latest Buddhist cave, where nine Buddha images fill the side walls as Buddha images filled the galleries of Cave 2.

Less literally, the shrine *maṇḍalas* in Cave 6 give cogent proof of the development of "*maṇḍalic*" thinking at Ellora. They impel us to look at the entire programs of even the earliest Buddhist caves from a *maṇḍalic* perspective, to seek a source of conceptual unity for each cave as well as for the evolution of iconography and programs from cave to cave. Taking this broader view, I would suggest that all sculptures in Cave 6 be considered as parts of a *maṇḍala*, executed on a life-size, three-dimensional scale. Later *maṇḍalas*, and those described in texts usually are filled with many more figures.[8] I propose that in Cave 6 it was reduced to the few absolutely necessary to make the cave function as the core of a *maṇḍala*. This could be in part because it is so early but also, given the significant incomplete sections especially in the front of the cave, it also could be the case that additional sculptures (which would have formed the outer sphere of the *maṇḍala*) may have been planned but never carved. For these reasons the Cave 6 *maṇḍala* is limited to the central shrine area. Aurangabad Caves 6 and 7, where iconographic programs were fully realized, provide examples of the way cave temples could be completed to represent all components of a *maṇḍala*.[9]

The worshiper originally should have approached the shrine/*maṇḍala* through the central opening of the cave. Today, with the front part of the cave eroded away, the visitor must start sideways from stairs carved into the front of the right (south) wing of the hall. This wing, and the one on the left of the central hall, are large, pillared but otherwise empty spaces (more similar in plan to Cave 21 than any Buddhist excavation) with cells cut along their perimeter.

A unique addition to the "architecture" of

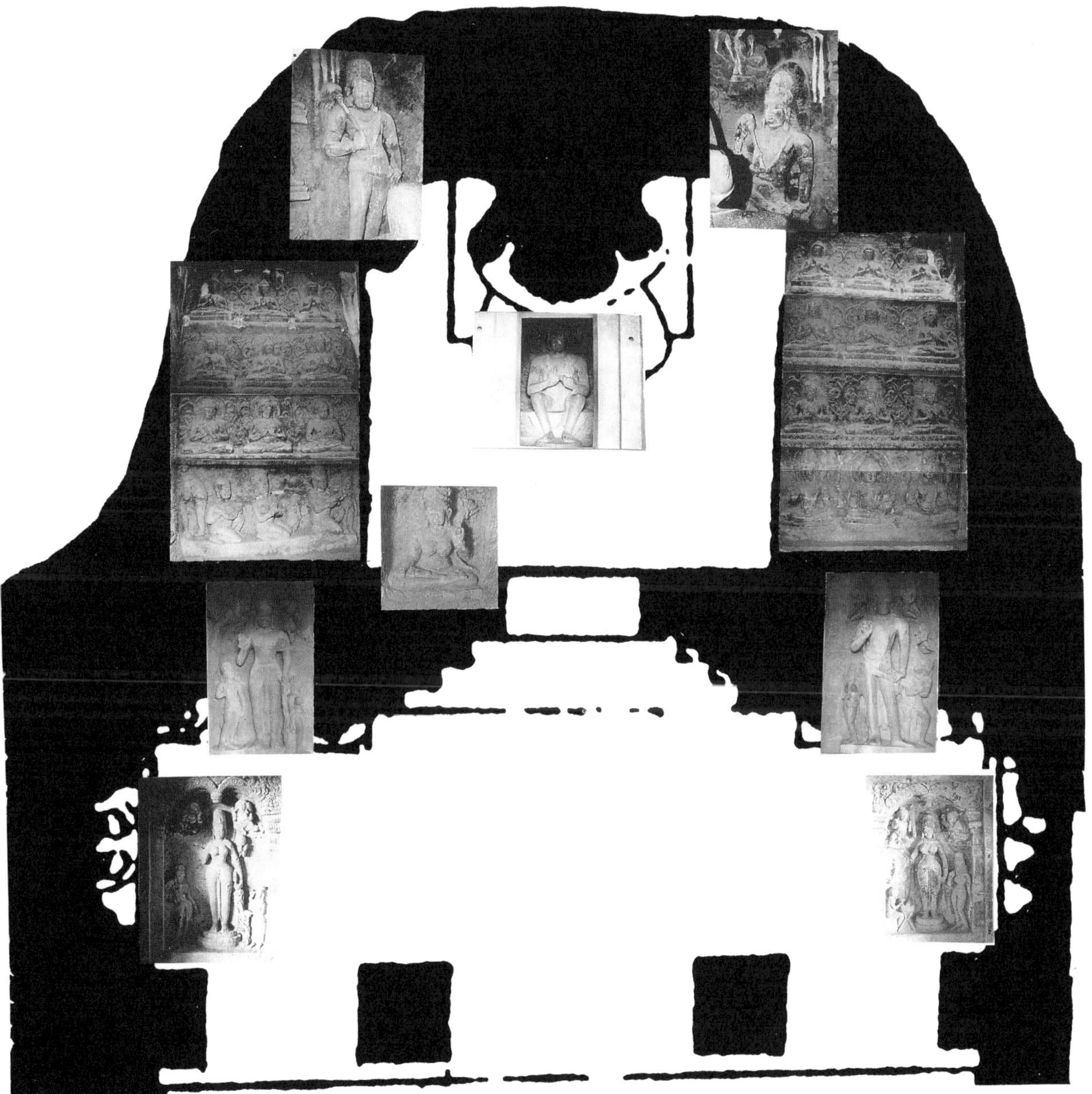

Text fig. 2–1   Cave 6 iconographic plan

Cave 6 is the presence of symmetrically carved, square niches above each hall pillar on the side facing the central hall, most probably contemporary with work on the pillars themselves (Fig. 25). They may have been placed there to hold wooden cross-beams, in order to support a sort of ceiling. This recalls the description given by the Chinese pilgrim-monk, I-tsing, of worship in a seventh-century north Indian monastery, where a canopy was stretched over the courtyard before the morning worship of the shrine image.[10]

Facing the antechamber (Fig. 28) the worshiper can see Bodhisattva or door guardians and the central Buddha image within the shrine. Hidden from direct view, at either end of the antechamber are large-scale relief panels depicting female deities, Bhṛkuṭī to the left (Fig. 31) and Mahāmāyūrī to the right (Fig. 32), forming the outermost "ring" of the core *maṇḍala*. Their importance as framing devices, shared with Hindu goddesses in Cave 21 (Fig. 22, 23) and 14, has been amplified in the new *maṇḍala*. Here, the image of Bhṛkuṭī—one of the earliest in India—with her stylized ascetic's knotted hair arrangement and animal skin shawl, seems to represent a feminine emanation of asceticism.[11] The meaning of the Mahāmāyūrī image at the other end of the antechamber (literally, "The Great Pea Hen"), a protective deity, who was most popular in China, also unprecedented in the western caves, is underscored by the relief carving of a peacock in this composition. (See chapter 5 for a discussion of the iconography of these images). The association of Bhṛkuṭī and Mahāmāyūrī is unusual elsewhere but, as will be described here, consistent at Ellora and, thus, a key to the idea of a single *maṇḍala* as the inspiration for its iconography.

At the Cave 6 shrine doorway, the worshiper next encounters larger than life-size images of Avalokiteśvara (left) (Fig. 33, 34) and Maitreya (right) (Fig. 21, 35). Iconographically these figures have clear Buddhist identities, but compositionally they are direct descendants of the Ellora style of *dvārapāla* (door guard) closely allied to their Hindu predecessors in Cave 21 (Fig. 19) and other early caves. Avalokiteśvara as *dvārapāla* and shrine attendant to the Buddha remains almost unchanged throughout the history of Ellora. As

dvārapāla he stands upright, hair arranged in a tall *jaṭāmukuṭa* (knotted or matted hair arrangement), with a small image of the Jina Buddha, Amitābha, in its center. Instead of jewelry he wears an *ajina* (antelope skin) draped over his left shoulder, with a lotus stalk supporting a large bud or open blossom twisted around his left arm. He holds an *akṣamālā* (rosary) in his upraised right hand. The identification of the right door guardian is not so secure, although the consistent pairing of him with Avalokiteśvara as guards to a *dharma-cakramudrā* shrine Buddha, suggests that this Bodhisattva should always be the same. Here in Cave 6, the *stūpa*-like crest jewel in his ornate *jaṭāmukuṭa* and his right hand held in *vitarkamudrā* (gesture of argumentation) are clues to his identification as Maitreya (see chapter 5 for a more detailed discussion of Bodhisattva iconography at Ellora).[12] Despite this uncertainty, the conventional Bodhisattva composition is clearly designed to focus the worshiper's attention before entering the shrine. Thus, the cherubs flying at shoulder level toward the viewer, the male attendants turned to look up at the Bodhisattva, and the voluptuous females at their feet entice the worshiper to stop at each image before approaching the sanctum. This profusion of detail, a carry-over from the style of earlier Brahmanical caves, will become muted in the succeeding Buddhist caves. Similarly, the river goddesses tucked into niches at either end of the shrine door lintel (Fig. 20) continue an older tradition that subsides after this.

As one faces the shrine in Cave 6 (Fig. 36) the Buddha image overwhelms all other impressions, but this should be the image considered last, at the center of the *maṇḍala* and, thus, the culminating point in its worship. First, to the left on the front, inside wall of the shrine are carved two small cross-legged, *dharmacakramudrā* Buddha images above a cross-legged image of the Buddhist goddess, Tārā, holding a lotus in her upraised left hand (Fig. 37). Carved roughly, these appear to be afterthoughts, and may not be a part of the original *maṇḍala*. Moving around clockwise, on the left shrine wall is the nine-part Buddha *maṇḍala* described above. Below the *maṇḍala* is a group of worshipers, accompanied by an elephant, making offerings to the shrine image.

Much reduced, this group carries forward a tradition established at Ajanta and extended at Aurangabad of placing carved images of worshipers in the shrines, another technique that startles the worshiper into a sense of involvement in the immanence of the *maṇḍala*.[13] Across the shrine, on the right wall, is the second *maṇḍala*, below which is a triad composed of the deities Avalokiteśvara, Jambhala, and Mañjuśī (Fig. 30). This may prefigure Jambhala's increasing prominence in later caves, together with Tārā or other female figures, as consistent and important internal door guards in the shrines.

The central shrine image, on the back wall, is guarded by two "generic" Bodhisattva figures. Holding fly whisks in their right hands, with left hands resting on the knots of their belts, they have no attributes that would suggest a more specific identification. They guard the Buddha, who sits in *pralambapādāsana* on a lion throne, hands held in *dharmacakramudrā*. The throne's square back is carved to represent a relatively standard variety of animal and human figures, a design widespread and persistent through the history of Buddhist art in India. *Makaras* serve as corner pieces of the throne; a long-necked bird emerges from their mouths. Beneath the *makaras* are rearing *vyālas* ridden by dwarfish men. The *vyālas* rear over elephants that form the bases of the throne back. The throne itself is supported by chubby lions that clearly identify the *siṁhāsana*. Such imagery, appearing as early as at Ajanta, one hundred and twenty-five years earlier, illustrates the conservative nature of the iconography of the Buddha image.[14]

Despite the traditional iconography of the throne area, it seems likely that the Buddha image was intended to represent a specific Buddha whose identification would help identify the *maṇḍala* as a whole. The focus of worship in nearly every shrine throughout the Mahāyāna Buddhist cave sites of the western Deccan is a Buddha image, almost always portrayed with hands held in *dharmacakramudrā*. This icon had remarkable longevity, from the late-fifth-century caves at Ajanta[15] to the sixth-century caves of Kanheri, Nasik, and Aurangabad,[16] to Ellora's early seventh-century excavations. Although the appearance and dissemination of Buddha images displaying the *dharmacakramudrā* gesture is familiar,[17] there is no consensus about the identity of those images. The "historical" interpretation, that it is a symbol of Śākyamuni delivering his first sermon, may be too narrow outside a context that includes depictions of other events in the life of the Buddha. It therefore seems likely that these images follow a trend that developed from the sixth or seventh century onward, when the historic Buddha (Śākyamuni) ceased to be as important an object of meditation as were his emanations in the form of the five *tathāgatas*: Vairocana, Akṣobhya, Ratnasambhava, Amitābha, and Amoghasiddhi.[18] These figures are most commonly identified by the position of the hands (*mudrā*). For instance, Vairocana holds his hands in *bodhyagrīmudrā*,[19] a variant of the *dharmacakramudrā* so common in Buddha images from Ajanta to Ellora. In eastern India, the whole system of five Buddhas was portrayed, but in the Western cave sites it was not represented systematically.

At Ellora, the changing *mudrās* of the shrine images, especially in the later Buddhist caves, implies that some version of a multi-*tathāgata* system did have at least limited influence.[20] Thus, with *dharmacakramudrā*, the Cave 6 Buddha image might be seen as representing Vairocana, who in early tantric texts like the *Mañjuśrīmūlakalpa*, is usually described in a triad that includes the attendants Avalokiteśvara and Vajrapāṇi.[21] Identification of the proper right attendant as Avalokiteśvara is clear. However, the proper left attendant is not so easily identified since in Cave 6, as in Ellora's other early Buddhist caves, the figure does not hold the *vajra*, Vajrapāṇi's usual attribute. Here, based on the *stūpa*-like jewel in the *jaṭāmukuṭa* and right hand in *vitarkamudrā*, and on the likely connection between Cave 6 and Cave 5 (see below), I suggest that the Bodhisattva is Maitreya. Thus, the core of the earliest *maṇḍala* can be outlined schematically this way:

<pre>
                Buddha/Vairocana
         Nine Buddhas   Nine Buddhas
(Tārā)   Avalokiteśvara/Jambhala/Mañjuśri
     Avalokiteśvara   Maitreya
Bhṛkuṭī   Mahāmāyūrī
</pre>

29

This, the earliest expression of the *maṇḍala* here, immediately shows Ellora's uniqueness—a combination of deities not described together in any known text nor portrayed in a similar pattern at any other site.

Cave 5

Cave 5 (Fig. 4), an ambitious project excavated immediately to the south of Cave 6, seems not to have had extensive *maṇḍalic* importance although the iconography of its shrine area gives important clues for reading the iconography in Cave 6. (Images in its front "right wing" shrine, probably carved later than the central Cave 5 shrine, illustrate the development toward the *maṇḍala's* middle period.) This excavation, 117 feet long from the veranda to the back wall, is the largest of all the early Buddhist caves. It was most likely designed to be a recitation or instruction hall, similar to the so-called Darbar Cave 32 at Kanheri near Bombay,[22] with long, low ledges running down the center of the hall, that may have served as benches or desks for study (Fig. 38). The cave is arranged more symmetrically than its predecessor at Kanheri, with empty cells placed all around its perimeter, suggesting an active refinement process for a "new" plan.[23] Such functional differentiation as this is unusual in the western caves

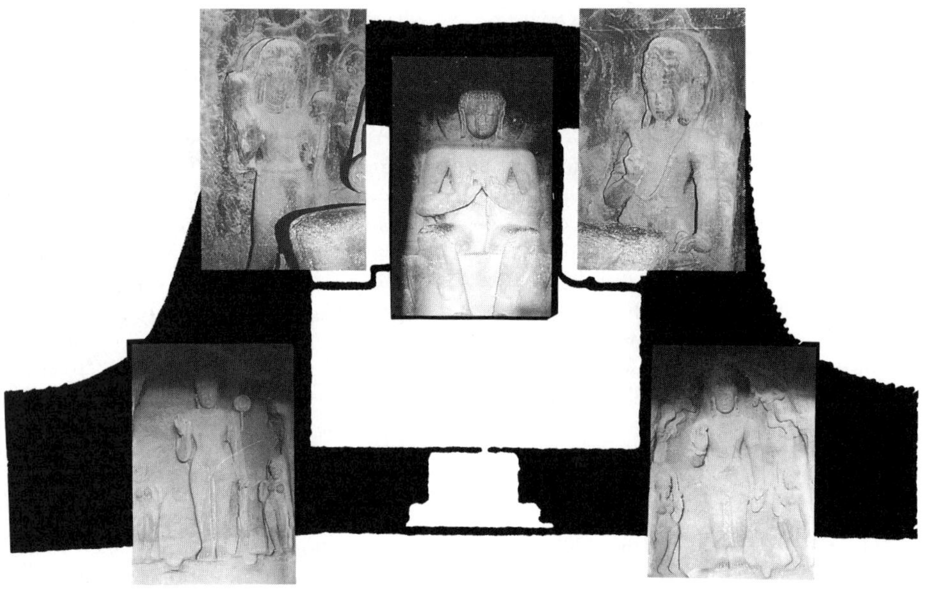

Text fig. 2–2   Cave 5 iconographic plan (shrine area only)

which, up to this period were generally divided into *vihāra* (residence) and *caitya* (worship) halls. The setting, planning, and architectural distinction of lecture and/or refectory halls, is more typical of Japanese temples of the Nara and Heian periods.[24]

Because of its proximity to Cave 6, the front shrines were not symmetrical. Instead, a small Buddha image was begun in the first cell on the left aisle inside the hall (Cell A in the plan). Here, only a *pralambapādāsana* Buddha and his right hand attendant were carved; blocks were left above for flying figures. This must have been part of the original plan of the cave since sufficient stone was left in front of this cell for a small pillared porch and an elaborate plinth whose moldings follow the pattern used in plinths of early Hindu Caves 17 and 14 and Buddhist Caves 2 and 3. Across the hall, another ambitious front shrine (Cave 5RW, see below) was excavated. Its style suggests that it was not contemporary with the original work in Cave 5, although its iconography relates it in part to Cave 6 as well as other early and middle period caves.

Despite these inconsistencies, the focal

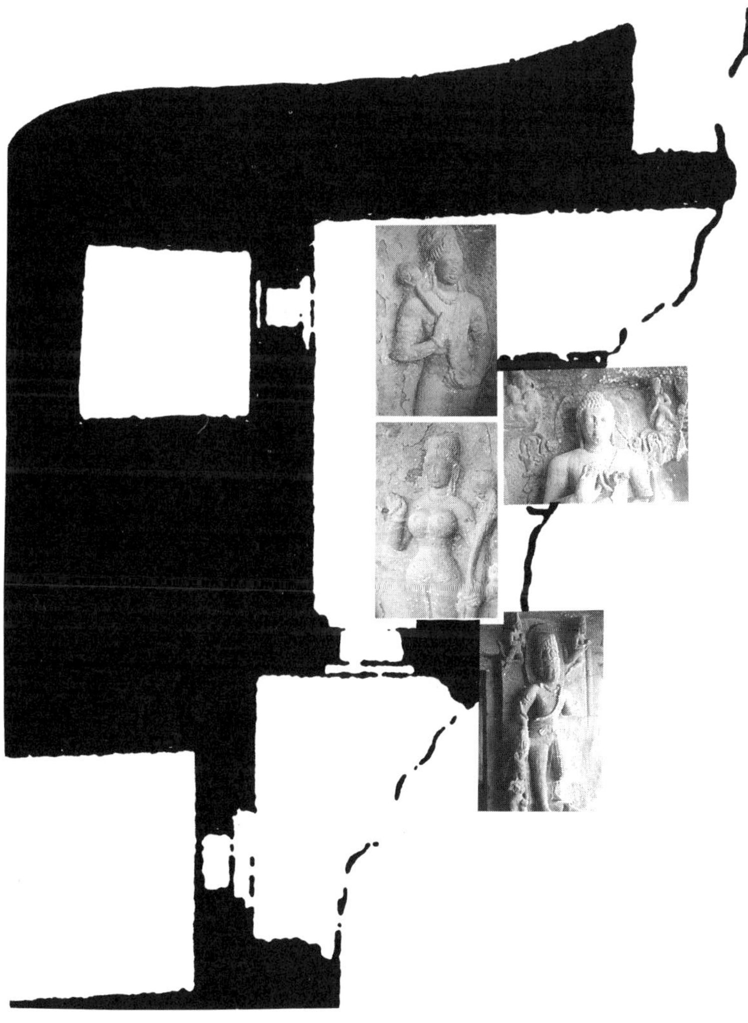

Text fig. 2–3   Cave 5RW iconographic plan

point of Cave 5—its shrine area—provides key information on the earliest stage of Ellora's core *maṇḍala.* Here, the program is limited to Bodhisattva shrine door guardians, and the Buddha image within, attended by a similar Bodhisattva pair. The shrine door guard groups (Fig. 40–42) were carved in hastily excavated arched recesses. In contrast to the polished style of the Cave 6 images, these appear out of proportion, with relatively short legs and large, heavy heads. On the left is Avalokiteśvara, attended by two indistinguishable females. Of particular importance is the right Bodhisattva, whose attributes are depicted very clearly, and seem to offer strong support for identification of the attendant in this position as Maitreya. The image holds a small, pointed-leaf flower in his right hand, perhaps representing a *campaka* blossom (an attribute of Maitreya in later texts and images). And a tall crest jewel, composed of several small balls stacked vertically, decorates his crown. This ornament may be interpreted as a *stūpa,* another emblem of Maitreya. Clearest in this image, a *stūpa*-like crest jewel appears in the crowns of other early Bodhisattvas in this position, suggesting that they may all represent Maitreya. No subsidiary attendants were carved on the left and those in the right group hover clumsily over the Bodhisattva's shoulders, one barely separated from the stone behind it. Holding symbols of wealth, they are connected to *nidhi* imagery that is so characteristic of Ellora, and which provides a key link to other Buddhist sites, as will be discussed in chapter 5.

Inside the shrine, the central figure is the Buddha/Vairocana—as in the Cave 6 *maṇḍala* hands held in *dharmacakramudrā* and seated in *pralambapādāsana* on a rudimentary lion throne. Like the shrine door attendants, the Buddha image here was coarsely carved, its robe decoration only a rough version of the delicate, double-edged ruffle of the Cave 6 Buddha image. The two shrine attendants repeat the iconography of the shrine door, Avalokiteśvara (Fig. 43) to the left and Maitreya to the right (now identified only by the *stūpa*-jewel in his crown) (Fig. 44). Traces of plaster on the shrine Bodhisattvas and throne betray the haste with which the cave was "completed" with the absolute minimum of sculp-

ture necessary to give the shrine area meaning. And, outside in the hall, Cave 5 lacks even the intrusive panels added to so many other unfinished Buddhist caves.

Cave 5RW

Cave 5RW provides important, if only partial confirmation of the composition of Ellora's early *maṇḍala.* It is one of several transitional excavations that bridge the distance in style and iconography between the earliest and latest groups of Buddhist caves. Individual elements of their iconography and their architectural plans, although not their style, are more comparable to components of the late sixth-century Aurangabad caves than to any others at Ellora. Entered from the court of Cave 5, Cave 5RW opens to the north, perpendicular to the usual west opening shrines of the larger caves, including Cave 4 below it. This "archaeological" observation has an important functional implication: because of the incongruence of the shrine orientation in Caves 5RW and 4 it is not likely, as is commonly held, that Cave 5RW was meant to be an upper story of Cave 4.[25] Instead, entered from Cave 5, and with lingering stylistic relationships to that cave, it seems more accurate to label it as a wing of Cave 5. Cave 5RW could not have been started until after the court in front of Cave 5 was finished because Cave 5RW can only be entered from this direction. As noted in appendix A, it is possible that Cave 5 was meant to have two symmetrical front shrines, Cave 5RW and a parallel (hypothetical) Cave 5 Left Wing, but lack of space between Cave 6 and 5 made this impossible.

Cave 5RW consists of a detached shrine that could be circumambulated, with two cells cut on the left (east) wall of the *pradakṣiṇapatha* (path for circumambulation). If cells had been added symmetrically on the right side, the cave would have been approximately ten feet wider than it is now and would have extended partially over the courtyard of Cave 4. Its plan connects the cave to the later Aurangabad caves where shrines could also be circumambulated, just as the worshiper would meditate one-by-one on images within var-

32

ious sections of a *maṇḍala*.[26] The front of 5RW has eroded, exposing its shrine image to view from the outside (Fig. 45). It is likely that at least the cell doorways on the east side of 5RW and the shrine doorway were carved soon after the cell doorways in Cave 5 since they share the same pattern of round and flat jambs, but only the first cell in Cave 5RW was carved; the second cell door is plain. Here the moldings were completely carved with relief designs: lotus petals on the outside, diagonal geometric patterns over the round molding, and a diamond-and-bead design on the innermost section, comparable to the small piece carved on the first cell door in Cave 5. This overall design has a long history that can be traced back to Ajanta, for example, in the porch doorway of Cave 26;[27] it continued through to the Aurangabad Cave 7 veranda windows. The doorways in Ellora Cave 5RW, lacking the innermost band of figures in small niches, are a simplified version of the earlier form. The complete carving of the two doorways in Cave 5RW, and the fact that the entire shrine area had been plastered, show that work on this cave proceeded much more quickly and thoroughly than it did in Cave 5, perhaps an indication of the ritual importance of this mini-shrine, mediating the entrance to the site's only lecture hall.

The eclectic nature of Cave 5RW deserves emphasis, showing the *maṇḍala* was subject to flexible interpretation at this early stage of its development, and utilizing artistic ideas tied to a number of sources at Ellora and beyond. For instance, the left *dvārapāla*'s high, smooth, cylindrical crown with its round crest jewel (Fig. 46) is most comparable to that of the right *dvārapāla* in Cave 6. In other respects, however, these images differ, for example, the *yajñopavīta* (sacred thread) of the Cave 5RW *dvārapāla* drapes down only to his waist, like *yajñopavītas* of other middle period images, whereas the Cave 6 *dvārapāla*'s *yajñopavīta* hangs down to his hip. Instead of the flat, wide, jeweled necklace worn by earlier *dvārapālas*, the figure in Cave 5RW wears a simple, single strand necklace of thick beads. This necklace, together with his tall crown, circular crest jewel and short *yajñopavīta* connect this image to the left (north) *dvārapāla* (Fig. 79) in Cave 4 as well as to the

proper left attendant of the Cave 4 shrine Buddha. The Cave 5RW *dvārapāla* is also comparable to a door guard on the porch of the Durgā temple at Aihole, datable to the late seventh century.[28] Both wear thick beaded necklaces, serpentine arm bands and waist-level "cloth" belts whose ends hang in flat bands down their thighs. The Cave 5RW *dvārapāla* probably also wore an upper belt like the one worn by the Durgā temple image; its traces are evidence in the lighter strip of stone above his waist. Furthermore, the similar proportions and style of carving of these figures, for example, the gentle curve of the chest area into the arm, suggest a similar chronological position. Yet the Cave 5RW example, being stiffer and more upright, is probably earlier; the one from the Durgā temple is closer to the exaggerated angularity of eighth-century Cālukya sculpture.

Inside the shrine of Cave 5RW, the *dharmacakramudrā* Buddha image is seated on a throne (Fig. 47) whose back is most like those found in Caves 5 and 6. This design preserves the old pattern with *makaras* resting on *vyālas* that rear over small elephants that support the sides of the throne back. By contrast, in nearly every shrine image of the intermediate and later periods—Caves 8, 9, 10, 11, and 12—the throne back has a different design, in which the crossbar at the top projects beyond the side, forming a "T"; the *makaras* then are placed above the "T" which is supported by the *vyālas*' heads. The syncretistic quality of the shrine style in Cave 5RW is demonstrated by the carving of the throne base lion whose puffy upper lip, arched back, and jauntily raised forepaw are most like the lion at the base of the throne in the Cave 8 shrine, where the throne back is of the new "T" type (Fig. 48, 49).

Other comparisons illustrate more clearly the affiliation of Cave 5RW with Cave 5. The Bodhisattva (Fig. 51) standing to the proper right of the shrine image in Cave 5RW is similar to the comparably placed figure in the Cave 5 shrine where this Bodhisattva, Avalokiteśvara, holds a rounded lotus bud; his hair is arranged in a relatively naturalistic *jaṭāmukuṭa* bound with horizontal strands of hair. The image of Avalokiteśvara in Cave 5RW also holds a round lotus bud, with both hands

33

in this case, and his hair is arranged in the same way, although the top of the arrangement is squarer than in the Cave 5 image.

Iconographically, Cave 5RW confirms partially the composition of the core *maṇḍala* seen more completely in the Cave 6 shrine. On the left (east) wall of the shrine is a standing image of Bhṛkuṭī (Fig. 50), holding an *akṣamālā* (rosary) and a lotus bud, with her hair arranged in a *jaṭāmukuṭa* similar to that of the image of Avalokiteśvara in the same shrine. The position of the image, on the left shrine wall, underscores its *maṇḍalic* orientation, even as it differs from the Cave 6 Bhṛkuṭī image, depicted in a more complex composition, wearing a tall, cylindrical *jaṭāmukuṭa*, and standing outside the shrine. These similarities suggest that while Cave 5 itself was not part of the *maṇḍalic* scheme of the caves, its function for teaching *was* mediated by the *maṇḍala*, which monks would have encountered as they entered first Cave 5RW, and then Cave 5.

The Maṇḍala *in Three Levels: Caves 2, 3, and 4*

Linked in location, style, and iconography, Caves 2, 3, and 4 may be viewed as a three-part *maṇḍala*, arranged horizontally in separate excavations.[29] Among them, Cave 2 was the most ambitious project, one of the most "expensive" early caves. It was planned to be approached up steps cut through a decorated plinth (only partially finished). Above the entrance, traces of tentative carving remain, suggesting that a second storey of façade decoration, at least, was planned (Fig. 52). Inside, its elaborate character is revealed by ten, nearly life-size Buddha images placed along its galleries, where they replaced the residential cells found in most other "*vihāra*"-type caves. In complexity Cave 2 is surpassed only by the later Caves 10, 11, and 12, and it provides key evidence for the nature of Ellora's earliest *maṇḍala*. Together with Caves 3 and 4, it provides in skeleton form the idea of a three-dimensional, three-layered *maṇḍala* most elaborately realized more than fifty

years later in the last Buddhist Cave 12, a three-storied excavation.

Cave 2

Cave 2 is linked by iconographical and architectural features to Cave 6, most significantly by their very similar shrine Buddha images, among the earliest at Ellora. Yet, patterns of incomplete features in Cave 2, together with differences in style among shrine, gallery, and front wall images, show that work on this excavation continued in at least two phases, over a longer period than did work in Cave 6, where its few major images are carved in a consistent style and are generally complete. Appropriate to its pioneering nature, Cave 2, as one of the earliest Buddhist caves is relatively crude: the gallery Buddha images are partially obscured from view by the hall pillars, sculpture of its second phase was hastily added in shallow panels, and in general, the cave lacks a finished appearance.

Its pillar style links Cave 2 with Caves 6 and 5 (see appendix A), but the program of the cave included features that were carved in differing styles perhaps not even in one period of excavation. At the same time, its iconographical clarity expresses Ellora's early *maṇḍala* more completely than does Cave 6, and suggests that a coherent plan unified these efforts in a program that encompasses sculpture on the veranda, around the perimeter of the hall, and in the shrine area.

On the veranda, three iconographical focal points remain. At the left end, tucked into a niche and surrounded by intrusive panels depicting Buddha images, is a figure of Jambhala (Fig. 56). Stylistically, this image has more in common with an image of Pāñcika in Aurangabad Cave 7 (see chapter 5 for a discussion of its iconography), but its location to the left of the entrance connects it to later images of Jambhala, which were placed to the left of the shrine door in Caves 11 and 12, and to a Pāñcika/Hārītī panel carved outside Cave 8. Across the veranda, at the right end, the only remaining sculpture is a female *chowrie*-bearer (Fig. 57), again closer in style to Aurangabad sculptures than to female figures in Ellora's earliest Buddhist caves. We can only

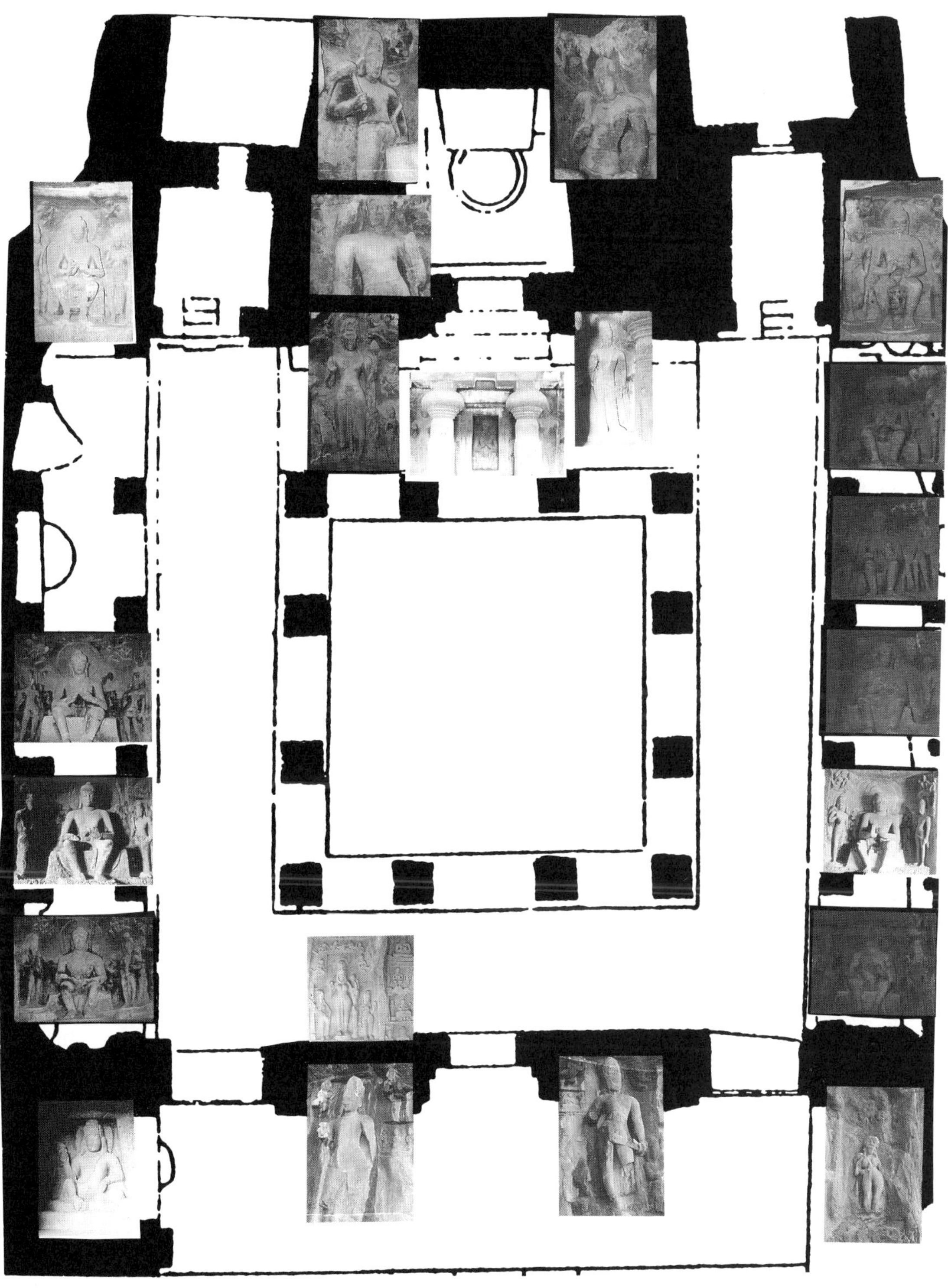

Text fig. 2–4   Cave 2 iconographic plan

postulate that the image originally attended a sculpture of Tārā, who is paired with Jambhala at entrances to the later Cave 11 and 12 shrines, positioned as guardians of the "central ring" of the *maṇḍala*. At the veranda door, imposing but iconographically indistinguishable Bodhisattvas serve as guardians, now much abraded, but originally attended by flying figures and standing attendants.

Immediately to the left of the door as one enters the Cave 2 hall is an image of Bhṛkutī (Fig. 58), surrounded by many intrusive panels. The image is not as polished as its counterpart in Cave 6, nor is the setting as elaborate, but her wide hips and the projecting fold of cloth between her legs illustrate their stylistic connections. In Cave 6, the Bhṛkutī image was placed at the left end of the shrine antechamber. In Cave 2, lacking this architectural feature, the image was moved to the front of the cave. Surrounded by intrusive panels, the Bhṛkutī in Cave 2 may appear to have been an afterthought. But, in Caves 6 and 5RW, the image was certainly part of the original plan. In Cave 2, if one circumambulates in the normal, clockwise direction, one passes first Bhṛkutī, then a row of seated Buddha images, and then confronts the image of Avalokiteśvara as *dvārapāla* before entering the shrine. Similarly, circumambulating Caves 6 and 5RW, one first encounters Bhṛkutī, then Avalokiteśvara and then the central shrine image. These similarities suggest that while the image may have been carved late, it was part of an original iconographical conception of Cave 2.

The most startling feature is the looming presence of ten Buddha images, carved in shallow recesses along the left and right galleries of the hall, three-dimensional counterparts of the Buddha-*maṇḍalas* in the Cave 6 shrine and precursors of the Buddhas flanking the hall on the third floor of Cave 12. These Buddhas are seated in *pralambapādāsana*, and all except the front, left image, were portrayed with hands held in *dharmacakramudrā*. This iconographical unity is not matched by style or state of completion. All five images carved along the right gallery were completed, each attended by two Bodhisattvas and flying figures (Fig. 60). Across the hall along the left gallery, only the first three of

the five images, whose narrow faces and broad, square shoulders suggest work by the same sculptor, were brought close to completion (Fig. 59). In the rearmost two niches the Buddha images themselves were begun but no cutting had started on attendant figures or throne decoration. By contrast, the ceiling moldings were finished to the back on the left side, while ceiling moldings on the right were not. In other words, sculptural and architectural features were being carved at different paces in different sections of the cave.

Such discontinuities are exemplified by the second Buddha image in the left gallery (Fig. 61). Here, neither flying figures nor throne bases were finished, but clearly discernable traces of plaster show that images could have been plastered, and presumably painted, as soon as sculptors stopped their work—even before all details had been carved.[30] Moreover, the style of the gallery Buddha images differs from that of the shrine group. For example, in the shrines of Caves 6, 5, and 2 the Buddha image wears a ruffle-edged robe, whereas the gallery Buddha images wear plain robes (like the robe worn by the Cave 3 shrine image, Fig. 68). The Buddha images carved along the left gallery in Cave 2 and the Cave 3 shrine image also have similar, long, narrow heads. And, the long-legged, slim flying figures inside the Cave 2 shrine are most like those in the Cave 6 shrine, while the shorter-limbed, fatter flying figures attending the second right gallery Buddha are more like those in the Cave 3 shrine. Here, iconographical organization is not matched by stylistic consistency.

The imposing shrine *dvārapālas* in Cave 2 are most similar to those in Cave 6, another key to its relatively early position in Ellora's development. As in Cave 6, in Cave 2 the right figure (Fig. 63) stands in a stiff *ābhaṅga* (bent) pose, legs held quite close together. The belts draped over the right leg of the Cave 2 image imitate, but do not duplicate the profusion of decorative garb on the Cave 6 guard, a carryover from the style of the earlier Brahmanical caves. Female attendants of the Cave 6 and 2 *dvārapālas* occupy a similar position, but in Cave 2 the integration of the composition has been lost, as the woman is closer to the doorway than to the guard, and no longer stands on a pedestal with the other figures. This group was never completed, showing that work must have been interrupted during an important phase in the sculptural elaboration of Cave 2. Where a cross-armed male attendant to the *dvārapāla* would be expected by analogy to the Cave 6 group, and to balance the outer attendant of the left *dvārapāla* in Cave 2 itself (Fig. 62), there are only small, instrusive, crudely carved panels. Nor was the shrine door frame finished; only the right (south) door frame is decorated, with a diamond-and-foliage pattern carved in low relief.

Within the shrine the program is relatively simple, repeating only some of the features of the early Cave 6 *maṇḍala*. Apart from the central Buddha image and its Bodhisattva attendants, the only other major figures are larger than life-size standing images of the Buddha as monk, carved on the right and left walls. Next to them, in the left and right front corners, groups of four worshipers, now rotated ninety degrees from their position in the Cave 6 shrine, were carved vertically, facing the main Buddha image. (Their position is most comparable to the groups of three Buddhas carved immediately to the left and right of the shrine Buddha image in Aurangabad Cave 7.)[31] The shrine Bodhisattva attendants to the Buddha are, again, Avalokiteśvara to the left (Fig. 65), holding a stylized, round, open lotus, and to the right, Maitreya (Fig. 66), holding no distinguishing attribute, but wearing a distinctive, high, peaked crown with a *stūpa*-like crest jewel (almost identical to the one in the Cave 3 shrine; see below).

The Cave 2 shrine Buddha image (Fig. 64), like the one in Cave 6, has a double-ruffled robe edge with narrow folds near the hem. The closeness of their stylistic, as well as iconographic, relationship can also be seen in the throne backs, supported by relatively small figures and sharply rearing *vyālas*. Other small details connect its style to Aurangabad Cave 7 such as the upright posture and relatively small head of the throne base lion, and the throne back, where a long-necked bird emerges from the *makara*'s mouth.

A last component of the Cave 2 program with possible significance for the *maṇḍala* was barely begun: dual subsidiary shrines cut several steps up at ends of the left and right aisles. On both sides, a double cell, or perhaps vestibule and cell were roughly cut, but no sculptures were carved in the left one. In the right cell, relief panels were carved on the left and right walls of the vestibule, depicting cross-legged Buddha images with hands held in *dharmacakramudrā*, attended by identical monks, similar to the intrusive panels carved in the front of Cave 2 and on the veranda. Unfortunately the main image, which should be on the rear cell wall, was not carved, so it is not possible to determine what the meaning of these shrines might have been. However, even these incomplete signs suggest some connection to the programs of Caves 6 and 7 at Aurangabad, where similar dual subsidiary shrines were placed in the rear corners of both excavations, holding seated images of the Buddha/Vairocana, but so small as to make entrance very difficult. In Ellora Cave 2, by contrast, despite their incomplete state, these shrines appear to have had greater importance since they are large enough to enter more easily.

The outline of the Cave 2 *maṇḍala* may be depicted as below, a condensed preview of the *maṇḍala* as it was to unfold into the three-tier complexity of Cave 12:

<pre>
[Buddha?]   [Buddha?]
          Buddha/Vairocana
          Avalokiteśvara   Maitreya
          Buddha monk   Buddha monk
          Avalokiteśvara   Maitreya
     Five Buddhas   Five Buddhas
       Bhṛkuṭī
       Bodhisattva   Bodhisattva
     Jambhala   [Tārā?]
</pre>

Cave 3

Like Cave 2, Cave 3 was planned on an impressive scale (see reconstruction, plan Fig. 3), and represents core elements of the same *maṇḍala*, but with significant additions and differences. Its veranda extends down to the present cliff edge in an elaborate series of plinth moldings and steps (Fig. 67). But only the right side of the plinth was completed; as was the case with Cave 2, in Cave 3 the exterior area was never finished. The large scale

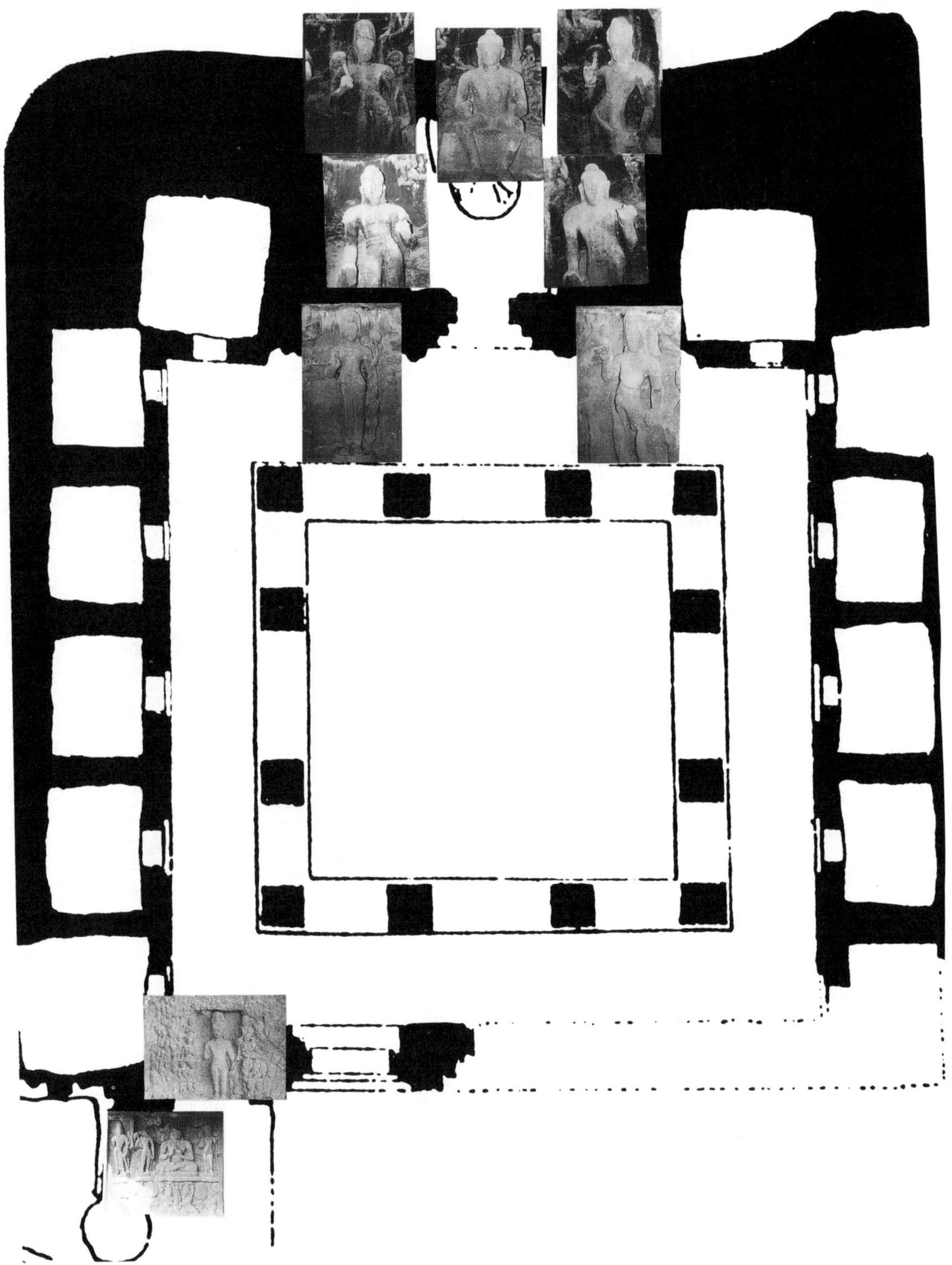

Text fig. 2–5   Cave 3 iconographic plan

of this approach area, together with a massive central door, of which only the left jamb remains, and marks where pillars would have supported a porch roof, show that the cave entrance was conceived, but not finished, to match the grandeur of the entrance to Cave 2.

Despite its ambitious start, Cave 3 was not carried as far as Cave 2. Five cells were cut along its left wall, while only four were cut into the right side, which is missing the frontmost cell. There might have been room for the fifth, although it would have come very close to the left end of the Cave 2 veranda, a sign that Cave 3 was blocked out after Cave 2. Instead, a cistern was excavated in this space.

Work on Cave 3 probably began shortly after major work on Cave 2 ended. The similarity between the shrine image in Cave 3 (Fig. 68) and the Buddha images carved along the left gallery of Cave 2 has already been mentioned. Only the most important sculptures in Cave 3 were completed, probably to make the cave functional as soon as possible. Once this stage was reached, no further work was carried out, as in Cave 5, which by this time had been brought to a similar functional if not aesthetically complete state. Apart from the shrine, there are no other programmatic features in Cave 3 and there, the program of sculptures duplicates the shrine program in Cave 2. The shrine *dvārapāla* groups are the first to reveal this similarity: the hairstyle, lotus, and attendant figure of the left door guardian, Avalokiteśvara, (Fig. 69) are nearly identical to their counterparts in Cave 2, although the figures in the Cave 3 group are spaced further apart. The right group around Maitreya as *dvārapāla* is more complete (Fig. 70); instead of panels to the guard's left as in Cave 2, in Cave 3 the right guard has cherubs and attendants on both sides. Perhaps in Cave 3, where work concentrated only on the shrine area, the iconographic scheme could be completed while in Cave 2, where more projects were underway, it was more difficult to finish everything. This Bodhisattva (Fig. 71) holds a rounded bud in his upraised right hand, perhaps a blossom of the *nāgakesara* tree, his later cognizance.

The similarity between the shrines in Caves 3 and 2 is revealed by even small de-

tails. For example, the left Bodhisattva attendants to the shrine Buddha, images of Avalokiteśvara, hold stylized flat, open lotuses (Fig. 65, 72). And the right attendants (Fig. 66, 73), probably Maitreya, wear distinctive straight-sided, peaked crowns. The rest of the shrine program repeats that of Cave 2, too: standing monk-Buddhas on the side walls, and worshipers carved vertically into the front shrine corners.

The concentration on the Cave 3 shrine area occurred at the expense of architectural details in the hall. Not one of the twelve pillars in this area was completely carved. This is another case, like that of Cave 6, where sculptural programs were completed before pillars. Those that went beyond initial blocking had rather heavy, square bases and a narrow, round fluted neck that supported a plain pot-and-foliage capital; this design is related to that of the side cell pillars in Cave 5. Cave 3, unlike Cave 2, did have cells cut around the central hall, but their doorways were only roughly blocked out, giving the cave a utilitarian atmosphere.

A significant, if roughly cut, addition to the Cave 3 veranda is a panel depicting Aṣṭamahābhaya Avalokiteśvara (Fig. 74). Here, the poor proportions of the central Bodhisattva, especially his overly large head, are like those of a small image of the same deity added to the right (south) wall of the cell cut between Caves 3 and 4 (marked "A" on the plan of Cave 4, Fig. 3), and called "Cave 3A" here. This large-headed style may also be compared to that of the right *dvarapala* in Cave 5 with its large head, tall but flat hair arrangement, and open lotus. Work on these poorly executed images was probably close in time.

This form of Avalokiteśvara as savior from the "eight great perils" was common in Buddhist caves of western India, appearing first at Ajanta,[32] and then in the sixth century at Kanheri[33] and Aurangabad where the simpler image of Avalokiteśvara as *dvārapāla* was replaced by a colossal, formal Aṣṭamahābhaya composition.[34] The larger scale Aṣṭamahābhaya Avalokiteśvara (Fig. 75) found in Ellora Cave 3A appears to have been a component of this cell's original program, but the main figure is so damaged that its style is not clear and, to further ruin it, a door was cut into the wall through what must have been the right side of the scene. This suggests that the cell was carved before the court of Cave 4, which is entered through this very low door, and that therefore, Cave 3A should be considered as a subsidiary part of the Cave 3 program, and the *maṇḍala* it represents, as Cave 5RW mediates the entrance to Cave 5. What is left of the composition, on its left side, depicts the perils of fire, sword, fetters, and shipwreck. This order, although not the style of carving, is also found on the left side of the Aurangabad Cave 7 image, linking these scenes more closely than others in the Western caves, where the order and even number of perils differ.[35] Yet the clumsy treatment of the Ellora images, and their placement in peripheral areas, contrasts with the carefully sculpted images from Aurangabad and earlier sites. This carelessness reflects the decreasing importance of this form of Avalokiteśvara, where in the new doctrine expressed at Ellora, other icons replaced it.

Next in clockwise order in Cave 3A is a small image of Bhṛkutī, located to the left of the main shrine group as are the Bhṛkutī images in Caves 6 and 2 (Fig. 76). Here, the sculptural style and proportions are most like the Cave 2 Bhṛkutī, with high breasts, and a thick fold of cloth between the legs. Across this cell, that is, on the right or south wall, images of Avalokiteśvara, the Buddha, and another Bhṛkutī were carved, but without apparent connection among them, an indication of the disrupted nature of these subsidiary areas in the Cave 2 through 4 group.

The central image of Cave 3A is a Buddha attended by two Bodhisattvas and four clumsy cherubs (Fig. 78). The proper right attendant to the Buddha (Fig. 76) wears a neater version of the hair arrangement worn by the image of Avalokiteśvara in the Cave 3 veranda. The knotted hair of the right attendant (Fig. 77) has no precedent at Ellora nor is it like crowns of Bodhisattvas from other sites of this period although a somewhat similar arrangement is found on an attendant figure in Aurangabad Cave 7.[36]

Combining this small outer section with Cave 3, this part of the *maṇḍala* holds:

Cave 3
Buddha/Vairocana

Avalokiteśvara	Maitreya
Buddha monk	Buddha monk

Avalokiteśvara Maitreya

Cave 3A
Buddha/Vairocana

Avalokiteśvara   Mañjuśrī
Aṣṭamahābhaya Avalokiteśvara   Bhṛkutī

Cave 4

Like Cave 5RW (and Cave 8, to be discussed in the next section), Cave 4 has both a unique plan and new iconographic features, presented in a style developed at Ellora itself. Its style is connected to Cave 5RW, while its plan and iconography anticipate, as do parts of Cave 8, elements found in the latest Buddhist Caves 11 and 12.

Cave 4 appears to be squeezed into the space under Cave 5RW and to the north of Cave 3. Set at a slight angle to Cave 3, it was not cut as deeply into the cliff as were Caves 2 and 3 and compared to them is relatively small, consisting of a high-walled square forecourt separated from a narrow vestibule by four pillars, with three cells cut into the back wall (Fig. 3). Lacking residence cells, Cave 4 could not have functioned as a *vihāra*, nor was it conceived on the scale of a worship hall like Cave 2 or 6. Its plan is most like that of the first floor of Cave 11 (Fig. 8), a much larger excavation, where again, a courtyard leads to a long, narrow vestibule with three cells cut in the rear wall. This is one of several features that connect Cave 4 with later caves.

Much of this cave is unfinished; most walls are still very rough and relief decoration on the pillars was never begun. On the back wall, just enough surface was cleared to accommodate the *dvārapālas*. The left (north) cell doorway was plain but neatly carved, while the right cell doorway was not even cut squarely. Only the left side of the central, shrine doorway has relief decoration although here, too, there are incomplete sections. In style, it is most like the shrine doorjamb of Hindu Cave 27 (Fig. 81, 82).

As one approaches the shrine area, the first

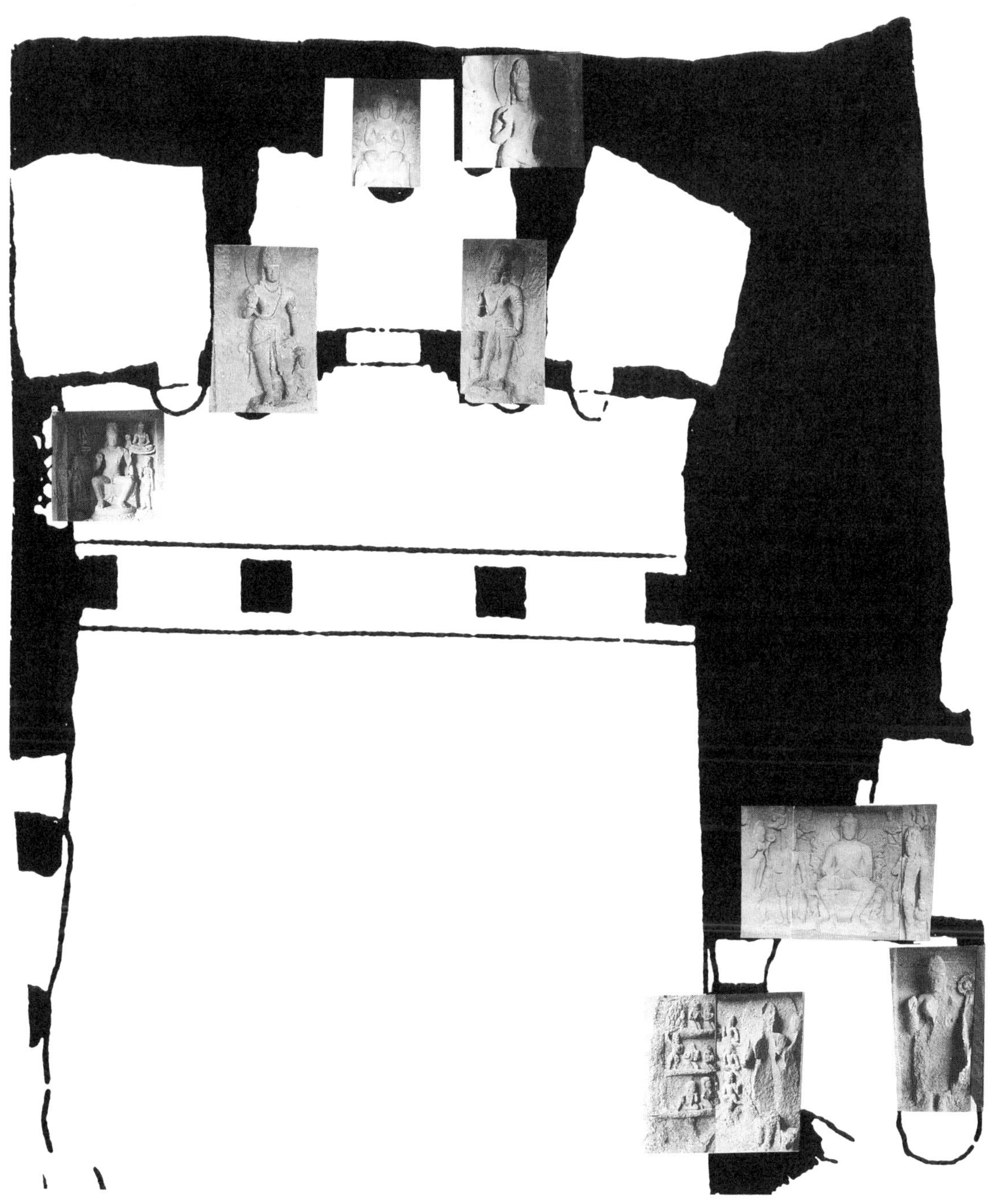

Text fig. 2–6   Cave 4 iconographic plan

image of note is an important and finely sculpted panel at the left end of the antechamber (Fig. 83) depicting Avalokiteśvara as Rakta-Lokeśvara. The earliest image to be carved in the Western caves, its composition, but not its style, is most comparable to early seventh-century sculptures from eastern India.[37] In location, it must be connected with the groups carved in the left courtyard cell of Cave 11 and on the second floor of Cave 12 (see below) but stylistically, this image is most similar to sculptures in Cave 8. For instance, the hairstyles of the female images are most comparable to similar images in Caves 5RW and Cave 8. (The nearly featureless faces reflect the growing importance of plaster as a finishing medium. No plaster remains in Cave 4, but in Caves 11 and 12, most facial features and ornaments were made of plaster, and where the plaster is gone, as in Cave 4, the facial contours of the sculptures have a distinctively flat appearance.)

The central image in this panel is Avalokiteśvara, seated in *pralambapādāsana*, a pose hitherto reserved for Buddha images. His right hand is raised in *abhayamudrā* and holds an *akṣamālā*. His left hand, resting on his knee, holds the stem of a large lotus bud. His hair is arranged in a tall *jaṭāmukuṭa* with a small Jina Buddha seated in the center. A standing Buddha image is carved at his left shoulder; another sits cross-legged on the left. At ground level, an image of Bhṛkuṭī (Fig. 84) stands on the left (her position in Caves 6, 5, and 2), holding the ascetic's pot (*kamaṇḍalu*) in her left hand, and the ascetic's *akṣamālā* in her right. Her hair also is arranged in a neat *jaṭāmukuṭa*. To the right is an image of Tārā (Fig. 85), holding a bouquet of flowers in her right hand. The care with which this panel was carved, and its position in the *maṇḍala* "ring" around the Cave 4 shrine image, contrasts strongly with the clumsy Aṣṭamahābhaya Avalokiteśvara images in Caves 3 and 3A, and suggests that Rakta-Lokeśvara replaced Avalokiteśvara, the savior from perils, as the icon used to guide meditation on this important Bodhisattva.

At the shrine door, the *dvārapālas* are comparable in style to the *dvārapāla* in Cave 5RW, with their extremely high, elaborate, cylindrical crowns, simple necklaces, and short

yajñopavītas. The right Bodhisattva image inside the shrine also shares this style (Fig. 79, 80). The curly hair of the dwarf next to the left *dvārapāla* reflects a coarsened version of the naturalism in the Cave 5RW hairstyles. These figures are most significant because they are not the usual pair of Avalokiteśvara on the left and Vajrapāṇi or Maitreya on the right. Instead, they are nearly identical. In the first floor of Cave 12 (Cave 12.1) a similar pair guards the shrine door, another connection between Cave 4 and the latest Buddhist caves.

Inside the shrine, the main sculptures are the *dharmacakramudrā* Buddha image (Fig. 86) and its proper left attendant (Fig. 87), both carved in the rear wall. The other three shrine walls were left in extremely rough condition. The base of the Buddha's throne is a plain block, but the throne back was carved in flat relief, decorated in the "old" style pattern like the one in Cave 5RW, without a "T"-shaped crossbar. Here, large *chowrie*-bearers stand behind the throne, in a similar position to that held by *nāgas* behind the throne in the Cave 12.1 shrine. Above the Buddha's head is a tree with frothy foliage, an anomaly in the early and middle period caves at Ellora although, in Cave 12.3, images of seven Buddhas seated under trees were carved on the back, left side of the hall. The Bodhisattva, with a *stūpa*-like jewel in his hair, and hand closed over the stem of a flower, is probably Maitreya.

This important "first level" of the *maṇḍala* contains the following elements:

Buddha/Vairocana

Maitreya

Bodhisattva   Bodhisattva

Rakta-Lokeśvara

Bhṛkuṭī   Tārā

Caves 2, 3, and 4: A Three-Part *Maṇḍala*

Returning to the connection between Ellora's earlier and latest caves, it is significant that in some ways the shrine area of Cave 4 is more like the first floors of Caves 11 and 12 than any other excavation. As in Cave 12.1, Avalokiteśvara and Vajrapāṇi/Maitreya are conspicuously missing as shrine attendants of the Buddha. Instead, in both shrines, large *chowrie*-bearers or *nāgas* stand behind the throne. Furthermore, the Cave 4 shrine *dvāra-pālas* are not the usual, differentiated pair; instead they are nearly identical. In Cave 12.1, too, the *dvārapālas* are not Avalokiteśvara and Vajrapāṇi. Instead, to the left of the door is an image of Maitreya, and to the right, an image of Mañjuśrī. And, like the first floor of Cave 11, Cave 4 is little more than a veranda, whose approach is "mediated" by an image of Rakta-Lokeśvara to the left.

These similarities suggest that Cave 4 may have prefigured the program of Caves 11.1 and 12.1. This is important because it suggests that Caves 4, 3, and 2 may have been three tiers of a *maṇḍala* analogous to the three-floored *maṇḍala* in Caves 11 and 12. The similarity in the arrangement of Buddha images along the side walls of Caves 2 and 12.3 can then be seen to be part of a more systematic relationship between earlier and later caves. Even Cave 3 and Cave 12.2 (the middle levels) are loosely linked by the fact that the shrine programs of Caves 12.2 and 12.3 are nearly identical, as they are in Caves 3 and 2. Thus, Cave 4, not much more than an entrance hall, would have functioned as did the first floor of Cave 12; Cave 3, like the second floor of Cave 12; and Cave 2 as the top, or third floor.[38] With their unified programs and style, the conscious expression of the ritual connection among the three floors of Cave 12 is clear. By contrast, even if Caves 2, 3, and 4 were connected by a *maṇḍala*, there could have been a period of twenty or more years before all three "levels" could function simultaneously, since Cave 2 (the "top" floor) appears to have been started first and Cave 4, the "first" floor, was completed later in a different style. In other words, the order of excavation actually inverted the ritual order of the caves. This would generally have been the case in Cave 12, also, where excavation and then carving started at the top and moved down.

3. *CAVES OF THE MIDDLE PERIOD: THE MAṆḌALA GROWS*

Cave 8 and 8A

The transitional and syncrestistic qualities of Cave 8 make it one of the more interesting and important Buddhist excavations at Ellora. Sharing elements of its plan, shrine iconography and sculptural style with Cave 5RW, it is more complex than that relatively small shrine, and more completely reflects the middle stage of the *maṇḍala*'s development. Cave 8 is also noteworthy for numerous, if unsystematic, parallels between its imagery and that of Aurangabad Caves 6, 7, and 9, where another set of *maṇḍalas* is likely to have determined the layout of the temples.

Its three-part plan is unique among the Buddhist excavations (Fig. 6). In the frontmost of these sections is a small shrine (labeled Cave 8A here), cut in the north wall, not much larger than sculptural panels found in the antechambers of other caves. At the left (west) end of this section is an empty area with smoothly finished walls. It was, prepared to hold moveable sculptures, as may also have been the case in the empty cells in Cave 5.[1] Passing between two pillars one reaches the second section, an astylar, square hall with three cells cut into the left (north) wall. Two pillars also frame the entrance to the third section that contains the shrine with circumambulatory passage. Three more cells are cut in the left wall of this section, and the back (east) wall behind the shrine is extended into a wide, two-pillared cell, similar to the "wing" in Cave 5, but without subsidiary cells cut around it. As described in appendix A, cells could not be added to the right (south) wall of Cave 8 because they would have broken through to Cave 7.

The detached shrine in Cave 8 is the most distinctive element of its plan. Although the same idea was used in Aurangabad Caves 6 and 7, the plans of these caves are quite unlike the plan of Cave 8.[2] For example, both Aurangabad caves are entered through a narrow, four-pillared vestibule, they have three cells cut into the side walls of their main halls, as well as two cells in the *pradakṣiṇapatha* behind the shrine, and the shrine area is proportionately much larger there than in Ellora Cave 8. Instead, Cave 8 is most like Cave 14, where the detached shrine is set in the rear one-third of the cave, preceded by a large pillared hall. So, although Cave 8 shares with the Aurangabad caves the concept of a detached shrine used in a Buddhist context, the artisans who worked on Cave 8 most likely followed local architectural practices.[3]

Local architectural ideas are further illustrated by the pillar types in Cave 8, which follow the patterns used earlier in Cave 5. For example, the pillars at the front of the hall and the pilasters at the junction of the hall and shrine area are decorated with plain pot-and-foliage capitals, fluted neckings, and incised circular designs at the top of their square bases, like the rear and side-wing pillars in Cave 5. The pillars in front of Cave 8A and in front of the shrine in Cave 8, like those in front of the shrine in Cave 2, are fluted cushion capital pillars with petals draped over the top of each flute. Except for the petal overlay, these pillars are also comparable to those carved in the hall of Cave 5, with only two, not three, scalloped bands beneath the cushion, and a shorter fluted shaft. Similar pillars were also used to frame the shrine in Cave 9 where the exaggerated edge of the Cave 8 pillars' scalloped bands is duplicated. In Cave 8A, the fluted cushion capital pillars are slimmer and anticipate the court level cell pillars of Cave 10, where the cushions became more compressed and proportionately wider compared to their shafts. These features show the transitional nature of Cave 8, intermediate between early caves like Caves 5 and 2, and middle period caves like Caves 9 and 10.

The iconographic program of Cave 8 begins outside, to the left (west) of the entrance, with a relief panel depicting Pāñcika and Hārītī, holding a child on her knee (Fig. 88). This image is significant not simply as a new component of the Buddhist *maṇḍala* at Ellora, but also (as will be discussed in chapter 5) as a key marker in the diffusion of symbolism of wealth and fecundity in the *maṇḍala* across the central part of India. Ellora's Cave 8 composition is most likely inspired by the same beliefs that are behind a similar panel found in Aurangabad Cave 7, itself a reduction from the complex narrative of the Pāñcika-Hārītī panel in Ajanta Cave 2.[4] However, the locations of the Ellora and Aurangabad panels differ. At Aurangabad it is carved on the right side of the main hall of Cave 7, not outside the cave. Also, the style of the Ellora image is drier, characterized by hard, schematic ridges of fat under Pāñcika's neck and over his stomach, and by his thick rolls of hair. By comparison, the Aurangabad figures are corpulent, smooth-fleshed, and have a softer surface.[5] The style of the Cave 8 Pāñcika is, in fact, closer to that

of the small *nidhi* (auspicious being) placed to the left of the small female attendant of the left shrine door guard in Aurangabad Cave 6.[6] Like Ellora's Cave 8 Pāñcika, this small figure has a hard roll of flesh over his stomach, thick roll curls, a single-strand beaded necklace and flat-sided crown decorated with a pointed, arch-shaped front medallion. Even closer in style, however, is another image from Ellora, located to the left (north) side of the veranda of an unnumbered cave between Brahmanical Caves 19 and 20 (Fig. 89).[7] In both, the main figure has thick rolled hair curls, hard ridges of fat, a flat-sided crown and a single-strand, thick beaded necklace. Such similarities suggest that approximately contemporary work went on at Cave 8 and in the Brahmanical center of activity further north. The local continuity of these features is further illustrated by the smooth style and iconographic details: pot belly and mongoose-skin bag, of an early-eighth-century image of Kubera in Cave 25 (Fig. 91).

Cave 8A

As in Cave 4, another middle-period cave, the entrance to Cave 8 is emphasized by a small subsidiary shrine, Cave 8A, which shares the sculptural style of most images in the rest of Cave 8. In this shrine, attention focuses both on a *dharmacakramudrā* Buddha (Fig. 92) and also on an image of Avalokiteśvara serving not so much an attendant role to the Buddha as one of parallel importance. This image of Avalokiteśvara (Fig. 93), still in its traditional position to the left of the Buddha, occupies the entire left wall of the Cave 8A shrine. But first on the left, is an image of Tārā (Fig. 94) standing in a gentle *abhaṅga* pose whose crown, jewelry, and clothing are most similar to the image of Tārā inside the Cave 8 shrine (Fig. 102). This Tārā holds a small bouquet of buds and flowing leaves, probably an *utpalamañjarī* (bouquet of blue lotuses), mentioned in texts describing Tārā. The bouquet is most comparable to the one held by the small female attendant to the left *dvārapāla* in Aurangabad Cave 6 where three different buds[8] and a long, drooping leaf are clearly depicted. A similar, but larger

46

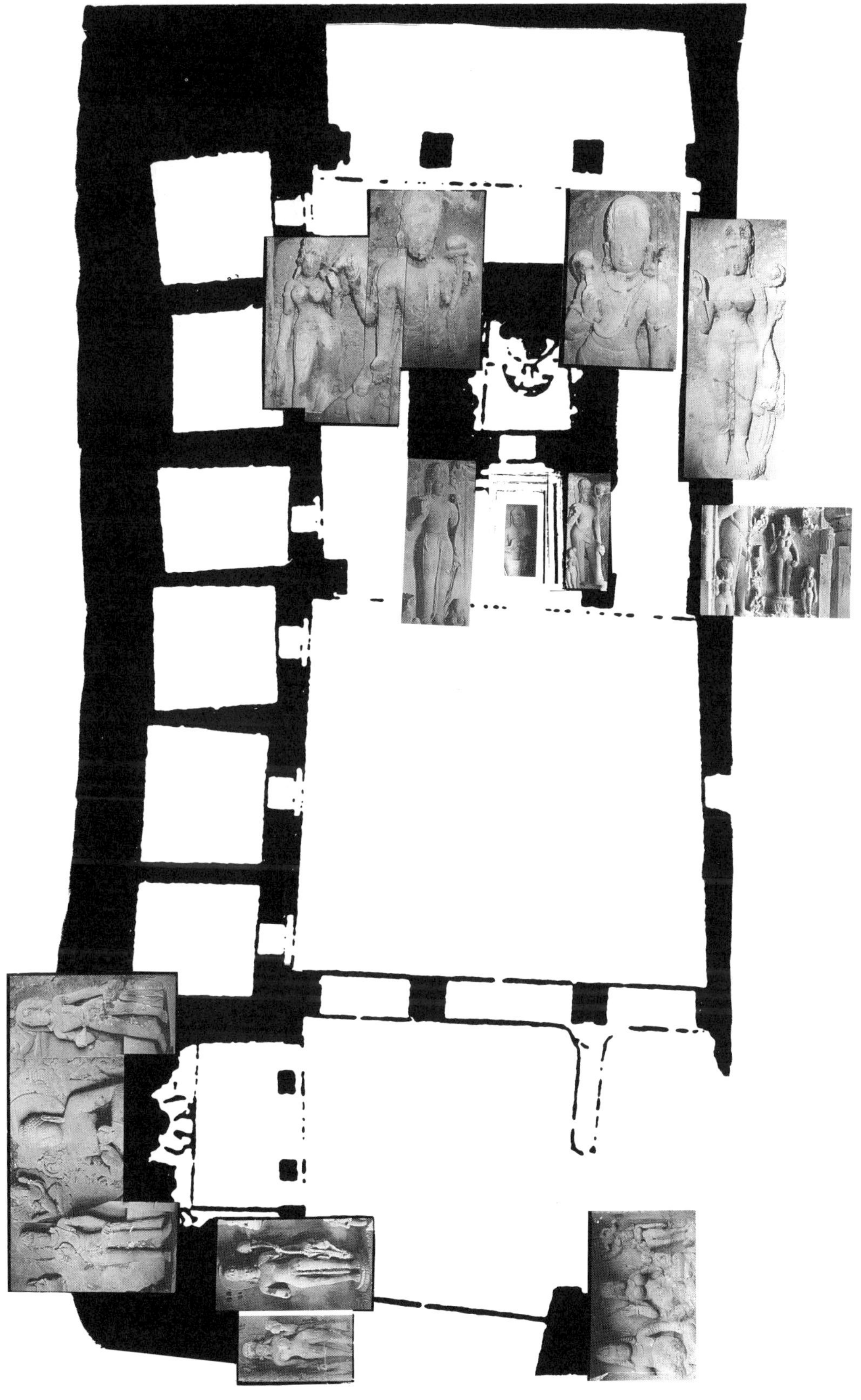

Text fig. 3–1   Cave 8 and 8A iconographic plan

bunch of flowers (without a leaf) is held by the female figure standing to the right of the shrine door in Aurangabad Cave 7,[9] and also by the image of Tārā in the Cave 4 Rakta-Lokeśvara panel (Fig. 85). Yet, while individual iconographic elements were passed from site to site, it appears that the style of the Aurangabad female images, with their extremely large bouffant hair arrangements and exaggerated *ābhaṅga* poses, was not transferred to Ellora.

The image of Avalokiteśvara holds a lotus bud with narrow pericarp, unlike the earlier buds which had no pericarp. The folds of cloth between the legs are depicted as a series of short, narrow, overlapping pleats, not the regular bumps of the images of Avalokiteśvara in Caves 2 and 5, or the larger, plain pleats worn by the image of Avalokiteśvara in Cave 6. This distinctive pleated garment is most comparable to that worn by the four-armed image of Avalokiteśvara carved on the left of the veranda in Aurangabad Cave 9.[10] The *jaṭāmukuṭa* has a round, smooth contour and the small Buddha image in the front sits in a smallar arched panel than does the one on the *jaṭāmukuṭa* of the image of Avalokiteśvara in Cave 2.

In the corner, between Avalokiteśvara and the Buddha group, is a kneeling female devotee whose long legs, flat, smooth hairstyle and pot are nearly identical to those of the female worshiper in the Cave 8 shrine (Fig. 104), one of many signs that work on these two areas was nearly contemporary. Such worshipers may be traced back to the much larger group in Aurangabad's Cave 6 shrine, whose source is the even earlier (early sixth-century) group of worshipers in Aurangabad Cave 3.[11]

Moving toward the Buddha image in Cave 8A, the worshiper would first see not the usual Avalokiteśvara, but another Bodhisattva, probably Maitreya, right hand held in *vitarkamudrā*, grasping a small flower bud between the thumb and forefinger (Fig. 95). And, on the viewer's right is one of the first clearly identifiable, large-scale images of Vajrapāṇi at Ellora, holding a *vajra*, literally a thunderbolt, but here a small, dumbbell-shaped weapon (Fig. 96). In Cave 2, a small

intrusive image of Vajrapāṇi is located in the top panel of the north jamb in the north window, where it is placed to the proper right of a Buddha image (Fig. 97). The image of Vajrapāṇi in Cave 8A, the next in chronological order at Ellora, holds the *vajra* in his right hand.[12] Significantly, it is on the first floor of Cave 11 (Fig. 152), one of the latest Buddhist caves, that a figure most comparable to the one in Cave 8A is found, again holding the *vajra* in his right hand. In later sculptures in Caves 11 and 12, the *vajra* is almost always held in the left hand.

Despite the shift in Bodhisattva attendants, the Buddha image in Cave 8A is still the standard *dharmacakramudrā* type found throughout Ellora's early and middle-period Buddhist caves. Stylistic changes in the throne, however, reveal the varied sources of style in Cave 8 and hint at more significant iconographical shifts that will occur in the latest caves. Instead of the older, square back, the throne is now topped by a horizontal bar that projects beyond the vertical side posts in a "T" shape. A *makara* spitting a long-necked bird rests above this crosspiece, while a rearing *vyāla* supports it from below, standing on the back of an elephant at the bottom of the post.[13] This, and the similar throne in the Cave 8 shrine, are the first examples of the use of this design at Ellora, where in earlier caves a design without projecting crosspieces was used, following the old Ajanta and Aurangabad type. In the Western caves, the design appears first in Kanheri Cave 32 and in Nasik Caves 16 and 23, both sixth-century excavations.[14] It is possible that the design was imported from Kanheri, as was the plan of Cave 5, both altered slightly in the years intervening between work at these two sites, one on the coast and the other further inland. Elsewhere in India, the "T"-shaped crossbar was a feature of Buddhist thrones of the fifth century from Sarnath, and it became common throughout India from the eighth century onward, so that the Cave 8 throne backs can be seen as early examples of an even more widespread "late" motif, one that was to be used in Caves 9, 10, 11, and 12.

Moving into Cave 8 and facing the shrine (Fig. 98), the worshiper would see the standard *dvārapāla* pair, Avalokiteśvara on the left (Fig. 99) and Maitreya on the right (Fig. 100), who are most similar to their counterparts in Cave 8A. Here, devotees kneel at the feet of Avalokiteśvara, a unique addition to the composition of such groups. Further to the right, cut into the wall of the aisle around the shrine, is a panel depicting Mahāmāyūrī (Fig. 101). Bhṛkuṭī, the companion we would expect by analogy to Caves 6 and 10, is absent across the hall on the left. This image may have been among the last to be carved in Cave 8; it was added both as a partial solution to the problem of the empty south wall of the *pradakṣiṇapatha* (lacking cells because it is so close to Cave 7) and to imitate the image of Mahāmāyūrī placed in a similar position in Cave 6 (Fig. 32). There is a clear difference in style between the Cave 6 and 8 figures although their iconographic features are nearly identical. In Cave 8 the figure has a narrower face, smaller breasts, slimmer hips, and longer legs. Also the schematic composition of the group is less unified than in Cave 6. The panel is cut abruptly from the wall, unlike the Cave 6 panel with its graceful pilaster and *makara*-arch frame. Inside the Cave 8 panel, cherubs, a female attendant, and scribe are rather literally placed in the four corners, whereas in Cave 6, all such secondary figures are harmoniously linked to the main figure. Stylistically the relatively stiff main image is like the Bhṛkuṭī image of Cave 2 (Fig. 58), and her female attendant is nearly identical to the one attending the right *dvārapāla* at the shrine door in Cave 8 whose small head, short legs and wide hips link them to the female figures carved in the balcony niches of Cave 10, another sign of the transitional position of Cave 8.

Inside the Cave 8 shrine, the expected *maṇḍalic* positions of the female figures is reversed. Here, an image of Tārā is carved on the left wall, with the Bhṛkuṭī image carved across the shrine, on the right. As noted earlier, this image of Tārā (Fig. 102) is stylistically comparable to the Cave 8A Tārā, although this figure holds a small bud, not a bouquet of lotuses. The Cave 8 shrine Bhṛkuṭī (Fig. 103) holds an *akṣamālā*, open lotus blossom and water pot, with her hair arranged in

a wavy, naturalistic *jaṭāmukuṭa* most like the style of the Cave 5RW figure. These images of Bhṛkuṭī, with their similar hairstyles and positions inside the shrine, link Cave 5RW with Cave 8, and contrast with Caves 6 and 2, where images of Bhrkuti wear tall, cylindrical *jaṭāmukuṭas* and stand outside the shrine.[15] The shift from the left side to the right side of the cave is first seen here; Bhṛkuṭī was always placed to the viewer's right in later excavations.

As usual, Avalokiteśvara stands on the left, as attendant to the *dharmacakramudrā* main shrine image, close in sculptural style to that of Cave 5RW and even the somewhat earlier Cave 5 shrine. The image has four arms, another parallel to Aurangabad Cave 9, where a four-armed Avalokiteśvara stands on the left end of the veranda.[16] In the left rear corner of Cave 8, between the feet of the Avalokiteśvara image and the Buddha's throne, are images of two kneeling devotees (Fig. 104) whose style, as noted above, is most like that of the devotee in Cave 8A. Beyond differences in style—the Ellora figures are placed closer to the wall and carved in flatter relief—there is an important difference in the kind of people being portrayed. At Aurangabad the figures probably represented laymen, wearing jewelry, elaborate headdresses, and presumably clothes that were painted on. By contrast, the Ellora Cave 8 worshiper is a monk, wearing his hair tied in a simple top-knot, dressed in a typically Buddhist robe draped over his left shoulder. This might symbolize a new stage in development of tantric sites, where only the initiated were allowed into the sanctum to participate in esoteric rituals.

On the viewer's right, the Bodhisattva attendant is Maitreya (Fig. 105), carved in the same style as the left attendant in Cave 8A, and similar to the Cave 5 right attendant (Fig. 44). Both wear crowns in whose center is an arched crest jewel enclosing a round emblem. Their empty left hands rest on their hips, while they hold conventional fly whisks in their upraised right hands. The Buddha image is portrayed in traditional *dharmacakramudrā, pralambapādāsana* pose but, as in Cave 8A, the throne back uses the new "T"-shape, that was to become standard in Ellora's later Buddhist caves.

49

In outline, the *maṇḍala* in Cave 8 and 8A would appear as follows:

Buddha/Vairocana
Avalokiteśvara   Maitreya
Tārā   Bhṛkuṭī
Avalokiteśvara   Maitreya
Mahāmāyūrī

Buddha/Vairocana
Maitreya   Vajrapāṇi
Avalokiteśvara
Tārā
Pāñcika/Hārītī

Thus, Cave 8 had a number of stylistic antecedents: its shrine attendants and the robe of its shrine image follow the Cave 5 shrine style; its female figures are closest to those in Cave 5RW, while its plan and some of its images, notably those depicting Avalokiteśvara, are closer to elements of Aurangabad's latest caves. Minor elements, like its throne backs and flying figures seem to reflect the influence of earlier examples from Kanheri. Furthermore, the styles of the throne backs and female images show that Cave 8 anticipated the style of later caves.

The presence of female figures in Caves 8 and 8A offers a particularly compelling parallel to Aurangabad Caves 7 and 9, although there is identity of neither style nor position. In Aurangabad Cave 7, major female figures with attendants replace the usual male *dvārapālas* on either side of the shrine door, and another female stands to the left of the Buddha image's proper left attendant inside the shrine, in the same position as the image of Bhṛkuṭī inside the shrine of Ellora Cave 8. In Aurangabad Cave 9, a similar group was placed on either side of the entrance to the central shrine, where women holding lotuses were carved at the sides and in the rear corners.

This pattern of partial similarity among several images suggests that a systematic transfer of ideas from Aurangabad to Ellora did not occur, as one would expect if a single teacher or teaching moved directly from one site to the other. Instead, it appears that certain elements were used interchangeably, perhaps because requirements for iconography and shrine programs had not been strictly

conventionalized by that time, or because more than one workshop was active at the same time. This eclectic use of motifs is further illustrated by the throne backs in Cave 8, whose style is related not to that of Aurangabad, but to Buddha images at Western cave sites like Kanheri and Nasik.

The problem of Cave 8 is to explain the meaning of such diversity. Its physical position and awkward direction of entry show that it was started after Caves 6, 5, 7, and 10 were underway. This alone places it in a transitional position between earlier and later groups of caves. Its unique mixture of styles provides additional evidence for this position, placing it near the midpoint in the relative chronology of the Buddhist caves, but making it difficult to establish its relative date. Spink placed it in the same period as Cave 2, later than Caves 6 and 5, but contemporary with Caves 3, 4, 9, and 10, and the beginning of work on Cave 11.[17] Debala Mitra, on the other hand, thought it could be earlier than Cave 6 because she believed the image of Mahāmāyūrī in Cave 8 preceded the one in Cave 6.[18] I believe the evidence supports a chronology closer to Spink's. If Caves 6 and 5 were started at about the same time, and if Cave 5RW followed Cave 5 (as did Cave 7), then, following the archaeological argument made above, Cave 8 must follow all of those. At the same time, after Cave 6 was completed, Cave 2 was begun, probably by artisans who moved from Cave 6 to work at the south end of the site. Work on Cave 8 may have begun after Cave 2, but work on Cave 2 did not continue evenly, so that the last images added there, like the image of Bhṛkuṭī on its front wall, could be close in time to the addition of the stylistically similar Mahāmāyūrī panel in Cave 8.

Thus, in both style and iconography Cave 8 is a pivotal excavation, connecting the latest phase of work on Ellora's earliest Buddhist caves with the beginning of work on the latest Buddhist excavations. Such as assemblage of different styles in Cave 8 reflects the heterogenous advent of new ideas to the site, after the more traditional early caves were underway. And these changes, brought about by the gathering from different places of the teachers and artisans, who must have carried these ideas with them, portended the even greater innovations to come in Ellora's latest Caves 11 and 12.

The Culmination of the Middle Period in Caves 9 and 10

Cave 10, the only *caitya* at Ellora—and, thus, an important ritual focal point—is probably best known for its dramatic façade (Fig. 116), and the large *stūpa* inside its apsidal hall (Fig. 117). Generally assigned a date around 650, space for it must have been reserved earlier, and work on it may have continued over several decades.[19] Its location seems particularly appropriate, since at this point the scarp projects forward, suggesting a mountain within a mountain, especially apt for a *stūpa* with its cosmographic connotations.[20] After the main program of pillars and sculptures was completed in Cave 10 near the mid-seventh century, sculptures of a different style and iconography were added in panels on the balcony and in the southeast courtyard cell. This latter phase of work was contemporary with work on Cave 11. Thus, the entire period of work on Cave 10, from initial clearance to additions could have lasted for much of the seventh century.

Cave 9 must have been started after Cave 6 since the only means of entry is through the latter (Fig. 5). Its location, façade, pillar and sculptural style connect it closely with Cave 10 and show its derivation from Cave 8. Although we call it Cave 9, this excavation may have been envisioned as a three-dimensional extension of Cave 10's second storey, making its entire southern "wall" into a massive architectural feature.

Cave 9

Facing south, Cave 9 is little more than a vestibule with three deep relief panels carved along its back wall. A shallow excavation whose small size was dictated by the presence of Cave 10 behind it, its vestibule-like quality reinforces the impression that it may have

been a symbolic side entrance to Cave 10. Further supporting this theory is its elaborate façade (Fig. 106) which depicts the roof of a three-storied building. Although not identical to the façade of Cave 10, it is at the same level and can be imagined to be the side or end of the building symbolized by the Cave 10 façade. Their close date is shown, for example, by similarities between *gavākṣas* (small arched niches) on the Cave 9 façade and those above the left (north) balcony niche of Cave 10, sharing double scroll finials, bosses in the top center of the arch, and half arches at the sides of the "roofs." At the same time, small details offer a prelude to later developments; for instance, the four-armed dwarfs supporting the middle tier of *gavākṣas* anticipate dwarfs supporting the throne bases in Cave 11 and 12 shrines (Fig. 170, 255).

Despite the absence of a large *candraśālā* (arched window), the façade provides a link between the reduced elegance of the Cave 10 façade and the complex façades of Ajanta's *caityas*, Caves 19 and 26.[21] In these late-fifth-century excavations the façades are cut into horizontal registers dominated by large niches enclosing *yakṣas* and Bodhisattvas on each side. The Ellora Cave 9 façade, with its unified mesh of *gavākṣas* carved in deep relief, creates a more realistic impression of a structural edifice.[22] This form was meant to represent a *phāṃsanā* (pent-roof structure), a common decorative motif on many seventh-century Hindu monuments throughout much of India.[23] In Cave 9 the motif was adapted carefully to its Buddhist context, with a balanced and complete application of Buddhist imagery in all open spaces. For instance, the lowest tier of the façade is cut into niches housing seven Buddhas alternating with six Bodhisattvas, while the upper three levels, dominated by the six, Buddha-filled *gavākṣas*, is a seeming reference to the large *candraśālā* that opens on to the major Buddha image on the *stūpa* in Cave 10. The primary Bodhisattva figures are not as prominent as they are at Ajanta or in Cave 10, raised here to the second storey, and carved on small pedestals instead of in prominent niches (Fig. 107).

In keeping with the increasing prominence of female imagery, this façade also introduces female figures, both as attendants to the Bodh-

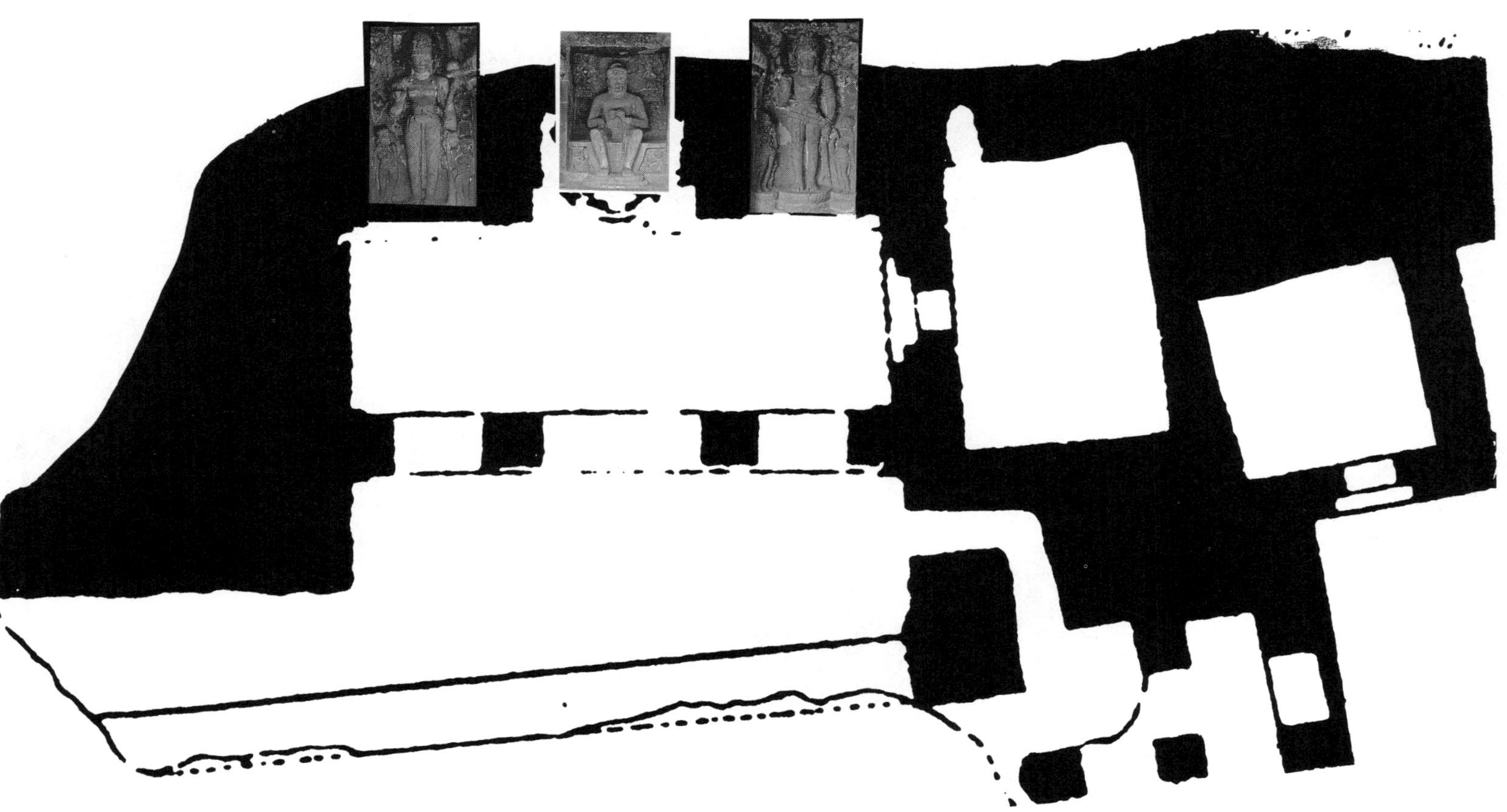

Text fig. 3–2   Cave 9 iconographic plan

isattvas on the second tier, and, on the left, as a free-standing image on the third storey (Fig. 108). This figure, now much abraded, has been identified in earlier studies as an image of *Aṣṭamahābhaya* Tārā,[24] supposedly framed by three scenes on each side, depicting (on the right) the perils of fire, shipwreck, and (on the left) snake, enemy, and elephant. This form of Tārā, parallel to Aṣṭamahābhaya Avalokiteśvara, is found nowhere else in the western caves, but later images demonstrate her popularity in Orissa and eastern India. In those cases, she holds an *utpala*, not apparent here, and is surrounded by eight "perils." Although this identification is difficult to corroborate, especially if only six instead of eight perils were included, even as a solitary image of Tārā it emphasizes the growing importance of female imagery at Ellora, permeating the traditional iconography of the *caitya* façade.

Careful attention to detail in the Cave 9 façade was carried over to the shrine and pillars. Its pillars show both its derivation from the Cave 5 and 8 tradition as well as its close relationship to Cave 10. Pilasters flanking the Cave 9 shrine, with their fluted, petal-topped cushion capitals (Fig. 114, 115) are most like the rear pillars in Cave 8 (Fig. 100), while the pillars of the small veranda in Cave 9 (Fig. 109) derive their plain pot-and-foliage capitals and incised, empty circle motifs from the Cave 5 pillars. Now the basic form has been modified: the ends of the foliage in Cave 9 have exaggerated curls, above each "branch" is a geometric, trapezoid-shaped cut, and the shaft has been lengthened to accommodate niches with loving couples on each of its eight facets. Similar niches, unfilled, are found on the right (south) aisle pillars of the Cave 10 courtyard (Fig. 110). The empty, incised medallion elaborated with small, pointed-leaf blossoms of the right (east) pilaster of the Cave 9 veranda (Fig. 111) is nearly identical to the design on a pilaster in the rear (southeast) corner of the Cave 10 courtyard aisle (Fig. 112), so similar that they may be the work of the same artisan.

The shrine image is still—at mid-century—the traditional *dharmacakramudrā* Buddha seated in *pralambapādāsana* on a lion throne (Fig. 113). The robe, hanging in bumpy pleats follows the robe style of the Cave 8

shrine Buddha image, as does the robe of the Buddha image on the *stūpa* inside Cave 10 (Fig. 117). Similar connections are to be found among the throne base lions, nearly identical in Caves 9 and 10, which share the energetic style of Cave 8, and the Cave 9 and 10 throne backs are the "T" type first used in Cave 8.

In the left (west) niche of Cave 9, is an image of Avalokiteśvara (Fig. 114), portrayed holding a lotus with a very large pericarp, similar to the type found in Cave 8 and on the Cave 10 *stūpa*. Also, as in Cave 10, here a small image of Amitābha sits directly against the *jaṭāmukuṭa*, not in the small panel found in earlier shrines.

To the right of the Buddha image is a panel depicting Vajrapāṇi (Fig. 115), the first appearance of this Bodhisattva as attendant to a major shrine image at Ellora. He holds the *vajra* (thunderbolt) in his left hand, as it is held by a small image of Vajrapāṇi carved in a window panel in Cave 2 (Fig. 97). The plain, flat belt above his waist is a late design in Ellora's Buddhist caves, found on the right Bodhisattva on the Cave 10 *stūpa*, and on many eighth-century guardian figures in the later Brahmanical caves.

Although Cave 9 is a small excavation, its façade and interior sculpture reflect well-organized planning and skillful craftsmanship, with only a few details of its veranda pillars and pilasters left incomplete. This contrasts strongly with the incomplete nature of all preceding temples. The entire shrine area was plastered and painted, and considering its relatively well-exposed location, a remarkable amount of paint has survived. This is especially obvious in the panel depicting Vajrapāṇi, where the painted design of the halo and the circular decoration on the molding above the head are quite distinct. These characteristics, together with the close stylistic relationship between Cave 9 and 10, show that it was the product of an intensive period of patronage near the middle of the seventh century, when artisans, who had worked on Cave 8, turned their now-perfected skills to Caves 9 and 10 where their work was uninterrupted until basic and new components of the sculptural programs, plastering, and painting of both caves were finished.

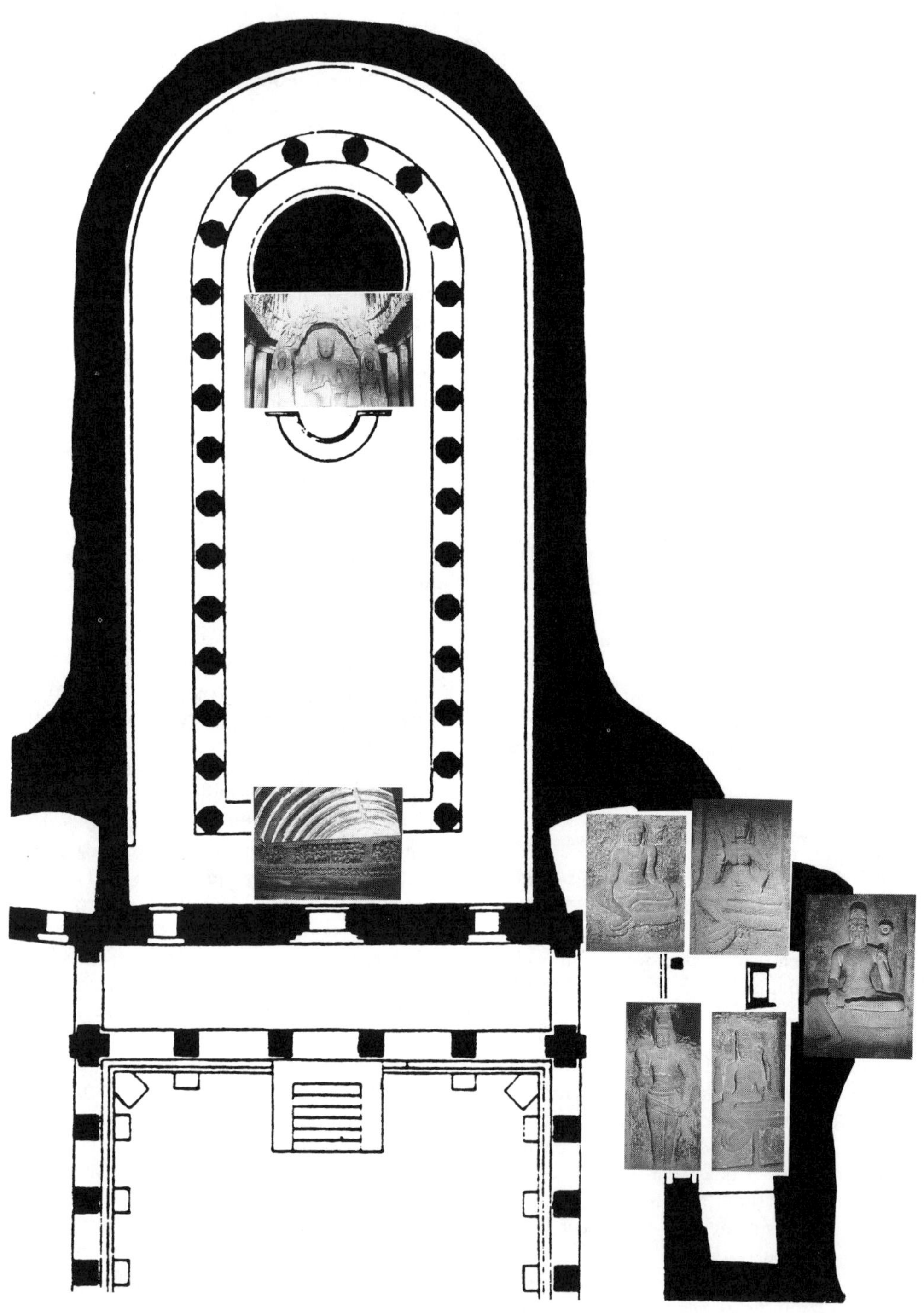

Text fig. 3–3   Cave 10 iconographic plan

Cave 10

Cave 10 marks the culmination of the site's middle period. Housing the site's *stūpa*, a key feature of a Buddhist cave temple site, it is likely that space for it would have been blocked out early in Ellora's development, while actual excavation, carving and painting could have been carried out later (Fig. 7).[25] Its central Buddha image follows the stylistic and iconographic tradition developed in earlier caves but Cave 10 was the last one in which typical seventh-century architectural designs and sculptural style were used while it also includes features that anticipate the style of later caves. The elegant sculptures and graceful proportions of the *stūpa* area were certainly the work of experienced craftsmen guided by a clear, unified program. The *stūpa* and various pillar types and façade decoration display a wide range of designs, but are well integrated into the plan of the cave. This conscious use of multiple stylistic themes, seen for example, in the contrasting *śikhara* types over the left (north) and right (south) balcony niches (Fig. 116), was characteristic of other seventh- and eighth-century temples in the Deccan, for example, the rock-cut temples at Mahabalipuram and the temples erected at Pattadakal.

Because the *caitya*-hall was a traditional "structure," its iconography seems to have been relatively standardized. Its original program included few major sculptures: those on the *stūpa* and triforium inside the *caitya*, and the flying figures and Bodhisattva images of the façade niches. While Cave 10 preserves other vestiges of the oldest rock-cut *caityas*, such as its stone-ribbed ceiling and large façade window, at the same time, the changing iconography of mid-seventh-century Buddhism prevails, most dramatically exemplified by the emphasis on imagery of Bodhisattvas added to the *stūpa* itself and in the prominent façade niches of the exterior balcony, and in additions to the façade and courtyard that reflect the influence of the evolving *maṇḍala*.

The *stūpa* itself can also be viewed as a kind of *maṇḍala*, laid out in a ritual based on the principle of "squaring the circle."[26] In Vajrayāna Buddhism, the *stūpa* was explicitly identified with the *maṇḍala*, as at Barabudur,

where the *stūpa*-tower *is* a *maṇḍala*.[27] *Stūpas* of the five *tathāgatas* can be expressions of the *vajradhātumaṇḍala*, housing the Ādi-Buddha identified with Mahāvairocana, who is the center of that *maṇḍala*.[28] The *stūpa* may be viewed simultaneously as a mountain and as a cave: Barabudur, a stepped pyramid, exemplifies the expression of *stūpa* as mountain.[29] At the same time, the *stūpa* is a "cave" enclosing a Buddha, and may be identified with the body of the Buddha: the *Lalitavistara* says "Buddha is the *caitya* of the world."[30] The juxtaposition of a Buddha image on the *stūpa* shows their equivalence, and has parallels in portable "folding" bronze *stūpas* from South India, which unfold to reveal an inner Buddha image.[31] In esoteric Buddhism, the identity of the Buddha, the *stūpa*, and the teaching of *dharma* is revealed in the legend that recounts the origin of fundamental *sūtras*, which were originally preached by Mahāvairocana to Vajrasattva, who sealed them in an iron *stūpa* in South India, to be later recovered by Nāgārjuna, the great tantric teacher.[32]

The superimposition of Buddha image on a large-scale cave temple *stūpa*, first seen in the Deccan on smaller relief sculptures from Amaravati and Nagarjunakonda, was one of the major iconographical innovations at Ajanta in the late fifth century. In Ajanta Cave 19, the Buddha image is an older, standing image while, in Cave 26, the image is seated in *pralambapādāsana*, a position itself a first for this region, that was to become the standard pose of Buddha images into the mid-seventh century. At Ellora (Fig. 117) the Buddha is portrayed in *pralambapādāsana* on a lion throne, hands held in *dharmacakramudrā*, surrounded by flying celestial beings, "preaching" under a clearly depicted *aśvattha* (*Ficus Religiosa*) tree. Here the image no longer appears to sit inside the *stūpa* as at Ajanta but, instead, it was placed on a block of stone projecting forward from the front of the *stūpa* and dominating the composition. The *stūpa* itself, with only one tier of small Buddha images in panels at the viewer's eye level, is less elaborately carved than in either *caitya* at Ajanta. A second, upper level of niches was begun but never completed on the Cave 10 *stūpa*. This, together with the rather poor and sometimes incomplete carving of the Buddha panels, suggests that the *stūpa* itself was less important than the Buddha and Bodhisattva images in front whose carving is among the most refined of the Buddhist sculptures. They represent the core of Ellora's early *maṇḍala*, seen in all of the early shrines, centered on Buddha/Vairocana attended by Avalokiteśvara to the left and Maitreya (*stūpa*-like crest jewel visible in the crown) (Fig. 118) to the right, but now transposed to the *stūpa*'s core. The Bodhisattvas carved in the exterior balcony niches may also be considered the "*dvārapālas*" to this core. Their positions are reversed, Avalokiteśvara to the right (Fig. 120), and Maitreya (Fig. 119) to the left.

Details of sculpture reveal Cave 10's multiple affiliations. More than just stylistic details, these wide-ranging similarities suggest that ideas, or perhaps artisans themselves, came from several directions to work on this major excavation. The flying figures on the *stūpa* (Fig. 121) with their long, slim, tubular limbs are of the same type as the dramatic figures flanking the façade window (Fig. 122). These figures, partially detached from the flat, blank wall behind them, are comparable to the flying figures on the south wall of the Svarga Brahmā temple at Alampur, in Andhra Pradesh, of the late seventh century.[33] The flying figures of Cave 10 face forward, as do those inside the shrine of Cave 4, another mid-seventh century excavation. Also, part of the main phase of work on Cave 10, the loving couples at the top of the façade (Fig. 123) and on the triforium on the inside of the cave (Fig. 124) are twined in equally sinuous, if restrained passion.[34] This line of couples under the *makara*-arches, derived from the single *makara* arches of Cave 6, is an example of the way Cave 10 artisans effectively revitalized an old motif. In a similar way, the balcony railing (Fig. 125), with its panels depicting loving couples over a frieze of elephants and other animals, is carved in deeper relief, but is still reminiscent of the larger-scale reliefs carved on the porch of Cave 21.

Cave 10 pillars reveal its relationship to earlier caves at Ellora, its anticipation of pillars in later caves, and also its connections to a wider range of motifs from monuments in other regions. The similarity between its courtyard aisle pillars and the Cave 9 veranda pillars has already been mentioned. The square, fluted cushion capital pilasters of the left balcony niche framing Maitreya (Fig. 119) reflect the design of the antechamber pilasters in Cave 6 (Fig. 31). Partially connected to earlier examples are the front veranda pillars (Fig. 126), with a similar stylized, plain, pot-and-foliage capital design as that used in Caves 8 and 9. Other pillars introduce new motifs. Most notable are the corner pillars (Fig. 126, 127) and the pilasters on the veranda, which include a knotted design carved in deep relief on their upper shafts; a similar, but flatter design was carved in the center of the lintel above the left veranda window. This motif, with a more explicitly serpentine character, occurs as early as an Amaravati coping slab of the second to third centuries, where knotted snakes drape over a *stūpa*.[35] Later, in the early sixth century, the motif was added to pot-and-foliage pilaster bases on the Daśāvatāra temple at Deogarh, Madhya Pradesh.[36] *Nāga* imagery is also prominent in Aurangabad's later caves, as it was at Ajanta, but appears at Ellora only on these pillars. It seems evident that the three-dimensional design at Ellora symbolically represented snakes, as indicated by the very similar knots with explicitly portrayed cobra heads on a pillar from Sirpur in Madhya Pradesh, ascribed to the seventh century.[37] The motif appears on the bases of a stone *toraṇa* at the Mahābodhi temple, Bodhgaya, also of the seventh century. Shared by Buddhist and Brahmanical monuments, knotted snakes are also an important part of the design of the second floor veranda pillars of Ellora's Cave 15 (Fig. 198a,b).[38]

Inside the *caitya*, a basically old pillar design (Fig. 129) with plain, octagonal shafts, was used to frame the apsidal *pradakṣiṇapatha*.[39] The pillars, with their incised circular medallions, inset fluted necking and brackets with rounded ends and arched top moldings, have often been compared to the pillars erected around the apsidal hall of Sanci Temple 18 in Madhya Pradesh (Fig. 131).[40] Their similarity reinforces the picture of Cave 10 as a monument whose designs are typical of seventh-century temple architecture beyond Maharashtra. This design with its bands of rosettes above and below the necking, was repeated

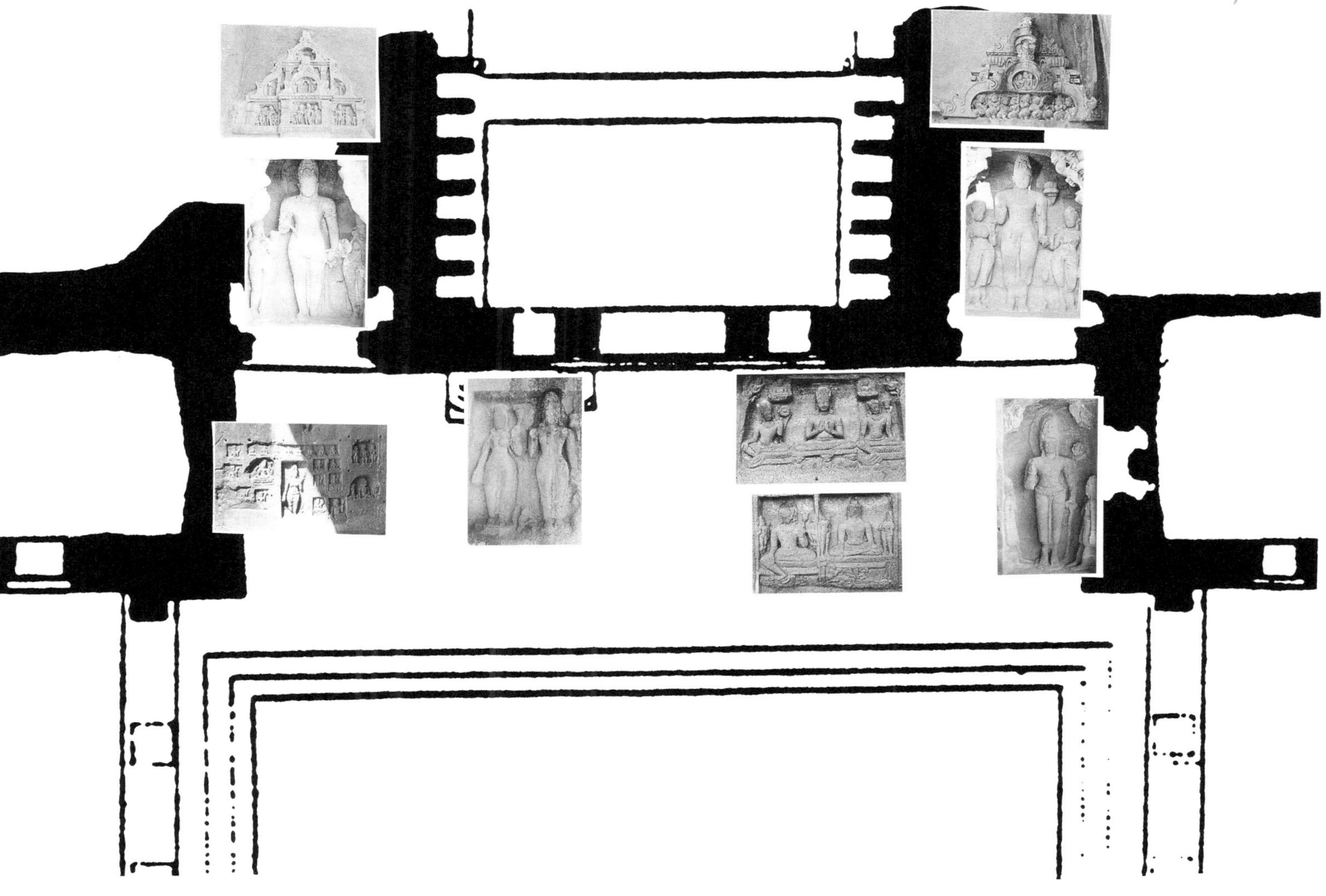

Text fig. 3–4 Cave 10 balcony iconographic plan

on the third storey veranda pillars of Cave 11 (Fig. 130), where the pillars are heavy, square blocks typical of all eighth-century caves at Ellora. Still, the sixteen-fluted necking, the eight incised circles and double rosette bands were carefully copied from Cave 10.

Beside the *stūpa* and façade niche figures, almost all other sculptures were added in a second phase of work, as their positions, style and iconography show. Any plastering of images probably occurred after the second sculptural phase ended. An important implication of this reconstruction is that large portions of the façade left blank in the original program were not painted, since the added panels would have been cut through existing paintings. This phase is most visible in the significant additions to the balcony of Cave 10 and its courtyard level Cell E, a shrine to Avalokiteśvara. New forms of female deities and Bodhisattvas, with iconography comparable to seventh- and eighth-century images from eastern India, are carved in a flat, functional style unrelated to images from any other site. This style persisted in the courtyard cell of Cave 11, but was soon replaced by the stiff, intricately crowned, heavily plastered treatment of images in Cave 11.2 and all of Cave 12.

Most prominent are the panels added on either side of the central balcony door. The panel on the left (north) side (Fig. 132) depicts Avalokiteśvara accompanied to his right by a female holding a book on an *utpala*, most likely a representation of the goddess Prajñāpāramitā. The intrusive nature of this panel is shown by the circular cut in the stone above the head of the Bodhisattva; clearly, the panel was not large enough for the sculptures, reflecting poor planning not seen in the first phase of work in Cave 10. The flat, stiff style of these images is typical of all late phase sculpture of Cave 10. On the opposite (right) side of the door, a double panel was added. The top half (Fig. 133) depicts a crowned Buddha with two Bodhisattvas; the bottom half (Fig. 134) portrays the Bodhisattva Mañjuśrī and a *bhumisparśamudrā* Buddha. The complex iconography of this group with its multiple Bodhisattvas, links it to the shrine iconography of Caves 11 and 12, another indication of the relatively late date and transitional nature of second phase sculpture in Cave 10.

Especially noteworthy is the top half of this panel, depicting a crowned, *dharmacakramudrā* Buddha/Vairocana seated on a three-lion *siṁhāsana*, attended by Avalokiteśvara to the left, and now with clear attributes, Mañjuśrī to the right, wearing the typical flat, triple-locked hair arrangement and tiger-claw necklace seen in the seventh- and eighth-century Mañjuśrī images from eastern India (see chapter 5 for further discussion of the iconography).[41] Images of crowned Buddhas were very common at Bodhgaya and were popular generally in Pāla-Sena art of the eighth century onward in Eastern India. The crown (and other ornaments) may signify the Buddha as *cakravartin* (literally, wheel-turner; figuratively, great king), who spread *dharma* from Bodhgaya where he was enlightened.[42] This iconography may also be linked to tantric literature where, at the center of the Diamond World *Maṇḍala* Mahāvairocana wears the headdress and ornaments of a monarch.[43] While these images are iconographically precise, the uneven sides of the upper panel and the careless manner in which the cherubs were detached from the surrounding stone are symptomatic of second phase sculptures throughout the cave. Yet, traces of plaster remain at the top of the panel showing that the façade was most likely painted at the end of this intrusive phase. It seems likely that even the original balcony niches were plastered at this time: in the left (north) niche blocks for cherubs were never carved (as they were in the right niche) but the blocks were heavily plastered. Since the façade walls were probably not painted before the second phase of sculpture began, it is likely that the niches were also not painted when work on their sculptures ended, but instead, that plaster and paint were added to the entire façade in one final stage of work that may be assigned a date in the late seventh century.

Panels added to the left (north) wall of the balcony provide good evidence for the relatively late date of the second phase of work on Cave 10. The wall is filled by a random collection of circular, square, and rectangular niches of varying sizes (Fig. 135). Among them, the dominant figure is a standing female holding an *utpala* (Fig. 136). Her thick, beaded belt, and roll of flesh hanging over it are like those of the image of Avalokiteśvara added to the opposite wall of the balcony. To the left of this figure is another female, now six-armed; to the right is a group of panels depicting Bodhisattvas similar to those carved in the intrusive panels to the right of the balcony's central door. Beneath a Buddha panel (Fig. 137) in this group is an inscription of the Buddhist "creed" carved neatly in letters of early eighth-century style. Its symmetrical placement beneath the panel suggests that it was planned, and therefore contemporary with the sculpture around it, thus providing an approximate data ca. 700 for this second phase of sculpture on the Cave 10 façade.

Most likely contemporary with these balcony additions are the sculptures of similar style carved below, in the right (southeast) corner cell of the courtyard aisle of Cave 10, the only part of the courtyard area that has sculpture, and one with great iconographical importance. There is nothing about the architecture of this cell, symmetrically matched in pillar form and plan to the cell at the opposite end of the veranda, that would suggest a late start. However, that cell has no carving, except for an incomplete frieze of seated Buddha images on the lintel above its pillared entrance.

Inside the right-end cell, the main image (on the back wall) is Avalokiteśvara, right hand in *varadamudrā*, holding an open lotus in the left, seated in *lalitāsana*, typical of eighth-century sculpture (Fig. 138). Except for the Rakta-Lokeśvara images in Caves 4 and 8, this Bodhisattva is rarely given such a prominent position in Ellora's early and middle period caves. The hair is arranged in a low *jaṭā-mukuṭa*. His eyes (most probably painted) are open very wide, and there is a subtle smile on his lips. These features are suggestive of the *Sādhanamālā* description of Vajradharma, a form of Avalokiteśvara, whose eyes are "dilated with joy."[44] According to the text, Avalokiteśvara as Vajradharma is seated on a peacock. In Cave 10, he sits only on a lotus throne but, perhaps, the image of Mahāmāyūrī in the antechamber (see below) indirectly carries the association made in the text. Outside the cell, all three walls of its small antechamber have relief panels. On the left (east)

wall is an image of the Bodhisattva Mañjuśri (Fig. 139), seated in *lalitāsana*, holding an *utpala*, and wearing the same youthful, triple-locked hairstyle and tiger-claw necklace as the façade Mañjuśrī. Across from Mañjuśrī on the right (west) wall of the courtyard cell antechamber, is an image of a standing male, possibly Maitreya, with his right hand raised in *vitarkamudrā*, difficult to read because the stone is not completely cut in this area (Fig. 140). His heavy, beaded belt and stiff legs show the connection between sculpture here and above in the intrusive balcony panels.

Flanking the shrine door in the courtyard cell are images of female deities. To the left (east) is an image of Mahāmāyūrī holding a peacock feather, seated in *lalitāsana* on a peacock supported lotus pedestal (Fig. 141). The *āsana* and the absence of attendant figures contrast markedly with the elaborately composed Mahāmāyūrī images of Ellora's earliest Buddhist caves. On the right (west) side of the door is a four-armed Bhṛkuṭī, also in *lalitāsana* (Fig. 142). The style and composition of this pair differ from their predecessors', but the pairing of Bhṛkuṭī and Mahāmāyūrī reflects iconographic practice found from the earliest Buddhist Cave 6 onward. At the same time, the image most comparable iconographically to the Cave 10 Bhṛkuṭī is an image seated to the left of an image of Avalokiteśvara in the north courtyard cell of Cave 11 (Fig. 147). However, the sculptural style of the Cave 11 image is closer to the shrines of Caves 11 and 12 than to the more simply carved additions to Cave 10, suggesting that this cell should be assigned a date transitional between the main phases of work on Caves 10 and 11. Taken as a whole, this Avalokiteśvara shrine occupies a position similar to panels depicting Rakta-Lokeśvara and, earlier, Aṣṭamahābhaya Avalokiteśvara, mediating the entrance to the shrine or center of the *maṇḍala*. But, here, it is applied to a *stūpa*, as a tantric and *maṇḍalic* overlay to this traditional feature of a Buddhist site.

A last connection between Cave 10 and the later Buddhist caves at Ellora are the cells added a level above the balcony, on either side of the façade. There is no formal means of access to these cells, but it is possible that ladders on the balcony aisles could have been used to reach them. In the right cell is a female image carved in a style like that of the additions below. These cells may represent an attempt to add a third storey to Cave 10, and thus reflect the new ideas more completely expressed in Caves 11 and 12, where three full stories were excavated. Such features offer poignant testimony to the changes taking place at Ellora, where the *maṇḍala* was influencing even the most traditional feature of the site, its *caitya* precinct.

The Cave 9/10 *maṇḍala* would appear as follows (second phase images included only where not intrusive):

<table>
<tr><td></td><td>Cave 10</td><td>Cave 9</td></tr>
<tr><td>third storey</td><td>female images</td><td>female image</td></tr>
<tr><td>second storey</td><td>Maitreya Avalokiteśvara</td><td>Buddha/Vairocana</td></tr>
<tr><td></td><td></td><td>Avalokiteśvara Vajrapāṇi</td></tr>
</table>

ground level   stūpa

Buddha/Vairocana

Avalokiteśvara   Maitreya

Avalokiteśvara/Vajradharma

Bhṛkuṭī   Mahāmāyūrī

Mañjuśrī   Maitreya

4. THE LATE BUDDHIST CAVES: THE MAṆḌALA UNFOLDED

History and Style

Iconographically, individual images carved during the final phase of Buddhist activity are comparable to images of the same period from eastern and central India. However, Ellora's unique style was not derived from this direction, but instead, appears loosely linked to seventh- and eighth-century Cālukya and Pallava sculptural style. This situation contrasts strongly with sculpture and architectural features in Caves 15 and 16, whose style and iconography were inspired directly by earlier Cālukya monuments that were themselves influenced by Pallava artistic tradition.

The latest Buddhist phase was not the result of influence from any single site but instead reveals a unique synthesis of architectural, iconographic, and stylistic elements characteristic of a broad range of monuments of the late seventh and early eighth centuries. This mixture of style and iconography suggests a cultural opening, which would have made possible, if not actually encouraged, exchange among various regions. The richness of the latest Buddhist caves, and the smooth transition to the mid-eighth-century Brahmanical excavations sponsored by the Rāṣ-

trakūṭas do not seem likely to be the result of the severe political turmoil one might expect if it were assumed that the Rāṣṭrakūṭas had to fight to gain control of the Ellora region in the early eighth century. The art and religious historical evidence leads to the historical conclusion that the Rāṣṭrakūṭas peacefully assumed control of the region around Ellora. And, even in its early stages, this political change resulted in an opening up of the region to religious and artistic ideas that circulated over much of the subcontinent in the late seventh and eighth centuries, including Buddhist sites like Nalanda, Bodhgaya, Ratnagiri, and Sirpur, that were being actively developed during this time.

As discussed above, Ellora's artisans were most probably part of local workshops, upon which the influence of southern style grew during the early eighth century. This may be connected more directly to politics. Since the Rāṣṭrakūṭas were still feudatories of the Cālukyas when the latest Buddhist caves were being excavated, it is possible that an attempt was made in them to emulate the practice of monument building by the Rāṣṭrakūṭa's overlords. This is to say that Ellora's latest Buddhist caves should be seen as early Rāṣṭrakūṭa-period monuments, although there is neither evidence nor need to assume that they were directly sponsored by the Rāṣṭrakūṭas themselves. When Dantidurga came to power, ca. 730, and sponsored major monuments at Ellora—Caves 15 and 16—the sculptural style changed to imitate Cālukya sculpture more explicitly, or even to be executed by imported Cālukya craftsmen, who no longer had work in the capital of the now defeated Cālukya kings.

Such changes in art paralleled changes in iconography that, in turn, represent changes in Buddhism. They were the result of a combination of internal development and a newly imported doctrine, still related in some respects to the one that inspired the earlier Buddhist caves. Thus, important features of the programs of Caves 6, 2, and 4 are repeated in the additions to Cave 10 and in the complex, late Caves 11 and 12. Changes in cave plan and iconography, especially the creation of three-storied excavations, the shift from *dharmacakramudrā* to *bhūmisparśamudrā* Buddha images, and introduction of multiple, differentiated Bodhisattvas in the shrines, suggest that a new doctrine was being propounded by a new sect. Yet, important features of the earliest caves are repeated in the complex, three-storied Caves 11 and 12, showing that the expression of new doctrine was to a certain extent integrated with the earlier, local teachings, in a synthesis that epitomizes Ellora's unique iconographic character. The shift occurs first in Cave 11, a largely unfinished and experimental excavation. Cave 12, the latest Buddhist cave at Ellora, reveals the full expression of a new, complex system of beliefs represented by the *maṇḍala*, tentatively illustrated in Cave 11.

Cave 11

Cave 11 was the first full-scale attempt at a three-storey excavation. It was set relatively close to the north side of Cave 10, but further back into the scarp, so that a flight of stairs was cut to reach its courtyard, as is also the case in Caves 12 and 15. Climbing them is a physical reminder of the symbolism of the mountain/cave. Although clearance for Cave 11 could have begun in the mid-600s, style and iconography suggest a date in the first

two decades of the eighth century for its sculpture.

The cave's plan reveals its experimental nature (Fig. 8). While the presence of three stories clearly connects it to Cave 12, where the three-part *maṇḍala* is fully expressed, in Cave 11, the floors were integrated neither in architectural nor iconographic details. Its courtyard, nearly twice as wide as the one in front of Cave 10, is rather asymmetrically excavated, with a rough cell cut on the right wall of the entrance area and another, containing important sculpture, cut half a storey up in the front, left (northwest) corner (hereafter termed Cave 11NC). The first two floors of the cave are merely long, narrow verandas with shrines cut into their back walls; the third floor is a deep, pillared hall, with a rear antechamber and central shrine, similar to the plan of the second floor of Cave 12 (Cave 12.2) (Fig. 10). Sculpture on the second floor (Cave 11.2) is most comparable to that of Cave 12, and is most significant in terms of the development of Ellora's *maṇḍala*. In the following discussion, Cave 11.2.1 will be discussed after the sculptures of the first and third floors, which are less finished and, thus, not as precisely linked to the *maṇḍala*.

Cave 11NC and 11.1

In plan and iconography, the first level of Cave 11 (Cave 11.1), including the courtyard cell, Cave 11NC, is connected to the earlier Cave 4. As a "mediating" space, it is also similar in position to Caves 5RW and 3A, encompassing abbreviated, but revealing aspects the *maṇḍalas* more fully depicted in the main caves. In Cave 11NC, at the same time, the worshiper would have encountered the new iconography of Ellora's latest Buddhist period. The main image, carved in extremely deep relief, is a now headless Buddha (Fig. 143) seated in *vajraparyaṅkāsana* (legs crossed with each foot on the opposite thigh) on a lion throne, right hand held in *bhūmisparśamudrā* (gesture of touching the earth). His robe drapes over his left shoulder in stiff parallel pleats, a style to be seen on Cave 12 Buddha images, and anticipated earlier on a small Buddha image in the upper right corner of the

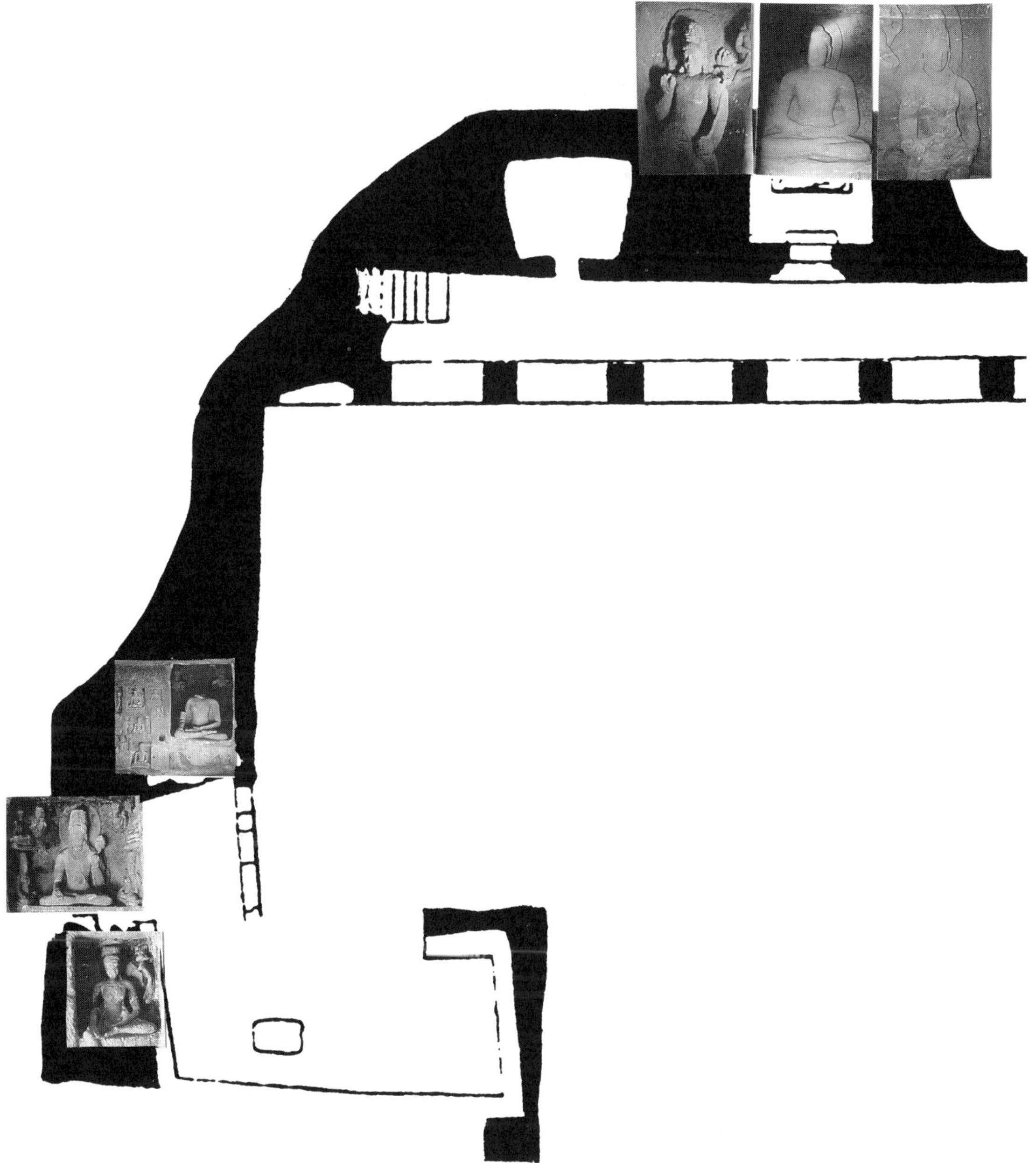

Text fig. 4–1   Cave 11.1 iconographic plan

Rakta-Lokeśvara panel in Cave 4 (Fig. 83). Bodhisattva attendants to the Buddha wear low-slung belts and *yajñopavītas* like other Cave 11 and 12 images (Fig. 144). On the left wall of the cell is an image of Rakta-Lokeś-vara, located in a parallel position to the earlier image in Cave 4 (Fig. 145). Tārā (Fig. 146), seated cross legged to the left, holds an *utpala* in her left hand, her right hand in *vara-damudrā* (gesture of granting a boon), attrib-

63

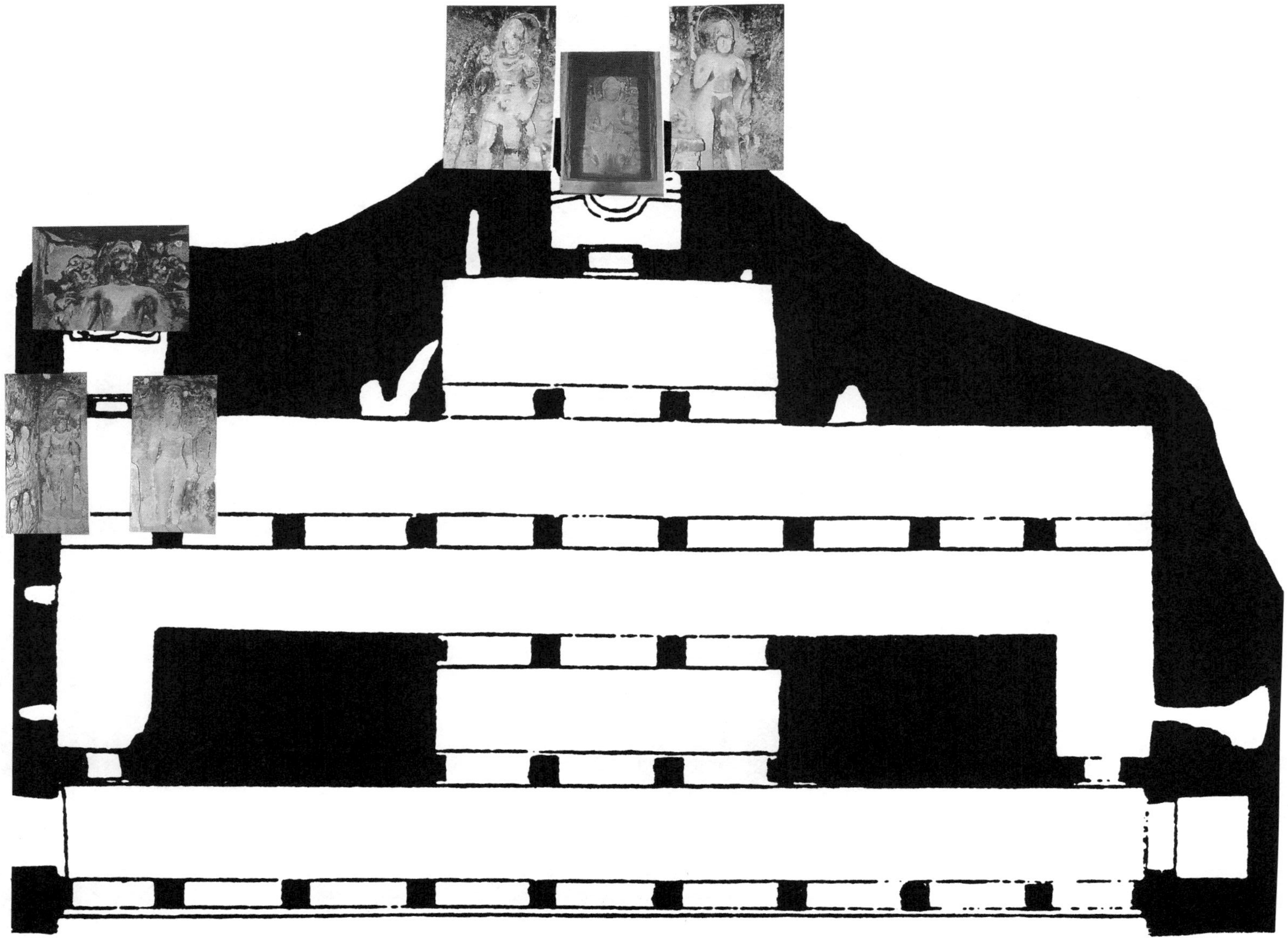

Text fig. 4–2   Cave 11.3 iconographic plan

utes most like those of an eighth-century stucco image of Tārā on the main *stūpa* at Nalanda in eastern India.[1] On the right is a four-armed image of Bhṛkuṭī (Fig. 147), marked with the same attributes she has in the Cave 10 courtyard cell: *stūpa* in her hair, staff, rosary, and flask. Both female figures here are carved in a flat, stiff style similar to that of the second phase sculptures in Cave 10. The remaining walls of Cave 11NC are filled with shallow, randomly carved panels. Most noteworthy are the several sections depicting a four- or six-armed female deity (Fig. 148), probably representing Cundā, a well-known tantric goddess, holding in her upraised hands a rosary and book on a lotus, with a begging bowl in her lap.[2] (See chapter 5 for further discussion of her iconography.)

Moving across the courtyard, the worshiper would first pass through the first floor of Cave 11, an elongated version of Cave 4, entered from the largest courtyard of any Buddhist cave except Cave 12. Three cells were cut along the back wall, but only the central one includes sculpture. The veranda is marked by large, square, roughly cut pillars that contrast strongly with the graceful, decorated pillars of the earlier caves (Fig. 149). The back wall of the veranda is also roughly finished, embellished only with the same kind of random, intrusive panels found in Cave 10. The central shrine was not centered, set too far to the left. Inside, the only sculptures were cut into the back wall; the remaining shrine walls were unfinished. The Buddha image (Fig. 150), seated in *vajraparyaṅkāsana*, holds his hands in *dhyānamudrā* (gesture of meditation). This is new at Ellora where, up to this point, the main shrine Buddha images were always seated in *pralambapādāsana*, hands held in *dharmacakramudrā*. The Bodhisattva attendants are Avalokiteśvara on the left (Fig. 151) and Vajrapāṇi on the right (Fig. 152). Here, as mentioned earlier, Vajrapāṇi holds a *vajra* in his right hand, comparable to the image of Vajrapāṇi in Cave 8A. The flat, somewhat coarse style of these images links them to both the style of sculpture in the middle-period caves, and also to that of the intrusive fifth cell images of the second floor of Cave 11 (see below).

Cave 11.3

"Architecturally" the third floor of Cave 11 (Cave 11.3) is the most complex floor of the cave, with a veranda connected to its long, pillared, very dark hall by narrow side doors and a wide, central, pillared passageway. This plan, with large, uncut blocks of stone left on either side of the central passage, is most like the plan of Cave 12.2 where, in addition, cells were cut into the back of the solid areas (see plans, Fig. 8, 10). Cave 11.3 was not carried far beyond the excavation of this ambitious plan. Only the veranda pillars (Fig. 153), that imitate the design of the Cave 10 *caitya* pillars, were given extra ornamentation; all others on all three floors of Cave 11 are plain, heavy, square columns (Fig. 154). Shallow marks on the walls reveal the tentative beginning of cells along the north and south walls of Cave 11.3, but the only two completely cut areas are the two shrines set into the back wall, the central shrine with the main Buddha image of this floor (11.3.2), and a smaller shrine cut in the left end of the back wall (11.3.1). All of its hall walls were only roughly finished, and those in the north half were filled with many small, randomly arranged relief panels. Despite their rough execution, the relief panels confirm the iconographical preoccupations of this time, including images of the goddess Cundā, standing eight-Bodhisattva groups, and *bhūmisparśamudrā* Buddhas.[3] As do the panels of Caves 2 and 10, these show that large wall surfaces were probably not painted as part of the original work on the cave since the relief carving would have been cut into painted surfaces.

Suggestive of the shifting iconographic ground, Bodhisattvas as doorguards to the shrine 11.3.1 *dvārapālas*, the only door guardians in any floor of Cave 11, have switched position. Avalokiteśvara, on the right (Fig. 156) wears a very tall, cylindrical *jaṭāmukuṭa*, similar to the style of the Cave 11NC image of Rakta-Lokeśvara. His companion on the left side of the door, holding a flower, is probably Maitreya (Fig. 155).[4] Inside 11.3.1, the sole image is the Buddha seated in *vajraparyaṅkāsana*, right hand held in *bhūmisparśamudrā*. The central shrine of Cave 11.3   65

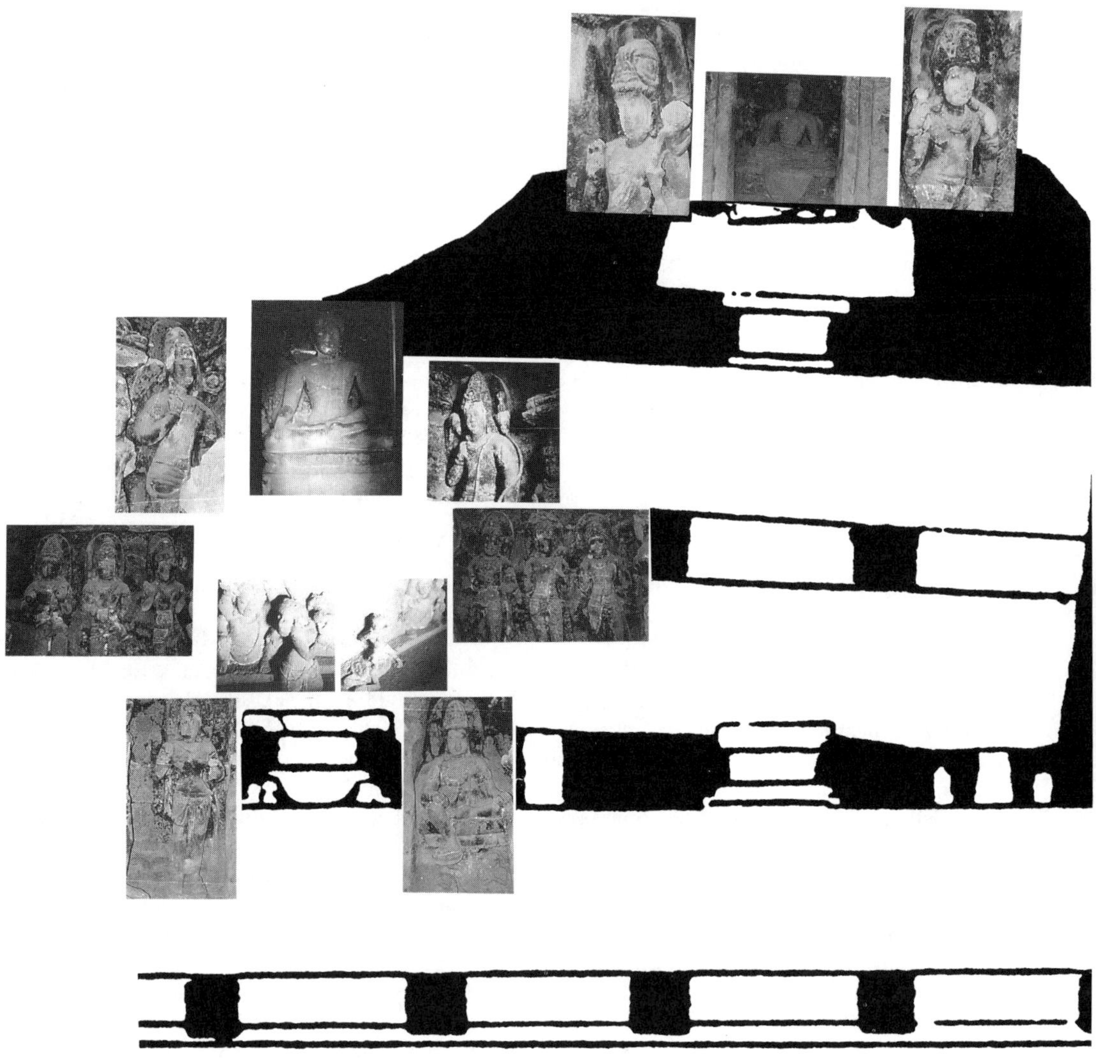

(11.3.2) includes only a traditional *dharma-cakramudrā* Buddha image (Fig. 157) seated in *pralambapādāsana*, attended by typical Bodhi-sattvas, but dressed in late-style robes and jewelry (Fig. 158, 159). Despite the empty, unfinished appearance of the Cave 11.3 shrines, both were heavily plastered and painted, an indication that even in this incomplete state the cave was put into use as soon as possible. The main images in Cave 11NC and the shrines of the second floor of Cave 11 were also finished with plaster and paint. None is evident in Cave 11.1, but as it was buried for many years, the plaster may have disintegrated.[5]

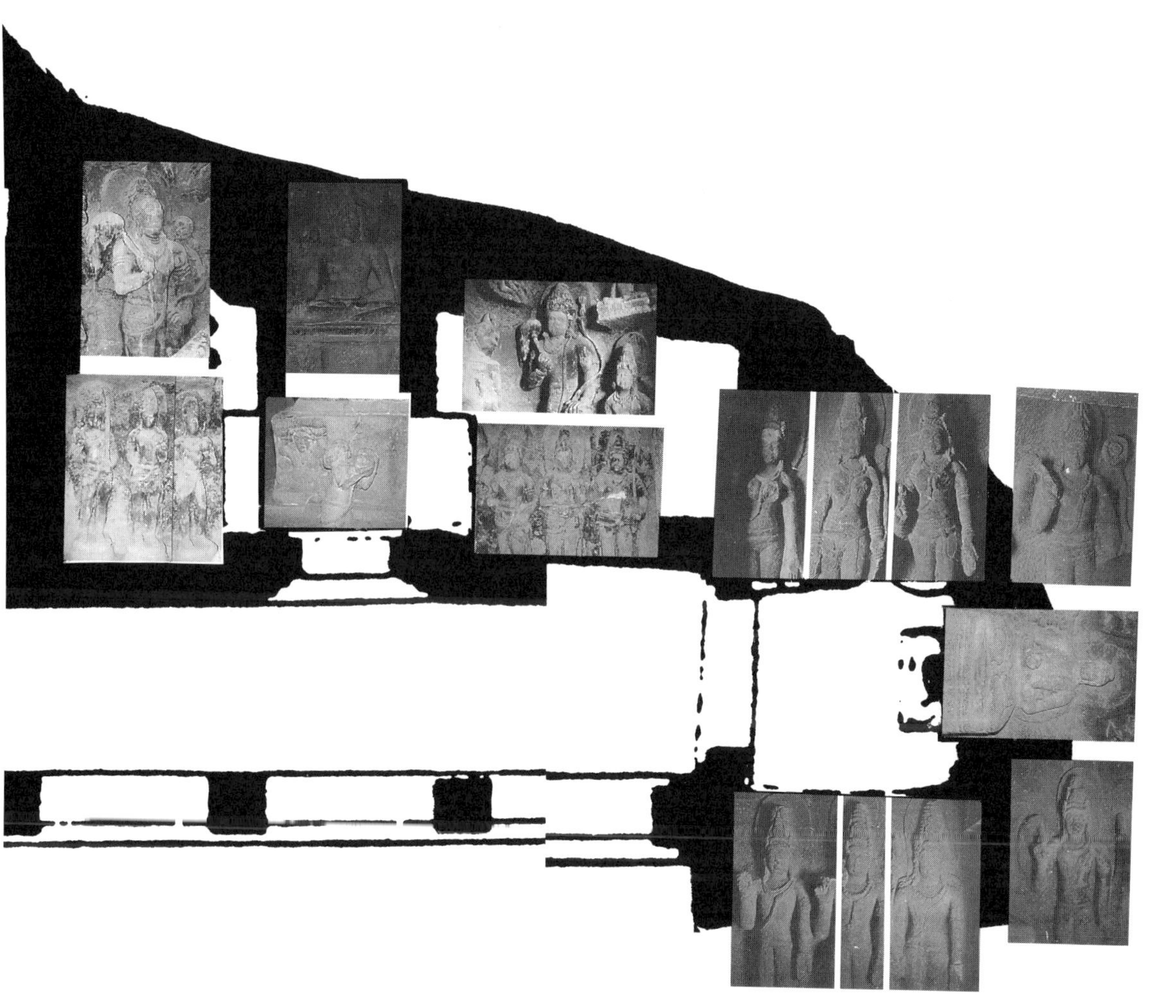

Text fig. 4–3   Cave 11.2 iconographic plan

Cave 11.2

It was the second floor of Cave 11, probably the last to be worked on, that received the greatest attention from sculptors, just prior to the beginning of sculptural work on Cave 12. Its plan is not much more complex than Cave 11.1 (Fig. 8), with five instead of three shrines cut without great precision into the back wall of the veranda. The central shrine (11.2.2) is flanked by two others (11.2.1 and 11.2.3) filled with sculpture, while the fourth (11.2.4) is empty. A fifth shrine (11.2.5) was cut into the right (south) end of the veranda. The

67

shrine iconography of Cave 11.2 moved a large step beyond earlier programs to include multiple Bodhisattva images carved in a style indirectly connected to eighth-century sculpture of south India. These attributes make Cave 11.2 one of the most important Buddhist excavations, showing the first confident use of its most elaborate *maṇḍala*, portrayed in a new sculptural style. Equally important, numerous features, some to be discussed here and others in chapter 5, connect these shrines to Buddhist art from eastern and central India.

The central shrine (11.2.2) has the simplest program on the floor, and may have been the first to be carved. The main image (Fig. 160) is a *dhyānamudrā* Buddha seated in *vajraparyaṅkāsana* on a lion throne, attended by two Bodhisattvas. All others walls of this shrine are plain. Several details connect this shrine to middle-period sculpture. The image of Avalokiteśvara on the left (Fig. 161) wears his hair in a *jaṭāmukuṭa* of thick locks similar to the images of Avalokiteśvara in the middle-period caves. The image of Vajrapāṇi on the right (Fig. 162) holds the *vajra* in his right hand, as do Vajrapāṇi images in Caves 8A and 11.1, but here the hand is raised, not held at hip level as in earlier examples.

By contrast, the shrines to the left (11.2.1) and right (11.2.3) include most of the elements found in the latest Buddhist shrines of Cave 12. The first, shrine 11.2.1, is the most elaborate, entered through the only completed doorway in Cave 11. Here, the inner two of four jambs (*śākhā*) were "supported" by miniature structures housing attendant figures (Fig. 163, 164). These miniature buildings, topped by three-storey *śikharas*, rest on tall, molded plinths. The roofs were carved to represent the *śikharas* typical of seventh- and eighth-century monuments, with small round windows on each storey and a large *candraśālā* filled with a blossom in front. Couchant lions rest at the doorsill on either side of a *candraśaila* decorated with elaborate, conch-shaped corner spirals. The figure in the niche closest to the doorway leans on a large *gadā* (club), a common pose of seventh- and eighth-century Cālukya *dvārapālas*, seen for example at the Svarga Brahmā temple at Alampur.[6] At Ellora this type of figure appears on a large scale

only in mid-eighth century Brahmanical caves, for example, as *dvārapālas* to the shrine on the second floor of Cave 15 (Cave 15.2).

This door treatment is the first indication of the close connection between shrine 11.2.1 and shrines of Cave 12. In Cave 12.2 the *śikharas* at the base of the door jambs are surmounted by large *āmalakas* (flat, fluted circular discs) (Fig. 165); on the inside of these moldings the design includes large *candraśālās*, as in 11.2.1. Here, also, the small attendants in the innermost niches lean on large *gadās*, one leg crossed behind the other. And couchant lions rest on either side of an elaborate *candraśaila*, like the one in 11.2.1. This device also appears on the third floor of Cave 12 (12.3) where the shrine door composition was elaborated further to incorporate an additional niche with pot-bearing attendant (Fig. 166, 167) on either side of the miniature shrines. These figures are not found elsewhere in the Buddhist caves, but similar pot-bearing images were carved on a larger scale beside the shrine door in the ground level cell cut into the south (right) wall of the Cave 16 courtyard (Fig. 168). Although not identical to the small-scale images in Cave 12.3, the Cave 16 pot-bearers, indisputably part of a mid-eighth-century excavation, show another association of Caves 11 and 12 with relatively late features. Like the miniature *śikharas* at the base of the 11.2.1 door, the ones in Cave 12.3 are portrayed without crowning *āmalakas*, and like the niches of both 11.2.1 and Cave 12.2., the composition of the Cave 12.3 shrine door bases includes inner figures resting on large *gadās* but here they lean with both hands on the club.

This ornamental feature of Caves 11 and 12 helps to place Ellora's latest Buddhist caves in the broader context of seventh- and eighth-century temples across India. The building type represented in the Cave 12.2 shrine door moldings, with its large *āmalaka* and mesh of small *gavākṣas*, is most comparable to seventh- and eighth-century temples of central India, such as an eighth-century Śiva temple at Mahua in Madhya Pradesh.[7] More specifically, keyhole niches are found on the Muṇḍeśvarī temple of ca. 636 at Ramgarh, Bihar, and other monuments in eastern India.[8] Across India, at the Śitaleśvara Mahādeva temple at Chandravati in Rajasthan, probably contemporary with the Muṇḍeśvarī temple, the innermost *śākhā* of its shrine door is supported by a simple, square niche housing a *nadīdevatā* (river goddess) with her attendants.[9] Variants of keyhole-shaped niches are also found in late-seventh-century and early eighth-century temples from Orissa and Karnataka, as in the doorways of the Jambulinga temple, dated 699 at Badami,[10] or in the door frame of the Kalikamata temple at Chitorgarh in Rajasthan of ca. 725, where the outermost guardians stand in small pavilions supported by pillars.[11] Yet, in every respect the latter is more complex than the Ellora examples. A closer comparison for the Ellora Cave 11 and 12 door frame niches is a free-standing stone door frame from Bodhgaya, now in the Indian Museum.[12] Divided into three *śākhās*, the base of each is filled by small attendants standing on blocks, over whose heads are placed small *śikhara*-like designs. On the left, the outermost figures stand under *gavākṣas*, while the innermost guardian is placed in a niche surmounted by a five-tiered *nāgara śikhara*. On the right, the *dvārapāla* and attendant are protected by *gavākṣas* while the outermost figure, a river goddess, stands under another *nāgara śikhara*. As already noted, Cave 11.2 and 12 shrine doorways share a similar variation in "roof" design.[13]

These comparisons show that Ellora shared similar "architectural" developments seen in western and eastern India during the seventh and eighth century. If the door frames appear crudely executed by comparison, the lack of finesse may be attributed to inexperience working with these new, uncommon forms. More important, these connections to the west and east contrast sharply with the trend from the mid-eighth century onward, when the Rāṣṭrakūṭa sponsored excavations included many architectural, stylistic, and iconographic elements characteristic of southern, Cālukya monuments.

The Central Buddha Image

Inside shrines 11.2.1 and 11.2.3, the innovations of this period are even more striking,

pointing to the advent of a new stage in the evolution of Ellora's *maṇḍala*. The central Buddha image (Fig. 169) sits in *vajraparyankāsana*, right hand held in *bhūmisparśamudrā*, attended by Avalokiteśvara and Vajrapāṇi, who also form part of the eight-Bodhisattva groups in these shrines. Just as the Buddha/Vairocana shrine images of Ellora's earlier Buddhist caves were identified by their *dharmacakramudrā*, it is Śākyamuni or, in more esoteric tradition, the Tathāgata Akṣobhya, who is commonly identified by the *bhūmisparśamudrā* gesture, personifying Vajrāsana Buddha or Māravijaya Buddha.[14] Striking changes were made in the throne iconography to emphasize the changed meaning of the Buddha image, now supported not by lions but instead by four-armed dwarfs (Fig. 170, 171).

The imagery of the shrine 11.2.1 throne was repeated in Cave 12.2, although there the throne base is plain, and again in the shrine of Cave 12.3 (Fig. 255, 256) where all elements of the 11.2.1 design are present. Four-armed dwarfs were first noted on the façade of Cave 9, but as throne-bearers they occur only in eastern Indian Buddhist sculpture from the eighth century and later.[15] These figures, sometimes found in compositions that also include a female figure offering food in a bowl, are always associated with images of *bhūmisparśamudrā* Buddhas, icons representing the *Māravijaya* and *Mahābodhi*, that is, the triumph over evil and enlightenment of the Buddha at Bodhgaya.[16]

According to the *Sādhanamālā*, the four Māras (who attempted to prevent the enlightenment of Śākyamuni) are shown supporting the throne of this Buddha (explicitly called Śākyamuni in one *Sādhana*), seated in the *vajrāsana* pose with his right hand held in *bhūmisparśamudrā*, symbolizing the final meditation before enlightenment, when the Buddha-to-be touched the earth in testimony to his righteousness. This type of Vajrāsana Buddha, according to the text, corresponds to a miraculous statue at Bodhgaya that represented the Buddha at the moment of enlightenment.[17]

To make the Ellora iconography even more explicit, in front of the throne, to the left, a woman rises from the stone floor to offer a bowl to the Buddha (Fig. 170, 171, 227, 255) while, to the right, another female figure stands on a prostrate man's back (Fig. 172, 228, 256).[18] The bowl offering female has been identified as Bhūdevī or Pṛthvī, the earth goddess of the enlightenment episode.[19] However, the image might alternatively represent Sujātā, who offered food to the Buddha at another juncture in the enlightenment episode.[20] In another collection of *Sādhanas*, the earth goddess is equated with Vasudhārā (another Buddhist Sanskrit name for "Earth"), shown holding a pot and standing as witness against Māra.[21]

The female astride the prostrate figure most likely represents Aparājitā ("Invincible"), whose conquest of Gaṇeśa, or figurative conquest over evil, is not a narrative element in the enlightenment story but is recognized in the iconographic texts on Māravijaya Buddha and is clearly portrayed in eastern Indian representations of this icon.[22] Although Gaṇapati (Gaṇeśa) seems to be portrayed as a human, not an elephant, in the Ellora images, the identification of Aparājitā seems clear. In the 11.2.1 shrine (Fig. 172) and the Cave 12.2 shrine (Fig. 228) Aparājitā's stance, lunging with a hand raised in an aggressive slap (*capeṭamudrā*), while the other appears to cup a breast but elsewhere is in *tarjanīmudrā* (gesture of danger), is quite similar to the poses of later, eastern Indian and Orissan Aparājitā images.[23] With such extraordinary iconographical detail, these images have few counterparts from other regions. In certain respects, the closest source of comparison to this new Buddha imagery is a stele from Kurkihar (Gaya District, Bihar) (Fig. 173), that depicts a *bhūmisparśamudrā* Buddha.[24] As iconographic texts prescribe, the image is attended by Maitreya, a *stūpa* in his hair and a branch of *nāgakesara* flowers in hand; and Avalokiteśvara, holding a lotus in his left hand and marked by a small image of Amitābha in his hair. The throne is supported by elephants and pillars, between which are images of the earth goddess offering a bowl to the Buddha, and Aparājitā astride Gaṇapati, depicted as a dwarfish elephant. This image is one of the very few from eastern India that

depict both female figures. Despite the difference in Bodhisattva attendants (including Vajrapāṇi instead of Maitreya at Ellora) and throne supports (dwarfs instead of elephants), the parallel between this image and Ellora's latest Buddhist shrine images is all the more striking given the relative rarity of iconographically "complete" representations.

Ratnagiri, in Orissa, offers a different, but equally compelling source of comparison for these new shrine images. Like Ellora's late caves, this site reveals a concentration on *bhūmisparśamudrā* Buddha images: of sixteen large-scale images, thirteen are portrayed in this position, many of these attended by Avalokiteśvara and Vajrapāṇi.[25] Several include images of Bhūdevī or Māra on the throne base, and one includes an unusual grouping of Bhūdevī, Aparājitā, and Māra.[26] The latter offers the best iconographical parallel to the Cave 11 and 12 shrine images, although the representation of the icon is stylistically quite different. Here, Bhūdevī emerges from the earth, hands held in *añjalimudrā*. To her left is Aparājitā, right hand flung out to slap Gaṇeśa, whom she pins down with her left leg. Her left hand is cupped at her breast. To her left is a ghoulish Māra, turning away in defeat. As in the case of Ellora, these images seem to refer explicitly to the enlightenment episode and, thus, indicate that the image as a whole should be viewed, on one level, as a representation of the historic figure of Śākyamuni.[27] Taken together, the corpus of Buddha images at Ratnagiri seems to emphasize this form of the Buddha, instead of his later tantric transformation into Akṣobhya.[28] Each image varies slightly, revealing a creative application of iconographic principles.

Ellora's Cave 11 and 12 Buddha images and Bodhisattva companions are so similar to those at Ratnagiri, that it seems most likely that they represent the same icon. But here, the images could be transformed into three dimensions, with the earth goddess and Aparājitā placed forward from the throne, a unique innovation that used to best advantage the rock-cut cave medium. They may have been interpreted in tantric ritual as Akṣobhya, but given evidence only from external appearance, they should be identified as Śākyamuni. This rules out the *anuttarayoga* tradition as the basis for Ellora's *maṇḍala*, a conclusion sustained by the conspicuous absence of the horrifying or erotic deities that belong to that tradition, as discussed in chapter 1.

Bodhisattvas in the New *Maṇḍala*

Even more than the door jambs and Buddha images, it is the Bodhisattva iconography of Cave 11.2 that establishes the appearance of the new *maṇḍala* in the early eighth century. At no other place in India has a sculpted *maṇḍala* been preserved *in situ* so completely and on such a large scale at such an early date. It will be introduced here, and explored in greater detail in the discussion of Cave 12, below.

In shrines 11.2.1 and 11.2.3 three Bodhisattva images are placed on each shrine wall, a significant change over the traditional pattern, with only the Avalokiteśvara/Vajrapāṇi pair attending the central Buddha image (Fig. 178–181). The style of these graceless, broad-shouldered, wide-faced, narrow-hipped figures, exemplified by Avalokiteśvara images in 11.2.1 and 11.2.3 (Fig. 178, 180), with their thickly plastered jewelry and high, sloping *jaṭāmukuṭas*, differs considerably from that of earlier Bodhisattva images. They are, instead, more like *dvārapālas* of Ellora's mid-eighth century Cave 15. Vajrapāṇi, on the right, (Fig. 179, 181) holds the *vajra*, not in his right hand, as in some earlier images at Ellora, but up-ended on a lotus in his left hand, a trait of eighth-century Vajrapāṇi images from eastern and central India.[29] Such changes as these suggest that work on shrines 11.2.1 and 11.2.3 (as well as 11.2.5, to be discussed below) began after 11.2.2 and the shrine in 11.3, probably by a new group of artisans, who moved on to Cave 12 when work ended on these latest Cave 11 shrines. Even then, Cave 11 remained incomplete: only shrine 11.2.1 received its full complement of figures. Architecturally, the cave was also left incomplete: center sections of all veranda pillars on this floor were unfinished, but smoothed out

more in the center than at top and base, as if they were in the process of being prepared for further carving when Cave 11 was abandoned.

The 11.2.1 shrine program (the most complete of the entire cave) begins to the left of the door, with an image of Jambhala paired with an image of Tārā on the right (Fig. 182, 183). From left to right along the left wall of the shrine (Fig. 174) are the Bodhisattvas: Kṣitigarbha, holding a large bud,[30] Samantabhadra, holding a sword,[31] Maitreya with a *stūpa* in his *jaṭāmukuṭa* and holding a branch of the *nāgakesara* tree,[32] and Avalokiteśvara holding an open lotus, with an image of Amitābha in his hair (Fig. 178). Along the right wall, from left to right, are the Bodhisattvas Vajrapāṇi holding a *vajra* on a lotus (Fig. 179), with (Fig. 175) Mañjuśrī, holding a book on a lotus, Ākāśagarbha holding a large jewel,[33] and Sarvanivaraṇaviṣkambhin holding a banner.[34] (See Text Fig. 4–7 for a diagram of this arrangement.) These identifications are based on attributes where clear, and generally correspond to lists of eight Bodhisattva groups and representations in Orissa.[35] In shrine 11.2.3, the same Bodhisattvas are present, but positions of the first two Bodhisattvas on the left wall are reversed, and images of Jambhala and Tārā were not added to the front shrine wall. As discussed above, the central image is a *bhūmisparśamudrā* Śākyamuni attended by Avalokiteśvara and Vajrapāṇi. In both shrines, small images of the Mānuṣi Buddhas were placed above the Bodhisattva groups, three on each side wall and one on either side of the shrine door (Fig. 184), distinguished by varying *mudrās* and leaves of the trees hanging over their heads.

The Cave 11.2 multi-Bodhisattva groups, like the *maṇḍalas* carved on the walls in Cave 12, represent the core of the *maṇḍala* and are comparable to representations from other regions (see below). Given the general standardization of these lists across diverse iconographic texts it is doubtful that the Ellora groups would deviate considerably. However, text and images, especially early ones, seldom correspond precisely. This problem has several aspects. Attributes are not always clear or well-preserved and where skin color is a key feature of a Bodhisattva's identity, this is a crucial problem.[36] Moreover, an object may be held by more than one Bodhisattva, for instance, certain forms of Samantabhadra, Mañjuśrī, and Sarvanivaraṇaviṣkambhin may all hold a sword.[37] Last, even if all attributes are perfectly clear, it is still possible that the *maṇḍala* represented would not correspond to one recorded in a recorded text. The absence of perfect parallels between text and image has frustrated attempts to decode Ellora's iconography. This is why it is argued here that Ellora should be considered a "text" of its own *maṇḍala*.[38] This approach can indicate the closest textual parallels to Ellora's *maṇḍala*, but more important, it will provide a grid that explains the fundamental unity of the *maṇḍala* and later shrine programs.[39]

Shrine 11.2.5

Although it is tempting to view all five shrines of Cave 11.2 as connected iconographically, it seems more likely that only the first three shrines were part of the original iconographical plan. The remaining two cells, 11.2.4 and 11.2.5 appear to be afterthoughts. Cell 11.2.4 was squeezed into the right corner of the veranda, and contains no sculpture. Shrine 11.2.5 presents a very different—and difficult to decipher—iconography and style of sculpture from the main 11.2 shrines. Here, three female deities were carved on the left wall; the central figure, holding a narrow *utpala*, may be Tārā (Fig. 188). Across the shrine, on the right wall, are three Bodhisattvas, including Maitreya with a large *stūpa* in his headdress (Fig. 189). He stands next to Vajrapāṇi (Fig. 186) who, with Avalokiteśvara (Fig. 185), serve as standard attendants to the central image, a *dharmacakramudrā* Buddha.

Despite its obscure iconography, Shrine 11.2.5 is important for its style, which suggests a connecting thread between Ellora's new *maṇḍala* and sculpture from the south. The Bodhisattva attendants to the Buddha image are carved in stiff, low relief, perhaps derived from the style of intrusive panels on the Cave 10 veranda but even closer in style to a triad of Brahmanical deities (Fig. 187) added to the porch in Cave 27. Most notable is the similarity among the crowns of the Viṣṇu image in this triad, the central male Bodhisattva in shrine 11.2.5, and the third female figure on the opposite wall. In all three cases, the tall, narrow crown rests on a diagonally ribbed brim, upon which rests a large, blossom-like crest jewel. Above the jewel, the crown extends upward in a graduated series of smaller rolls.

The high conical crown appeared earlier in Cālukya art, and was most common as an early eighth-century crown type throughout the south. Perhaps its earliest use is documented in figures carved on pillars in Badami Cave 3, dated 578 C.E. A more cylindrical form is found in images of the Raval Phadi Cave at Aihole, also of the late sixth century. At Ellora, the Cave 5RW *dvārapāla* (Fig. 46) wears an extremely tall crown, but its style is not directly linked to the Cālukya examples. Later, this style appeared at the early eighth-century Kailāsanātha Temple at Kancipuram, on *vyāla*-riders,[40] and on *pratīhāras* (door guards) on many Cālukya temples, such as the Virupakṣa Temple at Pattadakal, dated around 740 C.E.[41]

These connections show that shrine 11.2.5—both stylistically and iconographically intrusive in Cave 11 and Cave 27—were probably works of the early eighth century and, further, that at least details of costume were influenced by contemporary southern style, even while architectural and iconographic features of the late Buddhist cave show stronger links to central and eastern India.[42] Clearly, Ellora was not cut off from southern influence although Cave 11.2 hardly presents a picture of systematic importation of a unified iconography and style.

The *Maṇḍala* in Cave 11

Cave 11 was the first attempt to unfold Ellora's newly elaborated *maṇḍala* into three dimensions and on three levels. It is not clear how literally the three floors of Cave 11 should be taken to be an iconographic unit. The three central Buddha images, displaying from bottom to top *dhyāna-, dhyāna-,* and *bhūmisparśamudrā,* would not appear to conform to symmetrical arrangements of such figures, where we would expect differentiated *mūdras* in each figure to represent some aspect of esoteric doctrine. One aspect could be the concept of Buddha bodies: *dharmakāya* (teaching body), *sambhogakāya* (enjoyment body), and *nirmāṇakāya* (transformation body),[43] or the three key concepts of *karuṇa* (compassion), *prajñā* (wisdom), and *bodhi* (enlightenment). It could be argued that the first floor Buddha displaying *dhyānamudrā* does symbolize Vairocana's embodiment of *karuṇa,* and that the third floor Buddha displaying *bhūmisparśamudrā* symbolizes the working together of *karuṇa* and *prajñā* to achieve *bodhi.*[44] However, we would then expect that the central shrine of the second level would represent *prajñā,* symbolized by some form of *dharmacakramudrā.* Since this figure displays *dhyānamudrā,* the literal argument does not work, even while the concept of "threeness" comes through clearly. It is worth noting, in particular, that in tantric realization, the *maṇḍala* is situated in a three-storey *kūṭāgāra* that houses the central deity (pavilion) on top of Mt. Sumeru, offering a possible source of inspiration for the three stories of Caves 11 and 12.[45]

The new iconography of the core *maṇḍala,* centered on a *bhūmisparśamudrā* Buddha and eight Bodhisattvas, also expressed in abbreviated form as relief *maṇḍalas* in Cave 12, was clearly represented in two shrines on the second floor of Cave 11. Here, the meaning of differentiated shrine Buddha images is unclear. If we assume, from the asymmetrical plan of Cave 11.2, that only three shrines were originally intended, then we would expect a three-Buddha group like the triad represented by the three floors of the cave. Instead, the central shrine image is a *dhyānamudrā* Buddha, while the two primary side shrines (11.2.1 and 11.2.3) focus on *bhūmisparśamudrā* Buddha images. Does this represent the odd case of a *maṇḍala* representing only *karuṇa* and *bodhi*? Or, was the original idea to include five shrines, only four of which were more or less completed? In this case, would

the shrines represent the five Buddhas (Akṣobhya, Vairocana, Ratnasambhava, Amitābha, and Amoghasiddhi) of the *pañcatathāgata* system? Again, they should be recognizable by differentiated *mudrās*; the double *bhūmisparśamudrā* Buddhas in 11.2.1 and 11.2.3 disturb the symmetry of this hypothetical reconstruction.

Based on the iconography of the images, it appears that Cave 11 is an expression of a *maṇḍala* that invokes forms of the Buddha as Vairocana and Śākyamuni, the latter perhaps also visualized as Akṣobhya, attended by eight Bodhisattvas. Related to teachings of the *kriyā* and *yoga tantras,* this pattern, as summarized below, was to be more elaborately portrayed in Cave 12.

Cave 12

As one approaches Cave 12, its difference from Cave 11 is immediately apparent. Instead of a wide, asymmetrical opening to the court, the entrance to Cave 12 begins on a wide platform, partially ornamented with geometric relief carving and intricate moldings (Fig. 190). A doorway with extremely wide jambs penetrates the full screen wall and leads to the courtyard (Fig. 191). Cave 16 is preceded by an even larger and more intricately planned screen wall; in comparison Cave 12 may be seen to be transitional between the poorly executed entrance to Cave 11 and the majestic mid-eighth century accomplishments of Rāṣṭrakūṭa patronage.

All three floors of Cave 12 are pillared halls, among which there are subtle differences in plan (Cave 12 plans, Fig. 9–11). For example, the pillared antechamber of Cave 12.1 is longer than in the other floors; blocks of stone were left on either side of the entrance to the hall of Cave 12.2 (as they were in Cave 11.3); and in Cave 12.3, niches with Buddha images and panels of Buddha and female groups replace the cells that line the walls of the first two floors. Despite these differences, the excavation of all three floors followed a unified scheme: from front to back on each floor there are six rows of eight pillars. Style and placement of pillars show the

Table: 4.1 *Cave 11 Maṇḍala Scheme*

<u>Level 3</u>

Śākyamuni/Akṣobhya — Vairocana — ?
Shrine 1 — Shrine 2 — Shrine 3

<u>Level 2</u>

Śākyamuni/Akṣobhya — Vairocana — Śākyamuni/Akṣobhya — ? — Vairocana

Śākyamuni/Akṣobhya				Śākyamuni/Akṣobhya				Vairocana	
Avalokiteśvara	Vajrapāṇi			Avalokiteśvara	Vajrapāṇi			Avalokit.	Vajrapāṇi
Maitreya	Mañjuśrī			Maitreya	Mañjuśrī			Prajñā #1	Maitreya
Samantabhadra	Ākāśagarbha			Kṣitigarbha	Ākāśagarbha			Tārā	Bodhi
Kṣitigarbha	Sarvanivaraṇa-viṣkambhin			Samantabhadra	Sarvanivaraṇa-viṣkambhin			Prajña #3	Bodhi
Jambhala	Tārā								

Māanuṣi Buddhas — Māanuṣi Buddhas
Shrine 1 — Shrine 2 — Shrine 3 — Shrine 4 — Shrine 5

<u>Level 1</u>

Vairocana
Avalokiteśvara Vajrapāṇi

Śākyamuni/Akṣobhya

Rakta Lokeśvara
Tārā   Bhṛkuṭī
       Cundā

unity of all three floors and the connection of Cave 12 to later caves. Except for the central hall pillars of 12.3, which are plain, square columns, all others in the cave are supported on molded bases (Fig. 192–195). More ornate than the plain pillars of Cave 11, this new type was to be used consistently in early to mid-eighth century Brahmanical caves such as Cave 25, 22, and all areas of Cave 15. And, with more elaborately molded bases, this type continued in use in Cave 16. The new pillar treatment lends Cave 12 a "Rāṣṭrakūṭa-period" ambience, albeit a restrained one compared to Cave 15 or Cave 16. The symmetry created by pillar placement not only reveals its organized planning, but also creates an atmosphere of well-balanced proportion.

Unlike Cave 11, whose first and third floors are incomplete, major images on all three floors of Cave 12 were completed, plastered, and painted, as was the ceiling at least in the front hall of 12.3. We can infer that an overall iconographic or *mandalic* scheme governed the cave's planning. Stylistic variations within the full-blown iconographic program suggest that work was carried out almost simultaneously on all three floors, by different groups of artisans working in related stylistic idioms. So, for example, the shrine of the second floor appears to have been carved by the same artisans who worked in the shrines of Cave 11.2.1 and 11.2.3; similarities include the *candraśaila* at the base of the 12.2 shrine door, the miniature buildings on the door jambs, and the dwarfs and female figures at the throne base. The image of Avalokiteśvara as *dvārapāla* at the 12.2 shrine door (Fig. 218) is stylistically most like the Avalokiteśvara images inside shrines 11.2.1 and 11.2.3, and the image of Vajrapāṇi at the Cave 12.2 shrine door (Fig. 219), holding the *vajra* in his upraised right hand, relates most closely to the composition of the Vajrapāṇi image in the central shrine of Cave 11.2.2. By contrast, the style of carving of the first floor shrine Bodhisattva images is closest to those in the third floor shrine.

Inside the screen wall, a wide, plain courtyard leads to the cave entrance. In the left courtyard corner is a cell cut in the back of the screen wall, reached by a shallow flight of stairs. Unlike its counterpart in Cave 11, this one is unrelieved by sculpture, but it does contain a rock-cut cistern. The main cave is entered up a short staircase, through the only two pillars of the entire excavation that are decorated with relief carving (Fig. 196, 197). Beneath their rectangular slab brackets the tops of these pillars were carved to represent square, stylized, fluted pot-and-foliage capitals. The pot-and-foliage design was a common feature of Ellora's seventh-century Buddhist caves, but this square, stylized design is an innovation in Cave 12. The bracket immediately above the capital is decorated with loving couples surrounded by foliage, with a *makara* at each end.[46] Chubby dwarfs support the foliage curling over the pots, a variant of the older design where dwarfs squatted at the corners of pillars, as in Caves 2 and 9. These pillars are most like the two pilasters and six pillars of the second floor veranda of Cave 15, a two-storey cave that may have been launched as a Buddhist temple, but was finished under the Rāṣṭrakūṭas as a Śaiva excavation, where the pillar decoration is more elaborate and varied than in Cave 12 (Fig. 198). This is yet another indication of both the eighth-century date of Cave 12 and its links to the workshop used by patrons of the Rāṣṭrakūṭa excavations in Caves 15 and 16.

The Eight-Bodhisattva *Maṇḍala* and Cave 12

On the first floor, three large, nine-square *maṇḍalas* are located on the left wall and in a cell cut into the right front corner of the hall. Their positions suggest that they were not part of the original iconographic scheme of the cave and may be, in some sense, intrusive. Two others, carved in a cell half a floor above ground level are identical, and appear to have been part of its original plan (see below). Yet, in all cases, their content—eight differentiated Bodhisattvas surrounding a *dhyānamudrā* Buddha image—connects them to the shrine programs in Cave 11.2 and all of Cave 12. These rock-cut *maṇḍalas*, whose essence pervades Cave 12, may be an intermediate step between manuscript or other pattern drawings and the three-dimensional sculptured *maṇḍalas* of the shrines.[47] Representations of similar groups have been found in northwest and eastern India, in Tibet, Central Asia, Java, China, and Korea, and most commonly in Japan.[48] Such groups are generally comparable to *maṇḍalas* of six, eight, or sixteen Bodhisattvas described in many tantric texts.[49]

In iconographic texts the groups of eight Bodhisattvas are nearly identical. This suggests that although there may be permutations in their order, variation in the form of their names, and in the attributes assigned to each, the same figures (or different manifestations of the same figures) should be expected. The following lists are representative:

Sādhanamālā 18	*Niṣpannayogāvalī 2* and *Piṇḍīkrama Sādhana*
Maitreya	Maitreya
Kṣitigarbha	Kṣitigarbha
Vajrapāṇi	Vajrapāṇi
Khagarbha	Khagarbha
Mañjughoṣa	Lokeśvara/Lokeśa
Gaganagañja	Mañjughoṣa
Viṣkambhin	Sarvanivaraṇaviṣkambhin
Samantabhadra	Samantabhadra

Aṣṭamahābodhisattvamaṇḍalasūtra and *Mahāvairocanābhisambodhisūtra*

Maitreya
Ākāśagarbha
Samantabhadra
Avalokiteśvara
Vajrapāṇi
Mañjuśrī
Kṣitigarbha
Sarvanivaraṇaviṣkambhin[50]

For the purposes of this study, the *Aṣṭamahābodhisattvamaṇḍalasūtra*, translated into Chinese by Śubhakarasiṁha in 725 C.E. and the *Mahāvairocanābhisambodhisūtra*, translated by Amoghavajra in the period between 746–774, are most interesting, since they are relatively close in date to Ellora's Bodhisattva groups. The latter text, of the *yogatantra* tradition, with Vairocana as the central Buddha, seems particularly close to Ellora's relief *maṇḍalas*, which portray a *dhyānamudrā* Buddha in the center square, the same *mudrā* Vairocana holds in the center of the *Mahākaruṇagarbhodbhavamaṇḍala* of this *sūtra*. This was a major component of the teaching of the Japanese Shingon tradition of esoteric Buddhism. On

the other hand, the eight-Bodhisattva *maṇḍalas* described in the *Niṣpannayogāvalī* and the *Piṇḍīkrama Sādhana* are centered on Akṣobhya who, identified by his *bhūmisparśamudrā*, may be closer to the central shrine images of Caves 11.2 and 12.

Comparable groups have also been identified at sites close in date to Ellora. Most important are the eighth- and ninth-century Bodhisattva groups found at the three Buddhist sites of Ratnagiri, Udayagiri, and Lalitagiri in Orissa. Although the groups differ slightly among themselves in terms of style, the identification of the Bodhisattvas is remarkably consistent, whether they accompany images of the Buddha/Akṣobhya, Vairocana or a central Mañjuśrī figure, as proposed in a recent study:

Orissan Bodhisattva groups	
Samantabhadra	Ākāśagarbha
Maitreya	Vajrapāṇi
Lokeśvara	Mañjuśrī
Kṣitigarbha	Viṣkambhin[51]

More distantly, but still close in date, ca. 800, is the eight-Bodhisattva group surrounding the Javanese temple at Candi Mendut, whose members are identified as:

Candi Mendut
Sarvanivaraṇaviṣkambhin
Maitreya
Samantabhadra
Kṣitigarbha
Vajrapāṇi
Mañjuśrī
Khagarbha
Avalokiteśvara[52]

Here, the central temple image is a *dharmacakramudrā* Buddha, identified as Vairocana. It has been suggested that this temple represents the *Garbhadhātumaṇḍala* whose source, the *Mahāvairocanasūtra*, is alluded to an inscription at the site which mentions the *tathāgata-kula*, a technical term of the *caryā tantras* that only appears in this *sūtra* and one other.[53] It is noteworthy that the entrance area of this temple, like the main temple at Ratnagiri in Orissa, and the shrines of Caves 11.2, 12.2 and 12.3, also includes images of Jambhala/Pāñcika, Hāritī, and other prominent female deities.

Comparisons with these texts and sites help identify the components of Ellora's *maṇḍalas*.

They may be best understood when reduced to a diagram in which each horizontal row corresponds to a wall inside a shrine. See Text Fig. 4–4. A comparison of attributes and positions of each figure in the *maṇḍala* and Bodhisattvas in the shrines, reveals the following relationship:

top *maṇḍala* row	=	left shrine wall
central *maṇḍala* row	=	rear shrine wall
bottom *maṇḍala* row	=	right shrine wall

MAṆḌALA

MAITREYA	SAMANTA-BHADRA	KṢITIGARBHA
AVALOKITEŚVARA	BUDDHA	VAJRAPĀṆI
SARVANIVARAṆA-VIṢKAMBHIN	ĀKĀŚA-GARBHA	MAÑJUŚRI

If the *maṇḍala* is divided into horizontal sections and the top and bottom sections are rotated ninety degrees, as shown below, each section then corresponds to a wall inside the later shrines:

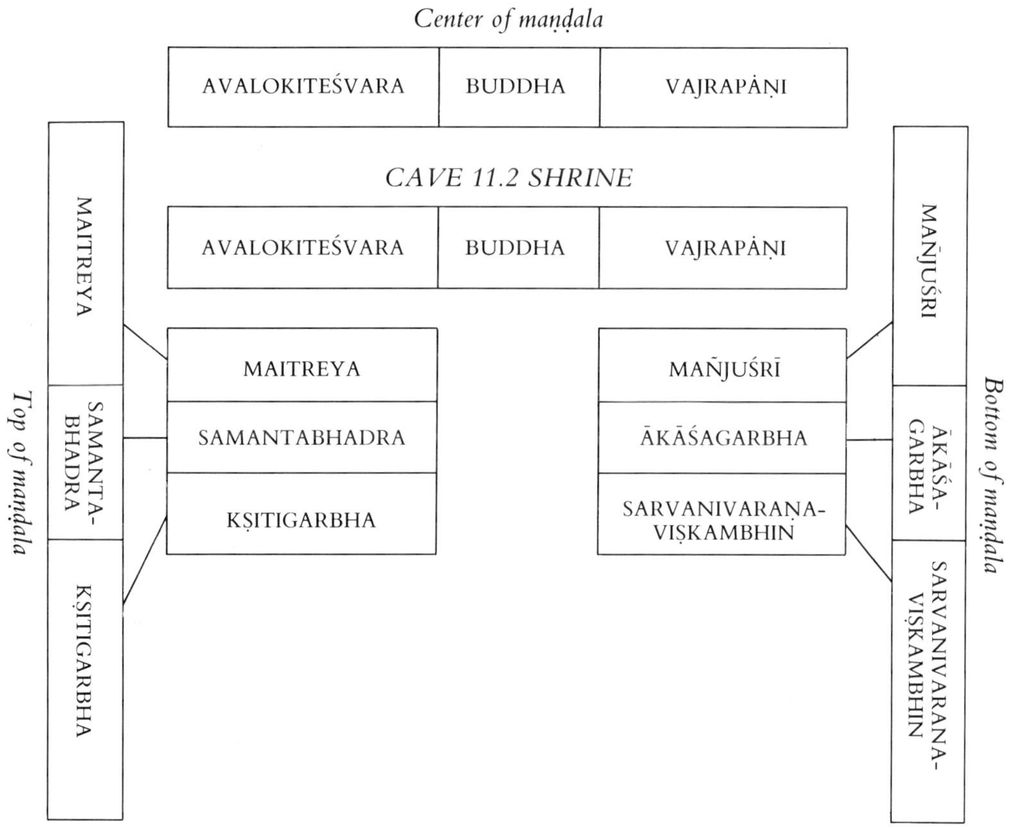

Center of maṇḍala

AVALOKITEŚVARA	BUDDHA	VAJRAPĀṆI

CAVE 11.2 SHRINE

AVALOKITEŚVARA	BUDDHA	VAJRAPĀṆI

Top of maṇḍala: MAITREYA / SAMANTA-BHADRA / KṢITIGARBHA

MAITREYA
SAMANTABHADRA
KṢITIGARBHA

MAÑJUŚRĪ
ĀKĀŚAGARBHA
SARVANIVARAṆA-VIṢKAMBHIN

MAÑJUŚRI

Bottom of maṇḍala: ĀKĀŚA-GARBHA / SARVANIVARAṆA-VIṢKAMBHIN

Text fig. 4–4   Cave 11 shrine and *maṇḍala* diagram

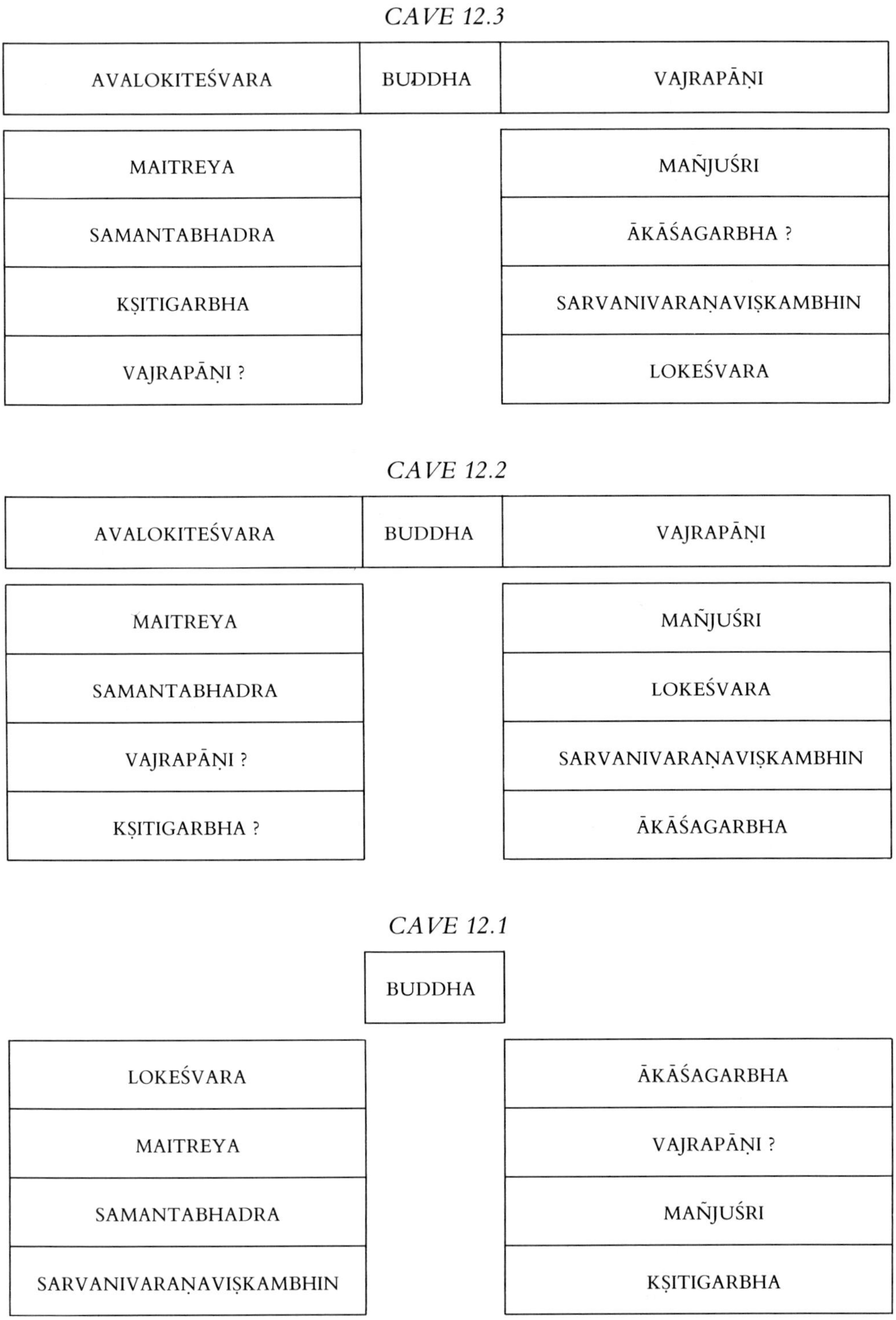

CAVE 12.3

AVALOKITEŚVARA	BUDDHA	VAJRAPĀṆI

MAITREYA		MAÑJUŚRI
SAMANTABHADRA		ĀKĀŚAGARBHA ?
KṢITIGARBHA		SARVANIVARAṆAVIṢKAMBHIN
VAJRAPĀṆI ?		LOKEŚVARA

CAVE 12.2

AVALOKITEŚVARA	BUDDHA	VAJRAPĀṆI

MAITREYA		MAÑJUŚRI
SAMANTABHADRA		LOKEŚVARA
VAJRAPĀṆI ?		SARVANIVARAṆAVIṢKAMBHIN
KṢITIGARBHA ?		ĀKĀŚAGARBHA

CAVE 12.1

BUDDHA

LOKEŚVARA		ĀKĀŚAGARBHA
MAITREYA		VAJRAPĀṆI ?
SAMANTABHADRA		MAÑJUŚRI
SARVANIVARAṆAVIṢKAMBHIN		KṢITIGARBHA

Text fig. 4–5   Cave 12 shrine/*maṇḍala* diagram

The relationship is clearest when the Cave 11.2.1 shrine is compared with the *maṇḍala*. Although the *maṇḍalas* are found on the first floor of Cave 12, it is on this floor that the shrine iconography actually differs the most from the *maṇḍala*. In Cave 12, there are four Bodhisattvas on each shrine wall, in addition to Avalokiteśvara and Vajrapāṇi as throne attendants in the second and third floor shrines. If the lists above correspond even generally to the eight-Bodhisattva *maṇḍala* at Ellora, we should expect to find a form of Vajrapāṇi and of Lokeśvara in the group of eight. Given the blanks caused by eroded attributes, the correspondence between texts, sites, and images is imperfect.

The diagrams show that the central *maṇḍala* row, like the rear shrine wall, encompasses the central Buddha image, attended by Avalokiteśvara and Vajrapāṇi. In the shrines of Caves 12.2 and 12.3, with four Bodhisattvas in addition to these traditional attendants, the latter may correspond to the small attendant figures within the central *maṇḍala* square. All relief *maṇḍalas* focus on a *dhyānamudrā* Buddha while, as noted above, the hand position of shrine Buddha images is *bhūmisparśamudrā* except in Cave 12.1, where it is *dharmacakramudrā*.

The top *maṇḍala* row and the left shrine wall both include a central sword-bearing Bodhisattva, identified here as Samantabhadra.[54] If the bouquet of small blossomed flowers (most visible in Fig. 199 and 213) held by the figure in the top left square is taken to represent a branch of the *nāgakesara* tree, then he may be identified as Maitreya, whose identity, with dishevelled hair adorned with a *stūpa*, on the right end of the left wall group, is clear. The attributes of the left, front shrine image and the top, left *maṇḍala* figure are not at all clear but, in the *maṇḍala*, the object may be a triple-bud stem. If so, it may represent Kṣitigarbha, who holds a branch of the *kalpadruma* tree, portrayed elsewhere as a three-budded flower.[55]

The bottom *maṇḍala* row corresponds more clearly to the right shrine wall. There, the foremost Bodhisattva holds a flag or banner, a symbol of Sarvanivaraṇaviṣkambhin. The central figure of the right shrine wall and in the *maṇḍala*'s bottom row holds a bud- or jewel-like object, here taken to label the figure as Ākāśagarbha.[56] The rearmost Bodhisattva on the right shrine wall, and the figure in the bottom right *maṇḍala* square both hold a book on a lotus, a clear indication that the image represents Mañjuśrī.

In each shrine, there are "blanks" where attributes are no longer distinct, or reversals in positions of some figures. Yet, as will be discussed in the following sections, the rear shrine walls (that is, the center of the *maṇḍala*), images of Mañjuśrī and Sarvanivaraṇaviṣkambhin on the right wall, and Maitreya and Samantabhadra on the left appear to be stable. Moreover, even "external" details connect the *maṇḍalas* to the general shrine program. For example, above the *maṇḍala* in the right-end cell in Cave 12.1 is a relief panel depicting a *dhyānamudrā* Buddha, attended to the left by a flower-bearing Bodhisattva (Maitreya or Avalokiteśvara) and to the right by Mañjuśrī (Fig. 200). At the left end of the panel is an image of Tārā and, at the right end, is an image of Cundā. This iconography is nearly identical to the front-wall program of the Cave 12.1 shrine, with Maitreya and Mañjuśrī as *dvārapālas*, and Tārā and Cundā on the wall just inside the door. Here, the figures above the panel "precede" the Bodhisattvas of the *maṇḍala*, as comparable images precede the Bodhisattvas on the shrine's side walls. (See Table 4–2 for a summary of the core *maṇḍala* diagrams and shrines.)

Cave 12.1

Moving into the first floor of the cave, panels depicting *dhyānamudrā* Buddhas were carved on both walls of the six-pillared antechamber (Fig. 201). Their attendants, Avalokiteśvara and Vajrapāṇi, are noteworthy for the style of their rather low, smooth-topped crowns, most like the Bodhisattvas inside the shrine of the same floor, suggesting that work on these areas was probably contemporary. These, in turn, are most like the Bodhisattvas wearing smooth, conical crowns in the Cave 12.3 shrine.

Iconographically, however, Cave 12.1 differs significantly from that shrine and also from the one in Cave 12.2. All elements of

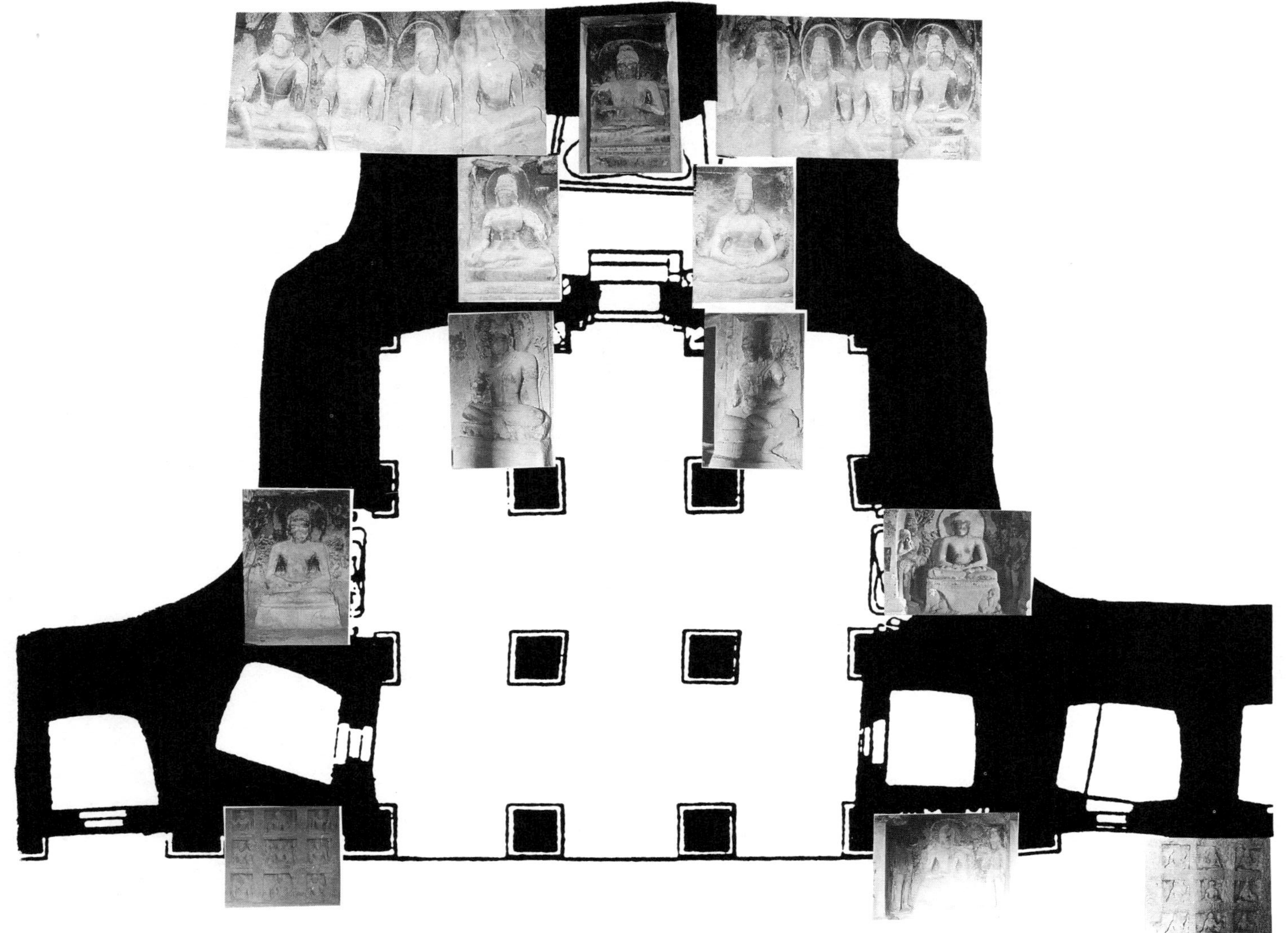

Text fig. 4–6 Cave 12.1 iconographic plan

the shrine program reinforce this difference. Instead of standing *dvārapālas*, seated figures flank the shrine door. And they are not the usual Avalokiteśvara/Vajrapāṇi pair, but instead, Maitreya to the left and Mañjuśrī to the right (Fig. 202, 203). This pair is unusual, although one form of Lokanātha is said to be attended by Maitreya and Mañjuśrī,[57] and another pair is represented in an early version in the Cave 10 courtyard cell. Here, Maitreya clearly holds a branch of the *nāgakesara* tree and on his hair, piled in a stylized *jaṭāmukuṭa*, is a small *stūpa*. The image of Mañjuśrī is seated in the same position as in the Cave 10 courtyard cell image (Fig. 139), but now it is carved in much finer detail. Here, the figure wears a tall, cylindrical crown, but a vestige of his more typical youthful hairstyle remains in the long, tubular, stylized curls hanging over his shoulders. The book and *utpala* are clearly depicted; traces of tiger claws are visible on his necklace. The twisted, jewelled *upavīta* is comparable to that of a Mañjuśrī image from Sanci, an indication that Mañjuśrī imagery at Ellora was part of a wider spread system of doctrine.[58]

Inside the shrine, an image of Tārā, holding an *utpala*, is placed to the left of the door, while opposite her, on the right, is a seated four-armed image of Cundā (Fig. 204, 205) instead of the Jambhala image we would expect by analogy to other Cave 11 and 12 shrines. This is the first "major" use of Cundā within the shrine *maṇḍala*, although, as noted above, she is paired with Tārā in a panel above one of the relief *maṇḍalas* in Cave 12, and she also appears in many intrusive images throughout Caves 10, 11, and 12.[59] Her natural hands are held in *dhyānamudrā* upon which rests the ascetic's bowl—a key feature of Cundā images. Her upper right hand holds a rosary, while her upper left holds a stoppered flask. These attributes are very close to textual descriptions and medieval sculptures representing Cundā.[60] The style of these images, with their heavy shoulders and round-topped crowns is closer to the style of sculpture in Cave 12.3 than 12.2, but in the 12.1 shrine the style appears more "southern" than sculptures in either area.[61] This style is also found in the Mātṛka group (Fig. 206) carved in the right courtyard cell of Śaiva Cave 22, a Rāṣṭrakūṭa-

period excavation, whose pillar bases and *candraśaila* are also comparable to architectural features in Cave 12 (and 15).[62]

Like the *dvārapālas* and shrine female figures, the eight Bodhisattvas inside the 12.1 shrine are now seated in *lalitāsana* instead of standing. Although a thick coat of plaster and paint was applied to all these images, the rather uneven arches carved above each give the shrine an appearance of careless or hastily completed work. Where their attributes are discernable, they show that the Bodhisattvas, still four on each wall, do not hold the same position as they do in the two floors above, or in the relief *maṇḍalas*. On the left wall (Fig. 207), the flag-bearing and sword-bearing Bodhisattvas (Sarvanivaraṇaviṣkambhin and Samantabhadra) are together in the first and second positions, respectively; each also holds a jewel-like object in the right hand, resting on the right thigh. The third position is held by Maitreya, holding a branch of the *nāgakesara* tree. The fourth Bodhisattva holds an open lotus, the emblem of Lokeśvara. On the right wall (Fig. 208), the front-most image holds a triple-bud branch of the *kalpadruma* tree, an emblem of Kṣitigarbha, similar to his portrayal at Lalitagiri in Orissa.[63] Next is an image of Mañjuśrī, holding a lotus supporting a book, locks of curly, "youthful" hair flowing over his shoulders. The attribute of the image in the third position has been destroyed (by process of elimination, this should be some form of Vajrapāṇi or Vajragarbha, who appears in *maṇḍalas* where Vajrapāṇi is otherwise absent).[64] The rearmost image on the right wall is nearly obliterated. However, the attribute remains, a frothy bud or elaborate jewel that should mark this figure as Ākāśagarbha.

Additional differences between the shrine of Cave 12.1 and other Cave 12 shrines are shown in the composition of the main shrine image, a *dharmacakramudrā* Buddha, seated in *vajraparyaṅkāsana* on a plain throne (Fig. 209), in contrast to the *bhūmisparśamudrā* Buddha images above and the *dhyānamudrā* Buddhas of the relief *maṇḍalas*. Also, instead of the usual throne-side attendants, Avalokiteśvara/Vajrapāṇi, here large *nāgas* stand behind the throne (Fig. 210), as did the large *chowrie*-bearers in Cave 4. And, the earlier rearing

81

vyālas under the "T" of the throne back have been transformed into streamlined leonine creatures that rest their forelegs on the elephants beneath them.

Cave 12.1–2

Between the first and second floors of the cave, a cell was cut into the right (south) wall of the courtyard, entered from a landing halfway up the stairs that lead from Cave 12.1 to 12.2, called Shrine 12.1–2 here (see plan). Although relatively small, it provides significant confirmation of the iconographic intent of the *maṇḍala* and main floor sculptural programs. On its ceiling is a large lotus medallion, a typical decorative device of eighth-century Brahmanical caves, for example, the west porch ceiling of Cave 16. The main image, carved on the back (in this case, south) wall, is a *bhūmisparśamudrā* Buddha, attended by Avalokiteśvara and Vajrapāṇi (Fig. 211), like the shrine images in Caves 12.2 and 12.3. Flanking this group are two nine-part relief *maṇḍalas* identical to those carved on the walls of Cave 12.1 below (Fig. 212, 213). Here, however, the *maṇḍalas* are effectively placed in the same position as the earliest ones in Cave 6, on either side of a central Buddha image. The position of the Cave 12.1–2 *maṇḍalas* provides the strongest confirmation that the eight-Bodhisattva groups in the shrines of Caves 11 and 12 were three-dimensional representations of the relief *maṇḍalas*, here placed where large-scale sculpture would not fit. Above the right-side *maṇḍala* is a small panel depicting a triad of female figures, most likely representing Cundā, Tārā, and Bhṛkuṭī.[65] Their presence here anticipates the much expanded group of female figures placed in the shrine antechamber on the third floor of Cave 12. The program of this cell also included a triad of deities carved on the right wall (Fig. 214). The central figure in this group is an image of Avalokiteśvara attended by Jambhala to the left, and to the right, an image of Tārā. Stylistically, these images are so similar to sculpture carved in the Cave 12.2 hall that it is likely that the same artisan may have been responsible for work in both areas (see below).

The left wall was not completed, but was filled in with randomly distributed panels.

Cave 12.2

All sculptures in the 12.2 hall are located along the central front-to-back axis. Many intrusive images were cut into pilasters at the junction of the veranda vestibule and the main hall, and at the junction of the main hall and the shrine vestibule. This location seems motivated by practical concerns: the wide stone blocks left at the front of the hall permit little light to enter the hall, so that only images along the main axis are lit by natural light from the front of the cave. On the left and right walls of the veranda vestibule are the only two major sculptures of this floor, apart from the shrine area. On the left is a panel depicting Rakta-Lokeśvara (Fig. 215), the figure of Avalokiteśvara marked by a small image of Amitābha in his *jaṭāmukuṭa*, attended to the left by Tārā and to the right by Bhṛkuṭī, with a *stūpa* in her *jaṭāmukuṭa*, and a flask dangling from her left hand.[66] The deep-cut relief, high crowns, and jewelry are characteristic of eighth-century Buddhist sculpture at Ellora, and, as mentioned earlier, nearly identical to the Cave 12.1–2 panel depicting Avalokiteśvara with Tārā and Jambhala. Less detailed iconographically than its predecessors, the location of this image, on the left of the approach to a shrine, connects it to Rakta-Lokeśvara images in Ellora's middle and transitional period Caves 4 and 11. This is one instance where a new iconographic form similar to images of eastern India appeared relatively early at Ellora and then evolved in a local style to become fully integrated into the full-blown *maṇḍala*.

In contrast to earlier caves where the Rakta-Lokeśvara images were asymmetrically solitary, in Cave 12.2 the group is paired with another composition directly across the vestibule on the right wall (Fig. 216). Here, a central male figure is accompanied by four female attendants. All sit in *lalitāsana*, right hands resting in *varadamudrā* on the knee, left hands holding a raised flower. Although the open lotus of the central male figure might suggest that it is some form of Avalokit-

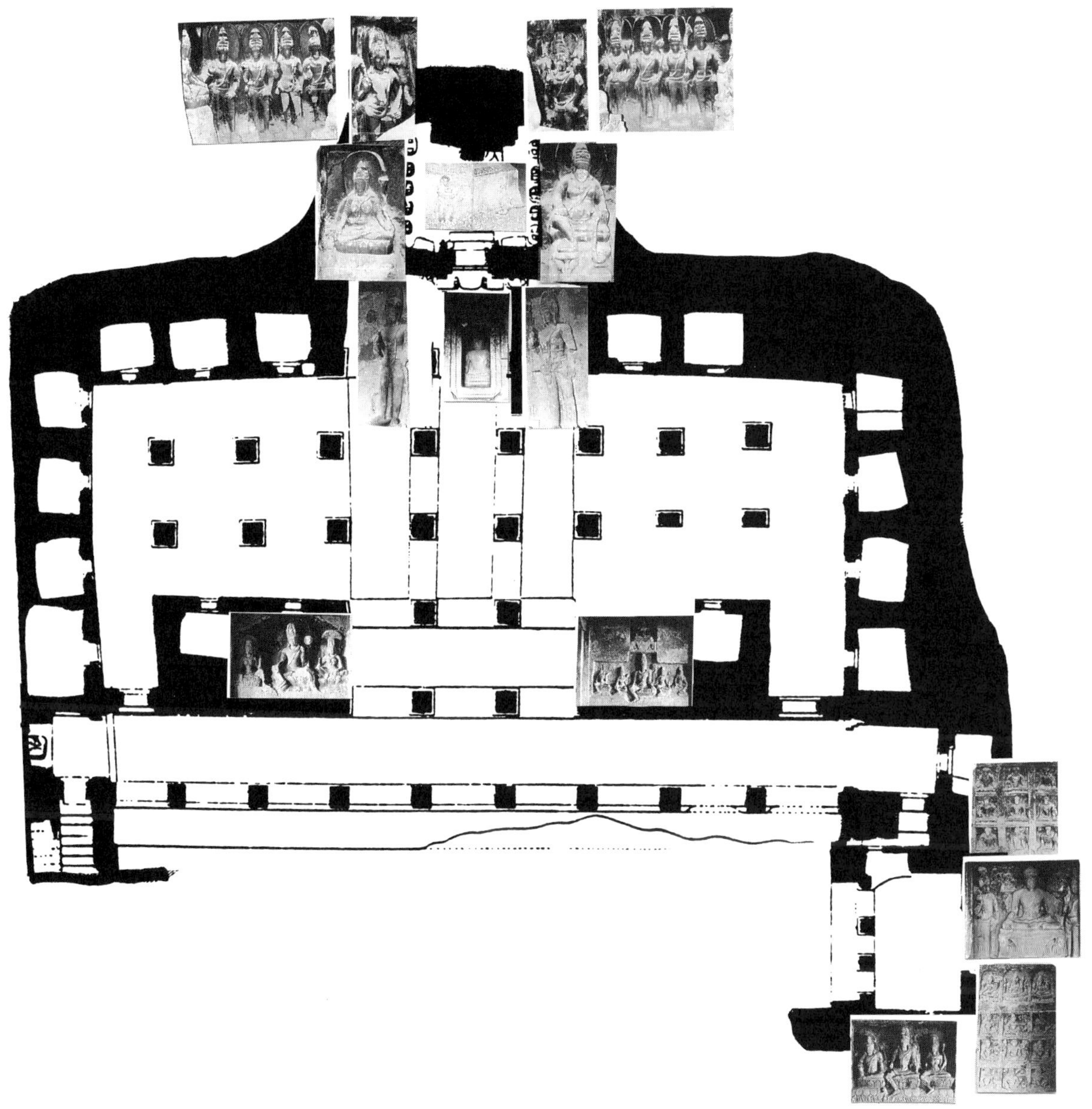

Text fig. 4–7   Cave 12.2 iconographic plan

eśvara, above his head is a neatly carved image of Akṣobhya, right hand in *bhūmi-sparśamudrā*, seated on a lion throne. Since Akṣobhya is the head of Mañjuśrī's lineage, another interpretation is that the image is intended to represent some form of Mañjuśrī.[67]

The four females, whose remaining attributes are identical (perhaps their color originally varied), are not easily identified, but may represent the four offering deities: Gītā (Song), Lāsyā (Enticing Dance), Mālā (Garland), and Nṛtyā (Exuberant Dance), who may occupy

83

outer circles of painted and textual *maṇḍalas*.[68] Alternatively, they may represent the "cult goddesses" who worship Mañjuśrī as Siddhaikavīra.[69] (See chapter 5 for further discussion of this image.)

Randomly placed, intrusively cut pilaster panels reveal and reinforce certain iconographic themes. For instance, at the front, left corner of the hall and veranda vestibule is a poorly carved replica of the better executed nine-square relief *maṇḍalas* found downstairs. Of more interest is an image of Vajradhara (Fig. 217), clearly marked by his hand position, and the *vajra* and bell he holds at chest level.[70] Vajradhara (or Vajrasattva) is considered a sixth Jina Buddha, or he may be a member of the "Sixteen Vajrabodhisattva" group, where he is located in the quarter of Akṣobhya, holding a *vajra* and bell over his heart.[71] The presence of this image here, even out of iconographic context, suggests that worshipers were aware of an even more complex *maṇḍala* than the one preserved in sculpture. And, several relief *stūpas* on this floor recall the much more numerous *stūpas* of the eighth century and later, found at eastern Buddhist sites like Bodhgaya and Ratnagiri.[72]

As described above, details of style and iconography of the shrine connect it closely with Cave 11.2. The *candraśaila* and miniature temples at the base of the door jambs show this relationship. It is underscored by the stylistic similarities between the *dvārapālas*, Avalokiteśvara and Vajrapāṇi (Fig. 218, 219), and images of these Bodhisattvas inside the Cave 11.2 shrines.

Inside the shrine of Cave 12.2, entered down two steps, the program first seen in the Cave 11.2 and 12.1 shrines is repeated with several iconographic and stylistic changes. For example, the positions of Jambhala and Tārā (Fig. 220, 221) are reversed on the front wall, Jambhala now on the right (south) of the doorway, Tārā on the left. And it is clear that the Jambhala image in Cave 12.2 is not a literal copy of the earlier one in shrine 11.2.1. Here, he holds a very long, thin-necked mongoose skin, the pot is under his left knee rather than his right foot, and he does not wear a garland, as does the image in 11.2.1.[73] The image of Tārā shares neither style nor position with her Shrine 11.2.1 counterpart; her peaked crown, sloping shoulders and

slim, crossed legs have more in common with the image of Lakṣmī carved on the base of the west wall of Cave 16.

Style and iconography also separate the Bodhisattva images in Cave 12.2 from those in 11.2 and 12.1 (Fig. 222, 223). Their crowns are tall, even more exaggerated than in the first floor of Cave 12, and covered in thick plaster that obscures all but their crest jewels. The large amount of paint preserved in the 12.2 shrine shows that details of clothing, like the folds draped over the Bodhisattva's legs, were painted. And, like the first floor shrine, here, too, there are four Bodhisattvas on the left and right shrine walls, excluding Avalokiteśvara (Fig. 224) and Vajrapāṇi (Fig. 225) who attend the central Buddha image. As suggested above, they may be viewed as standardized attendants, equivalent to the small attendant figures inside the central square of the relief *maṇḍalas*.

Complete identification of Bodhisattvas on the left wall is difficult, since attributes of those in the first and second positions are not clear. Looking first at the right wall (Fig. 223), where attributes are well-preserved, the group can be identified as (from front to back) Ākāśagarbha (holding a large bud or jewel), Sarvanivaraṇaviṣkambhin (pennant), Lokeśvara (open lotus), and Mañjuśrī (book). On the left (Fig. 222), the third figure holding a sword can be identified as Samantabhadra, and the fourth is clearly Maitreya, *stūpa* resting on his high-piled *jaṭāmukuṭa*. If the group corresponds to the textual lists, this leaves some form of Vajrapāṇi and Kṣitigarbha to be ascribed by process of elimination to the first two figures on the left. Since their attributes are not clear, these identifications are still hypothetical.

At ceiling level on the left front and side walls is a row of seven Buddha figures, seated in *vajraparyaṅkāsana*, right hands held in *bhūmisparśamudrā*. On the right is another group of seven Buddhas with hands held in *dhyānamudrā*. They correspond to the same groups found in the third floor shrine, and more loosely, to the two groups of seven large-scale Buddha images placed on either side of the back wall of Cave 12.3 (see below) although the *mūdras* differ.

As noted above, the central shrine image is a *bhūmisparśamudrā* Buddha/Śākyamuni (Fig.

226). In this shrine, the throne is plain, but figures of Bhūdevī and Aparājitā were carved in front, rising from the floor (Fig. 227, 228), confirming the identity of this Buddha image with those in Shrines 11.2.1, 11.2.3, and Cave 12.3.

Cave 12.3

The third floor of Cave 12 is an extraordinary creation, filled with light and major pieces of sculpture. Often the last Buddhist cave visited, it is a fitting conclusion to the

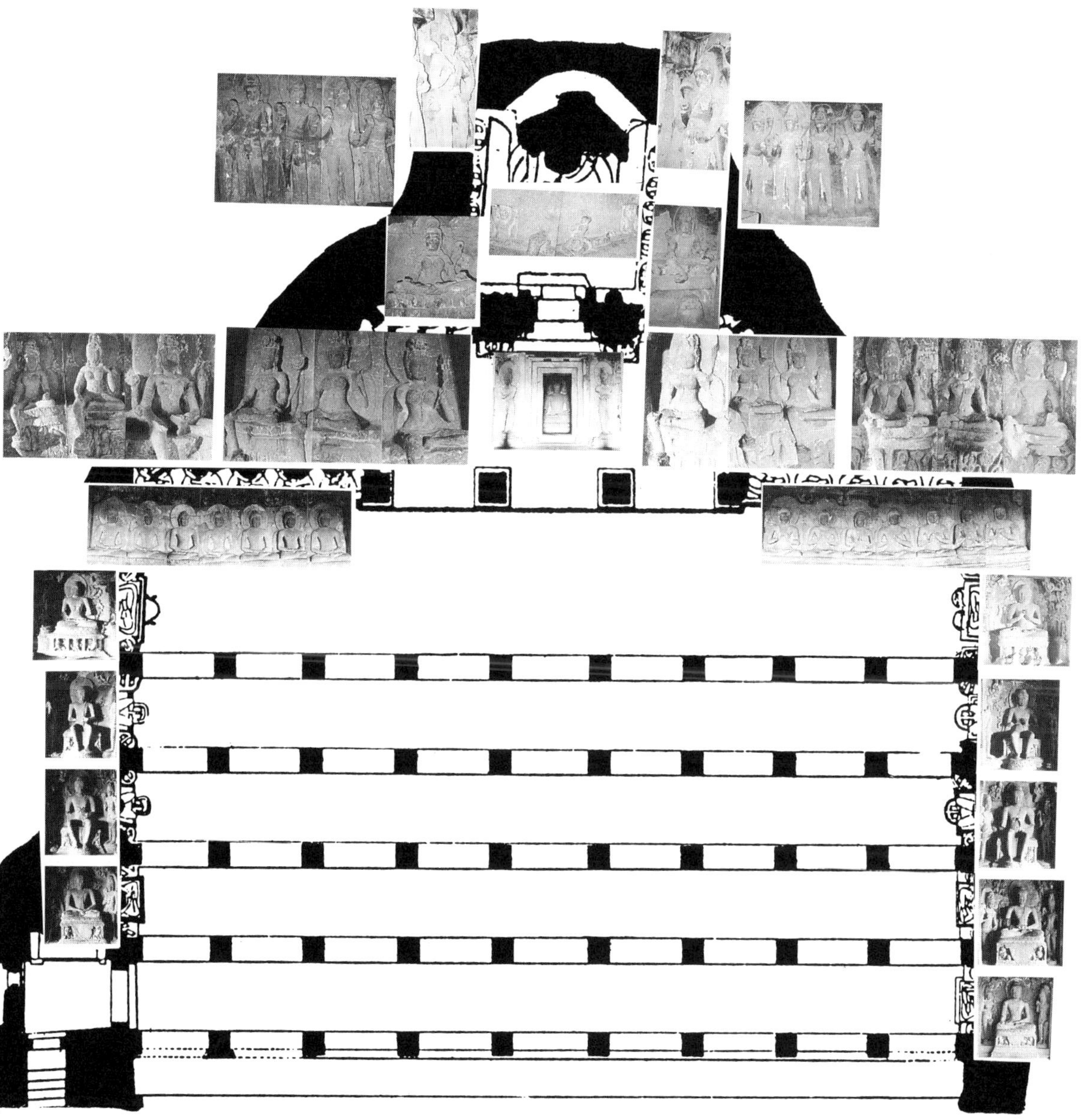

Text fig. 4–8   Cave 12.3 iconographic plan

experience of Buddhism at Ellora. The wide, pillared hall admits light all the way back to the shrine antechamber, a marked contrast with the dark, almost foreboding floors below (Fig. 229). This light was used to striking advantage, illuminating a sculptural program that completely covers every wall of the hall, antechamber, and shrine. The sculpture, distinguished by deep relief, symmetry, and formality relieved by individual variations in stylistic details, marks the mature unfolding of Ellora's *maṇḍala*.

Entering the hall, attention immediately focuses on nine Buddha images, carved in nearly three-dimensional relief in panels along the side walls, and, as in Cave 2, taking the place of cells usually cut into the *vihāra* walls. These images, four on the left (Fig. 230–233) and five on the right (Fig. 234–238) are separated by rows of pillars that lead the eye horizontally across the hall. All sit on lion thrones, attended by Avalokiteśvara and Vajrapāṇi, but their positions and *mudrās* vary, as do minor elements of style. As arranged around the hall, the pattern is:

Buddha 4	*dharmacakramudrā* *vajraparyaṅkāsana*	[rear wall] *dharmacakramudrā* *vajraparyaṅkāsana* [deer in front of throne]	Buddha 5
Buddha 3	*dharmacakramudrā* *pralambapādāsana*	*dharmacakramudrā* *pralambapādāsana*	Buddha 6
Buddha 2	*dharmacakramudrā* *pralambapādāsana*	*dharmacakramudrā* *pralambapādāsana*	Buddha 7
Buddha 1	*dhyānamudrā* *vajraparyaṅkāsana*	*bhūmisparśamudrā* *vajraparyaṅkāsana*	Buddha 8
[empty side shrine]		*bhūmisparśamudrā* *vajraparyaṅkāsana* [front of cave]	Buddha 9

Precisely portrayed, if not readily identifiable (groups of nine Buddhas are not mentioned in iconographic texts),[74] this group is most comparable to the ten Buddhas placed along the side walls of Cave 2. There, too, the left, front image is the only one portrayed with hands in *dhyānamudrā*. The importance of groups of nine Buddhas is reinforced by the two groups of nine small Buddha images placed at ceiling level in the shrine antechamber (see below), and earlier, by the nine-Buddha *maṇḍalas* in Cave 6. Here, in keeping with the articulation and thorough completion of the cave, the concept is expressed on a large scale—this part of the *maṇḍala* completely unfolded—in great and subtlely varying detail. Although unusual, such groups are not without precedent. For instance, a sixth- or seventh-century bronze finial from Central Asia portrays nine identical Buddhas seated in *vajraparyaṅkāsana*, hands held in *dhyānamudrā*.[75]

The stylistic variation among these images is noteworthy, displaying connections between Cave 12.3 and Buddhist art from elsewhere at Ellora and other sites and suggesting that several artisans with different backgrounds worked simultaneously on this part of the cave. For instance, the lions on the throne base of Buddha #5 (Fig. 234) appear to creep along the ground, reminiscent of lions in Ellora's earlier caves. By contrast, the lions at the base of Buddhas #1 and #4 (Fig. 239), carved in deeper relief, sit tensely upright and snarl convincingly. Their energy is comparable to the vivid ferocity of a lion in the Cave 16 Mātṛka shrine (Fig. 240). Moreover, the three-lion imagery of the fourth throne base is unprecedented at Ellora, but appears, for example, on the throne bases of Buddha images from Sirpur in Madhya Pradesh[76] and Bihar.[77] This stylistic relationship is underscored by the robe style of the Sirpur image that falls in ribbony folds over the left shoulder, as do robes on Buddha images from Ratnagiri, and those carved along the left rear wall of Cave 12.3.[78] Also, this panel, with small *parinirvāṇa* (deceased) Buddha images placed in the top right and left corners, may be seen as a nearly three-dimensional version of steles common in eastern India from the eighth century onward, where a similar *parinirvāṇa* Buddha may be placed at the top of the composition.[79]

In addition, the ornaments of the Bodhisattva attendants in these panels confirm their connection to mid-eighth century Rāṣṭrakūṭa sculpture at Ellora. For instance, the image of Avalokiteśvara with Buddha #1 (Fig. 241) wears belts that hang down in progressively longer loops, the longest to his knees. This design is seen in mid-eighth-century Brahmanical guardian images such as those in Cave 25, on the south veranda of Cave 22, and on the second floor veranda of Cave 15 (Fig. 241a). Its origin can be traced back ultimately to Cālukya prototypes, that likely influenced Ellora's Rāṣṭrakūṭa-period workshops.[80] A widespread convention, it appears, for example, on the ninth-century Bodhisattvas of Candi Mendut in central Java.[81]

On the back wall of the hall, two groups of seven Buddha images, seated in *vajraparyaṅkāsana*, were carved on a high, molded plinth. Those on the left (Fig. 242) hold their hands in *dhyānamudrā*; their robes are portrayed in a variety of stylized ribbon-like ends. These figures, representing, the six past Buddhas and the Buddha of this age, are distinguished by the different trees growing over their heads.[82] The Buddha images on the opposite (right) side of the rear wall (Fig. 243), all portrayed with hands held in *dharmacakramudrā*, have no distinguishing features, and have been more difficult to identify. They may represent an unusual group of seven Jina Buddhas.[83] Taken together, these groups are full-scale representations of the miniature groups carved at ceiling height in the Cave 12.2 and Cave 12.3 shrines. Such a large, formal display represents a great change from the much smaller and peripheral groups found even earlier, for instance on the veranda of Aurangabad Cave 1.[84] In Cave 12, they show how elements of earlier iconography were enlarged and completely integrated into this final, perfected example of Buddhist cave architecture. Slight variations in small details like the robes worn by Buddha images on the

left lend this floor an aesthetically lively atmosphere that would have been deadened if all images were identical in every detail.

Twelve female deities were carved, six on each side along the walls of the shrine antechamber (Fig. 244–247). As discussed earlier, large-scale female images framing the entrances to shrines are found from the earliest Brahmanical caves onward to the early Buddhist caves where, in Cave 6, prominent images of Bhṛkutī and Mahāmāyūrī were placed at the left and right ends of the shrine antechamber. Although most common at Ellora, a similar arrangement is also found at Aurangabad, where large female figures replace the usual Bodhisattva *dvārapālas* flanking the Cave 7 shrine door.[85] In Ellora Cave 10, Bhṛkutī and Mahāmāyūrī occupy a similar position, as *"dvārapālas"* to the small courtyard shrine to Avalokiteśvara. The precedent was thus set for the remarkable group in Cave 12.3.[86]

They wear nearly identical crowns and jewelry, and have the same proportions as the smaller-scale female figures in Cave 12.1–2 and the Cave 12.2 hall panels. They are single-faced, two are four-armed, the rest two-armed; all sit in *lalitāsana*, right hand held in *varadamudrā*. Distinguishing attributes were placed in the left hand and, in addition, beneath some of the figures are animals that might further assist in their identification. These attributes are not clear in every case, so it is not possible to ascribe a specific name to many of the figures, but several are clear and distinctive enough to suggest an identification for the group as a whole.

Most significant is the figure immediately to the right of the shrine door, who wears snakes in her hair and around her waist as a belt (Fig. 246a). Among Buddhist female deities, only the goddess Jāṅgulī (Lady of the Jungle), whose cognizance is the snake, wears such garb.[87] She appears in groups of females in only two places, a *maṇḍala* of Tārā, which Cave 12.3 clearly does not represent, or in groups of the ten or twelve Dhāraṇīs, embodiments of invocations found in two *maṇḍalas*: of Dharmadhātu Vāgīśvara Mañjuśrī[88] and of Mahāvairocana.[89] The presence of Jāṅgulī in the Ellora Cave 12.3 group of twelve suggests strongly that it should be regarded as a representation of the Dhāraṇīs, even though there is not a one-to-one correspondence between Dhāraṇīs named in the *maṇḍala* and the sculptures, and though the cave as a whole does not correspond systematically to either *maṇḍala*.[90]

In the Cave 12.3 group, in fact, we find some images now familiar from earlier caves at Ellora: a four-armed Cundā (also included in the lists of Dhāraṇīs) third from the left on the left side (Fig. 244c), Mahāmāyūrī (Fig. 246b) (perhaps Ellora's version of Parṇaśabarī, mentioned in the texts as holding a peacock feather), second on the right side, and a four-armed Bhṛkuṭī, third on the right side (Fig. 247a). The sixth figure on the left (that is closest to the shrine door) (Fig. 245c) holds a three-pointed *vajra* on an *utpala*. This corresponds closely to the description of Sarvakarmāvaraṇaviśodhanī in one of the iconographic texts on the Dhāraṇīs.[91] With these partial connections, it seems most likely that this group of twelve represents an early version of the Dhāraṇīs, part of a *maṇḍala* that shares some characteristics of those described in texts. Thus, like the Dhāraṇīs in these *maṇḍalas*, here they form part of the "outer circle" that the worshiper passes through in the approach to the central shrine image.

At the shrine door, the *dvārapālas* both stand cross-armed on lotus pedestals guarded by couchant lions (Fig. 248). Inside the shrine, as mentioned earlier, the program is a close copy of the Cave 12.2 shrine program, although there are stylistic differences. Here, the image of Jambhala (Fig. 249), again seated to the right of the shrine door, is a slim version of his more usual corpulent self, he wears no *yajñopavīta* (it may have been formed of now disintegrated plaster; remnants of thick plaster that would have filled out his form can be detected on both sides of the chest area as heavy white lines in the photograph), and he is seated directly over a large pot of overflowing jewels. His companion, Tārā, on the left side of the door (Fig. 250), is also slimmer than her counterpart in Cave 12.2, and her hair is arranged in a more rounded form. Both of these figures are too small to fit the colossal scale of the Cave 12.3 shrine, sug-

gesting that they may have been added by artisans different from those who worked on the massive Bodhisattva images.

Attributes still legible show that the Bodhisattva program of this shrine and that in Cave 12.2 are the same, although clearly, different artisans worked on them, too. Here, the left hands are raised, not resting on the hip, the crowns are somewhat shorter, and the shoulders are wider in proportion to the hips, features which make these figures more graceful and animated than those in the shrine below. On the left wall (Fig. 251), from front to back the first two positions are held by a baton- (or *vajra*-) holding Bodhisattva and one holding an oval object. Although unclear, these objects may identify them as Vajrapāṇi and Kṣitigarbha, who hold these positions in other shrines. Third on the left is the sword-bearing figure, Samantabhadra, and fourth is Maitreya, holding now a single bud of the *nāgakesara* tree. On the right (Fig. 252), the rearmost figure is Mañjuśrī, holding a book on an *utpala*, distinguished by its inverted triangular shape. The next figure holds an almost diamond-shaped bud or jewel, perhaps representing Kṣitigarbha. Third is Sarvanivaraṇaviṣkambhin, holding a banner that appears to fly up gracefully to the right, as if in a wind. Last (front-most) on the right, the Bodhisattva holds a large lotus bud, distinguishable by its rounded shape from Mañjuśrī's *utpala*, and thus, a sign that this figure is a form of Lokeśvara. Above them, groups of seven Buddhas, hands held in *dhyānamudrā* were carved at ceiling level on the left and right walls. The central shrine image is another *bhūmisparśamudrā* Buddha/Śākyamuni attended by Avalokiteśvara and Vajrapāṇi (Fig. 253, 254), the throne supported by dwarfs, and preceded by images of Bhūdevī (Fig. 255) (emerging out of the floor from her waist level, her head has been broken) and Aparājitā, now seated on her foe (Fig. 256). The area behind the throne was roughly cut out but not finished, as if being prepared for a small *pradakṣiṇapatha* inside the shrine.

Ellora's *maṇḍala*, fully unfolded, can be diagrammed as follows:

Level 3

Buddha/Śākyamuni

(Avalokiteśvara	Vajrapāṇi)
Maitreya	Mañjuśrī
Samantabhadra	Ākāśagarbha
Kṣitigarbha(?)	Sarvanivaraṇaviṣkambhin
Vajrapāṇi(?)	Lokeśvara

Tārā	Jambhala
Seven Buddhas/Akṣobhya	Seven Buddhas/Vairocana
Six Dhāraṇīs	Six Dhāraṇīs
Seven Mānuṣi Buddhas	Seven (Jina?) Buddhas
Four Buddhas	Five Buddhas

Level 2

Buddha/Śākyamuni

(Avalokiteśvara	Vajrapāṇi)
Maitreya	Mañjuśrī
Samantabhadra	Lokeśvara
Vajrapāṇi(?)	Sarvanivaraṇaviṣkambhin
Kṣitigarbha(?)	Ākāśagarbha
Tārā	Jambhala
Seven Buddhas/Akṣobhya	Seven Buddhas/Vairocana
Avalokiteśvara	Vajrapāṇi
Rakta-Lokeśvara	Siddhaikavīra(?)

Level 1

Buddha/Vairocana

Lokeśvara	Ākāśagarbha(?)
Maitreya	[Vajrapāṇi(?)]
Samantabhadra	Mañjuśrī
Sarvanivaraṇaviṣkambhin	Kṣitigarbha
Tārā	Cundā
Maitreya	Mañjuśrī
Buddha/Vairocana	Buddha/Vairocana

This pattern of similarity and difference suggests that the three floors of Cave 12 were programmatically related, with specific images rotating in position depending on the level of the *maṇḍala*.[92] The first level differs the most from the other two and, in this way, it may be most like Cave 4 which, as argued above, can be seen as the first level of a three-level *maṇḍala* presented in the Cave 2, 3, 4 group. The shrine in Cave 12.1 is also connected to Cave 4 in the absence of the conventional Avalokiteśvara/Vajrapāṇi pair as attendants to the shrine Buddha image. Instead, *nāgas* or large *chowrie*-bearers stand behind the throne. Moreover, in both cases, the shrine *dvārapālas* are not the usual Avalokiteśvara/ Maitreya or /Vajrapāṇi pair. In Cave 4 they are nearly identical; in Cave 12.1, they are Maitreya and Mañjuśrī.

These similarities suggest that Cave 4 may have prefigured the program of Cave 12.1. This is important because it suggests a more extensive relationship between earlier and later caves. Thus, Caves 4, 3, and 2 may have been components of a three-part set arranged horizontally, analogous to the three vertically aligned levels of Cave 12. The similarity in arrangement of Buddha images along the side walls of Cave 2 and Cave 12.3 are further evidence of this relationship. Even Cave 3 and Cave 12.2 are linked by the fact that the shrine program in Cave 3 is nearly identical to that of Cave 2, as are the programs of shrines in Caves 12.2 and 12.3.

Ellora presents an example unique in the Indian subcontinent of architectural attempts to transform a three-tiered *maṇḍala* into a structural form. The details may not correspond well to textual versions of *maṇḍalas*, sharing instead, elements of both *kriyā tantra* and *yoga tantra* texts, leaving Ellora and its rock-cut *maṇḍalas* as the best, if limited, text upon which to reconstruct the evolution of Buddhist belief and practice in the western caves. As the next chapter will show, the evolution is important because it preserves *in situ* imagery that is found out of programmatic context at important, contemporary Buddhist sites across the central part of India. It therefore can provide revealing clues to aid in reconstructing the development of early tantric Buddhism in places where religious monuments were not as well preserved as Ellora.

Table: 4.2 *The Core Maṇḍala in Diagrams and Shrines*

Cave 12 Maṇḍala ("folded")			Cave 12 Maṇḍala (unfolded)	
Maitreya	Samantabhadra	Kṣitigarbha	Vairocana	
Avalokiteśvara	Vairocana	Vajrapāṇi	Avalokiteśvara	Vajrapāṇi
Sarvanivaraṇa-viṣkambhin	Ākāśagarbha	Mañjuśrī	Maitreya	Mañjuśrī
			Samantabhadra	Ākāśagarbha
			Kṣitigarbha	Sarvanivaraṇaviṣkambhin

Cave 11.2.1 Shrine		Cave 11.2.3 Shrine	
Śākyamuni		Śākyamuni	
Avalokiteśvara	Vajrapāṇi	Avalokiteśvara	Vajrapāṇi
Maitreya	Mañjuśrī	Maitreya	Mañjuśrī
Samantabhadra	Ākāśagarbha	Kṣitigarbha	Ākāśagarbha
Kṣitigarbha	Sarvanivaraṇaviṣkhambin	Samantabhadra	Sarvanivaraṇaviṣkambhin

Cave 12.1 Shrine		Cave 12.2 Shrine		Cave 12.3 Shrine	
Vairocana		Śākyamuni		Śākyamuni	
Lokeśvara	Ākāśagarbha	Maitreya	Mañjuśrī	Maitreya	Mañjuśrī
Maitreya	[Vajrapāṇi?]	Samantabhadra	Lokeśvara	Samantabhadra	Ākāśagarbha(?)
Samantabhadra	Mañjuśrī	[Vajrapāṇi]	Sarvanivaraṇa.	Kṣitigarbha	Sarvanivaraṇa.
Sarvanivaraṇa-viṣkambhin	Kṣitigarbha	[Kṣitigarbha]	Ākāśagarbha	Vajrapāṇi(?)	Lokeśvara

5. A CENTER ON THE PERIPHERY: ELLORA'S PLACE IN BUDDHIST ART

Ellora is often regarded only as a peripheral regional Buddhist center, most worthy of mention as the end of the cave-temple tradition. Like other peripheral sites, it has been studied individually, without great concern for its place in the wider scope of Buddhist art. This situation applies to many sites in the area from Maharashtra south to Andhra Pradesh and east to Orissa. Unlike work on northern and eastern Indian art, where various models for diffusion of artistic styles and iconographic themes have emphasized both intra- and cross-regional relations,[1] little has been done to consider connections across the Deccan, or to seek interregional links.

As the previous chapters have suggested, Ellora reveals many significant connections to Buddhist art of other sites outside Maharashtra. Integrating these hints of pattern, this chapter will explore connections among a group of important Buddhist sites of the sixth to tenth centuries, covering a region from the western Deccan to eastern Orissa and south to Andhra Pradesh. Geographically, these sites are distributed along the periphery of the late classical-early medieval Buddhist heartland. Each preserves unique variations and even innovations in Buddhist art of the period.

Up to now, study of this material has proceeded region by region so that we know, for example, how the style of sculpture and architecture at Sirpur or Ellora developed. We know much less about the possible interrelationships between the two sites. Second, where relationships have been explored, they have usually been viewed as a dialogue between each peripheral site and some site in the heartland. This is not to suggest that developments in the Buddhist heartland were not a major influence on the periphery. Indeed, the regional sites that will be discussed here may preserve a record of central developments not as well preserved at major sites of northern and eastern India. Each site will be considered in the context of a group of sites that are not ordinarily discussed in detail together, as a kind of *maṇḍala* in its other sense of a circle or group of related entities, an inquiry that should both reveal unrecognized relationships within the regional system(s) and reflect on developments further north during an extremely fertile and dynamic period.

This approach will also call into question common assumptions about the transmission of ideas and religious practice. Clearly, the *style* of sculpture and architecture differ at the sites to be examined. Equally clear are the political boundaries that divided the northern Deccan and parts of central and eastern India during the period under consideration. Yet, are we to assume that these boundaries necessarily separated both religious practice and the *content* of sculpture and architecture that provide the evidence for those practices? Or, should we assume that political and religious influences moved simultaneously in the same direction? Was there a different pattern in which religious centers attracted and concentrated resources—public and private—which in turn attracted the teachers, who spread new ideas from center to center?

Without a specific Buddhist patron, it appears that Ellora, at least, was not the result of a single political or cultural shift. In its later Buddhist phase of the late seventh and early eighth centuries, there were distinctive stylistic and iconographic changes that have usually been associated with the advent of Cālukya influenced Rāṣṭrakūṭa patronage. However, the iconography of these caves—the Buddhism itself—is unlikely to have originated at Cālukya sites and instead, has parallels at Sirpur, Ratnagiri, Sanci, and Bodhgaya. Such connections suggest, if not direct cross-regional political alliances, at least the absence of obstacles to communication across the Deccan. Comparison of key features such as central Buddha images and female iconography, as well as minor stylistic details like pillar and throne base design are suggestive of relationships among these sites. At no other Indian site of this period, with the possible exception of Ratnagiri, is evidence for a *maṇḍala* so well preserved as at Ellora. Yet, iconographical features among all suggest a transregional diffusion of a teaching or teachings that shared a core of common belief.

This chapter will follow two paths to explore these questions. First, iconographical studies of key images will reveal with particular clarity its special position in Buddhist art. Taking apart the *maṇḍala*, these cross-sectional studies examine images important throughout Ellora's Buddhist period, comparing them as appropriate to material from other sites, to show both their unique character and their links to iconographical developments in the Buddhist world of the seventh and eighth centuries. Second, the threads of connection to sites throughout India will be gathered together in summaries that discuss the mutual relations among peripheral and more central Buddhist monuments. These are, then, members of the *maṇḍala* in which Ellora developed. Examining them together will, thus, put into perspective Ellora's place in Buddhist art.

Iconographic Studies

Bhṛkuṭī

Among the female deities that endow Ellora with its unique iconographical character, Bhṛkuṭī stands out as one of the earliest to be depicted with special clarity. Always found paired with Tārā or other deities, the features that make Bhṛkuṭī so important are described below.

Images of Bhṛkuṭī are found in several Buddhist caves, some identified earlier by Gupte.[2] However, an extremely important sculpture of this goddess, located in the left (north) end of the antechamber in Cave 6 (Fig. 31) was misidentified by him as Tārā. As the earliest Bhṛkuṭī image at Ellora, and one of the earliest known in India, this figure well illustrates the appearance of the deity in the early seventh century. The Cave 6 Bhṛkuṭī stands in *samapādasthānaka*, wearing her hair piled into an ascetic's stylized *jaṭā-mukuṭa*, upon which a *stūpa* rests. An antelope skin (*ajina*) hangs over her left shoulder. The right arm, now broken near the elbow, was most probably positioned in *abhayamudrā*. With her left arm, she holds the stalk of a fat lotus bud, growing from a clump of frothy foliage near her lotus pedestal. She is attended on her right by a female standing in *ābhaṅga* pose and holding a *chowrie* typical of female attendants throughout the western caves. On the left, the attendant also appears to be an ascetic wearing a *jaṭāmukuṭa*; she raises her right arm in *stutimudrā* to salute the main figure.

Many of these features were assembled from a local pool of symbols never before used to depict a female figure. Her attributes show that she should be identified as Bhṛkuṭī instead of Tārā, and therefore should not be confused with other female images identified as Tārā in the western caves.[3] Thus, her upright stance and plain costume are iconographic, not stylistic traits, and contrast strongly with the lush curves and elaborate ornaments of images such as the "Tārās" from Aurangabad Cave 7.[4] Specifically, the attributes of Ellora's Cave 6 female ascetic, Bhrkuti, her *jaṭāmukuṭa, ajina*,[5] lotus bud, and stance are most comparable to the images of Avalokiteśvara that guard the left side of the Cave 6 (Fig. 33) and Cave 2 (Fig. 62) shrine doors. Compositional aspects of the image, especially the *makara*-arch framing the panel, are also derived from local practice seen earlier in Brahmanical Caves 21 and 14. Moreover, in Cave 6 Bhrkuti is paired with Mahāmāyūrī who faces her from the opposite end of the antechamber. This pairing, repeated in Cave 10 (see below), is without precedent at other Buddhist sites, but may echo the earlier Brahmanical precedent of pairing Gaṅgā and Yamunā images on either end of verandas, as in Cave 21 (Fig. 22, 23).

Study of Bhrkuti images elsewhere in India has revealed that from the beginning she was portrayed as the ascetic emanation of Avalokiteśvara's *prajñā*, in contrast to the emanation of his *karuṇa*, the compassionate Tārā.[6] In eastern India, in the early seventh century, Bhrkuti was portrayed in triads with Tārā and Avalokiteśvara in the stucco panels of Nalanda's main stupa.[7] In these images, Bhrkuti's hair is arranged in a *jaṭāmukuṭa*; she wears plain clothes and no ornaments. In an eighth-century image from Sarnath; she is placed to the proper right of an image of Avalokiteśvara; she holds an *akṣamālā* in her right hand and a *kamaṇḍalu* in her left.[8]

In the *Sādhanamālā*, more complex attributes are ascribed to Bhrkuti, who appears in *maṇḍalas* or in compositions depicting individual deities.[9] The iconographic texts say nothing about her attributes when portrayed with one face and two hands. She is described with one face and four arms as assistant (with Tārā) to Avalokiteśvara Khasarpaṇa and Amoghapāśa—common representations in later art—where she has three eyes, wears a *jaṭāmukuṭa* adorned with a *stūpa*, and red clothes. Her two left hands hold the triple-staff (*tridaṇḍa*) and flask (*kamaṇḍalu*). One of her right hands holds a rosary, while the other may be in several different positions. She is generally placed to the left of Avalokiteśvara. She and Tārā may also attend Rakta-Lokeśvara.[10]

Although the earliest images are not so complex as the descriptions of Bhrkuti in the later *Sādhanamālā*, the consistent presence of ascetic traits such as the matted hair and rosary, confirm the identification of these early images as Bhrkuti. Moreover, where the Ellora Cave 6 image differs from other early examples from Nalanda and Sarnath, for instance, in wearing an *ajina* and holding a lotus bud, the attributes are to be found instead in local sculptures of Avalokiteśvara. More significantly, the *stūpa* found even in Ellora's earliest images is also mentioned in the *Sādhanamālā*, but does not appear in the earliest eastern Indian representations.[11] If similarity to a text or later images is accepted as a criterion of iconographic advancement, the Ellora Cave 6 Bhrkuti was more advanced than contemporaries in the Buddhist heartland. And, as examples to be discussed here show, the iconography of Bhrkuti developed rapidly from her earliest form to one that anticipated the elaborate images of the ninth century and later in eastern India and Orissa.

Ellora's Bhrkuti had two basic forms whose iconography changed gradually through the Buddhist period. The Cave 6 Bhrkuti exemplifies the first type, in which she stands alone or in a mediating position to a Buddha shrine group. In the second type, like the Nalanda, Sarnath and Orissan images, she accompanies Tārā as attendant to Avalokiteśvara. Both types appear in the earlier Buddhist caves at Ellora, but the standing form did not continue beyond the mid-seventh century, while the second type persisted into the early eighth century.

Images in Caves 2, 4, 5RW, and 8 show how the iconography evolved from the Cave 6 form, never duplicating but always reinterpreting her identifying attributes. In Cave 2, Bhrkuti was placed on the front (west) wall to the left (north) of the hall entrance (Fig. 58). Like the Cave 6 image, here she stands in *samapādasthānaka* on a lotus pedestal, right hand raised in *abhayamudrā*, with the stem of a fat lotus bud entwined around her left arm. Her hair is piled in a high *jaṭāmukuṭa* with a large *stūpa* on it. She, too, is attended by two

93

female figures. But there are differences as well. This figure wears a short necklace (perhaps a *rudramālā*), but she does not wear the *ajina*. Their positions differ, as well. The Cave 2 Bhṛkuṭī could have been added as an afterthought (as were the other panels in this location). The Cave 6 figure was certainly part of the original plan of the shrine area. Yet, if one circumambulates Cave 2 in a clockwise direction, one passes first Bhṛkuṭī, then a row of seated Buddha images, and then confronts the image of Avalokiteśvara as shrine *dvārapāla*. Similarly, circumambulating Cave 6, one first encounters Bhṛkuṭī, then Avalokiteśvara as *dvārapāla* before reaching the shrine. So, from the point of view of ritual, both the Cave 2 and Cave 6 figures may have served the same function, focusing the worshiper's attention prior to the approach to Avalokiteśvara and then the central Buddha image.

In Caves 5RW and 8, Bhṛkuṭī was not only sculpted in a different style but, also, she was placed inside the main shrine. In Cave 5RW she stands on the left (east) wall to the proper right of the main *dharmacakramudrā* Buddha (Fig. 50). As in Caves 6 and 2, here she is accompanied by two female attendants, and exhibits the same attributes of upright stance, *abhayamudrā*, rosary, fat lotus bud, and *jaṭāmukuṭa*. However, her hair is more naturalistically wavy than in the stiff, cylindrical arrangements of Caves 6 and 2. In this respect, the Cave 5RW Bhṛkuṭī resembles the image from Sarnath mentioned earlier.

Stylistically and iconographically related to the Cave 5RW image is the Bhṛkuṭī carved on the right wall of the Cave 8 shrine (Fig. 103). Again, the figure stands upright, holds a rosary and lotus and now, in addition, a *kamaṇḍalu*. She wears no jewelry, a feature accentuated by the elaborate ornaments worn by the female facing her on the left shrine wall (Fig. 102), most likely an image of Tārā who, in one verse of the *Sādhanamālā* is described as *nanālaṅkaravālī* (wearing various ornaments).[12] Her shifting position, from the Cave 6 antechamber to the Cave 2 front hall, to the Cave 5RW and 8 shrines suggests that by the mid-seventh century her iconography, or at least, *maṇḍalic* position, had not been rigidly codified. The shift from the left to right side of

the cave is seen first in Cave 8. After this, Bhṛkuṭī was always placed to the viewer's right.

Ellora's second group of Bhṛkuṭī images developed in a series of gradual changes that show the iconography evolving locally, not simply responding to imported alterations. This group includes Bhṛkuṭī in Rakta-Lokeśvara triads, and except for one example, these images belong to the later part of the Buddhist period in the late seventh and early eighth centuries.

First in this group is the Rakta-Lokeśvara panel (Fig. 83, 84) located in the left (north) end of the Cave 4 antechamber. The main image is Avalokiteśvara as ascetic, with *jaṭāmukuṭa*, *ajina*, *akṣamālā*, and lotus bud. To his right stands Bhṛkuṭī, in slight *ābhaṅga* pose, hair in a neat *jaṭāmukuṭa*, right hand raised in *abhayamudrā* and holding an *akṣamālā*; in her left is a *kamaṇḍalu*. Stylistically and iconographically, this image is most like the Bhṛkuṭī in Cave 8 than others of the first group. The group's composition, including an image of Tārā and two Dhyāni-Buddhas in the upper corners of the panel, is most comparable to one of the Nalanda stucco panels, although there Avalokiteśvara sits with legs crossed, not in *pralambapādāsana* as in Cave 4.[13]

The transitional quality of the Cave 4 Bhṛkuti is emphasized by comparing it with the Bhṛkuṭī in the south veranda cell of Cave 10. Here, Bhṛkuṭī (Fig. 142), on the right, is paired with Mahāmāyūrī on the left, flanking the entrance to this Avalokiteśvara shrine. For the first time, Bhṛkuṭī is four-armed, seated in *lalitāsana* on a lotus. Her upper right hand is in *abhayamudrā*, while the lower right is in *varadamudrā*. She holds a *tridaṇḍa* in her upper left hand and a *kamaṇḍalu* in the lower left. Her hair is arranged in a *jaṭāmukuṭa*, and she wears no ornaments. In most respects, this image corresponds to many examples of the eighth and ninth centuries from eastern India and Ratnagiri.[14] Ghosh, who did not take Ellora's earliest Bhṛkuṭīs into account, observed that while the exact date of appearance of a four-armed form is not known, finds of numerous images show that it became popular from the ninth century onward.[15]

The iconography of the Cave 10 image might suggest that it is equally late. However, its style does not differ dramatically from its predecessor in Cave 4 both of which, according to the relative chronology explained earlier, are mid-seventh century excavations. The images are carved in flatter relief than the earliest images in Caves 6, 2, and 8. They both have flattish faces, longer noses and *mukuṭas* that are neither cylindrical nor wavy. Their breasts are not as exaggeratedly spherical as in earlier sculptures. In other words, while the iconography of Bhṛkutī seems to have taken a sudden leap forward in Cave 10, the sculptural tradition developed along a more gradual path, away from the lush contours and relatively deep relief of early seventh-century sculpture at Ellora. And, even while her individual iconography changed, her position repeated, albeit in reverse, that of the very first Ellora Bhṛkutī paired with Mahāmāyūrī. To my knowledge, no text describes this association, nor are there images from elsewhere which illustrate it. It seems to have been a unique relationship, which was abandoned after completion of Cave 10 by the third quarter of the seventh century.

There are also important iconographic similarities between the Cave 4 Rakta-Lokeśvara group and its successor in the left (north) courtyard cell of Cave 11 (Cave 11NC) (Fig. 145). The main image of this cell is a *bhūmi-sparśamudrā* Buddha, located on the east wall. Thus, the Avalokiteśvara panel is in its expected place, as in Cave 4, to the left or north, of the main shrine image. As in the Cave 4 group, here Avalokiteśvara is attended by two females and two Dhyāni-Buddhas. His *jaṭāmukuṭa* is still cylindrical with a flattish top and clearly delineated locks of hair. Yet, his ornaments and sinuously twisted, jewelled *yajñopavīta* reflect the advent of a new style, reflected even more strongly in images of the main Cave 11 shrines. Four-armed Bhṛkutī (Fig. 147), seated to his left, holds the same objects as she has in Cave 10, although her staff does not appear to be three-pronged. In addition, a *stūpa* is clearly visible in her *mukuṭa*. The group as a whole corresponds well to Rakta-Lokeśvara images of the medieval period. Yet, stylistically, the Bhṛkutī image seems to be derived from the Cave 10 image, just as the style of the Cave 10 Bhṛkutī

evolved from the one on Cave 4. The relief is still low, the breasts are rather flat and her torso is stiff. Her *mukuṭa* is more schematic, with less attention paid to individual locks of hair. It should be assigned a date in the last quarter of the seventh century.

Finally, in Cave 12, Bhṛkutī appears in two important locations. On the second floor, she is again part of a Rakta-Lokeśvara panel (Fig. 215), carved on the left (north) wall of the front hall. As in Cave 11, she sits to the left of Avalokiteśvara. She is now two-armed; her right hand once raised is now broken. A stoppered *kamaṇḍalu* rests next to her left hand. Here, however, she is fully ornamented, as if the convention of portraying her as an ascetic had been forgotten. Last, on the third floor of Cave 12, Bhṛkutī is one of the twelve female deities flanking the shrine antechamber (Fig. 247), where she is on the right (south) wall, first from the left. Again, she is four-armed, holding an *akṣamālā* in her right hand, which is raised in *abhayamudrā*, her lower right held in *varadamudrā*. Her upper left hand holds a twisted stick and the lower left probably held a *kamaṇḍalu*.[16] The top of her hair preserves locks of a *jaṭāmukuṭa*, but as do the other eleven females in this group, she wears an elaborate headdress and a complete set of jewels. Although the style of both Cave 12 Bhṛkutī images approaches that of eighth-century sculpture from Ellora's Rāṣṭrakūṭa period, and of medieval sculpture in general, there are no images from outside Ellora which appear to have directly inspired these. Instead, it seems that Bhṛkutī's iconography developed at Ellora where its expression in stone was affected by the general changes in style that characterize both Caves 11 and 12. From this point of view the Cave 12.3 image is most important because, although it is found in a different context from others at the site, it preserves attributes found as early as the Cave 10 Bhṛkutī.

Bhṛkutī images at Ellora are significant for several reasons. First, the earliest ones preserve the nascent appearance of this deity, represented in the literally hieratic sense that conventional signs were used to indicate the meaning of the icon. Thus, Avalokiteśvara's ascetic attributes of *ajina*, *jaṭāmukuṭa*, *kamaṇḍalu*, were borrowed to represent Bhṛkutī, 95 just as early seventh-century Bhṛkuṭī figures from eastern India seem to have adapted the iconography of the Brahmanical female ascetic, Pārvatī, to a Buddhist purpose.[17] Yet, these images are far from hieratic; instead they appear to be entirely original creations in stone. It is of course possible that similar images preceded them but are no longer preserved. Meanwhile, no female figures in Aurangabad's later caves, which otherwise anticipate some stylistic and iconographic traits of Ellora's Buddhist sculptures, are depicted with such clearly identifiable traits. Suddenly, at Ellora soon after 600, the iconography became more specific, incorporating both local contextual themes like the *makara*-arch as a framing device, and features with very specific iconographic meaning, like Avalokiteśvara's *ajina*.

Second, differences among the Ellora images show that a single model was not faithfully copied each time. The icon did not remain static. Instead, at Ellora itself it developed and changed, in the direction of increasing conformity to later textual descriptions and images. At the same time, as the style of the Buddhist caves became more complex through the seventh and early eighth century, the iconography of the later images became relatively stable. Such continuity of iconography indicates that much of the change in Buddhism at Ellora could be due to internal development.

Finally, Ellora's Bhṛkuṭī images reveal parallels to contemporary images in eastern India and Orissa, but neither stylistic nor iconographic similarities suggest direct influence in either direction. Instead, they appear to have been part of a shared pool of new ideas, the physical manifestation of a changing doctrine that spread throughout much of India by the early seventh century. If Ellora's Bhṛkuṭī images seem to anticipate even later images in eastern India it is because the teachings, which inspired them, must have been similar, while the techniques used to express them remained regionally distinct.[18]

Mahāmāyūrī

As does Bhṛkuṭī, Mahāmāyūrī appears for the first time in the Western caves at Ellora.

But, unlike images of Bhṛkuṭī that are found at many Buddhist sites in India, images comparable to Ellora's Mahāmāyūrī are quite rare. Moreover, there appears to be no precedent for her pairing with Bhṛkuṭī in Caves 6 and 10, one of the unique features of Ellora's iconography and *maṇḍala*. According to later iconographic texts, this figure is described in various *maṇḍalas* as the head of one *sādhana*, and also as assistant to various forms of Tārā, but she is never mentioned in conjunction with Bhṛkuṭī. According to these texts, Mahāmāyūrī holds a peacock feather when two-handed. When six-handed, she may also hold a bow and arrow, the peacock feather, a bowl full of jewels (*ratnaghaṭa*) and a flask.[19]

At the south end of the Cave 6 antechamber, a panel representing Mahāmāyūrī (Fig. 32) was carved to face the Bhṛkuṭī image at the opposite end. Standing on a lotus pedestal in *samapādasthānaka*, Mahāmāyūrī (literally, "The Great Pea Hen") holds a peacock feather in her upraised right hand, and a fruit or jewel (*ratnaghaṭa?*) in her left. To make the iconography more precise, a peacock was carved to her immediate right. Also, in the foreground of the panel is a scribe seated at a small table, a feature unparalleled in other images or texts. The style and composition of this image are most like those of the Cave 6 Bhṛkuṭī panel. Both are framed by *makara*-arches, under which hover chubby flying figures, and both females are attended by small female figures. This is the earliest image of Mahāmāyūrī at Ellora and may well be the earliest extant image from India.

In Cave 8, the same iconographical devices were employed to depict Mahāmāyūrī (Fig. 101), again placed at the right (south) end of the shrine antechamber. Holding the peacock feather and *ratnaghaṭa*, she is accompanied by a scribe, peacock, and two flying figures, who now face her instead of the viewer. The dry carving style here differs from that of the Cave 6 figure and the composition is less unified than the Cave 6 panel, signifying that the Cave 8 image is the later of the two.[20]

Numerous Chinese translations of Sanskrit texts of the *Mahāmāyūrīvidya-rājñī* show that at least as early as the sixth century, Mahāmāyūrī was commonly invoked for protection, especially against snake poison.[21] Since the earliest date of these translations is 516 C.E., it is likely that in India she was popular at least as early if not earlier than the sixth century. However, such early texts do not describe images of Mahāmāyūrī. It is only the later Buddhist iconographical texts, such as the *Sādhanamālā* and *Niṣpannayogāvalī*, surviving from periods no earlier than the twelfth century, that include descriptions of this deity, where she may be discussed alone or as one of the five protective females, the Pañcarakṣas.[22] These texts, which assign two-armed Mahāmāyūrī a peacock feather, provide a sure way of distinguishing her from the Hindu goddess, Sarasvatī, whose *vāhana* is a *haṁsa* (goose). However, no text describes her precisely as she appears in Caves 6 and 8. Thus, Ellora's earliest images of Mahāmāyūrī present a unique iconography suggesting that, like Bhṛkutī, this figure may have been an original creation, interpreting for the first time a text not translated into stone sculpture before the seventh century.

The Mahāmāyūrī images of Caves 10 and 12.3 are clearly based on a different model than that used in Caves 6 and 8. At the same time, certain features, notably the peacock feather and peacock-*vāhana*, are consistent among all four. Also, as are the earlier images, the later ones are located in the antechambers of shrine areas. In Cave 10, Mahāmāyūrī (Fig. 141) occupies the left (east) side of the entrance to the Avalokiteśvara shrine in the south courtyard aisle. Here, as in Cave 6, she is placed opposite Bhṛkutī, although their positions are reversed. In Cave 12.3, Mahāmāyūrī is one of six female figures flanking the right (south) side of the shrine antechamber (Fig. 246), half of the twelve Dhāraṇīs located there. It is noteworthy that in three of her four appearances, Mahāmāyūrī is found to the right of the shrine entrance, a consistency that suggests some kind of textual (oral, if not written) source that provided consistency for her *maṇḍalic* position.

Both the Cave 10 and 12.3 images are seated in *lalitāsana*, right leg pendant and resting on a lotus. Beneath the lotus seat of each is a shallow, full-face relief carving of a peacock. In Cave 10, the figure holds a peacock feather in her upraised right hand; in Cave 12.3, the feather is held in the left hand. As Debala Mitra has pointed out, these seated images are comparable only to one other im-

age, carved on a plaque found at Nalanda,[23] which exhibits the same pose, peacock feather and peacock-*vāhana* as the later Ellora examples.

A further extension of the Nalanda-type image may be seen in a line drawing accompanying a diagram of a Mahāmāyūrī *maṇḍala* from the Japanese iconographical model book *Shosonzuzō* produced for Tendai Buddhist use in Japan.[24] Here, a four-armed Mahāmāyūrī sits on a peacock, holding a peacock feather in her upraised left hand, jewels in her lower left and upper right hands, and a lotus stalk in her lower right. Among known images of Mahāmāyūrī, only the Ellora, Nalanda, and *Shosonzuzō* examples share a simplicity of form that serves to emphasize their peacock emblems. Such features contrast with the multiple arms and attributes of later Tibetan images and textual descriptions of this deity.[25] The images of Ellora Caves 10 and 12.3 may be seen as relatively early examples of the type that was to be produced in eastern India and then exported to China and Japan in the eighth century and later. The consistently local style of carving shows no sign of influence from major images of another stylistic or regional tradition. In the seventh and early eighth centuries, when Ellora's Mahāmāyūrī images were carved, the sources for iconography there might instead have been orally transmitted texts whose interpretation was left to a local school of monks and artisans.

Cundā

Unlike Bhṛkutī and Mahāmāyūrī, recognizable images of Cundā only appear in the latest Buddhist period. Her presence connects Ellora more closely to Ratnagiri, where there are many images of Cundā, than to other eastern Indian sites where, except for Nalanda, more complex images are only seen from a later date.[26] Also, like the Mahāmāyūrī-Bhṛkutī pair, the pairing of Cundā and Tārā at Ellora as major interior shrine entrance "guardians" in Cave 12.1 appears to be unprecedented. The three major Cundā images to be discussed below show another aspect of Ellora's iconography, at once unique and linked to other Buddhist sites in India.

The earliest Ellora Cundā (Fig. 148) is a   97

four-armed figure carved in the midst of other panels to the right of the Rakta-Lokeś-vara group in Cave 11NC, identifiable by the characteristic begging bowl (*pātra*) held in her left hand, which rests in her lap.[27] Here she sits in *lalitāsana*, her natural right hand held in *varadamudrā*, her upper right raised to hold a rosary, while with the upper left, she holds a book on a lotus. In a panel carved by the door to Shrine 11.2.1, paired with Tārā, she holds an open lotus with no book, but her inner hands hold a bowl in her lap, corresponding closely to textual descriptions and to medieval sculptures representing her.

In Cave 12, Cundā is also paired with Tārā on opposite sides of the first floor shrine door (Fig. 205). She sits in *vajraparyaṅkāsana* with both natural hands held in *dhyānamudrā*, upon which rests a bowl. Her upper right hand holds a rosary, while her upper left holds a stoppered flask. Her position mediating the entrance to a shrine or central image is paralleled on a smaller scale above one of the relief *maṇḍalas* on the same floor, where a panel depicts a *dhyānamudrā* Buddha flanked by Tārā and Avalokiteśvara to his right, and Mañjuśrī and Cundā to his left (Fig. 200). She also appears in a triad with Tārā and Bhṛkuṭī, carved above the right side, nine-square relief *maṇ-ḍala* (Fig. 213) in the shrine between the first and second floors of Cave 12.

In the antechamber of Cave 12.3, where she appears as one of twelve *Dhāraṇīs* (as she does in texts describing these goddesses), Cundā again holds a bowl with her natural left hand (Fig. 244), while her natural right hand rests on her knee in *varadamudrā*; with her upper right she holds a rosary (the attribute in the upper left is unclear). In other Ellora images, the attribute held in the upper left hand varies between a lotus, a lotus supporting a book, and a flask. Where the goddess is six-armed (four of the twenty-seven images), she holds a flask in her lower left hand, and a lotus with a book in her upper left. It appears that the four-armed images reduced the more complete iconography of the six-armed figures through a varied selection of key attributes.

The six-armed images, it should be noted, are always found in small, probably intrusive panels, such as the one added to the balcony

of Cave 10 and another added to the left wall of the same cave inside the *stūpa* chamber, while the four-armed image predominates in other caves. The small scale and peripheral location of such figures suggests that this form was ritually less important than the larger, four-armed Cundā images, a variation reflecting a generally felt ambiguity about her iconography. For example, this icon can be confused with Prajñāpāramitā since they share several attributes, although they can be distinguished because in her four-armed form, Prajñāpāramitā holds her natural hands in *dharmacakramudrā*, not the *dhyānamudrā* of Cundā.[28] With a name itself difficult to etymologize, and appearing in many forms both in texts and in sculpture or painting, with four, six, twelve, sixteen, eighteen, and twenty-six hands, Cundā is a particularly variable figure whose variability is anticipated in her early images at Ellora.[29]

The iconography of these figures is comparable but not identical to that of many four-armed female figures at Ratnagiri where she is almost always represented on a small scale on many votive *stūpas*.[30] Here, also, her iconography varies to the extent that she may be portrayed with two or four hands (never six), and occasionally holds a flask in one hand. The rosary and *dhyānamudrā* are invariable, and provide the best clues to her identification at Ratnagiri. Ratnagiri Cundās never hold the book supported by a lotus, as they do at Ellora. This, together with the dissimilarities in sculptural styles, assures us that neither site had a direct influence on the other, even while they shared an emphasis on this particular deity.

Significantly, Candi Mendut in central Java provides a close parallel not only to Ellora's Cundā iconography, but also to her programmatic location, a sign that these two sites shared if not the same, at least a similar *maṇḍala* and teaching. At Candi Mendut, a four-armed image is carved in a panel on the outer wall of the temple, along with Bhṛkuṭī, Hāritī and Jambhala and eight Bodhisattvas.[31] This Cundā image, holding a book, is actually closer iconographically to the Ellora images than are those from Ratnagiri.

It should be noted that stone Cundā images are found at other key Buddhist sites in

India, but their complexity underscores their difference from those found at Ellora and Ratnagiri. An example is a finely carved tenth-century Cundā with eighteen arms from Bodhgaya.[32] Looking further south, a four-armed image from Amaravati, of the ninth or tenth century, shares the simpler iconography of Ratnagiri, portrayed with typically southern cylindrical crown, squinty eyes, and flattish contours.[33] Lacking the book, and carved in southern style, this image exemplifies the dissimilarities between Ellora and southern Buddhist sites.

Bodhisattvas in Pairs: Maitreya as Avalokiteśvara's Companion

The Buddha image is seldom represented alone but, instead, is accompanied by at least two Bodhisattvas. One of these, almost always on the viewer's left is Avalokiteśvara, whose iconographic representation as an ascetic appears to have stabilized relatively early in the western cave temples, including hair piled in a *jaṭāmukuṭa* upon which rests the small Jina Buddha Amitābha, absence of jewels and, sometimes, an *ajina* thrown over the left shoulder.[34] Avalokiteśvara was particularly important at Ellora, where, in addition to his roles as door guard and shrine attendant to the Buddha, several major sculptural panels and one small shrine were dedicated to him in his form of Rakta-Lokeśvara.

In the latest caves, his companion, usually on the viewer's right, is almost always Vajrapāṇi, but is more difficult to identify securely in the early and middle period caves. According to tantric texts such as the *Mañjuśrīmūlakalpa*, *Mahāvairocanasūtra*, and *Sarvatathāgatatattvasaṃgrahasūtra*, the Buddha/Vairocana should be attended by Avalokiteśvara and Vajrapāṇi.[35] However, it is precisely in the Ellora caves where the central Buddha image in *dharmacakramudrā* is most likely to be Vairocana, that the companion to Avalokiteśvara is not obviously Vajrapāṇi, elsewhere marked clearly by the *vajra* he holds. Attributes are unclear in some cases, have been broken in others, and in all cases correspond inexactly to those of other sculptures or textual descriptions of Bodhisattvas. Arguments can be made for identifying some of these figures as Vajrapāṇi, Mañjuśrī or Maitreya.

The argument for identifying Avalokiteśvara's companion as Vajrapāṇi even in the early caves where he does not hold a *vajra*, is based first on the fact that earlier, at Ajanta in the late fifth century, for example in Cave 1, Vajrapāṇi, holding that emblem, is Avalokiteśvara's companion.[36] A century later, in Aurangabad Cave 6, Vajrapāṇi appears as *dvārapāla*.[37] In these cases, the Buddha image is portrayed in *dharmacakramudrā*. Even in Ellora's Cave 2, this triad is present, but only in small, intrusive panels carved in the veranda area, where Vajrapāṇi's *vajra* is clearly depicted (Fig. 97). Appearing on a larger scale for the first time in Caves 8A (Fig. 96) and 9 (Fig. 115), Vajrapāṇi is to the viewer's right of the *dharmacakramudrā* Buddha. It would seem that in cases where companions of Avalokiteśvara do not hold the *vajra*, they could be identified as Vajrapāṇi only if a significant lapse in iconographical precision is assumed.

The problem in the earlier caves is further illustrated first at Aurangabad Cave 7, where the Bodhisattva *dvārapāla* across from Avalokiteśvara holds not a *vajra* but a small flower. This is not the rather tubular *utpala* held by Tārā or Mañjuśrī in later images,[38] nor is it the rotund bud or round open blossom of the *padma* held by Avalokiteśvara. If it were an *utpala*, this would present the possibility that the Bodhisattva should be Mañjuśrī, although this would be an unusual pairing for Buddha attendants.[39] Here, however, the flower type is different, as can be seen in the one relatively large-scale image, on the Ellora Cave 10 balcony, which includes a crowned Buddha/Vairocana attended by Avalokiteśvara and Mañjuśrī (Fig. 133). To the right, Mañjuśrī holds an *utpala*, rising over his left shoulder. The flat, triple-locked hairdo and tiger-claw necklace confirm the identification, attributes missing from the proposed Aurangabad Mañjuśrī image.

A third alternative, that the Bodhisattva in question is Maitreya, is supported by a number of factors: textual precedents, eastern Indian images, the kind of crown worn by these images and by the flowers some hold, and the hand gesture of a few, as well. Maitreya is one of the "oldest" Bodhisattvas, mentioned in Hīnayāna texts and portrayed in Kuṣāṇa art from the second century of our era. A multivalent figure, conceived as both a Bodhisattva and as the future Buddha who will succeed Śākyamuni, he became the subject of special cults outside India. Within India, and in esoteric Buddhism, he was not as popular as Avalokiteśvara, Vajrapāṇi, and Mañjuśrī, playing a relatively minor role in such important tantric texts as the *Guhyasamājatantra*.[40] *Sādhanas* 3, 4, and 5 of the *Sādhanamālā* name Maitreya as the right assistant to the Buddha/Śākyamuni, seated on the *vajrāsana*, with Lokeśvara to the left,[41] a composition found in many eastern Indian images.[42] In these images, however, the Buddha is portrayed in *bhūmisparśamudrā*, not the *dharmacakramudrā* of the compositions under consideration here.[43]

In the Ellora images, the crowns are decorated in some, but not all, cases with a large circular crest jewel that may look more or less like a *stūpa*; the Cave 6 right *dvārapāla* provides a good example of a more *stūpa*-like emblem (Fig. 21, 35). In later, eastern Indian images of Maitreya, one of the consistent identifying attributes is the so-called *caitya*- or *stūpa*-crest jewel, seen in sculpture but not often recorded in texts, which name the *campaka* or *nāgakesara* flower as his emblem.[44] Others have identified the circular crest jewel as a *stūpa*, and thus named the early Bodhisattvas as Maitreya.[45] According to Śubhakarasiṁha's *Mahāvairocanasūtra*, which does recognize the *stūpa* as the cognizance of Maitreya, it represents the *dharma*-body of all the Tathāgatas, that is, the *dharma*-body of Mahāvairocana who appears in the central mansion of the *garbhadhātu maṇḍala*.[46] However, the circular crest jewel is also found in crowns of Śaiva shrine *dvārapālas*, for example, in Cave 17. If it were a general kind of ornament, its presence alone would be weak proof that an image is Maitreya.[47] Other images make this identification more likely. The Cave 5 right *dvārapāla* (Fig. 41, 42) wears a tall crest jewel, composed of several small balls stacked vertically, that is similar to the *stūpa* in the headdress of the Bhṛkuṭī image in the courtyard cell of Cave 11 (Fig. 147). In the latter case,

there is no doubt that the jewel is meant to represent a *stūpa*. Moreover, the Cave 5 Bodhisattva's tall jewel is similar to those in crowns of later, Kashmiri and eastern Indian images of Maitreya, securely identifiable because each holds a branch of the *nāgakesara* tree.[48] In addition, the hairstyle of these images may be depicted as a *jaṭāmukuṭa* similar to Avalokiteśvara's, clear in the Cave 6 and Cave 8 *dvārapālas* (Fig. 100), for instance. This not only corresponds to Maitreya's earlier identity as an ascetic monk, but also to his portrayal in the Pāla-period Vajrāsana Buddha images.[49]

Other attributes strengthen this identification. First, as noted above the flower held by these images is probably not the *utpala*. The Cave 5 figure, whose attributes are very clearly depicted, well illustrates the flower in question. This image holds a small, pointed-leaf flower in his right hand. It may represent a single *nāgakesara* blossom, whose small flowers grow along branches, as portrayed in later images, or it may be a *campaka* blossom, attributed to him in the Tibetan tradition.[50] In another case, the Cave 3 right *dvārapāla* holds a small, somewhat rounder flower (Fig. 71) between the thumb and forefinger of his upraised right hand. This hand position is significant, connecting these images with flowers to others without flowers, but holding their hands in a kind of *vitarkamudrā* (gesture of argumentation). This is clearest in the Cave 6 right shrine *dvārapāla* (Fig. 35) (wearing the most clearly *stūpa*-like crest jewel), where the right hand is raised almost to shoulder level in a loose fist, with the tips of the thumb and forefinger just meeting. This *mudrā* is recorded in texts as a gesture of Maitreya and is depicted in much later Tibetan bronzes.[51] It is found in other Ellora Bodhisattvas who stand in what may be Maitreya's position: the right shrine *dvārapāla* in Cave 2 (Fig. 63) where the image also holds a small flower, and the right *dvārapāla* in Cave 8 (Fig. 100). Given these similarities, it is clear that the right Bodhisattva in the Cave 8A Buddha group (Fig. 95) also represents the same figure.

Taken together, these traits suggest that Avalokiteśvara's companion in the early and middle-period caves was Maitreya. His representation was not stabilized, however, so that each image differs somewhat from the others, and none of this period correspond completely to texts describing this Bodhisattva. Later, in the *aṣṭabodhisattva maṇḍalas*, in the Cave 11 and 12 shrine groups, and at the doorway of Cave 12.1, Maitreya is portrayed in the form he has throughout eastern India, Orissa and the greater Buddhist world from the eighth century onward—hair decorated with a *stūpa*-crest jewel and holding a branch of the *nāgakesara* tree, covered with small, round blossoms.

Avalokiteśvara and Maitreya thus attend the *dharmacakramudrā* Buddha/Vairocana images of Ellora's earliest and middle-period caves, where we might expect Vajrapāṇi, instead. Later, Avalokiteśvara and Vajrapāṇi attend the *bhūmisparśamudrā* Buddha images where, by analogy to the eastern Indian *vajrāsana* images, we would expect Maitreya. The transition from one to the other is clearcut. In Cave 8A (Fig. 96), Cave 9 (Fig. 115) and in panels added to Cave 2 (Fig. 97), Vajrapāṇi is depicted holding a *vajra*, as attendant with Avalokiteśvara to *dharmacakramudrā*, *pralambapādāsana* Buddha images. They correspond most closely to the icon discussed earlier in which Vairocana is attended by Avalokiteśvara and Vajrapāṇi. Vajrapāṇi also attends *dharmacakramudrā* Buddha images located in peripheral positions in the latest caves, for example, in Shrine 11.2.5 and at the left (north) end of the Cave 12.2 veranda. There, the main shrine image was no longer the old *dharmacakramudrā* Buddha, but a new form in which the Buddha sits in *vajraparyaṅkāsana*, right hand held in *bhūmisparśamudrā*, attended by Avalokiteśvara and Vajrapāṇi. Thus, the Vajrapāṇi images with *dharmacakramudrā* Buddhas provide a link between earlier Buddhas with Maitreya and the later images with Vajrapāṇi. And, if all *dharmacakramudrā* Buddhas were meant to represent the same form of Vairocana, then his attendants must have shared a similar function that shifted from Maitreya to Vajrapāṇi. In this, as in much else, Ellora appears to be a unique example of iconography in progress.

Mañjuśrī

Mañjuśrī, together with Avalokiteśvara and Vajrapāṇi, was one of the most popular Bodhisattvas of early tantric literature and art. Yet, unlike female deities who appear relatively early, large-scale images of Mañjuśrī appeared for the first time at Ellora only in the second phase of work on Cave 10 (Fig. 133, 134) of the late seventh century (the only exception is the small Mañjuśrī seated with Avalokiteśvara and Jambhala beneath the right shrine *maṇḍala* in Cave 6, Fig. 30). In Cave 10 he is depicted as a youth, seated in *lalitāsana*, hair parted in three locks, wearing a necklace strung with two tiger claws, and holding a lotus which supports a book. The iconography of these images, and the later ones in Caves 11 and 12, is comparable to Mañjuśrī sculptures from Nalanda, Sirpur, and Orissa of the seventh, eighth, and later centuries. Thus, Ellora's Mañjuśrī images add to the evidence that Buddhist iconography there kept up with contemporary developments elsewhere in India, even while its sculptural style remained unique.

Several verses in the *Sādhanamālā* describe the Bodhisattva Mañjuśrī, listing attributes found even in Ellora's earliest images.[52] His hair is parted into three locks (*tricīra*), the hairstyle of a young boy. He wears a necklace with two tiger claws and a central amulet. These are also attributes of the archetypal Hindu youths, Kṛṣṇa and Kārttikeya.[53] In addition, Mañjuśrī holds an *utpala* upon which rests a book (the *Prajñāpāramitā*), whose teaching is his responsibility, an attribute that helps to distinguish his images from those of Kṛṣṇa and Kārttikeya.

The simplicity of these images is most comparable to an early seventh-century stucco Mañjuśrī from Site Three at Nalanda.[54] Here, he is seated in *vajraparyaṅkāsana* rather than the *lalitāsana* of the Ellora images. His hair is arranged in a low, flat style, there are two tiger claws and an amulet in his necklace, and he holds an *utpala*. However, the style of this image, typical of eastern Indian art of this period, has nothing in common with those at Ellora. This comparison shows that Mañjuśrī's iconography was conventionalized relatively early, but that one site was not the source of inspiration for the sculpture itself. Furthermore, these images are iconographically similar to much more elaborate, eighth-century images, such as the Mañjuśrī from Site Eight at Nalanda[55] and Bodhgaya,[56] the differences among them being almost entirely stylistic.

The iconography of Mañjuśrī appears to have spread rapidly and to have become established in central India and the western Deccan at about the same time. At Sirpur, (in the seventh century) Mañjuśrī's iconography may not initially have corresponded completely to that of images from other sites. This is shown by a small stone image of a *lalitāsana* Mañjuśrī from Sirpur, now in the M.G.M. Museum in Raipur,[57] holding the characteristic *utpala*, with hair arranged in a low style with curls over his shoulders, a variant on the triple-locked style of other regions. The Sirpur image holds its hands in *dharmacakramudrā*, as described in the *Sādhanamālā*.[58] It is, however, an eighth-century bronze image from Sirpur that displays all the attributes of the Ellora images, and shows that Ellora's late seventh-century iconography was comparable to images of a later date from central India.[59] This bronze Mañjuśrī has its hair arranged in a low style, its necklace includes two tiger claws and an amulet, and a clearly depicted palm-leaf manuscript is supported by the *utpala* held in the left hand. Also, as do the Ellora images, this one is seated in *lalitāsana*, with the right hand held in *varadamudrā*.

The wide provenance of this iconography is further illustrated by an eighth-century image of Mañjuśrī, seated above a peacock from Sanci.[60] The *utpala* rising over the left shoulder distinguishes the image as Mañjuśrī, even though the presence of the peacock might suggest that it represents Kārttikeya.[61] Noteworthy in this image is its thick, twisted *yajñopavīta*, not found in eastern Indian examples of Mañjuśrī, but typical of all Bodhisattvas in Ellora's Buddhist caves, and specifically of Mañjuśrī in Caves 11 and 12.

In Caves 11 and 12, Manjusri appears as one member of the *aṣṭabodhisattva* shrine groups and *maṇḍalas*. His presence in these groups is confirmed by widespread textual traditions, where Mañjuśrī as Mañjughoṣa, one of his other names, is one of the six, eight, or sixteen Bodhisattvas.[62] In the shrines of Cave 11.2 (Fig. 175), Cave 12.2 (Fig. 223), and Cave 12.3 (Fig. 252), Mañjuśrī always stands to the proper left of Vajrapāṇi, on the

right wall of the shrine. In the shrine of Cave 12.1, already noted above for its differences from other shrines, Mañjuśrī (Fig. 208) sits in *lalitāsana*, third from the left on the right wall. It is this shrine where he is also paired with Maitreya as *dvārapāla* (Fig. 203). The iconography of these images is uniform: as do the other Bodhisattvas in these groups, Mañjuśrī wears an intricately jeweled, conical crown instead of his usual triple-locked hairstyle. But his necklace is ornamented with tiger claws, and in every case he holds an *utpala* supporting a book.[63] Even in the smaller scale relief *maṇḍalas* of Cave 12 (Fig. 199, 212, 213), the *utpala* and book are clearly depicted.

The style of these images, with their conical crowns, narrow eyes, wide cheeks, and heavy shoulders, is superficially similar to eighth-century sculpture from south India. However, when they are compared to a specific image, for example, the Mañjuśrī from Amaravati of ca. 700 now in the British Museum,[64] it is clear that the style is not the same, even though the images are comparable iconographically. As do Mañjuśrī images at Ellora, the Amaravati figure holds an *utpala* supporting a book, and it may have had a single tiger claw in the center of its necklace. But its hair is arranged in a top knot, not the typical triple-parted style of northern images. The puffy cheeks, heavily outlined eyebrows and eyelids, and multiple folds of flesh around the neck further distinguish the style of the Amaravati image from the flatter-surfaced Ellora images.

Orissan Buddhist sites, particularly Ratnagiri, provide the widest range of comparable Mañjuśrī images. At Udayagiri and Lalitagiri, Mañjuśrī appears among the eight-Bodhisattva groups, where he stands holding a lotus, supporting a book in his left hand, and wearing his typical three-parted hairdo.[65] At Ratnagiri, like Ellora, he has several forms. He is portrayed as a boy, seated in *lalitāsana* on several votive *stūpas* and on a freestanding sculpture,[66] as well as in the *aṣṭabodhisattva maṇḍalas* surrounding Śākyamuni/Akṣobhya.[67] He is portrayed as a standing youth, as at Udayagiri and Lalitagiri.[68] And, unlike images from other sites, he is also represented as a crowned figure, like those in the Cave 11.2 and 12 shrines.[69] Here, the iconographical range links the sites even while style separates them.

Beyond individual iconographical features, which are relatively standard, Ellora's Mañjuśrī images occur in less common associations with other figures. In Cave 6, he appears with Avalokiteśvara and Jambhala (Fig. 30). In Cave 10, Mañjuśrī is part of a triad, attending Vairocana together with Avalokiteśvara (Fig. 133). Although no texts describe such a group, these two Bodhisattvas attend an eleventh-century Buddha image from Bodhgaya.[70] In Cave 12.1, Mañjuśrī (Fig. 203) is paired with Maitreya as *dvārapālas* to the shrine, where a vestige of his youthful hairstyle remains in the long, stylized, tubular curls hanging over his shoulders. Although images of Lokanātha may be attended by Maitreya and Mañjuśrī,[71] no text or other images replicate the unique association of this pair with a Buddha image. This pairing may reflect the links between these two Bodhisattvas, described in such texts as the *Suvarṇaprabhāsasūtra*, *Gaṇḍavyūhasūtra*, and the *Saddharmapuṇḍarīkasūtra*, where Mañjuśrī is Maitreya's teacher.[72]

Also unique to Ellora is an image in Cave 12.2 (Fig. 216) that has been identified as Siddhaikavīra, a special form of Mañjuśrī.[73] A central male figure sits in *lalitāsana*, right hand held in *varadamudrā*. He wears jewelry typical of Bodhisattvas in the later caves, and holds the stem of an open, round lotus blossom. Above him is a small image of a Buddha, right hand held in *bhūmisparśamudrā*, representing Akṣobhya. Four female figures, two on either side of the central image, also sit in *lalitāsana*, wearing identical ornaments and holding lotuses. They may represent the four cult goddesses said to attend this emanation of Mañjuśrī,[74] or they could even be the four goddesses said to surround Nāmasaṁgīti Mañjuśrī, a more elaborate form of the Bodhisattva.[75] But, they might as well represent the four *prajñās* who may accompany images of Avalokiteśvara, but not Mañjuśrī,[76] who are represented in several steles and *stūpas* at Ratnagiri where, however, they are iconographically distinct, unlike the group here.[77] The identity of this composition is highly ambiguous since the open lotus—always an attribute of Avalokiteśvara and never

of Mañjuśrī—suggests that this image is some form of Avalokiteśvara. Given the widespread use at Ellora and elsewhere of features to signify Mañjuśrī—the triple-lock hairdo, tiger-claw necklace, and book—their absence here must be assumed to be deliberate. Thus, while the image of Akṣobhya, the chief Buddha of Mañjuśrī's line and never of Avalokiteśvara's, suggests that this is a form of Mañjuśrī depicted with characteristics not yet completely stabilized at this early stage,[78] it is difficult to accept such an identification. Taken in its broader programmatic context, paired with a panel across the hall of Cave 12.2, depicting Rakta-Lokeśvara, a form of Avalokiteśvara, this image could present another case of an Avalokiteśvara-Mañjuśrī pair as distant "attendants" to a Buddha image, in this case, the shrine image in Cave 12.2. Although this is unusual, it is not as unusual as an Avalokiteśvara-Avalokiteśvara pair would be. In either case, a definitive identification cannot be made, an example of the difficulty of Ellora's relatively early, "experimental" tantric iconography.

Pāñcika and Jambhala

The development of the iconography of Pāñcika and Jambhala at Ellora provides an excellent example of the way in which older icons, derived from sculptures at earlier Buddhist cave sites, evolved at Ellora into forms approaching the iconography of medieval tantric Buddhist images across India. Pāñcika (with his consort, Hārītī) and Jambhala are different personifications of the old concept of the *yakṣa*, an anthropomorphized symbol of abundance, wealth, and fecundity, well-known in Hindu contexts as Kubera.[79] The evidence from Ellora suggests that the transition in iconography from Pāñcika to Jambhala occurred during the seventh century, when Jambhala becomes the common personification of wealth, portrayed with symbols similar to those belonging to Kubera. Images of Pāñcika seem to be based on a legend describing him and his consort Hārītī. By contrast Jambhala, represents, as do most other later Buddhist images, a concept—in this case, of wealth, symbolized by his attributes. At

Ellora, similarities in physical traits, ornaments, and position suggest that Jambhala's iconography was based at least partially on that of Pāñcika. Seen much earlier at Ajanta, Pāñcika at Ellora shows clear connections to the contemporary iconography of Kubera.

The Pāñcika-Hārītī couple, well-known in Kuṣāṇa period sculpture from Gandhara,[80] appeared in the western caves first at Ajanta, then at Aurangabad, and finally outside Cave 8 at Ellora. These images represent a legend recounted in the *Lalitavistara*[81] and repeated by the Chinese pilgrim I-tsing.[82] Pāñcika was a general in Kubera's army of *yakṣas* (the interconnection of Buddhist and Hindu mythology immediately becomes apparent here). Pāñcika married Abhirati, whose name became Hārītī; together they had five hundred children. Hārītī, in order to feed them all, devoured the children of Rājagṛha, and as a lesson, the Buddha carried away her youngest child, Priyaṅkara. To get her favorite child back she pledged to give up eating the children of Rājagṛha, and in return, the people of the city promised to feed her and her children. For this purpose, food was always set aside for them in the *vihāra*s of northern India. I-tsing said that in the convents of India, either within the porch of the gates or by the side of the kitchen, they paint on the wall a figure of the mother holding a child and below sometimes five, sometimes three others in the foreground, to whom food was offered daily.[83]

The earliest of these images from the Deccan is the well known sculptured panel in the rear corner of the Ajanta Cave 2 hall, depicting Pāñcika and Hārītī as corpulent, peaceful deities.[84] Hārītī, now converted, holds a child on her lap, while others frolic beneath the throne. Behind the throne are worshipers and celestial beings. This is the most complex representation of this theme that we will see; from this time on, it becomes more and more reduced, as the focus narrows to the figures of Pāñcika and Hārītī, and then Tārā and Jambhala, alone. Also, the position of these figures changes after Ajanta—never again will they appear on the *back* wall of a shrine. Instead, they will be placed near an *entrance*, as were images I-tsing saw in the early eighth century.

By the time a comparable scene was carved on the right wall outside the hall in Aurangabad Cave 7, the icon was reduced to a portrait of the main characters in the episode, Pāñcika and Hārītī, with a child, probably Priyaṅkara, on her knee.[85] Here, the group is framed by two females and two cherubs, standard attendants in late sixth- and seventh-century sculpture, and therefore, probably without specific iconographic significance.

Iconographically comparable to the Aurangabad group is the one carved to the left of the entrance to Ellora Cave 8 (Fig. 88). Here, Hārītī, holding Priyaṅkara, sits to the left of Pāñcika, as she does in the Aurangabad image. Stylistically, however the two groups differ. The ridges of hair curls, flat-sided crown with double-arched center piece, and short necklace of the Pāñcika image are comparable not to attributes of the Aurangabad Cave 7 Pāñcika, but instead to the small *nidhi* seated to the left of the Aurangabad Cave 6 shrine door,[86] showing a generalization of traits used to depict images associated with fecundity and wealth.

An image located outside an unfinished excavation between Caves 19 and 20 (Fig. 89) may represent the first step in the transition from imagery of Pāñcika to Jambhala or Kubera and illustrates the universalization of symbolism of wealth. Whereas Pāñcika's presence was accounted for by the legend about his consort, Jambhala's appearance can be explained only in the context of the proliferation of many new Buddhist icons in the seventh century. This complex of new images is typical of early tantric Buddhist art from Ellora, developing at the same time in central and eastern India.

The style of the Cave 19–20 image is nearly identical to that of the Cave 8 Pāñcika. Both images have thick, rolled curls of hair, hard ridges of flesh, and both wear short necklaces composed of fat beads. The Cave 19–20 figure leans against a coiled object; the Cave 2 Jambhala (see below) has the same pose. And, the Cave 19–20 figure also holds a round object in his upraised right hand, perhaps a jewel, but also reminiscent of the citron (*jambhara*), another common attribute of Jambhala.[87] The image carved outside Cave

19–20, not obviously Hindu or Buddhist, may be the first step in the transition from Pancika to Jambhala imagery.

Small details suggest that the iconography here was beginning to shift to represent Jambhala. The round object held by the flying figure to the right of the Cave 19–20 image (Fig. 90) has been identified elsewhere as a *śankha* (conch), marking the figure as *śankhanidhi*.[88] Close examination reveals this object to be a bowl of fruit or other round objects. The flying figure to the left clearly holds a bouquet of flowers, earlier interpreted as representing the *padma*, attribute of *padmanidhi*. Similar figures, called Śankhamuṇḍa and Padmamuṇḍa in later texts, are placed at Jambhala's feet to personify the treasures he guards.[89] Stylistic similarities between these figures and the flying attendant of the Cave 8 Pāñcika, with their rolled hair style and left hands grasping the upper thigh, confirm the internal development of this imagery.

The Cave 19–20 cherubs, not yet literally representing *śankha-* and *padmanidhi*, should be viewed from a broader perspective on auspicious beings found in different contexts in the western caves. At Ellora itself, similar cherubs fly above the shoulders of Maitreya, right *dvārapāla* to the shrine in Cave 5 (Fig. 41, 42). Here, as in the Cave 19–20 image, the upper left figure holds a round object and the one on the right holds flowers (*utpalas?*) in both hands. As noted above, at Aurangabad, auspicious, chubby figures squat on either side of the veranda door and also on both sides of the shrine door in Cave 6. Similar figures on either side of the shrine door of Badami Cave 3, are also *nidhis* who specifically personify the *padma* and *śankha*.[90] Their presence in the Brahmanical Badami cave shows that this imagery was not specific to a single religion. Tartakov traces their iconography back to the façade of Ajanta Cave 19, where large *yakṣas* stand on either side of the *candra-śālā*.[91] The dwarf attendant of the left *yakṣa* has a "lotus"-shaped headdress and the dwarf attendant of the right *yakṣa* has a smooth, "conch" shell-headdress. He compares them to those found in Ceylonese sculpture, and suggests that the Ajanta figures are *āyuddha-puruṣas*, symbolizing the attributes, *padma* and *śankha*, that the *yakṣas* should hold. On the

façade of Ajanta Cave 26, the *yakṣas* were reduced to the kind of crouching figures later found in the sixth-century caves at Aurangabad and Dhokeśvara. Their presence in these varied contexts supports the idea that such figures were part of a general iconographic vocabulary dictated neither by specific texts nor religions.

In contrast to the Pāñcika-Hārītī of Ellora Cave 8 and the image of Cave 19–20, an image carved on the left end of the Buddhist Cave 2 veranda is more clearly a representation of Jambhala (Fig. 56). The image is now solitary, as later images of Jambhala would be. The only attribute now visible is a round object, perhaps a citron, held in his upraised right hand. His smooth, fleshy body is more like that of the Aurangabad Cave 7 Pāñcika than his counterpart in Ellora Cave 8. However, his flat-sided crown, the rolls of flesh on his neck, and the cushion on which his left elbow rests, show that this image is part of the tradition that produced Ellora's other early Pāñcika and Kubera figures.

The same smooth, relaxed style was applied to an early eighth-century figure, probably Kubera, located at the right end of Ellora's Cave 25 veranda (Fig. 91), a Brahmanical shrine. Here, the chest and neck are smooth with only a very thin ridge of flesh above the corpulent belly. Like the Cave 2 image, this one wears a *yajñopavīta* and also an above the waist belt characteristic of most late seventh- and eighth-century male figures at Ellora. His now broken, upraised right hand may have held an object to balance the clearly depicted money bag dangling from his left hand. His throne was carved in an elaborate relief, depicting lotus petals and jeweled swags, with small birds on the lower right. It appears that the lower left base may have had small pots, now only partially preserved. If so, they would correspond to the *aṣṭanidhis* represented by pots in many eighth-century images of Jambhala throughout India. The Cave 25 figure recalls I-tsing's description of an image carved outside monastery kitchens, holding a golden money bag and sitting with one foot hanging down, on a golden chair.[92] But Cave 25 is clearly a Vaiṣṇava shrine, with the base of a Garuḍa *stambha* in its courtyard, and an image of Surya carved on the ceiling in front of its shrine door. So, this image, most likely representing the Hindu deity, Kubera, supports the proposition that iconography of wealth had become similar in both Hindu and Buddhist contexts by Ellora's late seventh to early eighth century period.

From this perspective, the location of all such images in verandas or near cave entrances is not coincidental, but rather, confirms the idea of the unity of iconography proposed here. At Ajanta, the *yakṣa-nidhi* group was placed on the façade, at the entrance to the sacred area, separate from the Pañcika-Hārītī group inside. By the time of Ellora, there seems to have been a conflation of imagery, into a Jambhala/Kubera, now in an external, protective position, performing both earlier roles. It is thus significant that where images of Jambhala remain *in situ* at other Buddhist sites, they, too, are found in comparable entrance areas.

At Sirpur and Ratnagiri, notably, Jambhala or *nidhi* images have been recovered in frequency comparable to Ellora. For example, an image of Jambhala was placed in the right end of the vestibule of the Anandaprabha *vihāra* at Sirpur.[93] Moreover, the entrance to this structure was framed by four large images, two holding long, thin money bags, standing on bases supported by dwarf/*nidhis*. The outer member of each pair holds a round object (purse or jewel), the inner one holds a lotus, similar to the *śaṅkha-* and *padma-nidhi* pair found in other images of Jambhala.

Although not as prominent at Sanci, Jambhala images on the plinth of Temple 45, and on a stele now in the site museum, strengthen the sense that Jambhala was more popular among the peripheral sites than he may have been in the center of Buddhist India.

Images of Jambhala were most common at Ratnagiri, found loose and also *in situ* on the outer walls of the main *vihāra*.[94] Their prominence relates Ratnagiri to Ellora more closely than any other sites. The entrance, or "outer circle" of Monastery I reveals this connection most clearly. Small images of Jambhala were placed in niches at the base level of the east and west side walls of the front porch.[95] These small images are comparable to a small image of Jambhala carved on the *toraṇa* outside the Mahābodhi temple complex at Bodhgaya.[96]

They serve a "mediating" function on the very edge of the sacred compound. On the rear porch, a larger-scale image of Jambhala was placed on the west wall, paired with an image of Hārītī on the east wall, holding a child in her lap.[97] This pairing suggests that Jambhala should be identified as Pañcika, although his iconography is identical to that of other Jambhala images at Ratnagiri, and thus, illustrates the conflation of Jambhala/Pañcika imagery also seen at Ellora.

The iconography of the images from Sirpur and Ratnagiri closely resembles textual descriptions of Jambhala. They hold round objects, citrons, in their right hands; the Ratnagiri images wear garlands of *utpalas*, mentioned in texts. And, below their thrones are jewel-filled pots,[98] two in the Sirpur image, five or more at Ratnagiri. Such iconography was widespread, found also in images of the early eighth century from eastern India, and in later medieval images from India and Nepal.[99] Ellora's anticipation of such early images is shown by similarities between the Cave 19–20 Kubera and a tenth-century image of Jambhala from Ratnagiri found near the basement of Monastery I. This image holds a citron and mongoose skin, wears an *utpala*-garland, and sits above four pots.[100] In addition, above his right and left shoulders are figures holding a pot and banner; their position, if not their attributes, recalls that of the cherubs in the Cave 19–20 composition. This image is particularly important as the text and diagram of a *maṇḍala* guiding worship of Jambhala and Vasudhārā was incised on the back, the most concrete proof we have that *maṇḍalas* were used in worship at Ratnagiri.[101]

At Ellora images of Jambhala with comparable, if simpler, iconography were carved not outside the caves or shrines, but instead, inside on the front walls of shrines in Caves 11 and 12. For example, in Cave 11.2.1 (Fig. 183), Jambhala is seated in *lalitāsana* to the left of the shrine door; he holds a round object, the citron, in his right hand, and a mongoose-skin bag in his left. He wears a necklace, *yajñopavīta* and a garland of *utpalas*. Beneath his throne is a single large pot, tipped to spill its contents of jewels. In the shrine on the second floor of Cave 12, Jambhala, still on the front wall, is placed to the right of the door

(Fig. 221). Seated above an upright, jewel-filled pot, he holds the now familiar citron and mongoose bag whose length is most similar to the figure outside the Sirpur *vihāra*. He occupies the same position in the third floor shrine but is much less corpulent and sits above a much larger pot filled with copiously overflowing jewels (Fig. 249).

Jambhala also appears in groups of other deities, first in a triad with Avalokiteśvara and Mañjuśrī beneath the relief *maṇḍala* on the right wall of the Cave 6 shrine (Fig. 30). In the shrine of Cave 12.1–2, he is portrayed in a triad with Avalokiteśvara and Tārā (Fig. 214), most interesting because Jambhala here holds a *śaṅkha* in his right hand, and *padma* in his left, usually held or represented by attendant *nidhis*. This grouping is perhaps comparable to his presence on a votive *stūpa* from Ratnagiri together with a Buddha image, Avalokiteśvara and Bhṛkuṭī. Neither combination is specified in any extant text.[102]

With their pots of jewels, citrons, and mongoose skins, these images are closer to textual descriptions and eastern Indian images of Jambhala than was Ellora's earlier Jambhala in Cave 2. However, it was that earlier image whose location on the veranda recalls the facade *yakṣas* and *nidhis* of Ajanta Cave 19 and forecasts the position of the iconographically more complete (and later) images from Sirpur and Ratnagiri. If the shrines in Ellora's Caves 11 and 12 are viewed as mini-*maṇḍalas*, then Jambhala's location on the front wall might also be viewed as an "outside" position. And to reverse the argument, Jambhala images located on the outside of structural temples also sit on the outer edge of the *maṇḍala* that encompasses the entire temple.

Jambhala's companions must be noted, as well. In Ellora's Caves 11 and 12, Jambhala images are paired with images of Tārā, that were placed on the opposite side of the shrines' doorways. Together, the pairs appear to be inverse door guardians *inside* the shrines. According to iconographical texts,[103] Vasudhārā is Jambhala's usual consort, identified by her sheaf of jewels, corn or by an auspicious jar. The Ellora images paired with Jambhala all hold the same attribute—a clearly depicted, large *utpala*. Here, it seems, Jambhala presides with Tārā.[104] Significantly, elsewhere

only at Ratnagiri was an *in situ* pairing of Jambhala and a female figure preserved, and in this case, the female is Hārītī. Although images of Vasudhārā are found at Ratnagiri, none remain paired *in situ* with Jambhala.[105]

Jambhala iconography unites Ellora and Ratnagiri more closely than any other two sites. Their images share iconographical details that correspond to texts better than do images of most other deities at Ellora. At the same time, it is clear that Jambhala's presence is connected to earlier manifestations of a deity symbolizing wealth. The earlier images reveal stylistic connections that transcend the transformation from representations of Pāñcika to Jambhala. However, with the stabilization of the iconography came considerable stylistic variability both at Ellora and Ratnagiri. This evidence, taken together with the presence of images at Sirpur and Sanci, suggests that this deity was particularly important to the teachings disseminated along the central Indian periphery of the Buddhist world from the seventh to ninth centuries. Clearly an important figure in the "outer ring" of the *maṇḍalas* represented by the *vihāras* at Sirpur and Monastery I at Ratnagiri, and in the shrines of Ellora Caves 11 and 12, Jambhala is never mentioned in texts describing the *maṇḍalas* of tantric Buddhism. By default, Jambhala's clearly depicted representation suggests that teachings either not redacted in written form, or in texts now lost, governed the programs of these sites.

Site Studies

The Western Deccan

It has been argued here that to understand Ellora it is necessary to look beyond the western Deccani cave temple tradition most often used to explain it. However, certain features of its early Buddhist phase must be connected to this local tradition which, in the late sixth century, exhibited important traits of nascent tantric Buddhism. Equally important, several sites attest to the persistence of a Buddhist community in the northwest Deccan, one that maintained in later years at least some of the features established in the early 700s at Ellora.[106]

Aurangabad

The Aurangabad caves, located just outside the city of that name, are most closely related to Ellora in time and space, with a Mahāyāna/early tantric phase that ended by the late 500s.[107] Ironically, despite their proximity, the two sites are not related in any systematic iconographical or stylistic way, although there are connections among individual images and architectural features. They may have shared artisans from the same workshop, who moved from Aurangabad to Ellora in around 600. But, the specific teaching was not transferred from one to the other.

Like all Buddhist cave temples before the late seventh century, those at Aurangabad focus on the Buddha portrayed with hand held in *dharmacakramudrā*. It has been pointed out that subshrines in Cave 6 focus on Buddhas with different hand positions, similar to those portrayed in Japanese Shingon *maṇḍalas*. This variation, taken together with the extraordinary portrayal of multiple (if poorly differentiated) female deities in the adjacent Cave 7, suggests a relationship to the dual *maṇḍalas* of the *Mahāvairocanasūtra*, the key text of the Shingon sect.[108] The proliferation of female figures in this cave, and also in Cave 9, is a key similarity of Aurangabad and Ellora, more pronounced than at any other site in the Deccan. Yet, the females are distinguished by the most subtle of differences in hairstyle so that identification is quite difficult. By contrast, by the time of Ellora's earliest Buddhist caves, basic iconographic distinctions, like those between Tārā, Bhṛkuṭī, and Mahāmāyūrī in Cave 6, are clear cut.

In addition to its *dharmacakramudrā* Buddha images, Aurangabad exhibits other features that link it to a wider spread tradition. The portrayal of Aṣṭamahābhaya Avalokiteśvara in Cave 7, connects it to several sites in the Deccan, including Ellora.[109] The image of Pāñcika with Hārītī, also in Cave 7, links it, as noted in the previous section, to Ellora Cave 8 as well as Ajanta Cave 2. If Auran-

gabad represents the visualization of a new teaching, it would seem that its representation incorporated older themes into a new context. Moreover, its lush, polished sculptural style is relatively consistent, easily viewed as an extension of the western Deccani tradition. Here, too, iconography appears to have moved independently of style. It was only at Ellora that a new stylistic idiom would be introduced in the mid-seventh century.

These sites do, in fact, share certain elements of style and architecture. For instance, Ellora's Cave 5RW shrine, which could have been circumambulated, is most like the shrines of Aurangabad Caves 2, 6, and 7, although neither sculptural style nor iconography, including an image of Bhṛkuṭī, is the same. It is Ellora Cave 8 that shares the most in style with Aurangabad, as discussed in detail in chapter 3. Its shrine can also be circumambulated, although the cave plan is more like Ellora's early Hindu Cave 14 than the Aurangabad precedent. Outside the cave, the image of Pāñcika is stylistically most like one of the *nidhis* in a shrine door guardian group in Aurangabad Cave 6. A female figure in that cave also offers the best comparison for the bouquet held by the image of Tārā in Cave 8A. And, the Avalokiteśvara image in Cave 8A shares both iconographical features and even the small detail of garment pleating with its counterpart in Aurangabad Cave 9. But, reflecting the absence of systematic relationships, the central Buddha image of this small shrine has more in common with images from Kanheri (see below).

Two other contextual similarities between these sites are worth noting. Neither site includes dedicatory Buddhist inscriptions, so we cannot identify their Buddhist patrons. And, a Hindu cave temple was excavated at Aurangabad, attesting to a regional predilection for multiple use of sacred places.

Nasik

Nasik, located northwest of Ellora in the heart of the western ghats, was an important Hīnayāna Buddhist center in the early years of the common era. Several of its Hīnayāna excavations were converted to Mahāyāna use in the mid-sixth century. The sculptures of this period, neither plentiful nor well-known, offer a preview of some features that had parallels in Ellora's earliest Buddhist caves. As discussed earlier, Nasik may have been the Cālukya capital of Maharashtra in the seventh century. The caves, revealing no trace of influence from the south, show that its Buddhist period probably ended before the Cālukyas moved north and, equally important, that this dynasty was not involved in sponsorship of religious "building" projects in the region.[110]

Cave 23 is of most interest iconographically. As at Aurangabad, the central shrine image in the mid-sixth century was a *dharmacakramudrā* Buddha. At Nasik, the Buddha's thrones incorporate both plain throne backs and the "T"-type seen first at Ellora in the middle-period caves 5RW and 8. An image of Aṣṭamahābhaya Avalokiteśvara occupies a prominent position, accompanied to the left by a very early image of Bhṛkuṭī.[111] Panels depicting Avalokiteśvara and Vajrapāṇi offer a most interesting prelude to the iconographical development of female figures. Both images are flanked by vertically arrayed groups of female figures seated cross-legged on lotus pedestals.[112] To the left of both images is a column of four figures, alternating *abhaya-* and *varadamudrā*. To the right, the topmost figure is a portly male, perhaps an image of Pāñcika/Jambhala, seated in *mahārājalīlāsana* above three females with hands held in *abhayamudrā*. The bottom figures on both sides are quite abraded, but all others attending Avalokiteśvara wear their hair in neat *jaṭāmukuṭas*, as does the main image. The females attending Vajrapāṇi appear to wear a version of his ornate crown, including a distinctive tapered crest jewel.[113] These groups might be compared to the group of female figures attended by Avalokiteśvara and a standing Buddha image in the left veranda chamber of Aurangabad Cave 7.[114] There, a panel depicting Pāñcika and Hārītī is placed across the veranda on the right end, suggesting a connection to the portly figure in the Nasik groups. Even more distantly, the Nasik compositions may also anticipate the more elaborate

twelve-deity female group in Ellora Cave 12.3. Yet, stylistically, these images are not comparable to the more advanced compositions at Ellora or Aurangabad. Thus, Nasik provides another case where new iconography appeared in a unique form, expressing yet another variant of early tantric teachings.

Kanheri

Kanheri, a complex cave temple site just north of Bombay, was the seat of a long-lived Buddhist community that lasted at least to the eleventh century. Its sculptural production is divided between an early, Hīnayāna phase, and later Mahāyāna/early tantric phase of the mid-sixth century. The latter, probably contemporary with work at Nasik,[115] presents certain architectural, stylistic, and iconographic connections to Ellora, some close enough to suggest that members of the workshop moved from Kanheri to Ellora at the end of the sixth century when Cālukya expansion disrupted conditions on the coast. What is missing, however, are the systematic parallels we would expect if a single teacher or school had been transferred from one site to the other.

Noteworthy among these connections is Kanheri's "Darbar Hall," Cave 11, whose plan with long, low, rock-cut benches running down the center of the hall is most comparable to Ellora Cave 5. No other site, in fact, presents such a close comparison to this unusual structure. These two caves also share pillar design: a distinctive square type with narrow fluted necking and incised empty circular "medallions." Moreover, in Ellora Cave 8A, the slim, tubular limbs, neat *mukuṭas*, and slightly bulging eyes of flying figures above the central Buddha image are most comparable to those above the Kanheri Cave 32 Buddha image. These compositions also share use of the "T"-shaped throne back, not found in Ellora's earliest Buddhist caves. Less directly, the female deities accompanying the Aṣṭamahābhaya Avalokiteśvara image in Cave 90 show that at Kanheri, as at Nasik, Aurangabad, and Ellora, imagery of females was to receive increased emphasis across the Deccan in the late sixth and seventh centuries.[116]

Kanheri, like Nasik, displays important, early tantric images not found at Ellora. Illustrating the diversity of early esoteric iconography, they should be mentioned briefly. Iconographically most significant for the purpose here is a shallow, relief carving of a Buddha *maṇḍala* on the left wall of Cave 90, of the mid-sixth century.[117] The image portrays a *dharmacakramudrā* Buddha/Vairocana, attended by two Bodhisattvas and their female consorts. Four identical Buddha images in the corners of the main frame make up, with the central Vairocana, the *pañcajina* group often associated with esoteric *maṇḍalas* and shrines, but conspicuously missing from Ellora. The *maṇḍala* is framed by narrow bands, each holding four standing Buddhas arranged vertically—the eight *mānuṣi* Buddhas. This *maṇḍala* is paired with the image of Aṣṭamahābhaya Avalokiteśvara on the right wall, where Avalokiteśvara is attended by two female deities and surrounded by the eight perils or obstacles. The inclusion of female figures, and the portrayal of multiple Buddha groups resembles practices at Ellora, although the specific content of the *maṇḍala* differs considerably.[118]

These partial connections are not suggestive of an orderly transfer of ideas among these sites, yet they all reveal changes in iconography that, in the late sixth century, show that Buddhism through much of the northwest Deccan was evolving in the direction of tantric practice. New ideas were applied in different ways at each site, perhaps the result of the presence of different teachers in each place. At the same time, certain stylistic conventions in the portrayal of more minor features such as flying figures and throne backs, may be attributable to individual artisans who moved from site to site.

Although the art historical record of Buddhist activity here essentially ends in the sixth century, epigraphic material documents renewed use of the site in the ninth and tenth centuries.[119] Among these records is an 854 inscription of a monk from Gauda (eastern India) who endowed support for the monks at the Kanheri *mahāvihāra*,[120] a significant sign that the tradition of transregional circulation of devout Buddhists persisted even after Ellora's demise.

Sopara and Panhale-Kaji

After Ellora, organized Buddhism on a large scale ended in the northwest Deccan. Yet, as Kanheri shows, the Buddhist community did not disappear completely. Two other sites illustrate the persistence of ideas expressed earlier at Ellora.

Sopara, on the coast north of Kanheri, was the site of a small Buddhist community that existed into the ninth century. A *stūpa* deposit included a set, unprecedented for the Deccan, of eight small bronze images, seven depicting the Mānuṣi Buddhas, and one representing Maitreya, ascribed to the Rāṣṭrakūṭa period.[121] Although much smaller in size, and of a different medium, they may be compared with the Mānuṣi Buddha group portrayed in Ellora Cave 12.3. There, all seven figures hold their hands in *dhyānamudrā*; the Sopara group displays a variety of *mudrās*. In both groups, the figures sit in *vajraparyaṅkāsana* under a branch representing the species of tree particular to each one. All figures in the Sopara group wear a robe with the end folded in vertical, parallel pleats and hung over the left shoulder. This is a trait found on later Buddha images from eastern India,[122] but appears in the later seventh century at Ellora in the Buddha image in Cave 11NC (Fig. 143) and in more simplified form, on a small Buddha image in the Cave 4 Rakta-Lokeśvara panel. More elaborate variations of this style appear on later images at Ellora. The image of Maitreya is identified on the basis of the delicately formed *nāgakesara* branch in the left hand. Its elaborate, somewhat pointed crown design, ridged, arched eyebrows and rather puffy cheeks are comparable to Bodhisattva images in Ellora Cave 11.2, but are even closer to later, Rāṣṭrakūṭa-period sculpture, for instance door guards of the mid-eighth-century Kailāsa temple (Cave 16).[123] Somewhat later than comparable images from Ellora's Buddhist caves, the Sopara set offers a tantalizing glimpse of the way a composite iconography could be disseminated (and preserved) on a small scale.

Panhale-Kaji, a cave temple site near the coast of Maharashtra approximately 170 miles south of Bombay, represents the extreme end of the tradition begun in Ellora's latest Buddhist caves.[124] Originally a Hīnayāna monastic site, it housed a small Vajrayāna community in the tenth century, and later, in the thirteenth century, was taken over by Naths, a Hindu cult. The sparse sculpture of its Vajrayāna phase offers interesting connections to Ellora, as well as to later sites outside Maharashtra. Most significant are the five *bhūmisparśamudrā* Buddha images, seated in *vajraparyaṅkāsana* on thrones marked by *vajras*. Although identified as Akṣobhya in the site report,[125] they might also be interpreted as representing the Vajrāsana Buddha, especially in view of the clearly depicted *aśvattha* tree behind one of the images,[126] the tree beneath which Śākyamuni achieved enlightenment at Bodhgaya. If these are images of the Vajrāsana Buddha, then there would be a clear connection to the iconography of Ellora's latest Buddhist caves where, as discussed earlier, the iconography of the Māravijaya Buddha is plain. This would suggest that the primary focus of the teaching, if not the entire *maṇḍala*, expounded at Ellora in the eighth century was still current at Panhale-Kaji in the tenth century. At Ratnagiri, there also appeared to be an overlap of meaning in Śākyamuni/Akṣobhya images, portrayed with the identifying *bodhi* tree as at Panhale-Kaji where, in the later period it is more clearly Akṣobhya who is represented.[127] A small element of style supports the connections to Ellora and Ratnagiri: the images wear a robe with a vertically pleated end hanging over the left shoulder, as in the Sopara Buddha set, and in many images from Ellora's latest Buddhist caves. In this context, it is also noteworthy that a group of seven Mānuṣi Buddhas was carved in shallow relief in Cave 2. Coarse, and now much eroded, the subject connects Panhale-Kaji's iconography both to Ellora's Cave 12.3 group and to the Sopara bronze set discussed above.[128]

Of the remaining Buddhist sculpture at the site, most important is a rare image of Mahācaṇḍaroṣaṇa in Cave 10.[129] This figure, to whom an entire *tantra* is devoted, has no precedents in Maharashtra but, instead, is most comparable iconographically to an image carved on a votive *stūpa* at Ratnagiri,[130] fragmentary but explicit evidence of the advanced tantric affiliation of Panhale-Kaji and, even more, of continued connections between Maharashtra and Orissa.

The Maṇḍala *Across Central India*

Sanci

The links between Sanci, a complex and long-lived Buddhist center in Madhya Pradesh, and Ellora are quite specific, but also disappointingly unsystematic. Much of the site's monuments from the sixth century and later were considerably disturbed, with little sculpture remaining *in situ*. Most striking is the strong similarity between pillars in the Cave 10 *caitya* hall (Fig. 129), and pillars with the same kind of incised circle design that framed the apsidal hall of Sanci Temple 18 (Fig. 131). This monument, which originally housed a *stūpa*, is ascribed to the mid-seventh century and is, thus, contemporary with Cave 10.[131] No other site offers a closer parallel to the Cave 10 pillars, but this similarity is not repeated by other features at Sanci, which also display many connections to the early medieval art of eastern India.

Temple 45, the most intact structure, probably dates to the ninth century. Its central shrine Buddha sits in *vajraparyaṅkāsana*, left hand resting in the lap. The right arm, now broken at the shoulder, may have been held in *bhūmisparśamudrā*, indicated by the broken stone on the right knee, where the hand would have hung down. If this is the original shrine image, then its basic iconography can be connected to Ellora's latest shrines which focused on a similar icon.[132] Bodhisattvas carved in niches around the outer wall of the sanctum, including an image of Mañjuśrī, together with images of Mañjuśrī and other Bodhisattvas, and the female deities Tārā and Cundā,[133] now out of context, show that Sanci experienced many of the same developments of tantric Buddhism that took place earlier at Ellora and at other sites across central India. The Temple 45 plinth is decorated with a series of amorous and mythological panels, including one depicting a portly Jambhala holding his typical mongoose-skin money bag. Not a major image, its exterior position is still consistent with the location of similar images at other sites. A larger scale, loose image now in the site museum sits in typical *lalitāsana*, over five pots.[134] And, showing a connection even in the smallest of details, an image of Mañjuśrī, now in the site museum, wears a jeweled *upavīta*, twisted in a manner quite similar to the design of the ornament worn by the Ellora Cave 12.1 shrine doorway Mañjuśrī (Fig. 203).[135]

These scattered connections are suggestive of a loose relationship between the Buddhism current at Ellora in the seventh and eighth centuries and, later, at Sanci. The presence of images of Jambhala is of particular interest, a feature shared with Aurangabad, Sirpur, and Ratnagiri, across the central part of India. These images, together with the earlier Temple 18 pillars, hint at Sanci's relationship to other peripheral Buddhist centers where certain iconographic themes received an emphasis different than they did in the heartland further north. Ellora, so much better preserved than Sanci's seventh and eighth century monuments, may provide a clue to its iconographical programs now too disturbed to be adequately reconstructed.

Sirpur

Sirpur, ancient Srīpura, was an important religious center on the Mahanadi River in what is now the Chattisgarh region of eastern Madhya Pradesh. Its Hindu and Buddhist monuments were patronized by the Śarabhapurīya dynasty that ruled in the seventh and eighth centuries; the joint religious development in this area immediately recalls the situation at Ellora. The Mahanadi River was an important means of transportation, connecting Sirpur to the east coast of India, with tributaries flowing near important Buddhist sites of Ratnagiri, Lalitagiri, and Udayagiri in Orissa. Sirpur was also the site of a bronze workshop, whose Buddhist products are among the finest bronze sculptures from the early medieval period.[136]

Worship at Sirpur's two *vihāras*, Svastika and Ānandaprabhukuṭī, focused on images of *bhūmisparśamudrā* Buddhas.[137] As in the latest caves at Ellora, the images recline against large-buttoned bolsters on thrones supported by large elephants. Three lions support the Ānandaprabhukuṭī throne base, as they do on the base of the fourth hall Buddha in Ellora Cave 12.3. In the latter *vihāra*, the central shrine is flanked by two others, now empty, a vestige of a tri-partite plan similar to the one on the third floor of Ellora's Cave 11. *Bhūmisparśamudrā* Buddha images now out of context in the site museum, in the precinct of a nearby Hindu temple, and in the corpus of bronzes underscore the focus at Sirpur on his representation as Śākyamuni. This emphasis is corroborated by a dedicatory inscription found at the Ānandaprabhukuṭī *vihāra*, which describes the donor as one who has grasped the exalted *karuṇa* and who is the chastiser of the hostile Māra.[138] Like the shrines of Ellora's Caves 11.2 and 12 (where the message is even clearer), the Sirpur Buddhas invite the worshiper to meditate on the Buddha's triumph over Māra and, by extension, to emulate his enlightenment at Bodhgaya.

Given this striking and key similarity, other correspondences between Ellora and Sirpur would appear to be more than coincidental. Looking first at material still *in situ*, it is noteworthy that an image of Jambhala occupies a prominent position at the right end of the antechamber,[139] similar in location to the Jambhala at left end of the Ellora Cave 2 veranda, and to the Jambhala/Kubera between Caves 19 and 20. The latter image further secures the links between imagery of fecundity and wealth at both sites. At the corners of the doorway to the Ānandaprabhukuṭī *vihāra* precinct, four larger than life size images were installed, standing on bases supported by stocky dwarfs. The outer member of each pair holds a round object (purse or jewel?); the inner figures hold small lotuses. These attributes show that the pairs must be *nidhis*, often found attending images of Jambhala.[140] At Ellora, the Cave 19–20 Jambhala/Kubera is attended by flying figures who hold a *śaṅkha* (conch) or bowl of jewels (?) on the right, a bouquet of flowers on the left (Fig. 89, 90), most likely representing Śaṅkhanidhi or Śaṅkhamuṇḍa and Padmanidhi or Padmamuṇḍa, who may be placed at the feet of Jambhala images to personify the treasures he guards.[141] Their role at Sirpur as "vehicles" is unusual, but their position at the base of doorways is fairly common, found for example, at Aurangabad[142] and at Badami.[143] Although the figures they would have supported are not well preserved, it is clear that two were standing figures holding long, thin sacks, like the mongoose-skin moneybag Jambhala images from other sites hold.[144]

Other material now out of context lends support to the impression that the Buddhist teachings at Sirpur and Ellora shared some basic elements. In the corpus of Sirpur bronzes and small stone objects now in the M.G.M. Museum in Raipur, next to images of the Buddha, Mañjuśrī is the deity most often represented.[145] Iconographically complete, like those from Ellora, these images suggest that the iconography of Mañjuśrī had stabilized across the Deccan at a relatively early date,[146] disseminated in conjunction with the *bhūmisparśamudrā* Śākyamuni images that appear at the same time. Even relatively minor architectural details reflect this relationship. As mentioned in the previous chapter, veranda pillars in Ellora Cave 10 are decorated with a distinctive knotted design (Fig. 127). The serpentine character of this motif is clearer at other sites, notably at Sirpur, where a column (now in the M.G.M. Museum) is decorated with two bands of knotted cobras, part of a complex of Buddhist patterns that was carried across the central part of India in the seventh century.[147] This connection, it must be stressed, is iconographic only. From a stylistic point of view, the Sirpur material has much more in common with material from Ratnagiri (see below), showing that certain new iconographic ideas and stylistic idioms were moving along different paths.

Connections to the East and South

Eastern India

As the discussion in previous sections shows, through the period of Ellora's early-and middle-period caves, there appear to be only unsystematic connections to eastern India, the center of Buddhism in India. This section will not inventory the considerable Buddhist sculptural material not directly comparable to the Ellora corpus. Instead, specific comparisons have been sought for the appearance of new deities, like Bhṛkuṭī and Mañjuśrī. The dramatic changes in Caves 11 and 12 present the possibility of more direct connection in both iconography as well as "architectural" features.

Most compelling is the introduction in Caves 11 and 12 of a new shrine doorway design in conjunction with the new *bhūmisparśamudrā* Buddha image. As noted earlier, the doorways, decorated with base niches designed to resemble miniature temples, are most comparable to, although not an exact copy of a *toraṇa* from Bodhgaya. The central shrine images, depicting the Buddha's victory over Māra, refer explicitly to an event that took place at Bodhgaya. Images with similar iconography, unprecedented in the western cave temples, are most numerous in the Bodhgaya region, a relationship confirmed even by small details. For example, the dwarfs (the four Māras) supporting the Buddhas' thrones occur only in eastern Indian Buddhist sculpture of the eighth century and later. In the Orissan examples (see below), which otherwise parallel the iconography of these images, the Māras are not included. And the convention, seen in most of Ellora's latest Buddha images, of portraying the pleated robe-end draped over the left shoulder is seen also in eastern India, with, for instance, numerous examples from Bodhgaya itself.[148] Moreover, these images rest against bolsters embellished with an elaborate "button." This type of cushion was rare in earlier Deccani Buddhist sculpture, but was a common element in seventh-century images of the Buddha from eastern India.[149] Other design elements seem to have been adopted in modular fashion. For instance, a *dharmacakramudrā* Buddha image carved in a niche at the end of the Cave 12.2 veranda sits on a throne whose square back is decorated with unusually large corner roundels. Unlike other throne backs at Ellora, it is simpler but still most comparable to eastern Indian images, for instance, Buddha images from Bodhgaya[150] and the throne of a bronze Avalokiteśvara from Nalanda.[151]

Yet, the images from Ellora are not exact copies of the eastern Indian examples. They translate into Deccani style iconographic elements that convey a sense that the shrines may be viewed as Bodhgaya transposed to the cave temples. Lacking precise stylistic or fine iconographical correspondences, this is not a question of direct influence from eastern India. Instead, it appears that a conscious selection of features was made to convey the meaning of Bodhgaya, and to create an atmosphere in which worship could lead to enlightenment as profound as the Buddha's paradigmatic experience at Bodhgaya itself.

At the same time, the pantheon surrounding Ellora's latest Buddha images is more elaborate and varied than the pantheon that has been recovered even from later periods at key eastern Indian sites such as Bodhgaya, Nalanda, or Vikramaśila. From Bodhgaya,[152] come images of the Bodhisattvas Avalokiteśvara, Maitreya, Mañjuśrī, as well as images of two fierce associates of the latter, Yamāntaka and Trailokavijaya. Conspicuous by their infrequency in large-scale sculptural production—at least in comparison to Ellora—are Vajrapāṇi, groups of the eight Bodhisattvas, and Jambhala,[153] who appear in every shrine containing a *bhūmisparśamudrā* Buddha image. Female figures at Bodhgaya include Tārā, Prajñāpāramitā, Cundā, Marīcī, Nairātmā, and Bhṛkuṭī, as attendant to Avalokiteśvara. But no groups of female images comparable to the iconography of Cave 12.3 have been found at Bodhgaya or other eastern Indian sites.

Remains from other key, contemporary Buddhist centers offer important confirmation of the disparities between Ellora's pantheon (and by implication, *maṇḍala*) and those of other eastern India sites. For example, although we might expect Nalanda, the scholastic center of Buddhism during Ellora's Buddhist period, to have exerted some influence there, in fact, only piecemeal connections can be made.[154] Images of individual deities such as Avalokiteśvara (alone, and accompanied by Tārā and Bhṛkuṭī), Mañjuśrī, Tārā, Cundā, and a flag-bearing Bodhisattva show that some iconographic features were

shared by both sites.[155] However, even where groups of bronze images were discovered together at Nalanda, there has been no explanation for that particular grouping.[156] Moreover, it appears that the central teaching at Nalanda focused on the *pañcatathāgata* system, as revealed by the main temple with four corner shrines surrounding a *stūpa*,[157] quite distinct from the emphasis at Ellora on the *bhūmisparśamudrā* Buddha/Śākyamuni accompanied by eight Bodhisattvas, arrayed in three-tiered temples.

Nalanda's bronze workshop, the most prolific in the eighth century, could have been the source of ideas at other sites, for instance Sirpur, whose output resembles that of Nalanda in some respects.[158] However, specific stylistic differences suggest that Nalanda, despite its position as the most important monastery of its time, did not directly influence these other centers. Instead, it appears that bronze sculptures appeared simultaneously in various places.[159] This suggests that ideas about new iconography and media in which to express it diffused throughout the Indian Buddhist world independently of the movement of artisans who were more regionally bound. Under such circumstances, it is difficult to ascribe a one-to-one correspondence between Nalanda, or other Buddhist centers, and sites on the periphery. From this perspective, the relationship between Ellora and Orissan sites is all the more striking.

Orissa

The eastern Orissan sites of Ratnagiri, Lalitagiri, and Udayagiri straddle a tributary of the Mahanadi River that is a main route of communication between coastal Orissa and such inland sites as Sirpur. They are located within a half day's drive of the temple town and capitol, Bhubaneswar. This area provides by far the best parallels to the latest phase of Buddhist art at Ellora, the only ones in India that preserve comparable groups of eight Bodhisattvas centered on *bhūmisparśamudrā* Buddha images. The prominence of female deities, including Tārā, Cundā and Aparājitā, particularly at Ratnagiri, offer additional, if less exact analogies to Ellora. Moreover, at

Ratnagiri, sufficient epigraphical evidence has been preserved to suggest the textual basis, and thus, doctrinal affiliation for this iconographical distribution, providing a possible solution to the problem of identifying the teachings reflected in Ellora's latest Buddhist caves.

Udayagiri presents us with the most complex, large-scale multiple-Bodhisattva *maṇḍala* outside Ellora. The *stūpa* there, whose sculpture dates to the eighth century, is decorated with four niches in the cardinal directions, housing Tathāgatas each flanked by two Bodhisattvas. These Bodhisattvas are iconographically distinguishable as an *aṣṭabodhisattva* group comparable to those at Ellora.[160] The importance of this grouping at Udayagiri is corroborated by a series of eighth- and ninth-century relief "*maṇḍalas*" on stone steles that portray a *bhūmisparśamudrā* Buddha surrounded by groups of Bodhisattvas. Although not portrayed in geometric form like the Ellora *maṇḍalas*, the regular arrangement of images in the steles certainly suggests a *maṇḍalic* concept. Like the side walls of the Ellora Cave 11.2 shrines, however, these steles depict only six Bodhisattvas.[161] Despite these striking similarities, however, the iconography of the central image differs significantly, lacking the images of the dwarf Māras, Bhūdevī, and Aparājitā that make the meaning so clear at Ellora. It is noteworthy that similar *maṇḍalas*, centered on Mañjuśrī and Vairocana, also come from Udayagiri, showing a relatively early differentiation and development of this iconography, found in such texts as the *Niṣpannayogāvalī* and the *Mañjuśrīmūlakalpa*.

At Lalitagiri, seven miles southwest of Udayagiri, are preserved three extraordinary sets of the *aṣṭabodhisattva* group, dating from the eighth and ninth centuries.[162] These large-scale, standing figures are most comparable in dimension to the standing groups in Ellora Caves 11 and 12. However, each Bodhisattva was treated more individually, carved on a separate stone stele, accompanied by various subsidiary female and male deities that were only painted between the images at Ellora. Unfortunately, they were not preserved *in situ*, but the three groups of eight nevertheless offer invaluable information about the ico-

nography of the *aṣṭabodhisattvamaṇḍala*. Although the style of the images is typically Orissan and, thus, quite distinct from the images at Ellora, even small iconographical details confirm their relationship. Thus, the three images of the Bodhisattva Kṣitigarbha hold a three-stemmed "flower" with distinctive knobbed buds. This, a branch of the *kalpadruma* (the wish-granting tree), given as this Bodhisattva's attribute in the *Niṣpannayogāvalī*, appears quite clearly at Ellora in the Cave 12.1 shrine (Fig. 208).[163]

It is Ratnagiri, northeast of Lalitagiri, whose iconography most closely parallels Ellora's. Like Udayagiri and Lalitagiri, its remains include steles, representing *bhūmisparśamudrā* Buddhas encircled by an *aṣṭabodhisattvamaṇḍala* whose iconography corresponds to that of its sister sites, as well as to Ellora's.[164] In these steles, the Buddha image is identifiable only by the hand gesture, leaving open the possibility that it represents not Śākyamuni but Akṣobhya. However, other steles from Ratnagiri give more iconographic information. In one, below the throne is a small figure of Aparājitā crushing an even smaller Gaṇeśa, together with a grotesque Māra.[165] Although later, ascribed on epigraphic grounds to the ninth century, this image presents a relatively close parallel to the Ellora Cave 11 and 12 central shrine images. In another example, the Buddha is seated beneath the branches of an *aśvattha* tree. Small figures of Avalokiteśvara and Mañjuvajra attend him on the ends of the throne back while, below, a small scene depicts the attack of Māra.[166] Yet, in what may be regarded as the most important Buddha image of the site in the shrine of Monastery I, the *bhūmisparśamudrā* Buddha has no special iconographical markings, merely attended by Vajrapāṇi and Avalokiteśvara.[167] At the same time, the numerous *bhūmisparśamudrā* Buddha images at Ratnagiri (thirteen of sixteen large-scale sculptures) assure us that this icon was as important there as it was in Ellora Caves 11 and 12.[168]

Moreover, it is in Monastery I that *in situ* images of Jambhala, Pāñcika and Hārītī are found, connecting at least in outline the *maṇḍala* of Ellora's latest shrines with the layout at Ratnagiri. Images, no longer in context, of other Bodhisattvas and female figures—Mañjusrī, Avalokiteśvara (with Tārā and Bhṛkutī), and Cundā—illustrate a partial overlap with Ellora's iconography. Cundā appears at Ratnagiri only on votive *stūpas*, which appear to be among the later additions to the site.[169] By contrast, at Ellora, the images appear as early as the first phase of Cave 11. Other figures are notable by their absence, particularly large-scale images of Maitreya and Bhṛkutī. Still others, for instance Amoghapāśa and Aṣṭamahābhaya Tārā, demonstrating the emphasis on personifications of compassion at Ratnagiri, do not appear at Ellora. And, significantly, of the three Orissan sites, Ratnagiri is the one that seems to lack a large-scale *aṣṭabodhisattva* group. It would appear that even though the two sites have much in common, the emphasis differed at each. Are the similarities strong enough to suggest a common teaching?

At Ratnagiri, as Nancy Hock has explained, it appears that the predominant *bhūmisparśamudrā* Buddha images were intended to represent the more or less historic Śākyamuni, as distinguished from Akṣobhya, the focus of more advanced tantric teachings.[170] Although the specific text describing the configuration of images at Ratnagiri has not yet been recovered, Hock has shown that the pantheon seems most like that described in relatively early tantric texts such as the *Mañjuśrīmūlakalpa*, classified as a *kriyātantra* in the Tibetan canon.[171] Only in the *kriyātantras* is the central Buddha represented by Śākyamuni/Vairocana and only there is he said to be accompanied by Avalokiteśvara and Vajrapāṇi, a triad that seems to correspond to a tripartite scheme (*vajra* family, *padma* family, Tathāgata family) that distinguishes these early teachings from later ones that involve five-Buddha groups. According to this analysis, the first phase at Ratnagiri, which included Monastery I, belongs to this *kriyātantra* stage, also called *Mantrayāna* to distinguish it from the later, more esoteric practices of *Vajrayāna* Buddhism. At this stage, Buddhas, Bodhisattvas and female deities proliferated, but not in the horrific or overtly erotic forms to be seen in the last stages of tantric Buddhist art. From this perspective, the early tantric Buddhism of Ellora, like that of Ratnagiri, might be more precisely classified as belonging to the *kriyātantras* of Mantrayāna Buddhism.[172]

It was this form of tantric Buddhism that was disseminated in northwest India and Kashmir and throughout much of Central Asia, East Asia, and Southeast Asia.[173] In this context, the general connections that Ellora's *aṣṭabodhisattvamaṇḍala* seems to have to distant regions can be seen to be part of a broader pattern. It is, therefore, not entirely surprising that next to Ratnagiri, the most similar site in terms of relative simplicity of a nascent tantric Buddhist program is Candi Mendut in central Java, dated ca. 800, where a central Buddha image (here in *dharmacakramudrā*) is attended by Avalokiteśvara and Vajrapāṇi, with eight Bodhisattvas whose attributes match almost exactly those of Ellora's Bodhisattvas, placed in niches around the outside of the temple, and accompanied by Jambhala and Hārītī. There, however, they are positioned in groups of two (in a pattern more like that of the Udayagiri *stūpa*), separated by images of Cundā, Bhṛkutī, and Lokeśvara.[174] Contemporary with the Ratnagiri-area sites, and not too much later than Ellora, Candi Mendut appears to have preserved this stage, before it evolved with elaborations that make the Kashmiri sites and those in Japan appear so different.

The South

There are compelling reasons to consider Buddhist sites in the southern part of the subcontinent in a search for connections to Ellora. Cross-regional interest fueled the politics of the Deccan in the early medieval period when the Cālukyas in the seventh century, and the Rāṣṭrakūṭas in the eighth, fought to control the region from what is now Andhra Pradesh south through Tamil Nadu. The results of this interaction can be seen first at Cālukya temple sites in the seventh century, which show increasing influence of Pallava style, and then in eighth-century Rāṣṭrakūṭa monuments including Ellora, where the Kailāsa temple (Cave 16) shows clear evidence of its Cālukya/Pallava heritage. As noted earlier, sculpture in Ellora's latest Buddhist caves appears vaguely southern and, although no exact matches can be found, it appears that the south was at least indirectly the source of this style. The question is whether the new iconography represented in this new style came from the same source. Also, we know that sites along the southern coast were visited by the Chinese pilgrim monk, Hsüan-tsang, who journeyed through coastal Andhra Pradesh and south all the way to Kancipuram, and then turned northwest to travel through the Cālukya territory of Karnataka and thus north to Nasik.[175] We can only assume that he followed well-used routes and thus, that there was a direct line of communication that ran counterclockwise from Kalinga (with the major Buddhist centers of Ratnagiri, Udayagiri, and Lalitagiri), to Amaravati and neighboring sites, south to Kancipuram, and then west across the Deccan and north as far as the ghats just west of Ellora. Moreover, the economics and religious fervor that made Kancipuram a key staging point for sea journeys to Southeast Asia and on to China may have had spillover effects on the diffusion of Buddhist ideas inside India, as well.[176]

In this context, the absence of substantial material connections between the two regions is disappointing. At only a few sites in the south have sizeable bodies of sculpture been recovered, with little remaining *in situ*. Thus, from Amaravati, images of Cundā, Mañjuśrī, and Vajrapāni are similar in iconographic detail to their counterparts in Ellora Cave 12 but, coming from different periods, cannot be considered part of a single iconographic set.[177] Nor can a stylistic connection be made. For instance, the flat forehead, slit eyes, pinched lips, and sloping shoulders of the Amaravati Cundā is much more clearly in the Pallava tradition than the wider eyed, square-shoul-

dered Cundā in Ellora's Cave 12.1 shrine, the most "southern" stylistically of the Buddhist caves there. Several coarse images of *bhūmi-sparśamudrā* Buddha images, one flanked by Maitreya and Avalokiteśvara, and individual images of Maitreya, Jambhala, and Tārā do suggest that there was a teaching similar to that at Ellora at Amaravati but, given their tenth-century date, cannot be taken as a basis for ideas that diffused two centuries earlier.[178]

Salihundam, a site further north on the coast of Andhra Pradesh, offers a somewhat better analogy to the Ellora pantheon, including several images of *bhūmisparśamudrā* Buddhas, Maitreya, Avalokiteśvara in several forms, Mañjuśrī, Tārā, and Bhṛkuṭī.[179] However, with dates in the eighth century or later, this material is better viewed as parallel to, not a source of ideas for Ellora, more closely linked to Buddhist art of Orissa.[180]

Further south along the coast, at Nagapattinam in Tamil Nadu, an immense corpus of bronzes was recovered from several hoards. Ranging in date from the tenth to the sixteenth centuries, it includes images of *bhūmi-sparśamudrā* Buddhas, various forms of Avalokiteśvara, Maitreya, Tārā, Jambhala, and Vasudhārā.[181] Like the sites further north, it confirms the presence of a pantheon similar in some respects to that at Ellora but, with much later dates and of dramatically different style.

Taken together, this evidence is not sufficient to suggest direct contact with Buddhist establishments in the south and Ellora, although they appear to have shared parts of a general trend in Buddhism from the eighth to tenth centuries. This conclusion reinforces the picture of Ellora's latest caves as a relatively early expression of tantric Buddhism in the Deccan, whose nearest relations were the sites further north in Madhya Pradesh and eastern Orissa.

Ellora's Buddhist sanctuaries are the dramatic conclusion of a millennia long tradition of cave temple architecture in the western Deccan. But, they are even more than that. Carved at the site of an important regional Hindu *tīrtha*, they reflect its spiritual power that expanded during the seventh century Buddhist period, reaching its climax under the imperial Rāṣṭrakūṭas in the mid-eighth century. Although traditional in some respects, with a *caitya* hall, and caves laid out for residence and worship, in others, even the earliest caves reveal iconographic changes that portend a new form of Buddhism that was to be disseminated throughout the international Buddhist world from the eighth century onward. Ellora is important not simply because it was one of the earliest Indian sites to represent visually the beginning of this change. Equally important, it embodies the systematic application of *maṇḍalas*, assumed to be part of a complex of early tantric teachings, to the problem of creating iconographic programs for Buddhist shrines. Such creativity appears to have had no official, political sponsor, although it must have required powerful forces to aggregate the resources necessary to create the caves. Instead, the political conditions of the seventh and early eighth century appear to

have favored a dynamic mingling of regional and extra-regional styles and ideas.

Even the earliest caves anticipate these changes. Thus, both Caves 6 and 2 contain early images of the goddess Bhṛkuṭī who, paired with Mahāmāyūrī, appears in Cave 10 and later, in the company of ten other goddesses in Cave 12. Their position at entry points reflects both the importance of female imagery in many Buddhist and Hindu caves, and also the growing significance of female figures in tantric Buddhism. Cave 6, with the earliest relief *maṇḍalas* in its shrines, offers immediate evidence for the presence of "*maṇḍalic*" thinking at Ellora. The nine-part Buddha diagrams of its shrine specifically anticipate the sculptural groups of Buddha images in Cave 2 and, much later, on the third floor of Cave 12. On another level, it has been suggested here that the veranda-like Cave 4 may have prefigured the program of Caves 11.1 and 12.1, as the first level of a three-level *maṇḍala* encompassing Caves 2, 3, and 4, tiers analogous to the three-floored *maṇḍala* in Caves 11 and 12. The similarity in the arrangement of Buddha images along the side walls of Caves 2 and 12.3 are then comprehensible as part of a more systematic relationship between earlier and later caves. Even

Cave 3 and Cave 12.2 (the middle levels) are loosely linked by the fact that the shrine programs of Caves 12.2 and 12.3 are nearly identical, as they are in Caves 3 and 2. Thus, Cave 4, not much more than an entrance hall, would have functioned as did the first floor of Cave 12, Cave 3 and the second floor of Cave 12, and Cave 2 as the top, or third floor. This emphasis on "threeness" is confirmed by tantric literature, from elaborations of a three-part Buddha system, to descriptions of three-layered *maṇḍalas*, to tales of three-level meditations by tantric teachers.

In certain respects, Cave 8 can be seen as a pivotal excavation, connecting the latest phase of work on Ellora's earliest Buddhist caves with the beginning of work on the latest Buddhist excavations. Its assemblage of different styles reflects the advent of new ideas to the site, after the more traditional early caves were underway. These changes, brought about by the gathering from different places of the teachers and artisans, who must have carried these ideas to Ellora, portended the even greater innovations to come in Ellora's latest Caves 11 and 12. Unlike Cave 8, however, which was inspired by various trends in local and regional traditions, the latest caves introduce ideas from a much wider sphere, suggesting that a new teacher had appeared on the scene. At the same time, the style changed to reflect the growing influence of artisans from the southern Deccan.

The latest Buddhist phase was not the result of influence from any single site but instead reveals a unique synthesis of architectural, iconographic, and stylistic elements characteristic of a broad range of monuments of the late seventh and early eighth centuries. The richness of the latest Buddhist caves, and the smooth transition to the mid-eighth-century Brahmanical excavations sponsored by the Rāṣṭrakūṭas are not suggestive of the severe political turmoil one might expect if it were assumed that the Rāṣṭrakūṭas had to fight to gain control of the Ellora region in the early eighth century. Instead, it appears that political change resulted in an opening up of the region to religious and artistic ideas that circulated over much of the subcontinent in the late seventh and eighth centuries, including Buddhist sites like Nalanda, Bodhgaya, Ratnagiri, and Sirpur, that were being actively developed during this time.

Ellora's artisans were most probably part of local workshops, upon which the influence of southern style grew during the early eighth century. This may be connected more directly to politics. Since the Rāṣṭrakūṭas were still feudatories of the Cālukyas when the latest Buddhist caves were being excavated, it is possible that an attempt was made in them to imitate the style of the Rāṣṭrakūṭas overlords. This is to say that Ellora's latest Buddhist caves should be seen as early Rāṣṭrakūṭa-period monuments, although there is neither evidence nor need to assume that they were directly sponsored by the Rāṣṭrakūṭas themselves. When Dantidurga came to power, ca. 730, and sponsored major monuments at Ellora—Caves 15 and 16—the imperial sculptural style changed to imitate Cālukya sculpture more explicitly, or even to be executed by imported Cālukya craftsmen, who no longer had work in the capital of the now defeated Cālukya kings.

Such changes in art are overshadowed by contemporary changes in iconography that, in turn, represent changes in Buddhism. They were the result of a combination of internal development and a newly imported doctrine. While important features of the programs of Caves 6, 2, and 4 are repeated in the additions to Cave 10 and in the complex, late Caves 11 and 12, changes in cave plan and iconography, especially the creation of three-storied excavations, the shift from *dharmacakramudrā* to *bhūmisparśamudrā* Buddha images, and the introduction of multiple, differentiated Bodhisattvas in the shrines, suggest that a new doctrine was being propounded by a new sect. This expression of new doctrine was to a certain extent integrated with the earlier, local teachings, a synthesis that epitomizes Ellora's unique iconographic character. The shift occurs first in Cave 11, a largely unfinished and experimental excavation. Cave 12, the latest Buddhist cave at Ellora, reveals the full expression of a new, complex system of beliefs behind the *maṇḍala*, carved in relief on its walls and in more three-dimensional form in its shrine.

Ellora is often regarded only as a peripheral regional Buddhist center, most worthy of mention as the end of the cave temple tradition. Like other peripheral sites, it has been studied individually, without great concern for its place in the wider scope of Buddhist art. It does, however reveal many significant connections to Buddhist art of other sites outside Maharashtra, that may be regarded as a *maṇḍala* in the sense of a circle of related places. This *maṇḍala* encompasses a group of important Buddhist sites of the sixth to tenth centuries that cover a region from the western Deccan to eastern Orissa and south to Andhra Pradesh. They are located on the fringes of the late classical-early medieval Buddhist heartland, each preserving unique variations and even innovations in Buddhist art of the period.

Their shared ideas—the iconography—contrasts strongly with their stylistic differences. Equally clear are the political boundaries that divided them. Yet, it appears that these boundaries did not necessarily separate religious practice or the *content* of sculpture and architecture that provide the evidence for those practices. Religious centers attracted and concentrated resources—public and private—which in turn attracted the teachers who spread new ideas from center to center. The connections described here suggest that political and religious influences did not move simultaneously in the same direction.

Without an identifiable Buddhist patron, it appears that Ellora, at least, was not the result of a single political or cultural shift. In its later Buddhist phase of the late seventh and early eighth centuries, there were distinctive stylistic and iconographic changes that have usually been associated with the advent of Cālukya-influenced Rāṣṭrakūṭa patronage. However, the iconography of these caves—the Buddhism itself—is unlikely to have originated at Cālykya sites and, instead, has parallels at Sirpur, Ratnagiri, Sanci, and Bodhgaya. Comparison of key features such as central Buddha images and female iconography, as well as minor stylistic details like pillar and throne base design are suggestive of relationships among these sites. At no other Indian site of this period, with the possible exception of Ratnagiri, is evidence for a *maṇḍala* so well

preserved as at Ellora. Yet, iconographical features among all suggest a transregional diffusion of a teaching or teachings that shared a core of common belief.

Taken together, however, the comparative evidence is not sufficient to suggest direct contact between Buddhist establishments in the south and east with Ellora, although they appear to have shared parts of a general trend in Buddhism from the eighth to tenth centuries. This conclusion reinforces the picture of Ellora's latest caves as a relatively early expression of tantric Buddhism in the Deccan, whose nearest relations shared similar but not identical teachings. The cluster of sites in eastern Orissa—Lalitagiri, Udayagiri, and Ratnagiri—provides the geographically closest evidence for the use of *maṇḍalas* and specific texts in the construction of Buddhist monuments. At all three sites, steles and individual images represent an eight-Bodhisattva *maṇḍala* nearly identical to Ellora's. Equally important, images of *bhūmisparśamudrā* Buddhas, attended by Avalokiteśvara and Vajrapāṇi, are found at all three, again analogous to the central shrine images of Ellora's latest caves. Yet, Ellora differs in other important features, such as its prominent images of Bhṛkuṭī and Mahāmāyūrī, the Dhāraṇīs, and Rakta-Lokeśvara. The similarities between the earlier phase at Ratnagiri and the later Buddhist phase at Ellora might suggest that both were in the same tradition, while differences make it clear that the two sites did not share all the details of a single teaching.

Given these similarities, Ratnagiri offers the most promising evidence for the specific teaching and texts that might have inspired Ellora's latest caves. If, as has recently been proposed, the first of two tantric Buddhist stages at Ratnagiri depended on a *kriyātantra* text like the *Mañjuśrīmūlakalpa*, then it is possible that Ellora, too, shared this tradition. It emphasized the three Buddha families headed by Avalokiteśvara, Vajrapāṇi, and Śākyamuni, but excluded horrific or erotic representations of deities.

Among other examples analogous to Ellora, where a *maṇḍala* was systematically applied to the layout of a Buddhist monument, Barabudur, in Java, is perhaps the best known case. Recent studies have demonstrated connections between Barabudur and such tantric texts as the *yogatantra Mahāvairocanasūtra*. This teaching included the *Aṣṭamahābodhisattvamaṇḍalasūtra*, the text which perhaps best corresponds to the arrangement of Ellora's Bodhisattvas, although the central Vairocana figure does not correspond to the central Śākyamuni of the latest caves. Other suggestions for the textual basis of Barabudur include the *Gandhavyūhasūtra*, or the teachings of Vajravarman as reflected in the Tibetan tradition of the *Sarvadurgatipariśodhanatantra*, another *yogatantra*. These studies demonstrate that it is possible to go beyond the general statement that "Barabudur is like a *maṇḍala*," but at the same time, consensus has not yet been reached on *the* text or teaching that inspired creation of the monument. Moreover, Barabudur's structure and content differ from Ellora's Buddhist caves sufficiently so that we should not assume that they reflect a common literary tradition.

The case for connecting a written text with Ellora requires great caution. The relief *maṇḍalas* assure us that we should seek support from the tantric textual tradition on *maṇḍalas* in explicating the caves, even if they do not promise that a precise correlation will be made. Instead, there appear to be several lines of connection. With eight Bodhisattvas in the *maṇḍala* and in the shrines, perhaps Ellora was inspired by a teaching like the *Aṣṭamahābodhisattvamaṇḍalasūtra* of the *yogatantra* tradition prevalent in China and Japan. This *maṇḍala*, centered on an image of Vairocana with hands held in *dhyānamudrā* does not, however, correspond to the central shrine image in the latest caves. The central shrine image of

Śākyamuni in *bhūmisparśamudrā* may connect Ellora to the *Sarvadurgatipariśodhanatantra*, another text of the *yogatantra* school, known in two Tibetan versions, centered on Mahāvairocana/Śākyasiṃha, but this text involves the more complex five-Buddha system. With Avalokiteśvara and Vajrapāṇi as shrine attendants, and with no sign that the five-Buddha system was used systematically at Ellora, it may be that, like Ratnagiri's first phase, it reflects a simpler form of *kriyātantric* Buddhism, or a teaching that, earlier than the canonization of either *kriyā* or *yoga* tantra, preserves vestiges of both.

Like Ratnagiri and Barabudur, which remain uniquely complex expressions of the blossoming of esoteric Buddhist teachings, Ellora is also unique and remains the most satisfactory "text" about itself, preserving on the periphery of the tantric world a relatively early expression of a teaching not completely preserved into written form. Ellora presents a rare example of architectural attempts to transform a three-tiered *maṇḍala* into a structural form. The details may not correspond well to textual versions of *maṇḍalas*, sharing instead, elements of both *kriyā tantra* and *yoga tantra* texts, leaving Ellora and its rock-cut *maṇḍalas* as the best, if condensed, text upon which to reconstruct the evolution of Buddhist belief and practice in the western caves. The evolution is important because it preserves in context imagery that is found out of programmatic context at important, contemporary Buddhist sites across the central part of India. It therefore can provide clues in reconstructing the development of early tantric Buddhism in places where religious monuments were not as well preserved.

APPENDIX A. RELATIVE CHRONOLOGY OF ELLORA'S BUDDHIST CAVES

A Preliminary Sequence

The earliest excavations were begun in what is now the center of the site (Fig. 2). Brahmanical Cave 27, probably the first to be started, is located on the edge of the cliff overlooking the main water course, where a waterfall drops to a pool below the cave. From this pool, a stream flows west to the modern Ghṛṣṇeśvara *tīrtha* in Ellora village. Cave 29, the largest of the early Brahmanical excavations, was located across the pool from Cave 27, to the north, while all remaining early caves were strung out from Cave 27 south to Cave 17. Cave 17 is located close to what is now a large gully, formed by an intermittent stream. Cave 14, the latest of the early Brahmanical caves, is located not only to the south of this gully but also beyond Caves 16 and 15, both major works of the mid-eighth century and thus 150 years later than Cave 14. It is possible that Cave 14 was placed so far from its contemporaries because some kind of work was already underway in the area now occupied by the Cave 15 and 16 complexes.[1]

Buddhist activity commenced in the area south of Cave 14, not immediately adjacent to it, but approximately eight hundred feet further south along the scarp. Proximity to water was probably the most important consideration for the location of Cave 6, the earliest cave, and Cave 5, almost equally early, next to the watercourse that even today flows intermittently over Cave 5 (Fig. 14). This parallels the placement of Caves 27 and 29 among the earliest Brahmanical excavations, positioned to overlook the falls and pool at the north end of the scarp. Availability of water appears to have been important for both Hindu and Buddhist communities, and the presence of rock-cut cisterns outside several excavations, like Buddhist Cave 3 and Brahmanical Cave 27, shows that storage of water was an important element in the design of temples of both religions.

Proximity to water was not the only advantage these first caves had. From Cave 14, the scarp extends rather smoothly south, but then is cut back into the horseshoe-shaped gully in which Caves 5 and 6 were located. The "corner" formed where the gully cuts into the cliff screens Caves 5 and 6 from view from the north, giving a certain feeling of isolation from the rest of the site. This may have been desirable in the early seventh century when, as is argued here, Buddhist and Hindu activity went on simultaneously. Furthermore, Cave 10 was placed in this "corner" area; perhaps this prominent position was reserved for it, since the *caitya* is one of the most important features of a Buddhist monastic site.[2] However, although the area may have been reserved for Cave 10, as will be shown below, concentrated work on Cave 10 did not begin until after the earlier *vihāras* (residential caves) were completed.

The site plan only partially shows the problem of spacing between Caves 6 and 5. Cave 6 was placed higher on the scarp than Cave 5 (Fig. 15, 17), which was excavated at an angle instead of parallel to Cave 6. The right (south) front corner of Cave 6 was never completed; neither were cells added to the south end of the cave. An explanation for this is suggested by the broken stone visible above the cave; it is possible that it crumbled when work was begun there. Having seen the weakness of the stone at this level, probably due to the water course running above and between what are now Caves 6 and 5, workmen had to place Cave 5 slightly lower to avoid the same problem. But Caves 6 and 5 were not placed far enough apart, so that when the front wings of Cave 5 (Fig. 4, 5) were begun, there was only room to the south for Cave 5 Right Wing (here labelled Cave 5RW). The hypothetical "Cave 5 Left Wing" we would expect on the basis of symmetry was reduced to a much smaller single cell.[3] If "Cave 5LW" had been symmetrical with Cave 5RW, it would have weakened or even broken through the floor of the south wing of Cave 6 above it. These observations provide the beginning of a chronological sequence: Cave 6, Cave 5, Cave 5RW, with the inception of Caves 6 and 5 close in time. Cave 5's incomplete state shows that work did not proceed evenly in the main hall, and was abandoned relatively early. For instance, moldings were finished in only six out of twenty-one cell doorways. The rest are sometimes only roughly finished, as is the floor itself toward the back of the cave. Also, the bases of nearly all the hall pillars were left plain, although the few partially carved pillars suggest that additional relief treatment was intended.

Inconsistencies in Cave 5 betray the rushed, uneven pattern of work. Even more telling is the iconographical asymmetry in

cells cut in the front of the hall. It appears that entrance shrines were planned at both ends of the veranda (see plan, Fig. 4). However, Caves 6 and 5 were placed too close together, so that cells at the south end of the Cave 6 hall could not be excavated and, at the same time, a large-scale shrine could not be cut out on the front left end of the Cave 5 veranda.

From this point, work could have progressed both to the north and south of Caves 6 and 5, constrained only by plans for the *caitya*, Cave 10. Looking first to the south, at Caves 1 through 4 (Fig. 3, 16), the plan shows that Caves 3 and 2 are well-spaced, but Cave 1 is too close to Cave 2. Pillar style illustrates the links between Caves 6 and 2, and also Cave 5. For example, the coarse, lifeless pot-and-foliage type found throughout Cave 6 (Fig. 25–27) was used along the north and south galleries of Cave 2. In accordance with their less important position in Cave 2, these pillars are smaller, and the square bases are plain. The influence of Cave 21 is apparent in the fluted cushion capital pillars of the main hall, now more compressed, with a decorative rosette band (Fig. 53, 55). This type also connects Cave 2 with Cave 5, where such pillars appeared in the main hall (Fig. 54). These relationships indicate that like Cave 6, Caves 2 and 5 are among the earliest Buddhist excavations, still reflecting the influence of architectural details used in the late-sixth-century Brahmanical workshop.

Cave 4, one floor below Cave 5, was excavated on the same level but at a slight angle to Cave 3 (see Fig. 3). Cave 1 has cells on its right (south) and back (east) walls, and it would under normal circumstances have had cells symmetrically added to its left (north) wall as well. However, there are no cells there, and in addition, there is a hole in the back (east) end of the right (south) gallery in Cave 2. It appears that this hole was formed when work on Cave 1 weakened or broke through the right wall of Cave 2. Thus, Cave 1 must have been started after Cave 2 was excavated.[4]

Since the shrines of Caves 2 and 3 are nearly identical their dates are probably close. Cave 4 differs in plan, style, and iconography from Caves 2 and 3 but there are programmatic reasons for associating it with them, as is explained in chapter 2. Its placement below Cave 5RW suggests that it was started after the entire Cave 5 complex was excavated. Also, the sculptural style of images in Cave 5RW is related to that of Cave 4, so that the sequence to this point is Cave 6, Cave 5, Cave 2, Cave 3, Cave 5RW, and Cave 4.

Looking north, there is no direct access from Caves 2 through 4 to the area beyond Cave 5. The only approach is through stairs that have been cut to ascend to Cave 5 and then descend in front of Cave 7. Today, these stairs are protected by a high wall. A photograph taken in the mid-nineteenth century shows an old set of stairs leading up to Cave 5 outside a very deteriorated protective wall.[5] It seems likely, therefore, that there was never direct access between the Cave 1 through 4 group and caves north of Cave 5.

Directly below Cave 6 is Cave 7, excavated on the same level as Cave 8, which was placed below Cave 6 (Fig. 17). Cave 9 is on the same, upper level as Cave 6, but it was excavated in the south side of the hillock in which Cave 10 is located. Thus, Cave 9 is the only cave opening to the south; all others open to the west. Cave 9 can only be reached by passing first through Cave 6, one of many indications that Cave 9 is later than Cave 6. Caves 7 and 8 also follow Caves 5 and 6 chronologically because it is a common sense assumption that work would ordinarily begin at the top of an excavation to minimize problems of support and disposal of debris. An extension of this assumption is that, where possible, new excavations would be added under old ones to prevent debris from falling on people below and to shorten the distance it would have to be carried for disposal. So, if one imagines the site as it was before Caves 5 and 6 were begun, there would have been a path of some kind leading along the "ground" level from Cave 14 to what is now Cave 10, and then rising gradually to the level of Caves 5 and 6. These earliest Buddhist caves would have been at "ground" level, or close to it, not two stories above the path as they are today.

As stated above, Caves 7 and 8 were begun after Caves 5 and 6 (Fig. 6). There are architectural similarities between Caves 5 and 7 that suggest that work in Cave 7 was close in time to Cave 5. Cave 7 is largely unfinished, with only rudimentary work begun on cells around its walls. But it is important to see that cells were begun on all three sides. In Cave 8, by contrast, cells were placed only along the left (northern side). The cells of Cave 7 were too close to allow room for neighboring cells in Cave 8. Thus, Cave 7 must have preceded Cave 8, and the sequence in this direction would have been Cave 6, Cave 5, Cave 7, Cave 8.

Because it was oriented on an east-west axis, but was cut into the southern exposure of the hillside as it angles around from Cave 6 to Cave 10, one enters Cave 8 (Fig. 6) at a right angle to the main axis of the cave. A much simpler and more natural plan would have been to orient it on a north-south axis, like Cave 9 above, in which case it would have been under Cave 9 instead of Cave 6. I believe this was not done because at least the initial clearing for Cave 10 was already underway before Cave 8 was begun; if Cave 8 had extended north instead of east, it might have run into the south side of the Cave 10 court. This awkward position may be taken as evidence of the late start on its excavation, relative to surrounding caves. Yet a later start than for Cave 6 is suggested by its placement in the south side of the Cave 10 hillock perpendicular to the earlier caves. Work on Cave 9 (Fig. 5), as an upper level cave, could have begun as early as on Cave 6, but it may not have been planned until after Cave 10 was begun, as an attempt to provide an outer dimension for the *caitya*, that is, to create the impression that Cave 10 was a free-standing monument. The chronological sequence is thus extended to include Cave 6, Cave 5, Cave 7, Cave 8, Cave 10, and Cave 9. It must be emphasized that work on Cave 10, one of the largest excavations, must have continued longer after Cave 9 was completed. In other words, this sequence reflects only the beginning of work on each cave.

After Cave 10 (Fig. 7), two more Buddhist caves were added, not as afterthoughts, but as evidence of a surge in support for Buddhism of a new kind. There was room enough for more than two excavations between Caves 14 and 10, but Cave 11 was placed relatively close to Cave 10, while considerable space was left on either side of Cave 12. Since much of Cave 11 is experimental or unfinished (Fig. 8), its proximity to Cave 10 might be explained as the result of poor planning for the new idea of a three-storied excavation. By contrast, when Cave 12 was begun (Fig. 9–11), the problems of executing such a large project had been worked out. It is also likely that the first phase of concentrated work on Cave 15, a two-story Brahmanical excavation, commenced at this time, although as stated above, initial work there may have preceded excavation of Cave 14, and thus, all the Buddhist caves. The end of the chronological sequence is thus clear: Cave 10, Cave 11, Cave 12, Cave 15.

N O T E S

Introduction

1. M. Rahman, "A Rare Find," *India Today* (March 15, 1990), pp. 153–155, reports on the new discovery of twenty-eight Śaiva temples of the ninth to thirteenth centuries, up the hill from the Kailāsa temple. And Dr. B. N. Tandon, Director (Science), Archaeological Survey of India, has shared with me photographs of paintings, very recently revealed thanks to cleaning and preservation work, in the Buddhist caves (personal communication, April 1, 1990).

2. A recent international symposium, and the resulting publication, R. Parimoo et al, eds., *Ellora Caves: Sculptures and Architecture* (New Delhi: Books and Books, 1988) reflect the wide range of individual studies Ellora has engendered.

3. For a recent example of this methodology, see H. Maguire, *Earth and Ocean: the Terrestrial World in Early Byzantine Art* (University Park: Pennsylvania State University for the College Art Association, 1987), pp. 2–3.

4. G. Schopen, "On the Buddha and His Bones, The Conception of a Relic in the Inscriptions of Nāgārjunikoṇḍa," *Journal of the American Oriental Society*, 108.4 (Oct.–Dec. 1988), pp. 535–536. For a clear statement of the history of this methodological problem, see G. Schopen, "Archaeology and Protestant Presuppositions in the Study of Indian Buddhism," *History of Religions*, 31.1 (August 1991), pp. 1–23.

Chapter 1: Tīrtha *and* Maṇḍala

1. Muhammad Sāqī Musta'idd Khān, *Maāsir-i-'Ālamgīrī: A History of the Emperor Aurangzib-'Alamgīr (reign 1658–1707 A.D.) of Saqī Must'ad Khān*, trans. Jadunath Sarkar (Calcutta: Royal Asiatic Society of Bengal, 1947). I am grateful to Dr. Catherine Asher for this reference.

2. K. de B. Codrington, "Ancient Sites near Ellora, Deccan," *Indian Antiquary*, LIX (1930), p. 11; M. N. Deshpande, "The Rock-Cut Caves of Pitalkhora in the Deccan," *Ancient India*, No. 15 (1959), p. 68.

3. S. Dutt, *Buddhist Monks and Monasteries of India* (London: G. Allen and Unwin, 1962); B. N. Chaudhury, *Buddhist Centers in Ancient India* (Calcutta: Sanskrit College, 1969). They provide considerable information on these monastic communities.

4. C. Barbier de Meynard, ed. and trans., *Maçoudi—Les Prairies d'Or: Murūj-ul-Zahab*, Vol. IV (Paris: Imprimerie Impériale, 1869), pp. 95–96. (My translation.)

5. S. G. Tulpule, ed., Mhai Bhat, *Līḷācaritra*, Vol. I, part I (Nagpur and Poona: Suvicara Prakasan Mandala, 1964), pp. 22–26, 44. I am indebted to Dr. Tulpule, who assisted me in reading these passages.

6. J. Briggs, trans., *History of the Rise of the Mahomedan Power in India till the Year A.D. 1612*, Vol. I (London: Kegan Paul, Trench, Trubner and Co., 1829), pp. 366–368.

7. J. de Thévenot, *The Travels of Monsieur de Thévenot into the Levant*, trans. A. Lovell (London: H. Clark, 1687), p. 74.

8. Thévenot, *Travels*, pp. 75–76.

9. N. Manucci, *Storia do Mogor*, trans. W. Irvine, Vol. I (London: John Murray, 1907), pp. xvii–xix.

10. J. B. Seeley, *The Wonders of Ellora or the Narrative of a Journey to the Temples or Dwellings Excavated out of a Mountain of Granite at Ellora in the East Indies*, 2nd ed. (London: G. B. Whittaker, 1825).

11. For a discussion of patronage at Banaras, see Diana Eck, *Banaras, City of Light* (Princeton: Princeton University Press, 1982), pp. 2–43. For a summary of the international patronage at Bodhgaya, see G. H. Malandra, "The Mahabodhi Temple," in Janice Leoshko, ed., *Bodhgayā, The Site of Enlightenment* (Bombay: Marg Publications, 1988), pp. 16–25.

12. For Cave 16, V. V. Mirashi, "Vakataka Inscription in Cave XVI at Ajanta," *Hyderabad Archaeological Series*, 14 (Hyderabad, 1941); for Cave 17, V. V. Mirashi, "Inscription in Cave XVII at Ajanta," *Hyderabad Archaeological Series*, 15 (Hyderabad, 1949); for Cave 26, B. Ch. Chhabra, "The Incised Inscriptions," in G. Yazdani, *Ajanta*, Vol. IV (London: Oxford University Press, 1955), pp. 114–118. The chronology of Vākāṭaka rule, not entirely certain, is discussed in V. V. Mirashi, *Inscriptions of the Vākāṭakas*, Corpus Inscriptionum Indicarum, Vol. V (Ootacamund: Government Epigraphist for India, 1963), pp. v–xxxiii (hereafter, CII, V) and in W. Spink, "Ajanta's Chronology: The Crucial Cave," *Ars Orientalis*, X (1975), p. 143–170 and "Ajanta's Chronology: Politics and Patronage," in J. G. Williams, ed., *Kalādarśana* (New Delhi: Oxford and IBH Publishing Co. with A.I.I.S., 1971), pp. 116–121.

13. S. Weiner, *Ajaṇṭā: Its Place in Buddhist Art* (Berkeley: University of California Press, 1977), pp. 92–93, 102–103; J. G. Williams, *The Art of Gupta India* (Princeton: Princeton University Press, 1982), pp. 181–187.

14. V. V. Mirashi, *Inscriptions of the Kalachuri-Chedi Era, Corpus Inscriptionum Indicarum*, Vol. IV (Ootacamund: Government Epigraphist for India, 1955) (hereafter, CII, Vol. IV), pp. 29–32, 30; S. Gokhale, "Matvan Plates of the Traikūṭaka King Madhyamaseṇa, K. 256," *Proceedings of the All-India Oriental Conference, 26th Session, Ujjain, October 1972* (Poona: All India Oriental Conference, Bhandarkar Oriental Research Institute, 1975), pp. 267–269.

15. W. Spink, "The Great Cave at Elephanta: A Study of Its Sources," in Bardwell Smith, ed., *Essays on Gupta Culture* (New Delhi: Motilal Ba-narsidass, 1982), pp. 240–241; S. Gokhale, "Matvan Plates of Vikramāṣeṇa, K. 284," in M. S. Mate and G. T. Kulkarni, eds., *Studies in Indology: Medieval History (Prof. G. H. Khare Felicitation Vol.)* (Poona: Joshi and Lokhande Prakashan, 1974), pp. 86–94.

16. S. Gokhale, "Elephanta Hoard of Copper Coins of Kṛṣṇarāja," *Journal of the Numismatic Society of India*, XXXVIII, part 2 (1976), pp. 89–91; Spink, "Elephanta," pp. 236–238; Kṛṣṇarāja is called *paramamaheśvara* on his coins, the reverse type of which portrays Śiva's companion, the bull Nandi. See J. F. Fleet, "The Legends on the Silver Coins of the Early Guptas and Others Connected with Them," *Indian Antiquary*, XIV (1885), p. 68.

17. Spink, "Elephanta," p. 241; W. Spink, *Ajanta to Ellora* (Ann Arbor and Bombay: Marg Publications for the Center for South and Southeast Asian Studies, University of Michigan, 1967), pp. 9–10; W. Spink, "Ellora's Earliest Phase," *Bulletin of the American Academy of Benares*, I (1967), pp. 13–14. There is some evidence that Kalacuri power was recognized in Vidarbha, that is, eastern Maharashtra, in the late sixth century. The Nagardhan plates of Svāmirāja, found near Ramtek in Nagpur District, are dated in year 322, which Mirashi believes "must be referred to the Kalacuri era and corresponds to 573–574 A.C. This is the only record of the Kalacuri era found in Vidarbha. The use of this era indicates that the unnamed suzerain of Svāmidāsa was some Kalacuri king, probably Kṛṣṇarāja who flourished from circa 550 A.C. to 575 A.C." (CII, Vol. IV, p. xlvii.) However, this is not evidence enough to prove that a Kalacuri king, whether Kṛṣṇarāja or even his son, Śaṅkaragaṇa, definitely sponsored Ellora's early Śaiva excavations.

18. J. F. Fleet, "Mahakuta Pillar Inscription of Mangalesa," *Indian Antiquary*, XIX (1890), p. 10–19; the wealth of the Kalacuris was assigned by Maṅgaleśa's father and brother to the god Makuṭeśvaranātha, the god to whom the temple at Mahakuta was dedicated. Buddharāja is specifically called the son of Śaṅkarangaṇa in the Nerur plates: J. F. Fleet, "Sanskrit and Old Canarese Inscriptions," *Indian Antiquary*, VII (1878), pp. 161–162. Furthermore, Maṅgaleśa is said to have taken in marriage "the damsel, the Fortune of the Katachuris . . ." in the Aihole stone inscription of Pulakeśin II, dated S. 556 or 634, F. Kielhorn, "Aihole Inscription of Pulikeśin II; Śaka Saṁvat 556," *Epigraphia Indica*, VI (1900–1901), p. 8.

19. CII, IV, p. xlix. The first issued by Buddharāja himself is dated K. 360 or 609 C.E., from the "victorious camp pitched at Vidiśa," *CII*, IV, pp. 48, 51. The second, also issued by Buddharāja, dated K. 361 or 610 C.E., was issued from the

"victorious camp at Anandapura," modern Vadnagar, Mahesana District, Gujarat; *CII*, IV, p. 53.

20. Kielhorn, "Aihole Inscription;" G. C. Raychaudhuri, "History of the Western Cālukyas," *Journal of Ancient Indian History*, VII (1973–1974), pp. 1–124.

21. J. F. Fleet, in J. Burgess, "Rock Cut Temples at Badami, in the Dekhan," *Indian Antiquary*, VI (1877), pp. 363–364; G. M. Tarr, "The Chronology and Development of the Chāḷukya Cave Temples," *Ars Orientalis*, VII (1970), pp.155–157 and chart, p. 184.

22. A. S. Altekar, *The Rāshṭrakūṭas and Their Times* (Poona: Oriental Book Agency, 1934), pp. 31–48; A. S. Altekar, "The Rāshṭrakūṭas," in G. Yazdani, ed., *The Early History of the Deccan*, Parts I–VI (London: Oxford University Press, 1960), pp. 247–314. A compelling reconstruction of Rāṣṭrakūṭa history may be found in R. B. Inden, *Imagining India* (Oxford and Cambridge: Basil Blackwell, 1990), especially pp. 213–262.

23. Kielhorn, "Aihole Inscription," p. 10; Raychaudhuri, "History of the Western Cālukyas," pp. 64–65; D. C. Sircar, "The Chalukyas," in R. C. Majumdar, ed., *The Classical Age, The History and Culture of the Indian People,* Vol. III (Bombay: Bharatiya Vidya Bhavan, 1962), pp. 237–238.

24. In a grant of Bhogaśakti, a Cālukya feudatory, dated K. 461 or 709 C.E., from Añjaneri in Nasik District, the amount of taxes levied for the god Bhogeśvara is given in terms of Kalacuri currency, *Kṛṣṇarāja-rūpakas*. (CII, IV, pp. 146–147.)

25. J. F. Fleet, "Satara Copper-Plate Grant of Vishnuvardhana I," *Indian Antiquary*, XIX (1890), pp. 304, 310–311.

26. G. H. Khare, "Lohaner Plates of Chalukya Pulakesin II; Saka 552," *Epigraphia Indica*, XXVII (1947), pp. 37–39; CII, Vol. IV, p. lx.

27. K. A. Nilakantha Sastri, "The Chalukyas of Badami," in Yazdani, *Early History of the Deccan*, pp. 217–227; Raychaudhuri, "History of the Western Cālukyas," pp. 60–75.

28. S. Beal, *Si-yu-ki. Buddhist Records of the Western World Translated from the Chinese of Hieun Tsang (A.D. 629)* (London: Kegan, Paul, Trench, Trubner & Co., Ltd., 1884), vol. II, pp. 255–256; J. F. Fleet, "Hieun Tsiang's Capital of Maharashtra," *Indian Antiquary*, XXII (1893), pp. 113–116; Nilakantha Sastri, "The Chalukyas," p. 219; CII, Vol. IV, p. lx. Fleet's criteria are difficult to dispute. Nasik is 128 miles from Broach, in the far western region of central Maharashtra, to the far east of which Ajanta is located. "Hsüan-tsang described the Ajanta caves; see Beal, *Buddhist Records*, Vol. II, pp. 257–259. Sircar has suggested that the capital was at Ellora ("The Chalukyas," p.

239, note 2). However, if Ellora is taken as the far western city of some region, then it is difficult to find a mountain with a great rock-cut Buddhist establishment on the hypothetical eastern frontier of such a region, unless the region is so small that it only encompasses Ellora and Ajanta.

29. Some have read the date in the year 436 as 666 C.E. See Raychaudhuri, "History of the Western Cālukyas," p. 82. Mirashi, CII, IV, pp. liv–lv and 128–29, supports the 685 C.E. date. See also Sircar, "The Chalukyas," pp. 244–245.

30. M. S. Nagarajo Rao, "Jamalagama Grant of Chalukya Vijayaditya, Saka 619," *Epigraphia Indica*, XXXV (1966), pp. 313–316.

31. The identification of this Elāpura with Ellora has been questioned. See H. C. Chakladar, "Elāpura Grant of Western Cālukya Vijayāditya Śaka Saṁvat 626," *Indian Historical Quarterly*, IV (Calcutta, 1928), pp. 425–430 and the commentary of D. C. Sircar in Raychaudhuri, "History of the Western Cālukyas," pp. 83–89; in an editorial note to this article, Sircar suggests that Elāpura should be equated with Alampur, Mahbubnagar District (p. 88, note 77).

32. These feudatories included the Sendrakas and the family of Svāmirāja who controlled the coastal Konkan region in the late seventh century. For the Sendrakas, see CII, Vol. IV, pp. lxviii–lvix and 111–12; G. H. Khare, "Two Sendraka Grants: B. Kasare Plates of Sendraka Nikumbhallaśakti; Year 404," *Epigraphia Indica*, XXVIII (1950), pp. 197–205; for Svāmirāja, see CII, Vol. IV, pp. 147–152.

33. According to V. V. Mirashi, "Nagardhan Plates of Svāmirāja," *Epigraphia Indica*, XXVIII (1949–1950), pp. 2–46, there is an earlier record of this family, dated K. 322, or 573 C.E. The record refers to Svāmirāja and to his brother, Nannarāja. In Mirashi's view, these two people were ancestors in the lineage of Nannarāja of the Sangalooda, Multai, and Tiwarkhed plates. However, other than the similarity of names, there is no direct link to be made between the families. See Altekar, "The Rāshṭrakūṭas," p. 250 for another interpretation of the history of this family. For the individual records see: M. Venkataramayya, "Sangalooda Plates of Rashtrakuta Nannaraja: Saka 615," *Epigraphia Indica*, XXIX (1951), pp. 110–114; J. F. Fleet, "Multai Copper-Plate Grant of Nandaraja," *Indian Antiquary*, XVIII (1889), p. 230–236; R. B. Hiralal, "Tiwarkhed Plates of Rashtrakuta Nannaraja; Saka 553," *Epigraphia Indica*, XI (1911–1912), pp. 276–80.

34. Kielhorn, "Aihole Inscription," p. 9; Raychaudhuri, "History," p. 47; Venkataramayya, "Sangalooda Plates," p. 112. Only Svāmirāja, the hypothetical great-great-grandfather of Nannarāja,

according to Mirashi, bore the title *Bhaṭṭāraka-padānuddhyātaḥ*, in his Nagardhan grant; Mirashi suggested that the lord to whom he was devoted was the Cālukya king. See "Nagardhan Plates," p. 3.

35. Sircar, "Deccan in the Gupta Age," p. 202. This leaves open the question why they did not begin to use royal titles after Pulakeśin's death. As suggested below, they may have been feudatories of another Rāṣṭrakūṭa family, which would explain the absence of royal titles.

36. Venkataramayya, "Sangalooda Plates," p. 110.

37. Chhabra, "Incised Inscriptions," pp. 121–124.

38. K. Deva, "Indragadh Inscription of Nannapa, V. S. 767," *Epigraphia Indica*, XXXII (1957–1958), p. 114; H. V. Trivedi, "The Indragadh Stone Inscription of the Time of the Rāshṭrakūṭa King Naṇṇapa," *Journal of the Bihar Research Society*, XLI, Part 3 (1955), pp. 255–257; V. V. Mirashi, "Indragaḍh Stone Inscription of Rāshṭrakūṭa Nanna," *Studies in Indology*, Vol. II (Nagpur: Vidarbha Samshodhan Mandal, 1961), pp. 185–190; S. Gokhale, "Epigraphic Evidence for the Chronology of Ajanta," *Journal of Indian History*, LI (1973), p. 483; Weiner, *Ajaṇṭā*, p. 25.

39. Chhabra, "Incised Inscriptions," p. 122, believes he was a member of the Rāṣṭrakūṭa family. However, inscriptional evidence does not support this view, nor does the Ajanta inscription specifically describe him as an enemy of the Cālukyas. V. V. Mirashi, "A Note on Vajraṭa," *Indian Historical Quarterly*, XX (1944), p. 357, and CII, Vol. IV, pp. lx–lxii and p. 131, did not discuss the Ajanta Cave 27 inscription and does not seem to have noticed the possible connection between Vajjaḍa and Vajraṭadeva. Both Mirashi and N. Venkataramanayya, "Vajraṭa," *Indian Historical Quarterly*, XX (1944), p. 182, agree that Vajraṭa was a northern ruler. Mirashi believes that he is to be identified with the Maitraka king of Gujarat, Śilāditya II, who ruled from 662 to 684 C.E. According to other Rāṣṭrakūṭa records, Vajraṭa was defeated by the Cālukyas of Badami. In these records he is mentioned just after Harṣa, which suggests that they were both northern rulers of the seventh century. See D. R. Bhandarkar, "Alas Plates of the Yuvaraja Govinda II; Saka-Samvat 692," *Epigraphia Indica*, VI (1900–1901), pp. 210–212.

40. A more detailed discussion of the Ajanta inscription may be found in G. H. Malandra, "The Date of the Ajanta Cave 27 Inscription," *Wiener Zeitschrift für die Kunde Südasiens*, Vol. 26 (1982), pp. 37–46.

41. H. S. Thosar and T. V. Pathy, "Mahārāṣṭrakūṭa Karkarāja Yācā Bhindon Tāmrapaṭa,"

Pratishthan (July–August 1978), pp. 27–32. The genealogical order differs somewhat from that given in other inscriptions.

42. For a summary of Rāṣṭrakūṭa history, see Altekar, "Rashtrakūṭas," pp. 251–257. For the epigraphic evidence, see S. K. Dikshit, "Ellora Plates of Dantidurga," *Epigraphia Indica*, XXV (1940), p. 29; Altekar, *Rāṣṭrakūṭas and Their Times*, pp. 22–24.

43. These include the Anjaneri plates mentioned above and the 718 Bopgaon plates of Vijayāditya, published in the *Bhāratiya Itihāsa Samshodhana Mandal, Quarterly Journal*, IX (pp. 1 ff, as referred to in V. V. Mirashi, "The Date of the Ellora Plates of Dantidurga," *Studies in Indology*, Vol. II, pp. 4–7. The plates mention Samagiri-*viṣaya*, most probably the region near Nasik.

44. Cakladar, "Elāpura Grant of Western Cālukya Vijayāditya," pp. 425–430.

45. Altekar, "Rāshṭrakūṭas," p. 254; S. J. Czuma, "The Brahmanical Rashtrakuta Monuments at Ellora," (Ph.D. diss. University of Michigan, 1968), pp. 24–26, 101–102; James Burgess, *Report on the Elura Cave Temples and the Brahmanical and Jaina Caves in Western India*, Archaeological Survey of Western India, Vol. V. (1882; reprint, Varanasi: Indological Book House, 1971), p. 88, verse 23 (hereafter, Burgess, *Elura*); Kielhorn, "Aihole Inscription," pp. 9–11. In Dantidurga's last genuine record, the Manor plates of 749/50, none of his conquests or titles are mentioned. See V. V. Mirashi, "Dantidurga, the Founder of Rāshṭrakūṭa Imperial Power," *Studies in Indology*, Vol. II, p. 21. Although Dantidurga is assigned titles in the Samangad plates of 753, these plates appear to have been copies from another version of the record, and are thus an unreliable source (Ibid., pp. 18–19). See also Sircar, "Deccan in the Gupta Age," p. 202 for a discussion of Dantidurga's genealogy.

46. Dikshit, "Ellora Plates of Dantidurga."

47. Burgess, *Elura*, pp. 87–89, 251; J. Burgess and Bh. Indraji, "Elura Inscriptions," *Inscriptions from the Cave Temples of Western India* (Bombay: Central Government Press, 1881), pp. 99–100; Czuma, "The Brahmanical Rastrakuta Monuments of Ellora," pp. 25–27.

48. J. F. Fleet, "Sanskrit and Old Canarese Inscriptions, No. CXXVII," *Indian Antiquary*, XII (1883), pp. 156–165; R. G. Bhandarkar, "The Rāshṭrakūṭa Krishṇarāja and Ēlāpura," *Indian Antiquary*, XII (1883), pp. 228–230; D. R. Bhandarkar, "Epigraphic Notes and Questions, 8: The Kailāsa Temple at Elūrā," *Indian Antiquary*, XL (1911), pp. 237–238. See also Burgess, *Elura*, p. 26; Dikshit, "Ellora Plates," p. 29.

49. R. G. Bhandarkar, "The Rāshṭrakūṭa King Krishṇarāja and Ēlāpura," p. 229.

50. M. K. Dhavalikar, "Kailāsa—The Stylistic Development and Chronology," *Bulletin of the Deccan College Research Institute*, Vol. 41 (1982), pp. 33–45; see also Czuma, "Brahmanical Rashtrakuta Monuments," pp. 104–195. D. Chatham, "The Stylistic Sources and Relationships of the Kailasa Temple at Ellora" (Ph.D. diss., University of California at Berkeley, 1977), pp. 3–4 argues for an early start in the seventh century, and pp. 221–222, also believes work was completed by the end of the eighth century. H. Goetz, "The Kailāsa of Ellora and the Chronology of Rāshtrakūta Art," *Artibus Asiae*, XV (1952), pp. 84–107, argued for a much longer chronology in eight phases spanning the eighth to the thirteenth centuries under Rāṣṭrakūṭa and Pratihāra kings.

51. J. F. Fleet, "Pattadakal Pillar Inscription of the Time of Kirtivarman II," *Epigraphia Indica*, III (1894–1895), pp. 1–7.

52. This story is recounted by Dhavalikar, pp. 42–43 and p. 45, note 44. It comes from a medieval Marathi text discussed in R. C. Dhere, "Prācin Marāṭhī Vāgmāyatil Kailās Leṇe," *Jñāneshwar*, Vol. 7, No. 4 (Nov. 1975), pp. 1–10. These references are summarized in P. V. Ranade, "Echoes of Ellora in Early Marathi Literature," in R. Parimoo, et al., eds., *Ellora Caves: Sculptures and Architecture* (New Delhi: Books and Books, 1988), pp. 108–118. The prevalence of this legend is illustrated by the medieval Marathi *Līḷācaritra*, which includes Maṇikeśwar among the caves visited by the saint Cakradhāra. Tulpule, *Līḷācaritra*, p. 26.

53. Dhavilikar, p. 43; CII, Vol. IV, pp. 555, 557, 561, 563.

54. This cycle of twelve *liṅgas* of light is connected to Puranic accounts of the first appearance of Śiva's *liṅga*, but is unclear how a cycle of twelve acknowledged *jyotirliṅgas* evolved. (See Eck, *Banaras, City of Light*, pp. 107–110.) A list appears in the Śivapurāṇa, where Śiva claims to be especially in these twelve places: Somanātha, Mallikārjuna, Mahākāla, Amareśvara, Kedara, Bhimaśaṅkara, Viśveśvara, Tryambaka, Vaidyanātha, Nāgeśa, Rameśvara, and Ghuṣmeśvara (*Śiva-Purāṇa*, Pt. III. Delhi: Motilal Banarsidass, 1970, p. 1261). The last, called Guatameśvara in other places (Ibid., Vol. I, p. 148, note 153), is identified as modern Ghṛṣneśvara-*tīrtha*, located in Ellora village. This identification appears only in oral and local tradition; in the *Purāṇa*, the *tīrtha* is said to be at Śivalaya or Devaśaila (Ibid., Vol. I., pp. 1258, 1261, 1385.) In a Marathi text of the seventeenth century, the *tīrtha*, mentioned in a list of twelve that corresponds to the Puranic set, is called Ghusameśvara (Anne Feldhaus, "Maharashtra as a Holy Land: A Sectarian Tradition," *Bulletin of the School of Oriental and African Studies*, Vol. XLIX (1986), p. 544.

55. This temple was briefly described by J. Burgess, *Report on the Antiquities in the Bidar and Aurangabad Districts*, Archaeological Survey of Western India, Vol. III (London: William H. Allen & Co., 1878), pp. 82–83. It was built in the second half of the eighteenth century by Ahalyabai Holkar, a Maharashtrian queen renowned for her patronage of religious establishments throughout India, including shrines at Banaras and Gaya. According to Burgess, she also constructed a tank in the village, dedicated along with the temple to the worship of Ghṛṣneśvara. There is apparently no evidence of an earlier temple. The *Śivapurāṇa* refers only to a lake that came to be called Śivālaya (Vol. III, p. 1393). These facts, together with the shifting forms of the name, suggest that the *tīrtha* as it is known today developed rather late. For a recent study of the literary documentation for the Ellora *tīrtha*, see M. Soar, "The Tīrtha at Ellora," in Ratan Parimoo et al., eds. *Ellora Caves: Sculptures and Architecture* (New Delhi: Books and Books, 1988), pp. 80–103.

56. S. M. Bhardwaj, *Hindu Places of Pilgrimage* (Berkeley: University of California Press, 1973), Fig. 5–1, facing p. 80.

57. V. Turner and E. Turner, *Image and Pilgrimage in Christian Culture* (New York: Columbia University Press, 1978), p. 6.

58. Eck, *Banaras, City of Light*, p. 283.

59. Feldhaus, "Maharashtra as a Holy Land," p. 546.

60. Bhardwaj, *Hindu Places of Pilgrimage*, passim.

61. Ibid., pp. 87–90.

62. A prehistoric settlement, located above the cave temples, illustrates the long-term attractiveness of this water source. See K. V. Soundara Rajan and R. Sengupta, "Flake and Blade Industries from Ellora (Maharashtra)," *48th Proceedings, Indian Science Congress Association* (Calcutta: 1961), p. 449; and K. V. Soundara Rajan and R. Sengupta, "Microlithic Industries from Ellora," *Marathwada University Research Bulletin* (1962). According to the authors, the tools are characteristic of assemblages of the Middle to Late Stone Age. For the tank, see T. V. Pathy, *Elura, Art and Culture* (New Delhi: Sterling Publishers, 1980), p. 12; Codrington, "Ancient Sites," pp. 12–13.

63. Dikshit, "Ellora Plates of Dantidurga," pp. 29–30.

64. Fleet, "Sanskrit and Old-Canarese Inscriptions, No. CXXVII," pp. 156–157; R. G. Bhandarkar, "The Rāshtrakūṭa King Krishnarāja I and Elāpura," pp. 228–229.

65. Dikshit, "Ellora Plates of Dantidurga," p. 29; Burgess, *Elura*, p. 4. An earlier reference to the local *mahātmyā* is found in Burgess, *Report on the Antiquities in the Bidar and Aurangabad Districts*, p.

82. Burgess suggested that the *tīrtha* was originally located at Ellora's caves, but was transferred to the village after Aurangzeb "desecrated" the caves.

66. *Matsya Purāṇa* 22.50; referred to in S. G. Kantawala, *Cultural History from the Matsya Purāṇa* (Baroda: M.S. University, 1964), p. 322. A similar list appears in the *Skanda Purāṇa*, but Elāpura is not included there. See U. Thakur, "The Holy Places of West India as Mentioned in the Skanda Purana," *Purana*, XVIII (1976), pp. 162–196.

67. Kantawala, *Cultural History from the Matsya Purana*, p. 294; V. S. Agrawala, *Matsya Purāṇa—A Study: An Exposition of the Ancient Purāṇa-Vidya* (Varanasi: All India Kashiraj Trust, 1963), p. 115. This list was probably added to the chapter after 800 C.E.

68. Dikshit, op. cit., pp. 29 and 30.

69. For Tanjavur, see J. Heitzman, "Ritual Polity and Economy: The Transactional Network of an Imperial Temple in Medieval South India," *Journal of the Economic and Social History of the Orient*, Vol. XXXIV (1991), pp. 23–54. For Puri, see J. Rösel, "Sakralstädte als Krstallisatoren Regionaler Tradition—Das Beispiel der Indischen Tempel- und Pilgerstadt Puri," in H. Kulke and D. Rothermund, eds., *Regionale Tradition in Südasien* (Wiesbaden: Franz Steiner Verlag, 1985), pp. 149–170.

70. Spink, *Ajanta to Ellora*, pp. 8–10.

71. Beal, *Buddhist Records of the Western World*, Vol. II, pp. 19, 121; See also B. Barua, *Gaya and Buddha-Gaya*, Vol. II (reprint, Varanasi: Bharatiya Publishing House, 1975), pp. 55–56. The story of Śaśāṅka was also told in the *Mañjuśrīmūlakalpa*. See B. N. Srivastava, *Harsha and His Times* (Varanasi: Chowkhamba Sanskrit Series Office, 1976), pp. 157–159.

72. F. M. Asher, *The Art of Eastern India, 300-800* (Minneapolis: University of Minnesota Press, 1980), pp. 70, 75, 118, n. 14.

73. D. Mitra, *Buddhist Monuments* (Calcutta: Sahitya Samsad, 1971), p. 63. See also P. R. Myer, "The Great Temple at Bodh-Gaya," *The Art Bulletin*, XL (1958), p. 290.

74. Such eclectic use of religious centers seems to have been particularly common in the Deccan, as noted in Burgess, *Bidar and Aurangabad*, p. 10. At Nagarjunakonda, Andhra Pradesh, Hindu shrines were constructed during the late third century in the midst of a primarily Buddhist center. In Karnataka, from the late sixth and seventh centuries, the Cālukyas sponsored both Hindu (Śaiva and Vaiṣṇava), Jain, and possibly even Buddhist temple building at their capital, Badami, and at Aihole, nearby. H. Sarkar and B. N. Misra, *Nagarjunikonda*, 2nd ed. (New Delhi: Archaeological Survey of India, 1972), p. 25 and Pl. 3; Tarr, "The Chronology and Development of the Chāḷukya Cave Temples," pp. 155–184; G. M. Tartakov, "The Beginning of Dravidian Temple Architecture in Stone," *Artibus Asiae*, XLII (1980), pp. 39–99; S. Settar, "A Buddhist Vihāra at Aihoḷe," *East and West*, N.S. XIX (1969), pp. 126–138.

75. This is a standard identification. See, for example, Mitra, *Buddhist Monuments*, p. 186. The image may also be connected with a description of Vasudhāra found in the *Vajrāvalīnāmamaṇḍalopāyika* of Abhayākaragupta, where the goddess is described holding a pot and standing witness for Śākyasiṁha against Māra. See D. C. Bhattacharyya, "The *Vajrāvalī-nāma-maṇḍalopāyika* of Abhayākaragupta," in M. Strickman, ed., *Tantric and Taoist Studies in Honor of R. A. Stein* (Bruxelles: l'Institut Belge des Hautes Études Chinois, 1981), pp. 74–75.

76. According to the *Sādhanamālā*, Aparājitā is portrayed trampling on Gaṇapati; she is the destroyer of all wicked beings (M.-T. de Mallmann, *Introduction a l'Iconographie du Tântrisme Bouddhique* (Paris: A. Maisonneuve, 1975), p. 103), hereafter, de Mallmann, ITB. Images from eastern India clearly show the figure trampling on Gaṇapati. Although the Ellora images do not portray the elephant deity so clearly (rising as they must from the stone floors of the shrines), other details confirm the identification of Aparājitā, for instance the lunging posture and the upraised hand, identical to an eastern Indian image (see. B. Bhattacharyya, *The Indian Buddhist Iconography* (Calcutta: K. L. Mukhopadhyay, 1958), pp. 245–246, Figs. 189 and 190).

77. See, for example, A. C. Banerji, "A Buddhist Image from Kurkihar," *Journal of the Royal Asiatic Society of Bengal, Letters*, III (1937), pp. 53–54; A. Cunningham, *Mahābodhi; or the Great Buddhist Temple under the Bodhi Tree at Buddha-Gayā*, (1892; reprint, Varanasi: Indological Book House, 1961), Pl. XIV. The iconography of *bhūmisparśamudrā* Buddhas is discussed in detail in J. Leoshko, "The Iconography of Buddhist Sculptures of the Pāla and Sena Periods from Bodhgayā," (Ph.D. diss., Ohio State University, 1987), pp. 104–173.

78. R. C. Majumdar, ed., *The Age of Imperial Kanauj, The History and Culture of the Indian People*, Vol. IV (Bombay: Bharatiya Vidya Bhavan, 1955), pp. 10–11, 289–290; Czuma, "The Brahmanical Rashtrakuta Monuments at Ellora," pp. 38–40.

79. Burgess and Indraji, "Elura Inscriptions," pp. 99–100.

80. The best summary is still Spink, *Ajanta to Ellora*, passim. Greater detail is available in J. Fergusson and J. Burgess, *The Cave Temples of India* (London: W. H. Allen, 1880).

81. See B. G. Gokhale, *Buddhism in Maharashtra, A History* (Bombay: Popular Prakashan, 1976) for a description of these changes in Maharashtra.

82. S. B. Das Gupta, *An Introduction to Tantric Buddhism* (3rd ed., Calcutta: University of Calcutta, 1974), p. 2.

83. C. Yamamoto, *History of Mantrayana in Japan*, Sata-Pitaka Series, Volume 346 (New Delhi: Sharada Rani, 1987), p. 37.

84. T. Sawa, *Art in Japanese Esoteric Buddhism* (Tokyo, New York: Weatherhill/Heibonsha, 1972), p. 139.

85. This summary is based on the cogent discussion of D. Snellgrove, *Indo-Tibetan Buddhism*, Vol. I (Boston: Shambala Publications, Inc., 1987), pp. 117–194.

86. L. Chandra, "Borobuḍur as a Monument of Esoteric Buddhism," *South East Asian Review*, V (1980), pp. 2–3.

87. Some discussion of these relationships may be found in J. C. Huntington, "The Tendai Iconographic Model Book Shosonzuzō dated 1858," *Studies in Indo-Asian Art and Culture*, IV (1975), pp. 128–130; J. C. Huntington, "Cave Six at Aurangabad: A Tantrayāna Monument?" in J. G. Williams, ed., *Kalādarśana: American Studies in the Art of India*, (New Delhi: Oxford and IBH Publishers, Co. with A.I.I.S., 1981), pp. 47–55; R. S. Gupte, *Iconography of the Buddhist Sculptures (Caves) of Ellora* (Aurangabad: Marathwada University, 1964), pp. 77, 246–248; D. C. Bhattacharyya, *Studies in Buddhist Iconography* (New Delhi: Manohar, 1978), pp. 95–96.

88. C. D. Orzech, "Seeing Chen-Yen Buddhism: Traditional Scholarship and the Vajrayana in China," *History of Religions*, Vol. 29, no. 2 (1989), pp. 87–114, discusses the traditional "invisibility" of an early Chinese *vajrayāna* tradition, in which Hui-kuo is viewed as the "one moment" of Chinese *vajrayāna* (p. 110). Orzech shows clearly that Chinese *vajrayānists* had a more lasting influence on the ultimate configuration of Shingon *maṇḍalas* than is usually supposed. Yet, to date, there has not been sufficient exploration of the Chinese evidence to connect with what we see at Ellora. Hence, Japan still provides the most useful source of analogies.

89. At Ajanta 125 years earlier, evidence for sectarian affiliation is almost equally scarce, and is absent completely at Aurangabad. One epigraphic reference to a sect occurs in an inscription painted beneath an image of a standing Buddha, added in the late fifth century to the earlier Hīnayāna *caitya*, Cave 10. The inscription records the gift of the image by Parika of the Cetika school, considered to be a subsect of the Mahāsaṃghika sect, whose members were numerous further south at Nagarjunakonda. The Mahāsaṃghikas were associated with early worship of anthropomorphic Buddha images and their beliefs seem to have anticipated Mahāyāna tenets that developed in the early centuries of our era. See Weiner, *Ajaṇṭā: Its Place in Buddhist Art*, p. 55; N. Dutt, *Buddhist Sects in India* (Calcutta: K. L. Mukhopadhyay, 1970), pp. 60–61, 68–69.

90. Burgess, *Elura*, p. 13; E. Lamotte, *Histoire du bouddhisme indien*, Bibliothèque du Muséon, Vol. 43 (Louvain: Publications universitaires, 1958), p. 547; Mitra, *Buddhist Monuments*, p. 4; S. Dutt, *Buddhist Monks and Monasteries*, pp. 224–225, note 1.

91. Beal, *Buddhist Records of the Western World*, Vol. II, pp. 257–259.

92. According to N. K. Sahu, *Buddhism in Orissa* (Utkal: Utkal University), pp. 142–162, Uḍḍiyāna is to be identified with Orissa. However, D. C. Sircar, *Studies in the Geography of Ancient and Medieval India* (2nd ed., New Delhi: Motilal Banarsidass, 1971), pp. 182–184, shows that a distinction must be maintained between Uḍḍiyāna, located in northwest India, and Uḍḍiśa, which is the same as Orissa. See also H. V. Guenther, *The Royal Song of Saraha* (Seattle: University of Washington Press, 1969), pp. 4–12; L. Chimpa and A. Chattopadhyaya, trans., *Taranatha's History of Buddhism in India* (Simla: Indian Institute of Advanced Study, 1970), pp. 102–106.

93. Gupte, *Iconography of the Buddhist Sculptures*, p. 146, has pointed out that, according to the *Bstan-hgyur*, Saraha wrote two *sādhanas* on Rakta-Lokeśvara (*Sādhanamālā* numbers 37 and 38). It may more than coincidence that early representations of this form of Avalokiteśvara were placed in prominent positions in Caves 4 and 11 at Ellora. A large plaque depicting Rakta-Lokeśvara was among the four major images flanking the sanctum of Temple 4 outside Monastery 2 at Ratnagiri in Orissa (D. Mitra, *Ratnagiri (1958–61). Archaeological Survey of India, Memoirs*, 80 (New Delhi: Archaeological Survey of India, 1981), Vol. II, pp. 291–292). Gohkale, *Buddhism in Maharashtra*, p. 112, makes a similar connection between Orissa and Maharashtra, but admits that for determining the actual mode of cross-regional transmission, "The whole subject must be left open until such time more evidence on the migration of ideas and techniques becomes available."

94. A. Ghosh, "Khaḍipāda Image Inscription of the Time of Śubhākara," *Epigraphia Indica*, XXVI (1942), pp. 247–248; S. C. De, "The Orissan Museum Image Inscription of the Time of Śubhākaradēva," *Proceedings of the Indian History Congress, 1949* (Allahabad: 1950), pp. 66–74. The

inscription and image have been assigned on paleographic grounds to the seventh or eighth century.

95. S. Dutt, *Buddhist Monks*, pp. 278–279. Kālacakra is one of the most complex forms of Tantric Buddhism of the *anuttarayoga* class; see Das Gupta, *An Introduction to Tantric Buddhism*, pp. 63–67. These legends are corroborated by Hsüan-tsang's account: in the seventh century the monasteries of Dhanakaṭaka (Amaravati on the lower Krishna River) were largely deserted, but twenty were preserved. One thousand priests lived there, all studying the Great Vehicle (Mahāyāna).

96. Beal, *Buddhist Records*, pp. 97, 221.

97. A. Bareau, "Der Tantrismus," in *Die Religionen Indiens, II: Buddhismus, Jinismus, Primitivvölker* (Stuttgart: W. Kohlhammer Verlag, 1964), p. 173. These dates are not accepted by all scholars. For example, A. Wayman, *The Buddhist Tantras* (New York: Samuel Weiser, 1973), pp. 13–14, places Saraha and Nāgārjuna in the last half of the eighth century.

98. B. G. Gokhale, *Buddhism in Maharashtra*, p. 112.

99. A. Snodgrass, *The Matrix and Diamond World Mandalas in Shingon Buddhism* (New Delhi: Aditya Prakashan, 1988), p. 120.

100. G. Tucci, *The Theory and Practice of the Mandala* (New York: Samuel Weiser, Inc., 1970), p. 23.

101. L. Chandra, "Borobuḍur as a Monument of Esoteric Buddhism," p. 16. For an alternative explanation, based on the *Gaṇḍavyūha*'s description of the *kūṭāgāra* in the abode of Maitreya, see L. O. Gomez, "The Role of the *Gaṇḍavyūha* in the Design of Barabuḍur," in L. O. Gomez and H. W. Woodward, eds., *Barabudur, History and Significance of a Buddhist Monument* (Berkeley: University of California Press, 1981), pp. 173–194. Gomez, expecting rather precise correlations between text and monument, concludes (p. 185) that the "*kūṭāgāra* theory" fails since it is incomplete, explaining no more than "one fundamental aspect of the monument."

102. Snodgrass, *Matrix and Diamond World Mandalas*, p. 187.

103. Snellgrove, *Indo-Tibetan Buddhism*, Vol. I, p. 202.

104. Snodgrass, *Matrix and Diamond World Mandalas*, pp. 152–160 gives the Shingon version. Tucci, *Theory and Practice*, pp. 85–107, summarizes the Tibetan tradition, based on the *Guhyasamāja*.

105. Tucci, op. cit., p. 86.

106. de Mallmann, ITB, pp. 41–82.

107. Snodgrass, *Matrix and Diamond World Mandalas*, p. 555.

108. L. Chandra, "Borobuḍur as a Monument of Esoteric Buddhism," p. 24.

109. P. Granoff, "A Portable Buddhist Shrine from Central Asia," *Archives of Asian Art*, 23 (1968–1969), p. 88.

110. Snodgrass, *Matrix and Diamond World Mandalas*, p. 142.

111. Sawa, *Art in Japanese Esoteric Buddhism*, pp. 14–16, 135–150 (quote from p. 150).

112. L. Chandra, "Borobuḍur as a Monument of Esoteric Buddhism," pp. 15–16.

113. D. Klimburg-Salter, "Monastic Art of the Western Trans-Himalayas: Seventh to Seventeenth Centuries," in D. Klimburg-Salter, ed., *The Silk Road and the Diamond Path: Esoteric Buddhist Art on the Trans-Himalayan Trade Route* (Los Angeles: UCLA Art Council, 1982), p. 158.

114. D. L. Snellgrove and T. Skorupski, *The Cultural Heritage of Ladakh*, Vol. I (Warminster: Aris & Phillips Ltd., 1977), pp. 30–64; S. L. and J. C. Huntington, *The Art of Ancient India* (New York and Tokyo: Weatherhill, 1985), pp. 378–385.

115. Burgess, *Report on the Elura Cave Temples*, pp. 16–17.

116. Huntington, "Cave Six at Aurangabad: A Tantrayāna Monument?" pp. 47–55.

117. Less well known is the connection of *maṇḍala* and structural temple at Candi Jago, Java. See K. O'Brien, "Candi Jago as a Mandala: Symbolism of Its Narratives," *Review of Indonesian and Malayan Affairs*, Vol. 22.2 (summer 1988), pp. 1–61.

118. P. Mus, *Barabudur: Esquisse d'une histoire du bouddhisme fondée sur la critique archéologique des textes.* 2 Vols. (Hanoie: Imprimerie d'Extrême Orient, 1935).

119. The vast literature on Barabudur cannot be cited here but the following represent most recent studies: Chandra, "Borobuḍur as Monument of Esoteric Buddhism," pp. 1–41; L. O. Gomez and H. W. Woodward, eds., *Barabudur, History and Significance of a Buddhist Monument* (Berkeley: University of California, 1981), particularly A. Wayman, "Reflections on the Theory of Barabuḍur as a *Maṇḍala*," pp. 139–172; A. Snodgrass, *The Symbolism of the Stupa* (Ithaca, N.Y.: Southeast Asia Program, Cornell University, 1985).

120. See L. Chandra, op. cit., for the connection to the *Mahāvairocanasūtra*. For the connection to the *Gaṇḍavyūha*, see L. O. Gomez, "The Role of the Gaṇḍavyūha in the Design of Barabuḍur," in Gomez and Woodward, *Barabudur*, pp. 173–194. For the Nepalese-Tibetan connections, see A. Wayman, "Barabuḍur as a *Maṇḍala*," in Gomez and Woodward, pp. 139–172.

121. For illustrations of Ratnagiri's eight-Bodhisattva *maṇḍalas*, see Mitra, *Ratnagiri*, Vol. I, Plates CXXXVIII A & B.

122. N. Hock, "Buddhist Ideology and the Sculpture of Ratnagiri, Seventh Through Thirteenth Centuries" (Ph.D. diss., University of California-Berkeley, 1987), pp. 2–35.

123. L. Chandra, "Ellora as Śūnyatā and Rūpam," in R. Parimoo et al., *Ellora Caves* (New Delhi: Books and Books, 1988), pp. 134–136.

124. Wayman, "Barabuḍur as a *Maṇḍala*," note 25 on affiliation with the yogatantra school.

Chapter 2: Buddhist Caves of the First Period: The Beginning of the Maṇḍala

1. For an extensive discussion of this relative and absolute chronology see G. H. Malandra, "The Buddhist Caves at Ellora," (Ph.D. diss., University of Minnesota, 1983), Chapter I.

2. W. Spink, "Ellora's Earliest Phase," *Bulletin of the American Academy of Benares*, I (1967).

3. W. Spink, *Ajanta to Ellora* (Ann Arbor and Bombay: Marg Publications, 1967), p. 13. For example, two different pillar types might represent a temporal difference or a contemporary use of more than one motif. Spink's caution on this point is largely a reaction to the method used by scholars like Philippe Stern, who reconstructed the chronology from Ajanta to Ellora solely on the basis of changes in pillar types (P. Stern, *Colonnes indiennes d'Ajantā et Ellora* (Paris: Presses universitaires de France, 1972)). I believe that if changes even in "stereotyped" features of the caves are placed in a sequence, and if sequences of *several* features follow a parallel pattern, it is likely that the pattern so revealed reflects a genuine temporal development.

4. Spink, "Ellora's Earliest Phase," pp. 19, 21–22.

5. M. -T. de Mallmann, *Introduction a l'étude d'Avalokiteçvara*, Annales du Musée Guimet, Bibliothèque d'études, Vol. 57 (Paris: Civilisations du Sud, 1948), pp. 144–145, proposed these identifications, and observed that groups with similar iconography from eastern India post-date the seventh century.

6. T. Sawa, *Art in Japanese Esoteric Buddhism* (Tokyo and New York: Weatherhill, 1972), Fig. 7 and 10.

7. Sawa, *Art of Japanese Esoteric Buddhism*, Fig. 149 and pp. 130–131.

8. M. -T. de Mallmann, *Introduction a l'Iconographie du Tântrisme Bouddhique* (Paris: A Maisonneuve, 1975), pp. 41–82, provides a ready and thorough reference. Hereafter cited as de Mallmann, ITB.

9. J. Huntington, "Cave Six at Aurangabad: A Tantrayāna Monument?" In J. G. Williams, ed., *Kalādarśana: American Studies in the Art of India* (New Delhi: Oxford and IBH Publishers with A.I.I.S., 1981), Figs. 1, 6, 7.

10. J. Takakusu, trans., *A Record of the Buddhist Religion as Practiced in India and the Malay Archipelago (A.D. 671–695), by I-tsing* (1896; reprint, Delhi: Munshiram Manoharlal, 1966), pp. 147–148. Hereafter referred to as Takakusu, *I-tsing*.

11. M. Ghosh, *The Development of Buddhist Iconography in Eastern India. A Study of Tārā, Prajñās of Five Tathāgatas, and Bhṛkuṭī* (New Delhi: Munshiram Manoharlal, 1980), pp. 147–173.

12. For *vitarkamudrā* as the hand position of Maitreya, see de Mallmann, ITB, pp. 33, 244–248. The composition of this group is very similar to the right guard group in Aurangabad Cave 6. See C. Berkson, *The Caves at Aurangabad, Early Buddhist Tantric Art in India* (New York: Mapin International, 1986), p. 179.

13. Spink, *Ajanta to Ellora*, p. 29, Figs. 14, 15, 16; p. 30, Fig. 20.

14. J. Auboyer, *Le Trône et son symbolisme dans l'Inde ancienne* (Paris: Presses universitaires de France, 1949) presents the most complete study of the morphology and meaning of these symbols. As a conventionalized design the throne may not have had a specific meaning in a Buddhist context, as contrasted with a Brahmanical one. For a discussion of its Buddhist significance, see S. Weiner, *Ajaṇṭā: Its Place in Buddhist Art* (Berkeley: University of California Press, 1977), pp. 56–63.

15. Spink, *Ajanta to Ellora*, pp. 24–28.

16. Weiner, *Ajaṇṭā: Its Place in Buddhist Art*, pp. 98–100, 104–106; Spink, *Ajanta to Ellora*, pp. 29–31.

17. Weiner, op. cit., pp. 56–63.

18. de Mallmann, ITB, pp. 129–131.

19. Ibid., pp. 33, 392.

20. Huntington, "Cave Six at Aurangabad," p. 55, note 33 comments on the generalized, non-specific *mudrās* in early representations of this system. Also, L. Chandra, "Borobuḍur as a Monument of Esoteric Buddhism," *The South East Asian Review*, Vol. V., No. 1 (1980), pp. 26–29, points out that there was not an "immutable fixed standard" in describing them but, instead, there is considerable textual variation, so that each set of five *tathāgatas* may represent *a* system among many.

21. Huntington, "Cave Six at Aurangabad," p. 50 and p. 54, note 21. Texts describing this triad include the *Mañjuśrīmūlakalpa, Mahāvairocanasūtra*, and the *Sarvatathāgatatattvasaṁgrahasūtra*.

22. J. Fergusson and J. Burgess, *The Cave Temples of India* (London: W. H. Allen, 1880), pp. 353–355 and Plate LIV; D. Mitra, *Buddhist Monu-*

ments (Calcutta: Sahitya Samsad, 1971), pp. 167, 184.

23. The square pillars with narrow fluted necking and incised empty circular "medallions" of the Kanheri cave are comparable to the rear hall pillars of Ellora Cave 5. Such pillars seem to have had a general seventh-century Indian provenance, illustrated by portico pillars of the mid-seventh century Śiva temple at Mahua in Madhya Pradesh. See J. Williams, *The Art of Gupta India* (Princeton: Princeton University Press, 1982), Fig. 250; they recur in more elaborate form in Ellora Cave 10.

24. R. T. Paine and A. Soper, *The Art and Architecture of Japan* (Harmondsworth, England and Baltimore: Penguin Books, 1974), pp. 172–193, 210–228.

25. See, for example, R. S. Gupte and B. D. Mahajan, *Ajanta, Ellora and Aurangabad Caves* (Bombay: D. B. Taraporevala Sons & Co., 1962), p. 160.

26. For plans, see Berkson, *The Caves at Aurangabad*, pp. 102 (Cave 7), 174 (Cave 6), 188 (Cave 2).

27. Spink, *Ajanta to Ellora*, p. 41, Fig. 15.

28. O. Divakaran, "Le Temple de Jambulinga (daté de 690 ap. J.-C.) à Bādāmi," *Ars Asiatiques*, XXI (1970), p. 30.

29. A similar argument is made with regard to Aurangabad Caves 6 and 7 in Huntington, "Cave Six at Aurangabad."

30. Precedent for this functional approach to cave "completion" comes from Ajanta where, as Walter Spink has shown, in Cave 11 the shrine image was carved, plastered, and painted before the walls and ceiling of the main hall were plastered. There, the rear and side walls were decorated while the ceiling was only plastered. This would reflect time pressure on the end of work—presumably wall areas were more important than the ceiling in creating a functional monument. See W. Spink, "Ajanta's Chronology: The Problem of Cave Eleven," *Ars Orientalis*, VII (1968), pp. 162–163.

31. Huntington, "Cave Six at Aurangabad," Fig. 7.; Berkson, *The Caves at Aurangabad*, pp. 147, 152.

32. Walter Spink, "Ajanta's Chronology: Politics and Patronage," in J. G. Williams, ed., *Kalādarśana*, p. 123, note 6, lists three sculptures in Caves 2, 20 and 26, and five painted versions in Caves 2, 4, U6, 11, and 17.

33. Mitra, *Buddhist Monuments*, p. 165, lists three, in Caves 2, 41, and 90.

34. Berkson, *The Caves at Aurangabad*, pp. 124, 126–131.

35. For more detailed discussion of the Ellora images see M. E. Leese, "Ellora and the Development of the Litany Scene in Western India," in R. Parimoo, et al., eds., *Ellora Caves, Sculptures and Architecture* (Delhi: Books and Books, 1988), pp. 164–179.

36. See Huntington, "Cave Six at Aurangabad," p. 51, where the hair knots (pañcajaṭā) of a male attendant to the left female figure outside the shrine of Aurangabad Cave 7 are taken to indicate the maṇḍala of the five Jina Buddhas. Huntington acknowledges that this is a rare detail in Indian Buddhist art. The knots in the Ellora Cave 3A figure are not portrayed in the same manner so the identity of this figure remains in doubt. Some forms of Mañjuśrī are said to wear the hair in pañcacīra (five locks), but these would be hanging down, not knotted. See M.-T de Mallmann, *Étude Iconographique sur Mañjuśrī*, Publications de l'École Française d'Extrême-Orient, LV (Paris: École Française d'Extrême-Orient, 1964), pp. 13–15.

37. For example, an early seventh-century stucco panel on the main *stūpa*, Site Three, Nalanda. See Ghosh, *The Development of Buddhist Iconography in Eastern India*, Plates 5 and 6. Although Ghosh ascribes these images to the sixth century (p. 154), I follow the carefully reasoned chronology proposed by F. M. Asher, *The Art of Eastern India, 300–800* (Minneapolis: University of Minnesota Press, 1980), pp. 46–48, who assigns an early seventh century date to the Nalanda Site Three stuccos.

38. John Huntington, letter, October 14, 1980, suggested a similar interpretation to me.

Chapter 3: Caves of the Middle Period: The Maṇḍala Grows

1. An historical analogy is provided by the description by I-tsing of worship in a northern Indian *vihāra*, where moveable images were placed in windows or niches to be removed when the monks ate or slept. J. Takakusu, trans., *A Record of the Buddhist Religion as Practiced in India and the Malay Archipelago (A.D. 671–695), by I-Tsing* (1896; reprint, Delhi: Munshiram Manoharal, 1966), p. 113.

2. For plans and general discussion see D. B. Levine, "Aurangabad: A Stylistic Analysis," *Artibus Asiae*, XXVIII (1966), pp. 175–188; J. C. Huntington, "Cave Six at Aurangabad: A Tantrayāna Monument?" In Joanna G. Williams, ed., *Kalādarśana: American Studies in the Art of India* (New Delhi: Oxford and IBH Publishers, Co. with A.I.I.S., 1981), pp. 47–55; C. Berkson, *The*

Caves at Aurangabad, Early Buddhist Tantric Art in India (New York: Mapin International Inc., 1986).

3. The cave shrine with circumambulatory passage had its origin in the Śaiva Elephanta Cave 1, not Ajanta Caves 6, 16, and 17, where only the Buddha image, not the entire sanctum, can be circumambulated. The Elephanta-type plan was adapted in Caves 29, 26, 21, 17, and 14 at Ellora, as well as less literally in Aurangabad Caves 6 and 7. See W. Spink, "Ajanta and Ghatotkacha: A Preliminary Analysis," *Ars Orientalis,*" VI (1966), p. 143, note 13, and W. Spink, *Ajanta to Ellora* (Bombay and Ann Arbor: Marg Publications for the Center for South and Southeast Asian Studies, University of Michigan, 1967), pp. 18–22. Earlier, K. V. Soundara Rajan, "Beginnings of the Temple Plan," *Bulletin of the Prince of Wales Museum of Western India,* VI (1957–1959), p. 79, suggested that the development of the square, detached shrine in Buddhist caves coincided with the decline in *stūpa*-worship; the shrine would then have combined the functions of assembly hall and worship area into one structure. Since Ellora did have a major *caitya* hall housing a *stūpa,* this explanation seems unnecessary.

4. Spink, *Ajanta to Ellora,* p. 67, Figs. 15, 16, 17.

5. The style of the Pāñcika image in Aurangabad Cave 7 is closer to that of the Ellora Cave 2 veranda image of Jambhala.

6. Berkson, *The Caves at Aurangabad,* p. 178.

7. The cave might best be designated as Cave 19–20. K. Kumar, "The Buddhist Origin of Some Brahmanical Cave Temples at Ellora," *East and West,* N.S. XXVI (1976), pp. 363–364, identified this image as Jambhala and thus argued that this is a Buddhist excavation, even though there are no other Buddhist sculptures in it. He also assigned the image to the late fifth century, a date two hundred years too early, according to the chronology set forth here.

8. The *utpala* is identifiable by its distinctive, pointed petals. M.-T. de Mallmann, *Introduction a l'Iconographic du Tântrisme Bouddhique* (Paris: Adrien-Maisonneuve, 1975), pp. 17–18. See Berkson, *The Caves at Aurangabad,* p. 178. They are also held by the right attendant to the north court female figure in Aurangabad Cave 9. Ibid., p. 211.

9. Berkson, op. cit., pp. 135, 142.

10. Berkson, *The Caves at Aurangabad,* p. 208.

11. Spink, *Ajanta to Ellora,* p. 30, Fig. 22.

12. At Aurangabad, in Cave 6, there are images of Vajrapāṇi depicted with two different kinds of *vajras* but the Bodhisattvas standing in comparable positions in Cave 7 do not hold *vajras* at all. Huntington, "Aurangabad Cave Six," pp. 50, 54, and note 20.

13. Another example of this type comes from even further west, at the site of Mirpur Khas, in Gujarat, illustrated as the frontispiece in J. Auboyer, *Le Trône et son symbolisme dans l'Inde ancienne* (Paris: Presses universitaires de France, 1949). The projecting "T"-shaped crossbar was most probably derived from the fifth-century throne backs of north Indian Buddhist sculpture. A good example of a possible source is a stele from Sarnath, of the group dated ca. 475. See J. G. Williams, *The Art of Gupta India* (Princeton: Princeton University Press, 1982), Plate 94.

14. At Nasik, both throne back types are found in Cave 23.

15. See chapter 5 and G. H. Malandra, "Bhṛkutī at Ellora," *Journal of the Indian Society of Oriental Art,* Vol. 12 (1983), pp. 31–40, for a detailed discussion of the iconography of this image at Ellora.

16. Berkson, *The Caves at Aurangabad,* p. 208.

17. This reconstruction is summarized in the chronological chart in Spink, *Ajanta to Ellora;* evidence for it is not presented in any detail, however. According to John Huntington, the periods of excavation might have been even shorter, to meet astrologically determined deadlines; see J. C. Huntington, "Cave Six at Aurangabad," p. 55, note 35.

18. D. Mitra, "Iconographic Notes. A. An Image of Mahāmāyūrī in the Nalanda Museum," *Journal of the Asiatic Society,* Ser. 4, I (1959), pp. 37–38.

19. P. Brown, *Indian Architecture (Buddhist and Hindu Periods)* (reprint, Bombay: D. B. Taraporevala Sons & Co., 1976), p. 60; Spink, *Ajanta to Ellora,* chart.

20. J. Irwin, "The Axial Symbolism of the Early Stūpa: An Exegesis," and G. Roth, "Symbolism of the Buddhist Stūpa," in A. L. Dallapicolla and S. Zingel-Avé Lallemant, eds., *The Stūpa: Its Religious, Historical and Architectural Significance* (Wiesbaden: Franz Steiner Verlag, 1980), pp. 12–38 and 183–209; A. Snodgrass, *The Symbolism of the Stupa* (Ithaca, N.Y.: Southeast Asia Program, Cornell University, 1985).

21. S. Weiner, *Ajaṇṭā: Its Place in Buddhist Art* (Berkeley: University of California Press, 1977), Figs. 18, 19 and 84, 85.

22. S. Weintraub, "Viśvakarmā, Elurā: A Critical Analysis," *Marsyas,* XVII (1974–1975), pp. 49–57, also perceived the closer reference of the Ellora façades to structural buildings than to other rock-cut monuments, but made a strained connection between Cave 10 and seventh-century Pallava temples.

23. M. Meister, "Phāṁsanā in Western India," *Artibus Asiae,* XXXVIII (1976), p. 168. The *phāṁ-*

sanā is a "wedge"-shaped roof section of a pyramidal *śikhara*. Comparable features are found, for instance, on the Muṇḍeśvari temple in Bihar, dated around 636 C.E., and the late-seventh-century temples of Alampur in Andhra Pradesh and Aihole in Karnataka.

24. M. Ghosh, *Development of Buddhist Iconography in Eastern India: A Study of Tārā, Prajñās of Five Tathāgatas and Bhṛikuṭī* (New Delhi: Munshiram Manoharlal, 1980), pp. 20–24; R. Sen Gupta, "A Sculptural Representation of the Buddhist Litany to Tārā at Ellora." *Bulletin of the Prince of Wales Museum of Western India*, V (1955–1957), p. 12; D. Mitra, "Aṣṭamahābhaya-Tārā," *Journal of the Asiatic Society*, Ser. 3, XXIII (1957), pp. 19–20.

25. Spink initially placed Ajanta Cave 19 early in the sequence there because of its central place along the horseshoe-shaped cliff of the site; the corollary to this interpretation (central = early; peripheral = late) was that Cave 26, the other late-fifth-century *caitya* of Ajanta, had to be later because it was excavated at the end of the scarp. More recently, Spink has significantly altered this view by claiming solstitial orientation determined the positioning of Cave 19 and 26; 19 placed to meet the rising sun on the day of the winter solstice and 26 placed to meet the sun on the summer solstice. W. Spink, "Ajanta's Chronology: Solstitial Evidence," *Ars Orientalis*, XV (1984), pp. 97–117. His problem has been to explain the numerous cases of asymmetry relative to the solstitial axes of the caves. Thus, for Cave 19, he explains that the doorway was placed correctly, but the façade and inner *stūpa*, and the image on it, were laid off axis because it was one of the first caves excavated at Ajanta, with the typically imprecise work of inexperienced artisans. He furthermore claims that artisans noticed and tried to correct the asymmetry of the *stūpa* in Cave 19, adjusting it after it was initially blocked out. He acknowledges that the adjustment is subtle. Cave 26, Spink says, was much more precisely aligned than Cave 19 although, "admittedly, the *stūpa* is positioned a few inches to the right of [solstitial] center."

26. For a review of literature on *stūpas*, see R. L. Brown, "Recent Stupa Literature," *Journal of Asian History*, Vol. 20, no. 20 (1986), pp. 215–232. The following summary is based on the admirable compilation of information by Snodgrass, *The Symbolism of the Stupa*. On the connection of *stūpa* and *maṇḍala*, see pp. 104, 126–131 and also, G. Fussman, "Symbolism of the Buddhist *Stūpa*," *Journal of the International Association of Buddhist Studies*, Vol. 9, no. 2 (1986), pp. 37–53.

27. Snodgrass, *Symbolism of the Stupa*, p. 135.

28. Ibid., p. 147.

29. Ibid., pp. 201–226.

30. Ibid., p. 362.

31. Ibid., pp. 364–366.

32. Ibid., p. 376; Śubhakarasiṁha, a commentator on these *sūtras*, calls the iron *stūpa*, the "Buddha-*stūpa* in the mind."

33. See O. Divakaran, "Les temples d'Ālampur et de ses environs au temps des Cālukya de Bādāmi," *Arts Asiatiques*, XXIV (1971), Figs. 21a and 21b. Also, Ellora's *candraśālā*, flanked by two side niches, is comparable to the relatively plain *śikharas* with large *sukhanāsas* on Alampur temples, whose side walls include niches like those on the Cave 10 façade.

34. The identification of the central group is unclear. It has been suggested that it depicts the patron of the cave (R. S. Gupte and R. D. Mahajan, *Ajanta, Ellora and Aurangabad Caves* (Bombay: B. Taraporevala Sons & Co., 1962), p. 169. However, the small figures in the lowermost band stretch and cup their ears to hear, giving the impression that the scene may portray a proclamation in a sacred setting.

35. H. Zimmer, *The Art of Indian Asia*, Vol. II (New York: Pantheon Books, 1955), Plate 97.

36. Ibid., Plate 110.

37. Now in the Raipur Museum. According to D. Stadtner, "From Sirpur to Rajim: The Art of Kosala during the Seventh Century" (Ph.D. diss., University of California at Berkeley, 1976), p. 40, the Anandaprabhā *vihāra* at Sirpur can be dated roughly to the first two decades of the seventh century, while the Svastika *vihāra* may date to the end of the sixth century (p. 85). Stray sculpture is probably ascribable to the turn of the seventh century (p. 41). The well-known Sirpur bronzes, whose style is more elaborate than that of the *vihāra* stone sculpture, are ascribed to the eighth century. See M. G. Dikshit, "Some Buddhist Bronzes from Sirpur, Madhya Pradesh," *Bulletin of the Prince of Wales Museum of Western India*, V (1955–1957), pp. 1–11.

38. In several cases, the bust of the *nāga* (cobra) emerges above the fluted base. Such figures are reminiscent of the very common Cālukya *nāga* medallions found on monuments from the late sixth to early eighth centuries. See G. Michell, "Temples of the Early Chalukyas," in M. R. Anand, *In Praise of Aihole, Badami, Mahakuta, Pattadakal* (Bombay: Marg Publications, 1981), p. 95, Fig. 7 and p. 64. Kumar, "The Buddhist Origin of Some Brahmanical Caves," p. 369, says these capitals specifically symbolize the Rāmagrama *stūpa* guarded by *nāgas*, but this is difficult to interpret in the context of Cave 15, a clearly Śaiva temple.

Knots may represent the crossing points of the lines in a *maṇḍala*. A goal of Buddhism is to untie the knots of being, according to the *Suraṅgama*

Sūtra. In tantric practice, an aim is to untie (penetrate) such knots (*granthi*). See Snodgrass, *Symbolism of the Stupa*, pp. 111–114.

39. These occur as early as Ajanta Cave 17. See Spink, *Ajanta to Ellora*, p. 15, Fig. 7. At Ellora octagonal pillars appear only on the veranda of Cave 27, and are one of the early features of that excavation. See also Spink, "Ellora's Earliest Phase," pp. 12–13.

40. J. Marshall and A. Foucher, *The Monuments of Sanci*, Vol. I (London: Probsthain, 1940), p. 53, where they are assigned a date ca. 650.

41. An image with similar composition, the Buddha attended by Lokeśvara to his right and Mañjuśrī, with a low hair style, tiger claws and book on an *utpala*, to the left, is mentioned in de Mallmann, ITB, p. 255 and note 12.

42. M. Bénisti, *Contribution à l'étude du stūpa bouddhique indien: les stūpa mineurs de Bodhgaya et de Ratnagiri*, Vol. I (Paris: École française d'extrême orient, 1981), pp. 76–79.

43. Snodgrass, *Symbolism of the Stupa*, pp. 91–93. The initiation rites in Shingon Buddhism, which focus on this *mandala*, are performed in a *mandala* which is identified with a king's palace.

44. de Mallmann, ITB, p. 108. Alternatively, this may represent Khasarpaṇa, another form of Avalokiteśvara, who is accompanied by Tārā, Sudhanakumāra (Mañjuśrī), Bhṛkuṭī and Hayagrīva. Ibid., p. 107. However, the presence of Mahāmāyūrī makes this identification questionable.

Chapter 4: The Late Buddhist Caves: The Mandala Unfolded

1. F. M. Asher, *Art of Eastern India* (Minneapolis: University of Minnesota Press, 1980), p. 80, for the date of these images.

2. M.-T. de Mallmann, *Introduction a l'Iconographie du Tântrisme Bouddhique* (Paris: A. Maisonneuve, 1975), pp. 144–145.

3. Some of these are discussed and illustrated in R. S. Gupte, *Iconography of the Buddhist Sculptures (Caves) of Ellora* (Aurangabad: Marathwada University, 1964), p. 89 and Plates 14a–d.

4. A similar reversal is seen a century earlier at Aurangabad Cave 6, but there the central image is a *dharmacakramudrā* Buddha. C. Berkson, *The Caves at Aurangabad, Early Buddhist Tantric Art in India* (New York: Mapin International Inc., 1986), p. 182.

5. Because the first floor was buried, the cave appeared to have only two floors, hence its local name, Do Thal, meaning "two-storied." The first floor was cleared of debris in 1876; see R. Sengupta, "Repairs to Ellora Caves," *Ancient India*, XVII (1961), p. 50. Before this, Cave 11NC was level with Cave 11.2, as shown in the early nineteenth-century plans of T. Daniell, *Hindoo Excavations in the Mountain of Ellora near Aurangabad in the Deccan in Twenty-four Views* (London: 1803).

6. D. C. Chatham, "Pratīhāras from Paṭṭadakal to Ellora," in A. Krishna, ed., *Chhavi-2* (Banaras: Bharat Kala Bhavan, 1981), p. 76; O. Divakaran, "Les temples d'Ālampur et de ses environs au temps des Cālukya de Bādāmi," *Arts asiatiques*, XXIV (1971), Figs. 19 and 20.

7. O. Viennot, *Temples de l'Inde Centrale et Occidentale. (Étude stylistique et essai de chronologie relative du Ve au milieu de Xe siècle)* (Paris: École d'Extrême-Orient, 1976), Vol. I, p. 174; Vol. II, Plate 62.

8. G. Michell, "A Comparison of the Muṇḍeśvarī Temple at Ramgarh and the Meguṭi Temple at Aihole: Notes toward a Definition of Early Temple Style in India," *East and West*, N.S. XXVIII (1978)," Fig. 9; Asher, *Art of Eastern India*, p. 40 and Plates 45, 46, 47. Pillars with similar base niches also occur at Mahasthangarh in Bangladesh, assigned to the seventh century, as in Asher, Ibid., p. 62 and Plates 108 and 109.

9. C. Lin-Bodien, "The Chronology of Chandrāvatī, Kūsmā, Chitorgarh: A Case Study in the Use of Epigraphic and Stylistic Evidence," *Archives of Asian Art*, XXX (1980), p. 60 and Figs. 3 and 4.

10. See the door frame of the Bharateśvara temple at Bhubaneswar in C.L. Fabri, *History of the Art of Orissa* (Bombay: Orient Longman, 1974), Plate LXXXVII; O. Divakaran, "Le Temple de Jambulinga (daté de 699 ap. J.-C.) à Bādāmi," *Arts asiatiques*, XXI (1970), Figs. 24–27.

11. Lin-Bodien, "Chandrāvatī, Kūsmā, Chitorgarh," p. 53 and Fig. 7.

12. R. D. Banerji, *Eastern Indian School of Medieval Sculpture*, Archaeological Survey of India, Reports, N.I.S., LXVII (Delhi: Manager of Publications, 1933), Plate XCII(c).

13. This frame is comparable to, if more ornate, than an early-eighth-century door frame that serves as the entrance to a modern shrine in the Mahābodhi temple complex at Bodhgaya (Asher, *Art of Eastern India*, p. 71 and Plate 119). For example, both include alternating angular and semicircular meander patterns on their *śākhās*. And where the third *śākhā* extends across the top of the door frame, it is filled with flying figures converging on a small central image. Yet, the Indian Mu-

seum frame is more elaborate, including the base niches that the Bodhgaya frame lacks. Since the Ellora Cave 11 and 12 doorways are more complex than the seventh-century examples cited earlier, and similar to but less intricately composed than the Bodhgaya examples of the early to mid-eighth century, it seems most likely that the Ellora doorways should be assigned an intermediate date in the early eighth century.

14. See M.-T. de Mallmann, "Les bronzes népalais de la collection Sylvain Levi," *Artibus Asiae*, XXVII (1964), pp. 142–144. Her analysis is based on work done by Mus at Barabudur. It should be pointed out, however, that Mahāvairocana may also be portrayed as Śākyasiṁha, as in the *Durgatipariśodhana maṇḍala*; see de Mallmann, ITB, p. 62. It should also be noted that the more complex *maṇḍala* of the *Guhyasamājatantra* centers on Akṣobhya surrounded in the third circle by a group of eight Bodhisattvas, listed in the second *maṇḍala* of the *Niṣpannayogāvalī*. See A. Wayman, *The Yoga of the Guhyasamājatantra* (Delhi: Motilal Banarsidass, 1977), pp. 122–130; and de Mallmann, ITB, pp. 43–44. Here, however, Akṣobhya is three-faced and is accompanied by his *prajñā*.

15. For example, a stele from Bihar, illustrated in Banerji, *Eastern Indian School of Medieval Sculpture*, Plate XIX (b), where a single, four-armed dwarf squats in the center beneath the lotus-shaped throne base; and a Buddha image from Ujani, illustrated in N. K. Bhattasali, *The Iconography of Buddhist and Brahmanical Sculptures in the Dacca Museum* (Dacca: Rai S. H. Bhadra Bahadur, 1929), pp. 30–31 and Plate VIII, where four small figures squat below the throne, two on either side of a *vajra*.

16. Banerji, *Eastern Indian School of Medieaval Sculpture*, Plate XXI(b).

17. de Mallmann, ITB, p. 418.

18. The delicately looped belt of the bowl-offering figure is most comparable to belts worn by female figures guarding the entrance to the detached *maṇḍapa* in the Cave 15 courtyard (Fig. 274), a mid-eighth century structure. This similarity emphasizes the relatively late date and early Rāṣṭrakūṭa affiliation of Cave 11.2.

19. D. Mitra, *Buddhist Monuments* (Calcutta: Sahitya Samsad, 1971), p. 186.

20. de Mallmann, "Les bronzes nepalais," pp. 142–144.

21. This connection was suggested by Janice Leoshko, and documented in D. C. Bhattacharyya, "The *Vajravālī-nāma-maṇḍalopayika* of Abhayākaragupta," in M. Strickman, ed., *Tantric and Taoist Studies in Honor of R.A. Stein* (Brussels: 1981), pp. 74–75.

22. According to the *Sādhanamālā*, Aparājitā is portrayed trampling on Gaṇapati; she is the destroyer of all wicked beings. See de Mallmann, ITB, p. 103. Eastern Indian images clearly show the figure trampling on Gaṇapati. See B. Bhattacharyya, *The Indian Buddhist Iconography* (Calcutta: K.L. Mukhopadhyay, 1958), pp. 245–246 and figs. 189 and 190.

23. Bhattacharyya, *The Indian Buddhist Iconography*, Fig. 189; D. Mitra, *Ratnagiri (1958–61)*, Memoirs of the Archaeological Survey of India, No. 80 (New Delhi: Archaeological Survey of India, 1981), Plate LXXXIIIA. See also Asher, *Art of Eastern India*, Plate 144. Although the hand appears to cup her breast, according to iconographic texts, the left hand rests at the heart, holding the sacred thread and making the gesture of danger (*tarjanīmudrā*), see de Mallmann, ITB, p. 103. In Ellora Cave 12.2, it is the right hand that is in this position.

24. I am grateful to Janice Leoshko for directing my attention to this image. It was first discussed by A. C. Banerji, "A Buddha Image from Kurkihar," *Journal of the Royal Asiatic Society of Bengal, Letters*, 3 (1937), pp. 53–54.

25. See N. Hock, "Buddhist Ideology and the Sculpture of Ratnagiri, Seventh Through Thirteenth Centuries" (Ph.D. Diss., University of California-Berkeley, 1987), pp. 48–69, for a discussion of these images and their tantric meaning.

26. Mitra, *Ratnagiri* Vol. I, Plates LXXXIIIA (includes Aparājitā), Vol. II, Plates CCCXXIVa, CCCXXVa (includes Māra).

27. Hock, "Buddhist Ideology and Sculpture," p. 59.

28. Hock, Ibid., p. 69.

29. For instance, a bronze Vajrapāṇi from Sirpur; M. G. Dikshit, "Some Buddhist Bronzes from Sirpur," *Bulletin of the Prince of Wales Museum of Western India*, V (1955–1957), Plate 5a.

30. This figure epitomizes the problems inherent in identifying individuals in these groups. Looking at the relief *maṇḍalas* of Cave 12, Phyllis Granoff calls the figure in the corresponding position "Avalokiteśvara (Samantabhadra?)" ("A Portable Buddhist Shrine from Central Asia," *Archives of Asian Art*, 23 (1968–1969), pp. 88 and 90), but notes the "curious deviation" of two appearances of Avalokiteśvara in the *maṇḍala*. Gupte also identified the image as Avalokiteśvara/Lokanātha (*Iconography of the Buddhist Sculptures*, pp. 49–52). I would suggest that the figure may instead be Kṣitigarbha who, in some forms, holds a bottle, or a lotus supporting a branch of the *kalpadruma* tree, or simply a lotus (de Mallmann, ITB, p. 223).

31. de Mallmann, ITB, pp. 331–334. According to Granoff, "A Portable Buddhist Shrine," p.

88, this figure is Ākāśagarbha, assigned a flaming sword in the *Mahāvairocanābhisambodhisūtra*. However, Ākāśagarbha is portrayed elsewhere holding a *cintāmaṇi* (Ibid., p. 91; J. C. Huntington, "The Tendai Iconographic Model Book Shosonzuzō dated 1858," *Studies in Indo-Asian Art and Culture*, IV (1975), p. 302. And many other Bodhisattvas, including Samantabhadra and Sarvanivaraṇa-viṣkambhin also hold swords. Granoff identifies the sword-bearing Bodhisattvas in the Nelson Gallery *maṇḍala* as Samantabhadra, where Ākāśagarbha is portrayed holding a *cintāmaṇi* (Granoff, op. cit.), pp. 90–91.

32. The hair is a stylized *jaṭāmukuṭa* with a *stūpa*-like ornament resting on it. Maitreya's iconography at Ellora is further discussed in chapter 5.

33. de Mallmann, ITB, pp. 88–89, and note on Samantabhadra, above. Gupte, *Iconography of the Buddhist Sculptures*, pp. 44–45, identified the image as Samantabhadra. Granoff, "A Portable Buddhist Shrine," p. 88, identified the corresponding figure in the Cave 12 relief *maṇḍalas* as Kṣitigarbha, on the basis of the attribution to him of a lotus in the *Mahāvairocanābhisambodhisūtra* and in the *Amogha-pāśasūtra*. However, neither in the relief *maṇḍalas* nor in the Ellora shrine images does the figure hold a clearly depicted lotus.

34. Gupte, *Iconography of the Buddhist Sculptures*, identifies this figure as Jñānaketu, the only Bodhisattva besides Dhvajoṣṇīṣa assigned a *dhvaja* (see also de Mallmann, ITB, p. 157). However, if the object is recognized as a banner (*patākā*), the figure can be seen to represent Sarvanivaraṇa-viṣkambhin (Ibid., p. 12), although his banner is ordinarily surmounted by a *viśvavajra*, not evident in the Ellora images. Granoff, "A Portable Shrine," p. 88, identifies the figure as the latter on the basis of descriptions in the *Aṣṭamaṇḍalakasūtra* and the *Taizokai Jizoin*. This identification has the further, if not definitive, advantage that the name appears in several lists of Bodhisattvas, whereas Jñānaketu's does not.

35. de Mallmann, ITB, pp. 124–127. T. Donaldson, "The Buddhist Art of Orissa," manuscript, [1990], Chapter IV.

36. Some paint is preserved in the shrine areas of Caves 11.2 and 12, and is now undergoing cleaning and preservation by the Archaeological Survey of India. Unfortunately, mainly background paint remains, while the thick coat of plaster that was applied to the faces of the Bodhisattvas to fill out contours has disintegrated completely. The style of painting that remains is most comparable to the porch ceiling painting of Cave 16. I am indebted to B. N. Tandon, Director (Science) of the A.S.I. for recent photographs of the cleaned paint in Cave 12.

37. de Mallmann, ITB, p. 15.

38. de Mallmann acknowledged these difficulties, Ibid., p. 127.

39. Previous attempts at identifying the group and the *maṇḍala* have been handicapped by the same problems. Thus, Gupte, *Iconography of the Buddhist Sculptures*, pp. 44–52, was limited by his strict adherence to iconographic descriptions of individual Bodhisattvas. Huntington, "The Tendai Iconographic Model Book Shosonzuzō," p. 129, suggested that Ellora's *maṇḍalas* be compared to groups of Bodhisattvas in Tendai Japanese iconograpic texts. But, only a few images appear to have clear counterparts at Ellora. Granoff, "A Portable Shrine," pp. 92–93, suggested that "the power of the eight *bodhisattvas* lies not within their identity as one or another *bodhisattva*, but is more related to a general conception of the efficacy of a group of four or eight beings as protectors."

40. According to G. Tartakov, "The Chronology and Development of the Chālukya Cave Temples," *Ars Orientalis*, VII (1970), p. 177, note 67, such tall crowns are not used by the Pallavas before the reign of Rājasiṃha, that is, not before the early eighth century.

41. Chatham, "Pratīhāras from Paṭṭadakal to Ellora," Fig. 187. See particularly the crown worn by Rāvaṇa in the relief depicting the shaking of Mount Kailāsa, illustrated in G. Michell, "Temples of the Early Chalukyas," in M. R. Anand, ed., *In Praise of Aihole, Badami, Mahakuta, Pattadakal* (Bombay: Marg Publications, 1981), Fig. 8 on p. 126.

42. These connections have also been detected by M. A. Dhaky, "The Dravidian Sculptures in Pre-Imperial Rāṣṭrakūṭa Cave-Temples," in R. Parimoo et al., *Ellora Caves*, pp. 443–444, who says the Cave 12.3 *dvārapālas* are carved in "true Rāṣṭrakūṭa idiom."

43. A. Snodgrass, *The Matrix and Diamond World Mandalas in Shingon Buddhism*, Vol. I (New Delhi: Aditya Prakashan, 1988), pp. 187–188.

44. See J. Huntington, "Cave Six at Aurangabad: A Tantrayāna Monument?" in J. G. Williams, ed., *Kalādarśana: American Studies in the Art of India* (New Delhi: Oxford and IBH Publishers, Co. with A.I.I.S., 1981), for a similar proposal, which he summarized to me in an October, 1980 personal communication.

45. L. Chandra, "Borobuḍur as a Monument of Esoteric Buddhism," *South East Asia Review*, V (1980), p. 16.

46. The position of the couple on the front right pillar (Fig. 390), with heads together but bodies flying apart, is most like that of a couple from the Raval Phadi cave at Aihole, an example of Cālukya-like design incorporated into the Bud-

dhist work in Cave 12. See Michell, "Temples of the Early Chalukyas," p. 80, Fig. 9 for an illustration.

47. For a clear analogy, see D. Mitra, "Jambhala-maṇḍalas in Sculpture," *Journal of the Asiatic Society*, Ser. 4, III (1961), pp. 39–41 and Plates I, 1 and II. Here, an image of Jambhala is carved on the front of a stele from Ratnagiri, with a two-dimensional *maṇḍala* guiding meditation on Jambhala carved on the back. Chandra, "Borobuḍur as a Monument of Esoteric Buddhism," p. 3, notes the distinction among architectonic *maṇḍalas*, known as *pura-maṇḍala*, and those drawn with powdered colors, *rajo-maṇḍala*, or others painted on textiles, *paṭa-maṇḍala*.

48. Granoff, "A Portable Shrine from Central Asia," pp. 80–95, discusses several Central and East Asian examples. In a short response, Pratapaditya Pal noted several other examples of *aṣṭabodhisattvamaṇḍala* images, including a sixth-century circular terracotta plaque from Uttar Pradesh and a ninth-century bronze *stūpa* from Kurkihar ("A Note on the Mandala of the Eight Bodhisattvas," *Archives of Asian Art*, 26 [1972–1973], pp. 71–73). These examples show that Ellora's *maṇḍalas* are neither the earliest nor absolutely unique in the Indian context, yet the small number of others that can be cited underscores their relative rarity.

49. The *Niṣpannayogāvalī* describes many *maṇḍalas* that are conveniently summarized in de Mallmann, ITB, pp. 41–82. Other Sanskrit sources include the *Kriyāsaṁgraha* and the *Sādhanamālā*. Other important sources are known only in translation from east or central Asia, for instance, the *Aṣṭamaṇḍalakasūtra*, translated into Chinese by Amoghavajra in the mid-eighth century (Granoff, "A Portable Buddhist Shrine," p. 88).

50. de Mallmann, ITB, pp. 124–125, summarizes information from the *Sādhanamālā*, *Niṣpannayogāvalī*, and *Piṇḍīkramasādhana*. Information on the *Aṣṭamahābodhisattvamaṇḍalasūtra* comes from Granoff, "A Portable Buddhist Shrine," pp. 87–92 and L. Chandra, "Ellora as Śūnyatā and Rūpam," in R. Parimoo et al., *Ellora Caves*, pp. 134–136.

51. Donaldson, "The Buddhist Art of Orissa," mss., chapter 4, p. 254a. For an illustration of groups from Ratnagiri, see Mitra, *Ratnagiri*, Vol. I., Plate CXXXVIIIA and B. The Lalitagiri and Udayagiri images are not yet published.

52. N. J. Krom, "De Bodhisattvas van den Mendut," *Bijdragen tot de taal-, land- en volkenkunde, door Koninklijk Bataviaasch Gennotschapp van Kunsten en Wetenschappen*, Vol. 74 (1918), pp. 434. For the complete iconography of the temple, see also, J. S. Moens, "De Tjandi Mendut," *Tijdschrift voor Indische Taal-, Land, en Volkenkunde, door Bataviaasch Genootschap van Kunsten en Wetenschappen*, 59 (1921), pp. 529–600.

53. Chandra, "Borobudur as a Monument of Esoteric Buddhism," pp. 17–18.

54. For identifications, see section above on the Bodhisattvas and *maṇḍala* in Cave 11.2

55. Donaldson, *Buddhist Art of Orissa*, pp. 234–36. I am grateful to Professor Donaldson for making this identification.

56. de Mallmann, ITB, pp. 88–89.

57. de Mallmann, ITB, p. 255; illustrated in Banerji, *Eastern Indian School of Medieaval Sculpture*, Plate IX(b).

58. M.-T. de Mallmann, *Étude iconographique sur Mañjuśrī*, Publications de l'École Française d'Extrême Orient, Vol. LV (Paris: École Française d'Extrême Orient, 1964).

59. For instance, paired with Tārā, Cundā appears in a minor intrusive panel carved by the door to Shrine 11.2.1 (Fig. 426). Gupte, *Iconography of the Buddhist Sculptures*, pp. 100–104, identified many of these, on the basis of the characteristic bowl she holds in her hand(s), posed in *dhyānamudrā* in her lap.

60. de Mallmann, ITB, pp. 144–145, describes the iconography of Cundā.

61. For example, the Cundā image can be compared to a Cundā from Amaravati of late Cālukya style, clearly influenced by Pallava sculptural style, ascribable to a period no earlier than the mid-eighth century. See D. Barrett, "The Later School of Amarāvatī and its Influence," *Arts and Letters*, XXVIII (1954), Plates 1(b) and 3. The image of Cundā from Amaravati, with its flat forehead, narrowly slit eyes, pinched lips and rounded shoulders is more clearly a Pallava-style sculpture than the wide-eyed, square-shouldered Ellora female figures in the Cave 12.1 shrine.

62. For a discussion of Rāṣṭrakūṭa-period excavations, see S. J. Czuma, "The Brahmanical Rashtrakuta Monuments of Ellora," (Ph.D. Diss., University of Michigan, 1968), pp. 241–252. On the comparison of Caves 12 and 22, see pp. 191, and 253, note 14.

63. I am grateful to Thomas Donaldson for sharing unpublished illustrations of these images with me. The identification is made in his manuscript, "The Buddhist Art of Orissa," p. 239 and note 69.

64. See de Mallmann, ITB, pp. 405–406 and pp. 413–415.

65. Attributes are quite small. However, the left figure holds an *utpala*, the central figure holds a bowl in her natural hands, in *dhyānamudrā* in her lap, and the right figure holds a *kamaṇḍalu* in her upper left hand. They might correspond to the

three female figures on the left Cave 11.2.5 shrine wall.

66. These were already identified by Gupte, *Iconography of the Buddhist Sculptures*, pp. 78–79. The identification of similar images from eastern India is confirmed in M. Ghosh, *Development of Buddhist Iconography in Eastern India: A Study of Tārā, Prajñās of Five Tathāgatas and Bhrikutī* (New Delhi: Munshiram Manoharlal, 1980), pp. 151–63. According to the *Sādhanamālā*, Āryāvalokiteśvara-bhattāraka, or Rakta-Lokeśvara, is accompanied by Tārā and Bhrkutī (de Mallmann, ITB, p. 109). This is the only text in which Tārā and Bhrkutī are named as companions of Avalokiteśvara. In the text the attributes of the female images do not conform to earlier images, but their iconography is consistent with textual descriptions of them as individuals.

67. For discussion of this image, see Gupte, *Iconography of the Buddhist Sculptures*, pp. 86–87. Gupte called it Siddhaikavīra. However, it is Arapacana Mañjuśrī who is accompanied by four figures, Upakeśinī, Keśinī, Candraprabha, and Jālinīprabha and then, only the first two are female. For the problematic identification of this form of Mañjurśī, which can easily be confused with Lokanātha, see de Mallmann, ITB, pp. 251–252.

68. de Mallmann, *Mañjuśrī*, pp. 162–165.

69. Ibid., pp. 31–32; de Mallmann, ITB, p. 252 and note. 10.

70. de Mallmann, ITB, pp. 419–421. L. Chandra, "Ellora as Śūnyatā and Rūpam," pp. 136–137, has recently noted that this image represents Vajradhara, not Vajrasattva as earlier proposed (Gupte, *Iconography of the Buddhist Sculptures*, p. 30). They are distinguished by their hand positions, crossed over the chest in the case of Vajradhara images here and in Tibet.

71. de Mallmann, ITB, pp. 396–400.

72. See M. Bénisti, *Contribution à l'étude du stūpa bouddhique indien: Les stūpa mineurs de Bodh-Gaya et de Ratnagiri*, Publications de l'École Française d'Extrême-Orient, CXXV (Paris: l'École Française d'Extrême-Orient, 1981).

73. Similar variation is found among the numerous images of Jambhala at Ratnagiri. See Mitra, *Ratnagiri*, Pl. XLVIC; CLXXV, CLXXVI.

74. See Huntington, "Cave Six at Aurangabad," p. 55, note 33 on generalized, non-specific *mudrās* in Jina Buddha images. Chandra, "Borobudur as a Monument of Esoteric Buddhism," pp. 26–29, also notes the variability in representations and textual descriptions of the group.

75. D. Klimburg-Salter, *The Silk Route and The Diamond Path* (Los Angeles: UCLA Art Council, 1982), p. 123, Plate 53.

76. D. Barrett, *Mukhalingam Temples* and M. G. Dikshit, *Sirpur and Rajim Temples* (Bombay: N.M. Tripathi Private Ltd., 1960), Plate 52.

77. J. L. Davidson, *Art of the Indian Subcontinent from Los Angeles Collections* (Los Angeles: Ward Pritchee Press, 1968), Plate 39.

78. Mitra, *Ratnagiri*, Vol. I, Plates CLXV, CLXVIIA, CLXIXD.

79. Banerji, *Eastern Indian School of Medieaval Sculpture*, Plates Va, XXa, XXIa, b, c.

80. Seen as early as on the Varāha image in Badami Cave 3, but more common in seventh- and early eighth-century monuments, e.g., the Svarga Brahmā temple at Alampur and the Virupaksa temple at Pattadakal. See Chatham, "Pratīhāras," pp. 71–72.

81. Krom, "De Bodhisattvas van den Mendut," p. 434.

82. Burgess, *Elura*, pp. 19–20; R. S. Gupte and R. D. Mahajan, *Ajanta, Ellora and Aurangabad Caves* (Bombay: B. Taraporevala Sons & Co., 1962), p. 179. Left to right, they are: Vipaśyi, Śikhi, Viśvabhu, Krakucchanda, Kanakamuni, Kaśyapa, and Śākyamuni.

83. J. Burgess, *Report on the Elura Cave Temples and the Brahmanical and Jaina Caves in Western India*, Archaeological Survey of Western India, Vol. V (1882; reprint, Varanasi: Indological Book House, 1971), p. 20; Gupte and Mahajan, *Ajanta, Ellora and Aurangabad*, p. 179. Both sources identified these figures as seven Jina Buddhas, but ordinarily there are only five or six of these. The group would include the usual five: Vairocana, Aksobhya, Ratnasambhava, Amitābha, Amoghasiddhi, with the addition of Vajrasattva and Vajrarāga. L. O. Gomez, "Some Observations on the Role of the *Gandavyūha* in the Design of Barabudur," in L. Gomez and H. W. Woodward, eds., *Barabudur, History and Significance of a Buddhist Monument* (Berkeley: Berkeley Buddhist Series, 1981), p. 194, note 54, notes several lists of seven Buddhas that appear in the Chinese Tripitaka. Alternatively, L. Chandra, "Ellora as Śūnyatā and Rūpam," p. 142, suggests that they may be the "seven Medicine Buddhas."

84. Berkson, *The Caves at Aurangabad*, p. 60.

85. Ibid., pp. 134–135.

86. Previous guesses at their identification were based on a reliance on the well-known group of five female figures in Buddhism, the *prajñās* of the five Tathāgatas: Burgess, *Report on the Elura Cave Temples*, p. 21, and more recently, Gupte, *Iconography of the Buddhist Sculptures*, pp. 97–98.

87. de Mallmann, ITB, pp. 198–199. When described in *Sādhanas* specifically about her, she wears serpents; in the list of Dhāraṇīs, they are not mentioned.

88. Ibid., p. 60. The second enclosure of the *maṇḍala* includes four groups of twelve females: the Bhūmis, Pāramitās, Vaśitās, and Dhāraṇīs. Only the latter group includes Jāṅgulī and Cundā.

89. Ibid., p. 79. In this *maṇḍala*, however, there are four groups of ten, not twelve female figures.

90. Gupte, *Iconography of the Buddhist Sculptures*, p. 101, mentions the Dhāraṇīs, but does not connect them to these images, which he attempted to identify individually, not as a group.

91. de Mallmann, ITB, p. 151.

92. For the concept of rotation in a different *maṇḍalic* context, see Snodgrass, *The Matrix and Diamond World Mandalas*, Vol. I, p. 287; Vol. II, p. 597.

Chapter 5: A Center on the Periphery: Ellora's Place in Buddhist Art

1. F. M. Asher, *The Art of Eastern India, 300-800* (Minneapolis: University of Minnesota Press, 1980); J. G. Williams, *The Art of Gupta India* (Princeton: Princeton University Press, 1982).

2. R. S. Gupte, *Iconography of the Buddhist Sculptures (Caves) of Ellora* (Aurangabad: Marathwada University, 1964), pp. 104–106.

3. In M. K. Dhavalikar, "The Origin of Tārā," *Bulletin of the Deccan College Research Institute,* XXIV (1963–1964), Tārā is said to have been worshipped at all these sites. See also J. C. Huntington, "Cave Six at Aurangabad: A Tantrayāna Monument?" In J. G. Williams, ed., *Kalādarśana: American Studies in the Art of India* (New Delhi: Oxford and IBH Publishers, Co. with A.I.I.S., 1981), pp. 49–52, where the female figures are identified as Tārā and Māmakī on the basis of their positions, not their attributes, which are nearly identical. An earlier image of Bhṛkuṭī may appear in Nasik Cave 23, identified by her *jaṭāmukuṭa*.

4. C. Berkson, *The Caves at Aurangabad, Early Buddhist Tantric Art in India* (New York: Mapin International, Inc.: 1986), pp. 134–137.

5. To my knowledge, the *ajina* is a rare attribute, seen for example, in a tenth-century bronze image of Bhṛkuṭī from Achutrajpur in Orissa. M. Ghosh, *Development of Buddhist Iconography in Eastern India: A Study of Tārā, Prajñās of Five Tathāgatas and Bhṛikuṭī* (New Delhi: Munshiram Manoharlal, 1980), p. 168 and Plate 53.

6. Ghosh, *Development of Buddhist Iconography in Eastern India*, pp. 147–173.

7. Asher, *Art of Eastern India*, pp. 46–48 for date; Ghosh, *Development of Buddhist Iconography in Eastern India*, Plates 5 and 6.

8. Ghosh, op. cit., Plate 37 and 37a.

9. M.-T. de Mallmann, *Introduction a l'Iconographie du Tântrisme Bouddhique* (Paris: A. Maisonneuve, 1975), pp. 117–119.

10. Ibid., p. 109.

11. E.g., those portrayed at Sarnath and Nalanda. See Ghosh, *Development of Buddhist Iconography*, Plates 37, 37a, 39.

12. Ghosh, *Development of Buddhist Iconography*, p. 151.

13. Ibid., Plate 5.

14. Ibid., Plates 44, 47, 49; D. Mitra, *Ratnagiri (1958–61)*, Memoirs of the Archaeological Survey of India, No. 80 (New Delhi: Archaeological Survey of India, 1981), Vol. I., Plates XCIIIB, CLX-XIVA; Vol. II, Plates CCCXXXIVA and B.

15. Ghosh, op. cit., p. 160.

16. In an editorial note to G. H. Malandra, "Bhṛkuṭī at Ellora," *Journal of the Indian Society of Oriental Art*, Vol. 12 (1983), p. 40, note 20, Dr. Krishna Deva points out that many eastern Indian images of the ascetic Pārvatī hold such a twisted stick, which he identifies as *kuśaṅkura* (stem of *kuśa* grass). This confirms Ghosh's analysis (*Development of Buddhist Iconography*, pp. 155–158), which shows how the identification of Pārvatī's asceticism with that of Śiva could have carried over to the representation of Bhṛkuṭī.

17. Ghosh, loc. cit.

18. N. Hock, "Buddhist Ideology and the Sculpture of Ratnagiri, Seventh Though Thirteenth Centuries (India)," (Ph.D. diss., University of California-Berkeley, 1987), pp. 81, 166–167, suggests that at Ratnagiri, Bhṛkuṭī may have been portrayed as one of the *prajñās* of the Tathāgatas, although she does not appear in the usual lists of the female emanations of the five Buddhas. At Ellora, where the *pañcatathāgata* concept was not expressed, this seems unlikely and suggests that these two sites, so similar in many details, did not share the same teaching although both seem to focus on a central three-body system described in a *maṇḍala* in the *Mañjuśrīmūlakalpa* that does include Bhṛkuṭī among other female companions of Avalokiteśvara. See D. Snellgrove, *Indo-Tibetan Buddhism* (Boston: Shambala Publications, Inc., 1987), Vol. I, pp. 150–151 and 190–194.

19. de Mallmann, ITB, pp. 292, 295.

20. D. Mitra, "Iconographic Notes: A. An Image of Mahāmāyūrī in the Nalanda Museum," *Journal of the Asiatic Society*, Ser. 4, I (1959), p. 38,

says Cave 8 may be slightly earlier but offers few reasons to support this opinion.

21. K. Watanabe, "A Chinese Text Corresponding to Part of the Bower Manuscript," *Journal of the Royal Asiatic Society* (1907), pp. 261–266.

22. D. C. Bhattacharyya, "The Goddess Mahāmāyūrī and the Peacock," *Indian History Congress, Proceedings of the Twenty-seventh Session (1965, Allahabad)* (Aligarh: S. Nurul Hasan, 1967), pp. 45–46; D. C. Bhattacharyya, *Studies in Buddhist Iconography* (New Delhi: Manohar, 1978), pp. 5, 84–85, 91–92, 95–96; de Mallmann, ITB, pp. 289–290.

23. D. Mitra, op. cit., p. 37 and Plate IA.

24. J. C. Huntington, "The Tendai Iconographic Model Book Shosonzuzō dated 1858," *Studies in Indo-Asian Art and Culture*, IV (1975), pp. 172–173.

25. B. Bhattacharyya, *Indian Buddhist Iconography*, p. 234; de Mallmann, ITB, pp. 292–295.

26. See, for example, an eighteen-armed bronze Cundā from Nalanda in the Patna Museum, in P. L. Gupta, ed., *Patna Museum Catalogue of Antiquities* (Patna: Patna Museum, 1965), p. 123 and Plate XXVI, and D. Paul, *The Art of Nalanda, Development of Buddhist Sculpture 600–1200 A.D.* (Leiden: Quick Service Drukkerij, 1987), Plates 63, 78 and pp. 169–170.

27. de Mallmann, ITB, pp. 144–145; Gupte, *Iconography of the Buddhist Sculptures*, pp. 100–104.

28. D. C. Bhattacharyya, *Studies in Buddhist Iconography*, pp. 40, 52, 55, 60.

29. de Mallmann, ITB, pp. 143–145. Hock, op. cit., pp. 118–119, provides a useful summary of the literature on Cundā.

30. Hock, "Buddhist Ideology and the Sculpture of Ratnagiri," pp. 115–123. She identifies fourteen images. For a good source of comparison, see Mitra, *Ratnagiri*, Vol. I, Plate XCVIII and Vol. II, Plate CCCLB.

31. J. L. Moens, "De Tjandi Mendut," *Tijdschrift voor Indische Taal-, Land, en Volkenkunde, door Bataviaasch Genootschap van Kunsten en Wetenschappen*, 59 (1921), Plate 3 facing p. 581. Nancy Hock, loc. cit., has pointed out this connection. Although Moens identifies the image as Tārā, with the rosary, and *jaṭāmukuṭa*, it seems better identified as Bhṛkuṭī.

32. J. Leoshko, "Buddhist Sculptures from Bodhgayā." In J. Leoshko, ed., *Bodhgaya, the Site of Enlightenment* (Bombay: Marg Publications, 1988), pp. 52 and 55, Fig. 12.

33. D. Barrett, "The Later School of Amarāvatī and Its Influence," *Arts and Letters*, XXVIII (1954), Fig. 1b and pp. 44–45.

34. M.-T. de Mallmann, *Introduction à l'étude d'Avalokiteçvara* (Paris: Civilisations du Sud, 1948), pp. 120–124, 142–145. The Jina Buddha in the *jaṭāmukuṭa* is the primary marker, as described in the *Amitāyurbuddhānusmṛtisūtra*, translated into Chinese in the first half of the fifth century. The Buddha should be Amitābha, chief of Avalokiteśvara's lineage, who holds his right hand in *dhyānamudrā*, but the hand position varies in Avalokiteśvara images before the seventh century.

35. This has been pointed out by Huntington, "Cave Six at Aurangabad," p. 50.

36. W. Spink, *Ajanta to Ellora* (Bombay and Ann Arbor: Marg Publications for the Center for South and Southeast Asian Studies, University of Michigan, 1967), pp. 29 Fig. 13, and 50 note to Fig. 4.

37. Berkson, *The Caves at Aurangabad*, pp. 179, 182.

38. de Mallmann, ITB, pp. 251–252.

39. Huntington, "Cave Six at Aurangabad," p. 51 calls it an *utpala*, and thus identifies this figure as Vajrapāṇi-Mañjuśrī. However, the two floral types are quite distinct.

40. P. S. Jaini, "Stages in the Bodhisattva Career of the Tathagata Maitreya," in A. Sponberg and H. Hardacre, eds., *Maitreya, the Future Buddha* (Cambridge: Cambridge University Press, 1988), p. 65.

41. de Mallmann, ITB, pp. 106, 245.

42. See, for example, J. Leoshko, "The Vajrāsana Buddha," in J. Leoshko, ed., *Bodhgaya, the Site of Enlightenment* (Bombay: Marg Publications, 1988), p. 39, Fig. 12.

43. D. Paul, *The Art of Nalanda*, Plate 74 and pp. 158–160, illustrates and describes an unusual stone stele, portraying the Buddha in *dharmacakramudrā*, attended to the left by Avalokiteśvara and to the right, by Maitreya. The latter is identified in the donative inscription on the stele as Maitreyanātha, leading Paul to suggest that Avalokiteśvara represents Vasumitra, and that together the pair is a transformation into Bodhisattva form of famed propounders of the Vihāsaśāstra and Yogacāra schools.

44. de Mallmann, ITB, p. 246; G. Bhattacharya, "Stūpa as Maitreya's Emblem," in A. L. Dallapiccola and S. Zingel-Avé Lallemant, eds., *The Stupa. Its Religious, Historical and Architectural Significance*, Beiträge zur Südasien-Forschung, 55 (Wiesbaden: Franz Steiner Verlag, 1980), pp. 100–101.

45. Gupte, *Iconography of the Buddhist Sculptures*, pp. 59, 70.

46. Snodgrass, *Mandalas*, Vol. I, p. 250.

47. de Mallmann, *Avalokiteçvara*, pp. 149–150, recognized this problem, saying that the *stūpa*-like crest jewel would suggest an identification as Maitreya, whereas the *utpala* would suggest that the images should be identified as Mañjuśrī, even though Avalokiteśvara and Vajrapāṇi are normally

paired as heads of the two clans of Buddhist divinities.

48. Bhattacharya, "Stūpa as Maitreya's Emblem," pp. 106, 107 and Plates 8 and 10.

49. Leoshko, loc. cit.; de Mallmann, ITB, p. 245.

50. de Mallmann, ITB, p. 245.

51. de Mallmann, ITB, pp. 33, 244–248 and Fig. II.7. Here, it is illustrated with the three free fingers raised. This gesture is frequently portrayed, and may be confused with *abhayamudrā*, where the entire hand his raised in a gesture of reassurance. In later bronze images of Maitreya from Nagapattinam, in fact, the right hand gesture is *abhayamudrā*, while the *nāgakesara* branch is held in the left. The *stūpa*-like crest jewel is clearly depicted in these images, too. T. N. Ramachandran, *Nagapattinam and Other Buddhist Bronzes in the Madras Museum, Bulletin of the Madras Government Museum*, VII (1954), Plate VII.

52. de Mallmann, ITB, pp. 25 and 251; M.-T. de Mallmann, *Étude Iconographique sur Mañjuśrī*, Publications de l'École Française d'Extrême-Orient, LV (Paris: École Française d'Extrême-Orient, 1964), pp. 34–35.

53. de Mallmann, *Mañjuśrī*, pp. 44–46, shows that the iconography of Kārttikeya was transferred to Mañjuśrī; evidence of this is the presence together of these two deities in the *Mañjuśrīmūlakalpa*, where Kārttikeya is assigned attributes later ascribed to Mañjuśrī.

54. Asher, *Art of Eastern India*, Plate 71.

55. Ibid., p. 82 and Plate 164.

56. Leoshko, "The Iconography of Buddhist Sculptures," pp. 257–259.

57. American Institute of Indian Studies, Number 238.50.

58. de Mallmann, ITB, p. 251.

59. Dikshit, "Some Buddhist Bronzes from Sirpur," Plate 5b.

60. American Institute of Indian Studies, Number 228.76.

61. de Mallmann, *Mañjuśrī*, pp. 44–46, reidentified the image as Mañjuśrī, previously identified as Kārttikeya. See D. Mitra, "A Rare Type of Bodhisattva Image from Sanchi," *Indian Historical Quarterly*, XXXII (1956), pp. 286–289.

62. de Mallmann, ITB, pp. 124–125, 251.

63. With so many clearly distinguishable images of Mañjuśrī, it is difficult to understand why de Mallmann, *Mañjuśrī*, pp. 18–19, could categorically dismiss the relevance of early images on the grounds that they cannot be identified with certainty.

64. Barrett, "The Later School of Amarāvatī," pp. 42–44 and Plate 2.

65. Donaldson, "Buddhist Art of Orissa," pp. 242–245a.

66. Mitra, *Ratnagiri*, Vol. I, Plates LXXVID, LXVIIA-D, LXXVIIIA, CLXXIIB.

67. Mitra, *Ratnagiri*, Vol. I, Plates CXXVIIIA and B.

68. Ibid., Plate CCCLVIB.

69. Ibid., Plates CCXLVIIC, CCCXXXVIA. Hock, "Buddhist Ideology and Sculpture," pp. 101–106, discusses these images and their textual background.

70. Leoshko, "The Iconography of Buddhist Sculptures," pp. 187–188, 259–260.

71. Ibid., p. 255 and note 13.

72. P. Jaini, "Stages in the Bodhisattva Career of the Tathāgata Maitreya," pp. 59–69. His youthful appearance might appear contradictory to this role.

73. Gupte, *Iconography of the Buddhist Sculpture*, pp. 86–87.

74. de Mallmann, *Mañjuśrī*, pp. 31–32.

75. de Mallmann, ITB, p. 254.

76. Ghosh, *Development of Buddhist Iconography*, p. 131.

77. Hock, "Buddhist Ideology and Sculpture," pp. 163–167.

78. de Mallmann, ITB, pp. 251–252. This identification was first proposed by Gupte, *Iconography of the Buddhist Sculptures*, pp. 86–87. Avalokiteśvara in his various forms is *always* associated with Amitābha, never with Akṣobhya. de Mallmann, ITB, p. 106; *Mañjuśrī*, pp. 32–33.

79. de Mallmann, ITB, pp. 195–196; J. N. Banerjea, *The Development of Hindu Iconography* (New Delhi: Munshiram Manoharlal, 1974), pp. 337–344, 559–560.

80. J. Rosenfield, *The Dynastic Arts of the Kushans* (Berkeley and Los Angeles: University of California Press, 1967), pp. 245–249.

81. Gupte, *Iconography of the Buddhist Sculptures*, pp. 112–113.

82. J. Takakusu, trans., *A Record of the Buddhist Religion as Practiced in India and the Malay Archipelago (A.D. 671–695) by I-tsing*, (1896; reprint, Delhi: Munshiram Manoharlal, 1966), pp. 37–38.

83. S. Beal, trans., *Buddhist Records of the Western World Translated from the Chinese of Hiuen Tsang*, Vol. I (London: Kegan Paul, Trench, Trubner & Co., Ltd., 1906), pp. 110–111, note 96.

84. Spink, *Ajanta to Ellora*, Fig. 15, p. 67.

85. Huntington, "Cave Six at Aurangabad," pp. 50–51, suggests that the images represent the concept of *prajñā* and guard the outer ring of the *maṇḍala* the cave embodies. For an illustration, see Spink, *Ajanta to Ellora*, Fig. 16, p. 67.

86. Berkson, *The Caves at Aurangabad*, p. 178.

87. de Mallmann, ITB, p. 196.

88. K. Kumar, "The Buddhist Origin of Some Brahamanical Cave Temples at Ellora," *East and West*, N.S. XXVI (1976), p. 364.

89. de Mallmann, ITB, p. 196.

90. G. Tarr, "The Śiva Temple at Dhokeśvara and the Development of the Nidhi Image," *Oriental Art*, XV (1969), p. 269–280 and Figures 22, 23, 24.

91. Spink, *Ajanta to Ellora* p. 49, Figs. 1 and 2.

92. Takakusu, *Record*, p. 38. I-tsing called this figure Mahakala.

93. D. Barrett, *Mukhalingam Temples* and M. G. Dikshit, *Sirpur and Rajim Temples* (Bombay: N. M. Tripathi, 1960), p. 22; D. M. Stadtner, "From Sirpur to Rajim: The Art of Kosala during the Seventh Century" (Ph.D. diss., University of California, Berkeley, 1976), pp. 40–41, 86. Stadtner ascribes this structure and its sculpture to the first two decades of the seventh century. Iconographically, it appears to me to be later, comparable to material from Ratnagiri of the early eighth century. There is, of course, no a priori reason why Sirpur could not be earlier than Ratnagiri, but since its sculptural style is related to that of Ratnagiri, it is reasonable to expect a chronological relationship as well.

94. Mitra, *Ratnagiri*, Vol. I, pp. 28, 31, 61, 79, 93, 126, 161, 168, 229, 231, 232; Vol. II, pp. 278, 308, 309, 331, 371, 453.

95. Mitra, *Ratnagiri*, I, p. 161 and Plate CXI A.

96. Asher, *Art of Eastern India*, Plates 134, 135. A small image of Jambhala is also found on a lintel rebuilt into the wall of Cell 6 in Ratnagiri Monastery 2. See Mitra, *Ratnagiri*, Vol. II, p. 278 and Plate CCXVB.

97. Ibid., pp. 168–169, plates CXXA and B, CXXIA and B. Other major images at Ratnagiri are illustrated in Ibid., Plates CLXXV, CLXXVIA-D.

98. de Mallmann, ITB, p. 196.

99. For example, images from Nalanda and Kurkihar, in R. D. Banerji, *Eastern Indian School of Medieaval Sculpture*, ASI Reports, N.I.S., XLVII (Delhi: Manager of Publications, 1933), Plates XXXVI(a) and XXXV(c). Later examples include one from Vikrampur, and from Nepal, illustrated in B. Bhattacharyya, *Indian Buddhist Iconography* (Calcutta: K.L. Mukhopadhyay, 1968), pp. 286 and 287, Figs. 176 and 177.

100. Mitra, *Ratnagiri,* Vol. I, pp. 29–30 and Plate CLXXV.

101. Hock, "Buddhist Ideology and Sculpture of Ratnagiri," pp. 26–28. D. Mitra, "Jambhala-maṇḍalas in Sculpture," *Journal of the Asiatic Society*, Ser. 4, III (1961), p. 39 and Plate I.1.

102. Mitra, *Ratnagiri*, Vol. I., pp. 28, 93 and Plates XLVIA-D.

103. de Mallmann, ITB, p. 196; D.C. Bhattacharyya, *Studies in Buddhist Iconography*, pp. 22–23.

104. J. Huntington, "Shosonzuzō," pp. 129 and 184. He calls the Ellora Cave 11 and 12 images Kubera, although they obviously correspond to images called Jambhala elsewhere.

105. Mitra, *Ratnagiri*, I, pp. 189–190, Plate CXXVIIA. Another possible comparison was suggested by Huntington, "Shosonzuzō," p. 129 and Plate 183, to drawings in the Japanese iconographical pattern book, *Shosonzuzō*.

106. For an admirable and useful overview of Buddhist monuments throughout the subcontinent, see Mitra, *Buddhist Monuments*. Spink, *Ajanta to Ellora*, remains the best single source on the relative chronology of the western Deccani cave temple sites.

107. The tantric nature of the site has been discussed by Huntington, "Aurangabad: A Tantrayāna Monument?," pp. 47–55; and Berkson, *The Caves at Aurangabad*.

108. Huntington, op.cit.

109. M. E. Leese, "Ellora and the Development of the Litany Scene in Western India," in R. Parimoo, et al., eds., *Ellora Caves, Sculptures and Architecture* (Delhi: Books and Books, 1988), pp. 164–179.

110. Evidence of Buddhist activity in Karnataka, although confirmed by Hsüan-tsang, is extremely sparse. The corpus has been well summarized in S. Nagaraju, "Vestiges of Buddhist Art," *Marg*, 35 (1983), pp. 5–14. An argument has been made that an unfinished two-story excavation at Aihole was a Buddhist *vihāra* (S. Settar, "A Buddhist Vihāra at Aihole," *East and West*, N.S. XIX (1969), pp. 126–138 but, with almost no sculpture, it is not possible to determine its affiliation with any precision. A loose Buddha image, seated in *vajraparyañkāsana*, missing its head and right arm, was discovered outside another temple at Aihole; it may be of the same period as Ellora's latest caves. Several later images from South Kanara District attest to the presence of tantric Buddhists in the tenth century, probably connected to the later school of Buddhist art at Amaravati. Such meager evidence strengthens the argument that Buddhism at Ellora had nothing directly to do with the advent of the Cālukya dynasty in Maharashtra.

111. American Institute of Indian Studies photo archive, No. 630.13.

112. These seem most closely related to similarly positioned female figures in a seventh-century panel on the main Nalanda temple. See Asher, *Art of Eastern India*, Plate 70.

113. Archives of Asian Art, University of Michigan negative numbers 583/75, 584/75, 585/75, 586/75.

114. Berkson, *Aurangabad*, p. 120; Huntington, "Cave Six at Aurangabad," pp. 50–51, has identified these as "*saptamātṛkas*," but there are only six female figures in this group. A similar group of six females is found in the excavation he calls Cave Six-A, flanked by Śiva. Ibid., p. 50 and fig. 6.

115. Spink, *Ajanta to Ellora*, chart.

116. Mitra, *Buddhist Monuments*, p. 165 and photo 106. See also, Leese, op. cit., pp. 167–168.

117. S. L. Huntington, with J. C. Huntington, *The Art and Architecture of India, Buddhist, Hindu, Jain* (New York and Tokyo: Weatherhill, 1985), p. 263 and Fig. 12.25.

118. Ibid., p. 264 and Fig. 12.26. Huntington identifies the females as Tārā and Bhṛkuṭī but, as they are visually indistinguishable, this is not as clear as the differentiation is at Ellora, where iconographical traits make the identifications secure.

119. A small wooden image of Tārā was found at Kanheri forty-five years ago. Seated in *vajraparyaṅkāsana*, with a distinctive triangular profile, its proportions are most reminiscent of the Tārā image in Ellora Cave 12.1 and the Dhāraṇīs in Cave 12.3. It would appear on stylistic grounds to be of early eighth-century date. See H. D. Sankalia, "A Unique Wooden Image of the Buddhist Goddess Tara from the Kanheri Caves," *Marg*, 36 (1984), p. 84.

120. M. N. Deshpande, *The Caves of Panhale-Kaji*, Memoirs of the Archaeological Survey of India, 84 (New Delhi: Government of India, 1986), p. 12.

121. D. Barrett, "A Group of Bronzes from the Deccan," *Lalit Kala*, III-IV (1956–1957), pp. 39–45. Barrett noted the connection to Ellora Cave 12, p. 43.

122. This has been noted by Paul in *The Art of Nalanda*, p. 136.

123. See D. C. Chatham, "Pratīhāras from Paṭṭaḍakal to Ellora: The Early Western Chālukya Basis for the Sculptural Style of the Kailāsa Temple," in A. Krishna, ed., *Chhavi-2* (Banaras: Bharat Kala Bhavan, 1981), Figs. 197 and 198.

124. Deshpande, *The Caves of Panhale-Kaji*.

125. Ibid., pp. 153–154.

126. Ibid., p. 134.

127. Hock, "Buddhist Ideology and Sculptures," pp. 53–54.

128. Ibid., pp. 26, 156.

129. Ibid., pp. 47–50, 154–155 and Plate 21.

130. Mitra, *Ratnagiri*, Vol. I., pp. 125–126 and Plate LXXIIIA.

131. Sir J. Marshall and A. Foucher, *The Monuments of Sanchi*, Vol. I (London: Probsthain, 1940), p. 53.

132. Bodhisattva attendants are no longer *in situ*, but it has been argued that they may have been an Avalokiteśvara/Maitreya pair. A pair was found flanking the Buddha image in 1971. See J. Irwin, "The Sanchi Torso," *Journal of the Indian Society of Oriental Art*, New Series, VI (1974–1975), pp. 52–66.

133. Located in the site museum. Tārā, number 2902; Cunda, number 2638.

134. Sanci Site Museum Number 2781.

135. Identification of this image has varied although most recently, and most convincingly, it has been identified as Mañjuśrī. See de Mallmann, *Étude Iconographique sur Mañjuśrī*, pp. 44–46, for a review of the debate.

136. M. G. Dikshit, "Some Buddhist Bronzes from Sirpur, Madhya Pradesh," *Bulletin of the Prince of Wales Museum*, No. 5 (1955–1956), pp. 1–11.

137. According to Stadtner, "From Sirpur to Rajim," p. 40, the Anandaprabhā *vihāra* at Sirpur can be dated roughly to the first two decades of the seventh century, while the Svastika *vihāra* may date to the end of the sixth century (p. 85). Stray sculpture is probably ascribable to the turn of the seventh century (p. 41). The well-known Sirpur bronzes, whose style is more elaborate than that of the *vihāra* stone sculpture, are ascribed to the eighth through tenth centuries. See Dikshit, "Some Buddhist Bronzes from Sirpur," passim.

138. Noted by M. G. Dikshit, *Sirpur and Rajim Temples*, p. 22; see also, Stadtner, "From Sirpur to Rajim," p. 93; M. G. Dikshit, "No. 25—Sirpur Inscription of the Time of Balārjuna," *Epigraphia Indica*, XXXI (1955–1956), p. 198, verse 7.

139. Stadtner, op. cit., pp. 40–41, 86–87; Dikshit, *Sirpur and Rajim Temples*, p. 22.

140. Stadtner, op. cit., p. 88; Tartakov, "The Śiva Temple at Dhokeśvara and the Development of the Nidhi Image," pp. 269–280 and Figures 22, 23, 24.

141. de Mallmann, ITB, p. 196.

142. Caves 2 and 6; Berkson, *The Caves at Aurangabad*, pp. 177, 178, 193.

143. At the shrine doorway of Cave 3; M. K. Anand, ed., *In Praise of Badami, Aihole, Pattadakal* (Bombay: Marg Publications, 1981), p. 95, fig. 95.

144. Stadtner, op. cit., p. 88.

145. I am grateful to Mr. Parmar, M.G.M. museum director, for guidance and permission to study these images.

146. For illustrations of the bronze images, see Dikshit, "Some Bronzes from Sirpur," Plates 5B, 6A.

147. Links between western Maharashtra and the region to the east are found as early as the last quarter of the fifth century. See, for instance the compelling stylistic similarity between the *yakṣas* on the façade of Ajanta Cave 19 and a *yakṣa* from Manasar, near Ramtek in eastern Maharashtra. See J. Williams, "Vākāṭaka Art and the Gupta Mainstream," in B. Smith, ed., *Essays on Gupta Culture* (Delhi: Motilal Banarsidass, 1983), pp. 227–228 and Plates 2 and 16.

148. See J. Leoshko, "The Vajrāsana Buddha," in J. Leoshko, ed., *Bodhgaya, the Site of Enlightenment* (Bombay: Marg Publications, 1988), Plate 7.

149. It does appear rarely in the western caves, for instance in the shrine image of Ajanta Cave 17, See Spink, *Ajanta to Ellora*, p. 26, Fig. 5. For eastern Indian examples, see Asher, *The Art of Eastern India*, Plates 47, 78, 136.

150. Leoshko, "The Vajrāsana Buddha," Plates 9 and 12.

151. Asher, *Art of Eastern India*, Plate 170.

152. This material is discussed in detail in J. Leoshko, "The Iconography of Buddhist Sculptures of the Pāla and Sena Periods from Bodhgayā" (Ph.D. diss., The Ohio State University, 1987), pp. 228–327.

153. Except on the small scale of votive *stūpas*. See M. Bénisti, *Contribution à l'étude du stūpa bouddhique indien: Les stūpa mineurs de Bodh-Gaya et de Ratnagiri*, Publications de l'École Française d'Extrême-Orient, CXXV, Vol. 1. (Paris: l'École Française d'Extrême-Orient, 1981), pp. 54–58.

154. For summaries of material from Nalanda see Mitra, *Buddhist Monuments*, pp. 85–89; Asher, *Art of Eastern India*, pp. 46–50, 76–78, 80–86; Paul, *Nalanda, passim*.

155. Asher, op. cit., Plates 70, 71, 164, 165, 166, 171, 172.

156. Ibid., p. 83.

157. Ibid., pp. 46–47.

158. Ibid., pp. 83–85; Dikshit, "Some Buddhist Bronzes from Sirpur," pp. 10–11.

159. Asher, op. cit., p. 85.

160. T. Donaldson, "Buddhist Art of Orissa," mss. p. 214. Most of this material is unpublished. For illustrations of Udayagiri material see N. K. Sahu, *Buddhism in Orissa* (Utkal: Utkal University, 1958), Figs. 11, 13, 16, 17, 19, 20, 21.

161. Ibid., p. 281.

162. Donaldson, "Buddhist Art of Orissa," pp. 224–225. For partial illustrations see Sahu, op. cit., Figs. 23–28.

163. de Mallmann, ITB, p. 223. Credit is due to Donaldson, "Buddhist Art of Orissa," pp. 221, 234–236, for this identification.

164. Mitra, *Ratnagiri*, Vol. I, Plate CXXVIII a, b; Hock, "Buddhist Ideology and Sculpture," pp.

58–59; Donaldson, "Buddhist Art in Orissa," pp. 221–223.

165. Mitra, *Ratnagiri*, Vol. I, p. 140 and Plate LXXXIIIA.

166. Mitra, *Ratnagiri*, Vol. II, Plate CCCXXIVA; Hock, "Buddhist Ideology and Sculpture," pp. 54–56.

167. Mitra, *Ratnagiri*, Vol. I, Plate CXXVI.

168. Hock, op. cit., pp. 48–68.

169. Hock, op. cit., pp. 113–119.

170. Hock, op. cit., pp. 1–33, presents this argument in detail. See also D. Snellgrove, *Indo-Tibetan Buddhism*, Vol. I, pp. 117–152 for a lucid account of this distinction.

171. Snellgrove, Vol. I, pp. 190–191.

172. Hock, op. cit., pp. 35, 67–68, note 86.

173. Snellgrove, op. cit., Vol. I, p. 202.

174. Hock, op. cit., pp. 68–69; A. K. Bernet-Kempers, *Ancient Indonesian Art* (Cambridge: Harvard University Press, 1959), pp. 40–41 and Plates 58–61; N.J. Krom, "De Bodhisattvas van den Mendut," *Bijdragen tot de tall-, land- en volkenkunde, door Koninklijk Bataviaasch Gennotschapp van Kunsten en Wetenschappen*, Vol. 74 (1918), pp. 419–437; and Moens, "De Tjandi Mendut," pp. 529–600.

175. J. E. Schwartzberg, ed., *A Historical Atlas of South Asia* (Chicago: University of Chicago Press, 1978), p. 28.

176. V. Dehejia, "The Persistence of Buddhism in Tamilnadu," *Marg*, Vol. XXXIX, No. 4 (1987), pp. 53–74, documents the thriving late Buddhism of the south.

177. Barrett, "The Later School of Amarāvatī and Its Influence," pp. 41–45 and Figs. 1b, 2, 4a.

178. K. Krishna Murthy, *Sculptures of Vajrayana Buddhism* (Delhi: Classics India Publications, 1989), pp. 21–26 and Plates 1–4, 6–8.

179. Krishna Murthy, *op. cit.*, pp. 35–44 and Plates 13–28. Note that Plate 28, identified in the text as "Sitatārā," is more likely an image of four-armed Bhṛkuṭī, identifiable by the ascetic's flask in the lower left hand, and hair piled in a neat *jaṭā-mukuṭa*.

180. Mitra, *Buddhist Monuments*, p. 222.

181. Ramachandram, *Nagapattinam and Other Buddhist Bronzes*.

Appendix A: Relative Chronology of Ellora's Buddhist Caves

1. D. Chatham, "The Stylistic Sources and Relationships of the Kailāsa Temple at Ellora" (Ph.D.

diss., University of California at Berkeley, 1977), pp. 3–4.

2. Although the term *caitya*, meaning a Buddhist hall of worship containing a *stūpa*, is noncanonical, its use is attested in inscriptions, where it seems to mean simply "worship hall." See D. C. Sircar, *Indian Epigraphical Glossary* (Delhi: Motilal Banarsidass, 1966), p. 64. I follow conventional usage to distinguish the *stūpa*-containing Cave 10 from others, most of which have residence cells, commonly called *vihāras*.

3. A similar problem in planning occurred at Ajanta, when Cave 11 was inserted between older excavations, leaving no room for cells along its right wall. See W. Spink, "Ajanta's Chronology: The Problem of Cave Eleven," *Ars Orientalis*, VII (1968), p. 160 and Fig. 1.

4. Cave 1 has neither sculpture nor pillars so it is not relevant to a discussion of Buddhist art at Ellora.

5. J. Burgess, *Report on the Elura Cave Temples and the Brahmanical and Jaina Caves in Western India*, Archaeological Survey of Western India, Vol. V (1882; reprint, Varanasi: Indological Book House, 1970), p. 5.

REFERENCES

Agrawala, Vasudeva Sharana. *Matsya Purāṇa—A Study: An Exposition of the Ancient Purāṇa-Vidya.* Varanasi: All India Kashiraj Trust, 1963.

Alexander, James Edward. "Notice of a Visit to the Cavern Temples of Adjunta in the East Indies." *Transactions of the Royal Asiatic Society* [London], II (1830), pp. 362–370.

Altekar, Anant Sadashiv. *The Rāshṭrakūṭas and Their Times.* Poona: Oriental Book Agency, 1934.

————. "The Rāṣṭrakūṭas." In Gulam Yazdani, ed. *The Early History of the Deccan,* Parts I–VI. London: Oxford University Press, 1960.

Anand, Mulk Raj, ed. *In Praise of Badami, Aihole, Mahakuta, Pattadakal.* Bombay: Marg Publications, 1981.

Asher, Frederick M. *The Art of Eastern India, 300–800.* Minneapolis: University of Minnesota Press, 1980.

Auboyer, Jeannine. *Le Trône et son symbolisme dans l'Inde ancienne.* Paris: Presses universitaires de France, 1949.

Banerjea, Jitendra Nath. *The Development of Hindu Iconography.* 3rd Ed. New Delhi: Munshiram Manoharlal, 1974.

Banerji, A. C. "A Buddhist Image from Kurkihar." *Journal of the Royal Asiatic Society of Bengal, Letters,* III (1937), pp. 53–54.

Banerji, Rakhal Das. *Eastern Indian School of Medieval Sculpture.* Archaeological Survey of India, Reports, N.I.S., LXVII. Delhi: Manager of Publications, 1933.

Bareau, Andre. "Der Tantrismus." In *Die Religionen Indiens, III: Buddhismus, Jinismus, Primitivvölker,* pp. 173–187. Stuttgart: W. Kohlhammer Verlag, 1964.

Barrett, Douglas. "A Group of Bronzes from the Deccan." *Lalit Kalā,* III (1956), pp. 39–45.

————. "The Later School of Amarāvatī and Its Influence." *Arts and Letters,* XXVIII (1954), pp. 41–53.

————. *Mukhalingam Temples* and Moreshwar Gangadhar Dikshit. *Sirpur and Rajim Temples.* Bombay: Bhulabhai Memorial Institute, 1960.

Barua, Benimadhab. *Gayā and Buddha-Gayā.* 2 vols. 1931–1934; reprint, Varanasi: Bharatiya Publishing House, 1975.

Beal, Samuel. *Si-yu-ki, Buddhist Records of the Western World Translated from the Chinese of Hieun Tsang (A.D. 629).* 2 vols. London: Kegan, Paul, Trench, Trubner & Co., Ltd., 1884.

Bénisti, Mireille. *Contribution à l'étude du stūpa bouddhique indien: Les stūpa mineurs de Bodh-Gaya et de Ratnagiri.* Publications de l'École Française d'Extrême-Orient, CXXV. 2 Vols. Paris: École Française d'Extrême-Orient, 1981.

Bernet-Kempers, August Johan. *Ancient Indonesian Art* (Cambridge: Harvard University Press, 1959.

Berkson, Carmel. *The Caves at Aurangabad, Early Buddhist Tantric Art in India*. New York: Mapin International Inc., 1986.

Bhandarkar, Devadatta Ramakrishna. "Alas Plates of the Yuvarāja Govinda III; Śaka-Samvat 692." *Epigraphia Indica*, VI (1900–1901), pp. 208–213.

———. "Epigraphic Notes and Questions, 8: The Kailasa Temple at Elura." *The Indian Antiquary*, XL (1911), pp. 237–238.

Bhandarkar, Ramachandra Gopal. "The Rāshṭrakūṭa King Krishṇarāja I and Elā-pura." *Indian Antiquary*, XII (1883), pp. 228–230.

Bhardwaj, Surinder Mohan. *Hindu Places of Pilgrimage in India*. Berkeley: University of California Press, 1973.

Bhattacharya, Gouriswar. "Stūpa as Maitreya's Emblem." In Anna Libera Dallapiccola and Stephanie Zingel-Avé Lallemant, eds. *The Stupa. Its Religious, Historical and Architectural Significance*. Beiträge zur Südasien-Forschung, 55. Wiesbaden: Franz Steiner Verlag, 1980, pp. 100–111.

Bhattacharyya, Benoytosh. *The Indian Buddhist Iconography*. Calcutta: K. L. Mukhopadhyay, 1958.

Bhattacharyya, Dipak Chandra. "The Goddess Mahāmāyūrī and the Peacock." *Indian History Congress, Proceedings of the Twenty-seventh Session (1965, Allahabad)*. Aligarh: S. Nurul Hasan, 1967, pp. 45–46.

———. *Studies in Buddhist Iconography*. New Delhi: Manohar, 1978.

———. "*The Vajravālī-nāma-maṇḍalopayika* of Abhayākaragupta." In Michel Strickman, ed. *Tantric and Taoist Studies in Honor of R. A. Stein. Melanges Chinois et Bouddhiques*, XX. Bruxelles: l'Institute Belge des Hautes Études Chinois, 1981, pp. 70–95.

———. *Tantric Buddhist Iconographical Sources*. New Delhi: Munshiram Manoharlal Publishers, 1974.

Bhattasali, Nalini Kanta. *The Iconography of Buddhist and Brahmanical Sculptures in the Dacca Museum*. Dacca: Dacca Museum Committee, 1929.

Briggs, John, trans. *History of the Rise of the Mahomedan Power in India till the Year A.D. 1612*. Vol. I. Calcutta: Kegan Paul, Trench, Trubner & Co., 1829.

Brown, Percy. *Indian Architecture (Buddhist and Hindu Periods)*. 1965; reprint, Bombay: D. B. Taraporevala, 1976.

Brown, Robert L. "Recent Stupa Literature: A Review Article." *Journal of Asian History*. Vol. XX (1986), pp. 215–232.

Burgess, James. *Report on the Antiquities in the Bidar and Aurangabad Districts, 1875–76*. Archaeological Survey of Western India, Vol. III. London: William H. Allen & Co., 1878.

———. *Report on the Elura Cave Temples and the Brahmanical and Jaina Caves in Western India*. Archaeological Survey of Western India, Vol. V. 1982; reprint. Varanasi: Indological Book House, 1971.

———. and Bhagwanlal Indraji. "Elura Inscriptions," *Inscriptions from the Cave Temples of Western India*, pp. 99–100. Bombay: Central Government Press, 1881.

Chakladar, Haran Chandra. "Elāpura Grant of Western Cālukya Vijayaditya Śaka-Samvat 626." *The Indian Historical Quarterly*, IV (1928), pp. 425–430.

Chandra, Lokesh. "Borobuḍur as a Monument of Esoteric Buddhism." *South East Asian Review*, V (1980), pp. 1–41.

———. "Ellora as Śūnyatā and Rūpam." In Ratan Parimoo et al., *Ellora Caves*, pp. 131–144. New Delhi: Books and Books, 1988.

Chatham, Doris Clark. "Pratīhāras from Paṭṭadakal to Ellora: The Early Western Chālukya Basis for the Sculptural Style of the Kailāsa Temple." In Anand Krishna, ed. *Chhavi-2*, pp. 71–79. Banaras: Bharat Kala Bhavan, 1981.

———. "The Stylistic Sources and Relationships of the Kailasa Temple at Ellora." Ph.D. Diss., University of California, Berkeley, 1977.

Chaudhury, Binayendra Nath. *Buddhist Centers in Ancient India*. Calcutta: Sanskrit College, 1969.

Chhabra, Bahadur Chand. "The Incised Inscriptions." In Gulam Yazdani, ed. *Ajanta*, Vol. IV, pp. 112–124. London: Oxford University Press, 1955.

Chimpa, Lama and Alaka Chattopadhyaya, trans. *Taranatha's History of Buddhism in India*. Simla: Indian Institute of Advanced Study, 1970.

Codrington, Kenneth de Burgh. "Ancient Sites near Ellora, Deccan." *Indian Antiquary*, LIX (1930), pp. 10–13.

Cunningham, Alexander. *Mahābodhi; or the Great Buddhist Temple under the Bodhi Tree at Buddha-Gayā*. 1892; reprint, Varanasi: Indological Book House, 1961.

Czuma, Stanlislaw Jerzy. "The Brahmanical Rashtrakuta Monuments of Ellora." Ph.D. Diss., University of Michigan, 1968.

Daniell, Thomas. *Hindoo Excavations in the Mountain of Ellora near Aurangabad in the*

Deccan in Twenty-four Views [engraved from the drawings of James Wales]. London: 1803.

Das Gupta, Shashi Bhushan. *An Introduction to Tantric Buddhism.* 3rd ed. Calcutta: University of Calcutta, 1974.

Davidson, J. Leroy. *Art of the Indian Subcontinent from Los Angeles Collections.* Los Angeles: Ward Pritchee Press, 1968.

De, Susil Chandra. "The Orissan Museum Image Inscription of the Time of Śubhākaradēva." *Proceedings of the Twelfth Session of the Indian History Congress (1949).* Allahabad: 1950, pp. 66–74.

Dehejia, Vidya. "The Persistence of Buddhism in Tamilnadu." *Marg,* Vol. XXXIX, No. 4 (1987), pp. 53–74.

Deshpande, Madhusudan Narhar. *The Caves of Panhale-Kaji (Ancient Praṇalaka),* Memoirs of the Archaeological Survey of India, 84. New Delhi: Government of India, 1986.

———. "The Rock-Cut Caves of Pitalkhora in the Deccan." *Ancient India,* No. 15 (1959), pp. 66–93.

Deva, Krishna. "Indragadh Inscription of Nannapa, V.S. 767." *Epigraphia Indica,* XXXII (1957–1958), 112–117.

Dhaky, Madhusudan A. "The Dravidian Sculptures in Pre-Imperial Rāṣṭrakūṭa Cave-Temples in Ellora." In Ratan Parimoo et al., *Ellora Caves,* pp. 438–445. New Delhi: Books and Books, 1988.

Dhavalikar, Madhukar Keshav. "Kailasa: A Jyotirlinga at Ellora." *Indian Historical Quarterly* (March 1960), pp. 80–82.

———. "Kailāsa—The Stylistic Development and Chronology." *Bulletin of the Deccan College Research Institute,* Vo. 41 (1982), pp. 33–45.

———. "The Origin of Tārā." *Bulletin of the Deccan College Research Institute,* XXIV (1963–1964), pp. 15–20.

Dhere, R. C. "Prācin Marāṭhī Vāgmāyatil Kailās Leṇe." *Jnaneshwar,* Vol. 7, No. 4 (Nov. 1975), pp. 1–10.

Dikshit, Moreshwar Gangadhar. "No. 25— Sirpur Inscription of the Time of Balārjuna." *Epigraphia Indica,* Vol. XXXI (1955–1956), pp. 197–198.

———. "Some Buddhist Bronzes from Sirpur." *Bulletin of the Prince of Wales Museum of Western India,* V (1955–1957), pp. 1–11.

Dikshit, S. K. "Ellora Plates of Dantidurga." *Epigraphia Indica,* Vol. XXV (1940), pp. 25–31.

Divakaran, Odile. "Le temple de Jambulinga (daté de 699 ap. J.-C.) à Bādāmi." *Arts asiatiques,* XXI (1970), pp. 15–39.

———. "Les temples d'Ālampur et de ses environs au temps des Cālukya de Bādāmi." *Arts asiatiques,* XXIV (1971), pp. 51–101.

Donaldson, Thomas. "The Buddhist Art of Orissa." Manuscript [1990].

Dutt, Nalinaksha. *Buddhist Sects in India.* Calcutta: K. L. Mukhopadhyay, 1970.

Dutt, Sukumar. *Buddhist Monks and Monasteries of India.* London: George Allen and Unwin, 1962.

Eck, Diana L. *Banaras, City of Light.* Princeton: Princeton University Press: 1982.

Fabri, Charles Louis. *History of the Art of Orissa.* Bombay: Orient Longman, 1974.

Feldhaus, Anne. "Maharashtra as a Holy Land: A Sectarian Tradition." *Bulletin of the School of Oriental and African Studies,* Vol. XLIX (1986), pp. 532–548.

Fergusson, James and James Burgess. *The Cave Temples of India.* London: W. H. Allen, 1880.

Fleet, John Faithful. "Hieun Tsiang's Capital of Maharashtra." *The Indian Antiquary,* XXII (1893), pp.113–116.

———. "The Legends on the Silver Coins of the Early Guptas and Others Connected with Them." *The Indian Antiquary,* XIV (1885), p. 68.

———. "Mahakuta Pillar Inscription of Mangalesa." *The Indian Antiquary,* XIX (1890), pp. 7–20.

———. "Multai Copper-Plate Grant of Nandaraja." *The Indian Antiquary,* XVIII (1889), pp. 230–236.

———. "Pattadakal Pillar Inscription of the Time of Kirtivarman II." *Epigraphia Indica,* III (1894–1895), pp. 1–7.

———. In J. Burgess, "Rock Cut Temples at Badami, in the Dekhan." *The Indian Antiquary,* VI (1877), pp. 354–366.

———. "Sanskrit and Old-Canarese Inscriptions, No. CXXVII." *Indian Antiquary,* XII (1883), pp. 156–165.

———. "Satara Copper Plate Grant of Vishnuvardhana I." *The Indian Antiquary,* XIX (1890), pp. 303–311.

Fussman, Gerard. "Symbolism of the Buddhist *Stūpa.*" *Journal of the International Association of Buddhist Studies,* Vol. 9, No. 2 (1986), pp. 37–53.

Ghosh, A. "Khaḍipāda Image Inscription of the Time of Śubhākara." *Epigraphia Indica,* XXVI (1942), pp. 247–248.

Ghosh, Mallar. *Development of Buddhist Iconography in Eastern India: A Study of Tārā, Prajñās of Five Tathāgatas and Bhṛikuṭī.* New Delhi: Munshiram Manoharlal, 1980.

Goetz, Hermann. "The Kailasa of Ellora and the Chronology of Rashtrakuta Art." *Artibus Asiae*, XV (1952), pp. 84–107.

Gokhale, Balkrishna Govind. *Buddhism in Maharashtra: A History*. Bombay: Popular Prakashan, 1976.

Gokhale, Shobhana. "Elephanta Hoard of Copper Coins of Kṛṣṇarāja." *Journal of the Numismatic Society of India*, XXXVIII (1976), pp. 89–91.

————. "Epigraphic Evidence for the Chronology of Ajanta." *Journal of Indian History*, LI (1973), pp. 479–483.

————. "Matvan Plates of the Traikūṭaka King Madhyamaseṇa, K. 256." *Proceedings of the All-India Oriental Conference, 26th Session, Ujjain, Oct. 1972*, pp. 267–270. Poona: Bhandarkar Oriental Research Institute, 1975.

————. "Matvan Plates of Vikramāseṇa, K. 284." In M.S. Mate and G.T. Kulkarni, eds. *Studies in Indology and Medieval History (Prof. G. H. Khare Felicitation Vol.)*, pp. 86–94. Poona: Joshi and Lokhande Prakashan, 1974.

Gomez, Louis O. "Some Observations on the role of the *Gaṇḍavyūha* in the Design of Barabudur." In L. Gomez and H. W. Woodward, eds. *Barabudur, History and Significance of a Buddhist Monument*, pp. 173–194. Berkeley: Berkeley Buddhist Series, 1981.

Gomez, Louis O. and Hiram W. Woodward, eds. *Barabudur, History and Significance of a Buddhist Monument*. Berkeley: Berkeley Buddhist Series, 1981.

Granoff, Phyllis. "A Portable Buddhist Shrine from Central Asia." *Archives of Asian Art*, 23 (1968–1969), pp. 80–95.

Guenther, H. V. *The Royal Song of Saraha*. Seattle: University of Washington Press, 1969.

Gupta, Parmeshwari Lal, ed. *Patna Museum Catalogue of Antiquities*. Patna: Patna Museum, 1965.

Gupte, Ramesh Shankar. *Iconography of the Buddhist Sculptures (Caves) of Ellora*. Aurangabad: Marathwada University, 1964.

Gupte, Ramesh Shankar and R. D. Mahajan. *Ajanta, Ellora and Aurangabad Caves*. Bombay: B. Taraporevala Sons & Co., 1962.

Heitzman, James. "Ritual Polity and Economy: The Transactional Network of an Imperial Temple in Medieval South India." *Journal of the Economic and Social History of the Orient*, Vol. XXXIV (1991), pp. 23–54.

Hiralal, Rai Bahadur. "Tiwarkhed Plates of the Rashtrakuta Nannaraja: Saka 553." *Epigraphia Indica*, XI (1911–1912), pp. 276–280.

Hock, Nancy. "Buddhist Ideology and the Sculpture of Ratnagiri, Seventh Through Thirteenth Centuries." Ph.D. Diss., University of California-Berkeley, 1987.

Huntington, John C. "Cave Six at Aurangabad: A Tantrayāna Monument?" In Joanna G. Williams, ed. *Kalādarśana: American Studies in the Art of India*, pp. 47–55. New Delhi: Oxford and IBH Publishers, Co. with A.I.I.S., 1981.

————. "The Tendai Iconographic Model Book Shosonzuzō Dated 1858." In Perala Ratnam, ed., *Acharya Raghu Vira Commemoration Volume, Studies in Indo-Asian Art and Culture*, IV (1975), pp. 121–424.

Huntington, Susan L. with John C. Huntington. *The Art and Architecture of India, Buddhist, Hindu, Jain*. New York and Tokyo: Weatherhill, 1985.

Inden, Ronald B. *Imagining India*. Oxford and Cambridge: Basic Blackwell, 1990.

Irwin, John. "The Axial Symbolism of the Early Stūpa: An Exegesis." In Anna Libera Dallapicolla and Stephanie Zingel-Avé Lallemant, eds. *The Stūpa: Its Religious, Historical and Architectural Significance*, pp. 12–38. Wiesbaden: Franz Steiner Verlag, 1980.

————. "The Sanchi Torso." *Journal of the Indian Society of Oriental Art*, New Series, VI (1974–1975), pp. 52–66.

Jaini, Padmanabh S. "Stages in the Bodhisattva Career of the Tathagata Maitreya." In Alan Sponberg and Helen Hardacre, eds., *Maitreya, the Future Buddha* pp. 54–90. Cambridge: Cambridge University Press, 1988.

Kantawala, Sureshachandra Govindlal. *Cultural History from the Matsya Purana*. Baroda: M. S. Univeristy, 1964.

Kielhorn, F. "Aihole Inscription of Pulikeśin II; Saka Samvat 556." *Epigraphia Indica*, VI (1900–1901), pp. 1–12.

Khare, G. H. "Lohaner Plates of Chalukya Pulakeśin II; Saka 552," *Epigraphia Indica*, XXVII (1947), pp. 37–39.

————. "Two Sendraka Grants: B. Kasare Plates of Sendraka Nikumbhallasakti; Year 404," *Epigraphia Indica*, XXVIII (1950), pp. 197–205.

Klimburg-Salter, Deborah. "Monastic Art of the Western Trans-Himalayas: Seventh to Seventeenth Centuries." In Deborah Klimburg-Salter, ed. *The Silk Route and The Di-*

amond Path: Esoteric Buddhist Art on the Trans-Himalayan Trade Routes. Los Angeles: UCLA Art Council, 1982.

Krishna Murthy, K. *Sculptures of Vajrayana Buddhism.* Delhi: Classics India Publications, 1989.

Krom, N.J. "De Bodhisattvas van den Mendut." *Bijdragen tot de taal-, land- en volkenkude, door Koninkliijk Bataviaasch Gennotschapp van Kunsten en Wetenschappen,* Vol. 74 (1918), pp. 419–437.

Kumar, Krishna. "The Buddhist Origin of Some Brahmanical Cave Temples at Ellora." *East and West,* N.S. XXVI (1976), pp. 359–373.

Lamotte, Etienne. *Histoire du bouddhisme indien.* Bibliothèque du Muséon, Vol. 43. Louvain: Publications universitaires, 1958.

Leese, Marilyn Edwards. "Ellora and the Development of the Litany Scene in Western India." In Ratan Parimoo, et al., *Ellora Caves, Sculptures and Architecture,* pp. 164–179. Delhi: Books and Books, 1988.

Leoshko, Janice. "The Iconography of Buddhist Sculptures of the Pāla and Sena Periods from Bodhgayā." Ph.D. Diss., The Ohio State University, 1987.

———. "The Vajrāsana Buddha" and "Buddhist Sculptures from Bodhgayā." In Janice Leoshko, ed. *Bodhgaya, the Site of Enlightenment,* pp. 29–44, 45–60. Bombay: Marg Publications, 1988.

Levine, Deborah B. "Aurangabad: A Stylistic Analysis." *Artibus Asiae,* XXVII (1966), pp. 175–188.

Lin-Bodien, Carol E. "The Chronology of Chandrāvatī, Kūsmā, Chitorgarh: A Case Study in the Use of Epigraphic and Stylistic Evidence." *Archives of Asian Art,* XXX (1980), pp. 49–64.

Maguire, Henry. *Earth and Ocean: the Terrestrial World in Early Byzantine Art* (University Park: Pennsylvania State University for the College Art Association, 1987.

Majumdar, R. C., ed. *The Age of Imperial Kanauj, The History and Culture of the Indian People.* Vol. IV. Bombay: Bharatiya Vidya Bhavan, 1955.

Malandra, Geri Hockfield. "Bhṛkutī at Ellora." *Journal of the Indian Society of Oriental Art,* Vol.12 (1983), pp. 31–40.

———. "The Buddhist Caves at Ellora." Ph.D. Diss., University of Minnesota, 1983.

———. "The Date of the Ajanta Cave 27 Inscription." *Wiener Zeitschrift für die Kunde Südasiens,* Vol. XXVI (1982), pp. 37–46.

———. "The Mahābodhi Temple." In Janice Leoshko, ed. *Bodhgaya, the Site of Enlightenment,* pp. 9–28. Bombay: Marg Publications, 1988.

de Mallmann, Marie-Thérèse. "Les bronzes népalais de la collection Sylvain Levi." *Artibus Asiae,* XXVII (1964), pp.134–150.

———. *Étude Iconographique sur Mañjuśrī.* Publications de l'École Française d'Extrême-Orient, LV. Paris: École Française d'Extrême-Orient, 1964.

———. *Introduction a l'étude d'Avalokiteçvara.* Annales du Musée Guimet, Bibliothèque d'études, vol. 57. Paris: Civilisations du Sud, 1948.

———. *Introduction a l'Iconographie du Tântrisme Bouddhique.* Paris: Adrien-Maisonneuve, 1975.

Manucci, Niccolao. *Storia do Mogor, or Mogul India, 1653–1708.* Translated by William Irvine. Vol. I. London: John Murray, 1907.

Marshall, Sir John Hubert and Alfred Foucher. *The Monuments of Sanchi.* 3 Vols. London: Probsthain, 1940.

Meister, Michael. "Phāṁsanā in Western India." *Artibus Asiae,* XXXVIII (1976), pp. 167–188.

Meynard, C. Barbier de, trans. *Maçoudi—Les Prairies d'Or: Muruj-ul-Zahab.* Vol. IV. Paris: Imprimerie Imperiale, 1865.

Michell, George. "A Comparison of the Muṇḍeśvarī Temple at Ramgarh and the Meguṭi Temple at Aihole: Notes toward a Definition of Early Temple Style in India." *East and West,* N.S. XXVIII (1978), pp. 213–224.

———. "Temples of the Early Chalukyas." In M. R. Anand, ed. *In Praise of Aihole, Badami, Mahakuta, Pattadakal,* pp. 55–130. Bombay: Marg Publications, 1981.

Mirashi, Vasudev Vishnu. "A Note on the Tiwarkhed Plates of Nannarāja." *Studies in Indology,* II (1961), pp. 25–30.

———. "A Note on Vajraṭa." *The Indian Historical Quarterly,* XX (1944), pp. 353–359.

———. "Dantidurga, The Founder of Rāshṭrakūṭa Imperial Power." *Studies in Indology,* II (1961), pp. 16–24.

———. "The Date of the Ellora Plates of Dantidurga," *Studies in Indology,* Vol. II, pp. 4–7.

———. "Indragadh Stone Inscription of Rāshṭrakūṭa Nanna." *Studies in Indology,* Vol. II (1961), pp. 185–190.

———. "Inscription in Cave XVII at Ajanta." *Hyderabad Archaeological Series,* 15. Hyderabad, 1949.

————. *Inscriptions of the Kalachuri-Chedi Era. Corpus Inscriptionum Indicarum.* Vol. IV. Ootacamund: Government Epigraphist for India, 1955.

————. *Inscriptions of the Vākāṭakas.* Corpus Inscriptionum Indicarum, Vol. V. Ootacamund: Government Epigraphist for India, 1963.

————. "Nagardhan Plates of Svamiraja." *Epigraphia Indica,* XXVIII (1949–1950), pp. 1–11.

————. *Studies in Indology.* 2 Vols. Nagpur: Vidarbha Samshodhana Mandal, 1960, 1961.

————. "Vākāṭaka Inscription in Cave XVI at Ajanta." *Hyderabad Archaeological Series,* 14. Hyderabad, 1941.

Mitra, Debala. "A Rare Type of Bodhisattva Image from Sanchi," *Indian Historical Quarterly,* XXXII (1956), pp. 286–289.

————. "Aṣṭamahābhaya Tārā." *Journal of the Asiatic Society,* Ser. 3, XXXII (1957), pp. 19–22.

————. *Buddhist Monuments.* Calcutta: Sahitya Samsad, 1971.

————. "Iconographic Notes: A. An Image of Mahāmāyūrī in the Nalanda Museum." *Journal of the Asiatic Soceity,* Ser. 4, I (1959), pp. 37–38.

————. "Jambhala-maṇḍalas in Sculpture." *Journal of the Asiatic Society,* Ser. 4, III (1961), pp. 39–42.

————. *Ratnagiri (1958–61)* Memoirs of the Archaeological Survey of India, No. 80. 2 Vols. New Delhi: Archaeological Survey of India, 1981.

Moens, J. L. "De Tjandi Mendut." *Tijdschrift voor Indische Taal-, Land, en Volkenkunde, door Bataviaasch Genootschap van Kunsten en Wetenschappen,* 59 (1921), pp. 529–600.

Mus, Paul. *Barabudur: Esquisse d'une histoire du bouddhisme fondée sur la critique archéologique des textes.* 2 Vols. Hanoie: Imprimerie d'Extrême Orient, 1935.

Musta'idd Khan, Muhammad Sāqī. *Maāsir-i-'Ālamgīrī: A History of the Emperor Aurangzib-'Alamgīr (reign 1658–1707 A.D.) of Saqi Must'ad Khan.* Trans. Jadunath Sarkar. Calcutta: Royal Asiatic Society of Bengal, 1947.

Myer, Prudence R. "The Great Temple at Bodh-Gaya." *The Art Bulletin,* XL (1958), pp. 277–298.

Nagaraja Rao, M.S. "Jamalagama Grant of Chalukya Vijayaditya, Saka 619." *Epigraphia Indica,* XXXV (1966), pp. 313–316.

Nagaraju, S. "Vestiges of Buddhist Art." *Marg,* 35 (1983), pp. 5–14.

Nilakantha Sastri, Kallidaikurichi Aiyah Aiyar. "The Chalukyas of Badami." In Gulam Yazdani, ed. *Early History of the Deccan.* Parts I-VI, pp. 201–246. London: Oxford University Press, 1960.

O'Brien, Kathleen. "Candi Jago as a Mandala: Symbolism of Its Narratives," *Review of Indonesian and Malayan Affairs,* Vol. XX (1988), pp. 1–61.

Orzech, Charles D. "Seeing Chen-Yen Buddhism: Traditional Scholarship and the Vajrayāna in China." *History of Religions,* Vol. XXIX (1989), pp. 87–114.

Paine, Robert Treat and Alexander Soper. *The Art and Architecture of Japan.* Harmondsworth, England and Baltimore: Penguin Books, 1974.

Pal, Pratapaditya. "A Note on the Maṇḍala of the Eight Bodhisattvas." *Archives of Asian Art,* 26 (1972–1973), pp. 71–73.

Parimoo, Ratan et al., eds. *Ellora Caves, Sculptures and Architecture.* New Delhi: Books and Books, 1988.

Pathy, Tarigopula Venkata. *Elura, Art and Culture.* New Delhi: Sterling Publishers, 1980.

Paul, Debjani. *The Art of Nalanda: Development of Buddhist Sculpture 600–1200 A.D.* (Ph.D. Diss., University of Leiden, 1987.) Leiden: Quick Service Drukkerij, 1987.

Rahman, M. "A Rare Find,", *India Today* (March 15, 1990), pp. 153–155.

Ramachandran, T. N. *Nagapattinam and Other Buddhist Bronzes in the Madras Museum. Bulletin of the Madras Government Museum,* VII (1954).

Ranade, Phandarinatha Vishnupanta. "Echoes of Ellora in Early Marathi Literature." In Ratan Parimoo et al., eds. *Ellora Caves: Sculptures and Architecture,* pp. 108–118. New Delhi: Books and Books, 1988.

Raychaudhuri, G. C. "History of the Western Cālukyas." *Journal of Ancient Indian History,* VII (1973–1974), pp. 1–101; Vol. VIII (1974–1975), pp. 1–124.

Rösel, Jacob. "Sakralstädte als Krstallisatoren Regionaler Tradition - Das Beispiel der Indischen Tempel- und Pilgerstadt Puri." In Hermann Kulke and Dietmar Rothermund, eds., *Regionale Tradition in Südasien,* pp. 149–170. Wiesbaden: Franz Steiner Verlag, 1985.

Rosenfield, John. *The Dynastic Arts of the Kushans.* Berkeley and Los Angeles: University of California Press, 1967.

Roth, Gustav. "Symbolism of the Buddhist Stūpa." In Anna Libera Dallapicolla and Stephanie Zingel-Avé Lallemant, eds. *The*

Stūpa: Its Religious, Historical and Architectural Significance, pp. 183–209. Wiesbaden: Franz Steiner Verlag, 1980.

Sahu, Nabin Kumar. *Buddhism in Orissa.* Utkal: Utkal University, 1958.

Sankalia, Hasmukh Dhirajlal. "A Unique Wooden Image of the Buddhist Goddess Tara from the Kanheri Caves." *Marg*, 36 (1984), p. 84.

Sarkar, H. and B. N. Misra. *Nagarjunikonda.* 2nd ed. New Delhi: Archaeological Survey of India, 1972.

Sawa, Takaaki. *Art in Japanese Esoteric Buddhism.* Tokyo, New York: Weatherhill/ Heibonsha, 1972.

Schopen, Gregory. "Archaeology and Protestant Presuppositions in the Study of Indian Buddhism." *History of Religions*, 31.1 (August 1991), pp. 1–23.

———. "On the Buddha and His Bones, The Conception of a Relic in the Inscriptions of Nāgārjunikoṇḍa." *Journal of the American Oriental Society*, 108.4 (Oct.–Dec. 1988), pp. 527–538.

Schwartzberg, Joseph E., ed. *A Historical Atlas of South Asia.* Chicago: University of Chicago Press, 1978.

Seeley, John B. *The Wonders of Ellora or the Narrative of a Journey to the Temples or Dwellings Excavated out of a Mountain of Granite at Ellora in the East Indies.* 2nd ed. London: G. B. Whittaker, 1825.

Sengupta, R. "Repairs to the Ellora Caves." *Ancient India*, XVII (1961), pp. 46–67.

———. "A Sculptural Representation of the Buddhist Litany to Tārā at Ellora." *Bulletin of the Prince of Wales Museum of Western India*, V (1955–1957), pp. 12–15.

Settar, S. "A Buddhist Vihara at Aihole." *East and West*, N.S. XIX (1969), pp. 126–138.

Sircar, Dineschandra. "The Chalukyas." in R. C. Majumdar, ed. *The Classical Age, The History and Culture of the Indian People*, Vol. III, pp. 227–254. Bombay: Bharatiya Vidya Bhavan, 1962.

———. *Indian Epigraphical Glossary.* Delhi: Motilal Banarsidass, 1966.

———. *Studies in the Geography of Ancient and Medieval India.* 2nd ed. New Delhi: Motilal Banarsidass, 1971.

Śiva Purāṇa. Pt. III. Delhi: Motilal Banarsidass, 1970.

Snellgrove, David. *Indo-Tibetan Buddhism.* 2 Vols. Boston: Shambala Publications, Inc., 1987.

Snellgrove, David and Thadeusz Skorupski. *The Cultural Heritage of Ladakh.* 2 Vols. Warminster: Aris & Phillips Ltd., 1977.

Snodgrass, Adrian. *The Matrix and Diamond World Mandalas in Shingon Buddhism.* 2 Vols. New Delhi: Aditya Prakashan, 1988.

———. *The Symbolism of the Stupa.* Ithaca, N.Y.: Southeast Asia Program, Cornell University, 1985.

Soar, Micaela. "The Tīrtha at Ellora." In Ratan Parimoo et al., eds. *Ellora Caves: Sculptures and Architecture*, pp. 80–103. New Delhi: Books and Books, 1988.

Soundara Rajan, K.V. "Beginnings of the Temple Plan." *Bulletin of the Prince of Wales Museum of Western India*, VI (1957–1959), pp. 74–81.

———. *Cave Temples of the Deccan, Temple Architecture Series.* No. 3. New Delhi: Archaeological Survey of India, 1981.

Soundra Rajan, K. V. and R. Sengupta. "Flake and Blade Industries from Ellora (Maharashtra)." *48th Proceedings, Indian Science Congress Association*, p. 449. Calcutta: 1961.

———. "Microlithic Industries from Ellora." *Marathwada University Research Bulletin*, (1962).

Spink, Walter. "Ajanta and Ghatotkacha: A Preliminary Analysis." *Ars Orientalis,"* VI (1966), pp. 135–165.

———. *Ajanta to Ellora.* Bombay and Ann Arbor: Marg Publications for the Center for South and Southeast Asian Studies, University of Michigan. 1967.

———. "Ajanta's Chronology: The Crucial Cave." *Ars Orientalis*, X (1975), pp. 143–170.

———. "Ajanta's Chronology: Politics and Patronage." in Joanna G. Williams, ed. *Kalādarśana: American Studies in the Art of India*, pp. 109–126. New Delhi: Oxford and IBH Publishing Co. with A.I.I.S., 1981.

———. "Ajanta's Chronology: Solstitial Evidence." *Arts Orientalis*, XV (1984), pp. 97–117.

———. "Ajanta's Chronology: The Problem of Cave Eleven." *Ars Orientalis*, VII (1968), pp. 155–168.

———. "Ellora's Earliest Phase." *Bulletin of the American Academy of Banaras*, Vol. I (1975), pp. 11–22.

———. "The Great Cave at Elephanta: A Study of Its Sources." In Bardwell Smith, ed. *Essays on Gupta Culture*, pp. 235–284. New Delhi: Motilal Banarsidass, 1982.

Srivastava, Bireshwar Nath. *Harsha and His Times.* Varanasi: Chowkhamba Sanskrit Series Office, 1976.

Stadtner, Donald Martin. "From Sirpur to Rajim: The Art of Kosala during the Seventh Century." Ph.D. Diss., University of California at Berkeley, 1976.

Stern, Philippe. *Colonnes indiennes d'Ajantā et Ellora*. Paris: Presses universitaires de France, 1972.

Takakusu, J. trans. *A Record of the Buddhist Religion as Practiced in India and the Malay Archipelago (A.D. 671–695), by I-Tsing*. 1896; reprint, Delhi: Munshiram Manoharlal, 1966.

Tarr, Gary. "The Architecture of the Early Western Chalukyas." Ph.D. Diss., University of California, Berkeley, 1969.

————. "The Chronology and Development of the Chāḷukya Cave Temples." *Ars Orientalis*, VIII (1970), pp. 155–184.

————. "The Śiva Temple at Dhokeśvara and the Development of the Nidhi Image," *Oriental Art*, XV (1969), p. 269–280.

Tartakov, Gary Michael. "The Beginning of Dravidian Temple Architecture in Stone." *Artibus Asiae*, XLII (1980), pp. 39–99.

Thakur, Umakant. "The Holy Places of West India as Mentioned in the Skanda Purana." *Purana*, XVIII (1976), pp. 162–196.

Thévenot, Jean de. *The Travels of Monsieur de Thévenot into the Levant*. Translated by A. Lovell. London: H. Clark, 1687.

Thosar, H.S. and T. V. Pathy. "Mahārāṣtrakūṭa Karkarāja Yācā Bhindon Tāmrapaṭa." *Pratishthan*, July–August 1978, pp. 27–32.

Trivedi, H. V. "The Indragadh Stone Inscription of the Time of the Rāshṭrakūṭa King Naṇṇapa." *Journal of the Bihar Research Society*, XLI (1955), pp. 249–261.

Tulpule, Shankar Gopal, ed. Mhai Bhat, *Līḷācaritra*. Vol. I, part I. Nagpur and Poona: Suvicara Prakasan Mandala, 1964.

Tucci, Guiseppe. *The Theory and Practice of the Mandala*. New York: Samuel Weiser, Inc., 1970.

Turner, Victor and Edith Turner. *Image and Pilgrimage in Christian Culture*. New York: Columbia University Press, 1978.

Venkataramanayya, N. "Vajraṭa." *The Indian Historical Quarterly*, XX (1944), pp. 181–188.

Venkataramayya, M. "Sangalooda Plates of Rashtrakuta Nannaraja: Saka 615." *Epigraphia Indica*, XXIX (1951), pp. 109–115.

Viennot, Odette. *Temples de l'Inde Centrale et Occidentale. (Étude Stylistique et essai de chronologie relative du Ve au milieu du Xe siècle)*. 2 Vols. Paris: École d'Extrême-orient, 1976.

Watanabe, K. "A Chinese Text Corresponding to Part of the Bower Manuscript," *Journal of the Royal Asiatic Society* (1907), pp. 261–266.

Wayman, Alex. *The Buddhist Tantras*. New York: Samuel Weiser, 1973.

————. *The Yoga of the Guhyasamajatantra*. Delhi: Motilal Banarsidass, 1977.

————. "Reflections on the Theory of Barabuḍur as a *Maṇḍala*." In L. Gomez and H. Woodward, eds. *Barabudur, History and Significance of a Buddhist Monument*, pp. 139–172. Berkeley: Berkeley Buddhist Series, 1981.

Weiner, Sheila. *Ajaṇṭā: Its Place in Buddhist Art*. Berkeley: University of California Press, 1977.

Weintraub, Steven. "Viśvakarmā, Elurā: A Critical Analysis." *Marsyas*, XVII (1974–1975), pp. 49–57.

Williams, Joanna Gottfried. *The Art of Gupta India*. Princeton: Princeton University Press, 1982.

————. ed. *Kalādarśana, American Studies in the Art of India*. New Delhi: Oxford and IBH Publishing Col. with A.I.I.S., 1981.

————. "Vākāṭaka Art and the Gupta Mainstream." In Bardwell Smith, ed. *Essays on Gupta Culture*, pp. 215–233. Delhi: Motilal Banarsidass, 1983.

Yamamoto, Chikyo. *History of Mantrayana in Japan*, Sata-Pitaka Series, Volume 346. New Delhi: Sharada Rani, 1987.

Yazdani, Gulam. *Ajanta*. 4 Vols. London: Oxford University Press, 1931–1955.

————, ed. *The Early History of the Deccan*. Parts I–VI. London: Oxford University Press, 1960.

Zimmer, Heinrich. *The Art of Indian Asia*. 2 Vols. New York: Pantheon Books, 1955.

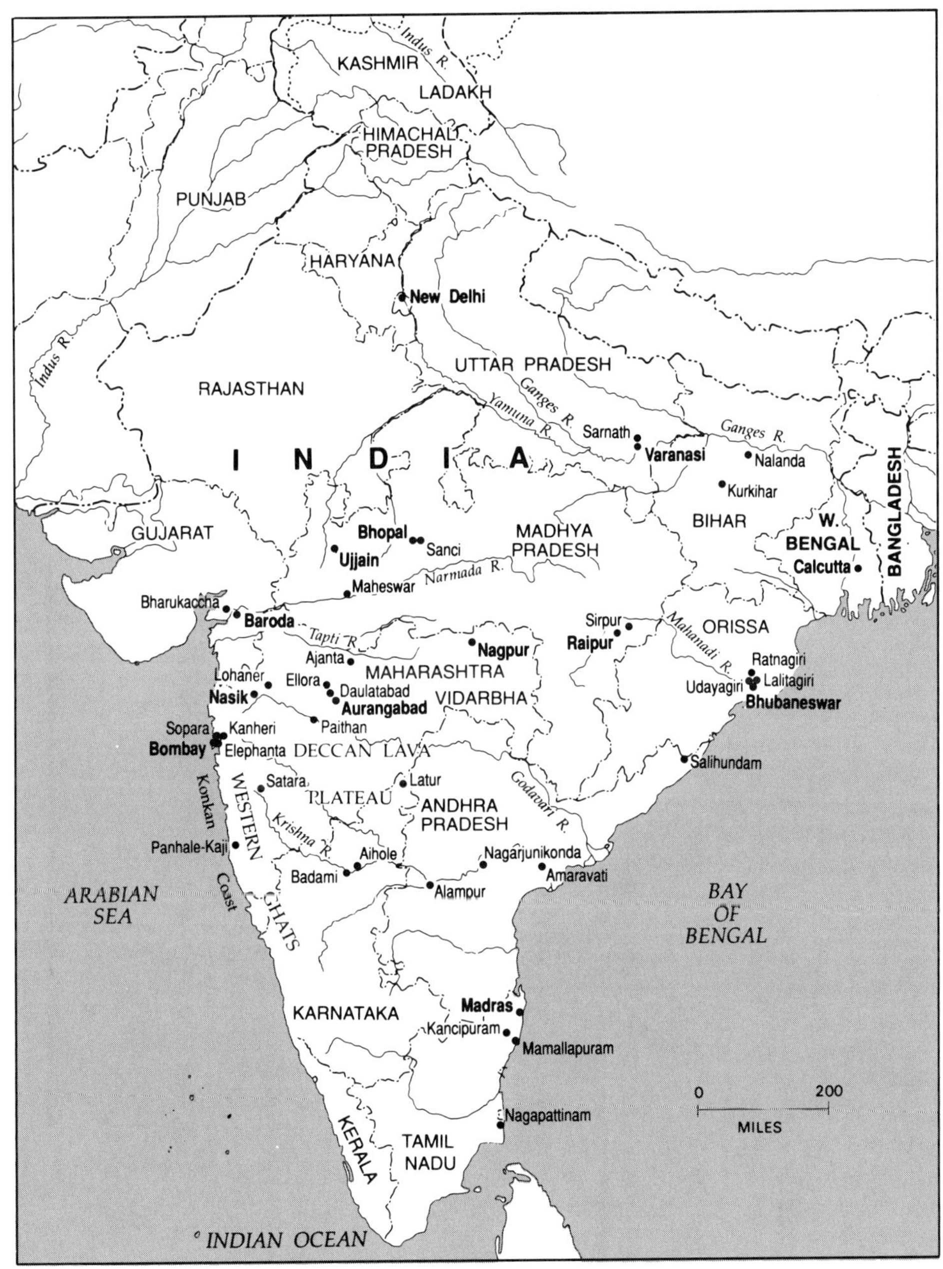

Fig. 1   Map Showing Locations Mentioned in Text

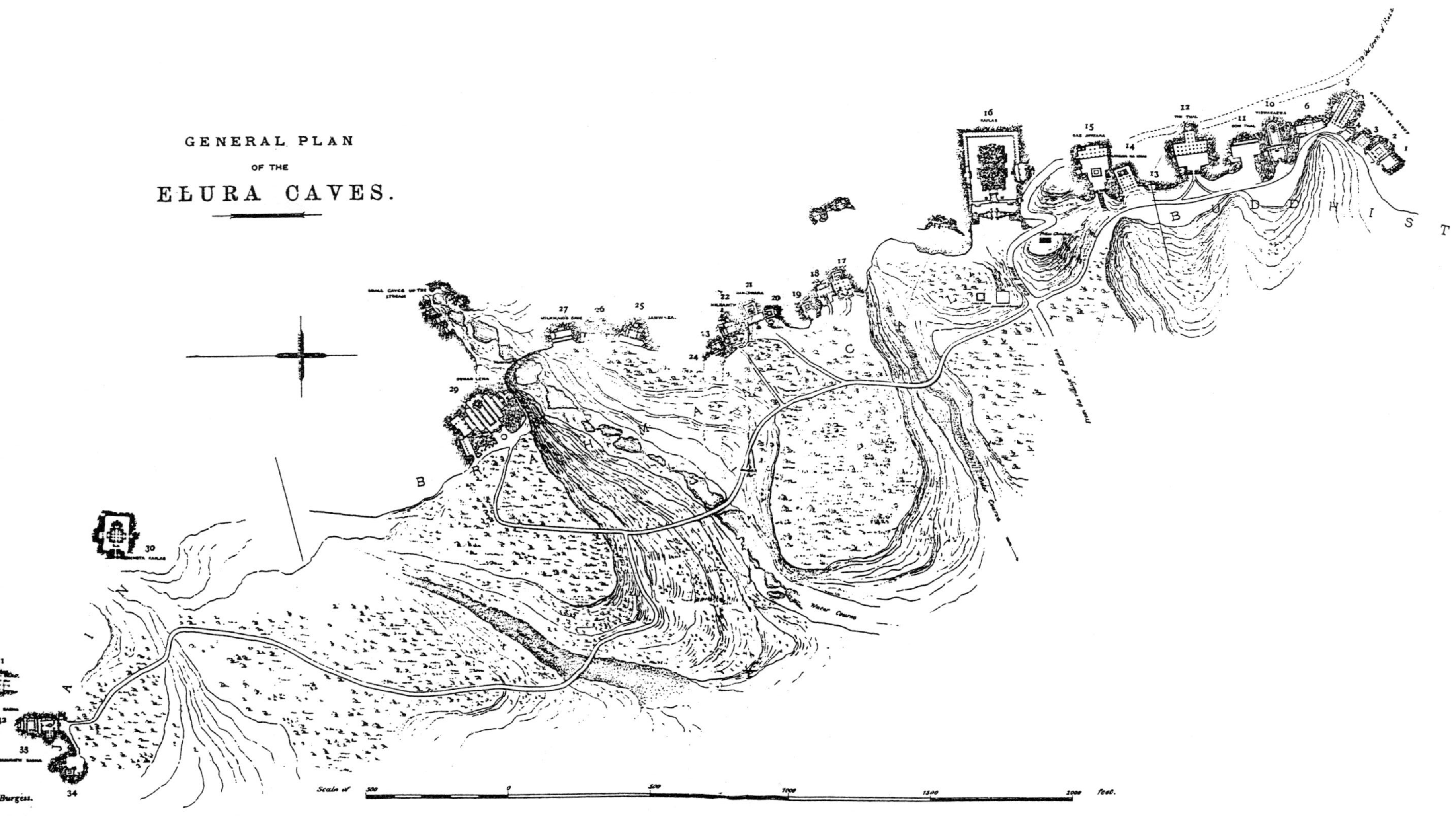

Fig. 2   Plan of Buddhist and Brahmanical Caves from Burgess, *Elura*

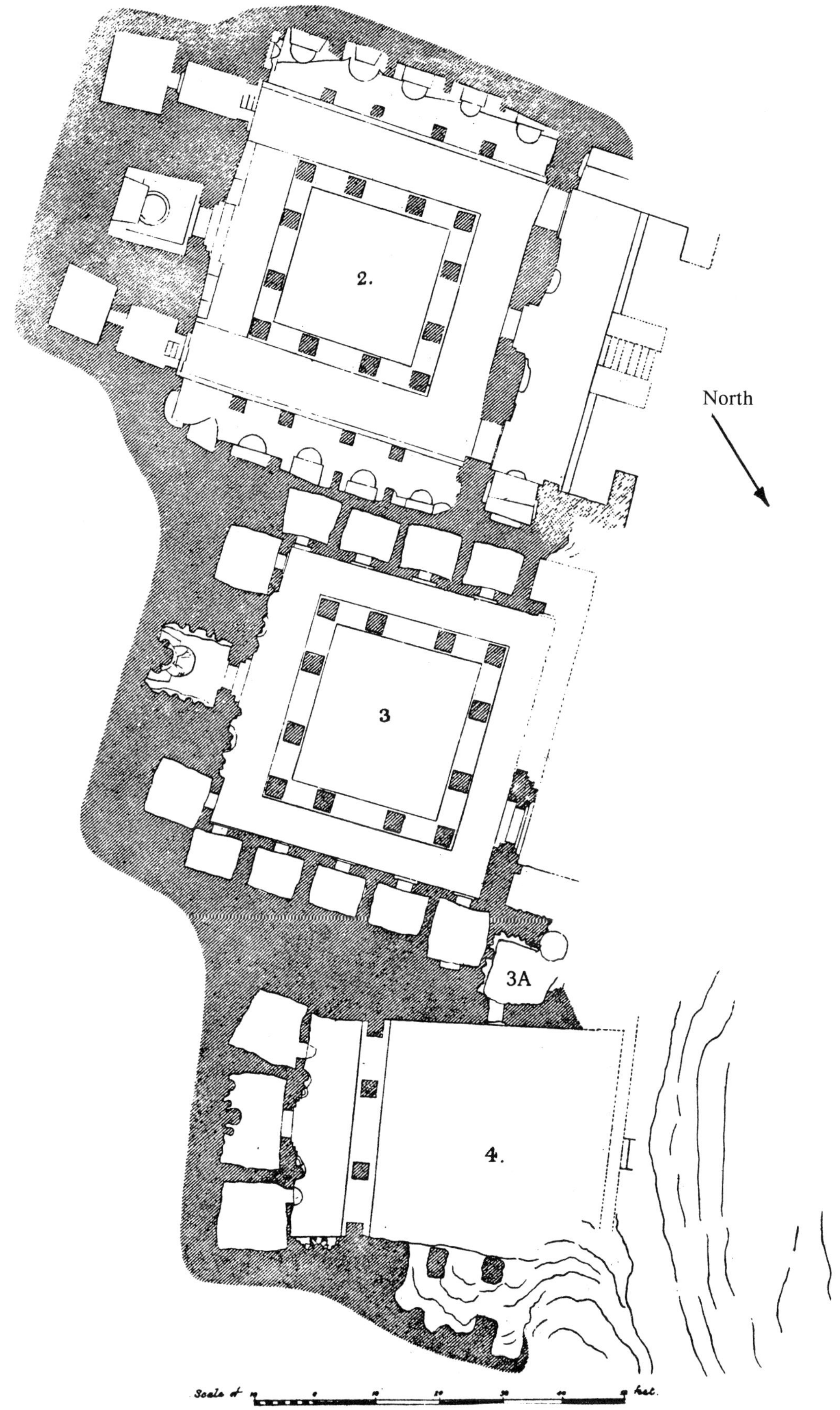

Fig. 3 Plans of Caves 2, 3, and 4, from Fergusson and Burgess, *Cave Temples of India*

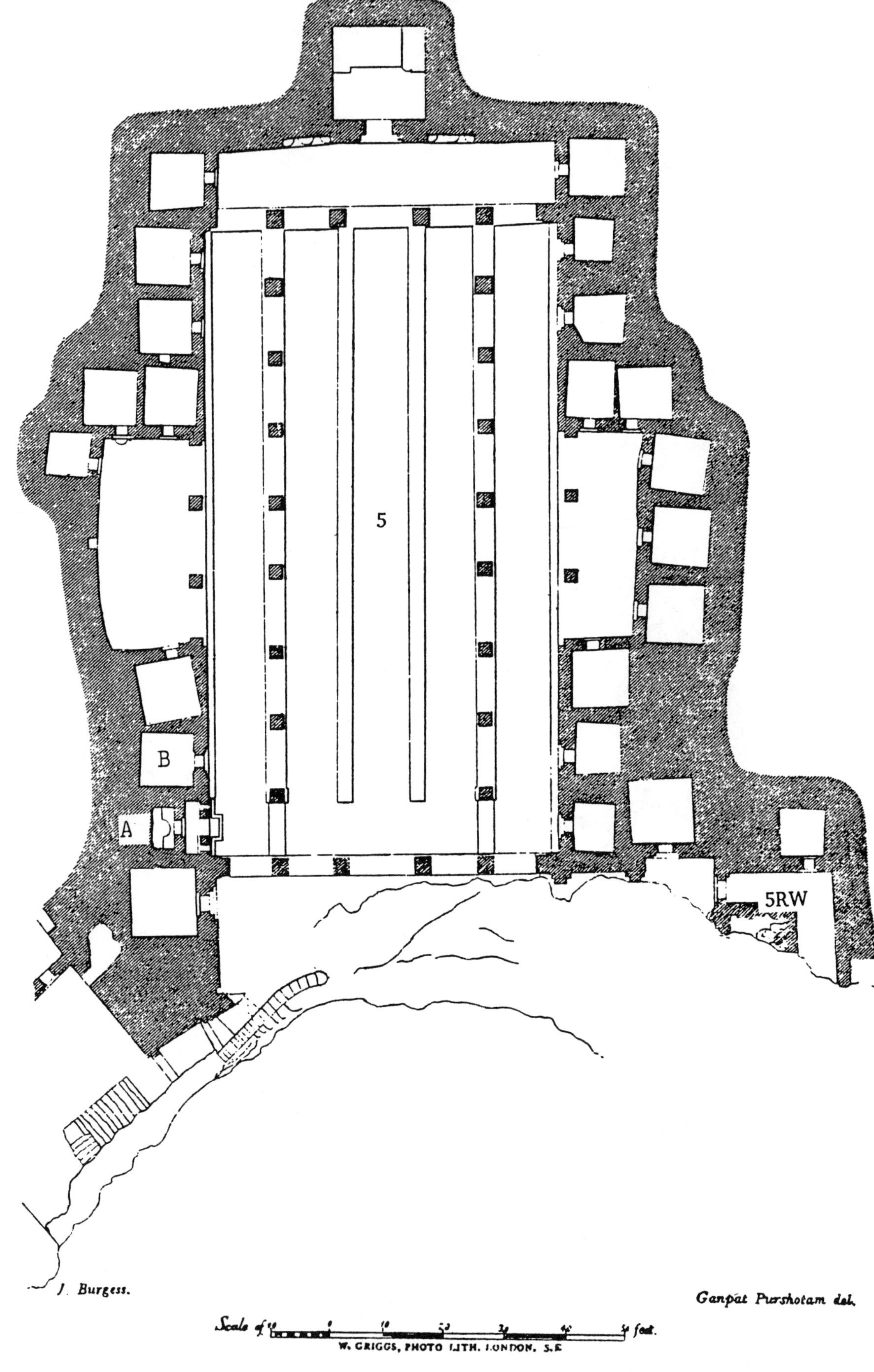

Fig. 4   Plan of Caves 5 and 5RW, from Fergusson and Burgess, *Cave Temples of India*

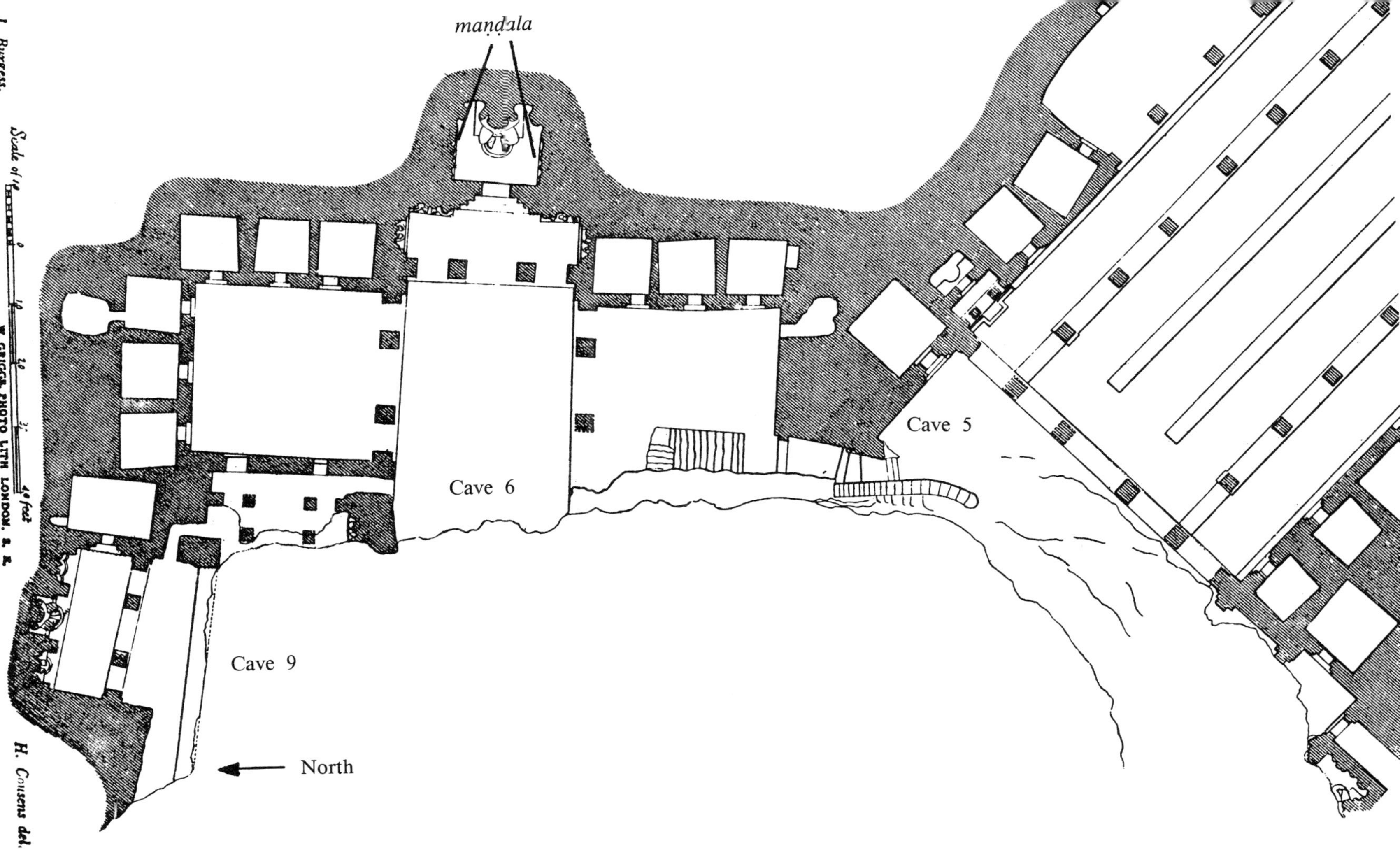

Fig. 5 Plans of Caves 6 and 9, from Fergusson and Burgess, *Cave Temples of India*

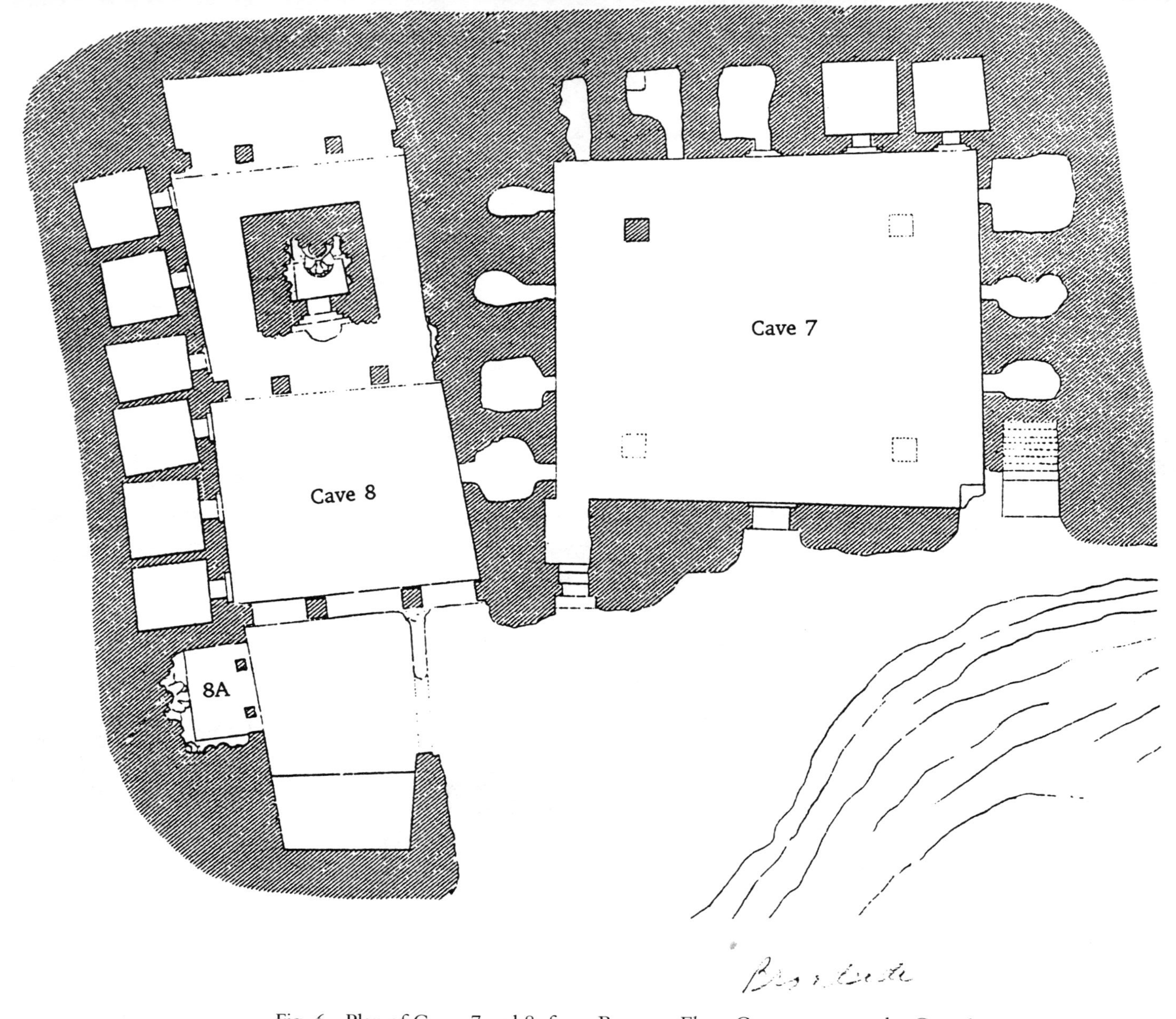

Fig. 6. Plan of Caves 7 and 8 from Burgess...

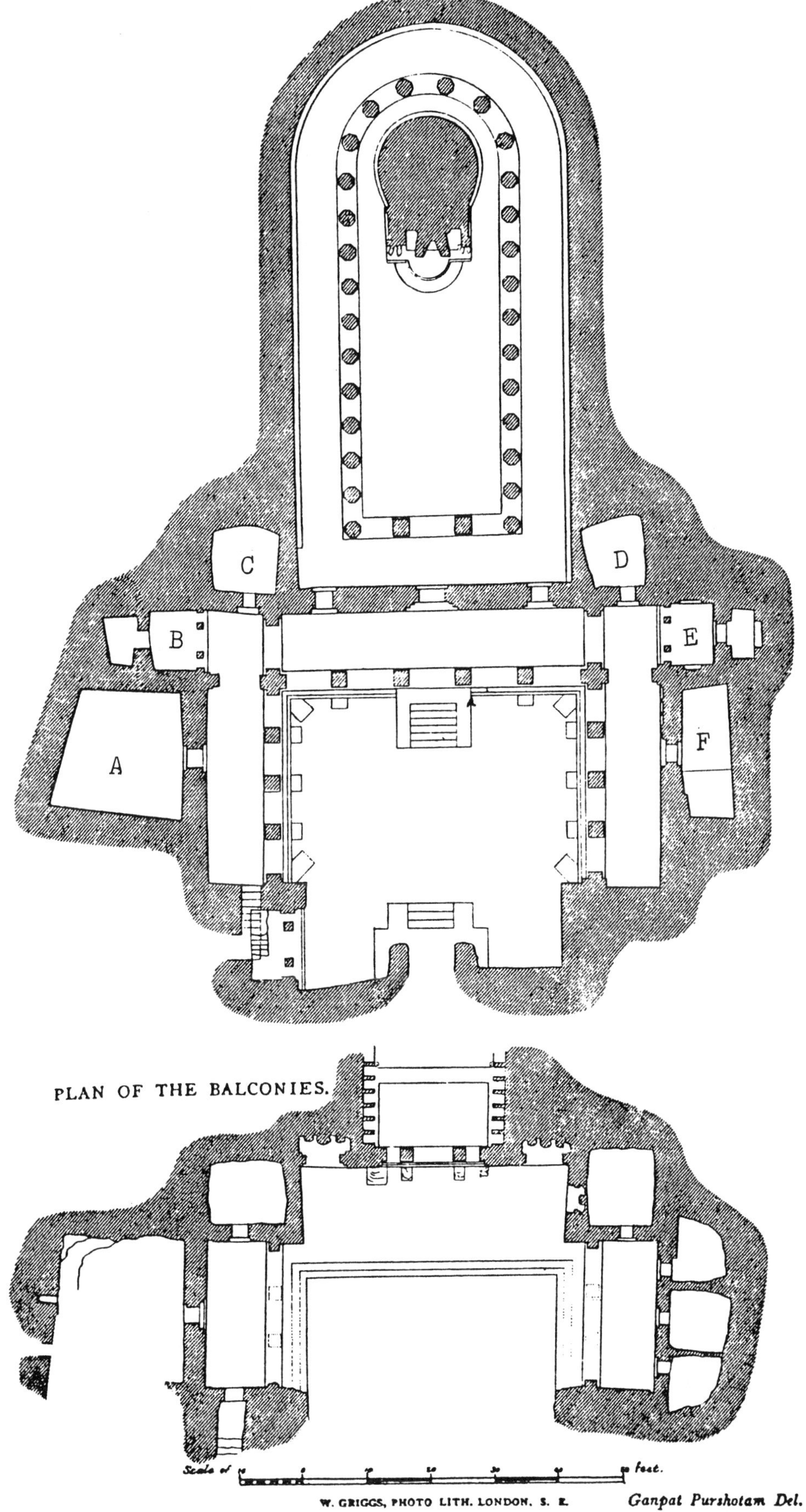

Fig. 7   Plan of Cave 10, from Fergusson and Burgess, *Cave Temples of India*

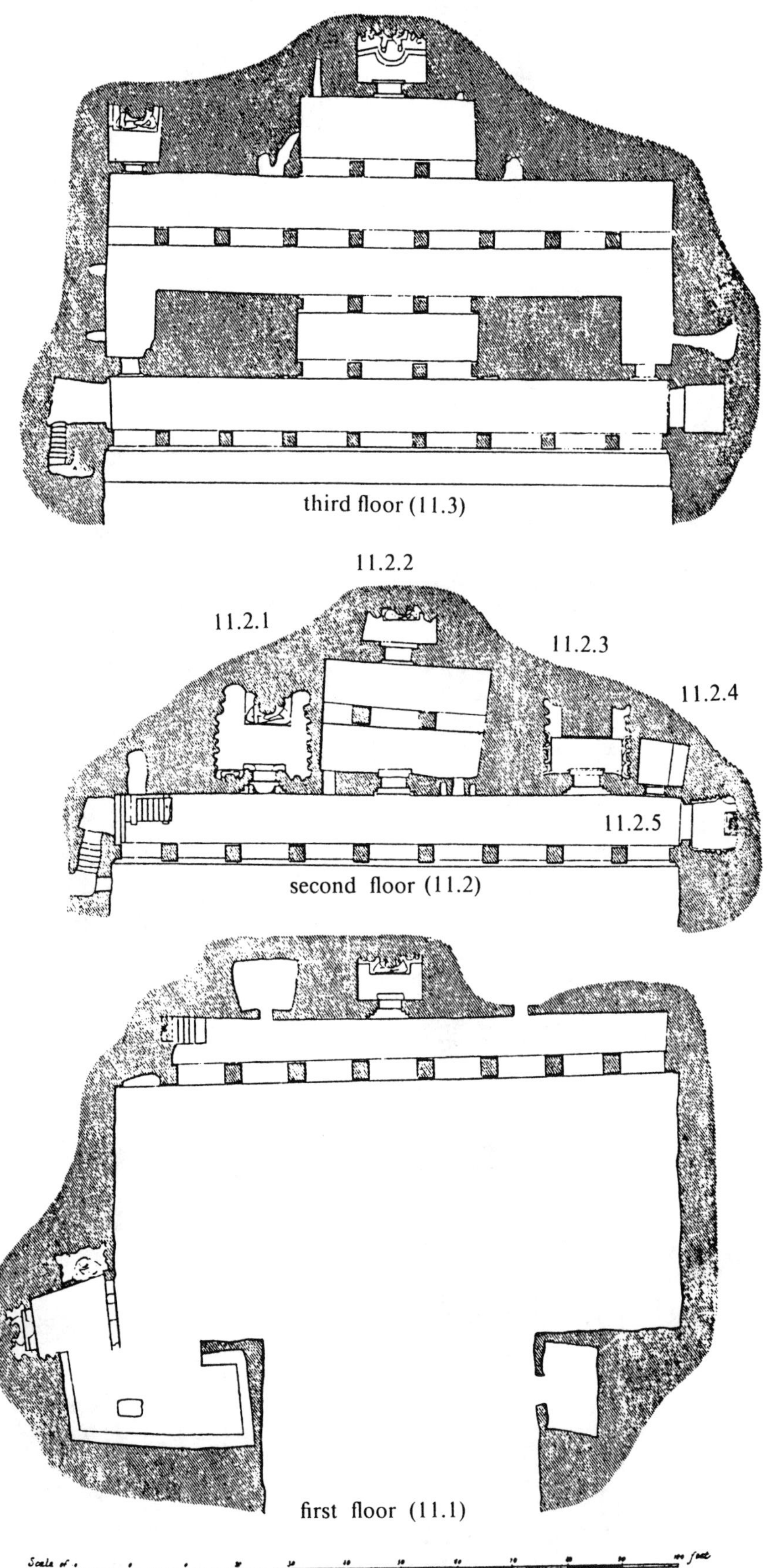

Fig. 8   Plan of Cave 11, from Burgess, *Elura*

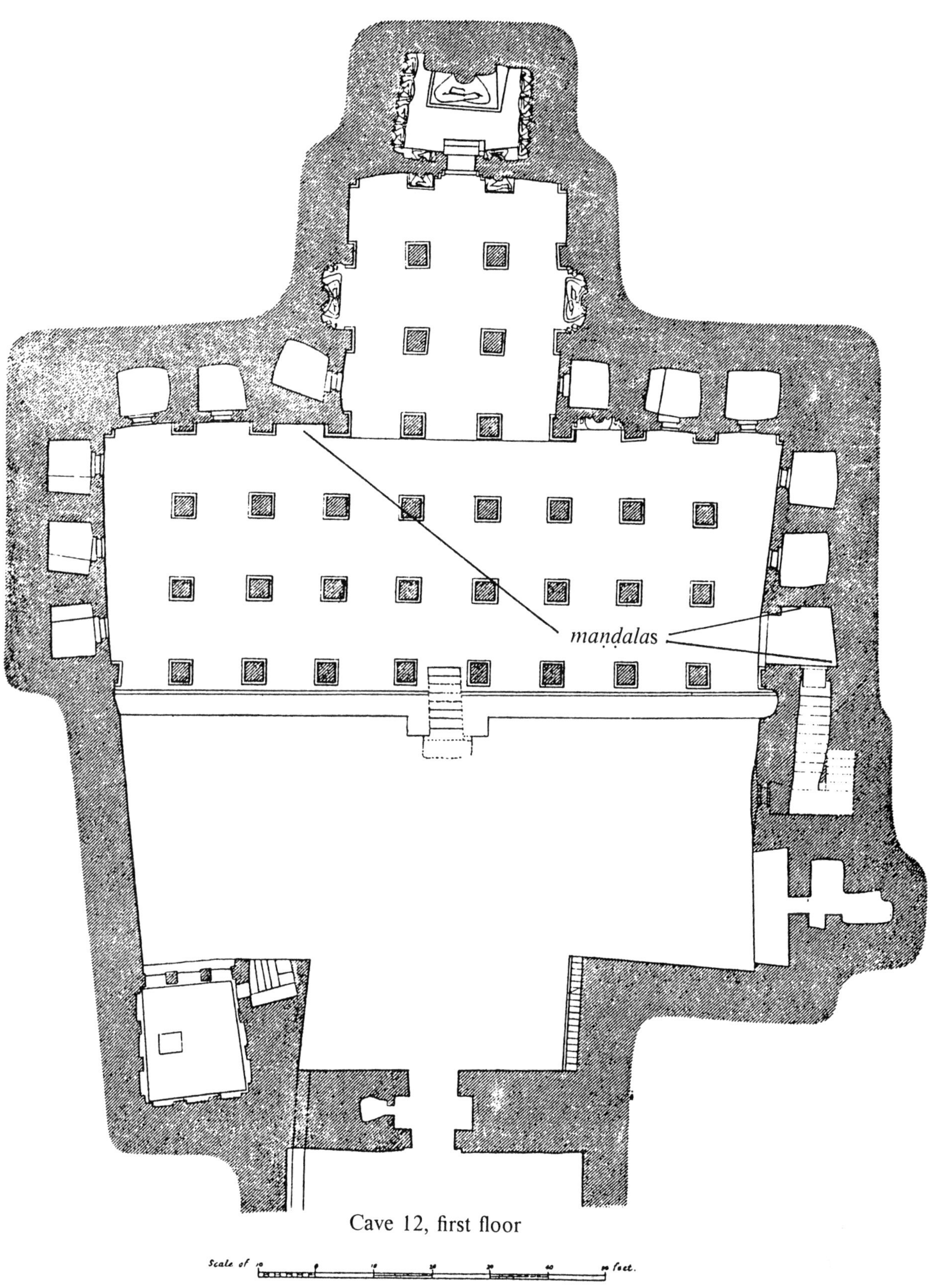

Fig. 9   Plan of Cave 12.1, from Fergusson and Burgess, *Cave Temples of India*

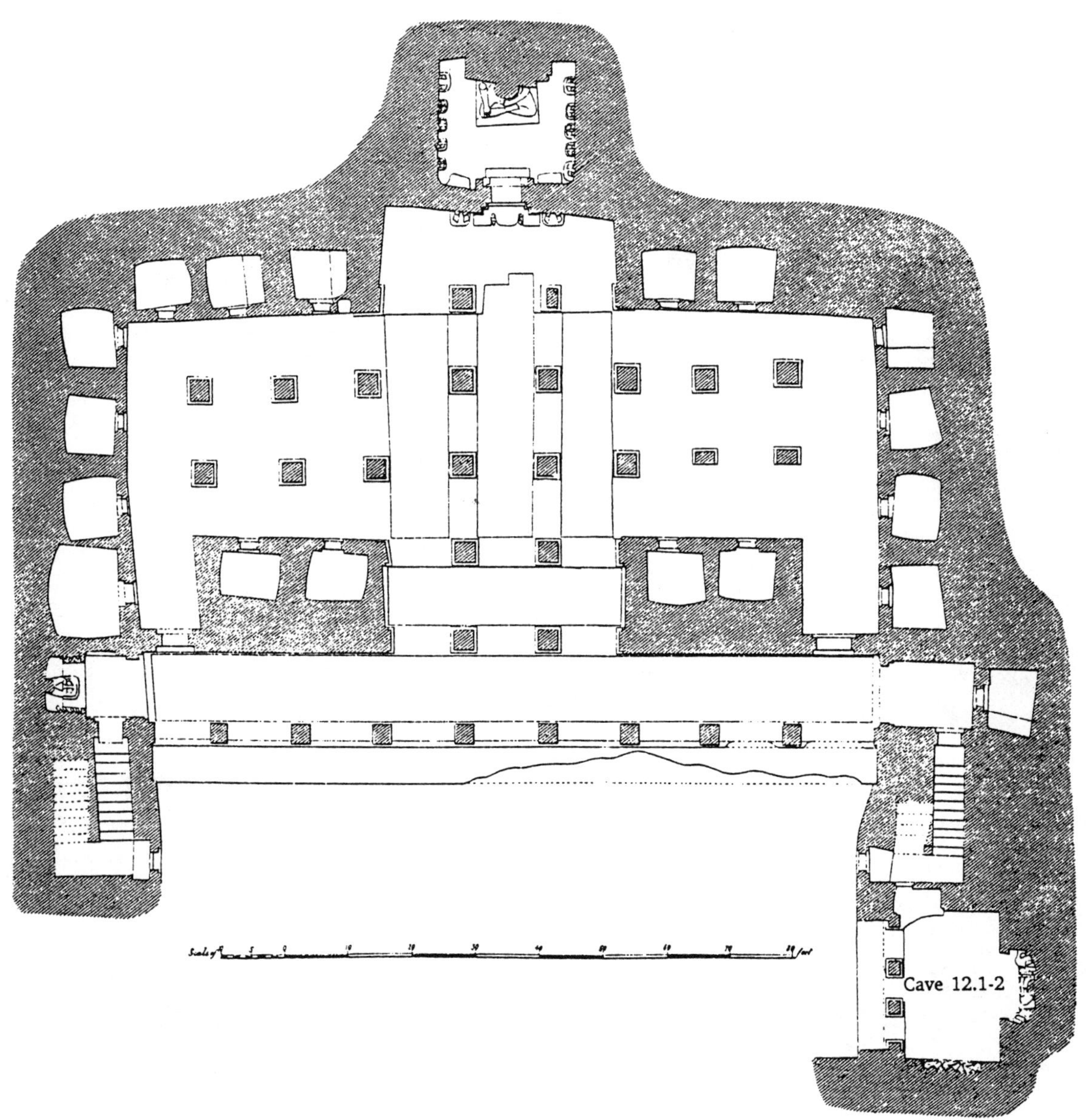

Fig. 10   Plan of Cave 12.2, from Fergusson and Burgess, *Cave Temples of India*

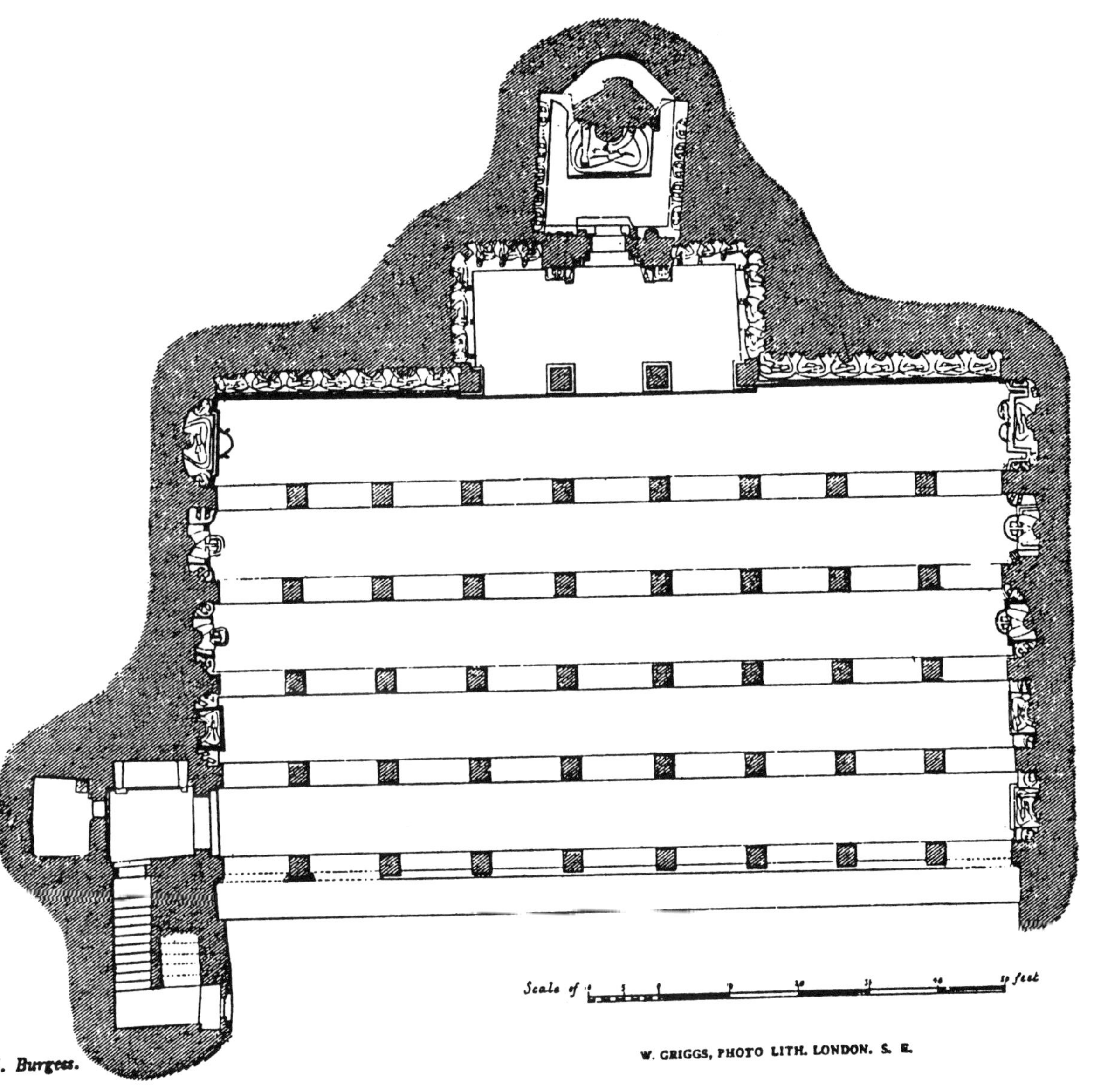

Fig. 11   Plan of Cave 12.3, from Fergusson and Burgess, *Cave Temples of India*

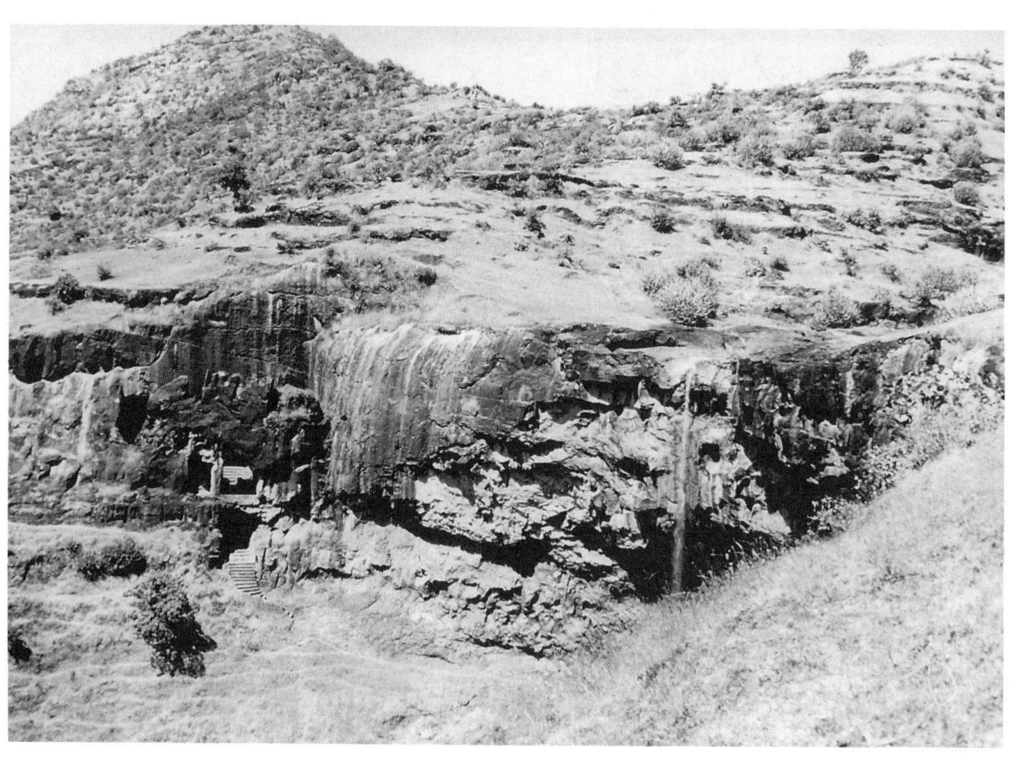

Fig. 12   Panoramic View of Caves and Waterfall

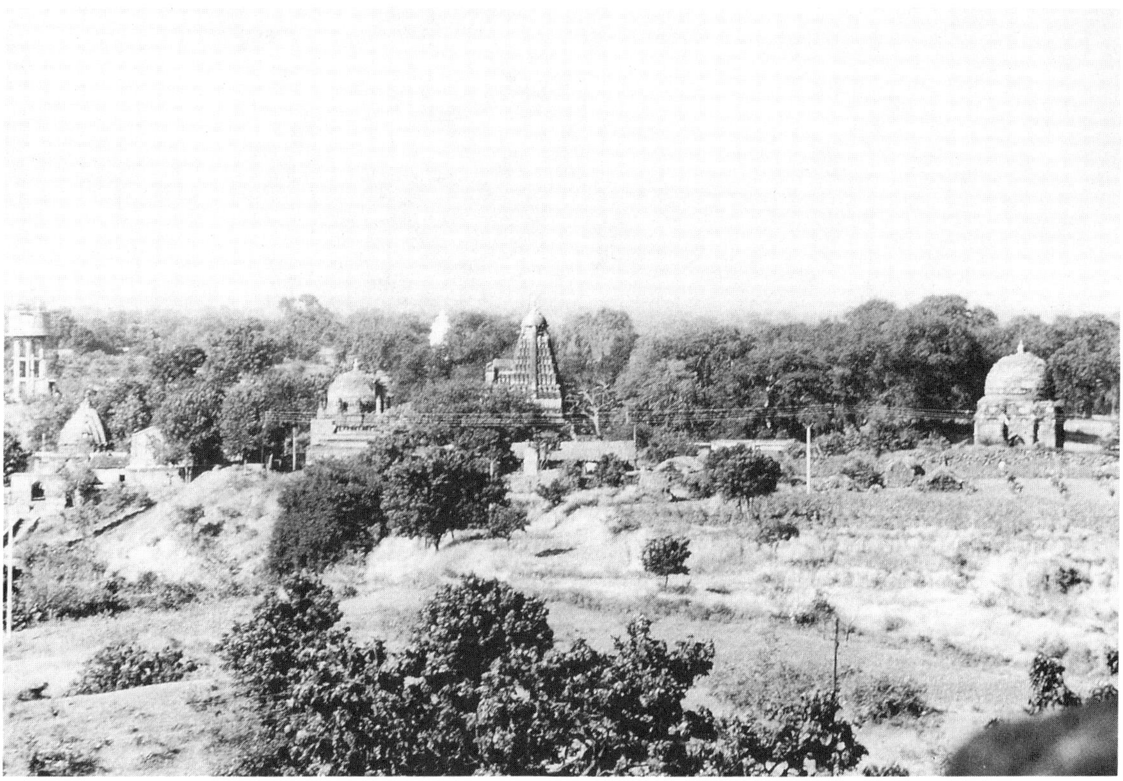

Fig. 13   Panoramic View of Ellora Village and Ghṛṣṇeśvara Temple

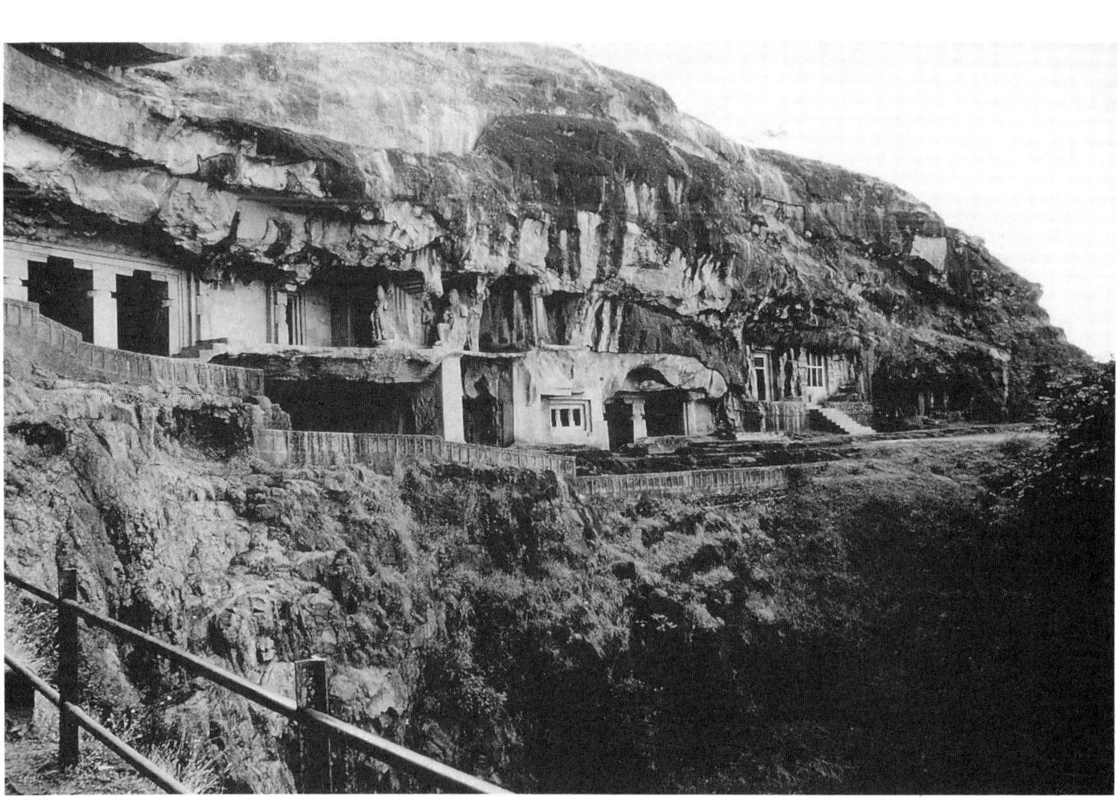

Fig. 14   Gully Cut by Waterfall over Cave 5

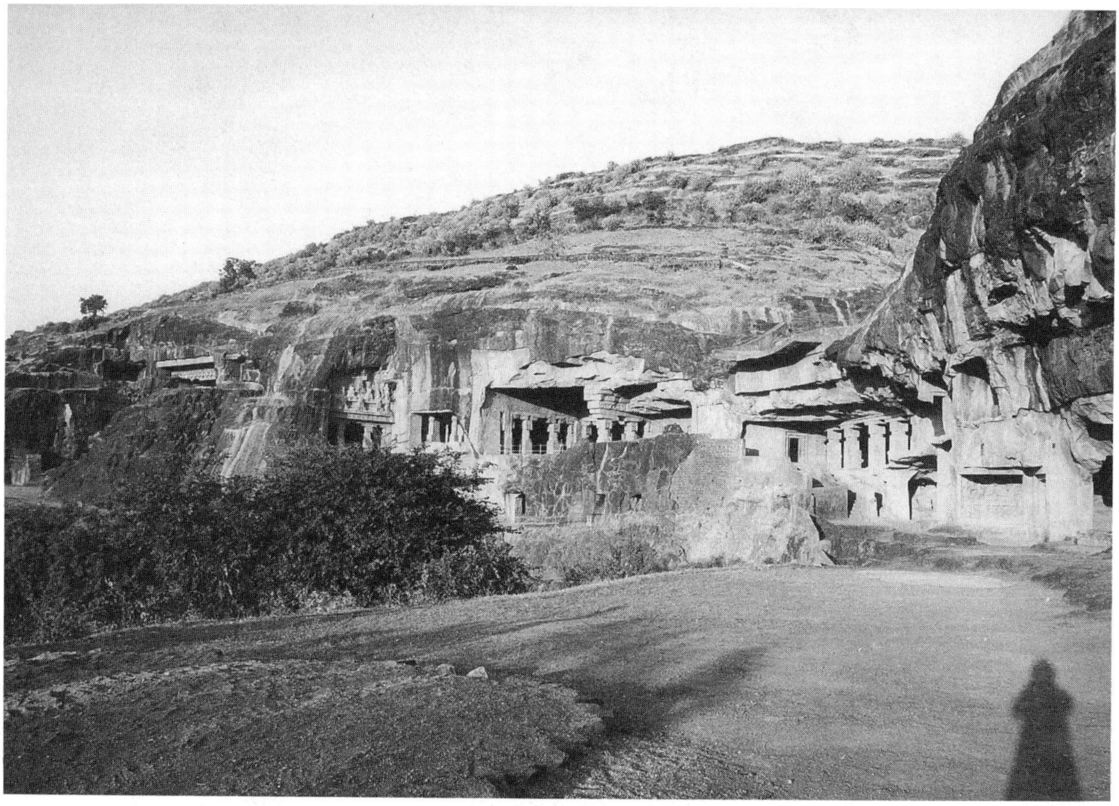

Fig. 15   View to northeast, from left, façades of Caves 10, 9, 6, 5, and 4

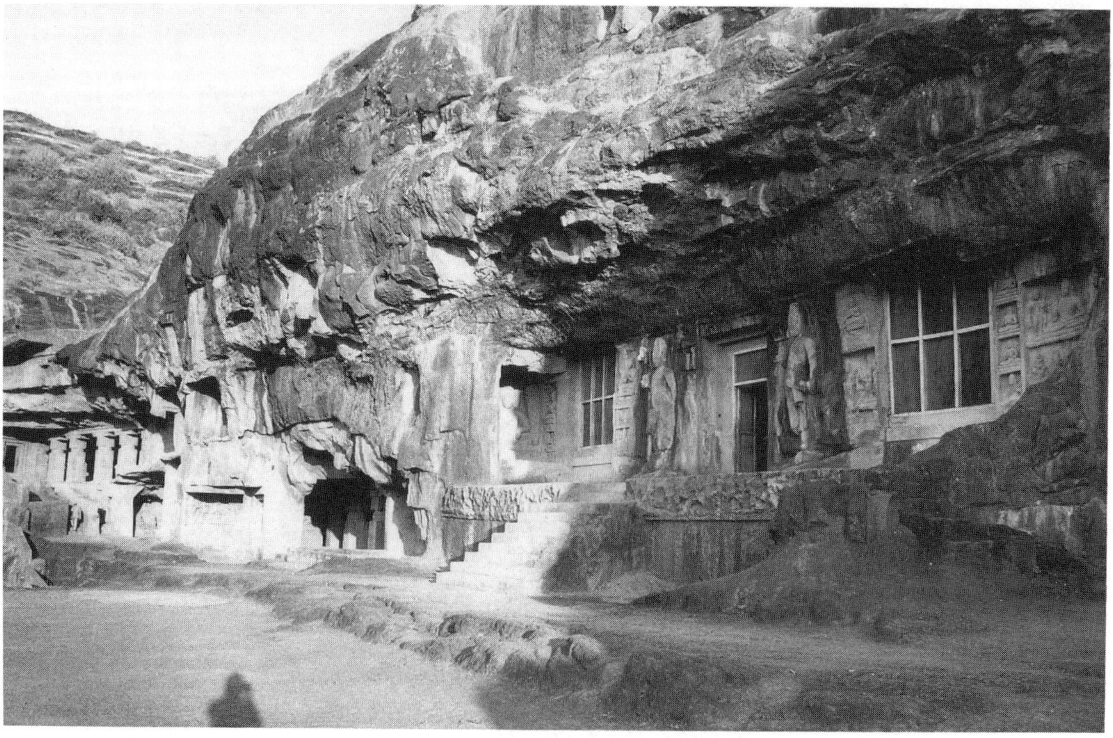

Fig. 16   View to northeast, from far left, Caves 5, 4, 3, and 2

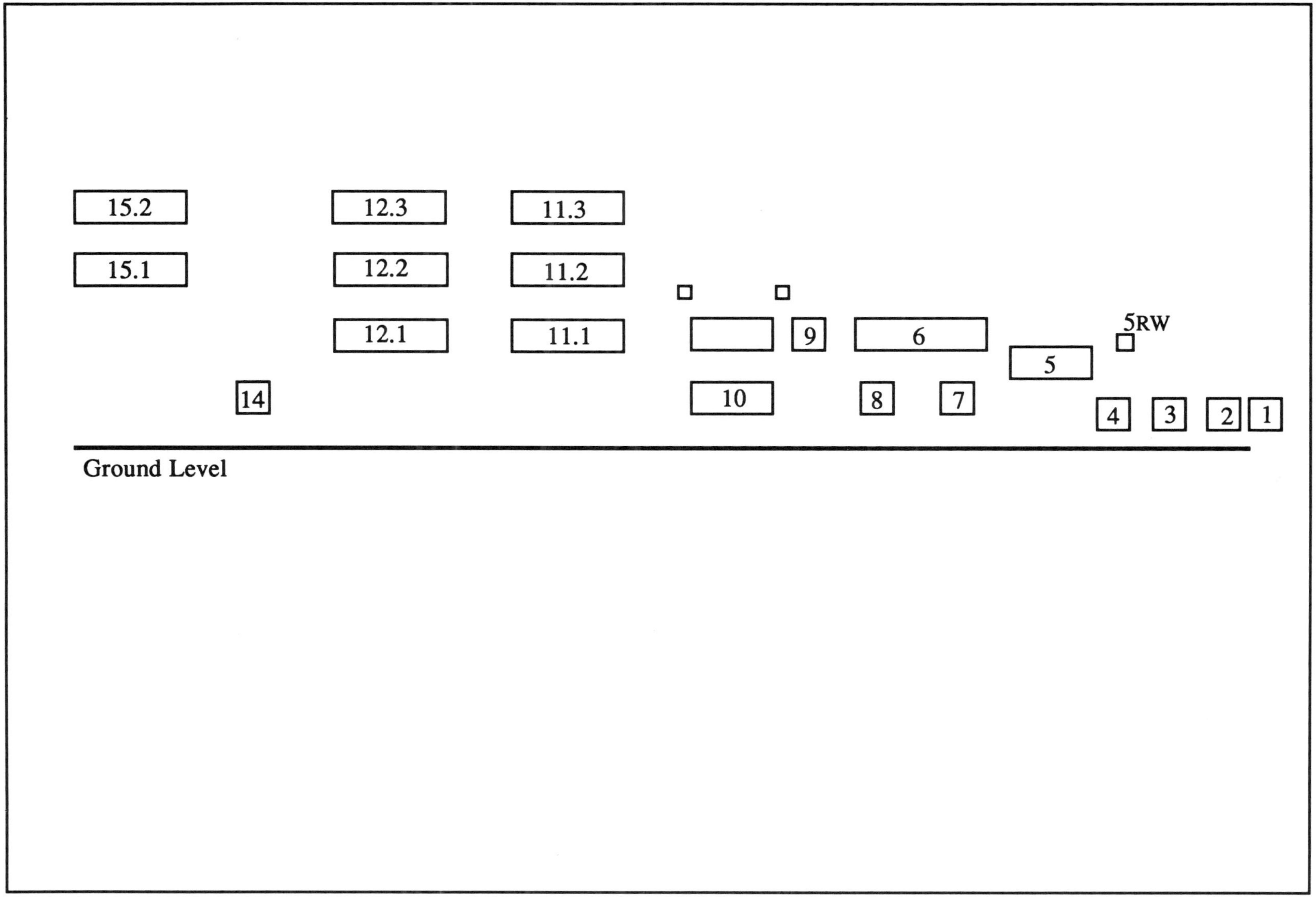

Fig. 17   Schematic plan showing relative vertical and horizontal positions of caves 1–15

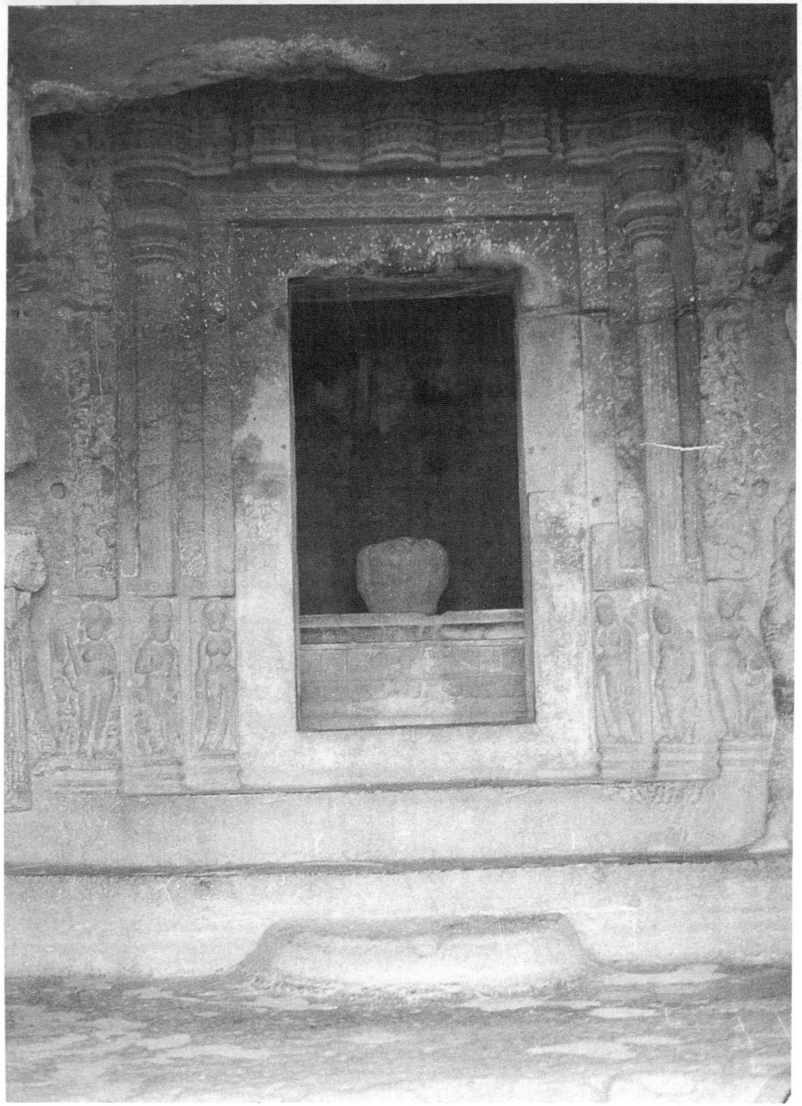

Fig. 18   Cave 21 doorway

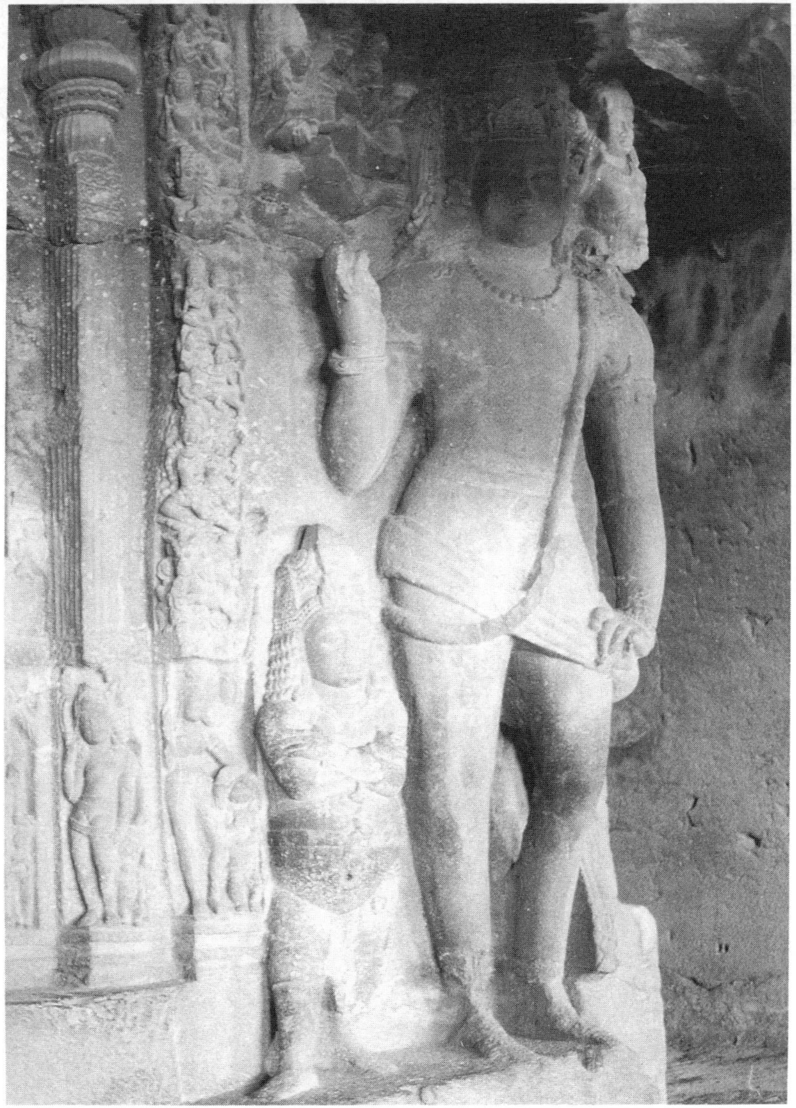

Fig. 19   Cave 21 right door guardian

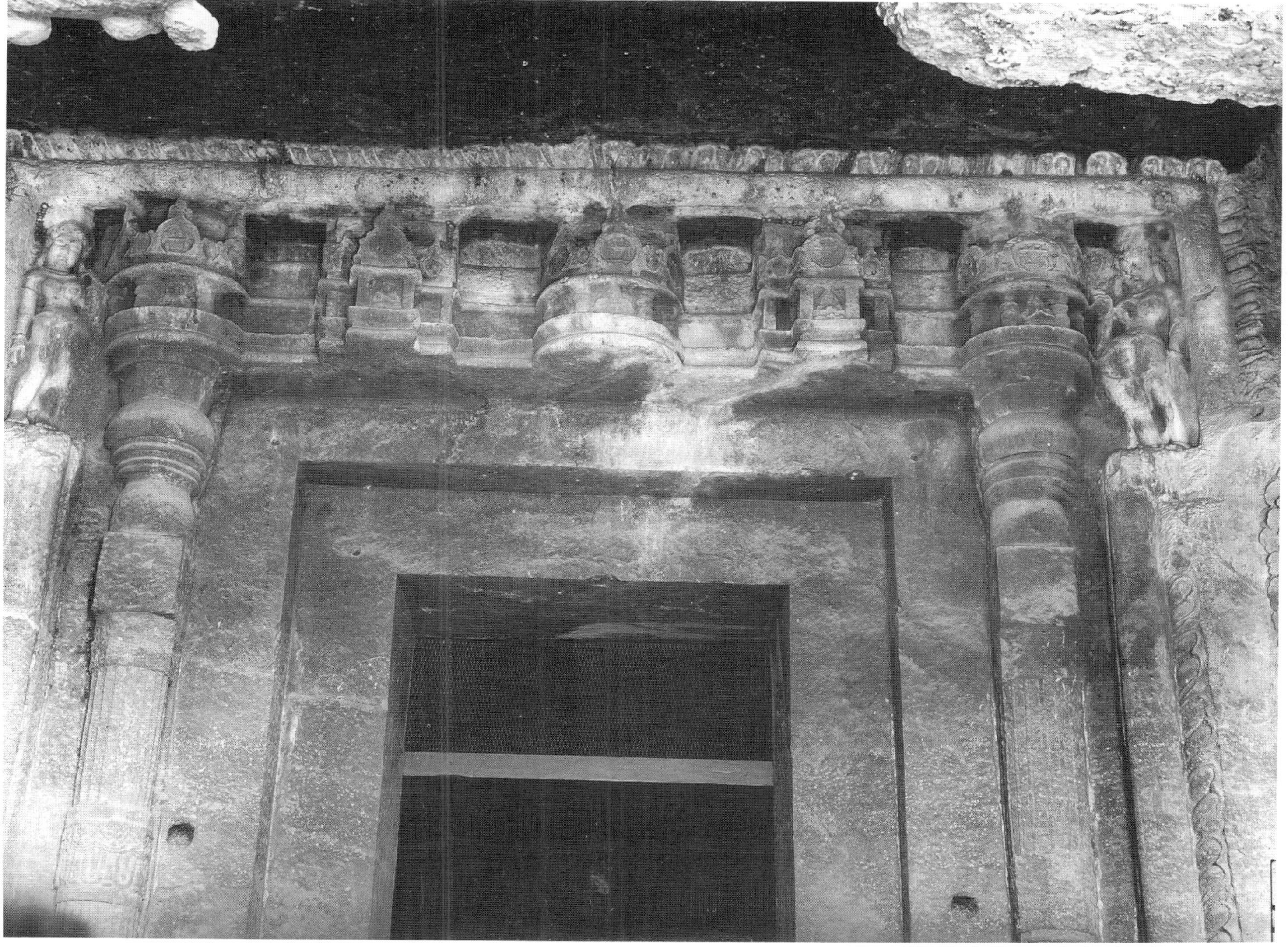

Fig. 20 Cave 6 shrine door lintel (AIIS)

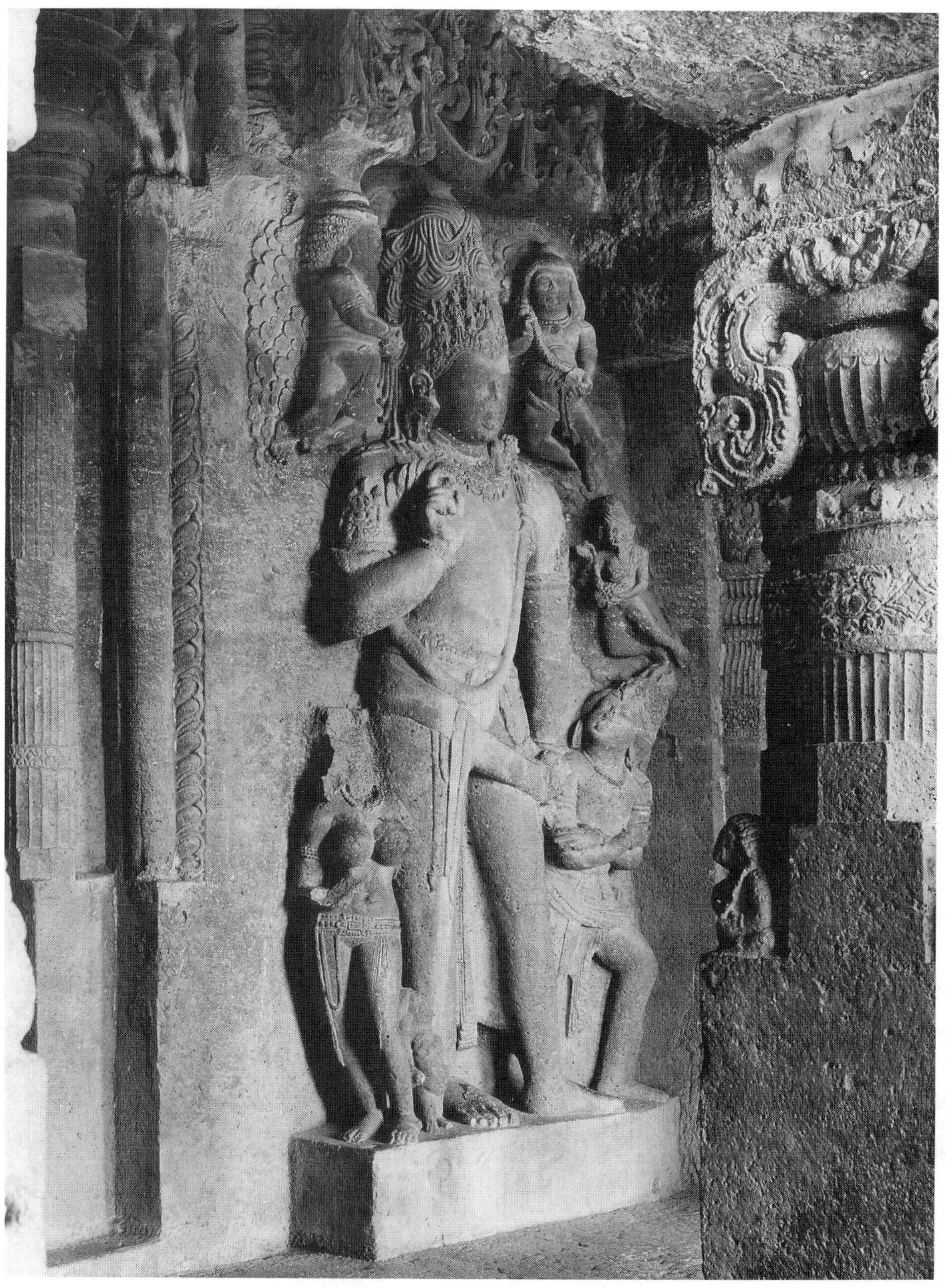

Fig. 21   Cave 6 right door guardian (AIIS)

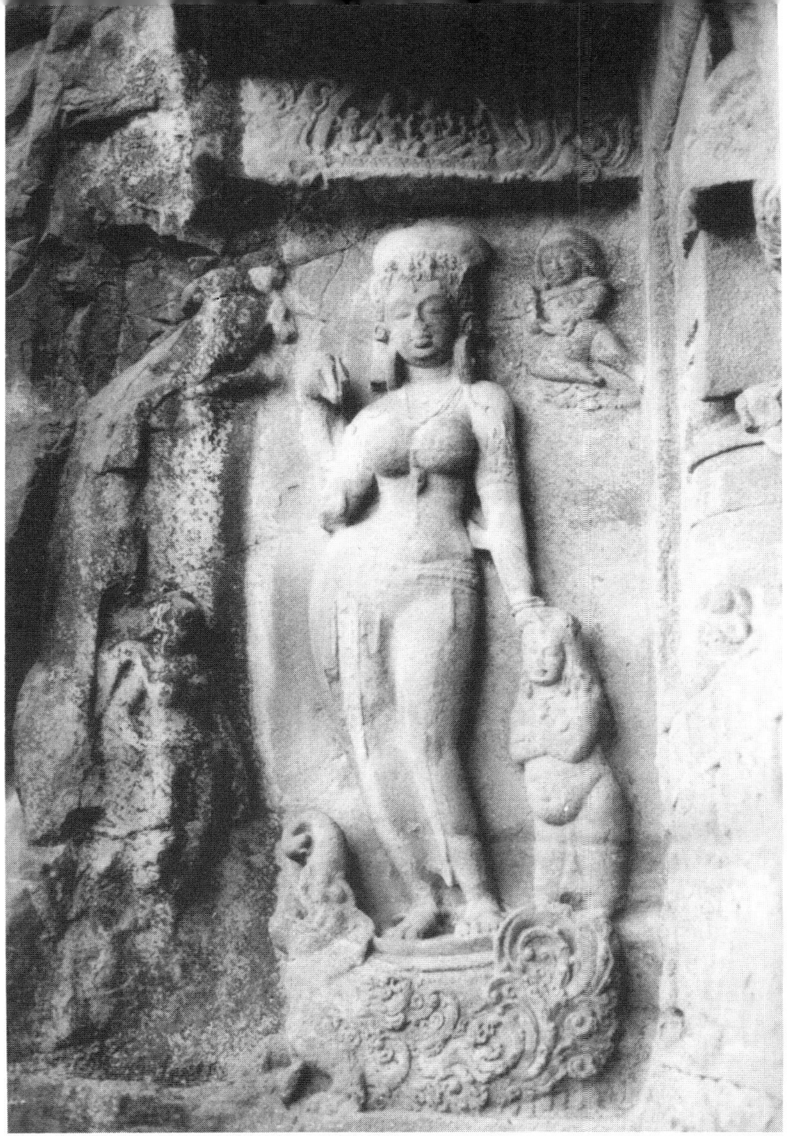

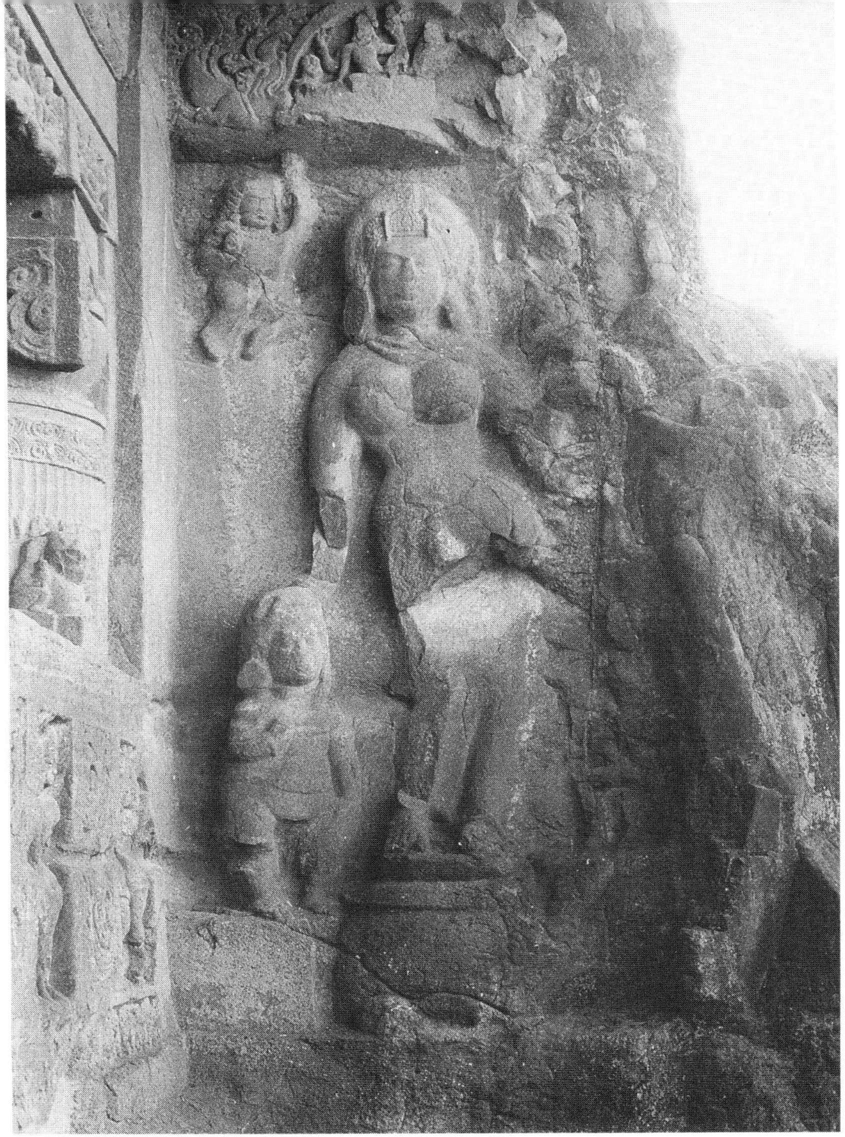

Fig. 23 Cave 21 Yamunā

Fig. 22 Cave 21 Gaṅgā

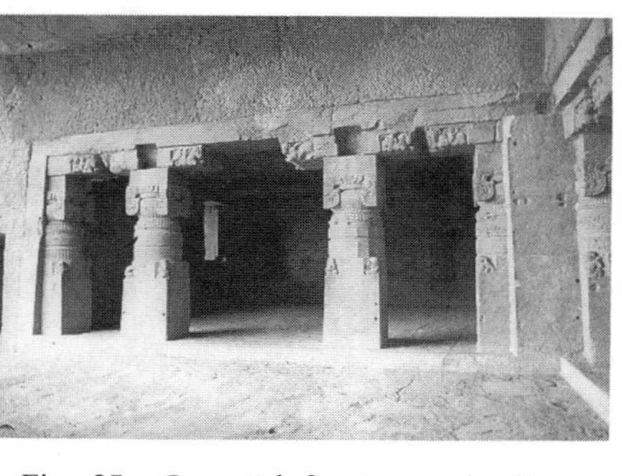

Fig. 24   Cave 21 corner pilaster

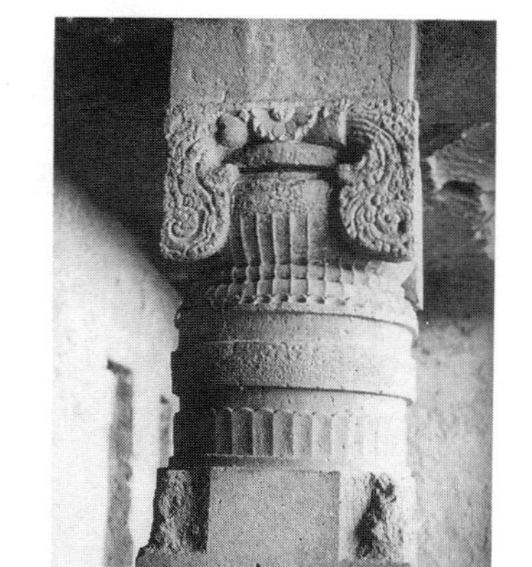

Fig. 25   Cave 6 left wing and pillars

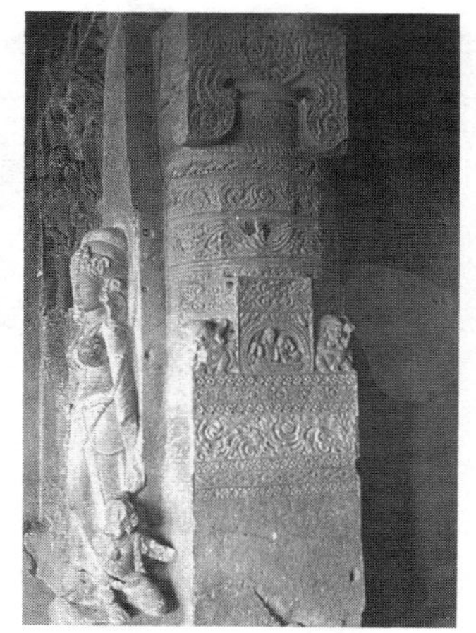

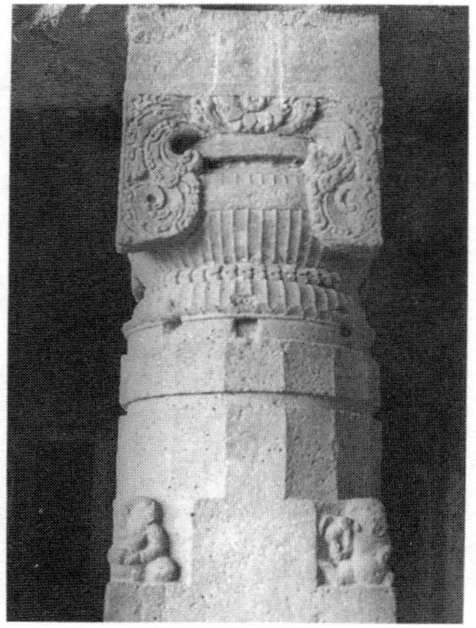

Fig. 26   Cave 6 pillar detail

Fig. 27   Cave 6 pillar detail

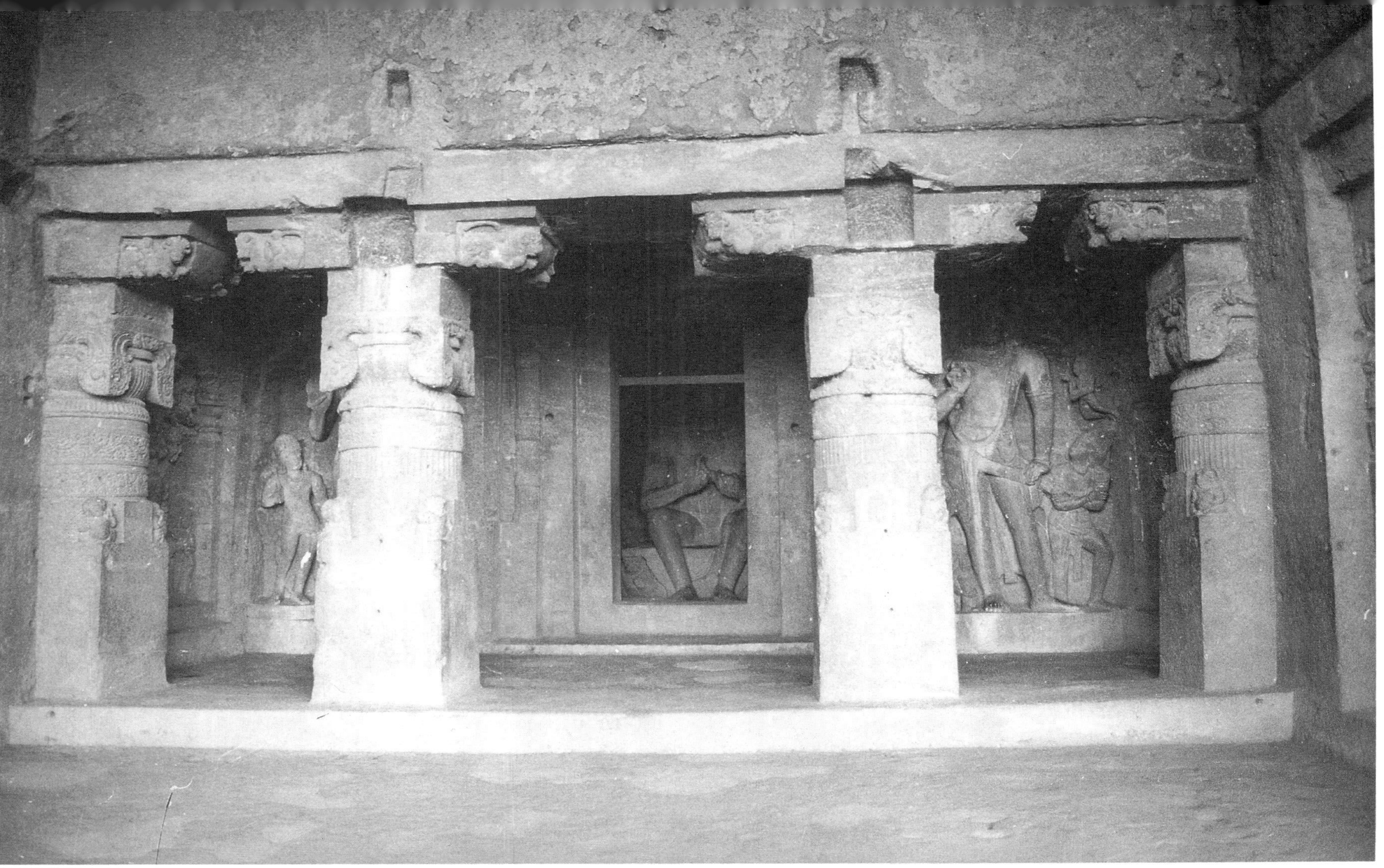

Fig. 28 Cave 6 view of antechamber and shrine image

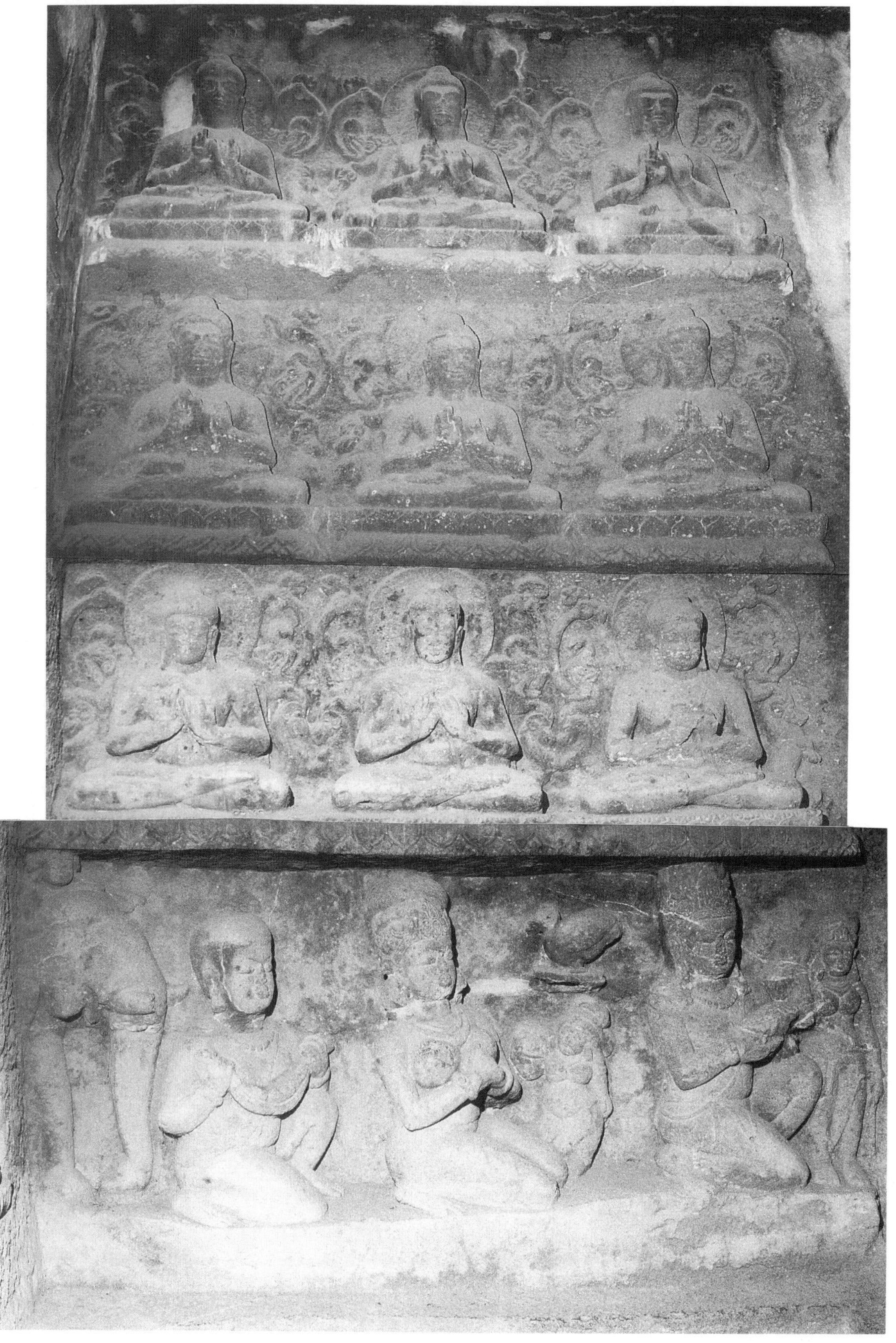

Fig. 29   Cave 6 shrine, left *maṇḍala*

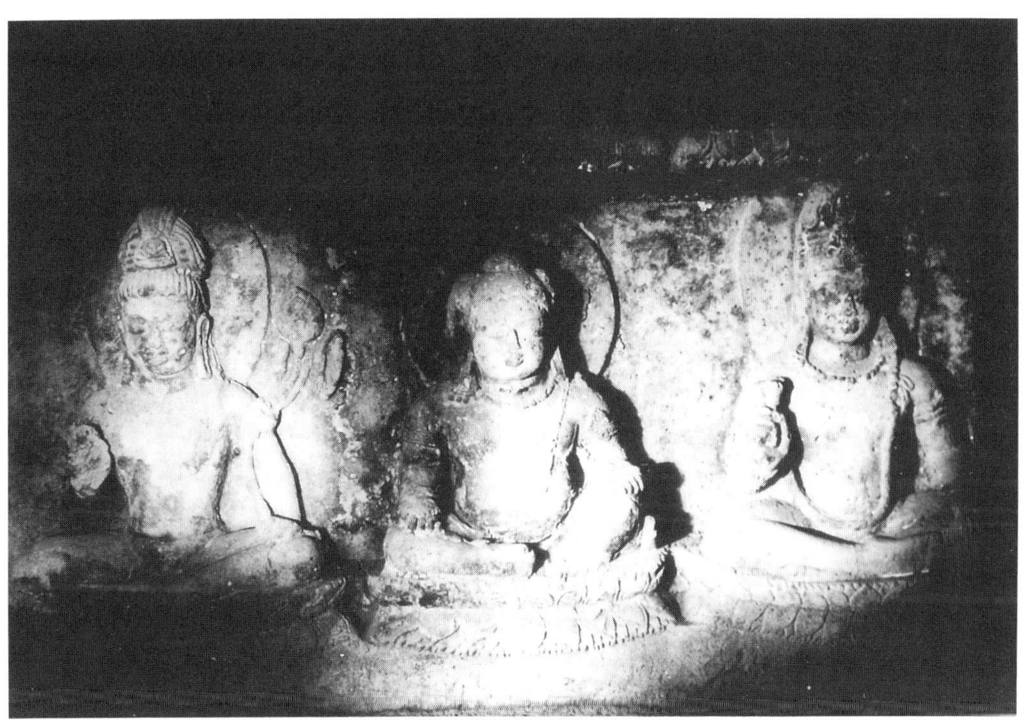

Fig. 30   Cave 6 shrine, right *maṇḍala*, lowest register

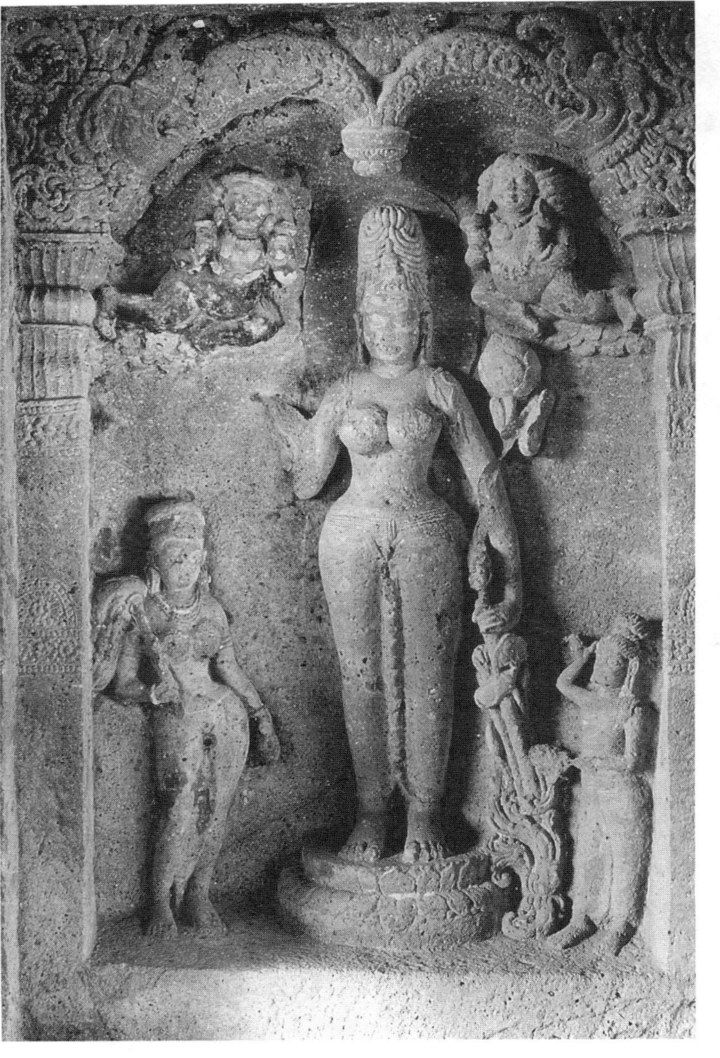

Fig. 31 Cave 6 antechamber, Bhṛkuṭī (AIIS)

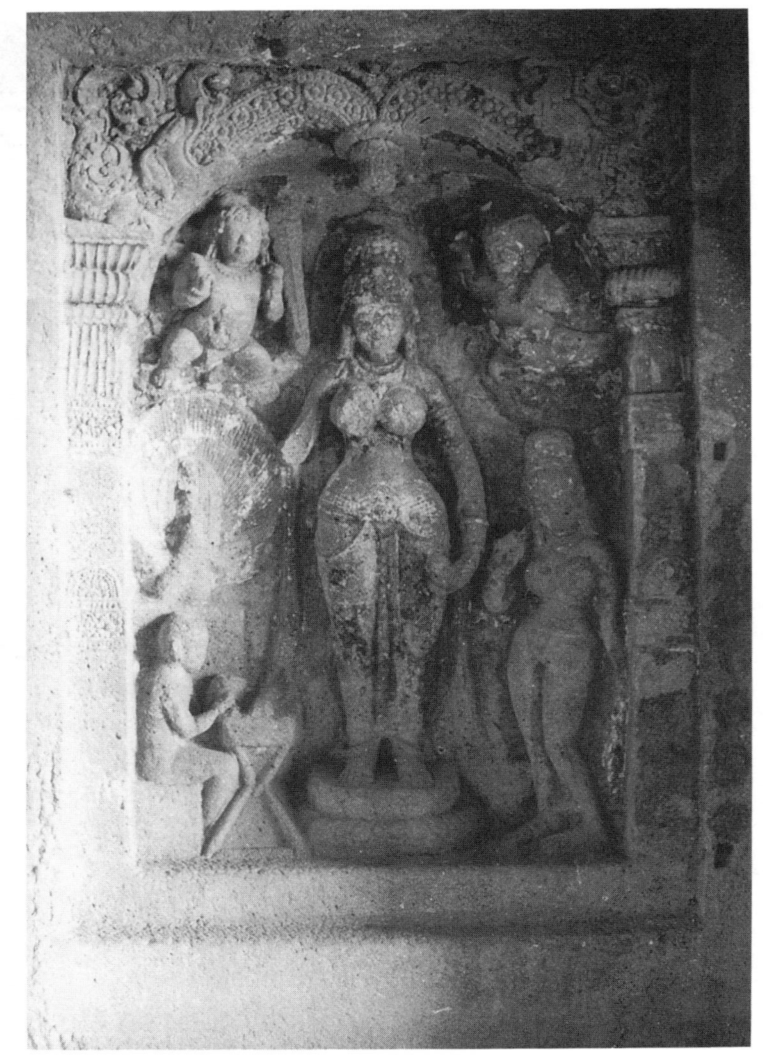

Fig. 32 Cave 6 antechamber, Mahāmāyūrī

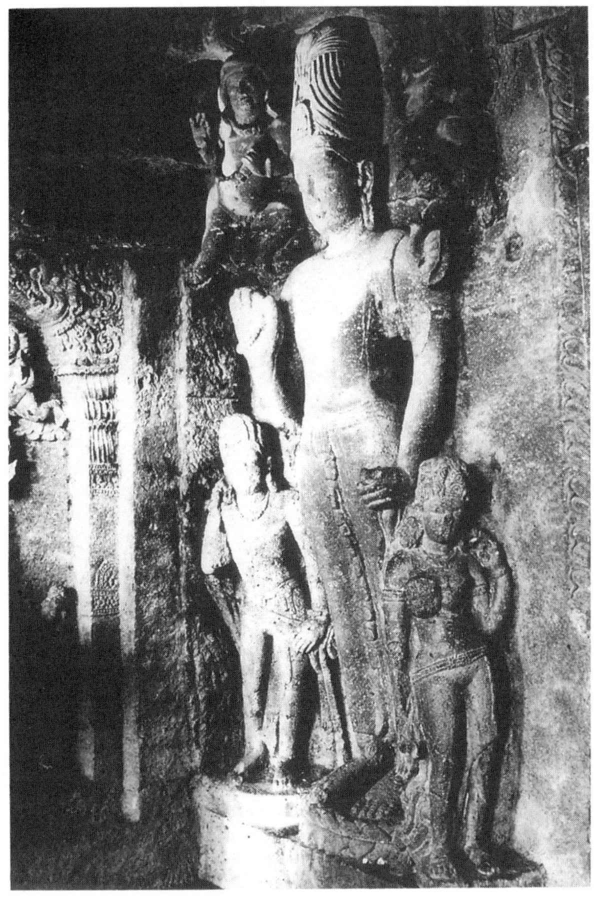

Fig. 33   Cave 6 shrine door, Avalokiteśvara (AAAUM)

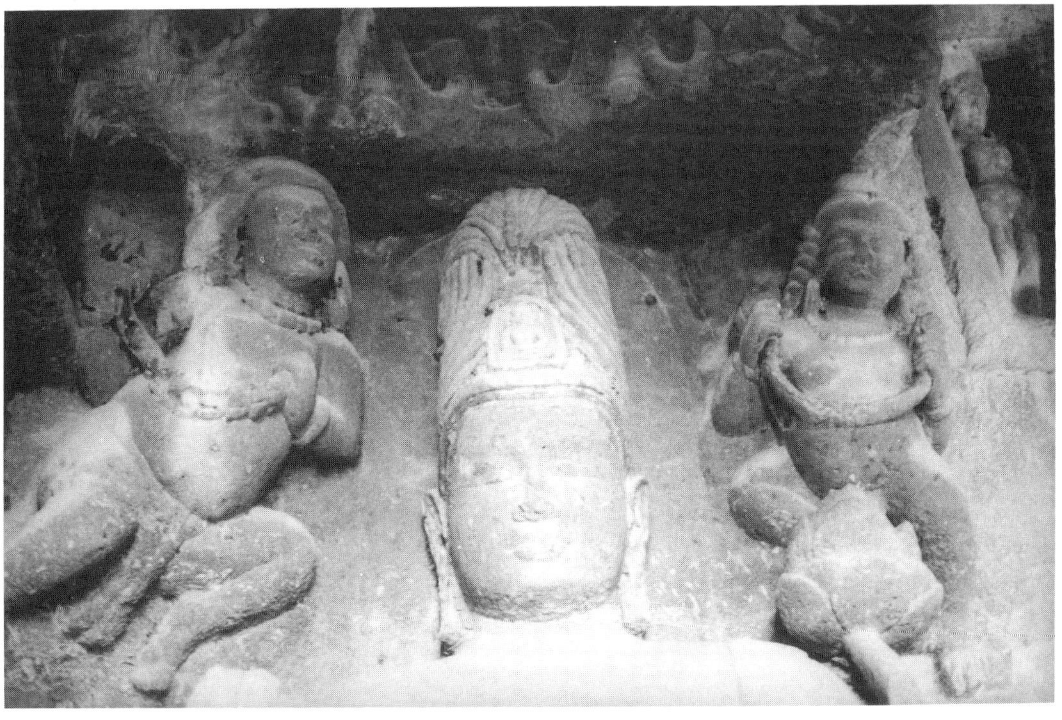

Fig. 34   Cave 6 shrine door, Avalokiteśvara, detail of headdress

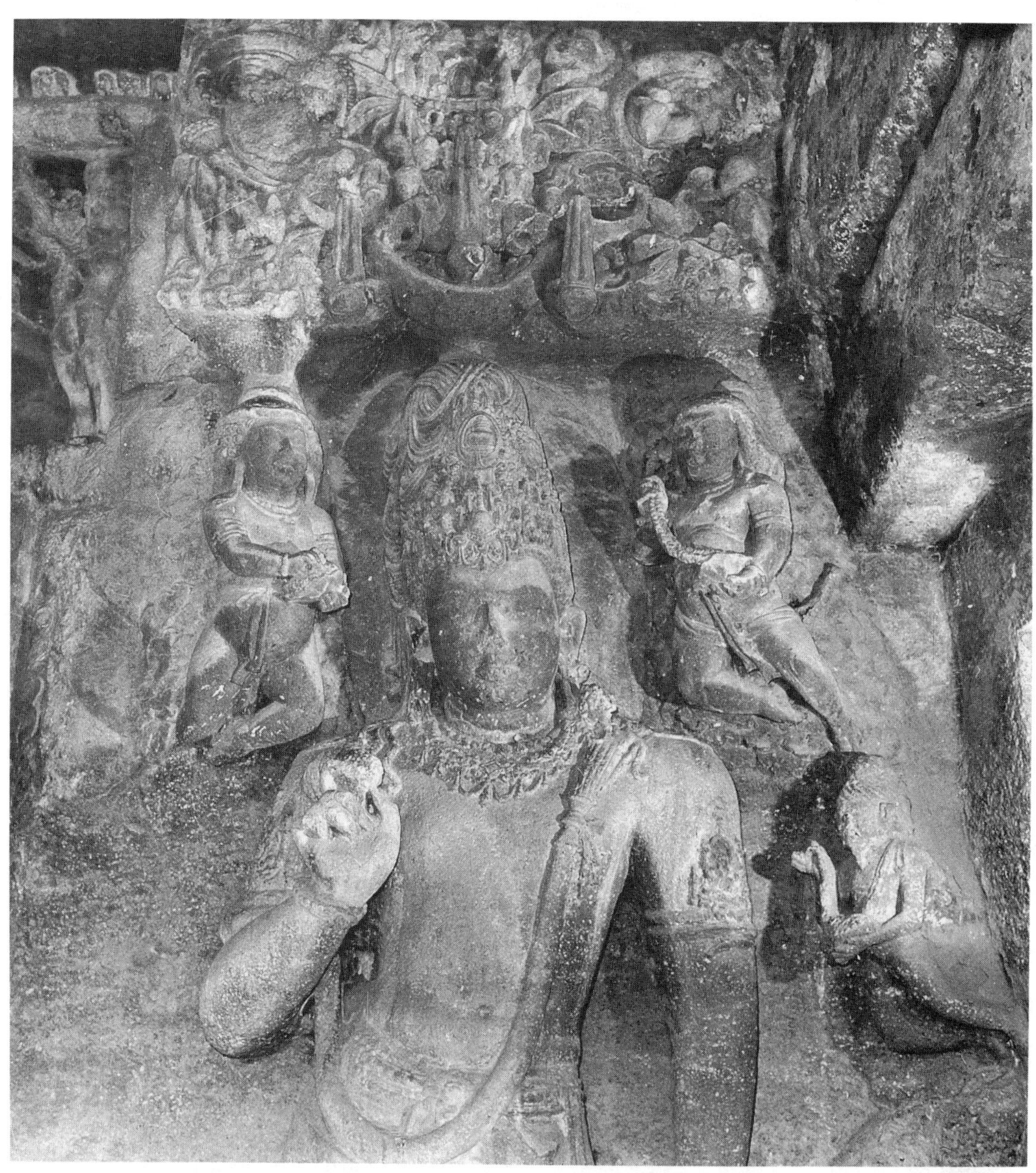

Fig. 35   Cave 6 shrine door, Maitreya (AIIS)

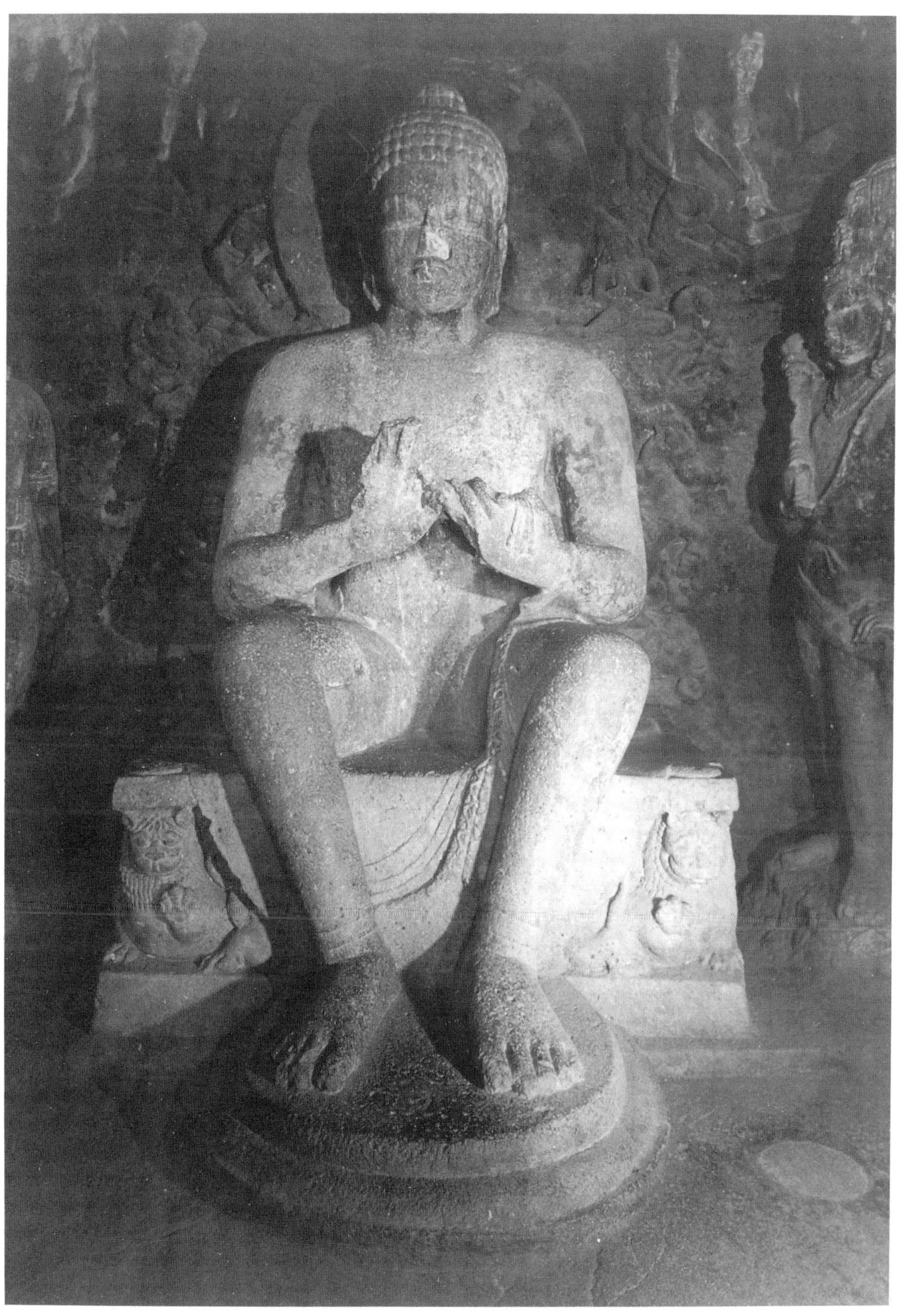

Fig. 36   Cave 6 shrine, Buddha (AAAUM, Suresh Vasant)

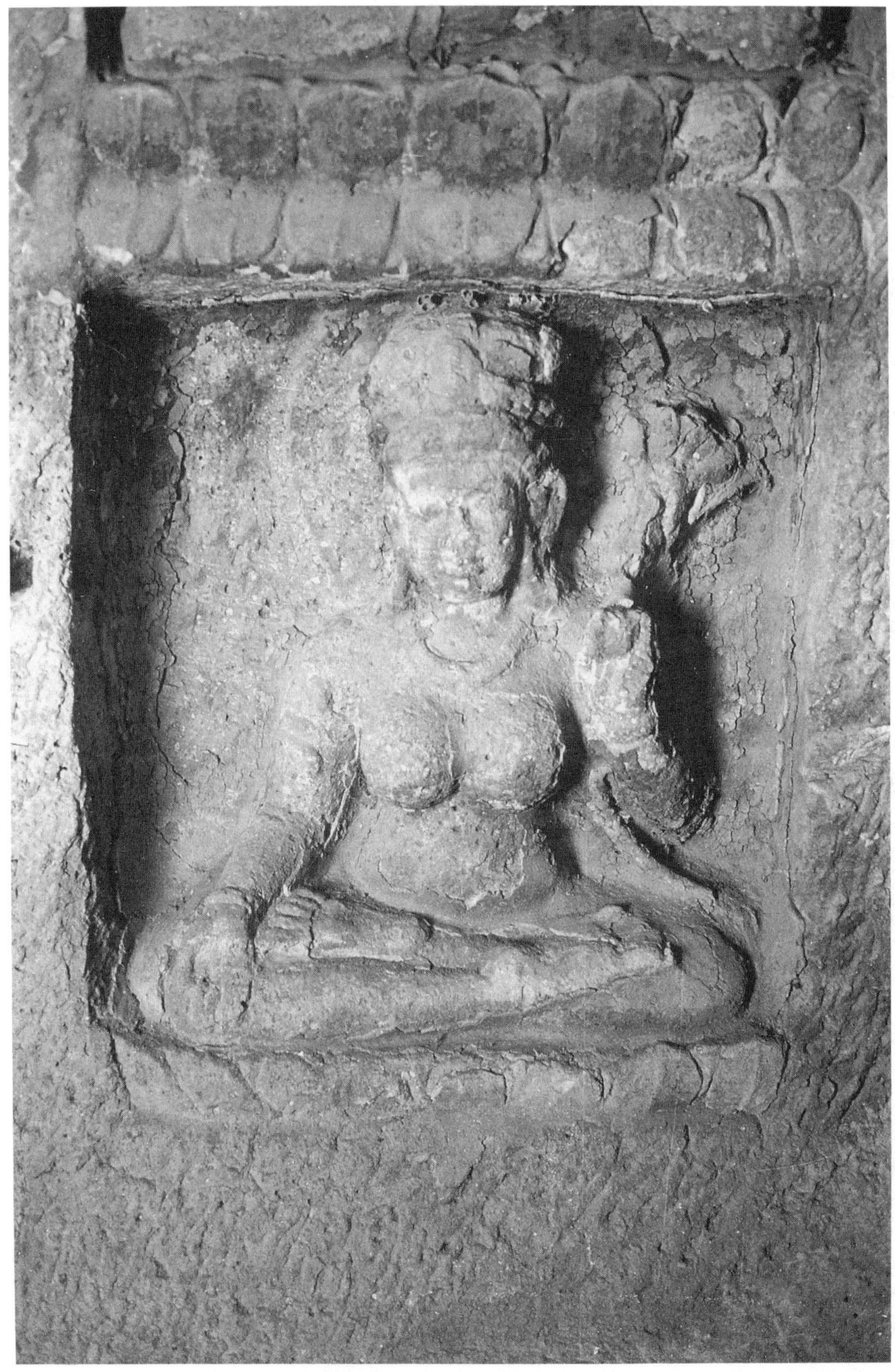

Fig. 37   Cave 6 shrine, Tārā

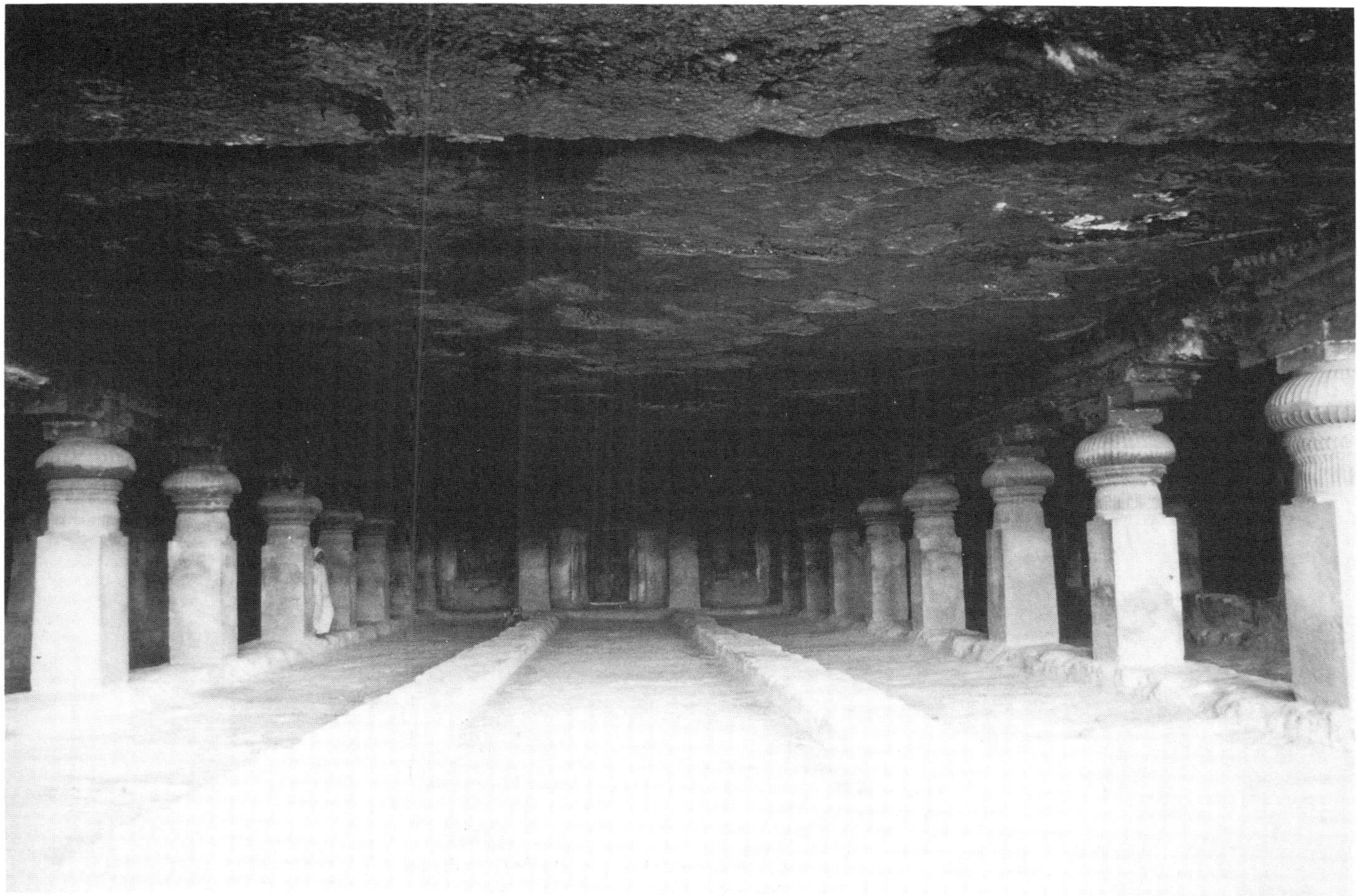

Fig. 38   Cave 5 view of hall

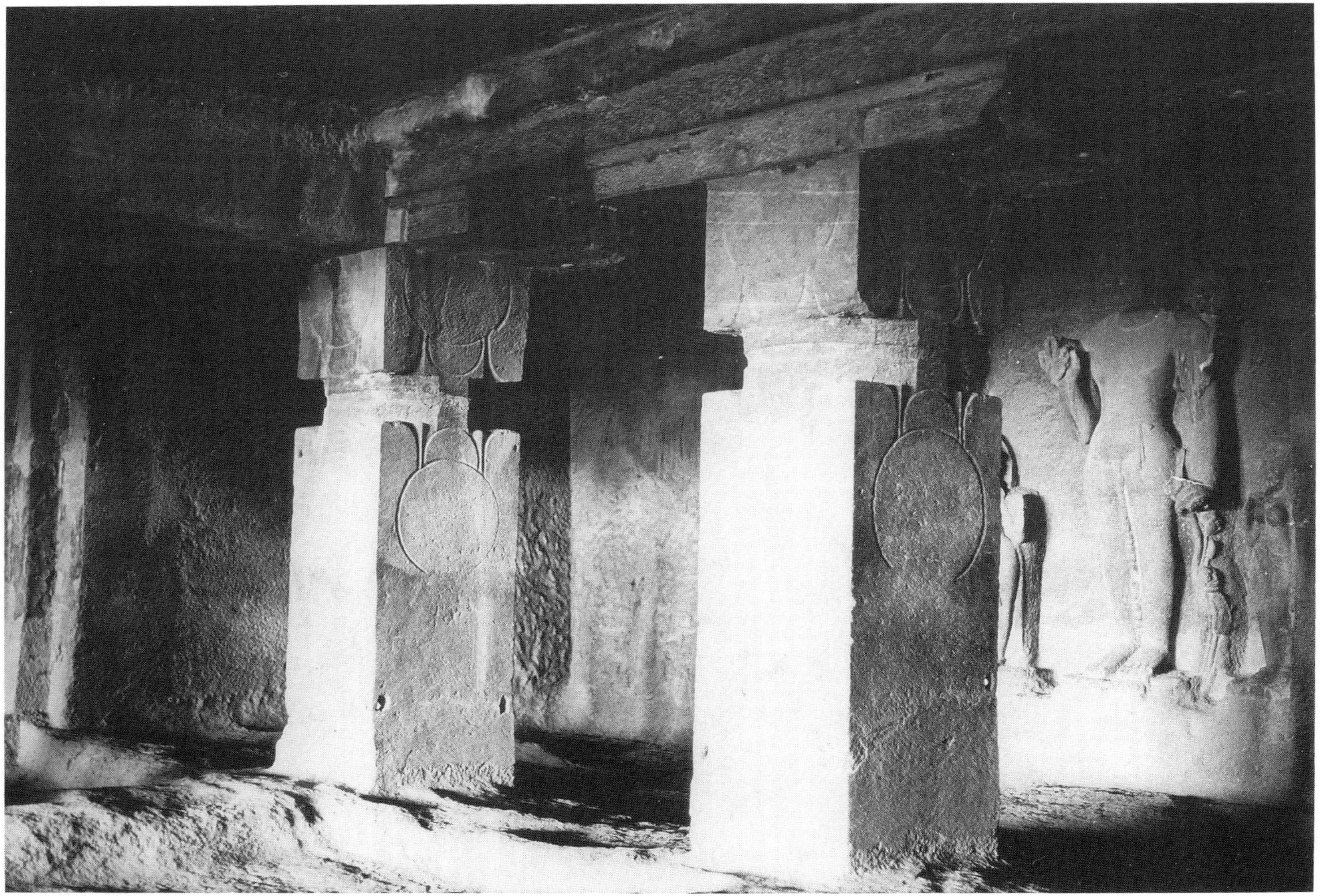

Fig. 39 Cave 5 rear pillars

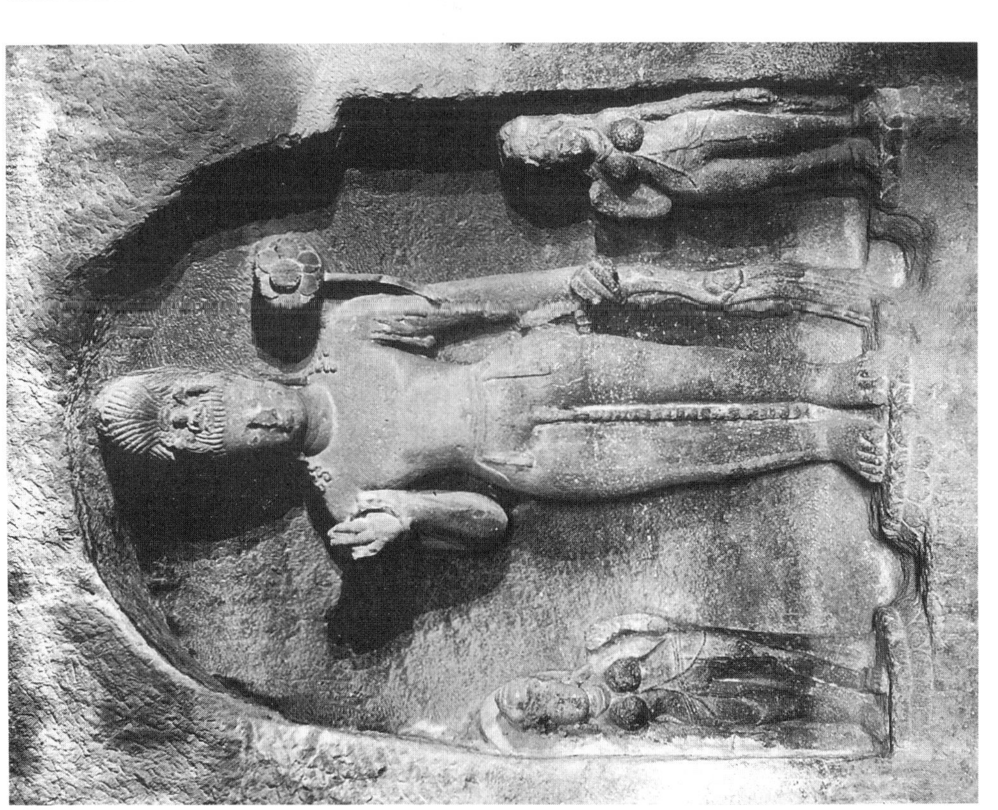

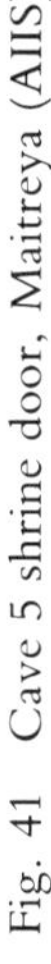

Fig. 41 Cave 5 shrine door, Maitreya (AIIS)

Fig. 40 Cave 5 shrine door, Avalokiteśvara (AIIS)

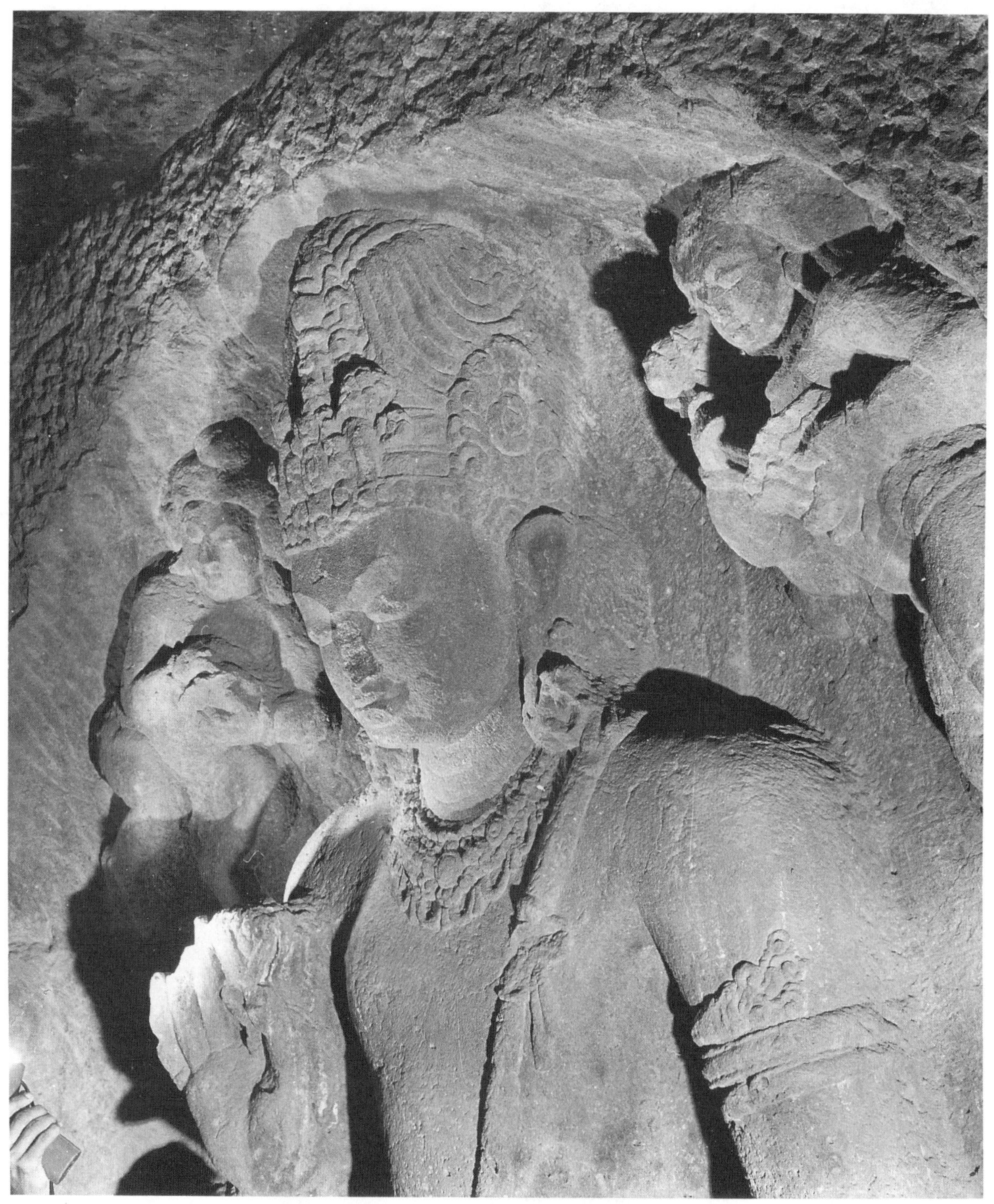

Fig. 42   Cave 5 shrine door, Maitreya close up (AIIS)

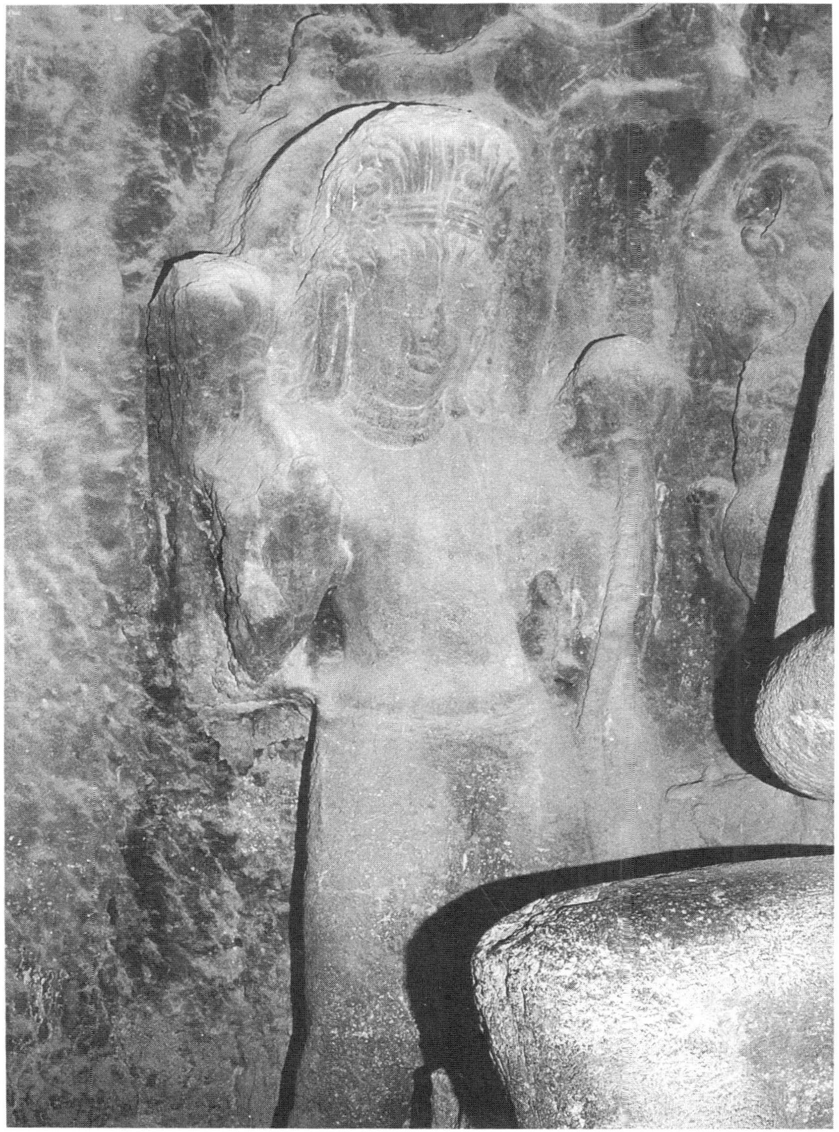

Fig. 43   Cave 5 shrine, Avalokiteśvara

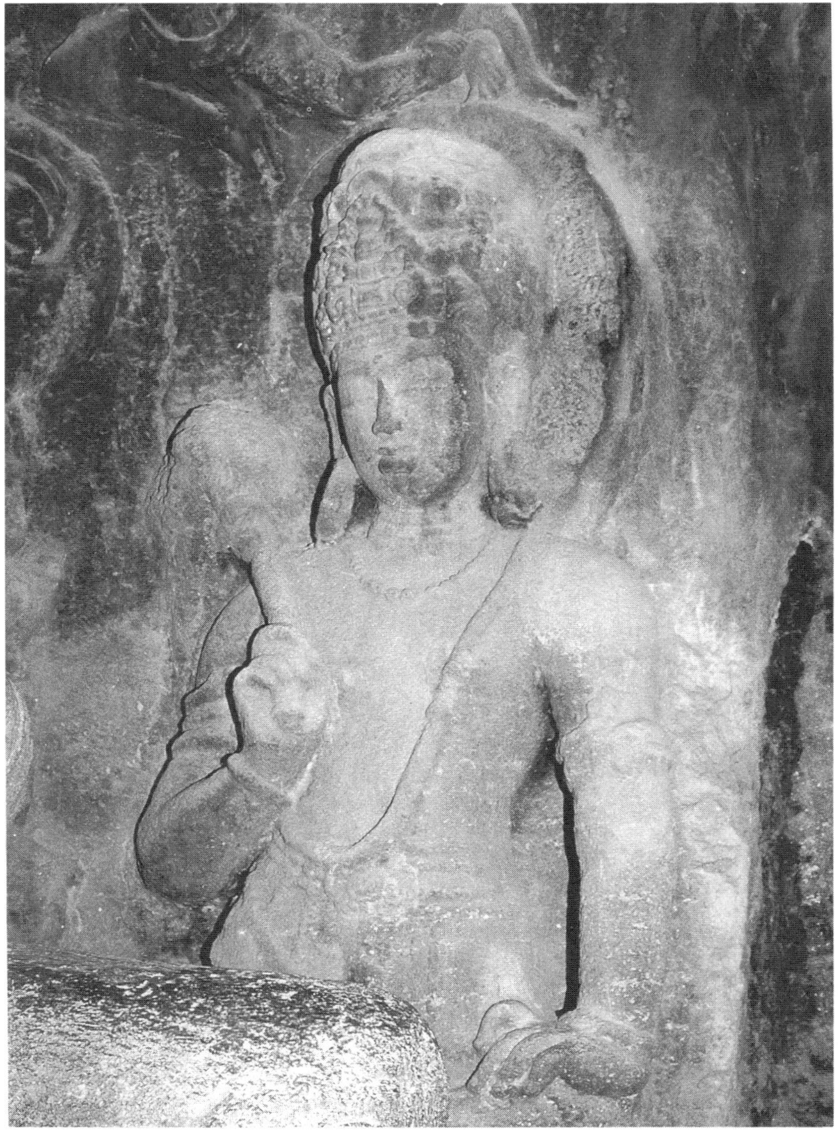

Fig. 44   Cave 5 shrine, Maitreya

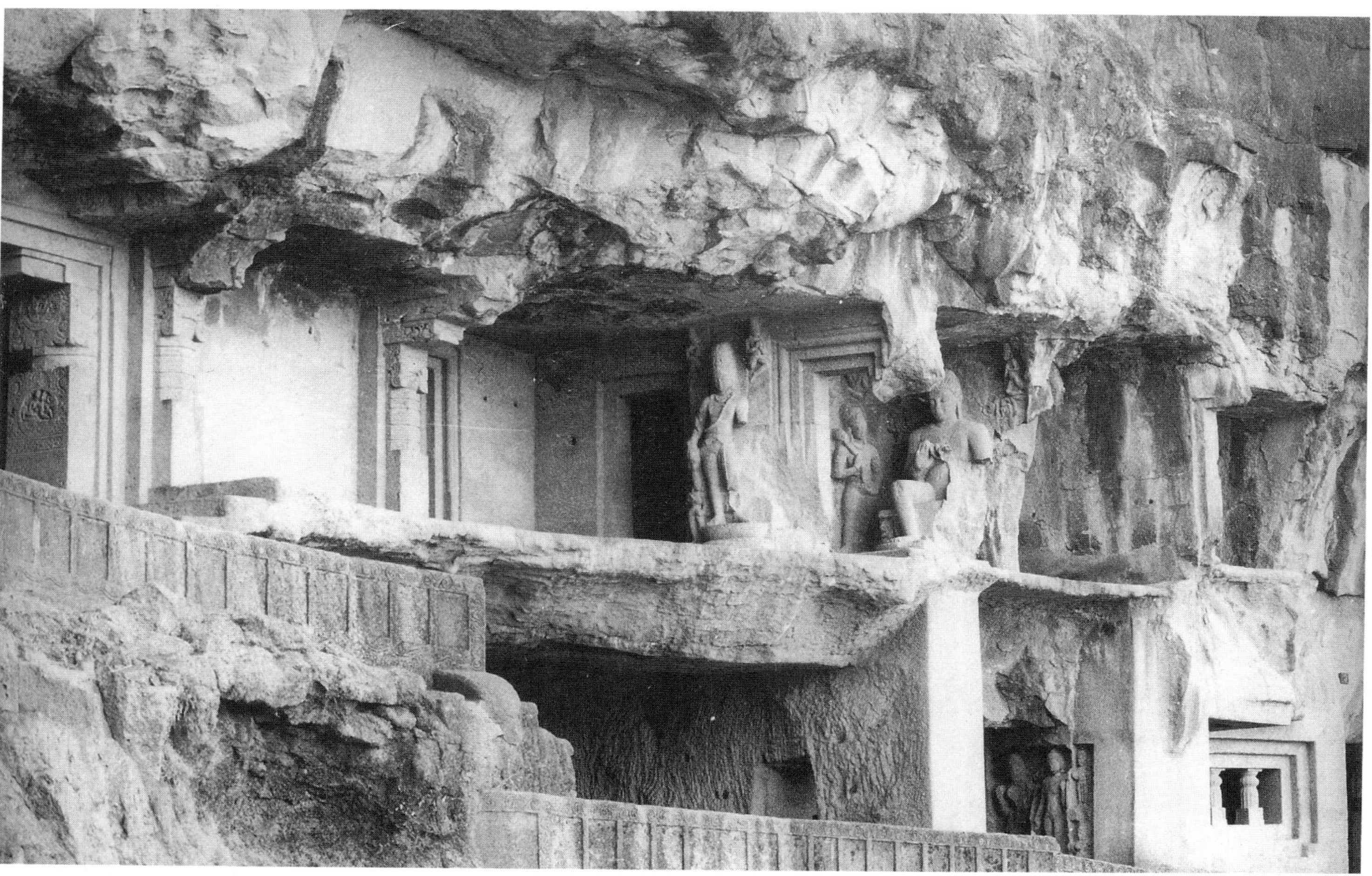

Fig. 45   View of Cave 5 Right Wing and Cave 4, below

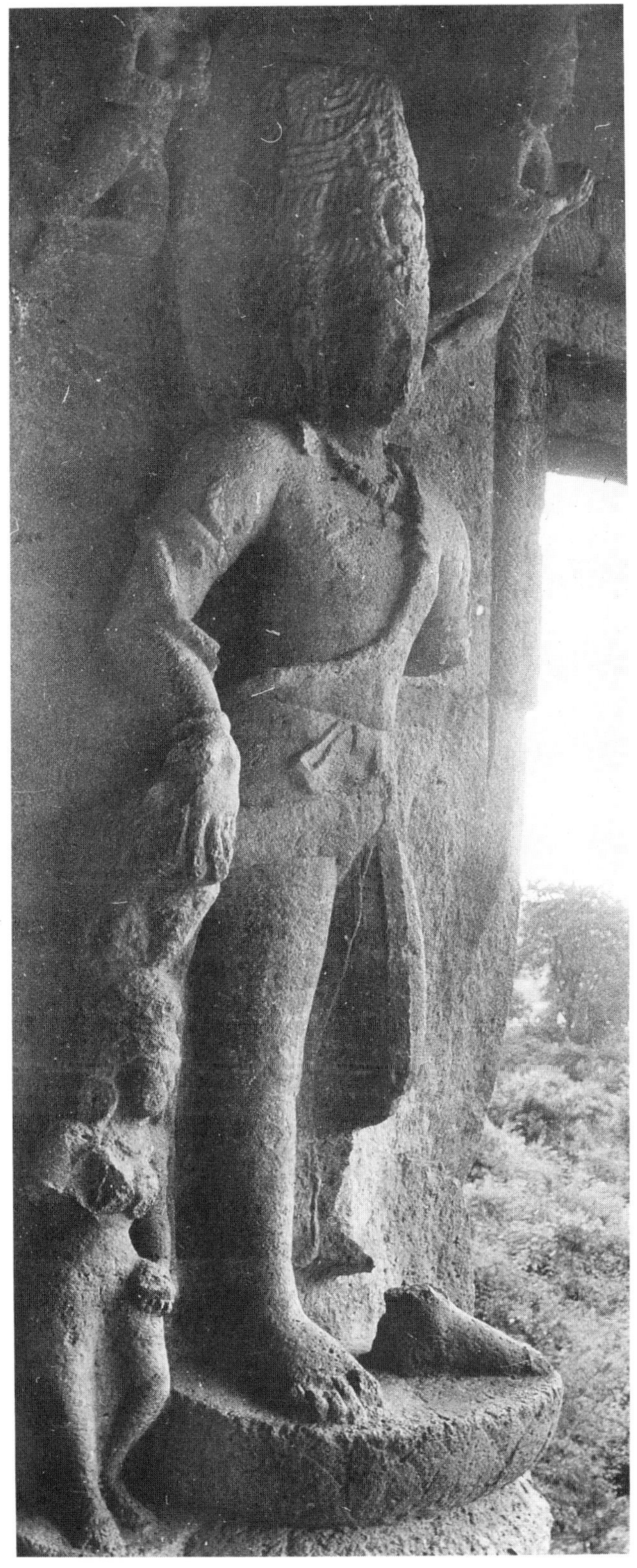

Fig. 46　Cave 5 Right Wing, Maitreya (AIIS)

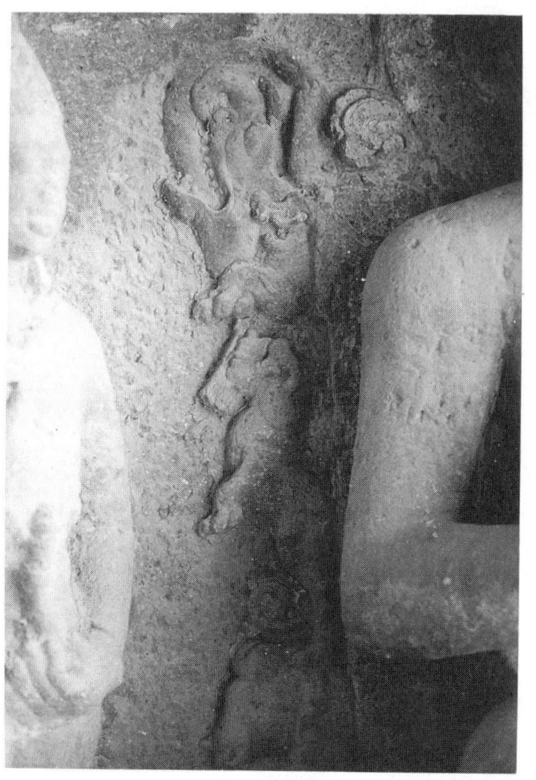

Fig. 47   Cave 5 Right Wing, throne back

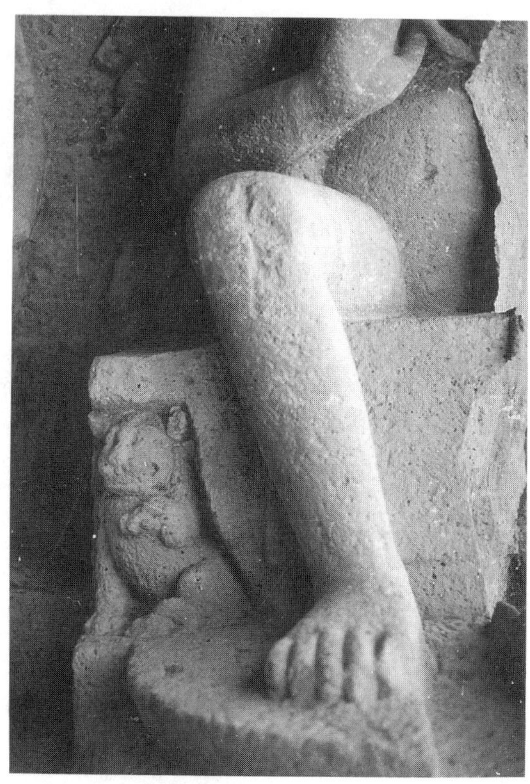

Fig. 48   Cave 5 Right Wing, throne base lion

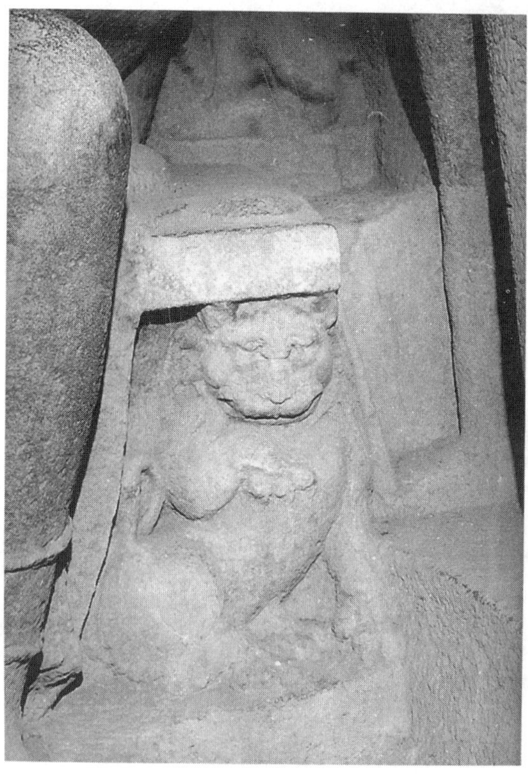

Fig. 49   Cave 8, throne base lion

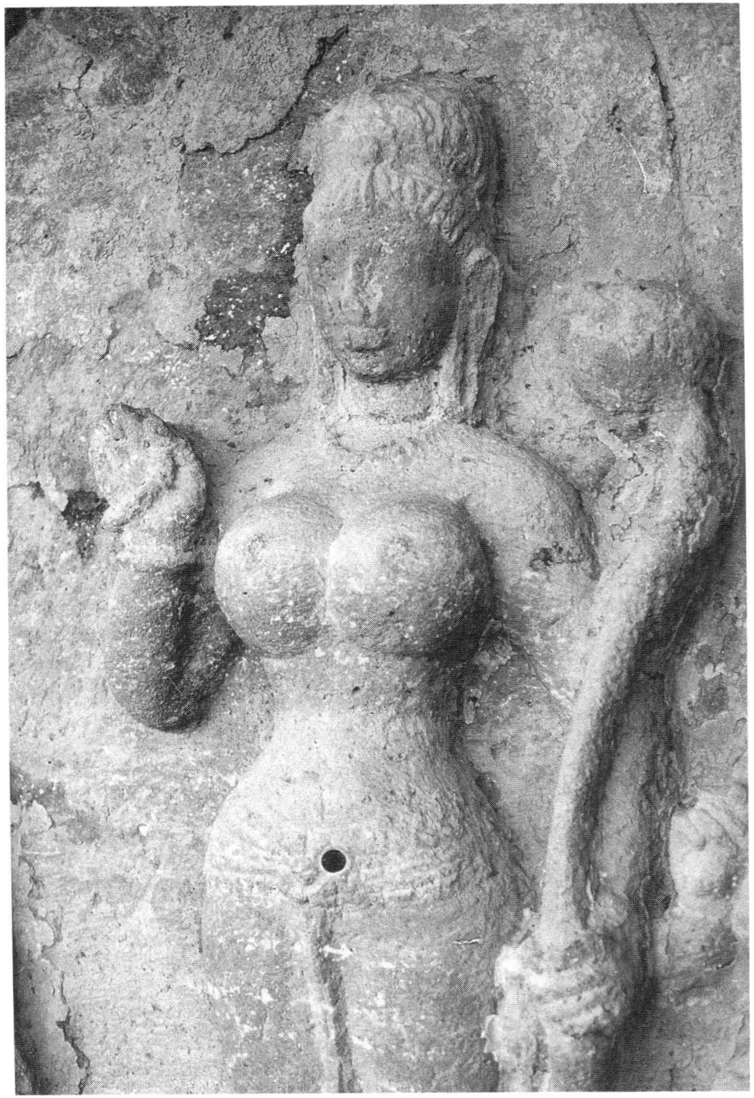

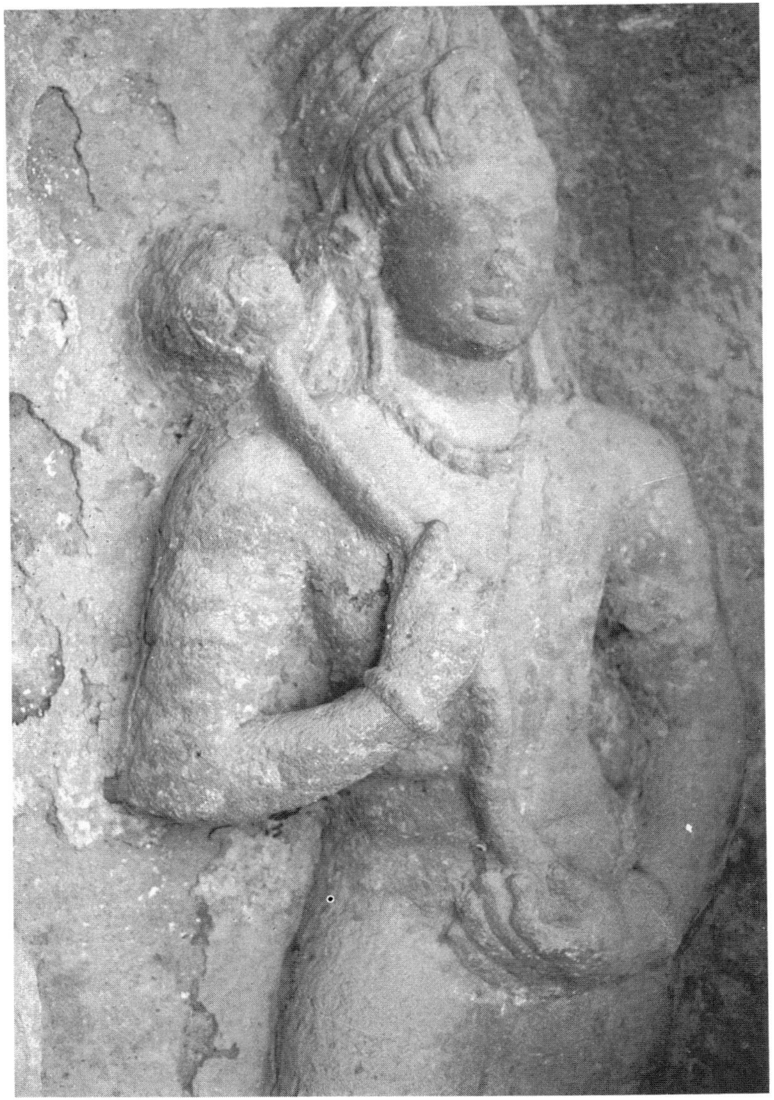

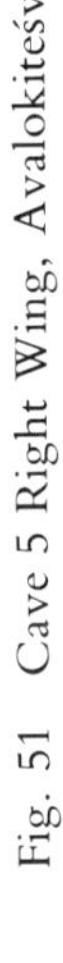

Fig. 51   Cave 5 Right Wing, Avalokiteśvara

Fig. 50   Cave 5 Right Wing, Bhṛkuṭī

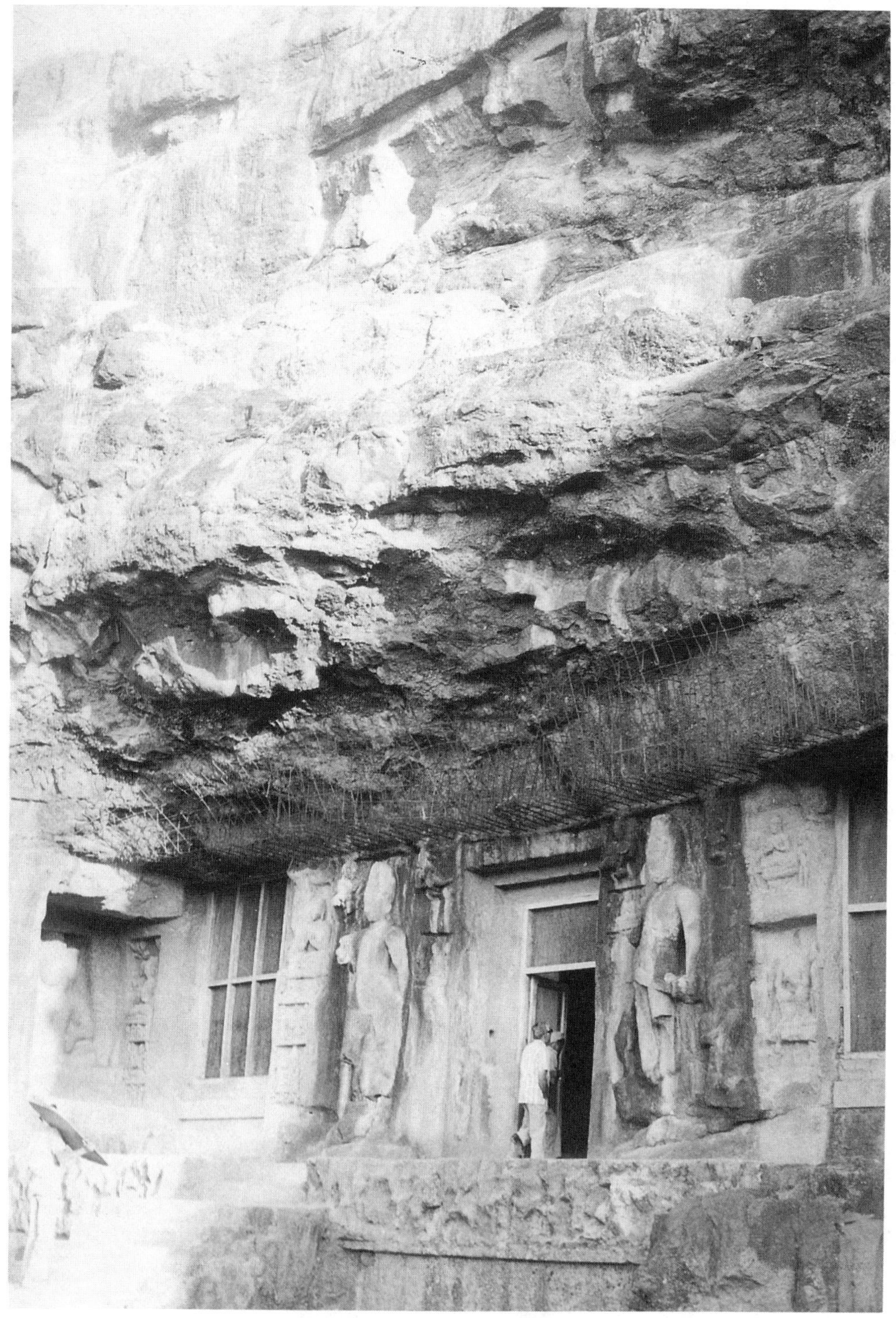

Fig. 52 Cave 2 façade

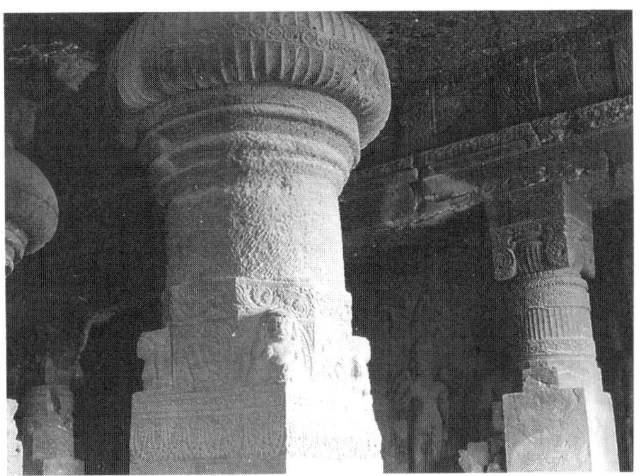

Fig. 53   Cave 2 pillars

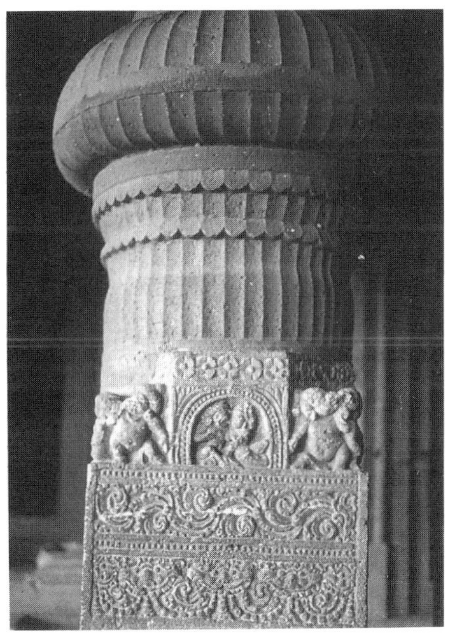

Fig. 54   Cave 5 pillar

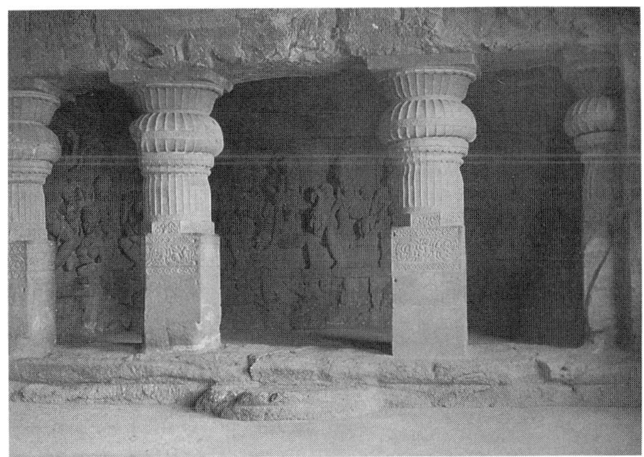

Fig. 55   Cave 21 pillars

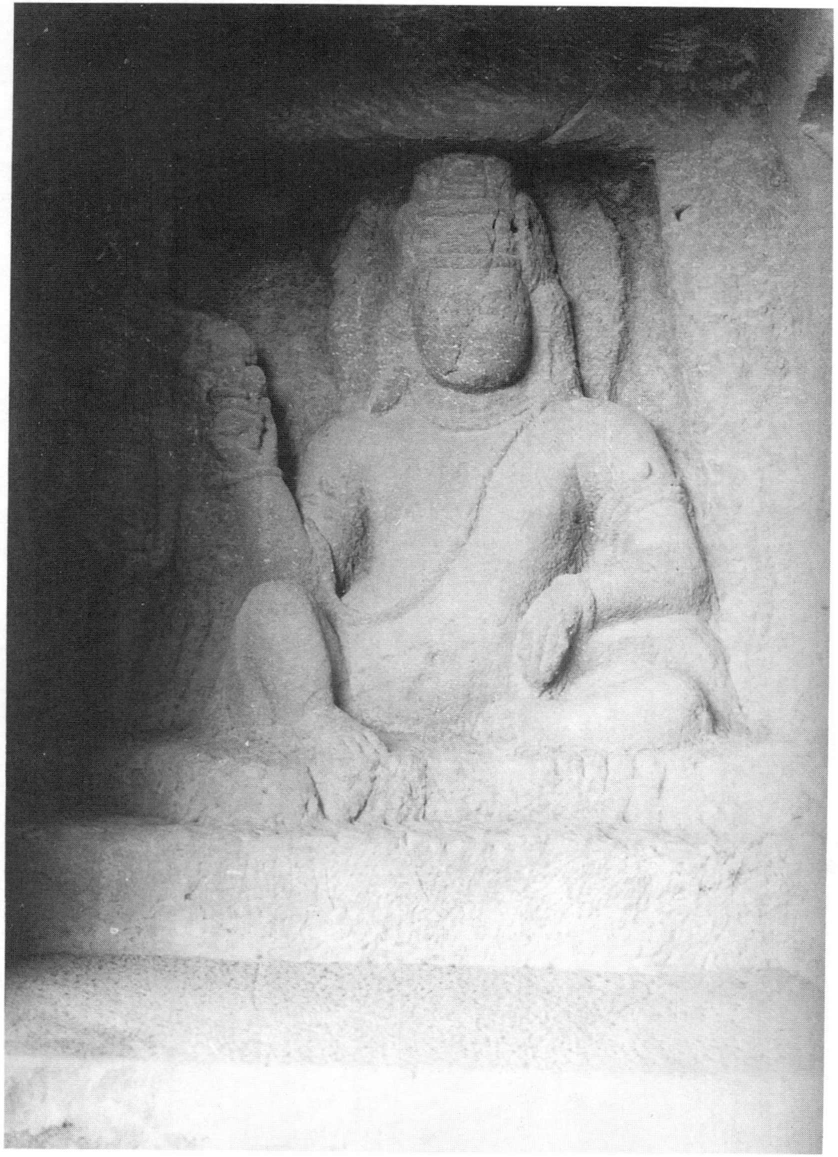

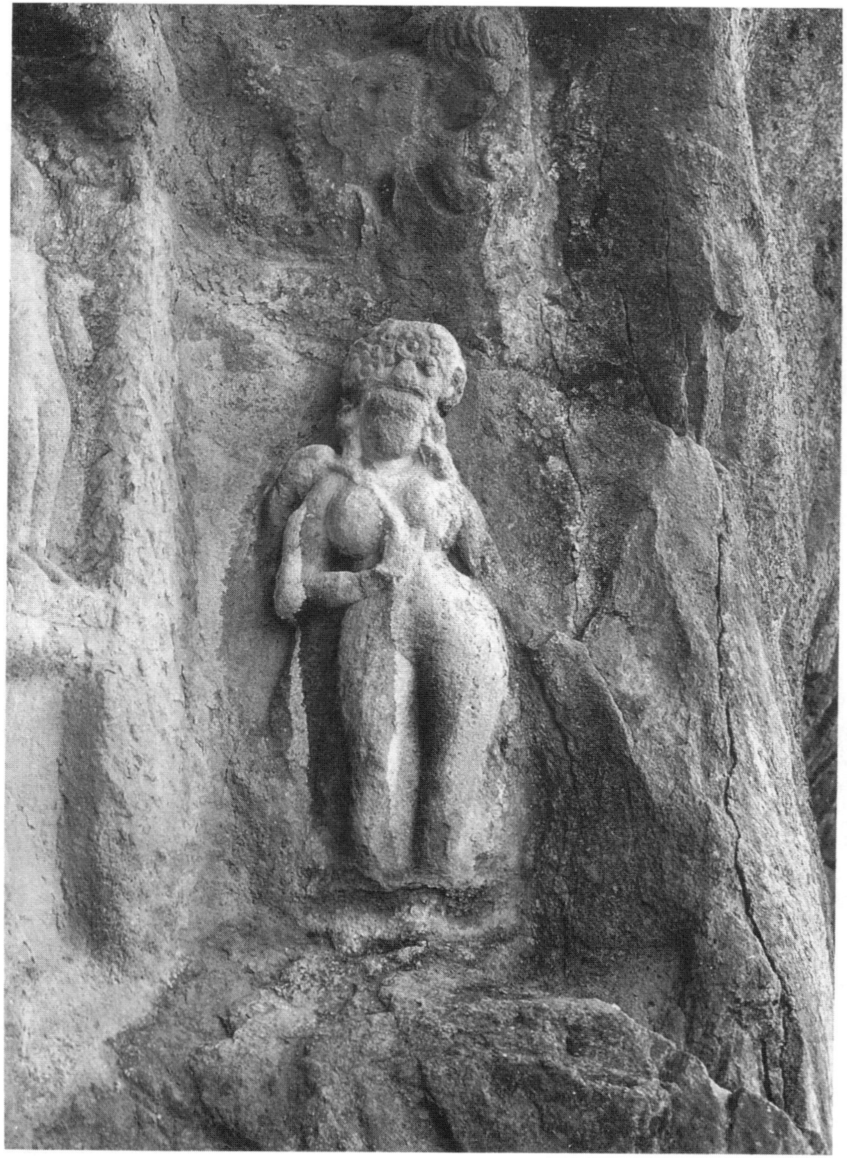

Fig. 57 Cave 2 verandah, female figure

Fig. 56 Cave 2 verandah, Jambhala

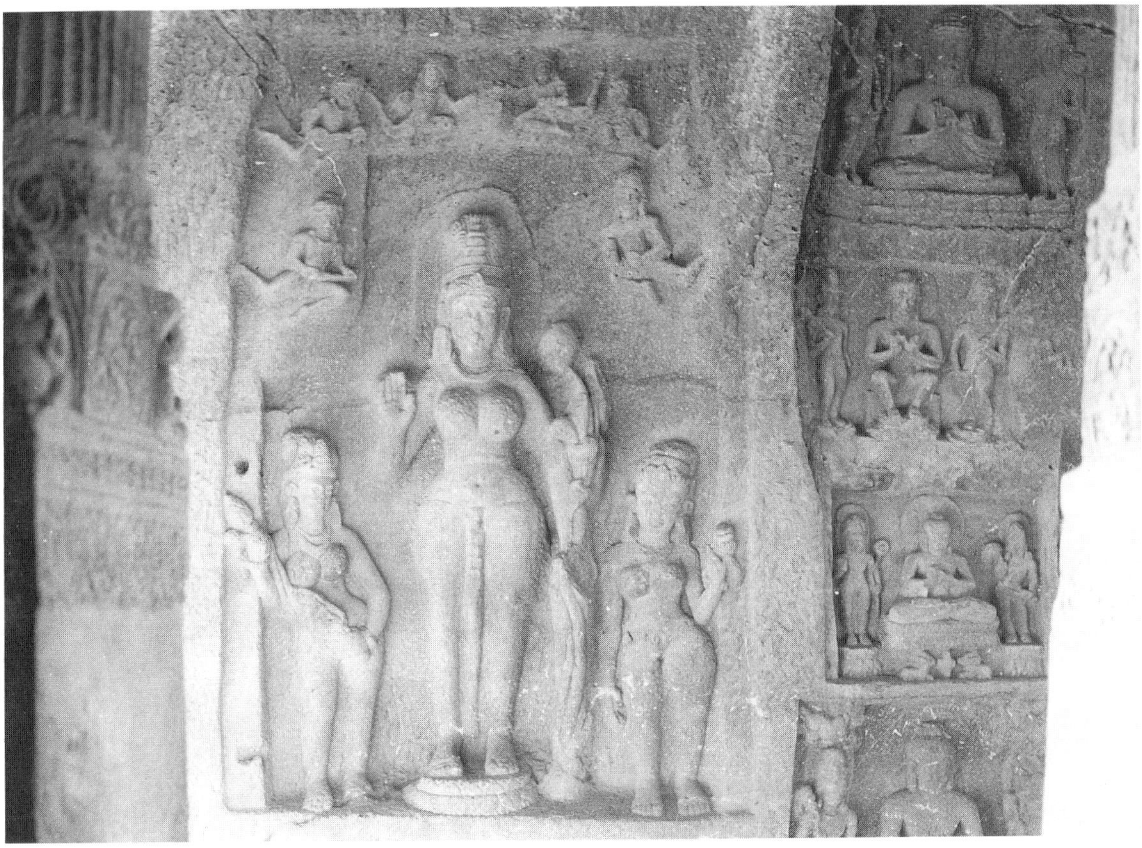

Fig. 58   Cave 2 Bhṛkuṭī

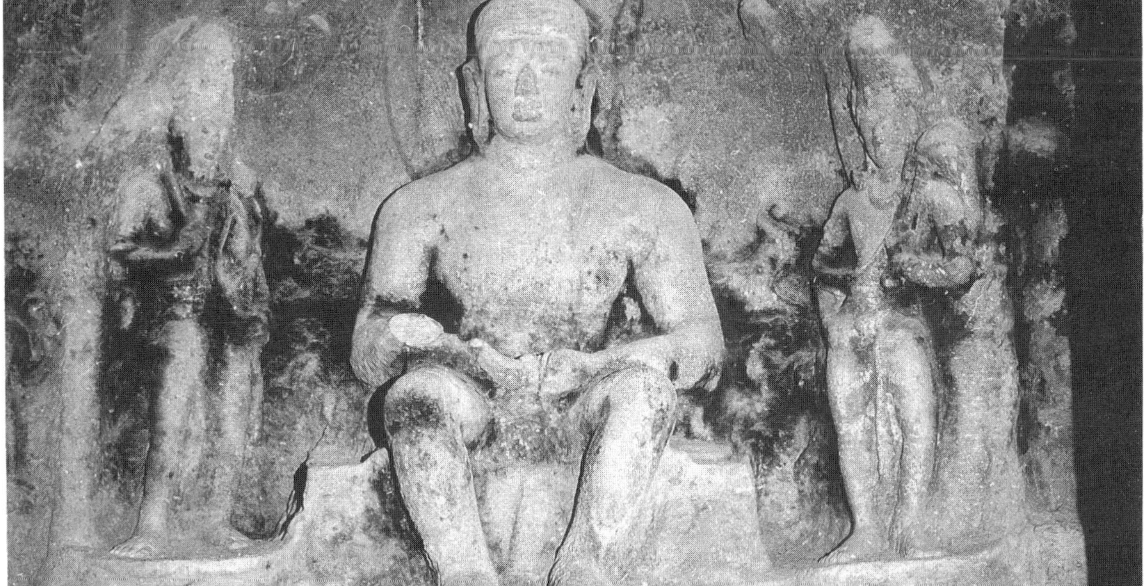

Fig. 59   Cave 2 left aisle, Buddha in first niche

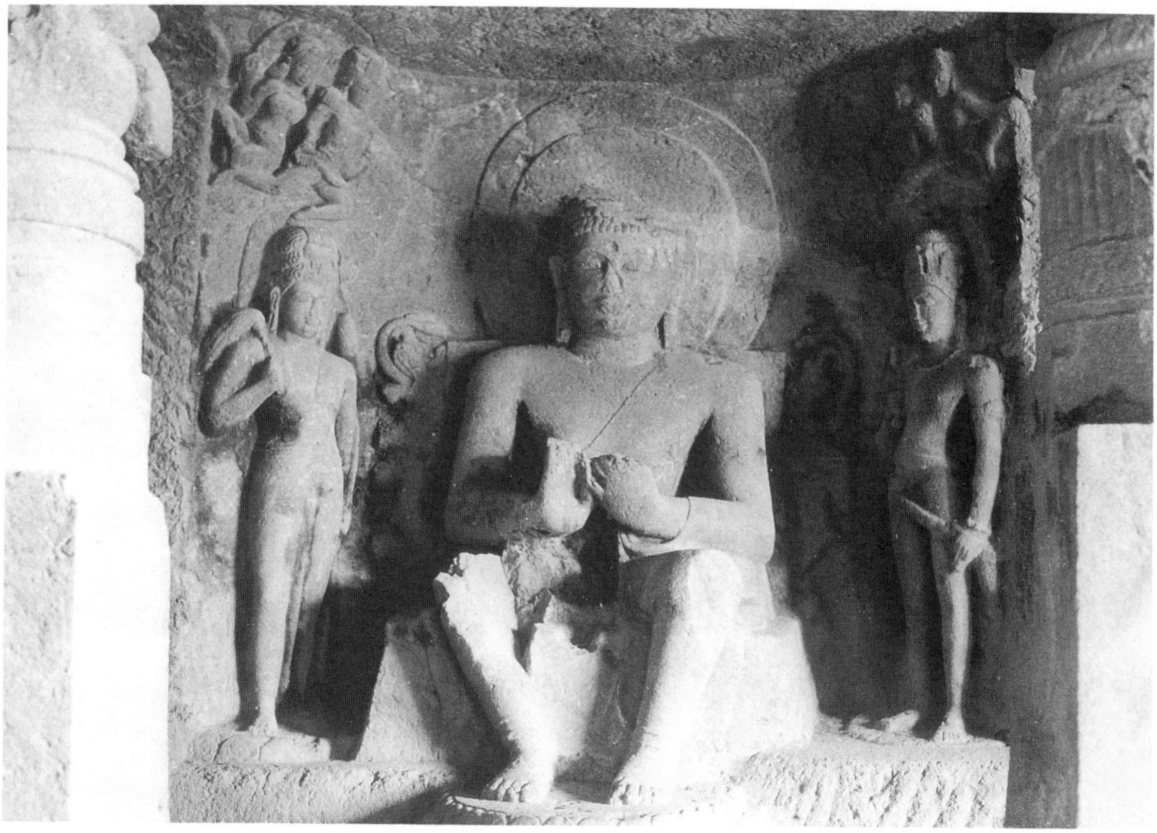

Fig. 60   Cave 2 right aisle, Buddha in first niche

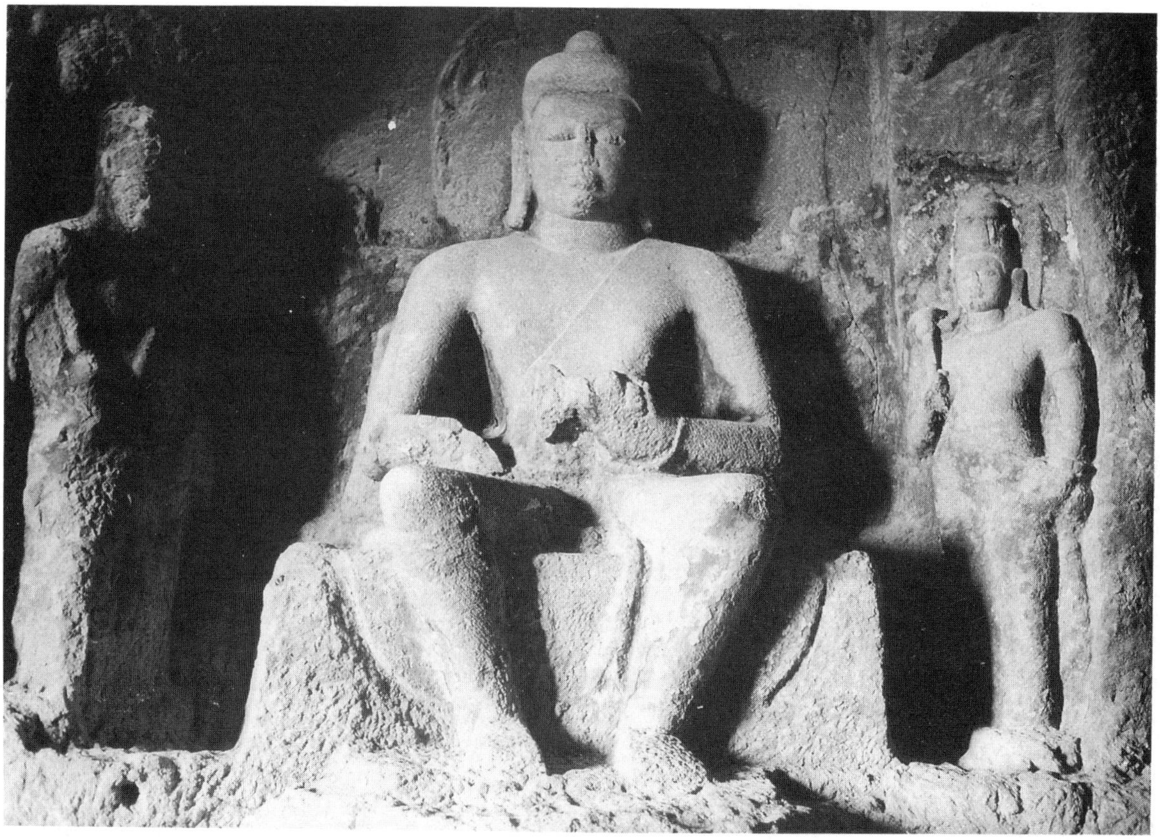

Fig. 61   Cave 2 left aisle, Buddha in second niche

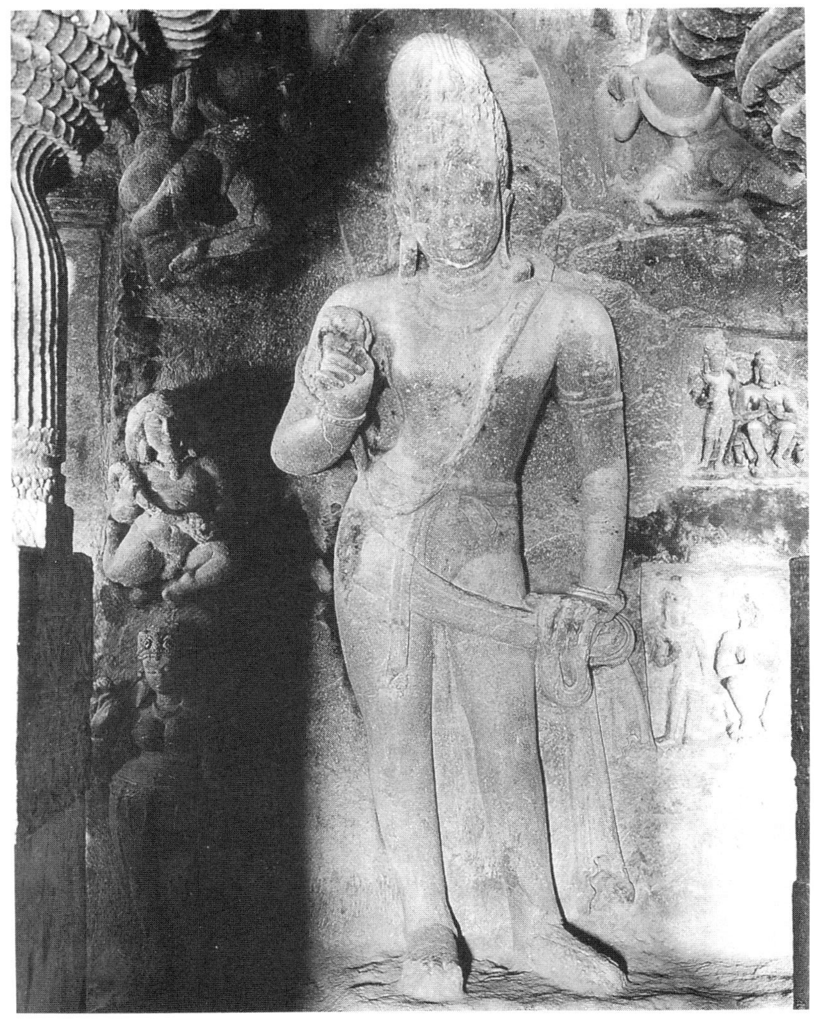

Fig. 62   Cave 2 shrine door, Avalokiteśvara

Fig. 63   Cave 2 shrine door, Maitreya (AIIS)

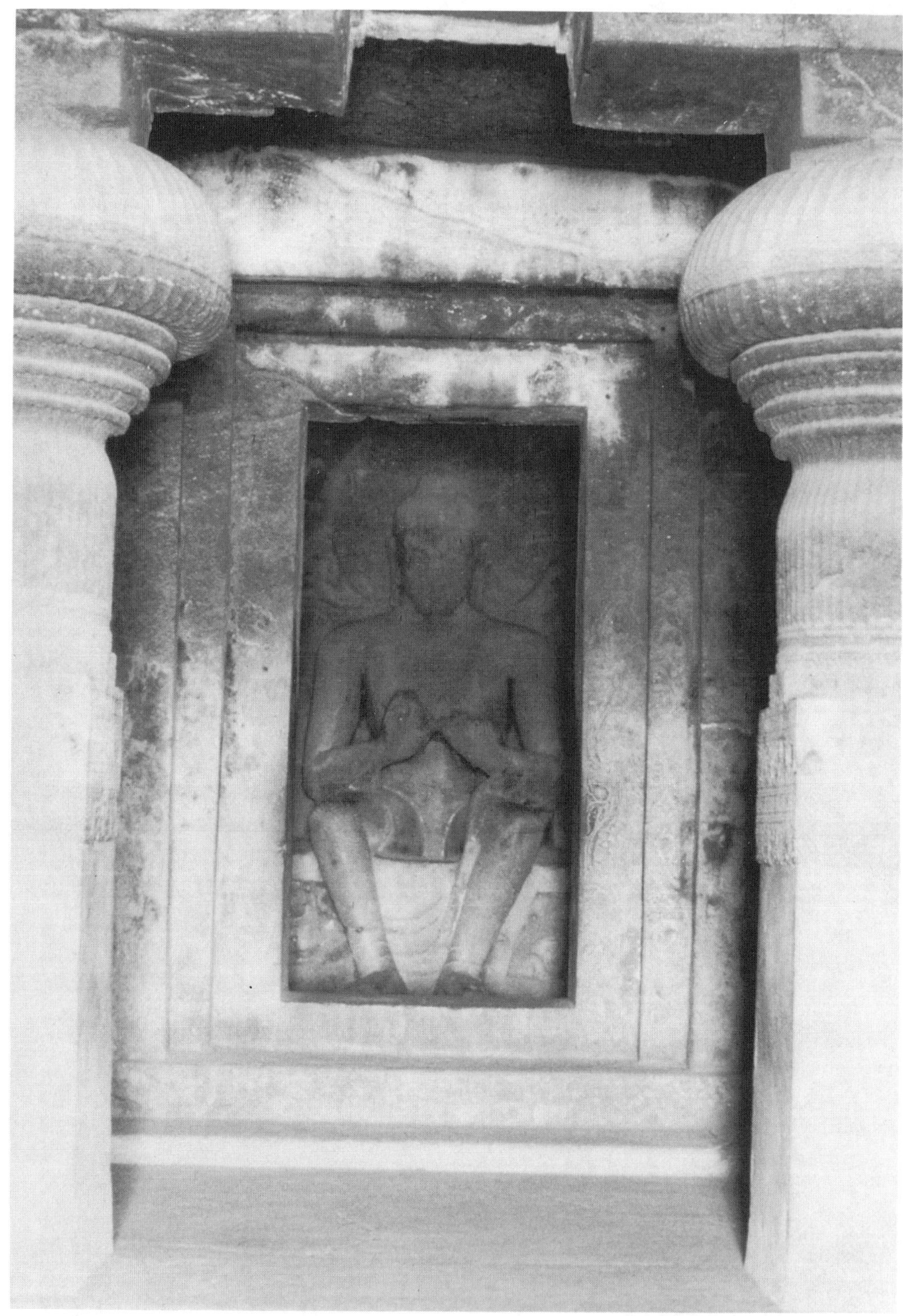

Fig. 64   Cave 2 view of shrine door and central Buddha

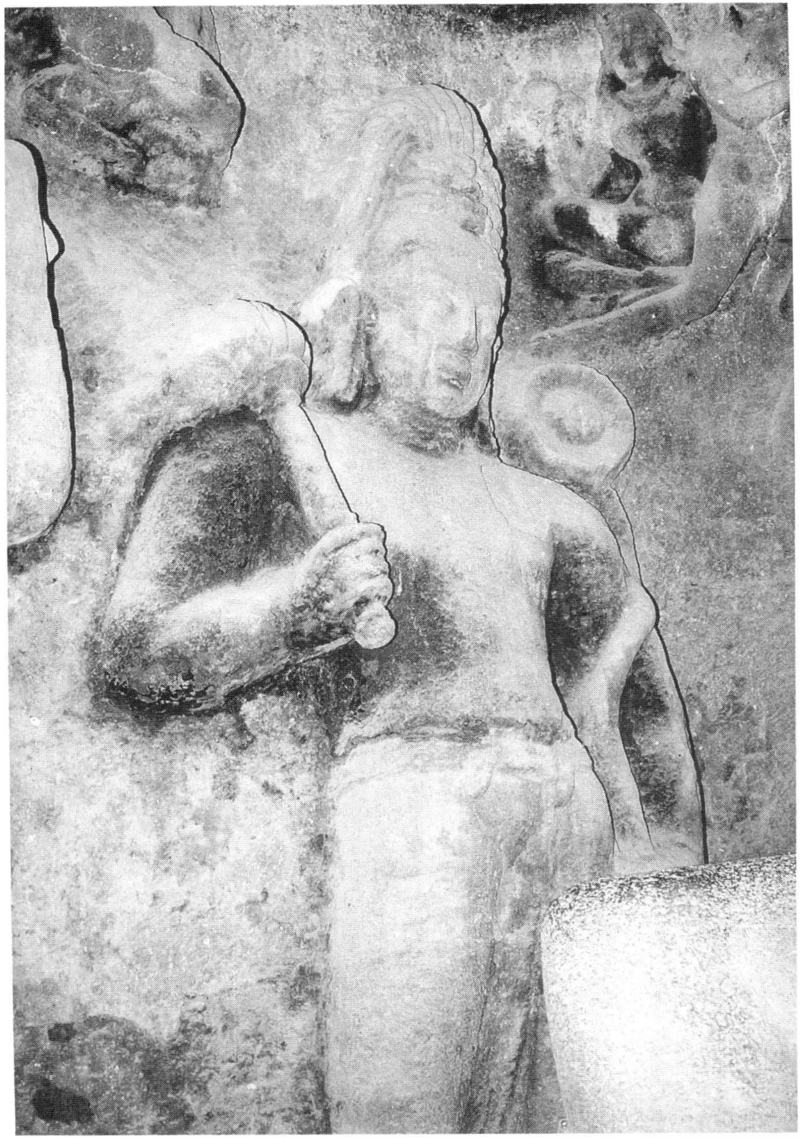

Fig. 65   Cave 2 shrine, Avalokiteśvara

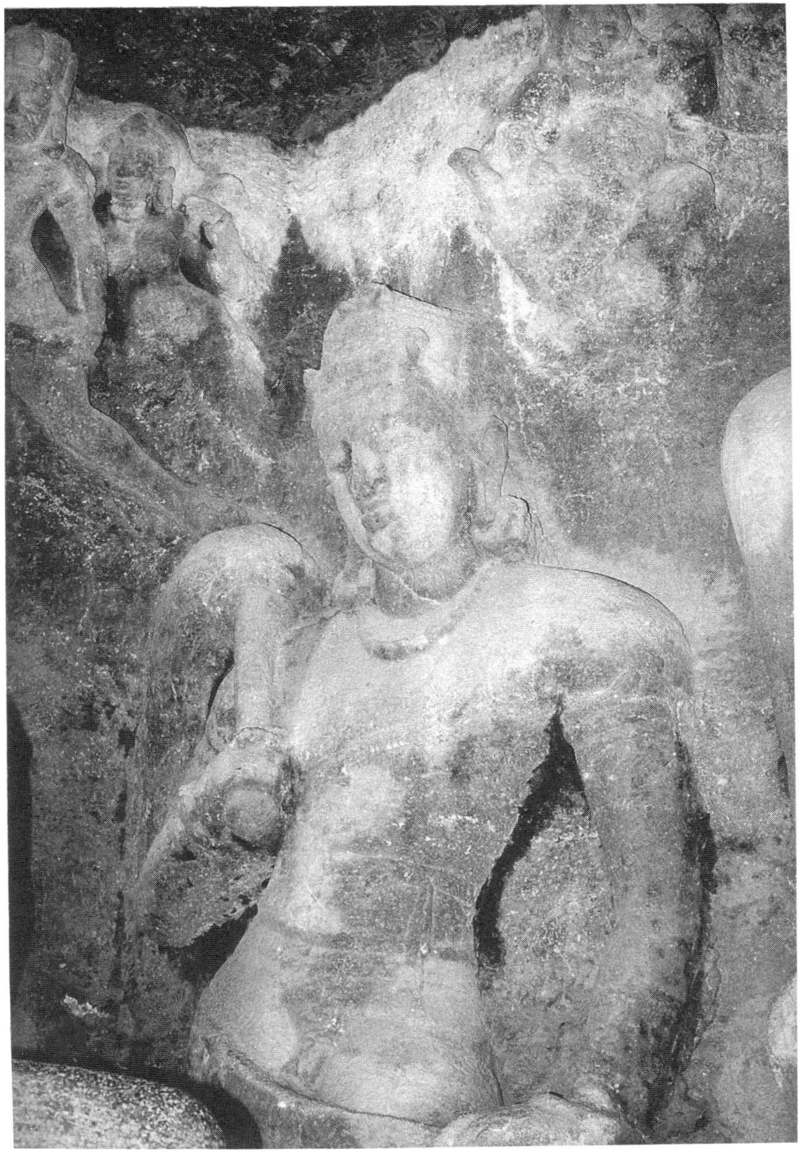

Fig. 66   Cave 2 shrine, Maitreya

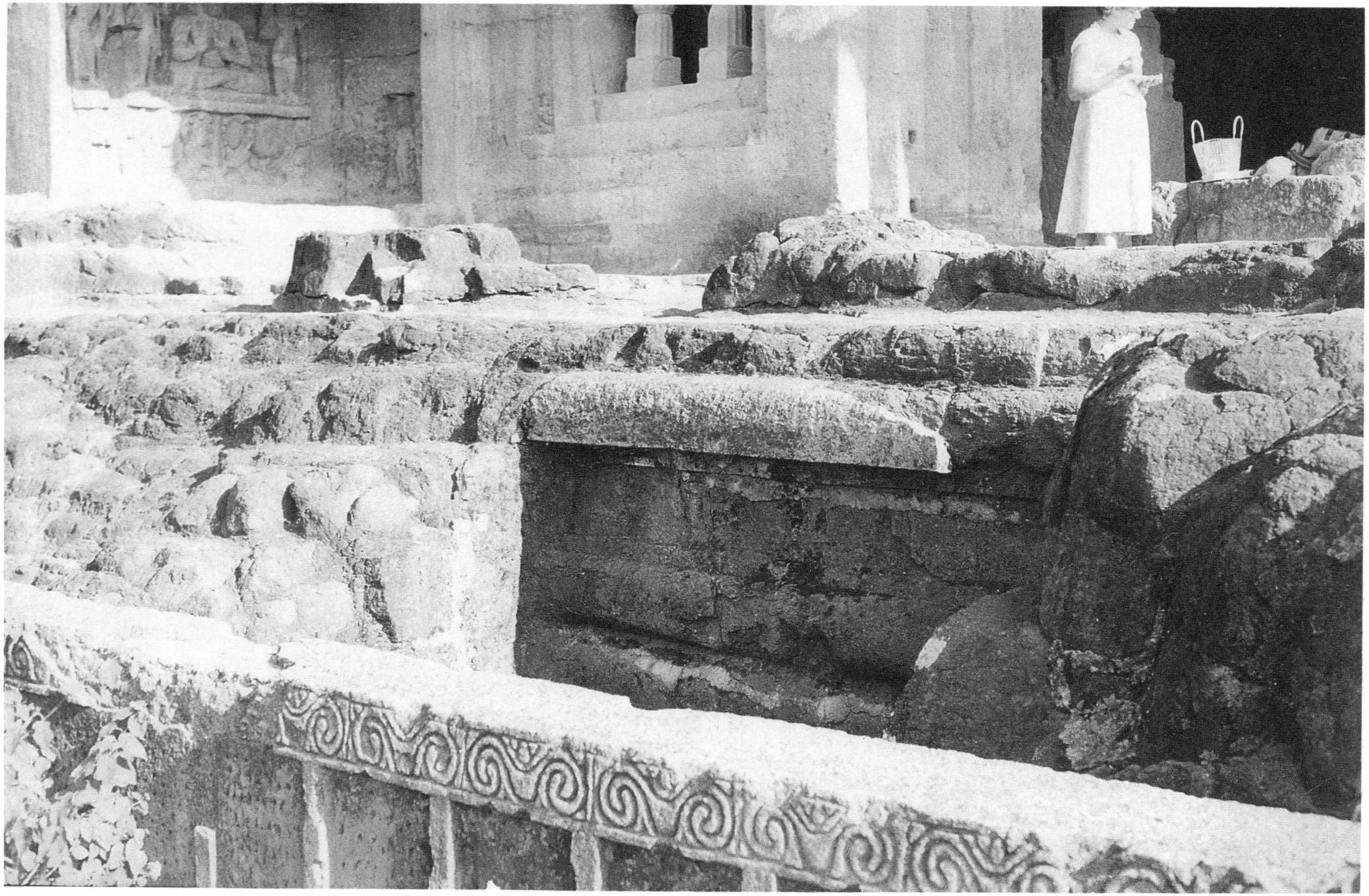

Fig. 67   Cave 3 plinth

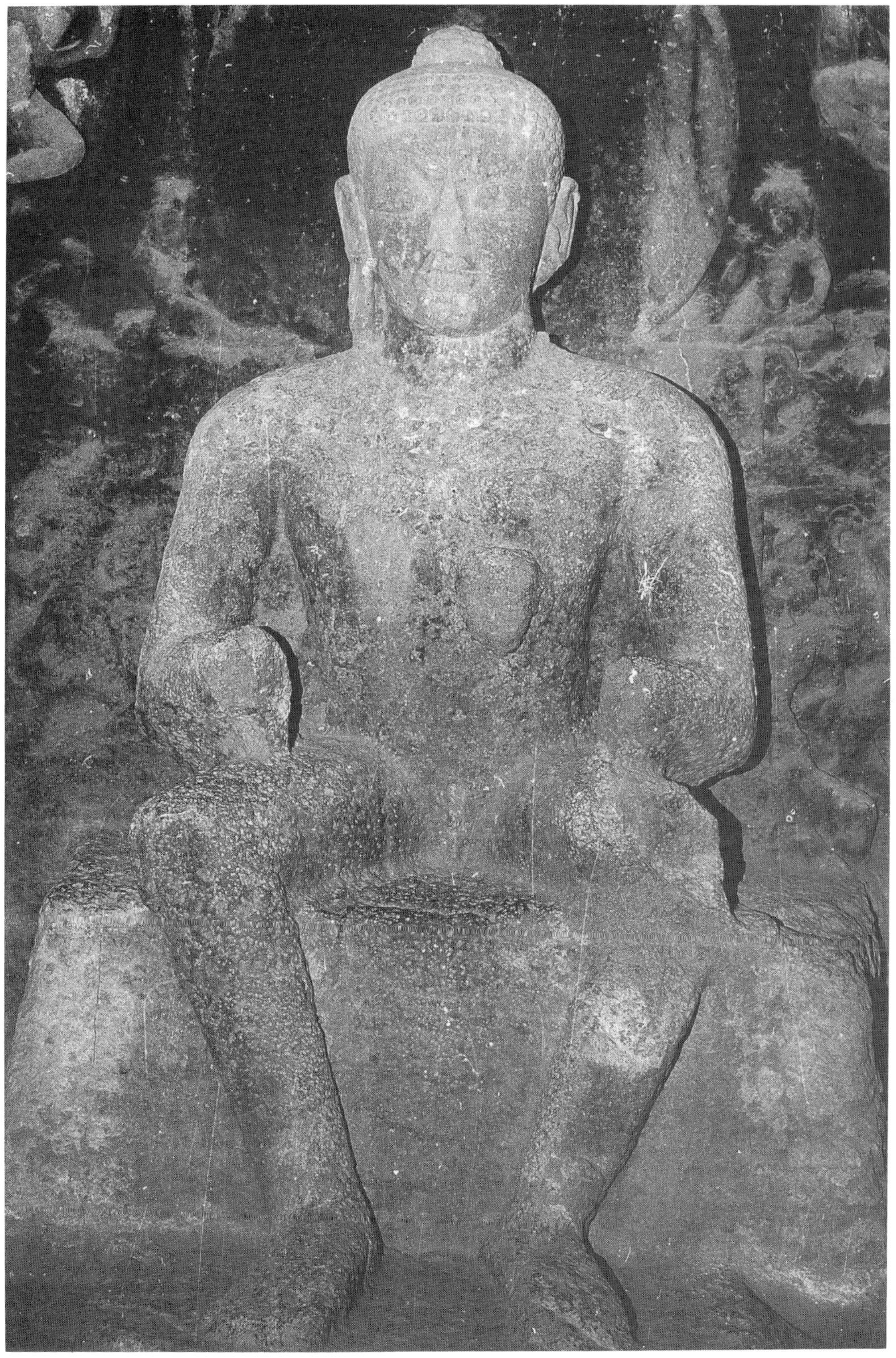

Fig. 68 Cave 3 shrine, Buddha

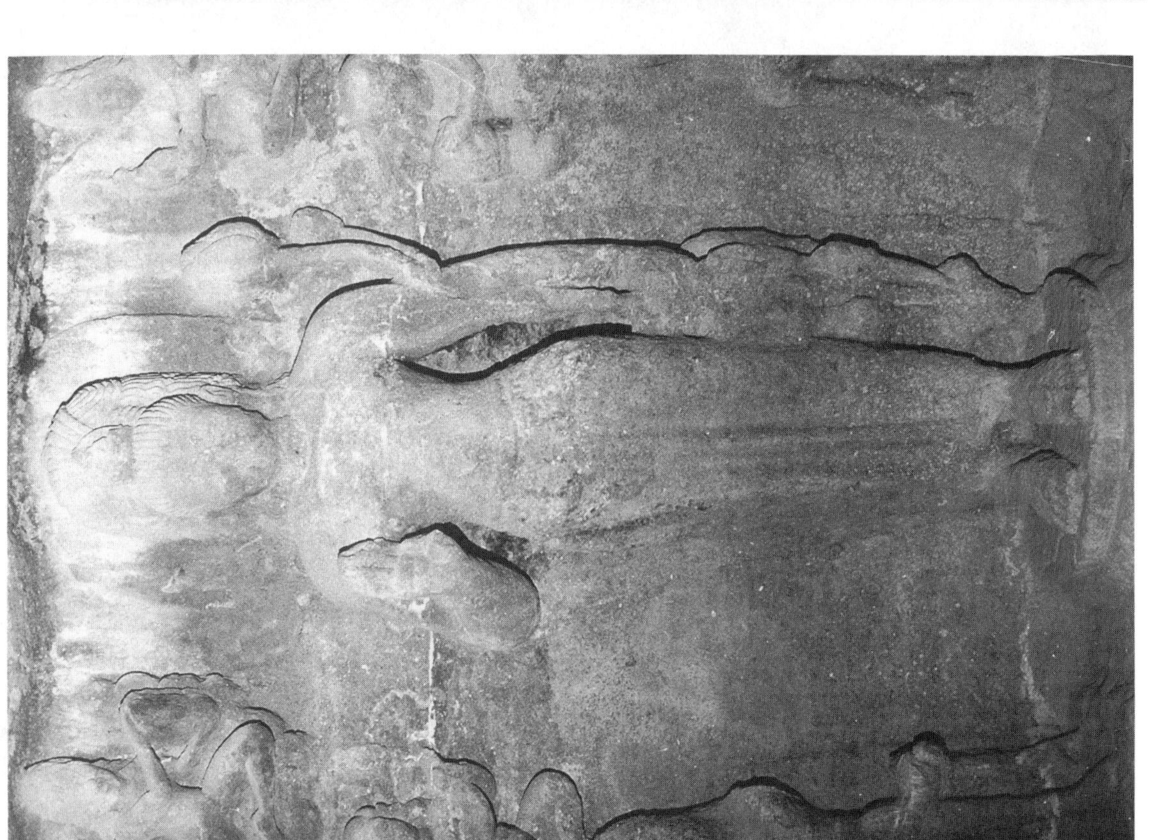

Fig. 70   Cave 3 shrine door, Maitreya

Fig. 69   Cave 3 shrine door, Avalokiteśvara

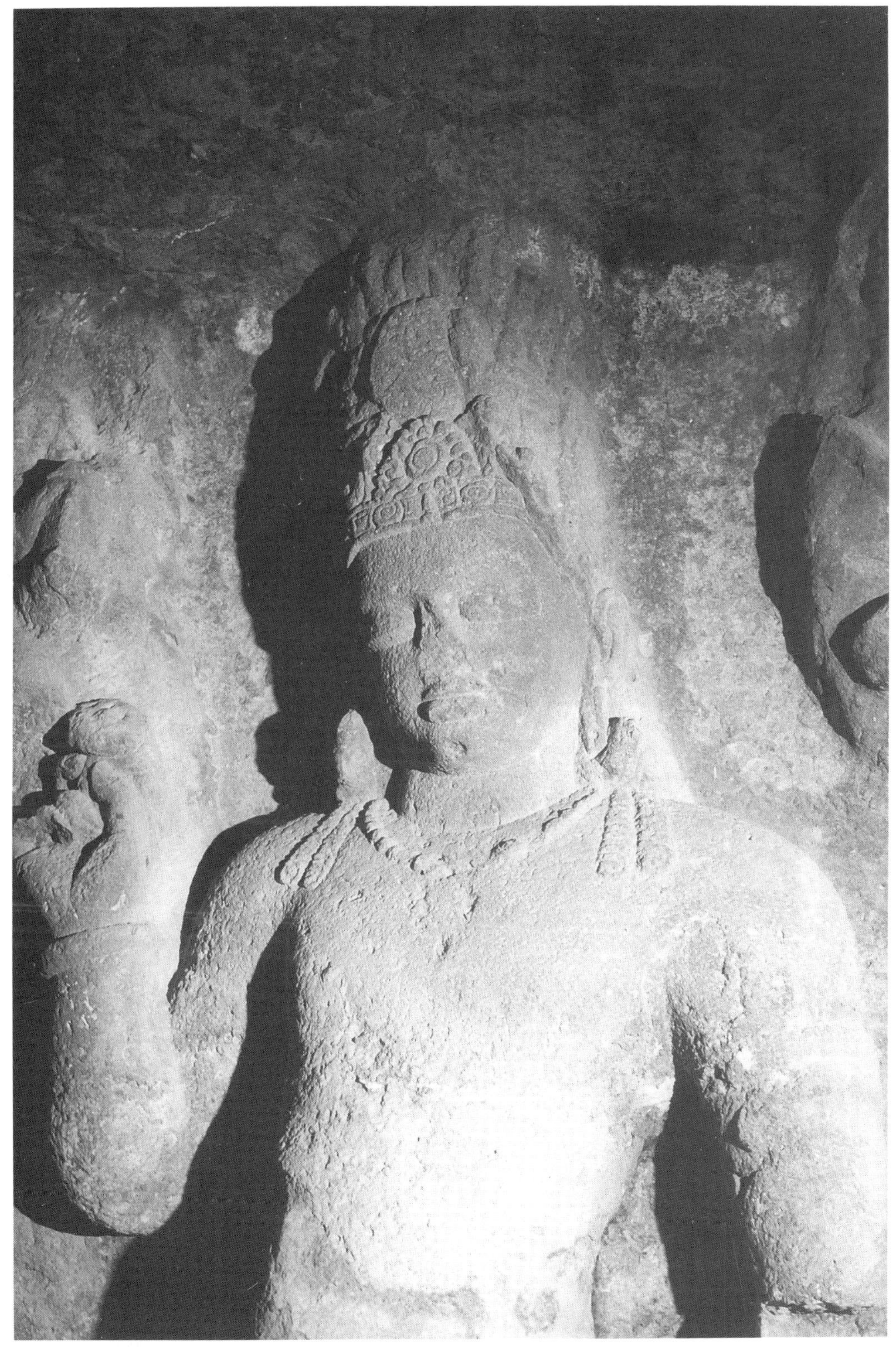

Fig. 71   Cave 3 shrine door, Maitreya closeup

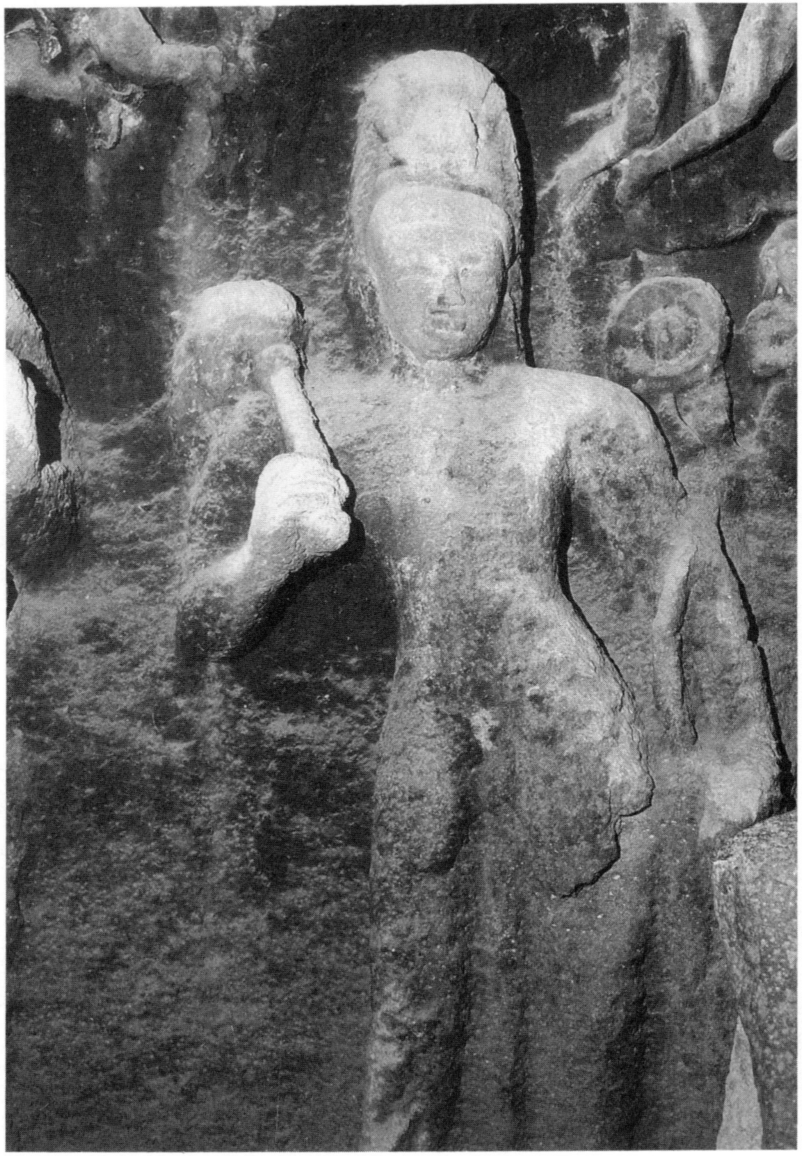

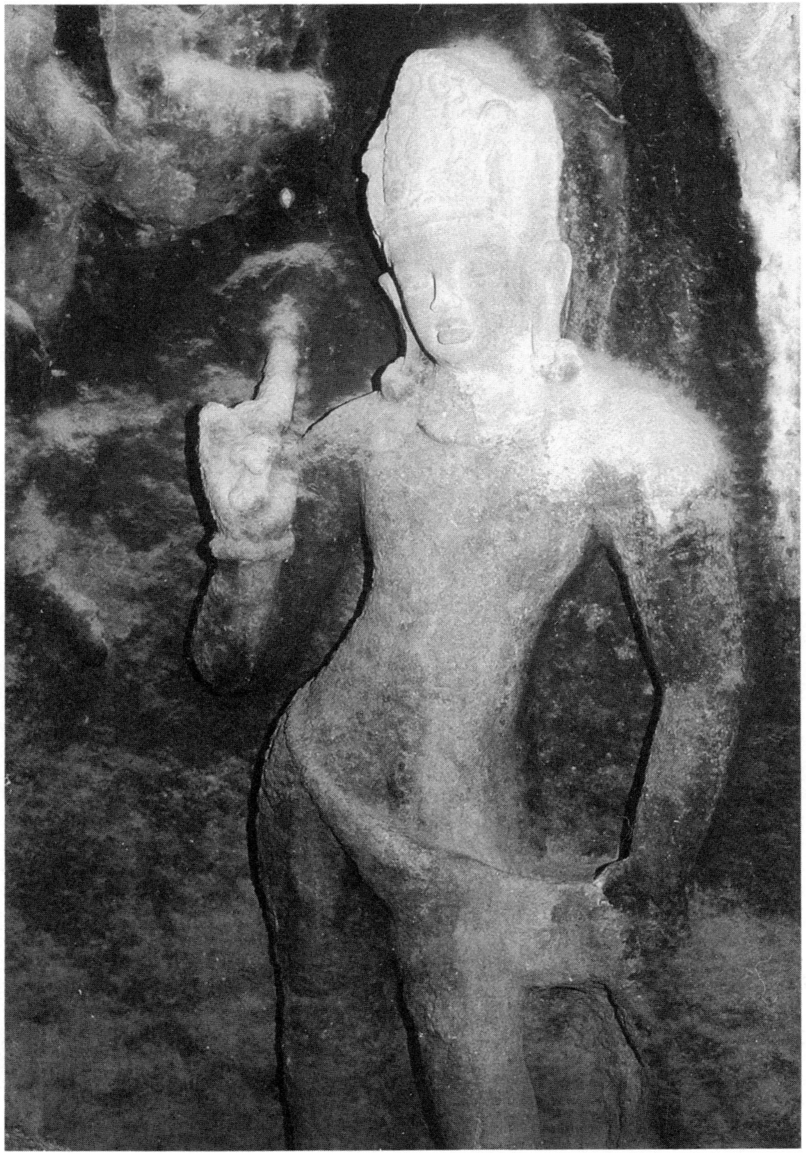

Fig. 73   Cave 3 shrine, Maitreya

Fig. 72   Cave 3 shrine, Avalokiteśvara

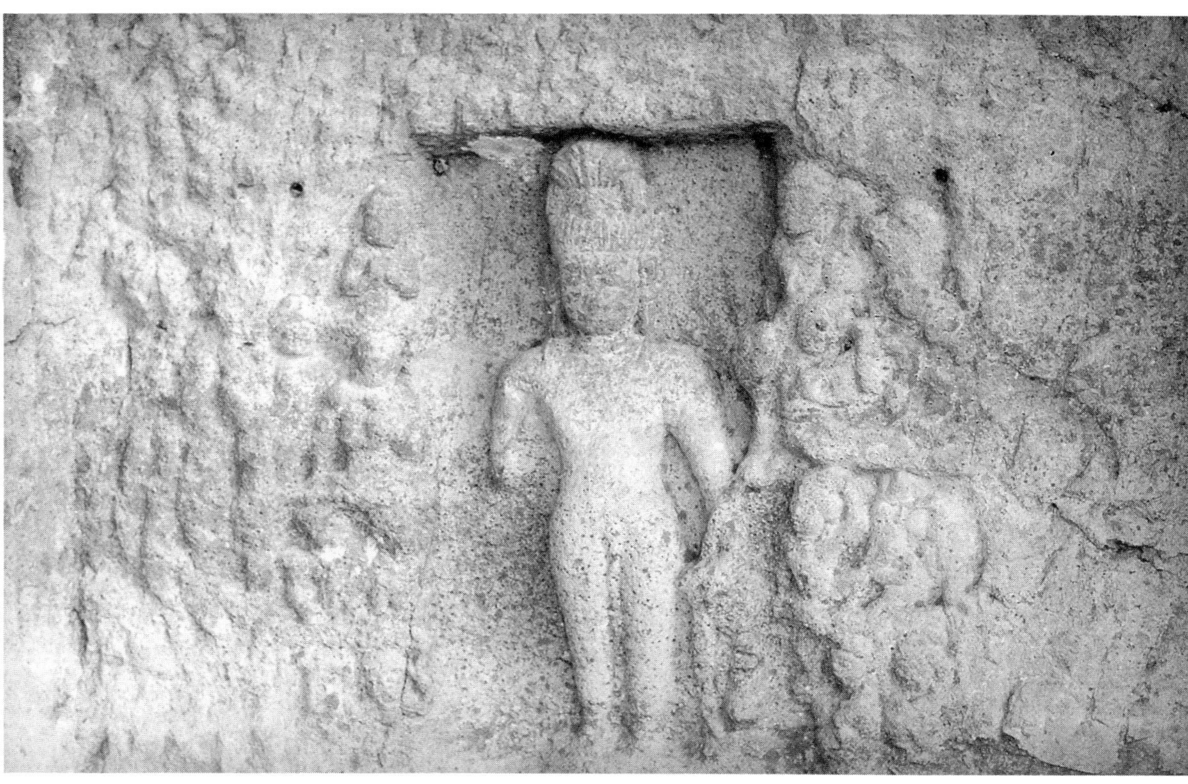

Fig. 74　Cave 3 Aṣṭamahābhaya Avalokiteśvara

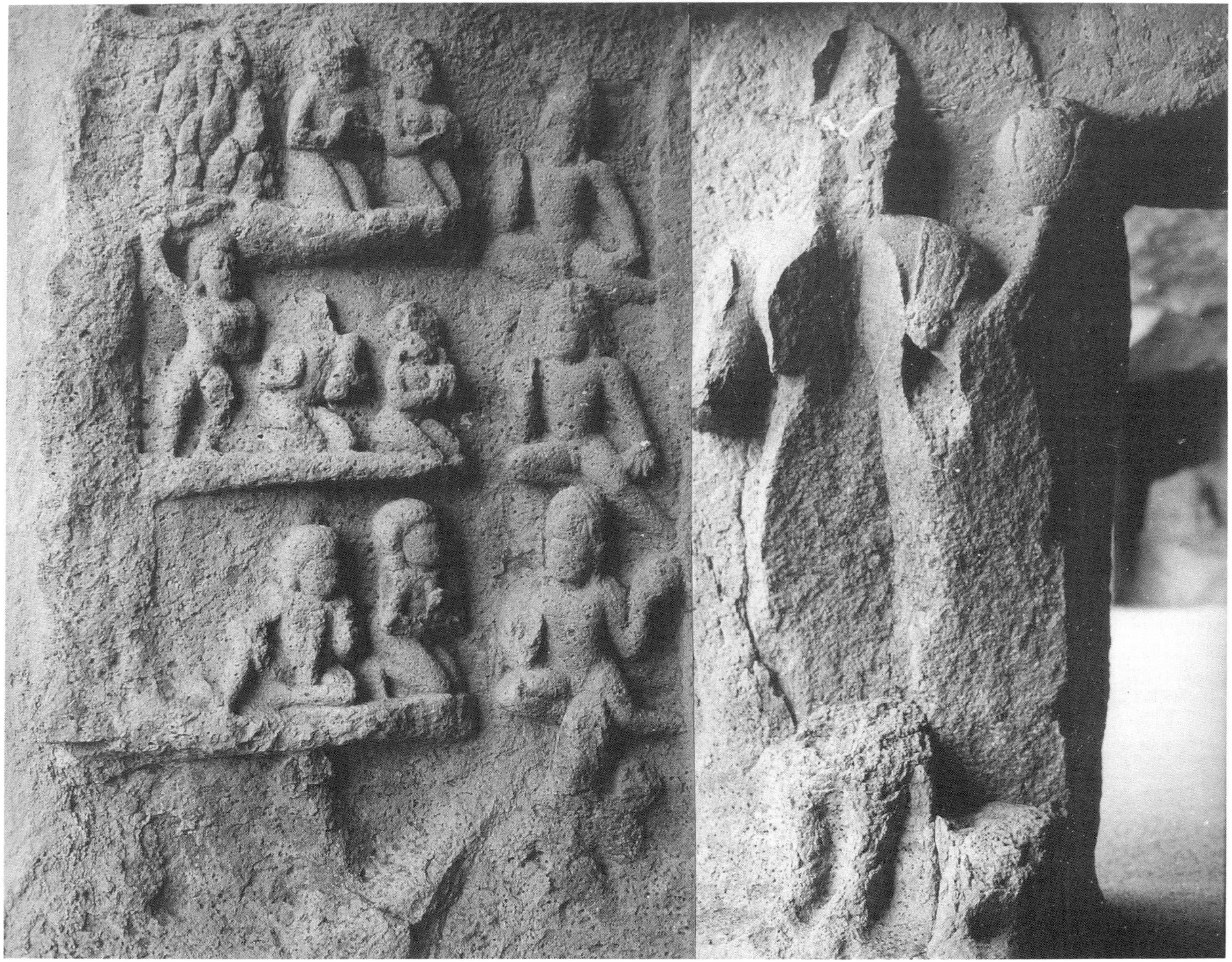

Fig. 75   Cave 3A Aṣṭamahābhaya Avalokiteśvara

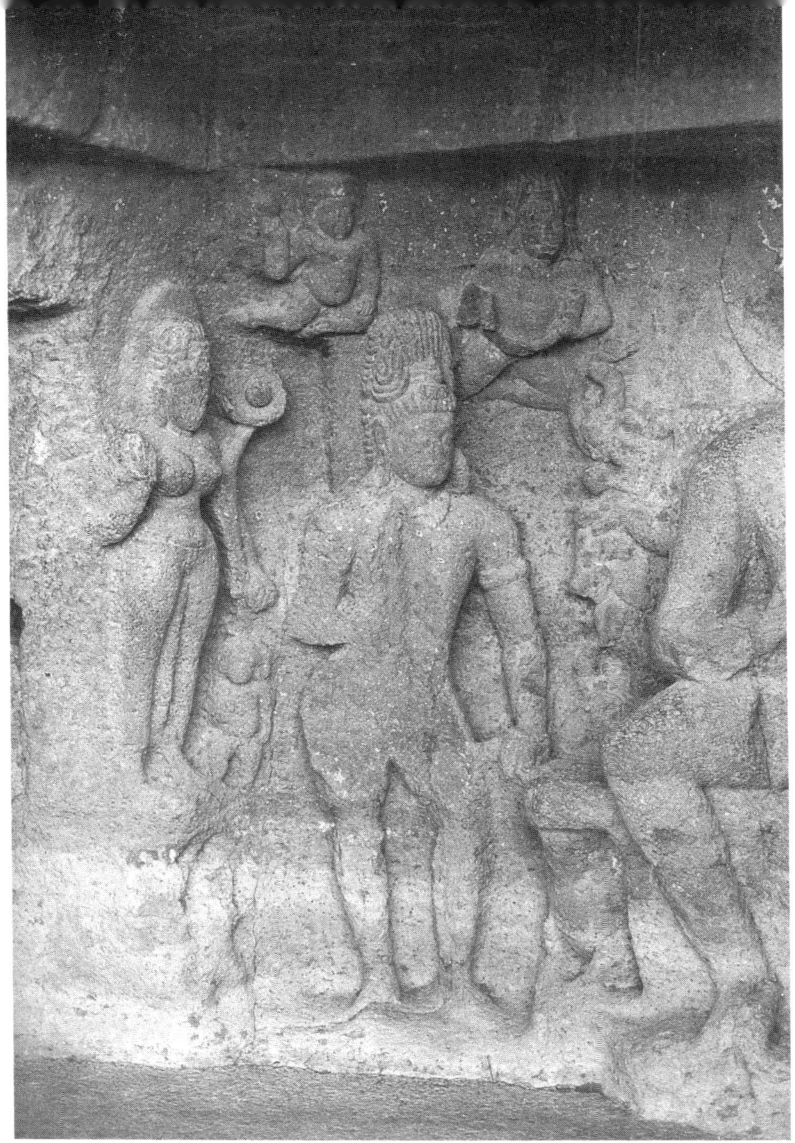

Fig. 76   Cave 3A Bhṛkuṭī and Avalokiteśvara

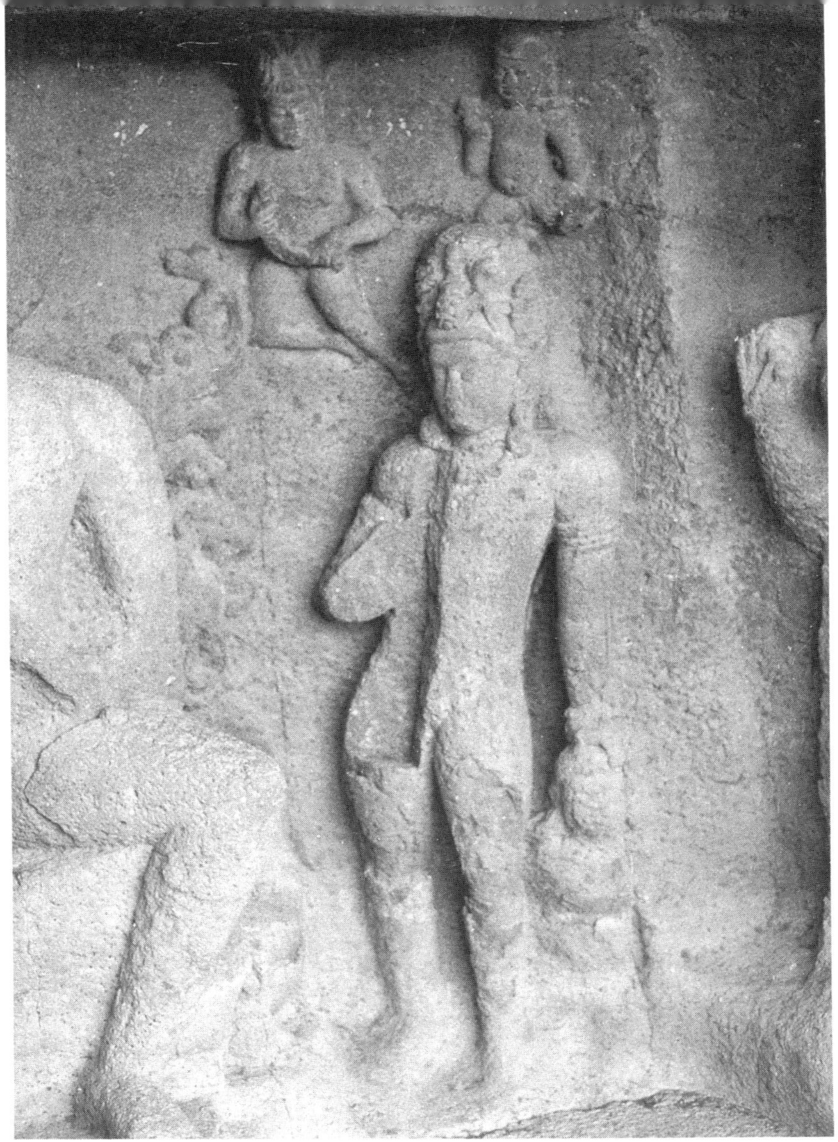

Fig. 77   Cave 3A Mañjuśrī

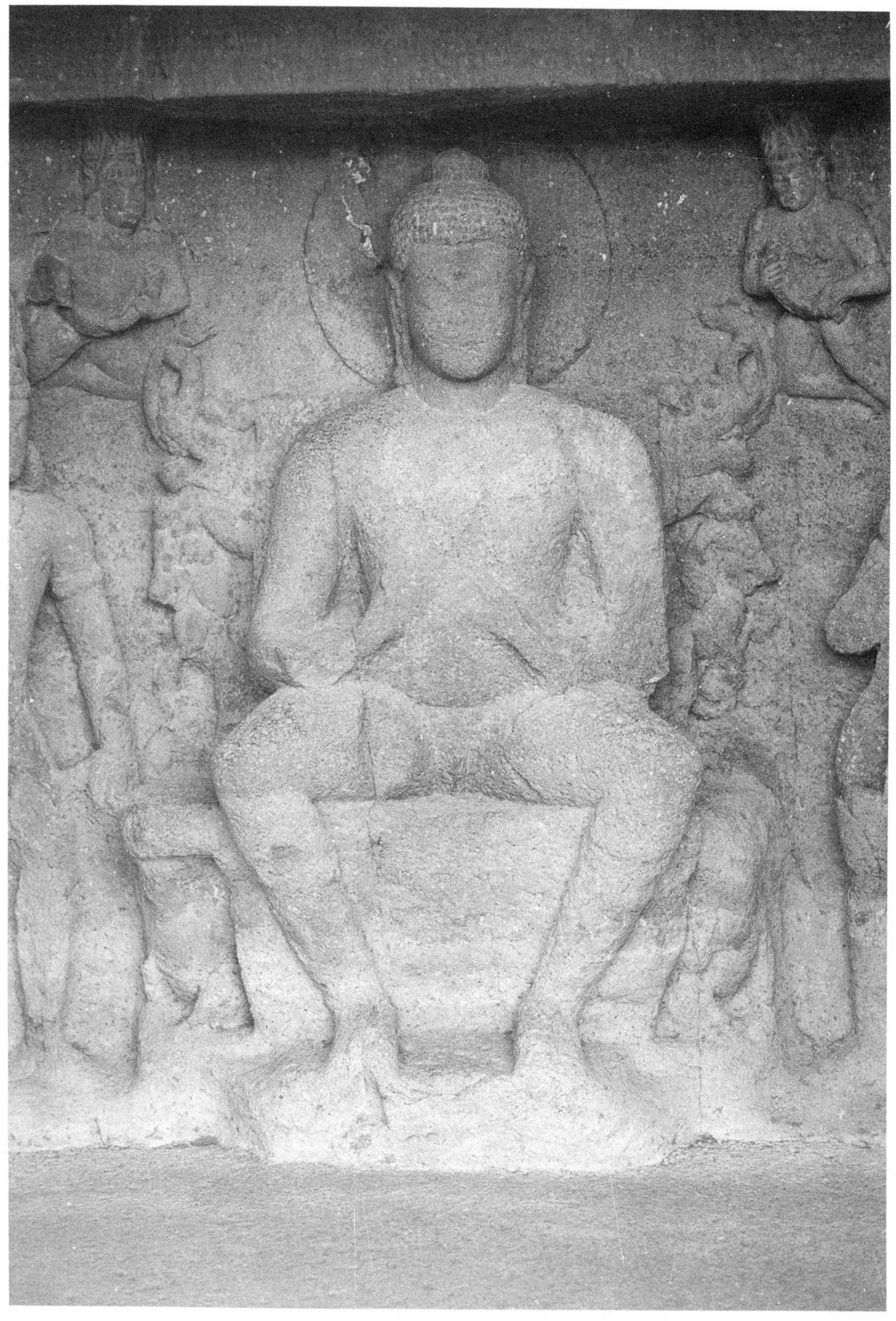

Fig. 78   Cave 3A Buddha

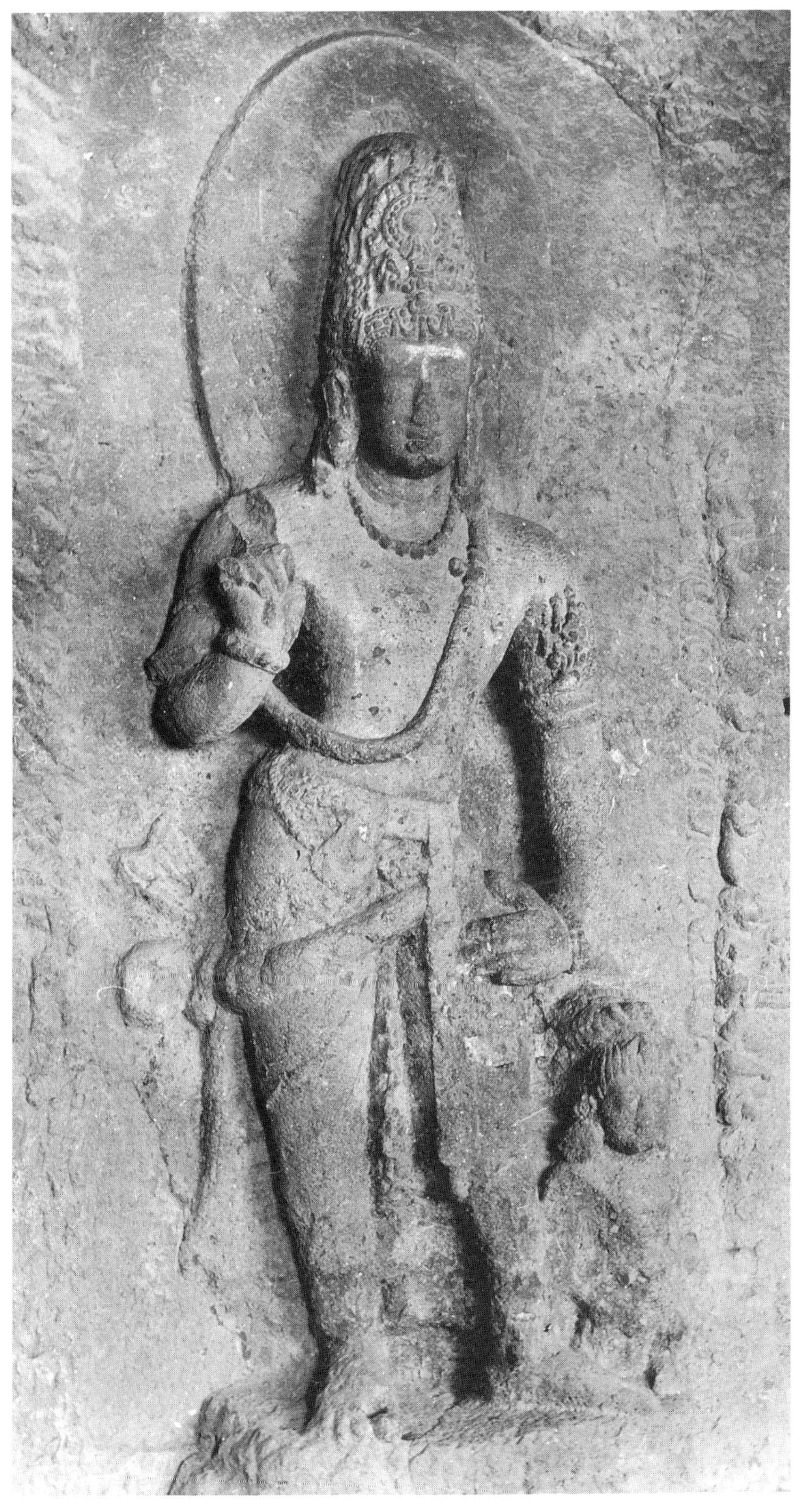

Fig. 79   Cave 4 shrine door, left guard (AIIS)

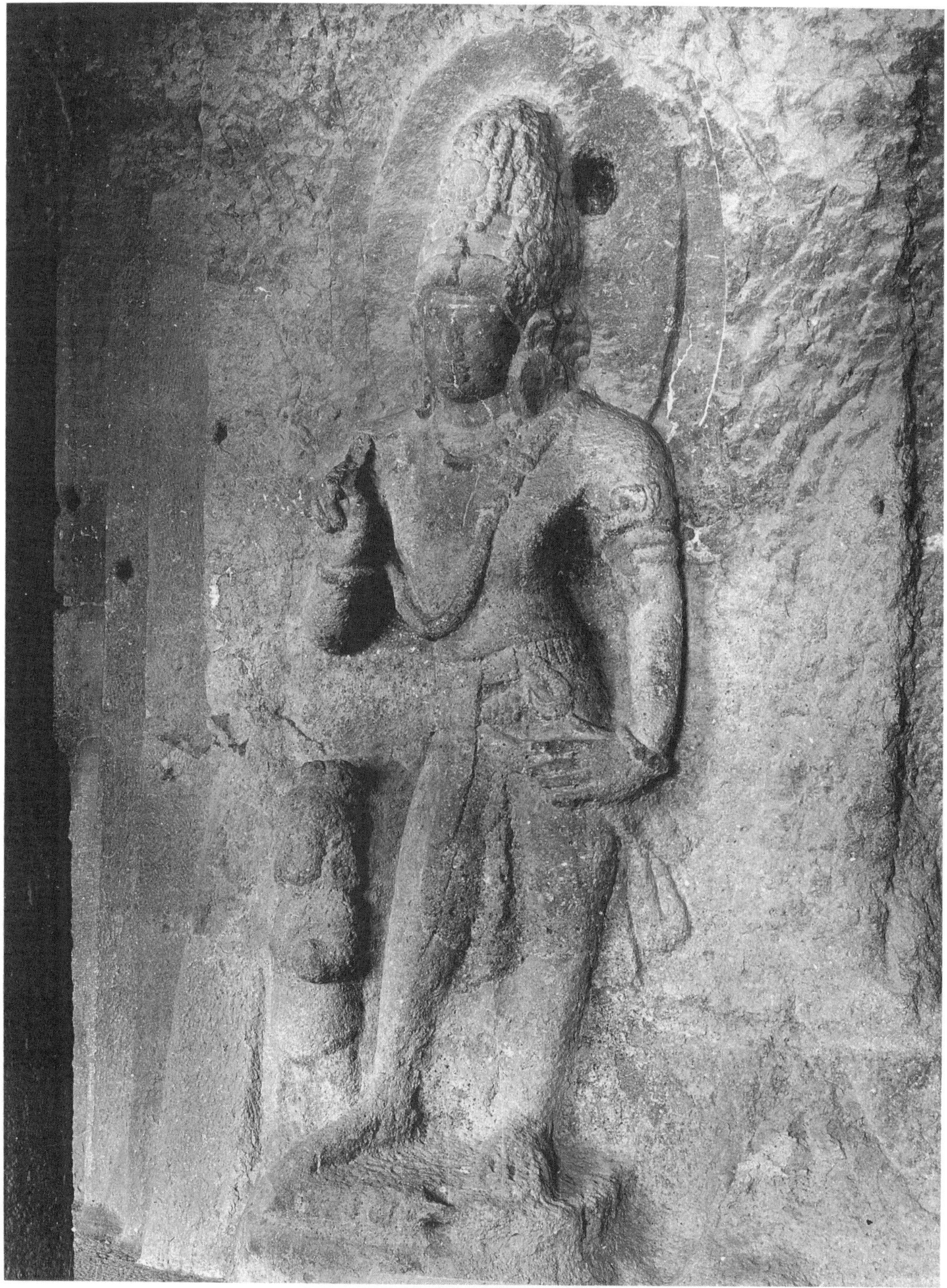

Fig. 80   Cave 4 shrine door, right guard (AIIS)

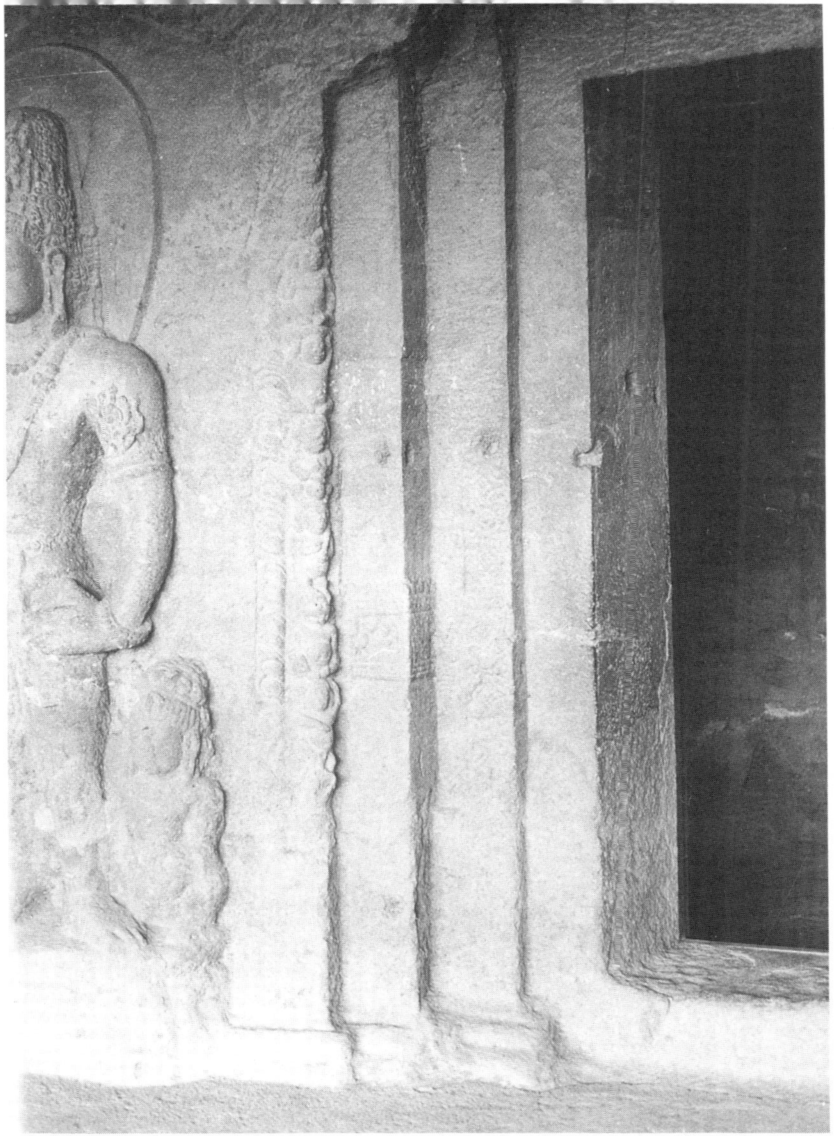

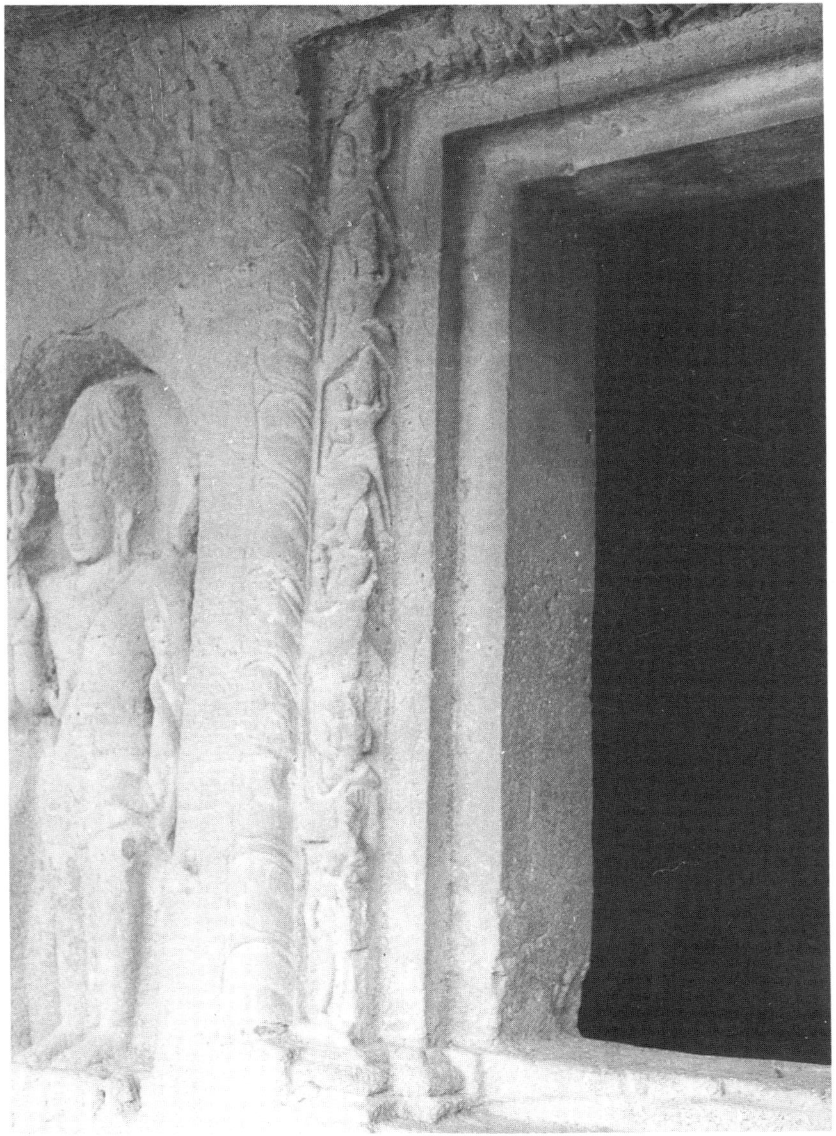

Fig. 82 Cave 27 shrine door frame

Fig. 81 Cave 4 shrine door frame

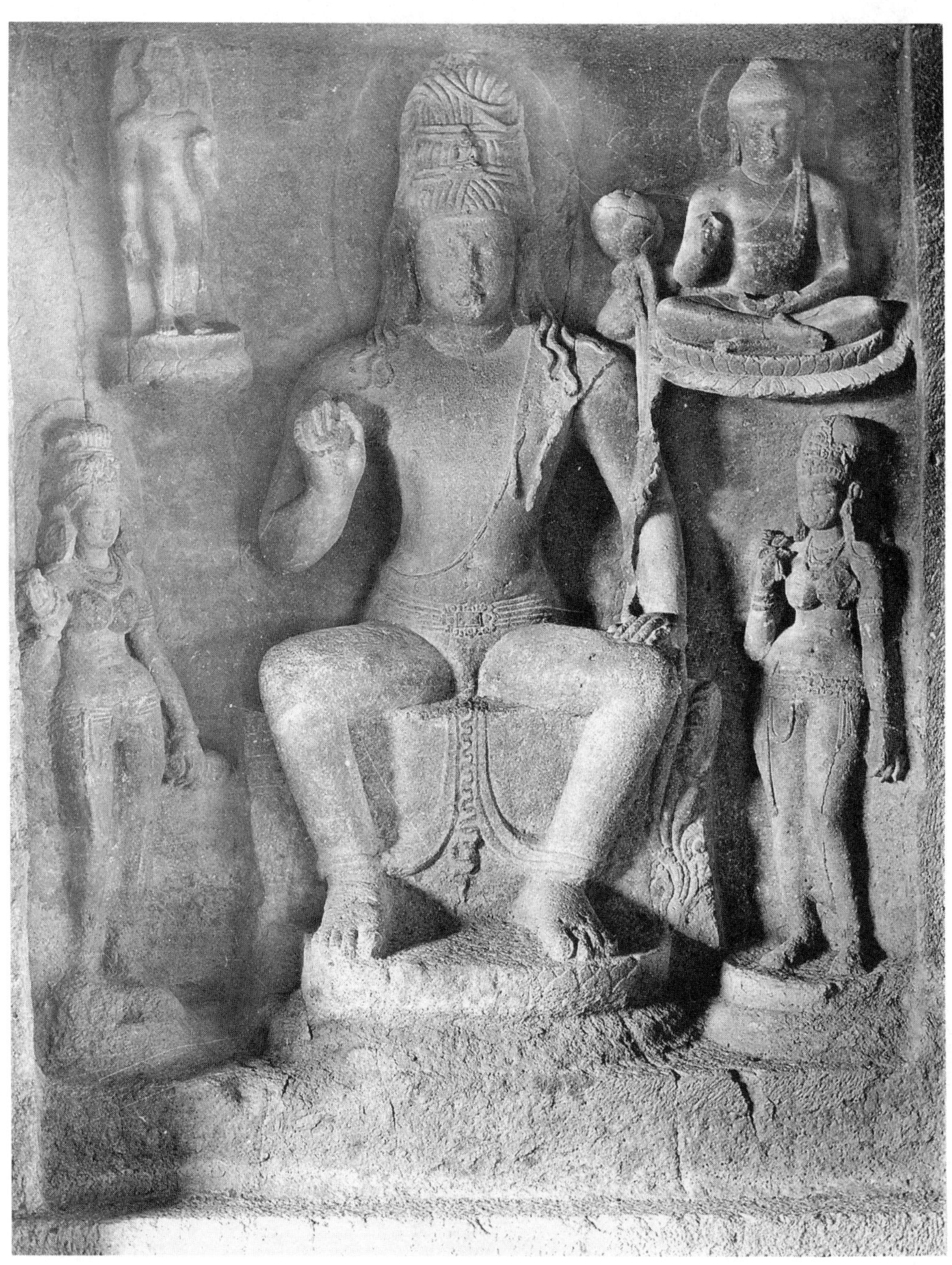

Fig. 83   Cave 4 antechamber, Rakta-Lokeśvara (AIIS)

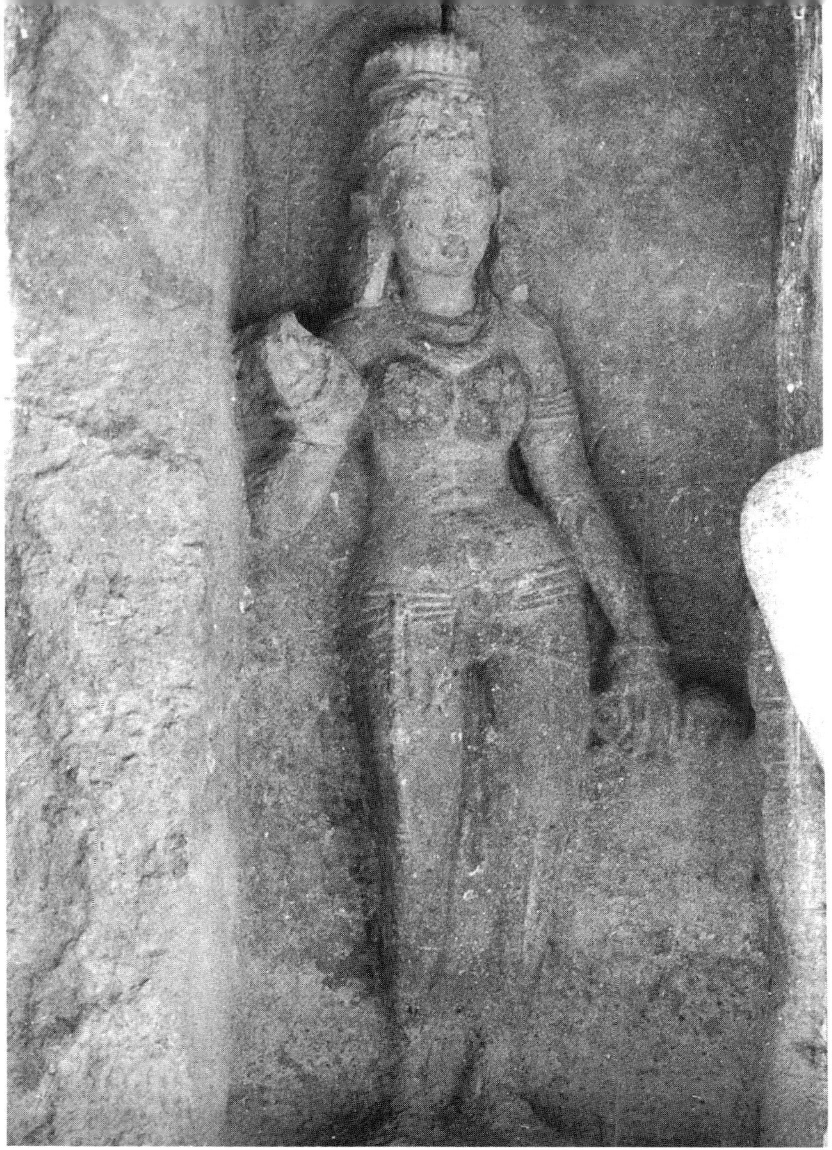

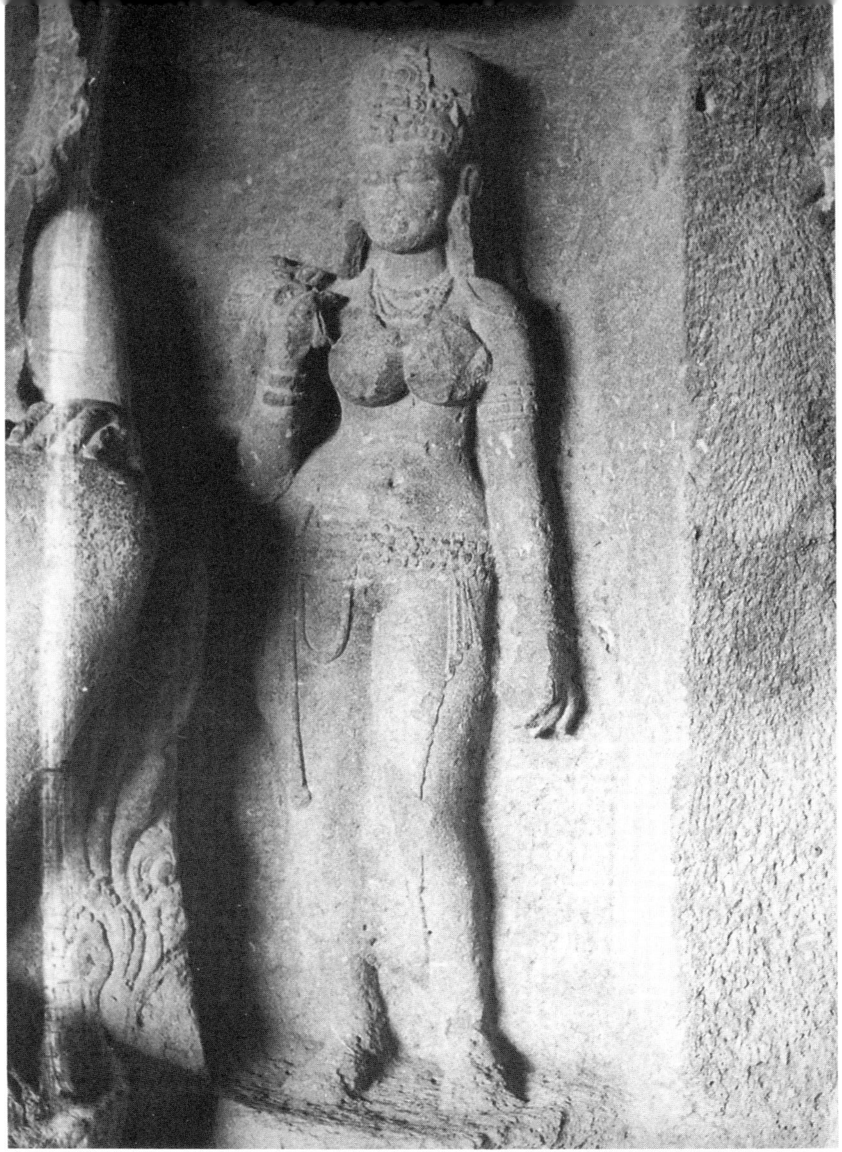

Fig. 85   Cave 4, antechamber, Rakta-Lokeśvara, Tārā closeup

Fig. 84   Cave 4 antechamber, Rakta-Lokeśvara, Bhṛkuṭī closeup

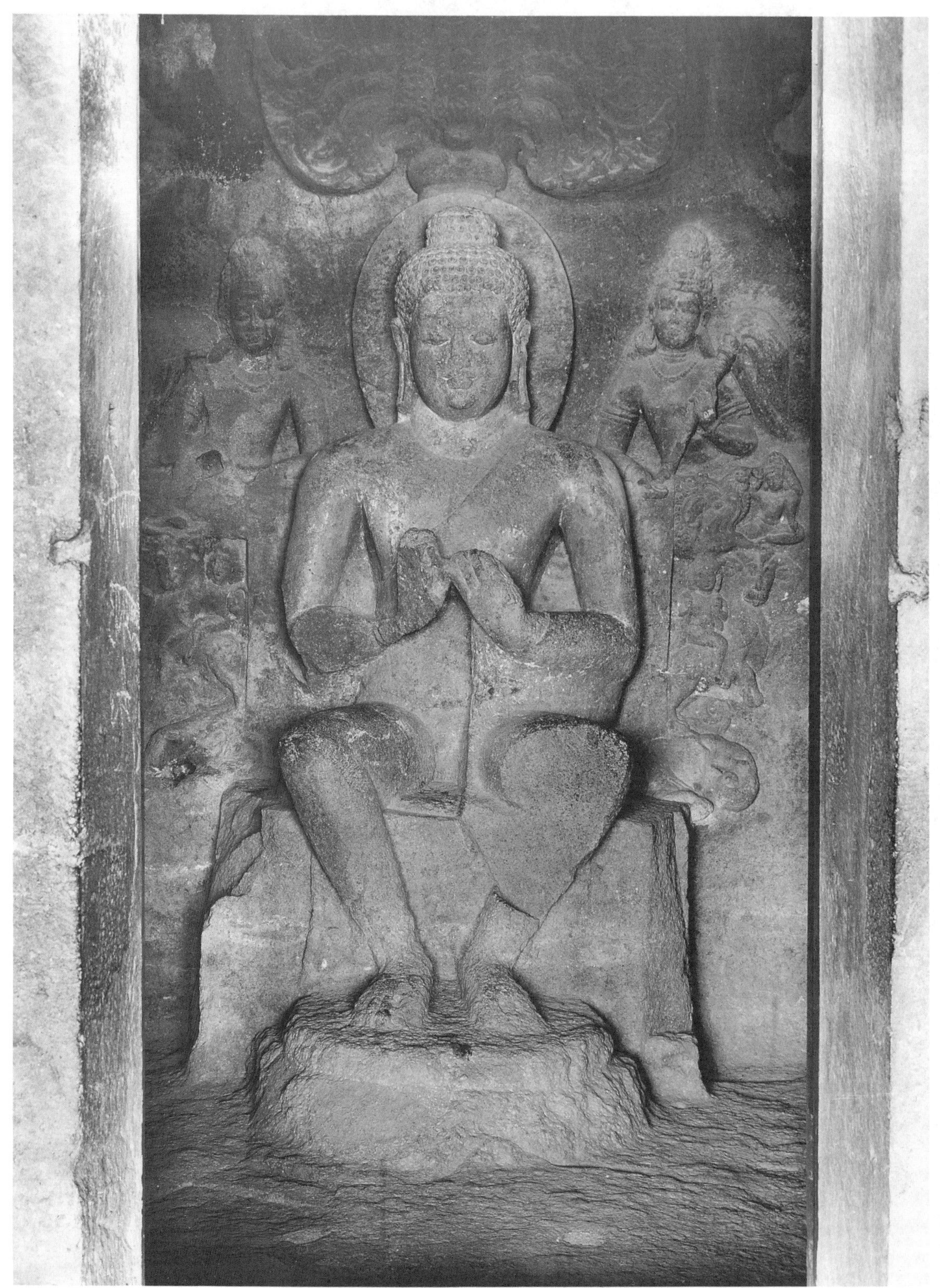

Fig. 86 Cave 4 shrine, Buddha (AIIS)

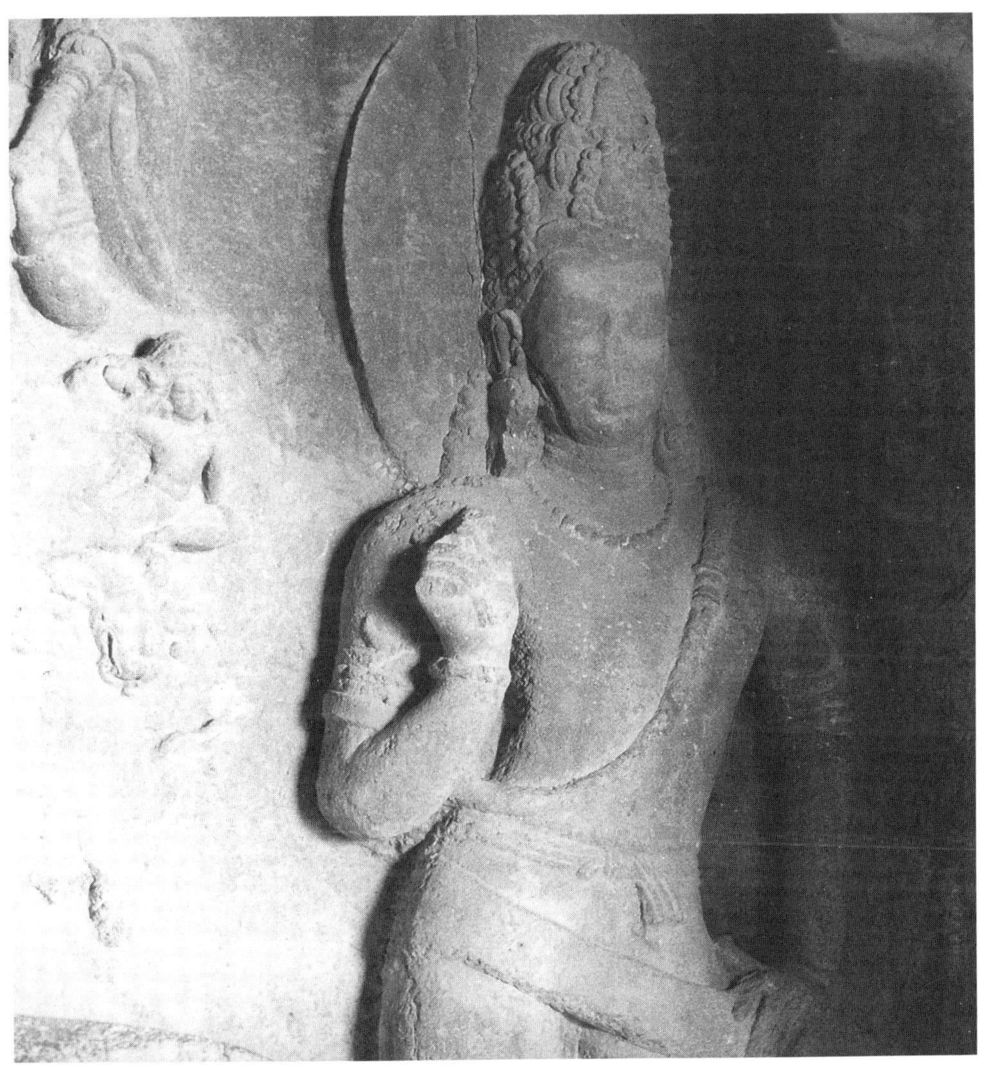

Fig. 87 Cave 4 shrine, Maitreya

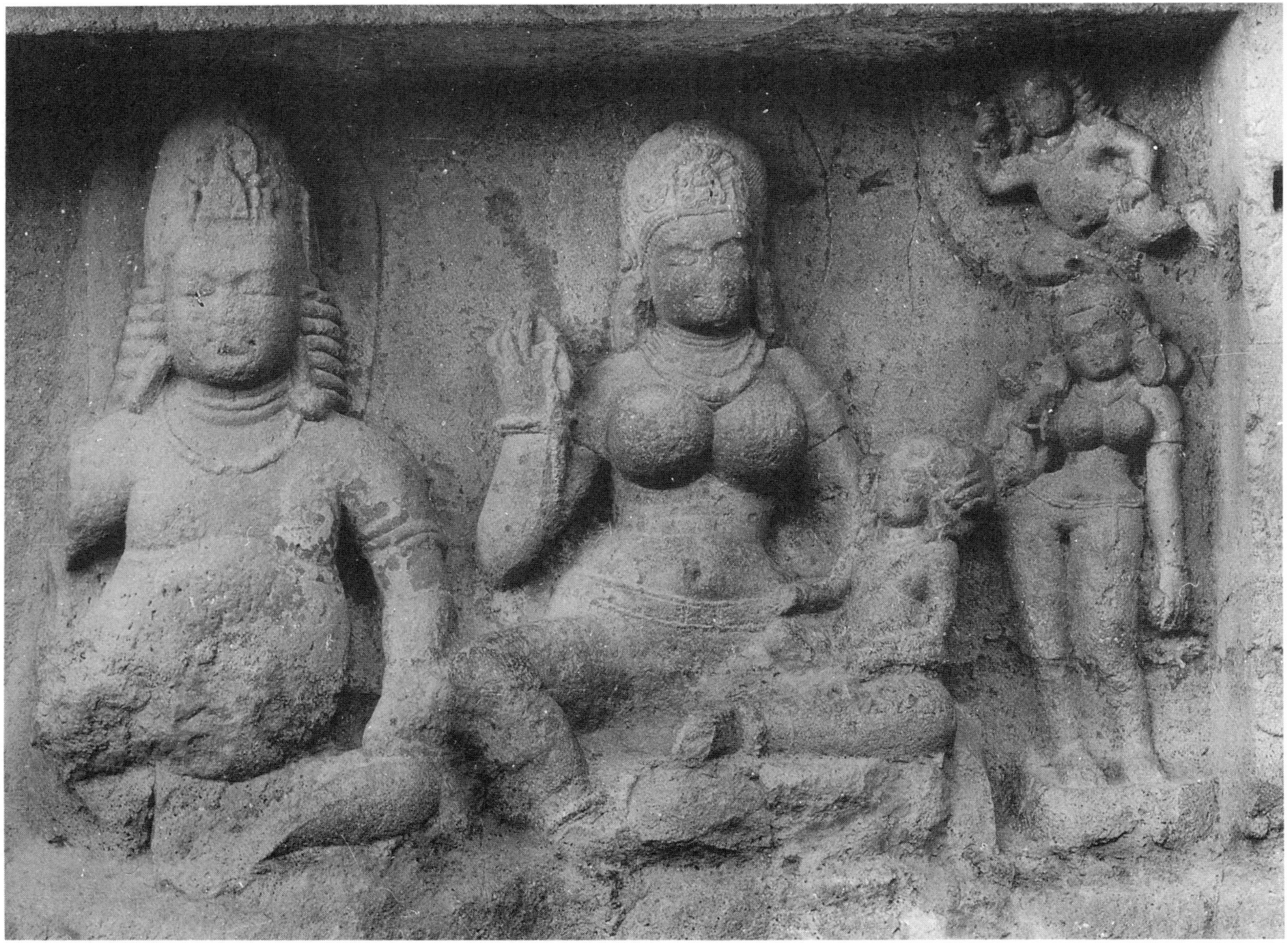

Fig. 88 Cave 8 Pāñcika and Hārītī (AIIS)

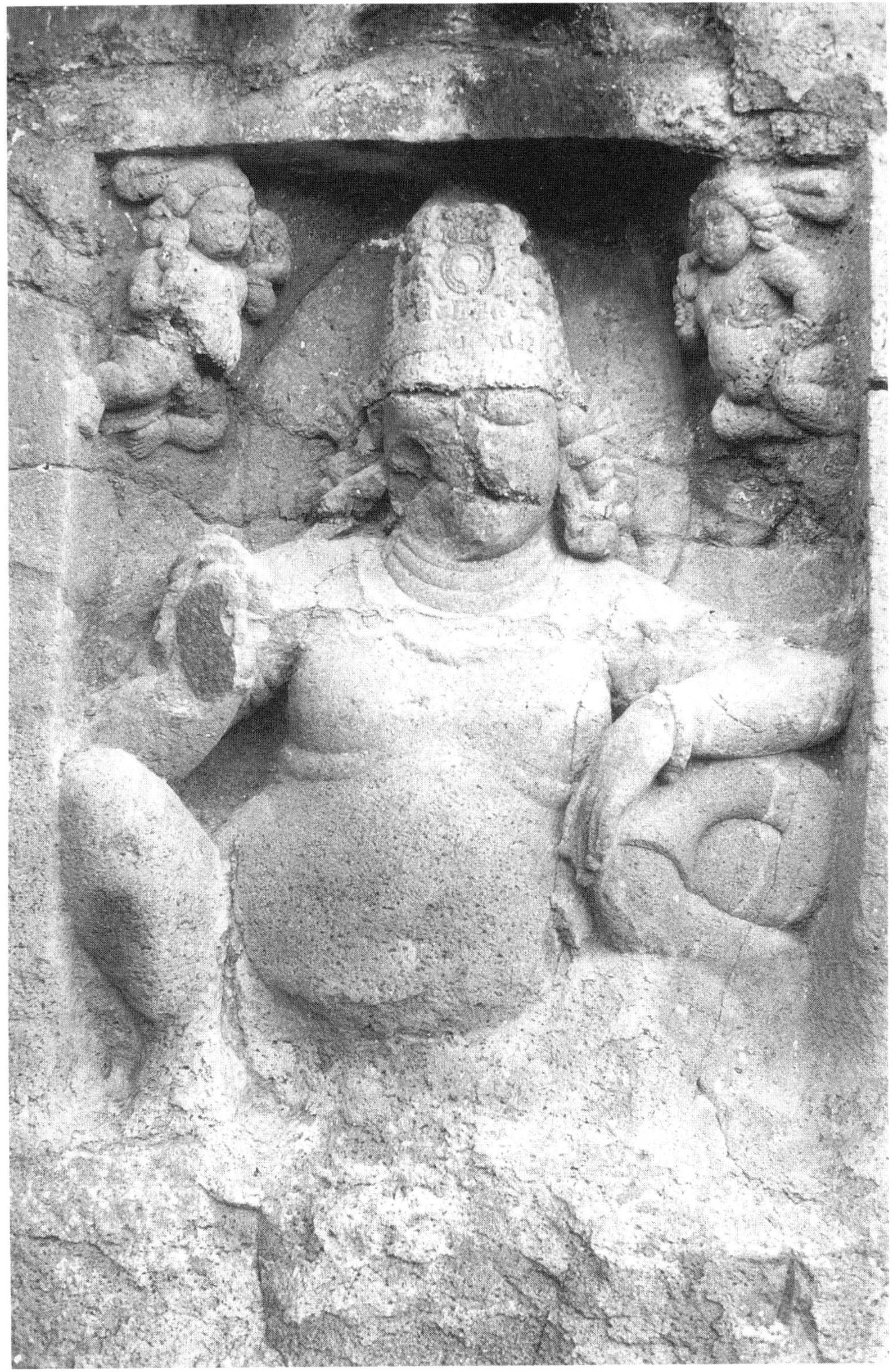

Fig. 89　Cave 19-20 Jambhala

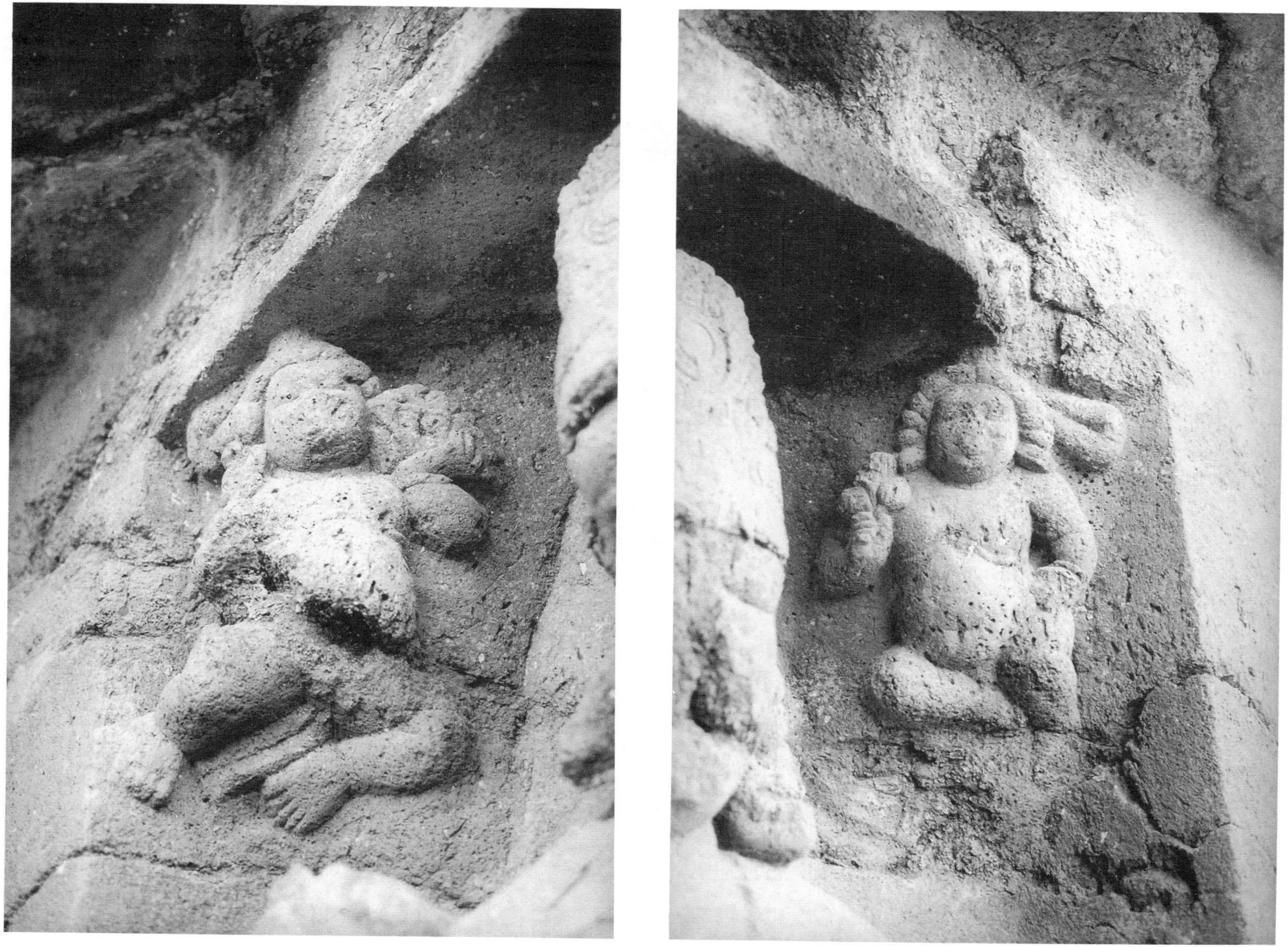

Fig. 90   Cave 19-20 Jambhala attendant figures closeup

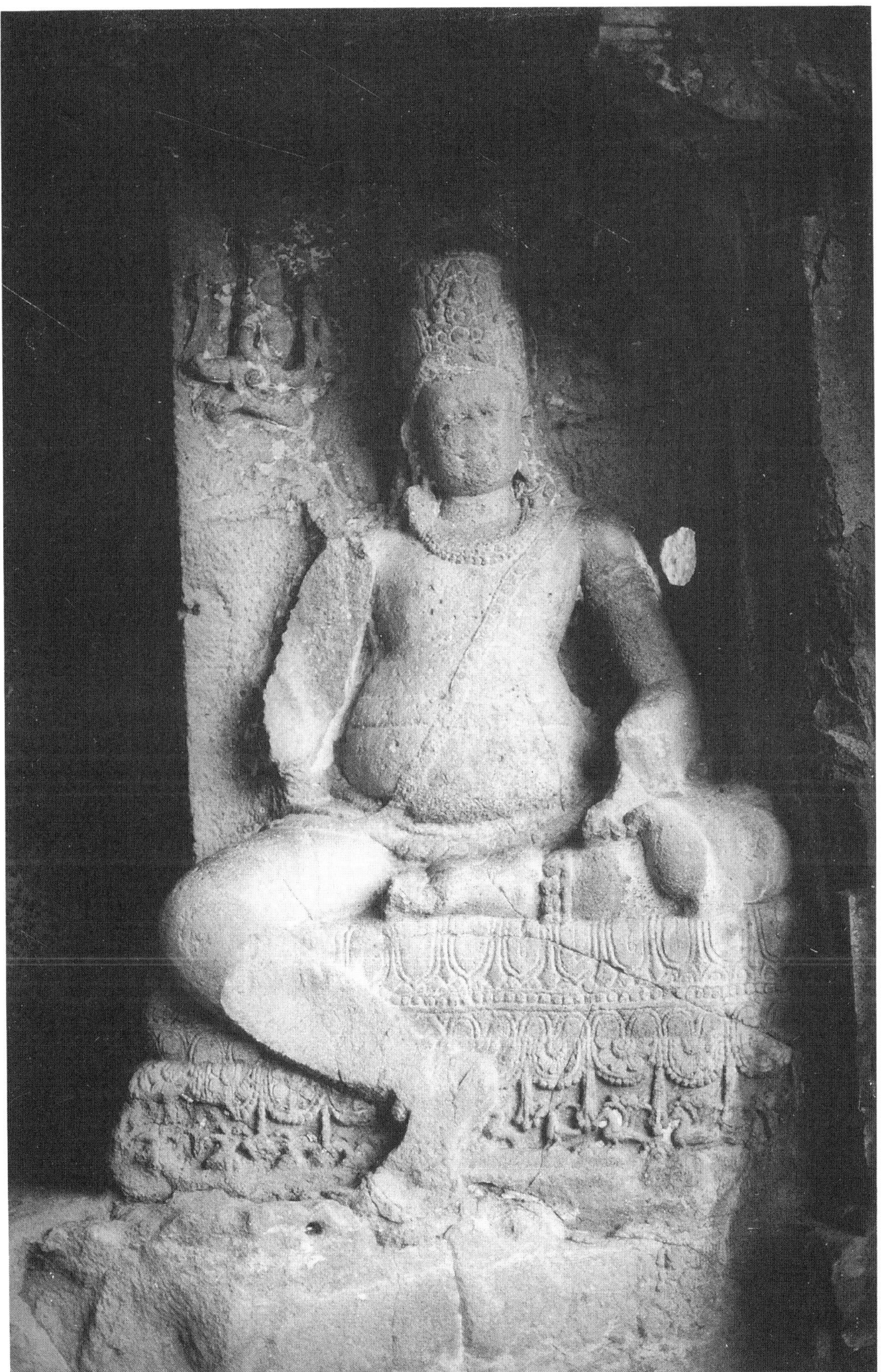

Fig. 91   Cave 25 Kubera

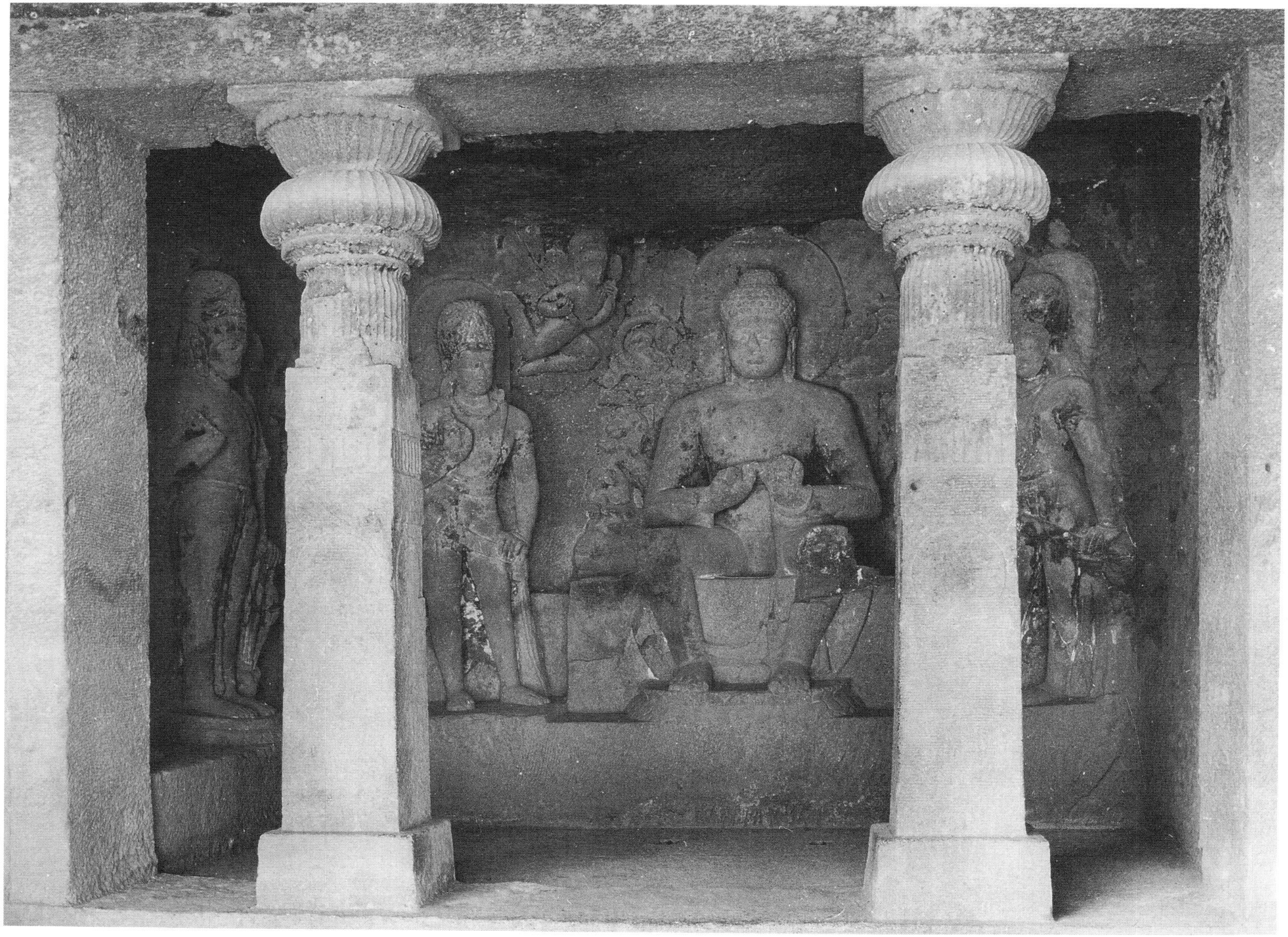

Fig. 92 Cave 8A Buddha (AIIS)

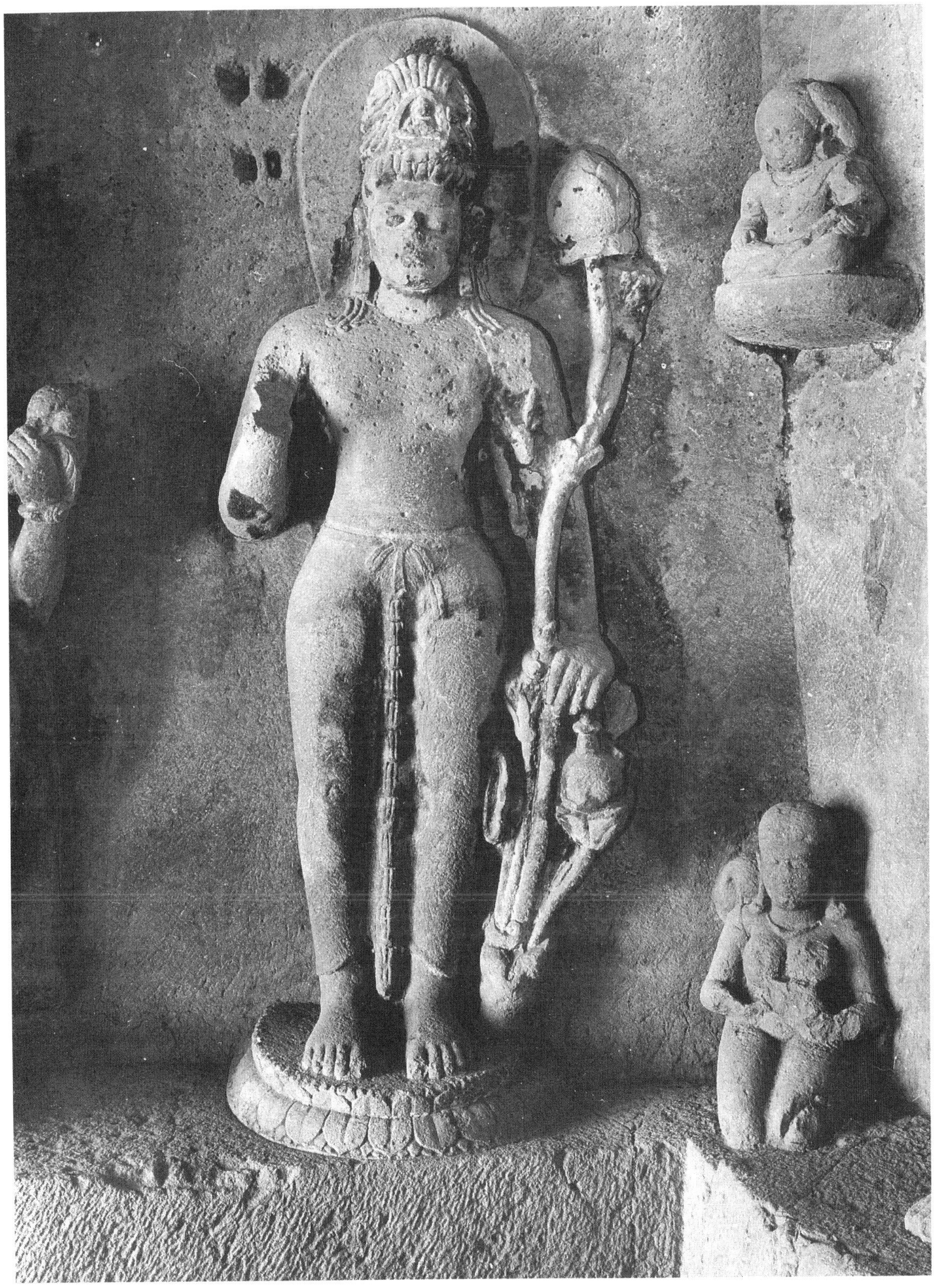

Fig. 93   Cave 8A Avalokiteśvara (AIIS)

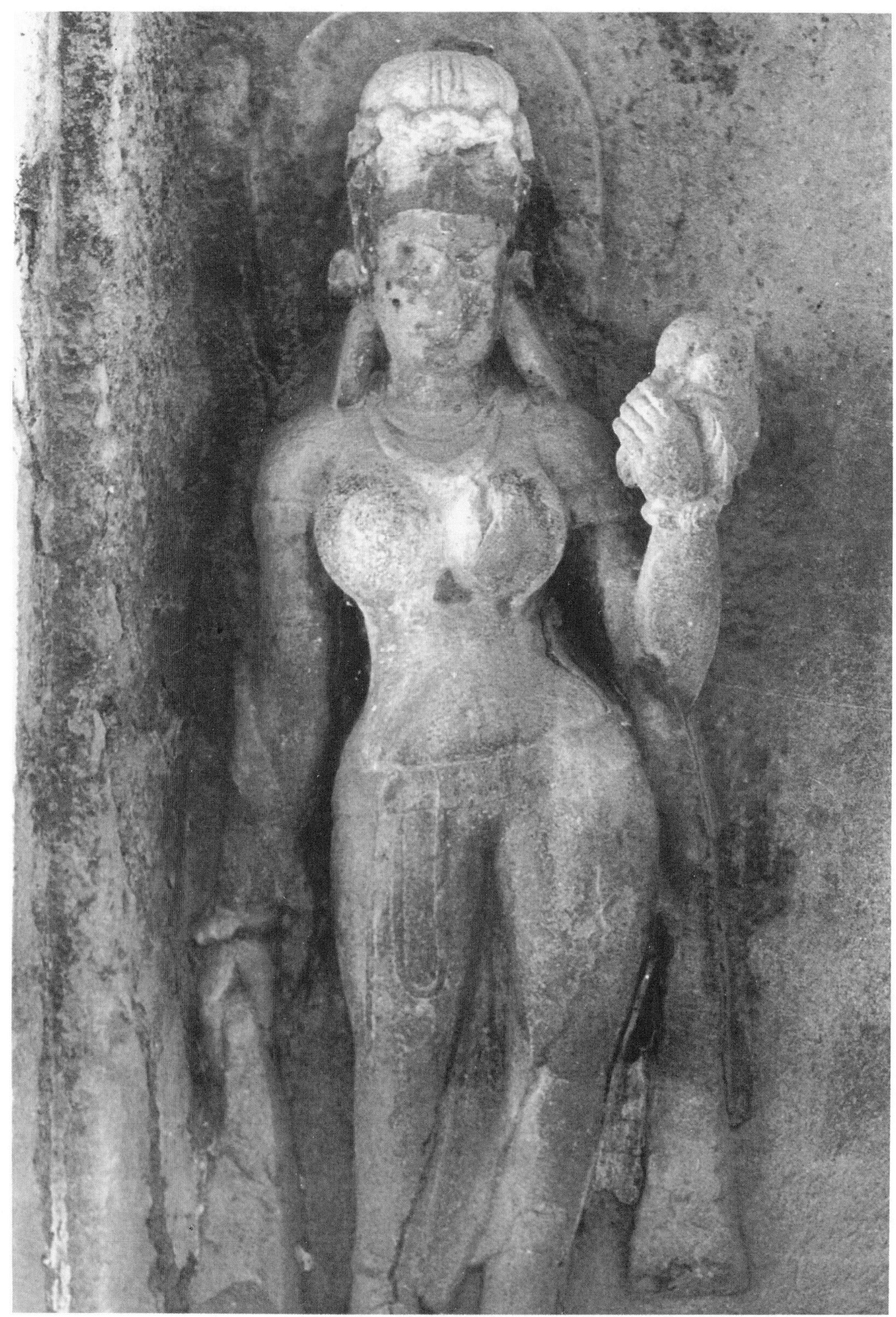

Fig. 94   Cave 8A Tārā

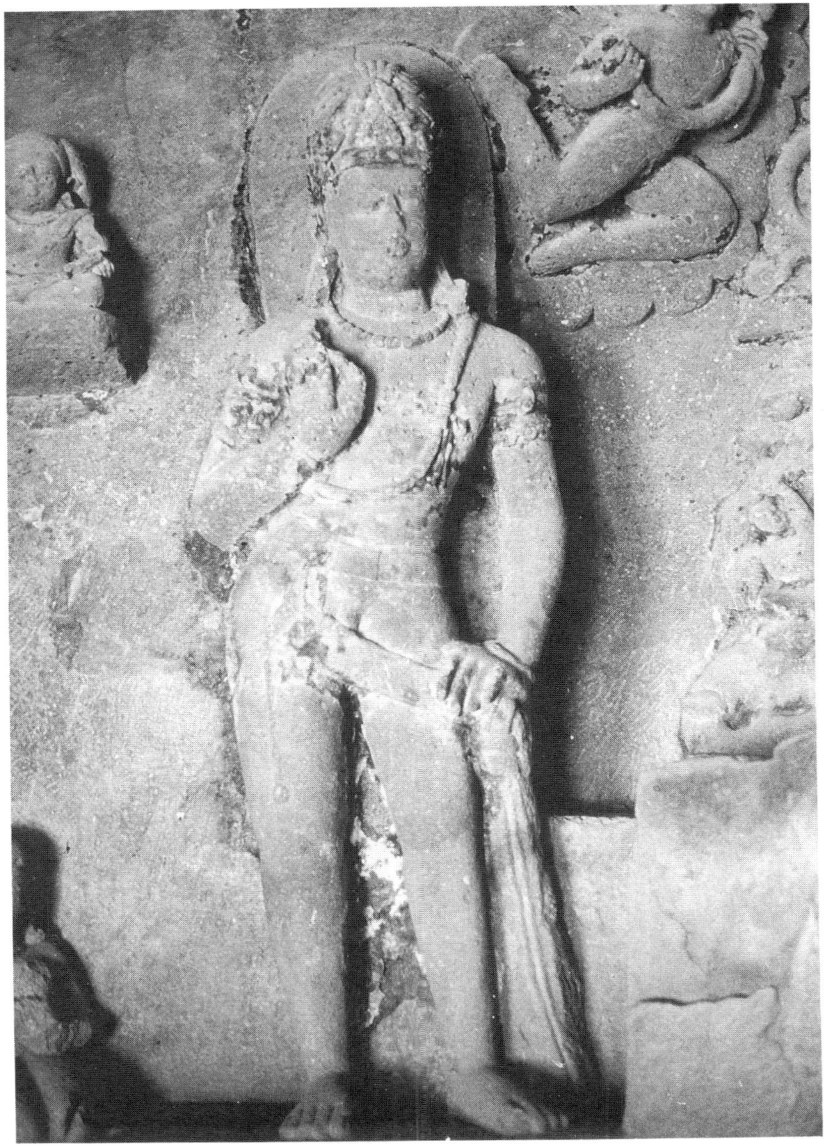

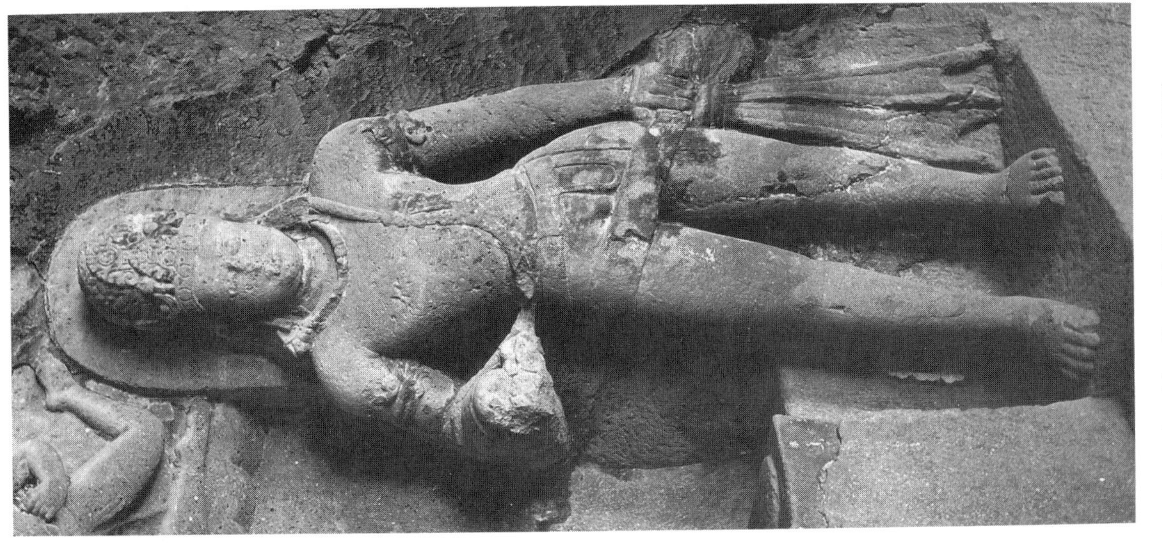

Fig. 96 Cave 8A Vajrapāṇi (AIIS)

Fig. 95 Cave 8A Maitreya

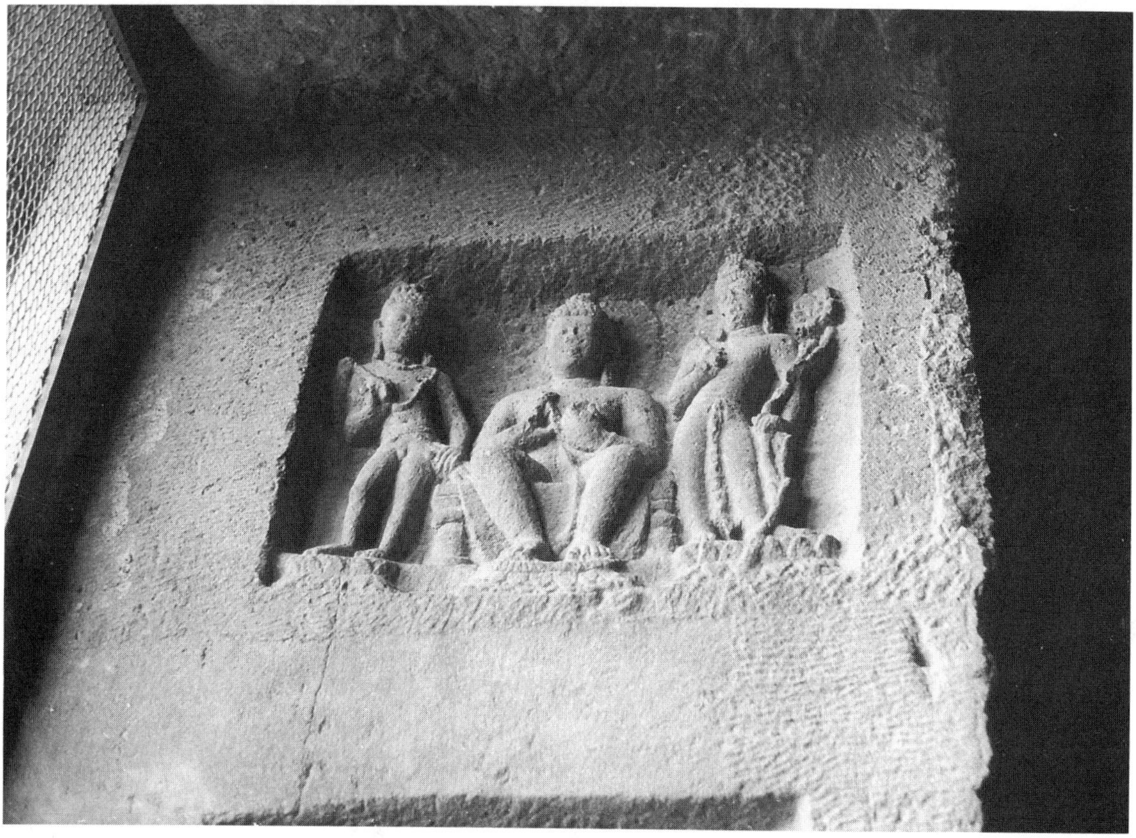

Fig. 97   Cave 2 Buddha panel with Vajrapāṇi on left

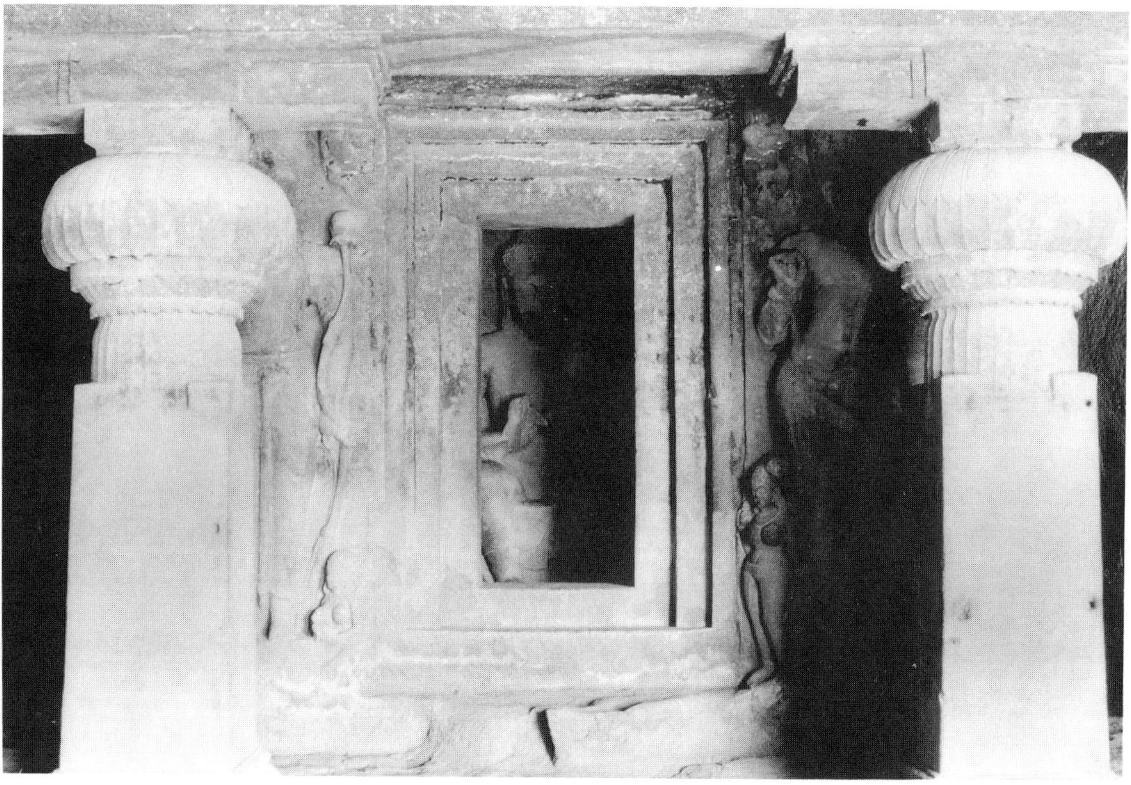

Fig. 98   Cave 8 shrine door and inner Buddha

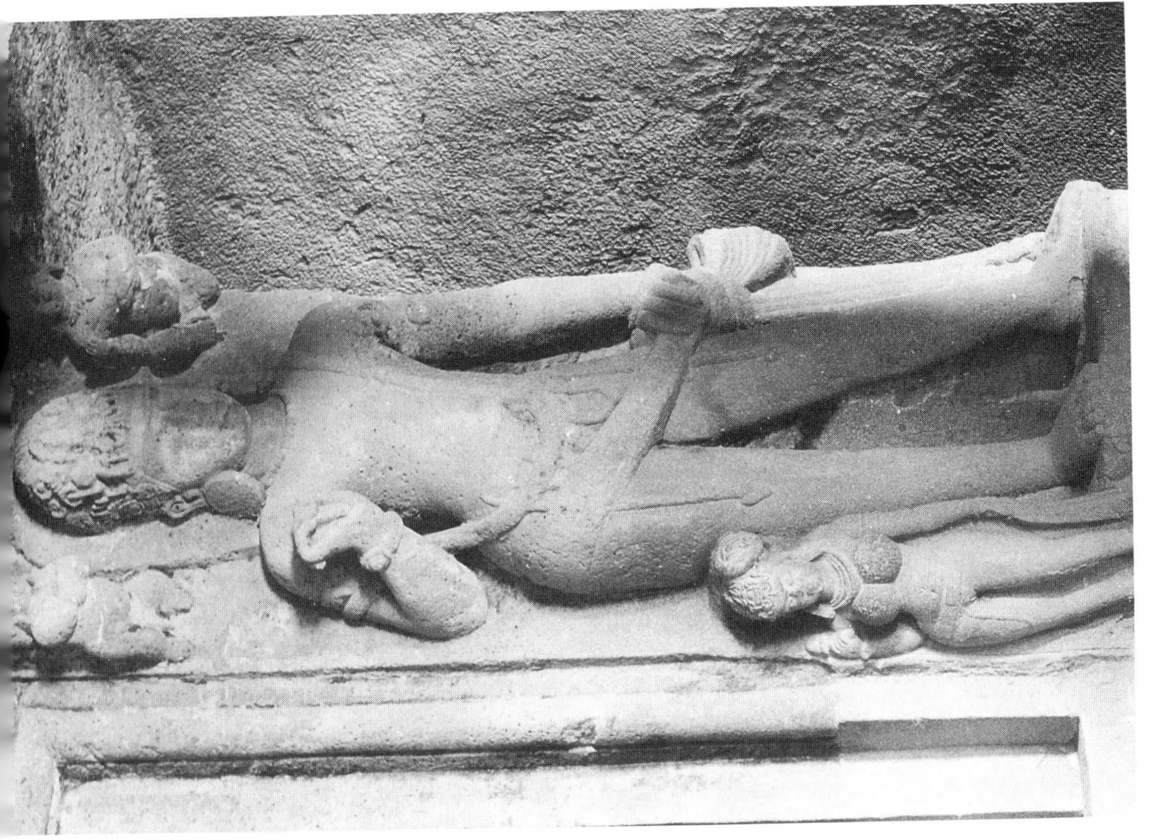

Fig. 100   Cave 8 shrine door, Maitreya

Fig. 99   Cave 8 shrine door, Avalokiteśvara

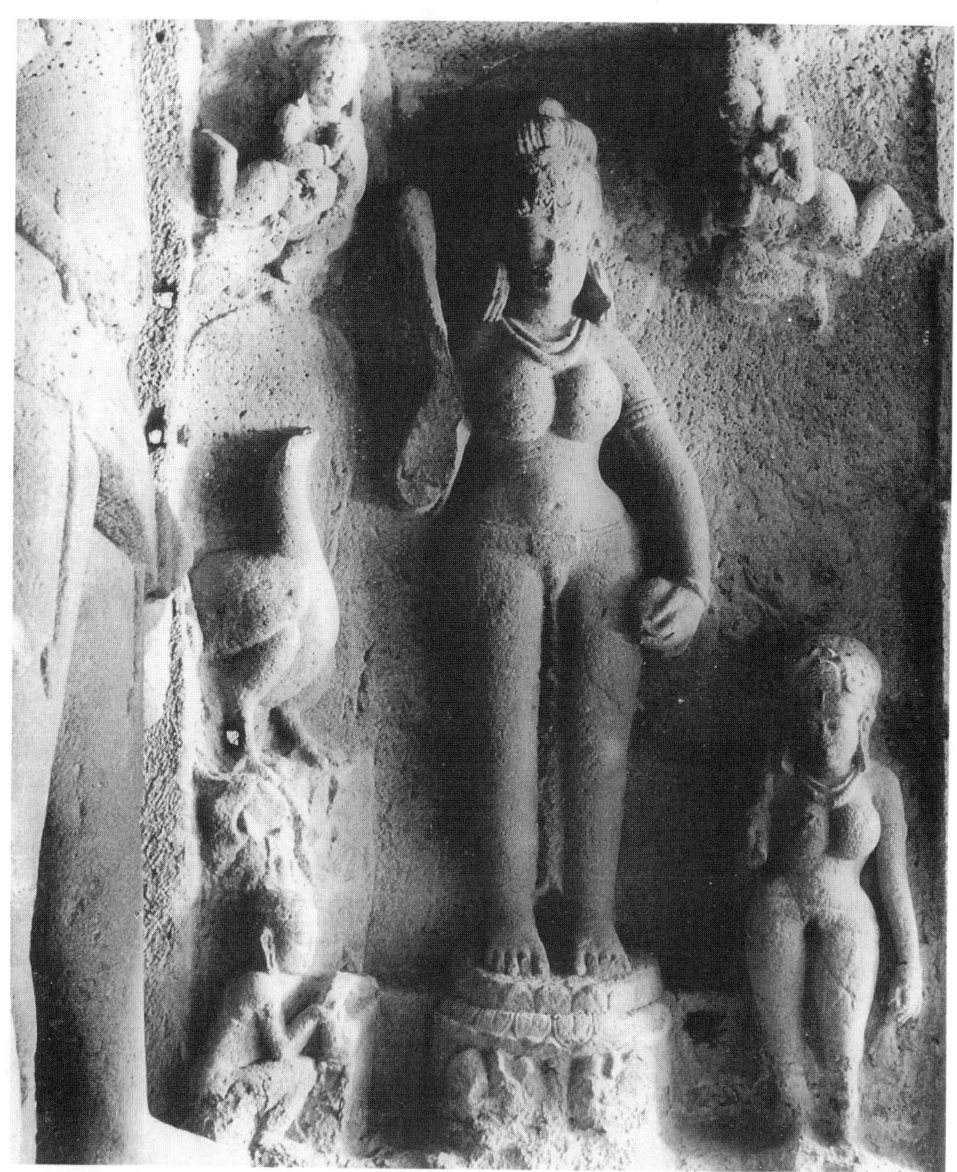

Fig. 101   Cave 8 antechamber, Mahāmāyūrī

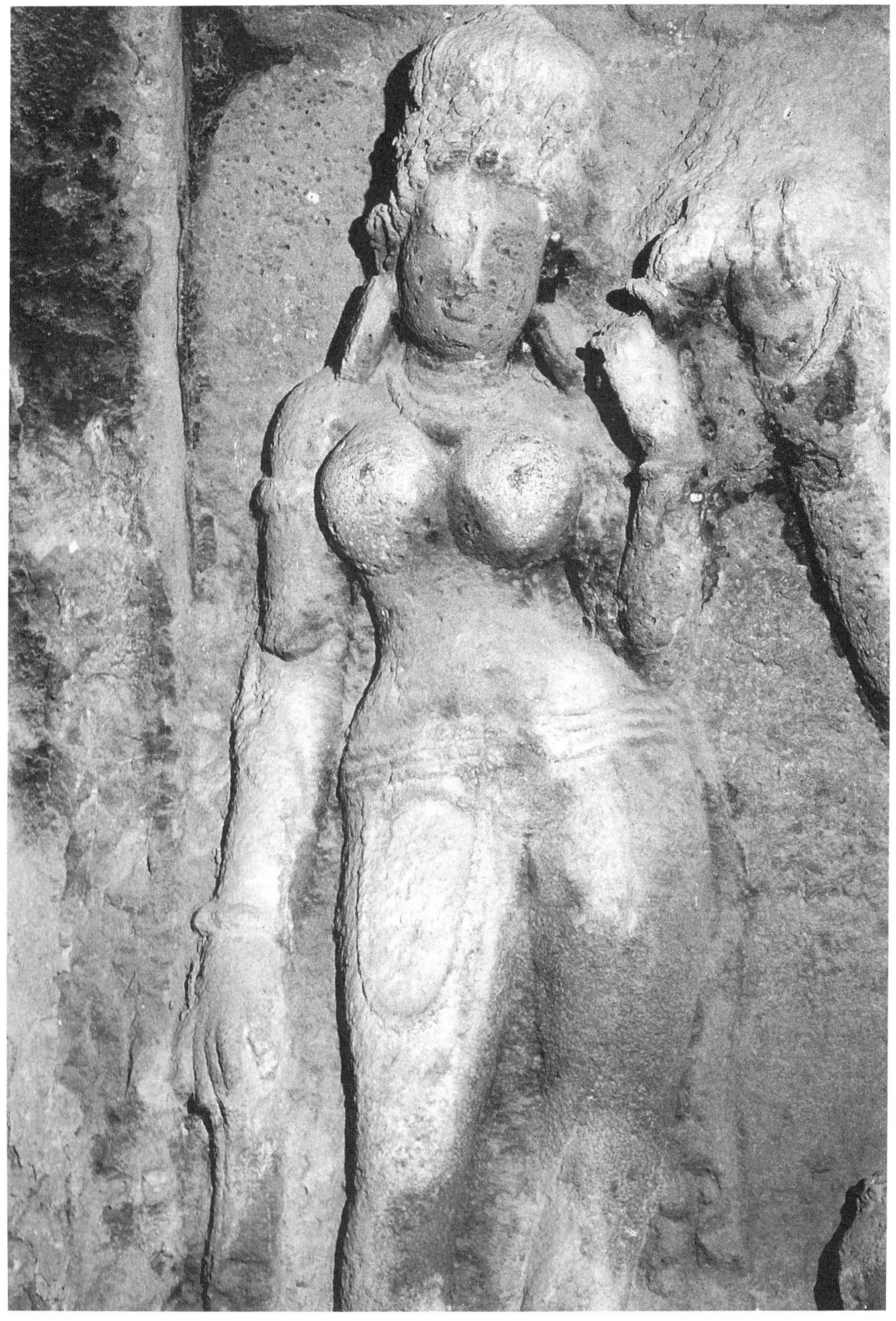

Fig. 102   Cave 8 shrine, Tārā

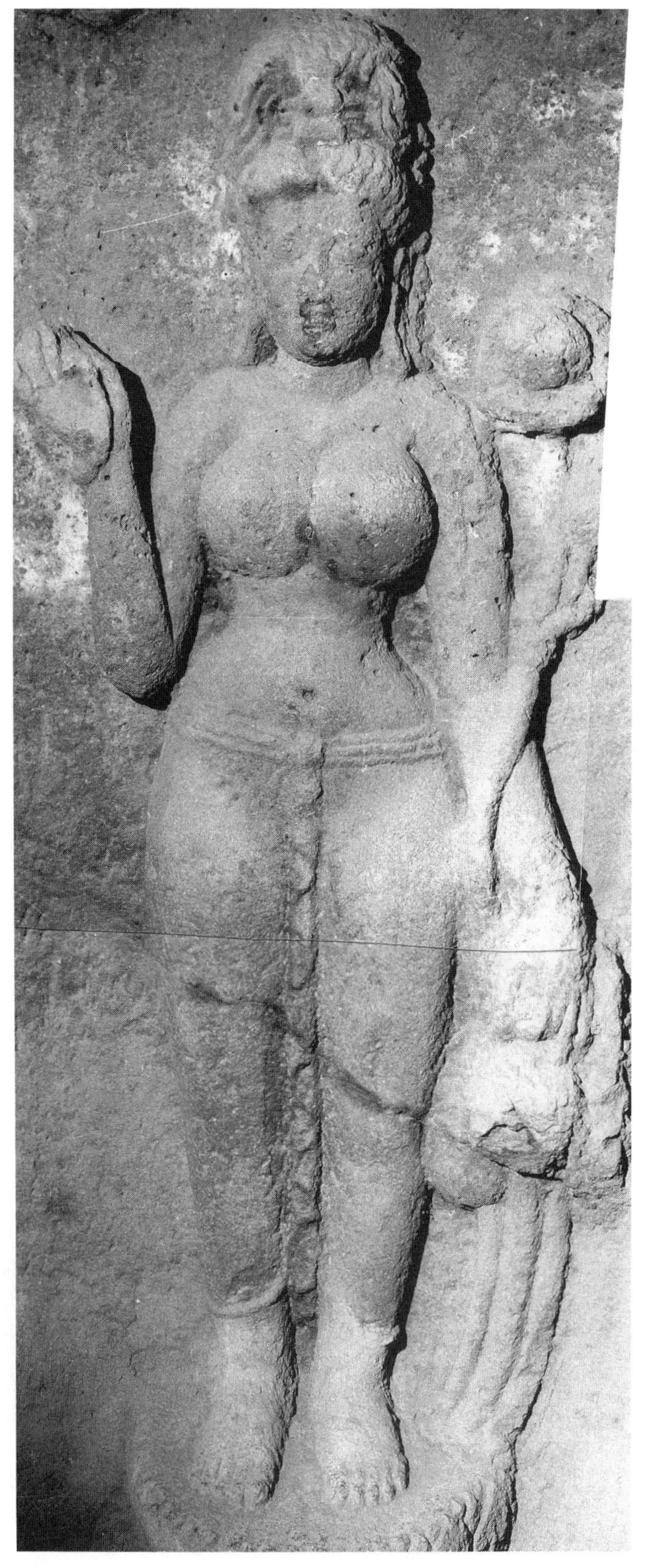

Fig. 103　Cave 8 shrine, Bhṛkuṭī

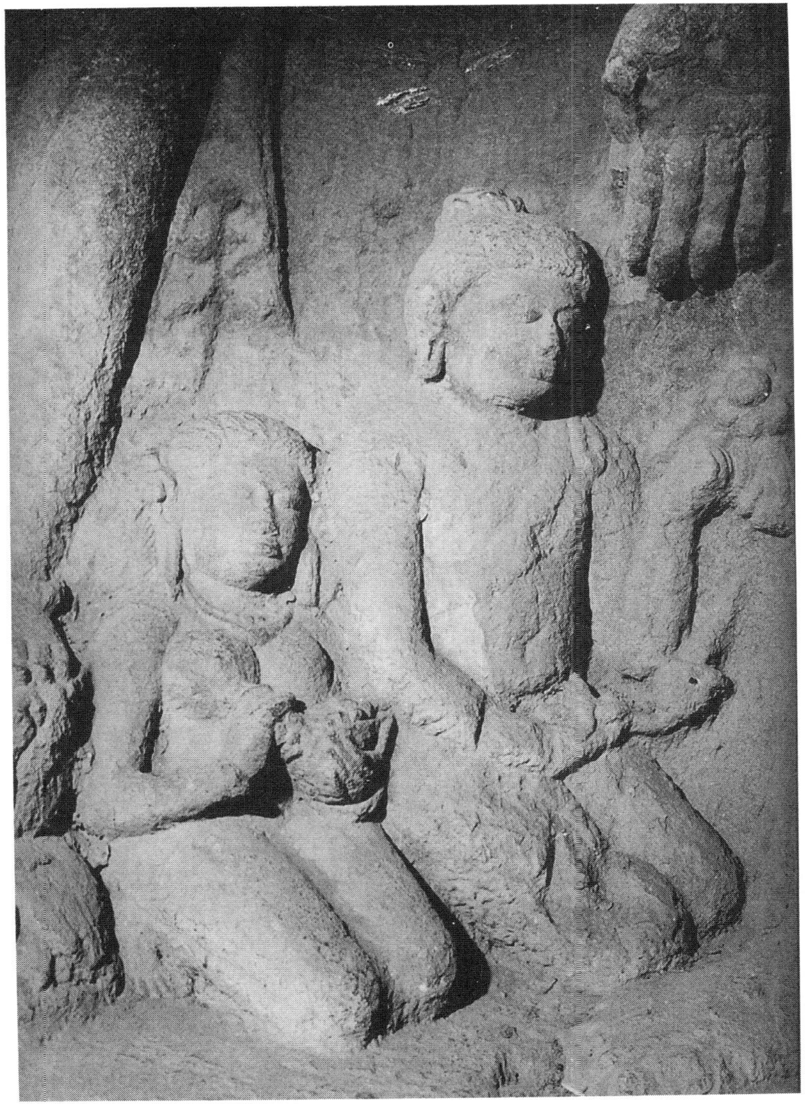

Fig. 104   Cave 8 shrine, devotees

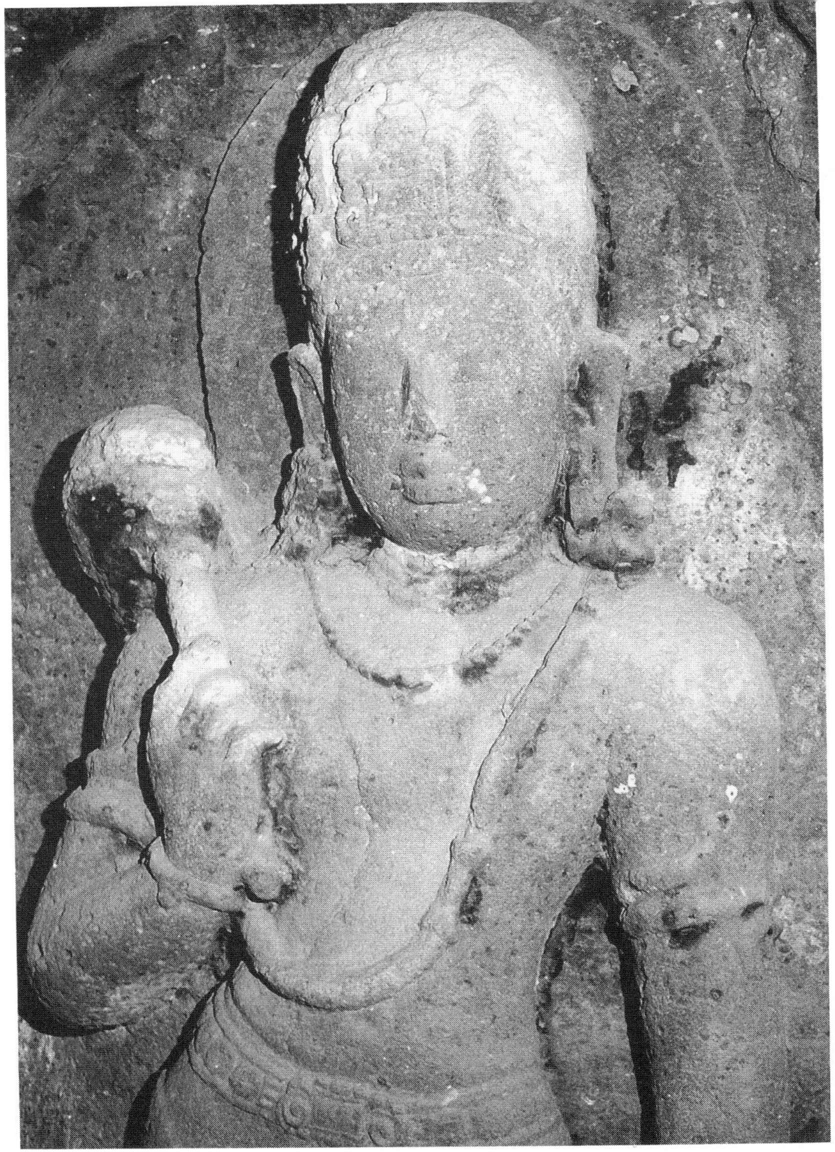

Fig. 105   Cave 8 shrine, Maitreya

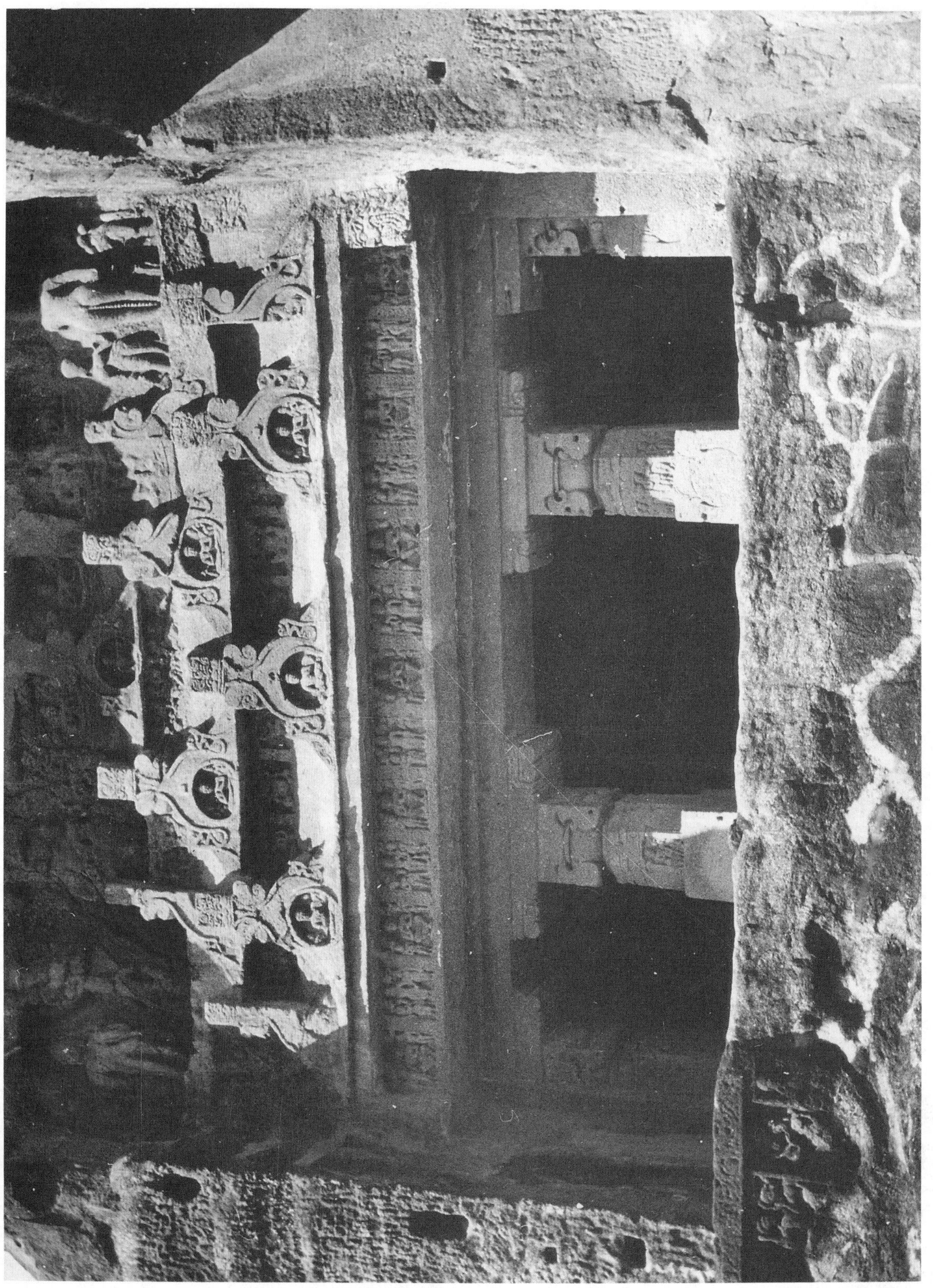

Fig. 106   Cave 9 façade (AIIS)

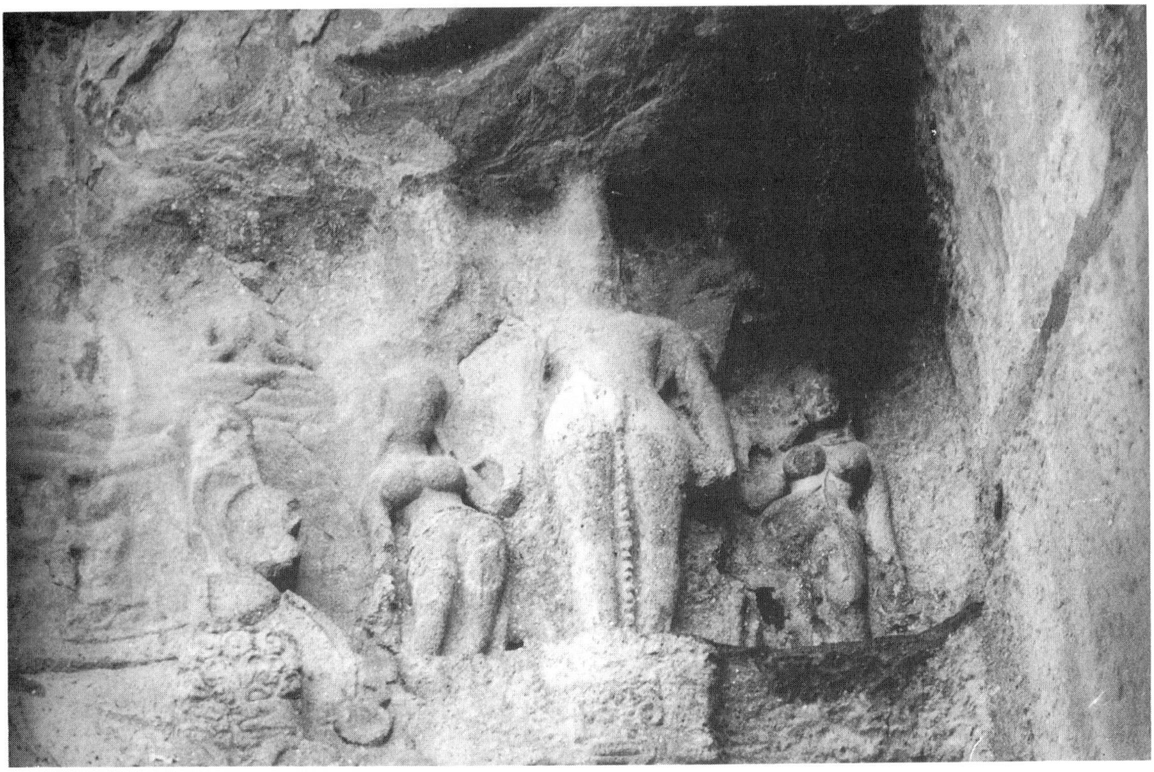

Fig. 107 Cave 9 façade, Bodhisattva closeup

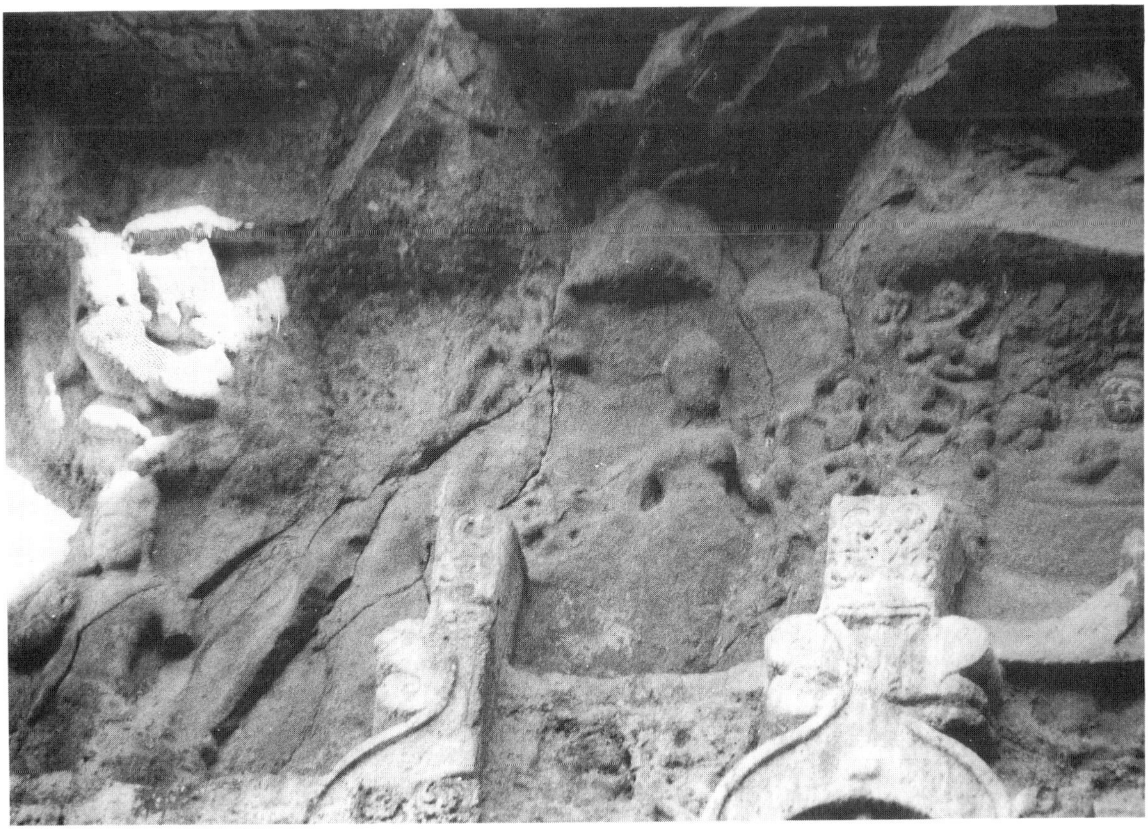

Fig. 108 Cave 9 façade, Tārā (?) closeup

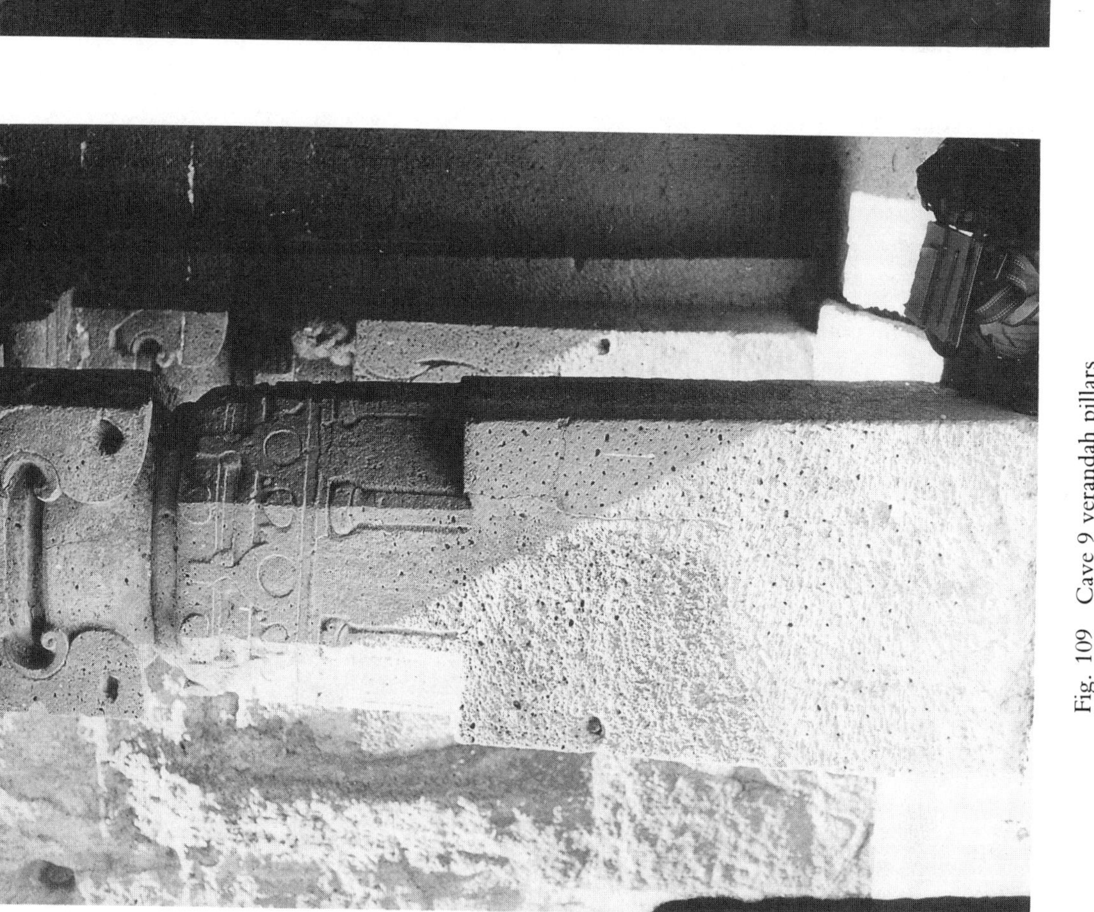

Fig. 110   Cave 10 pillar

Fig. 109   Cave 9 verandah pillars

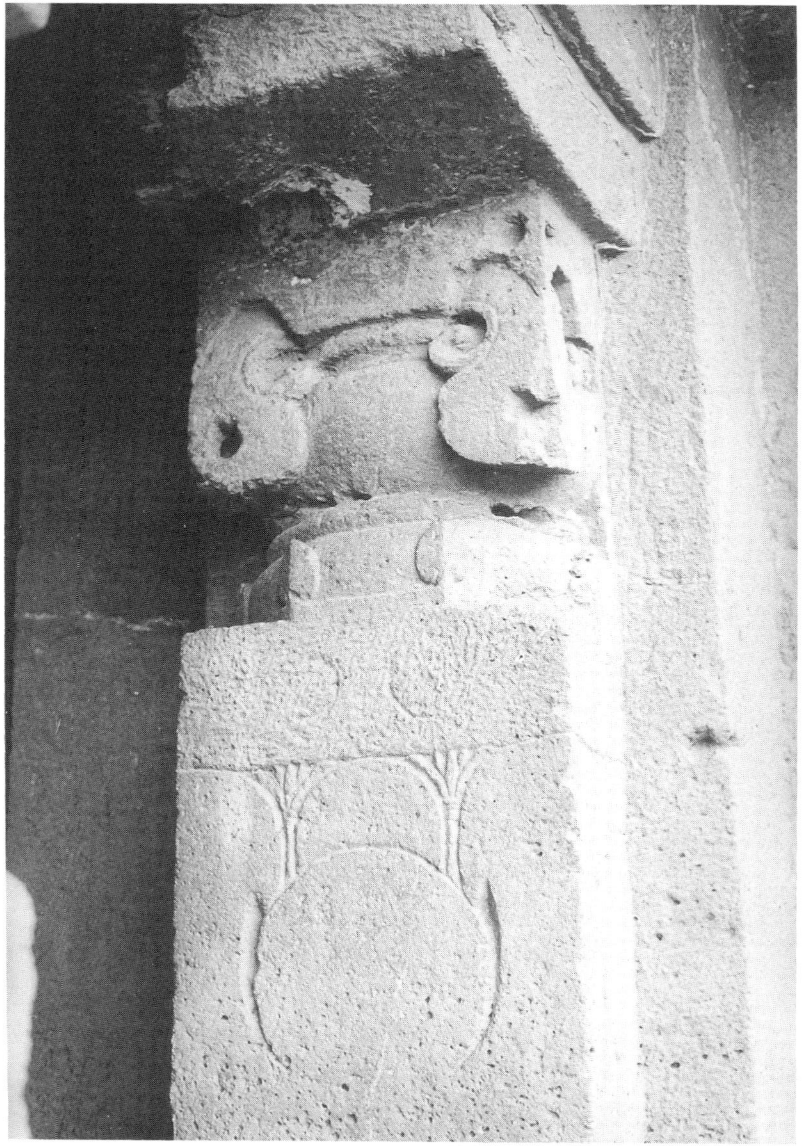

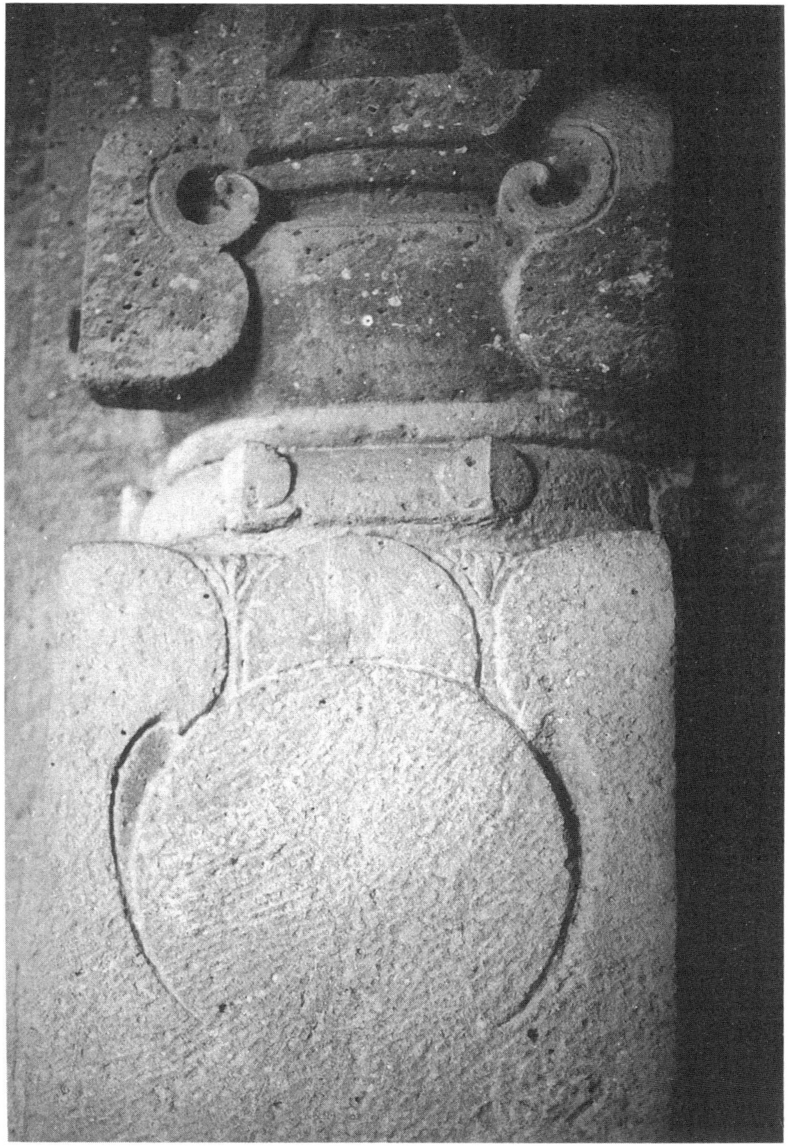

Fig. 112 Cave 10 piller

Fig. 111 Cave 9 pilaster

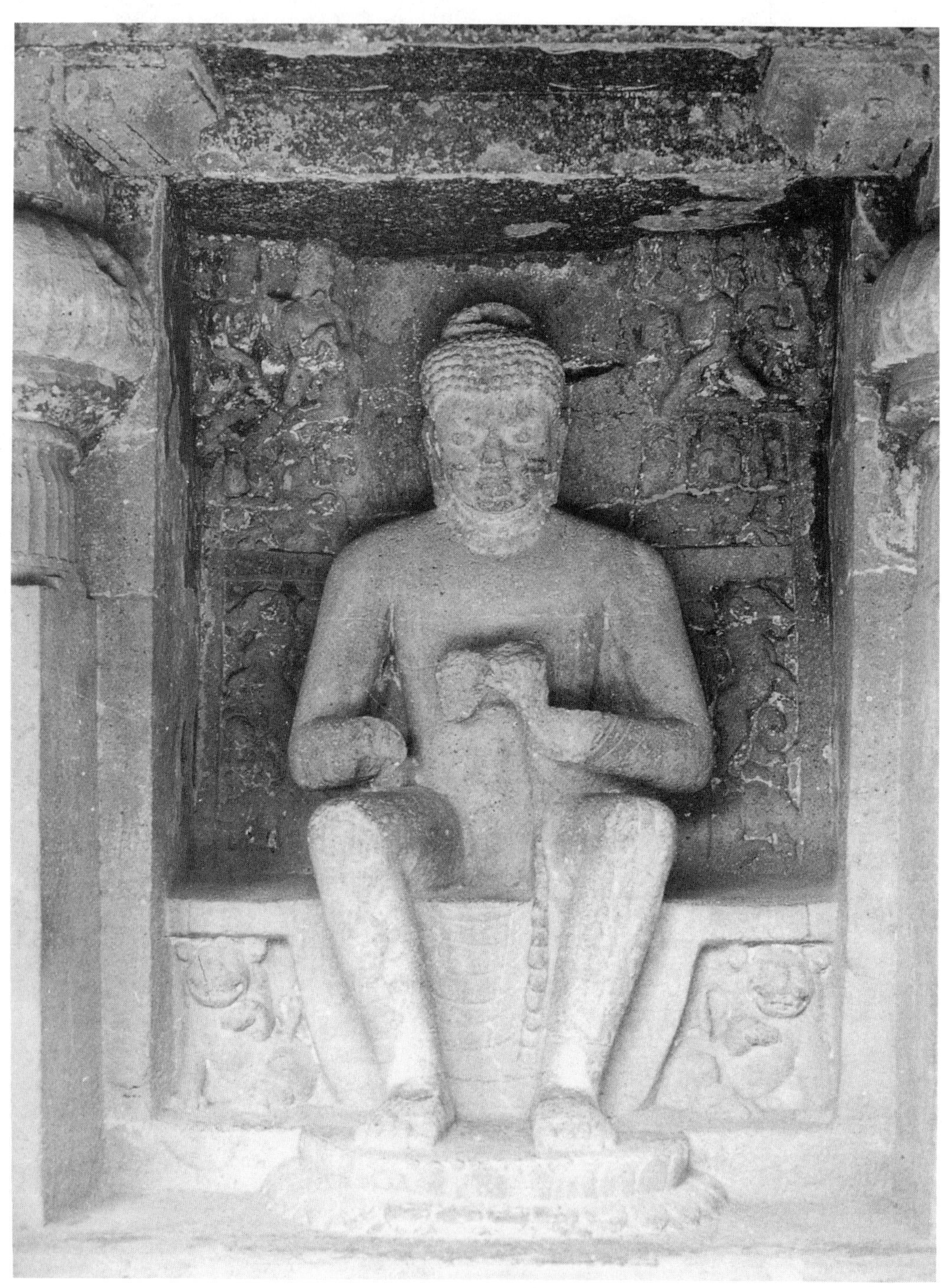

Fig. 113   Cave 9 Buddha

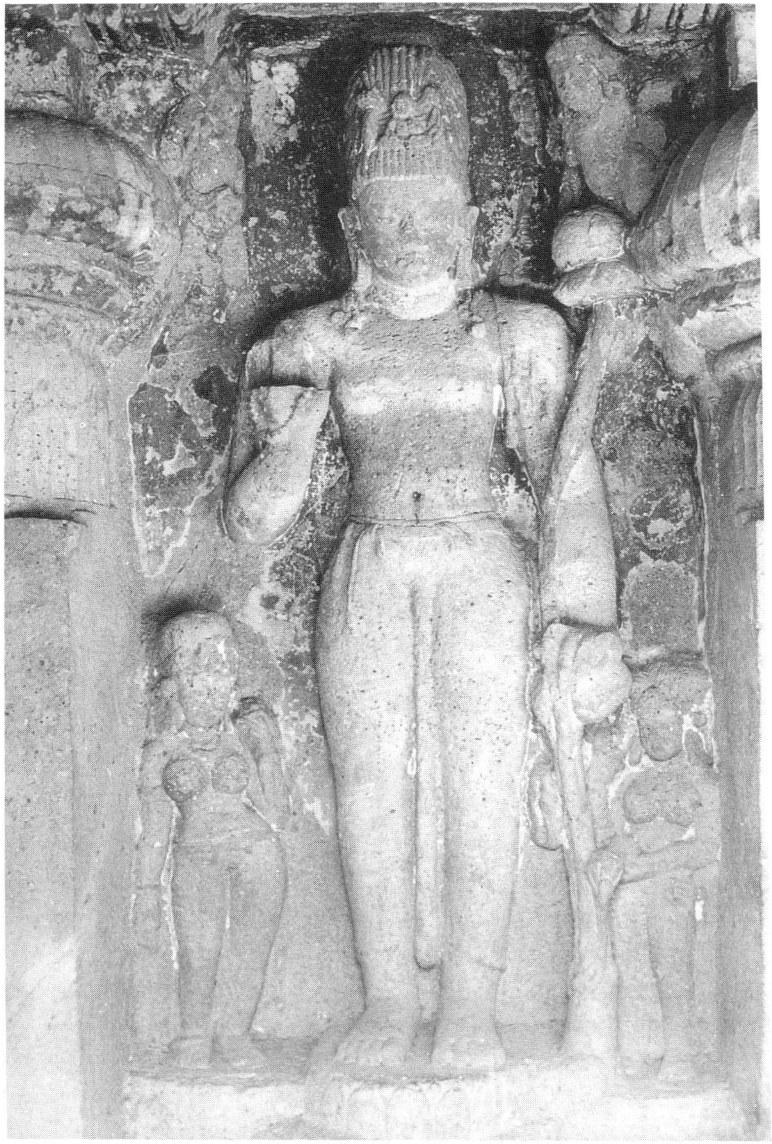

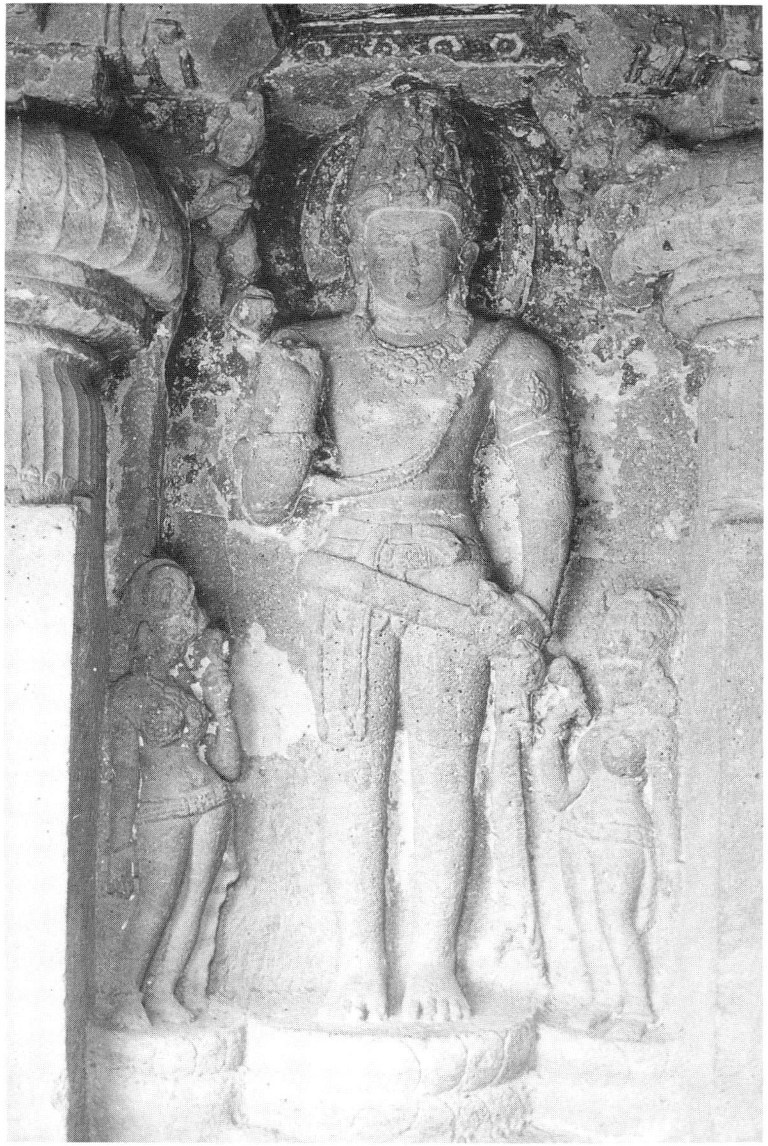

Fig. 115   Cave 9 Vajrapāṇi

Fig. 114   Cave 9 Avalokiteśvara

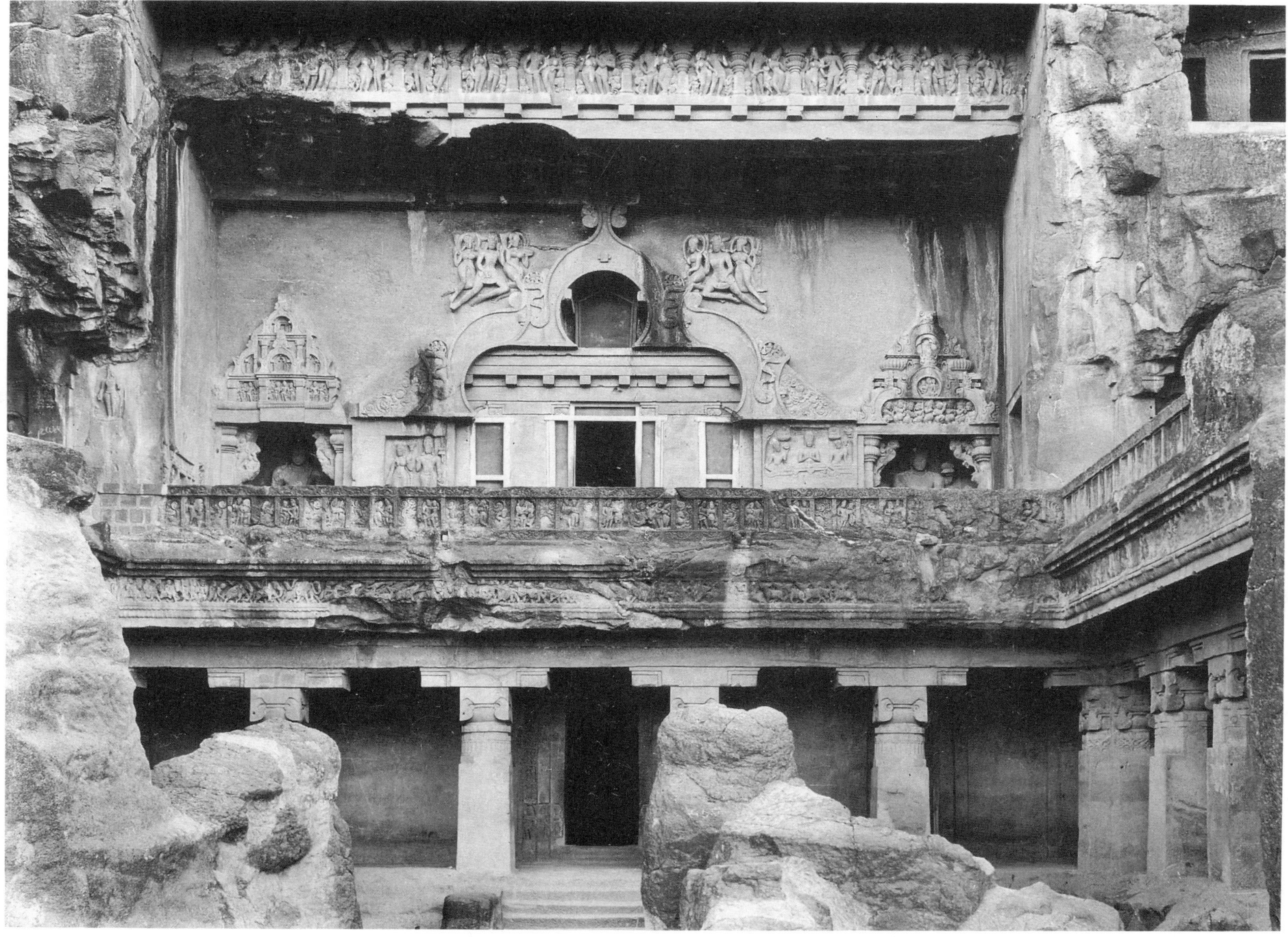

Fig. 116   Cave 10 facade (AIIS)

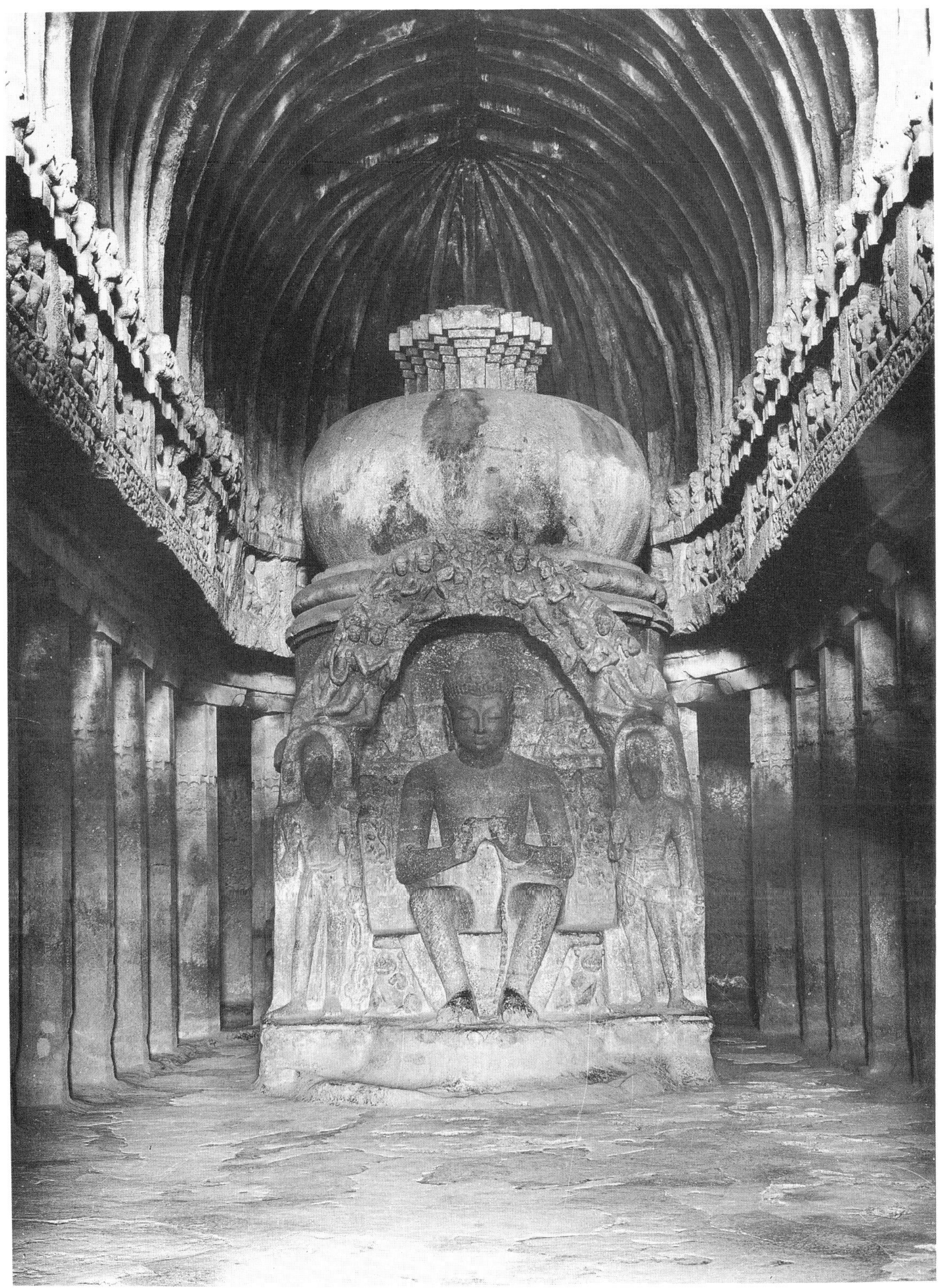

Fig. 117 Cave 10 *caitya* hall and *stūpa* (AIIS)

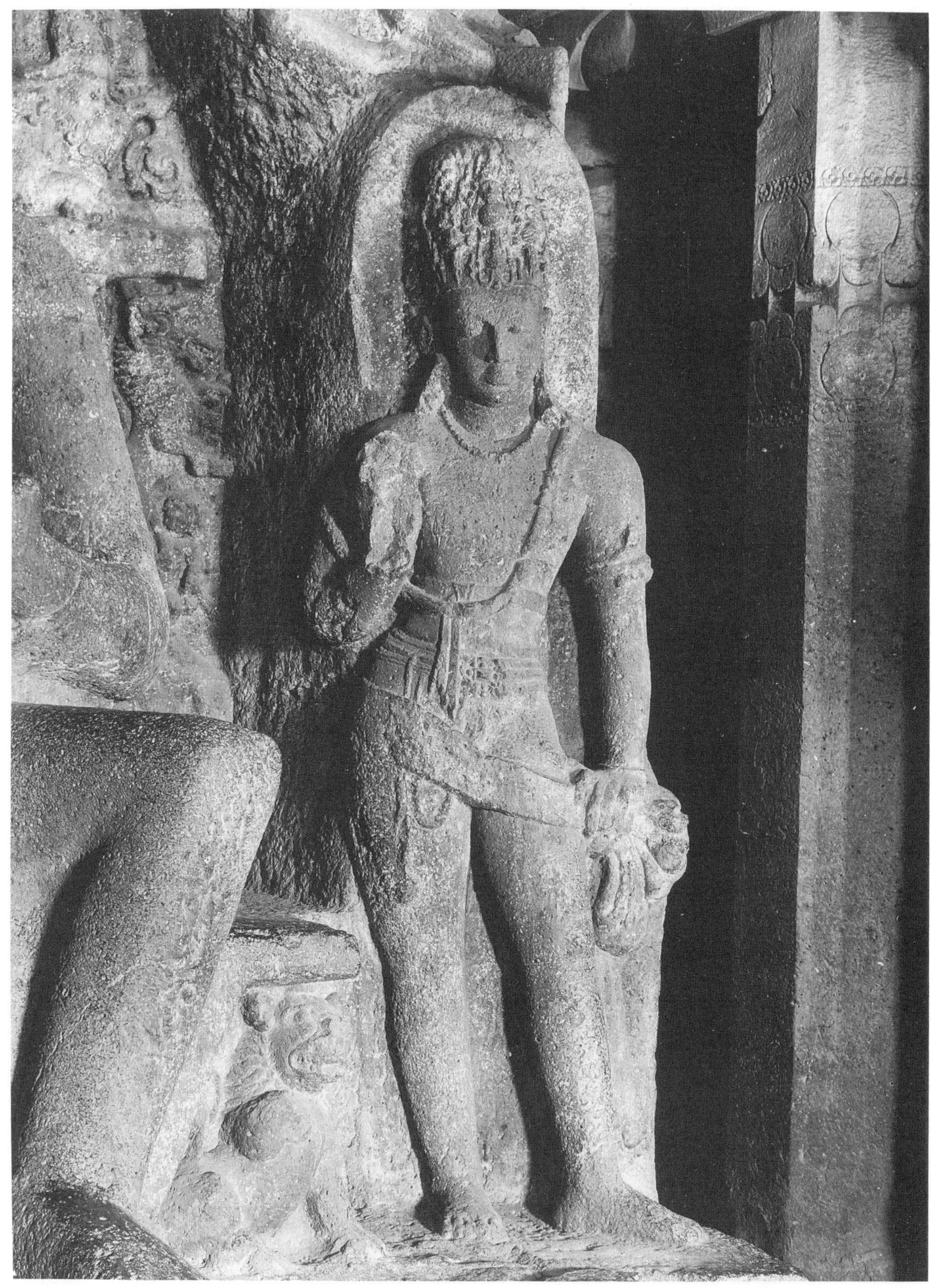

Fig. 118   Cave 10 *stūpa*, Maitreya closeup (AIIS)

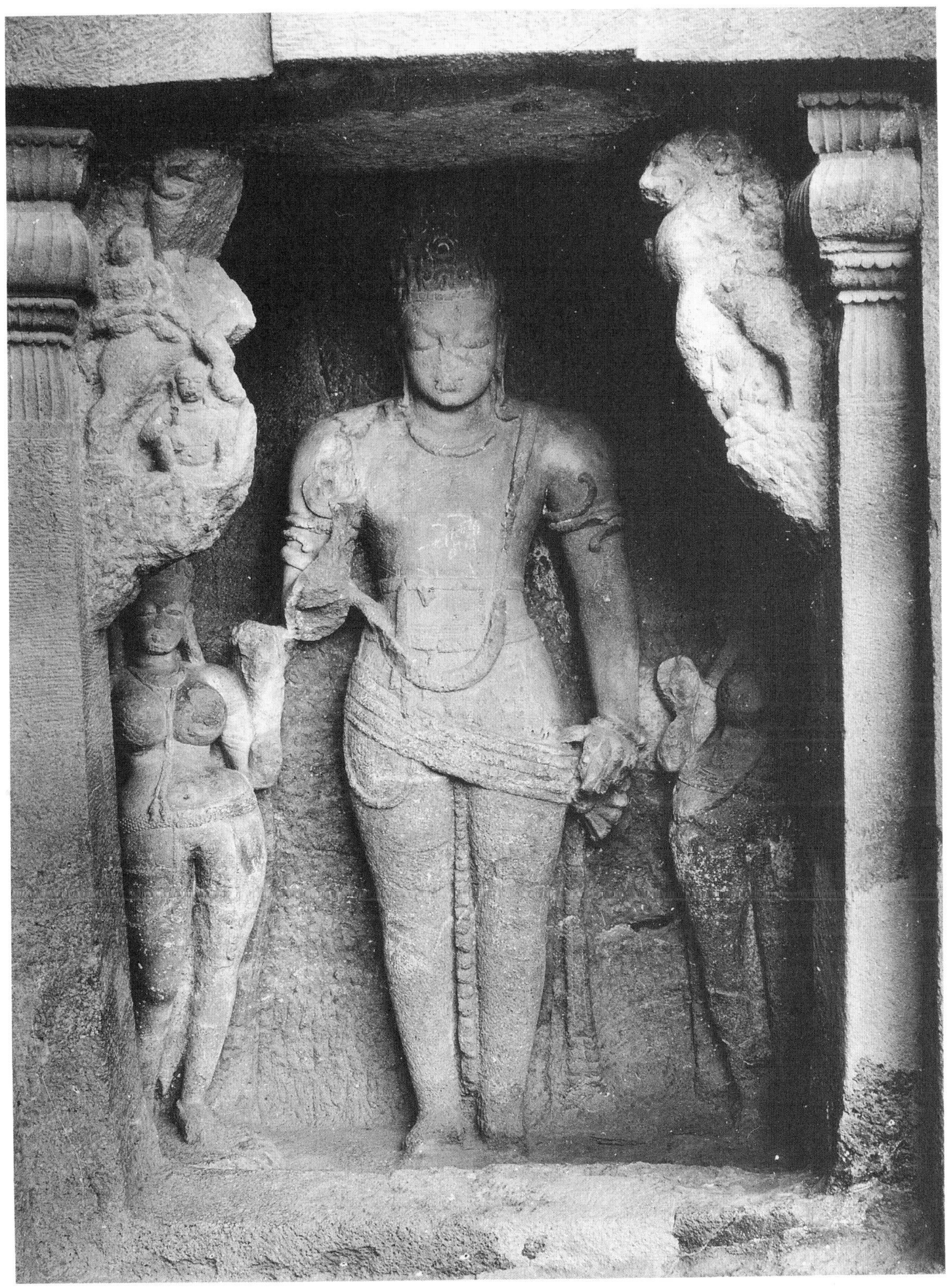

Fig. 119   Cave 10 balcony, Maitreya (AIIS)

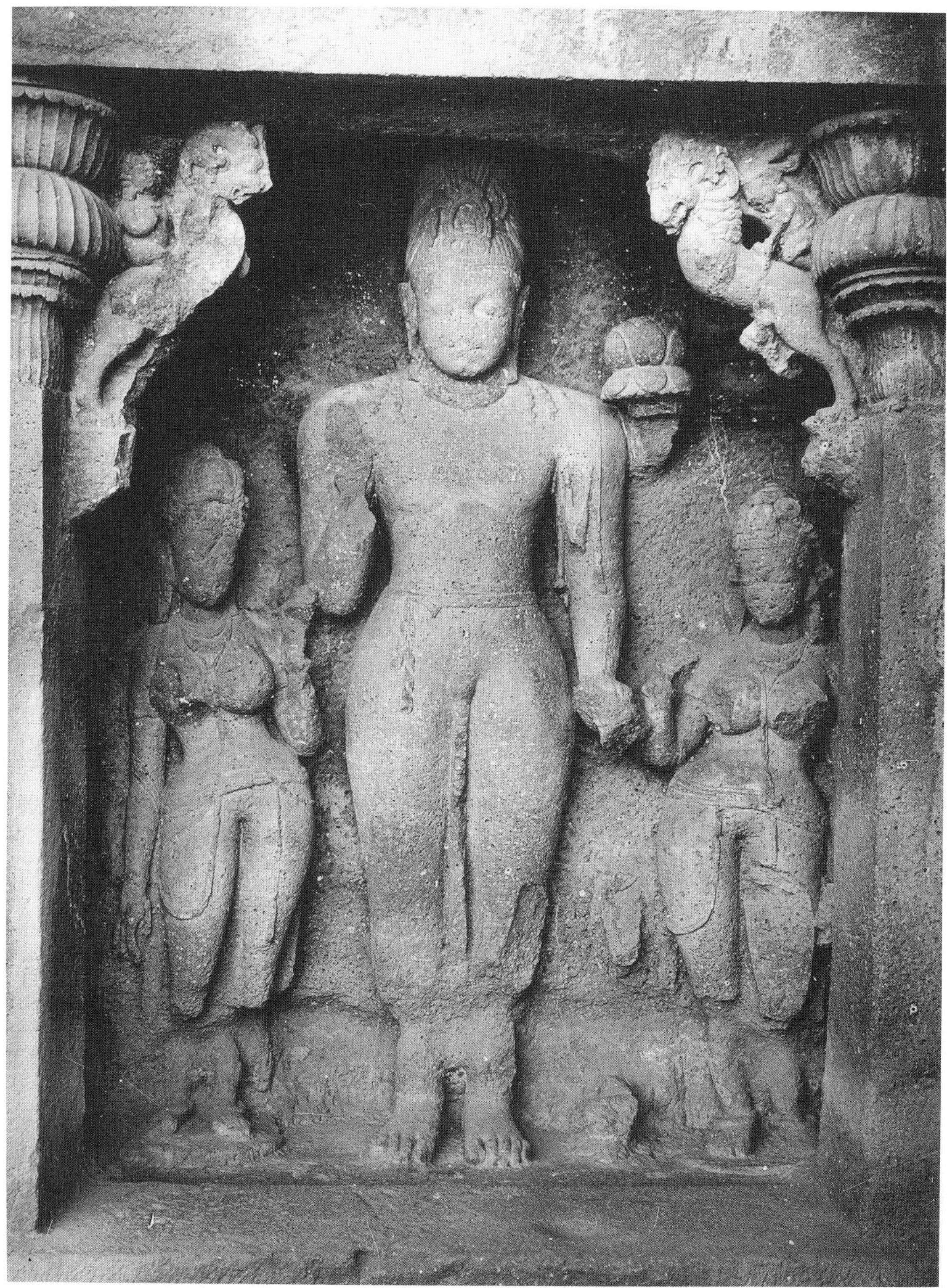

Fig. 120   Cave 10 balcony, Avalokiteśvara (AIIS)

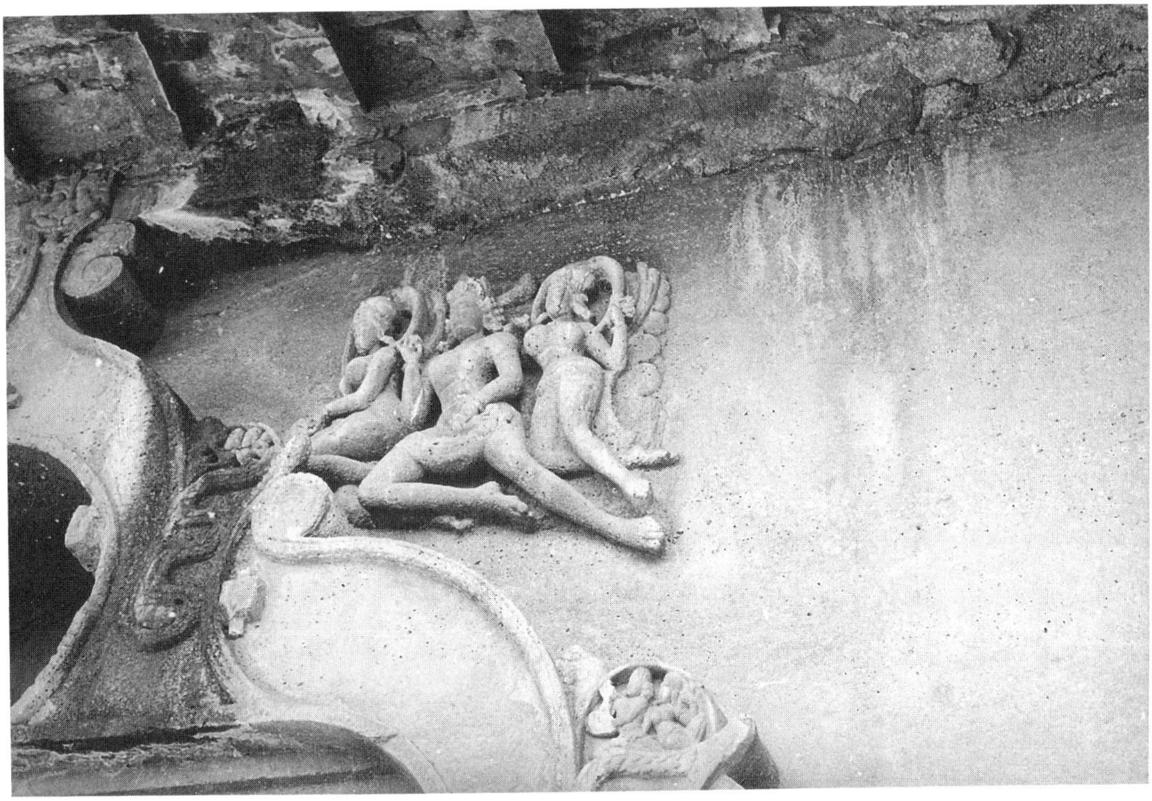

Fig. 121   Cave 10 façade, flying figures

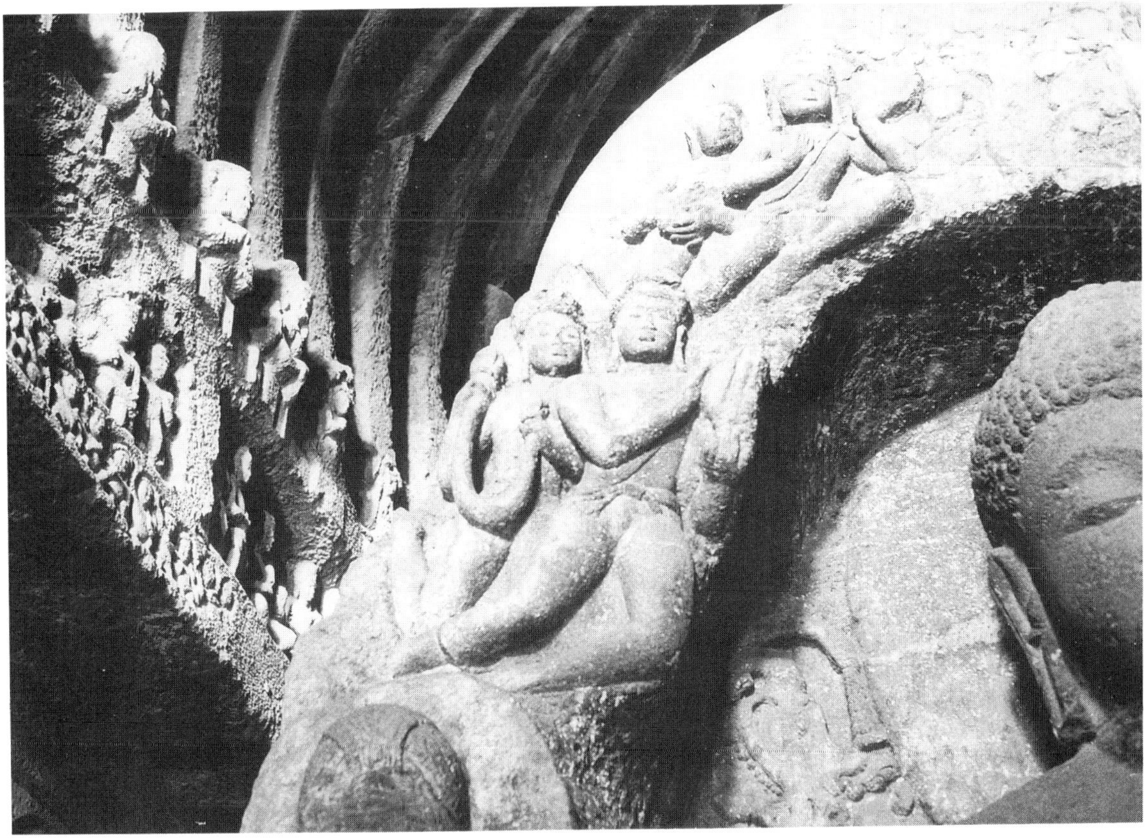

Fig. 122   Cave 10 *stūpa*, flying figures

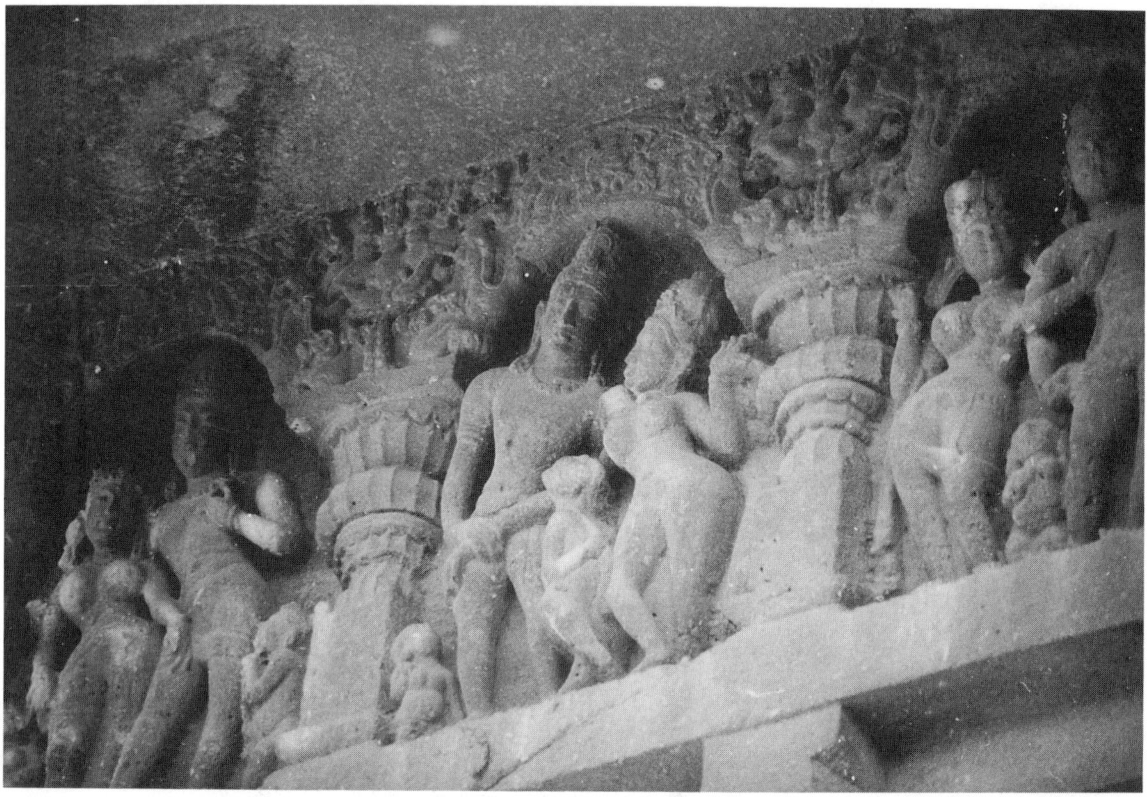

Fig. 123   Cave 10 façade, loving couples

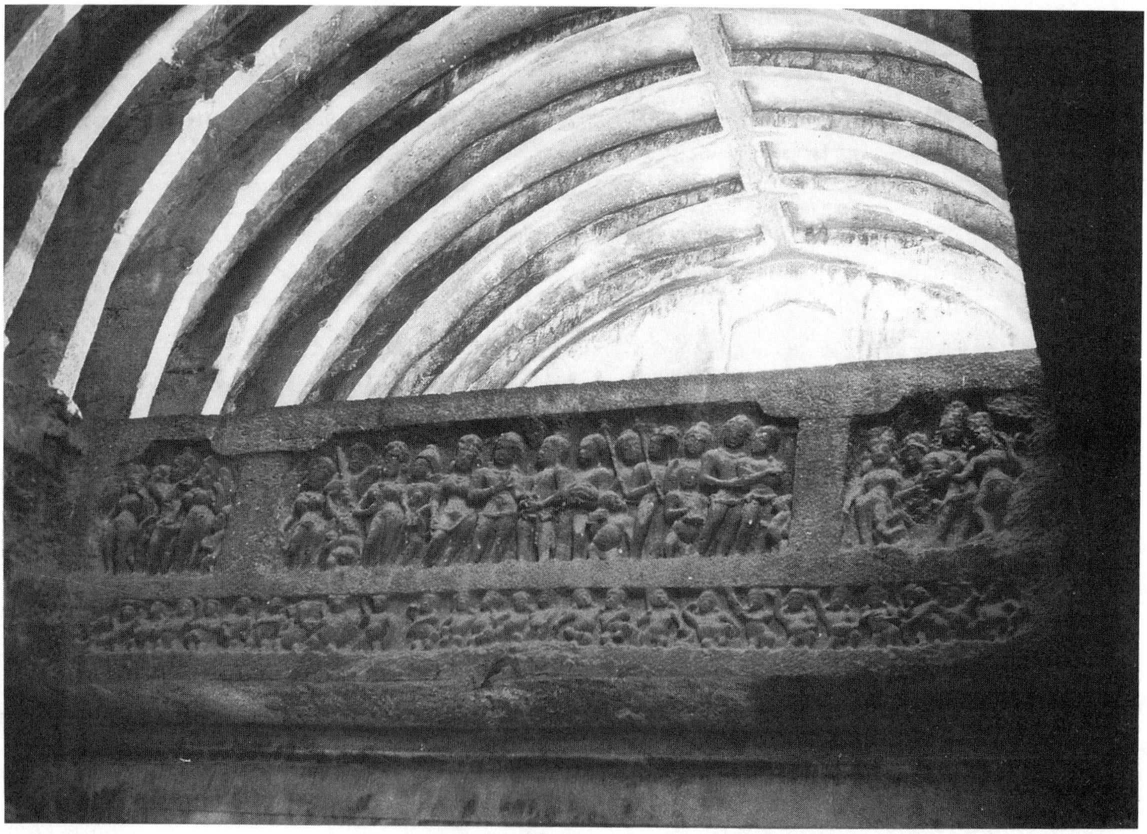

Fig. 124   Cave 10 *caitya*, triforium relief panel

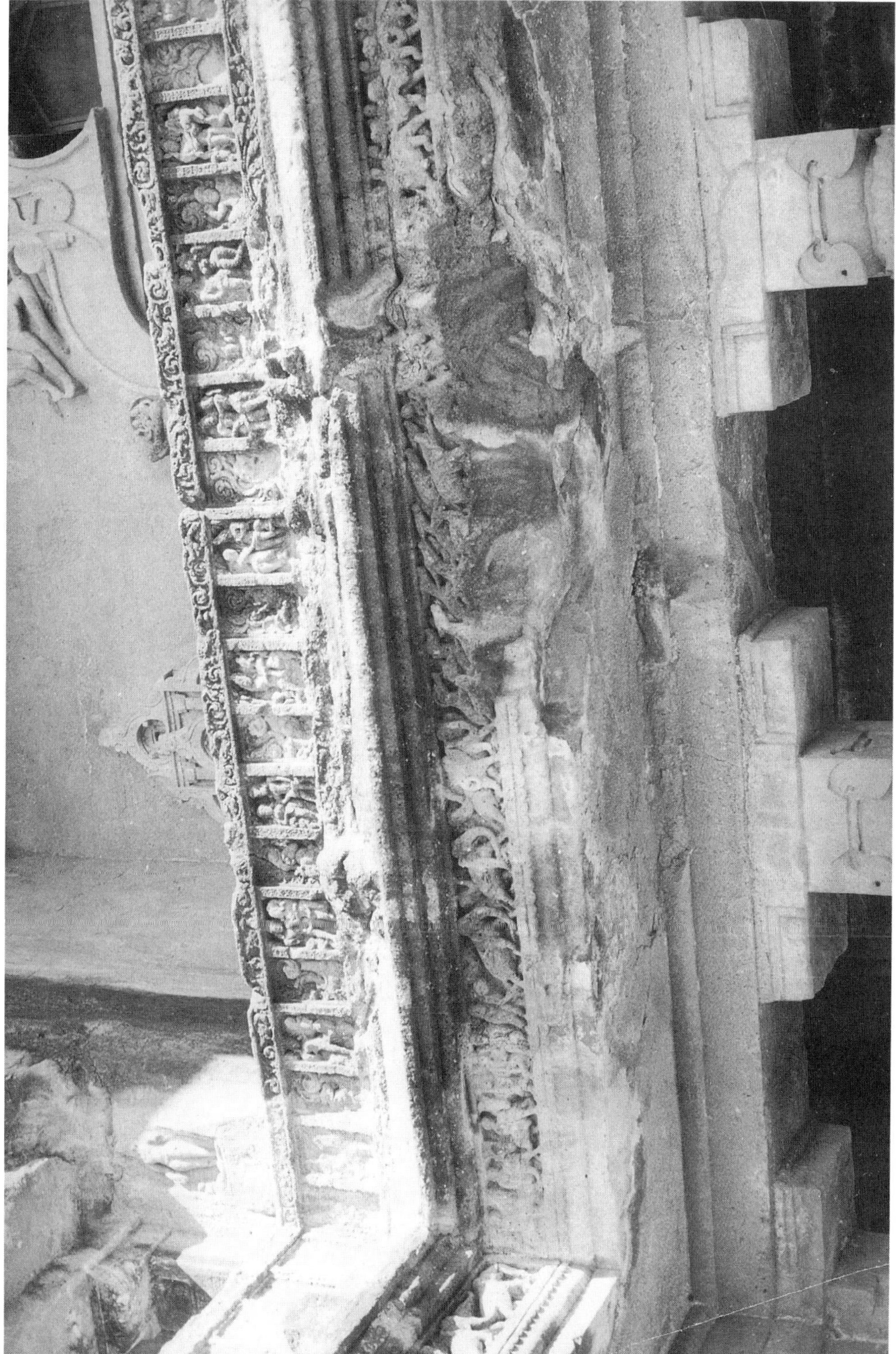

Fig. 125 Cave 10 façade, balcony railing

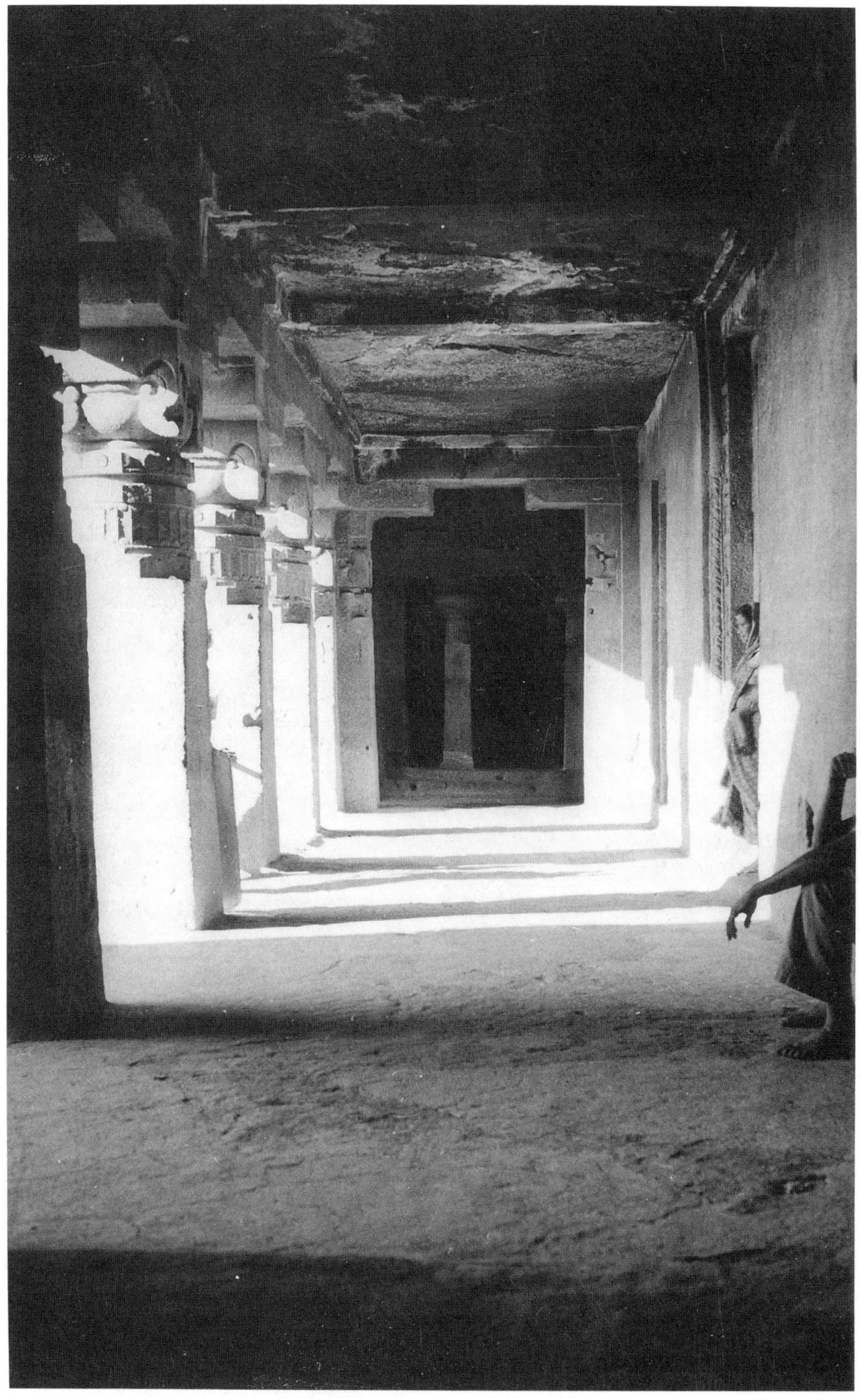

Fig. 126   Cave 10 verandah pillars

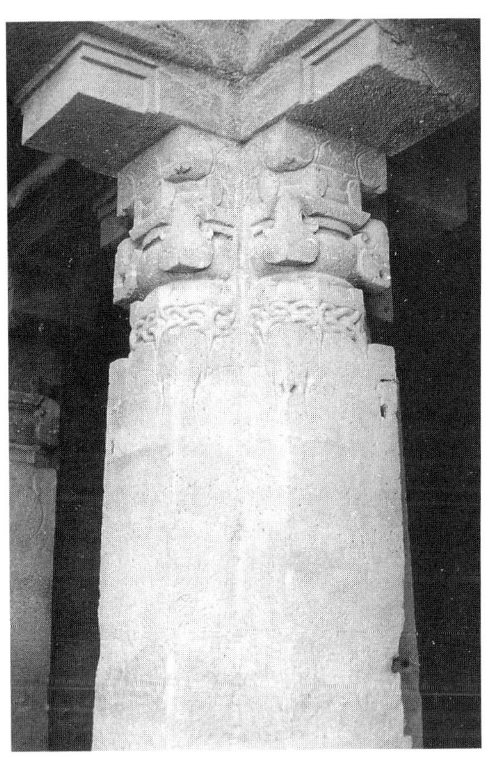

Fig. 127　Cave 10 pillar

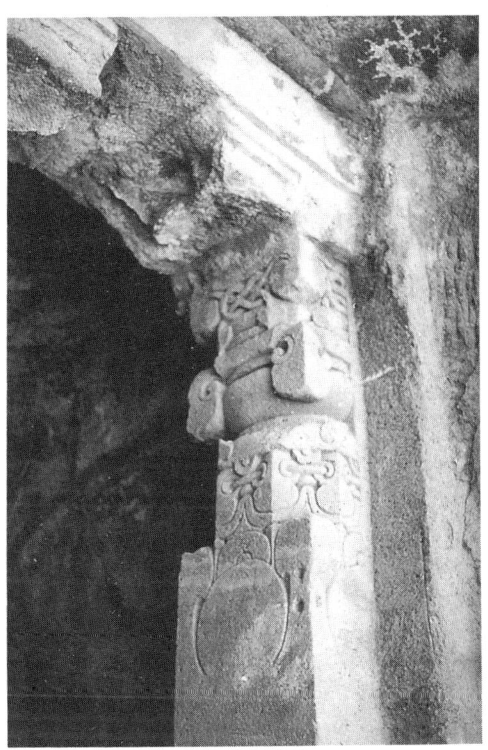

Fig. 128　Cave 10 pilaster

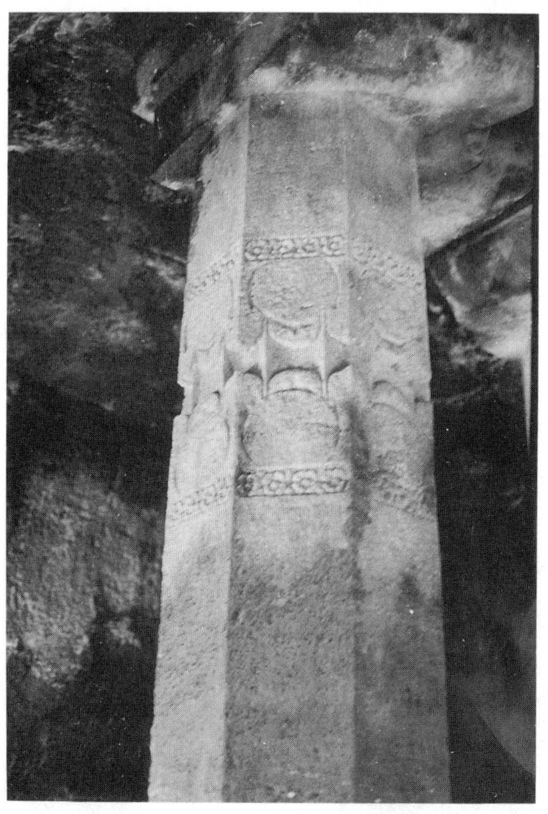

Fig. 129   Cave 10 *caitya* pillar

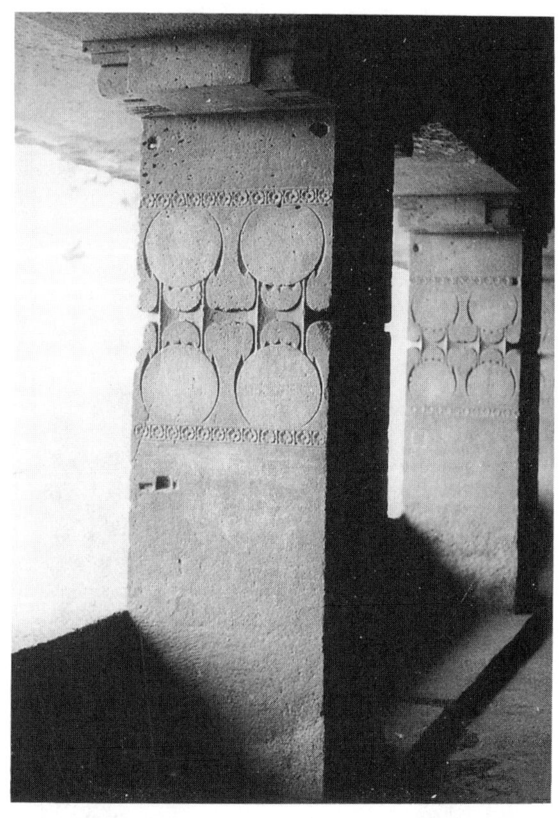

Fig. 130   Cave 11 third floor verandah pillars

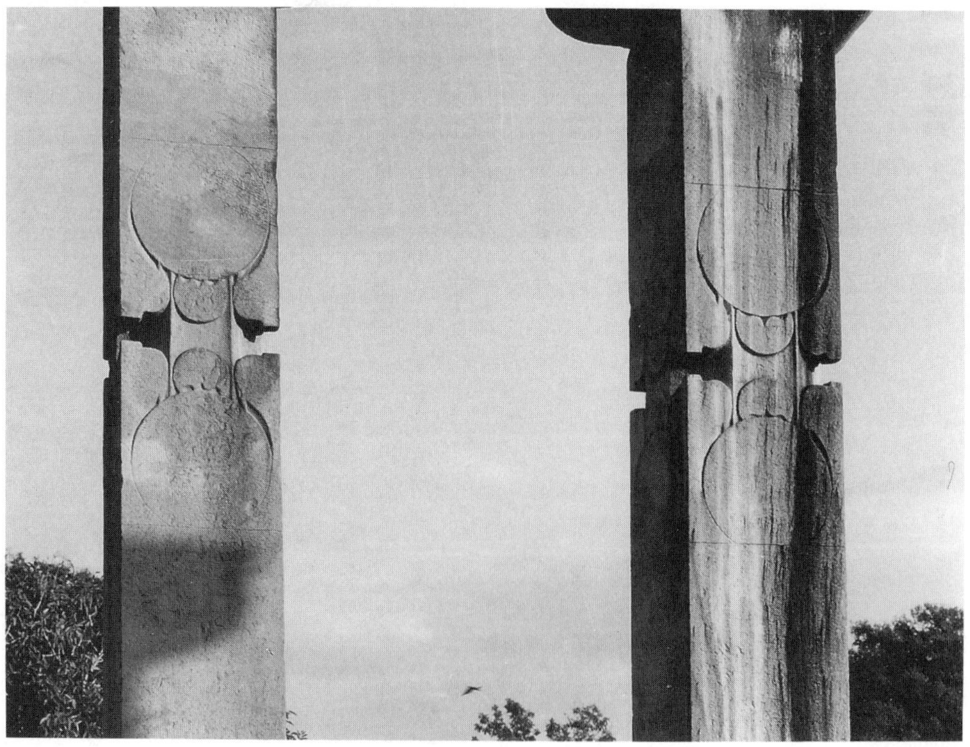

Fig. 131   Sanci Temple 18 pillars (AIIS)

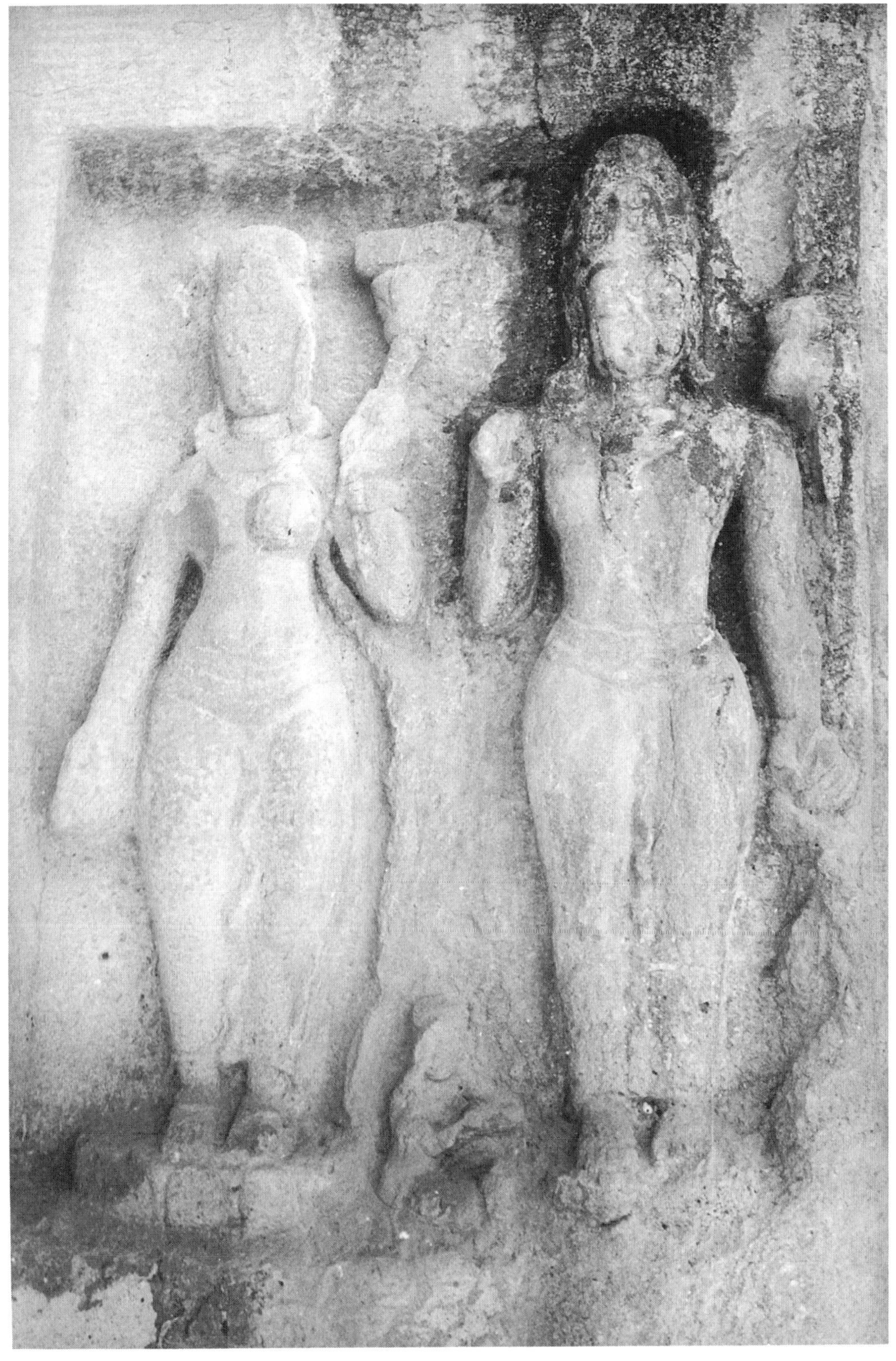

Fig. 132   Cave 10 balcony, Prajñāpāramitā and Avalokiteśvara

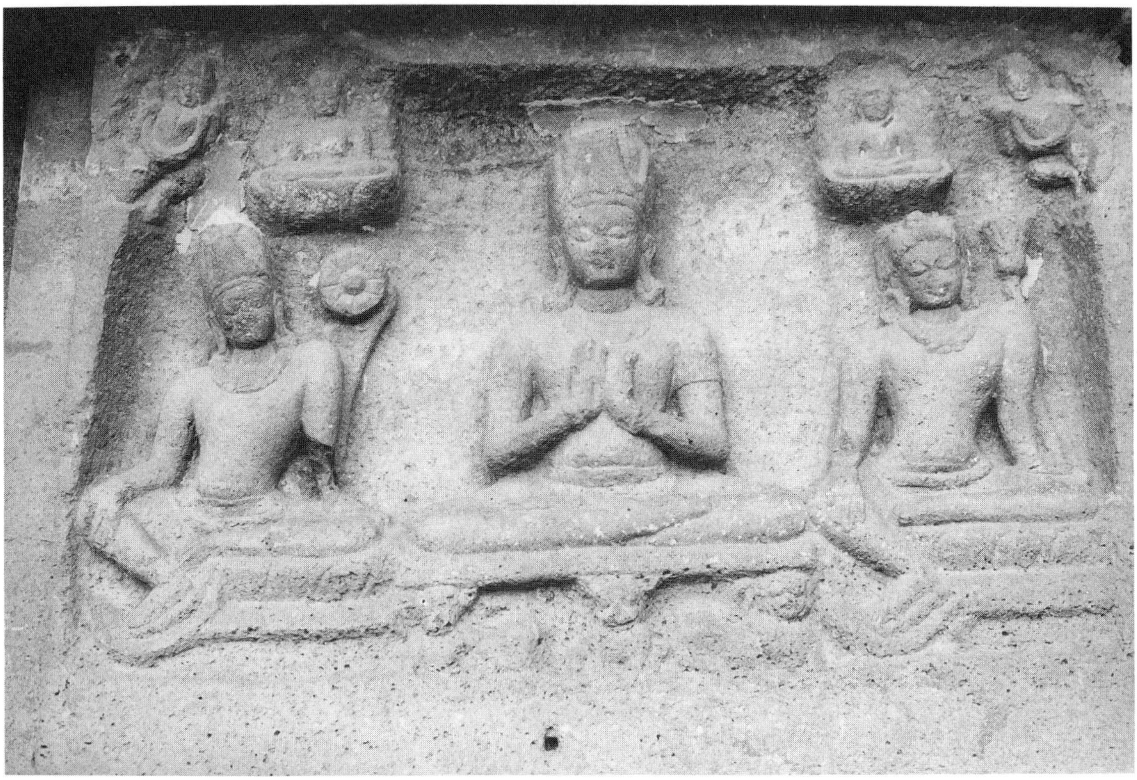

Fig. 133   Cave 10 balcony, Buddha with Avalokiteśvara and Mañjuśrī

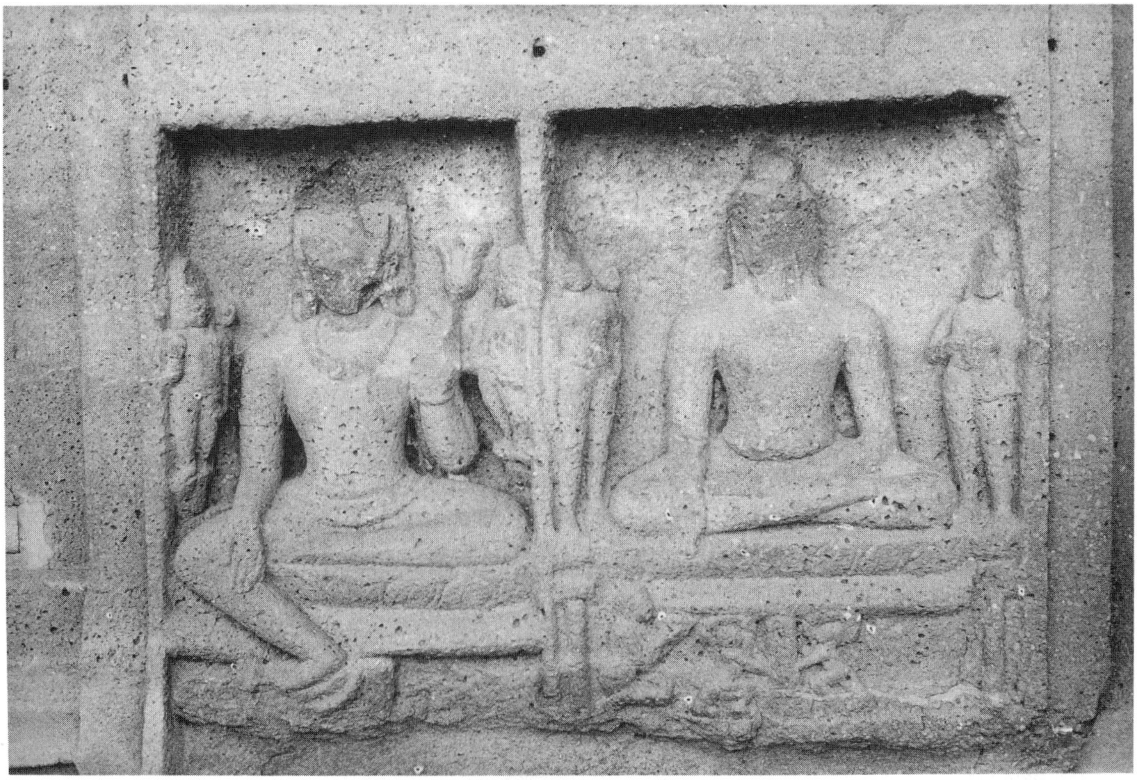

Fig. 134   Cave 10 balcony, Buddha with Mañjuśrī

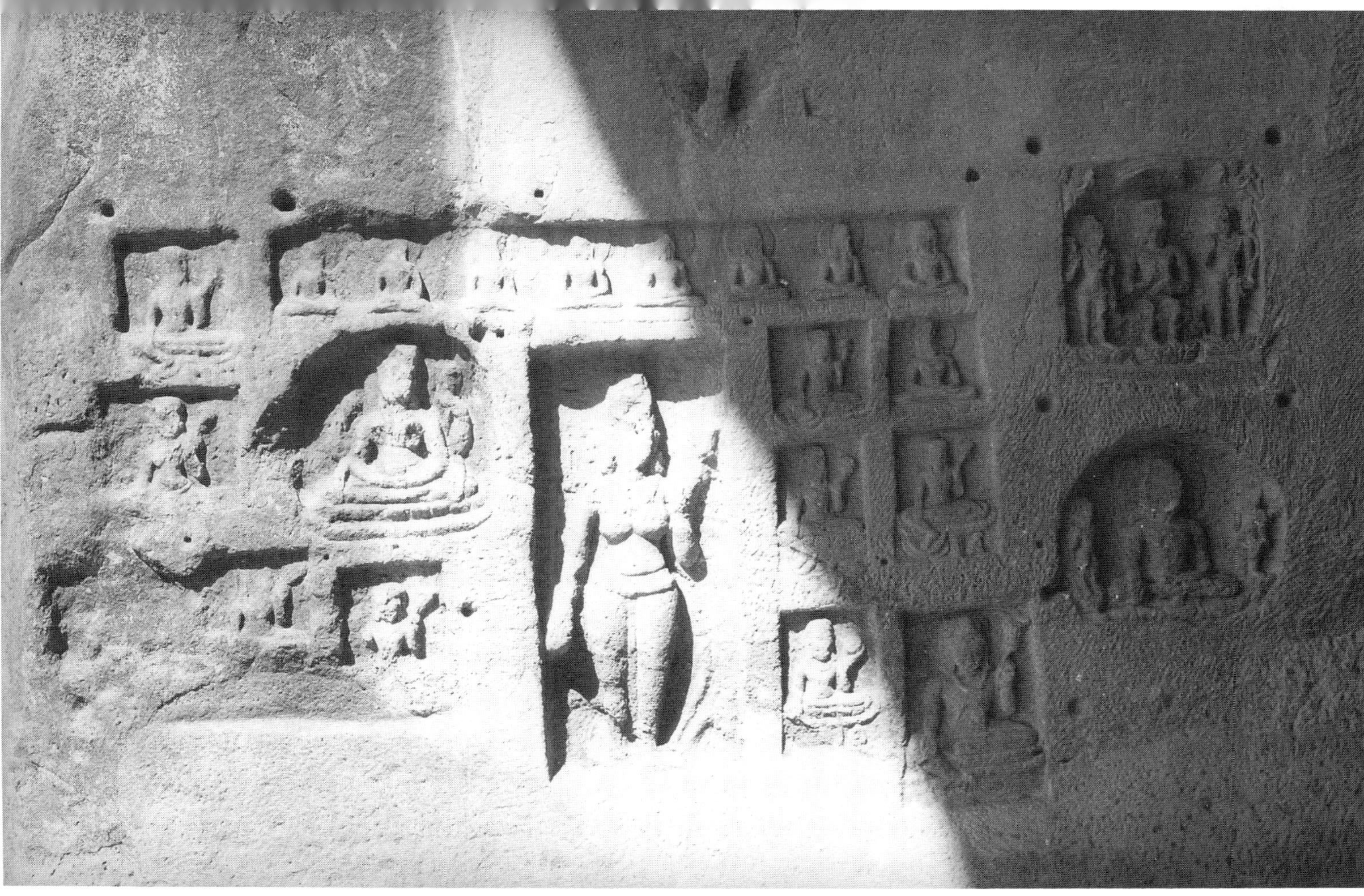

Fig. 135   Cave 10 balcony, north wall, intrusive panels

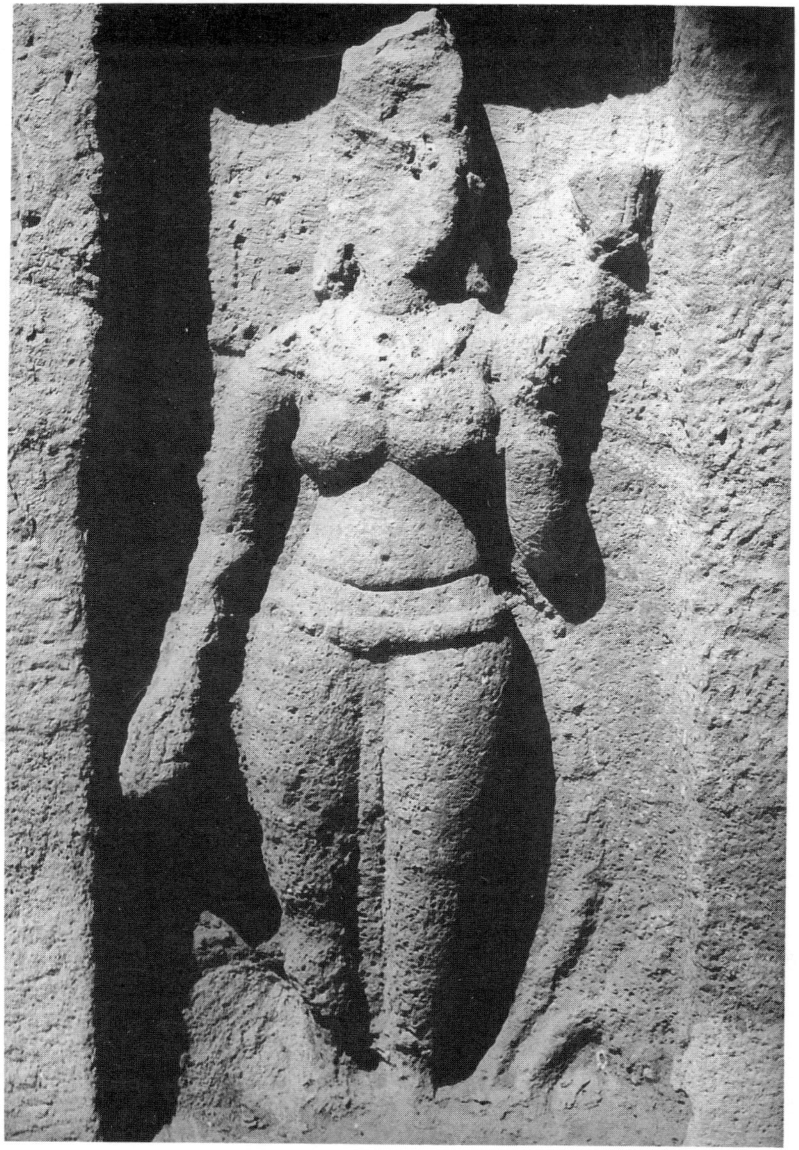

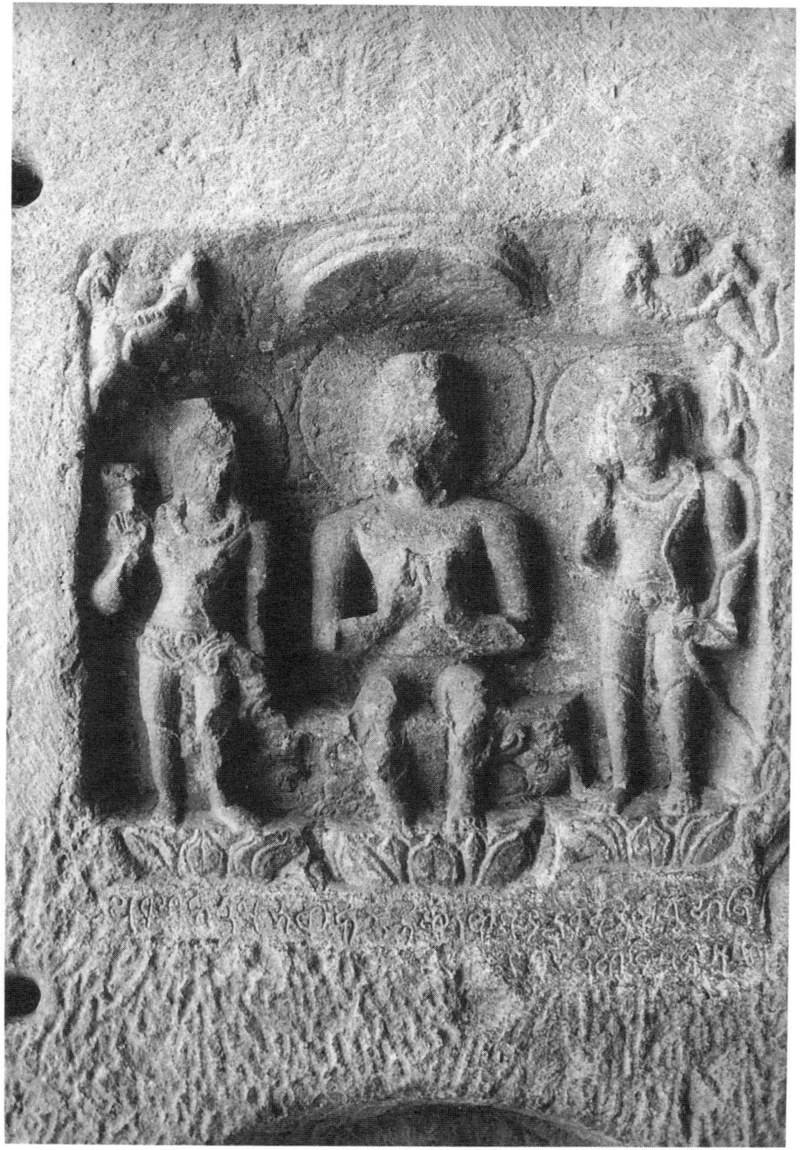

Fig. 137 Cave 10 balcony, north wall, Buddha panel with inscription

Fig. 136 Cave 10 balcony, north wall, Tārā

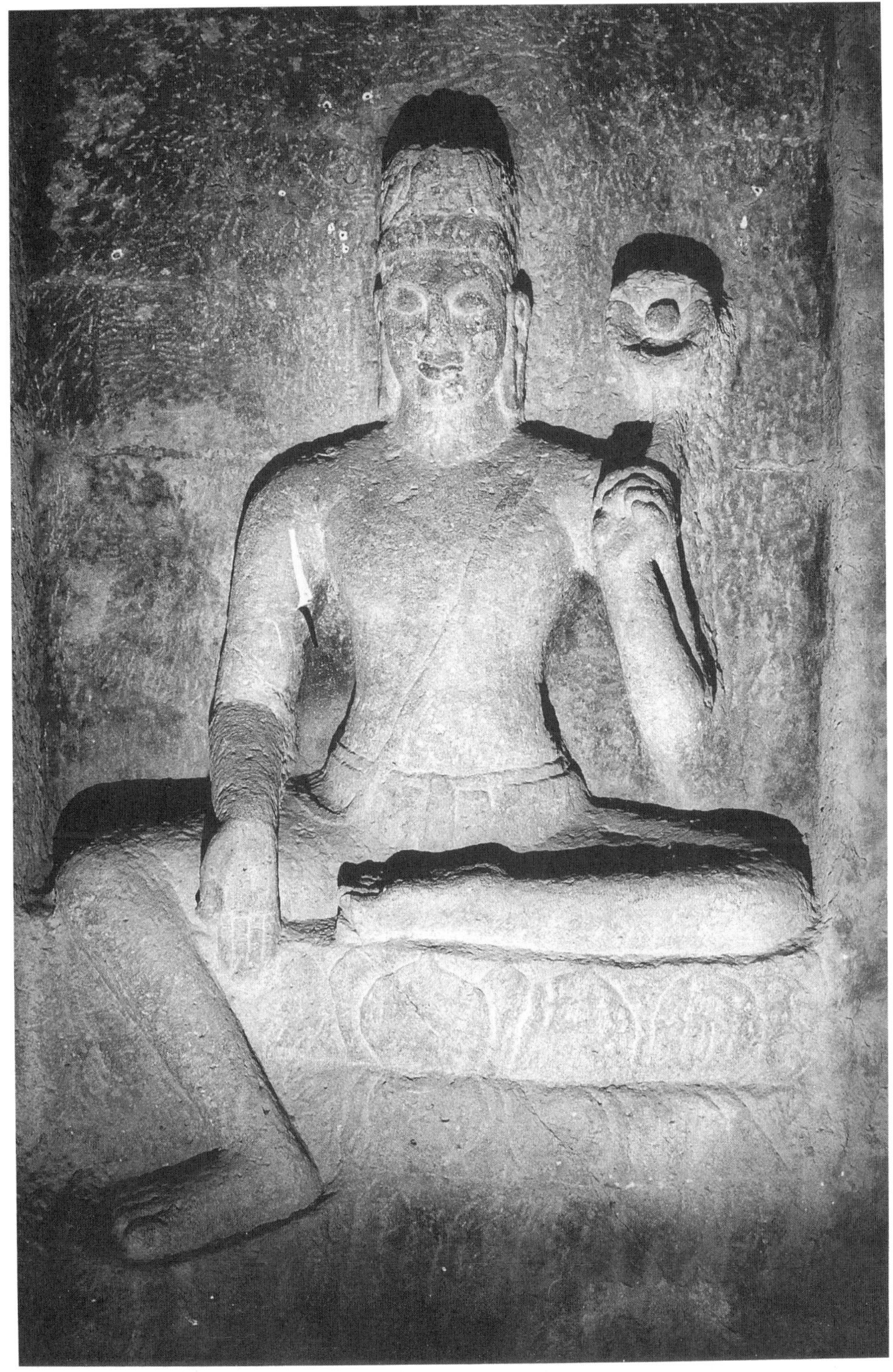

Fig. 138 Cave 10 courtyard cell E, Avalokiteśvara

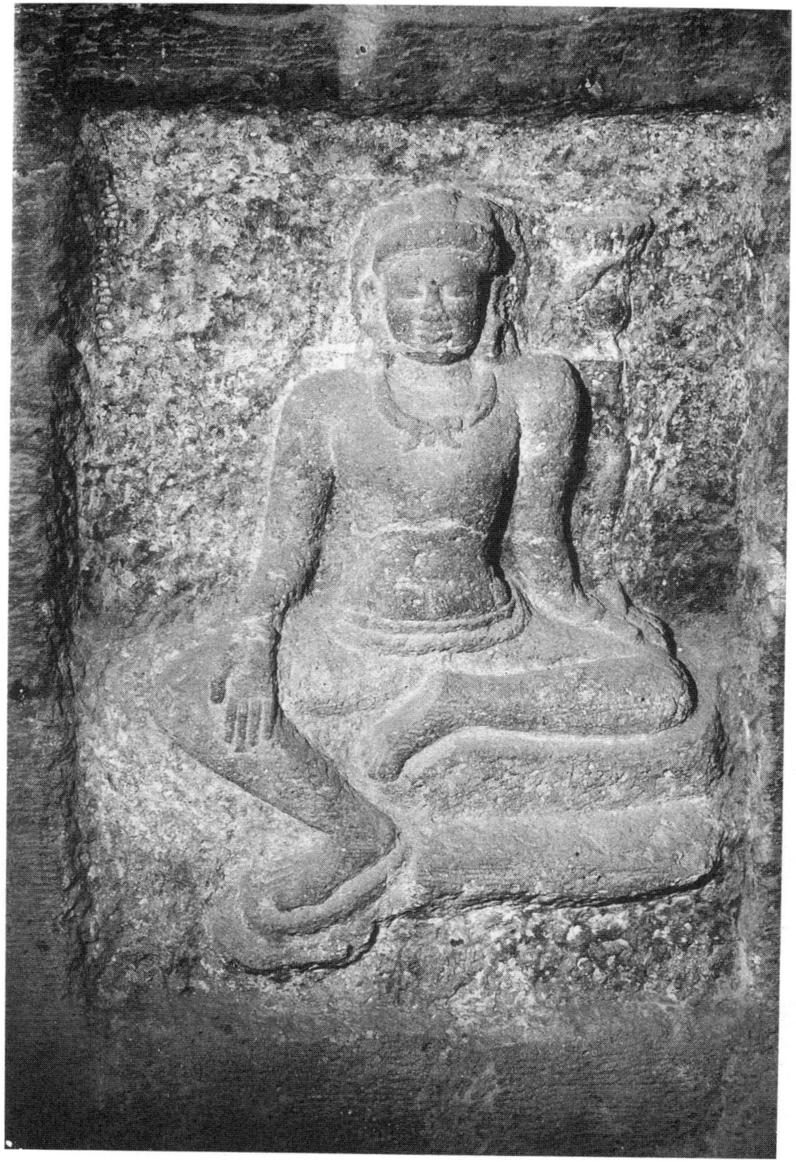

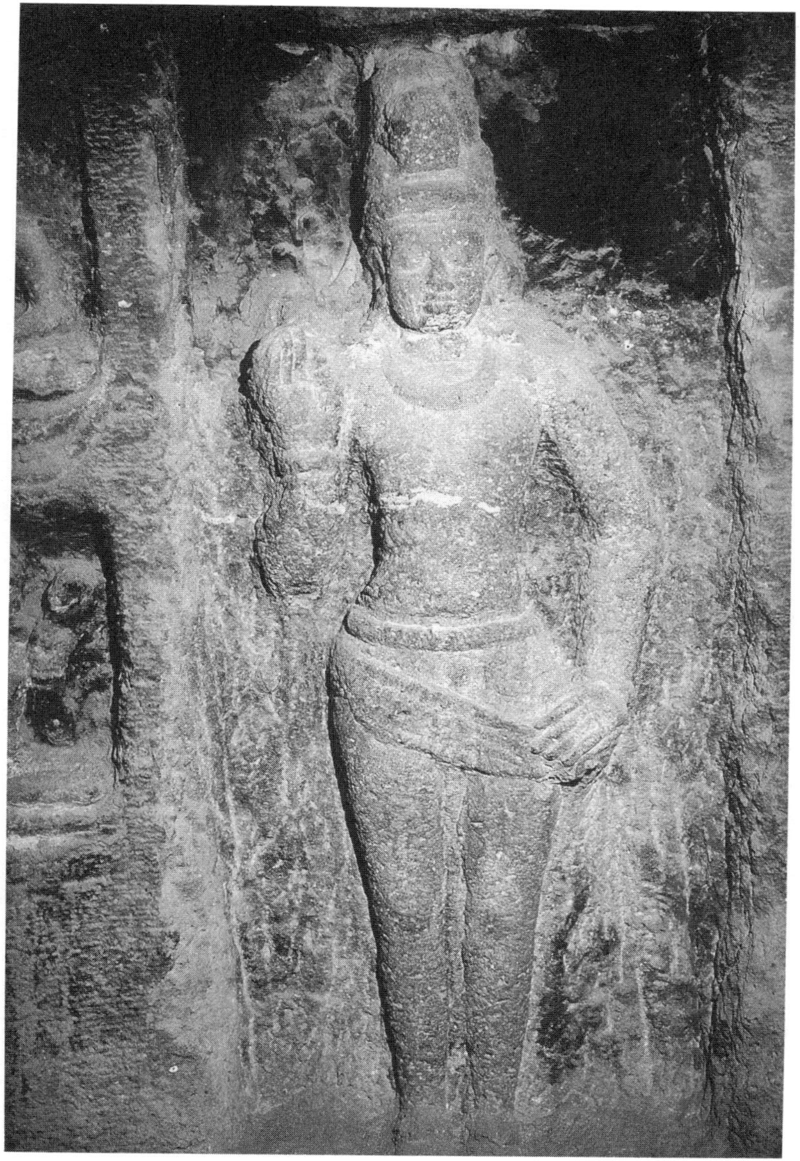

Fig. 140   Cave 10 courtyard cell E, Maitreya

Fig. 139   Cave 10 courtyard cell E, Mañjuśrī

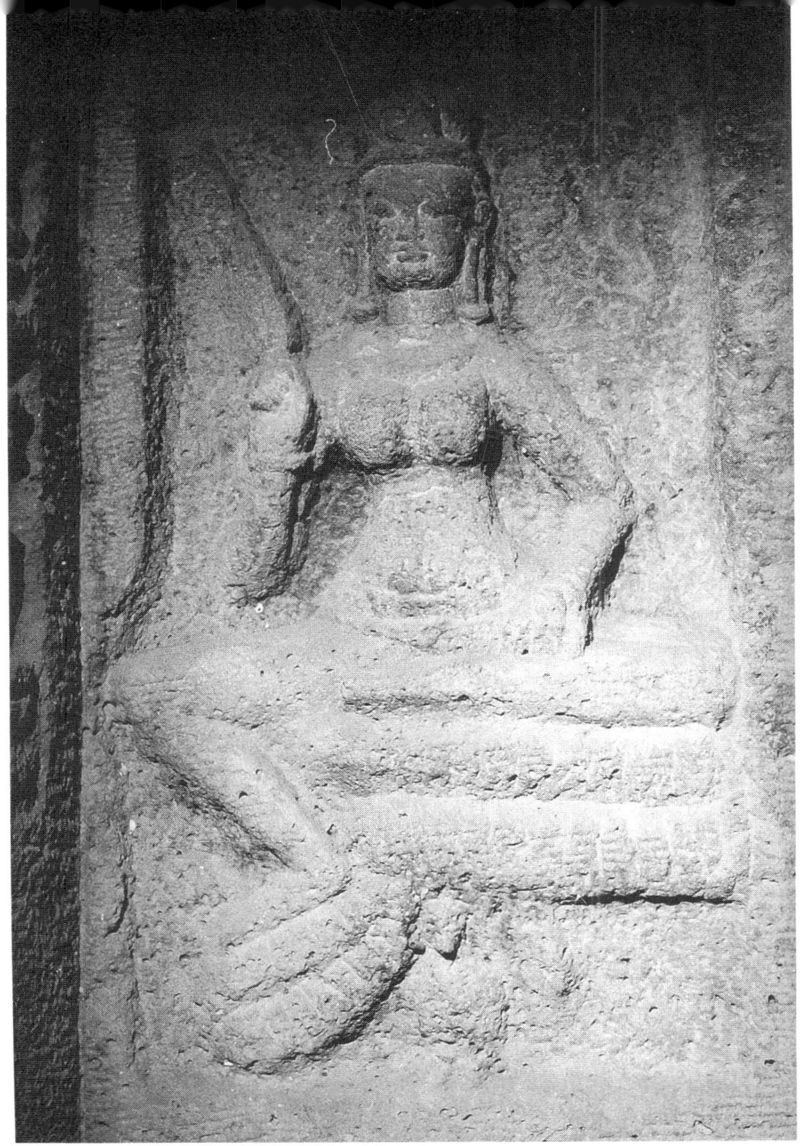

Fig. 141   Cave 10 courtyard cell E, Mahāmāyūrī

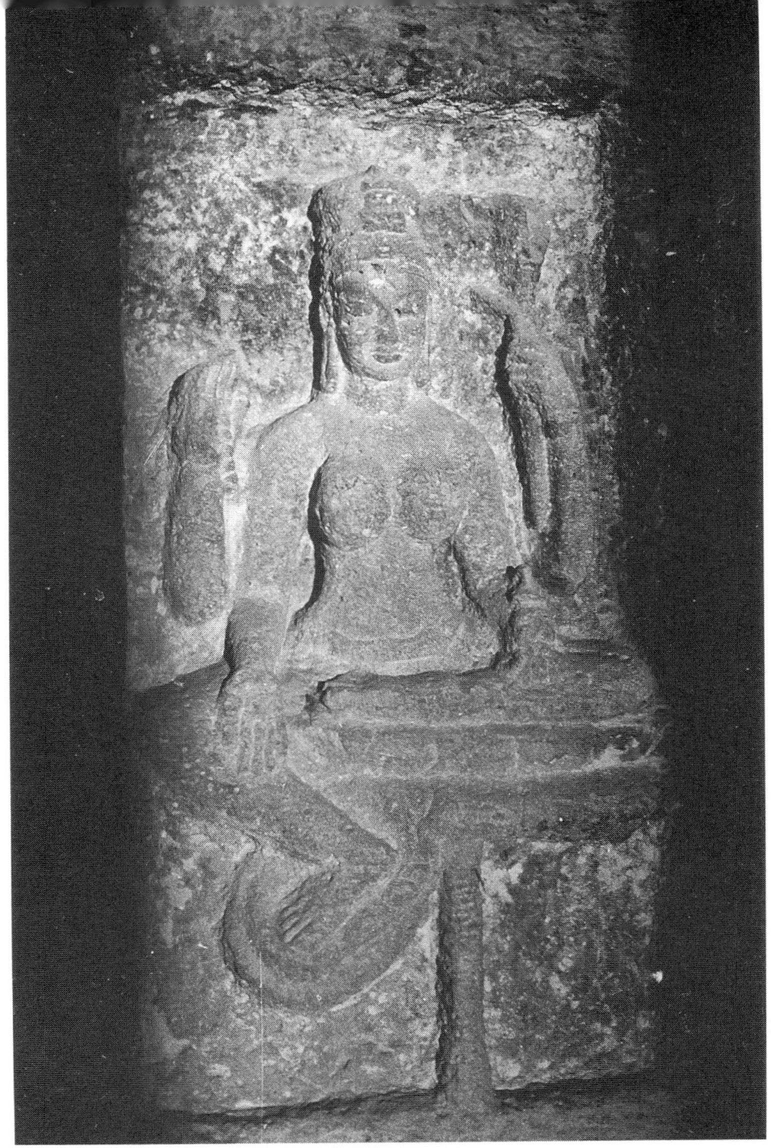

Fig. 142   Cave 10 courtyard cell E, Bhṛkuṭī

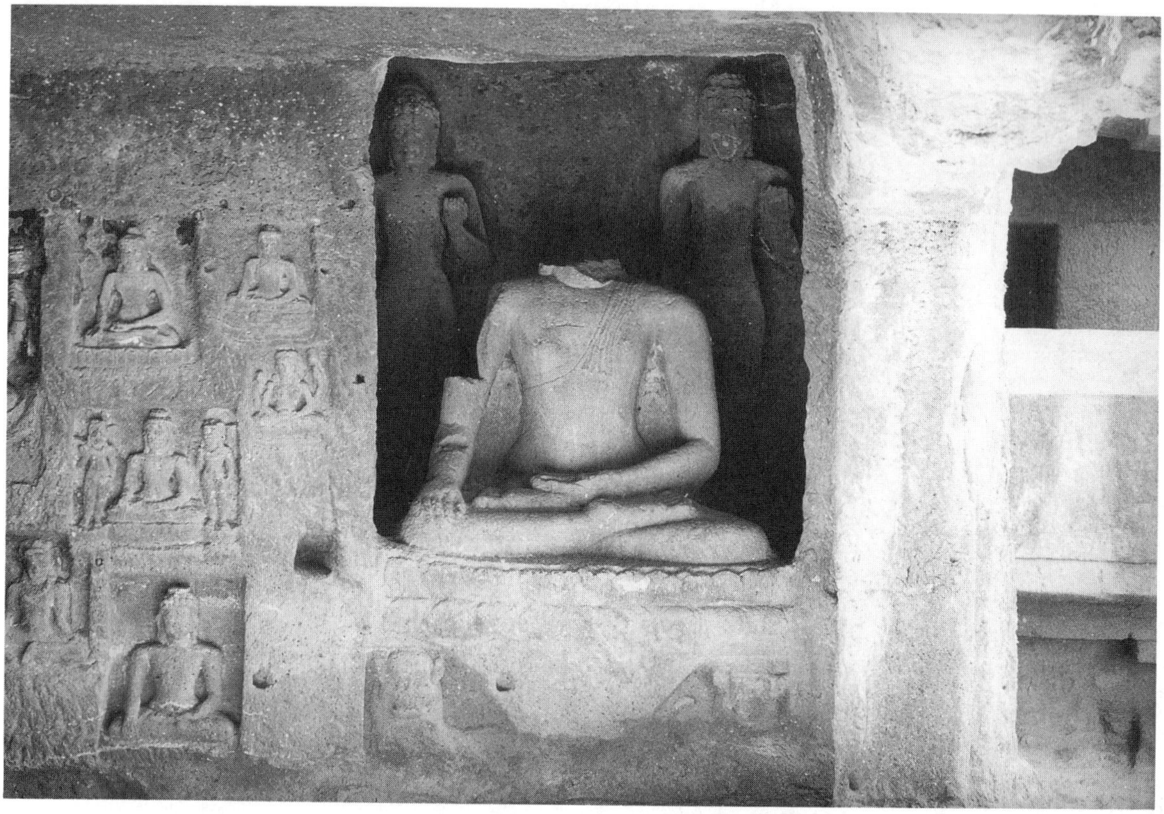

Fig. 143   Cave 11 north courtyard cell, Buddha

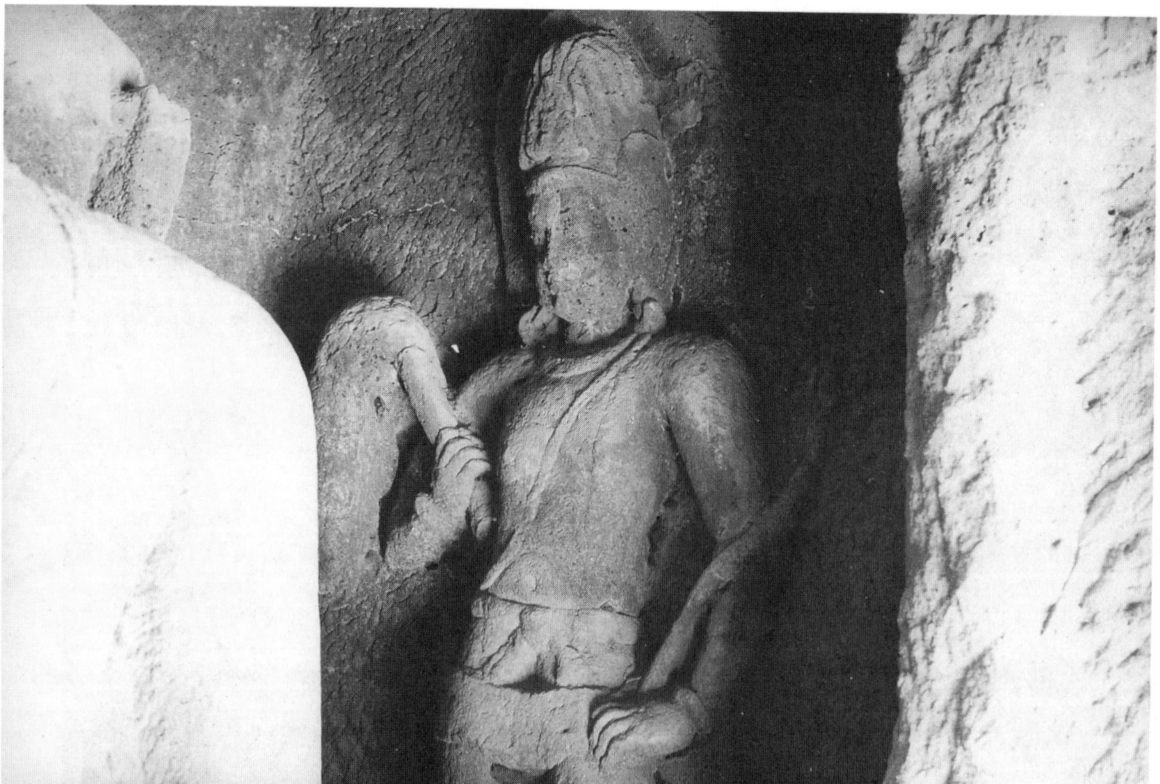

Fig. 144   Cave 11 north courtyard cell, Buddha panel, Bodhisattva

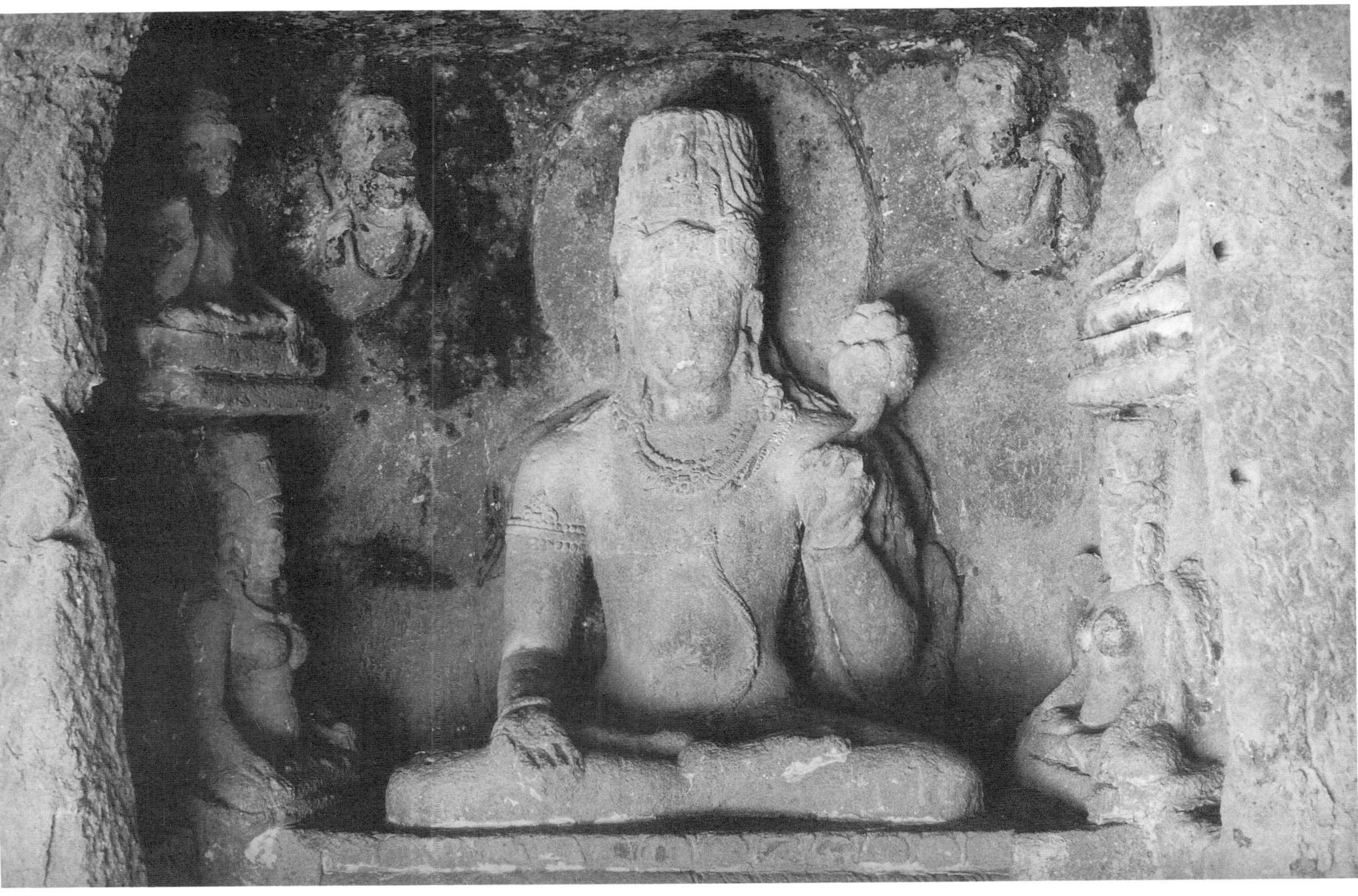

Fig. 145   Cave 11 north courtyard cell, Rakta-Lokeśvara

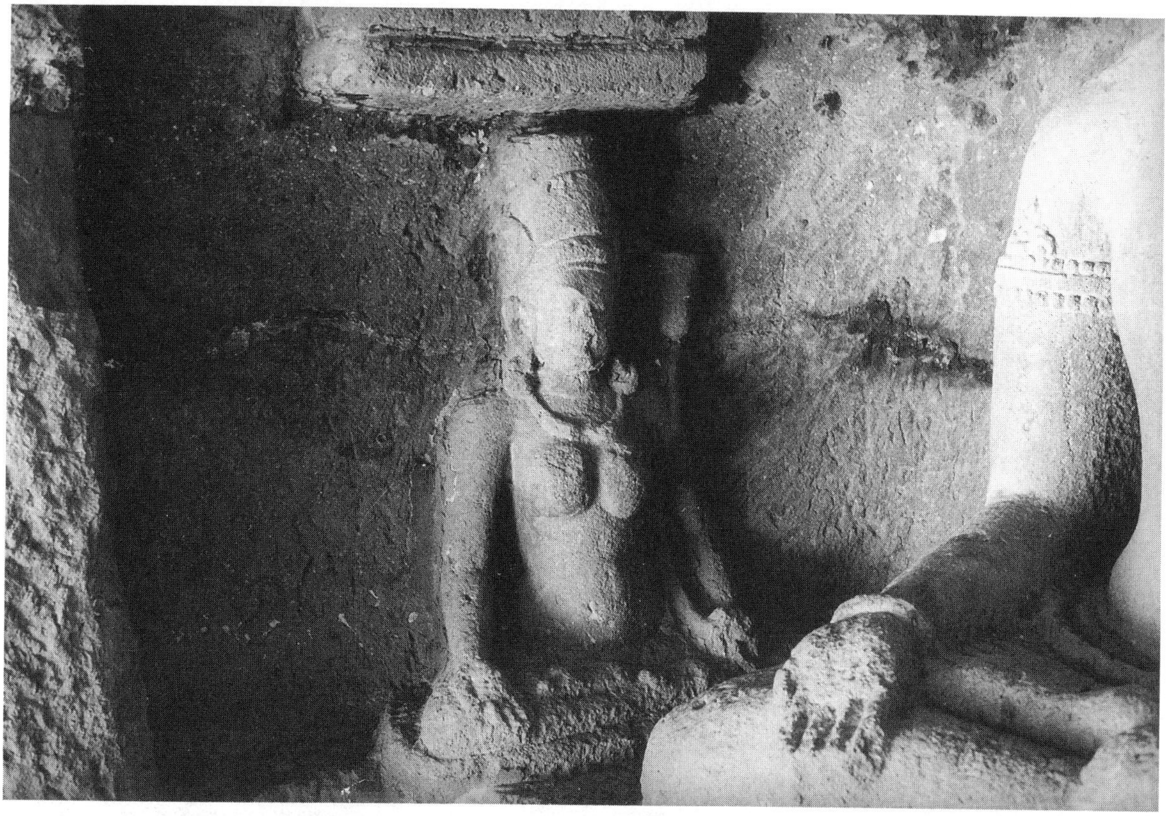

Fig. 146   Cave 11 north courtyard cell, Rakta-Lokeśvara, Tārā closeup

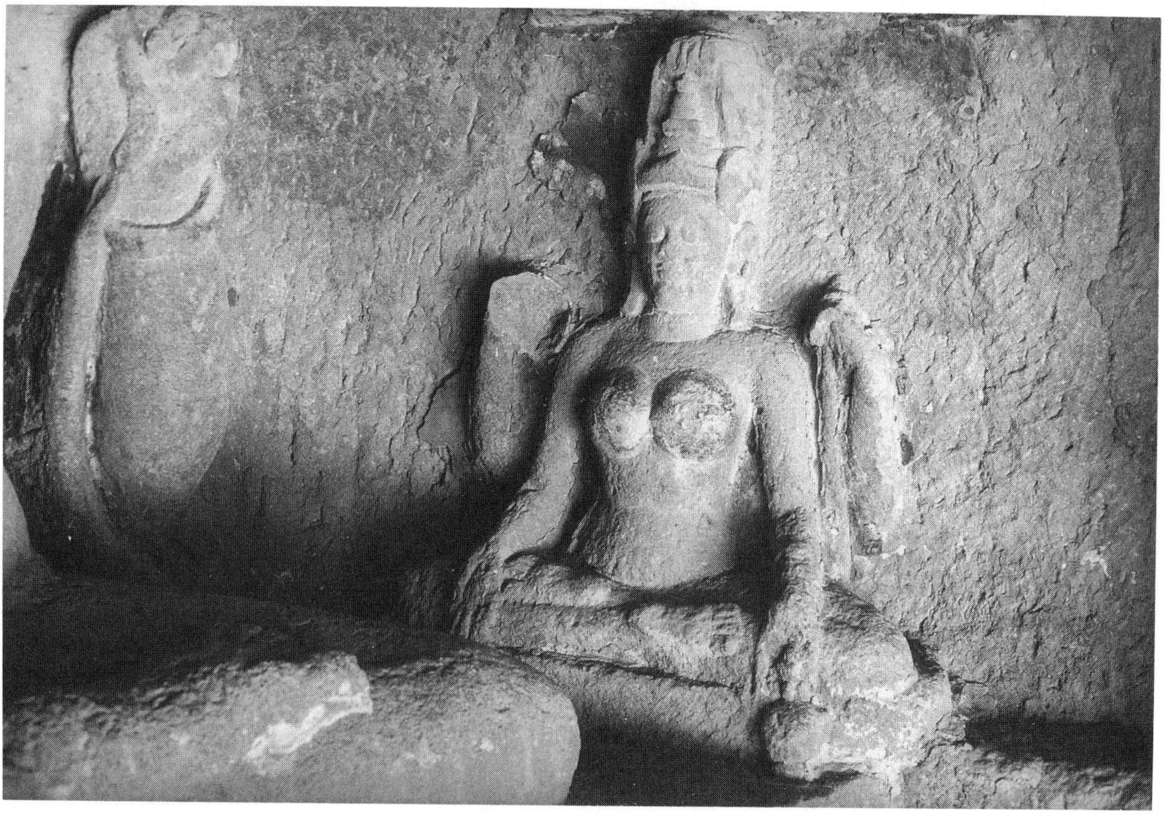

Fig. 147   Cave 11 north courtyard cell, Rakta-Lokeśvara, Bhṛkuṭī closeup

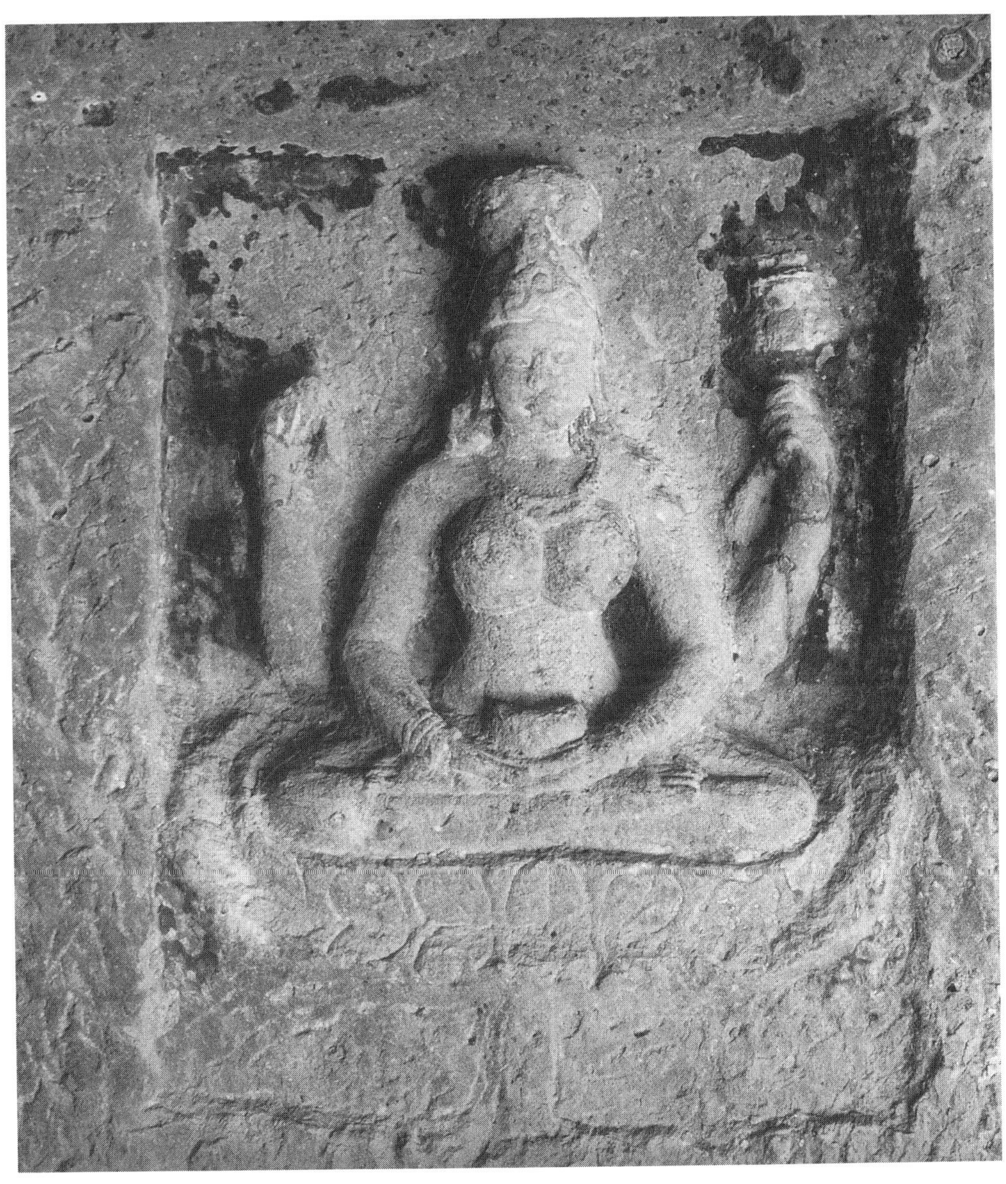

Fig. 148　Cave 11 north courtyard cell, Cundā

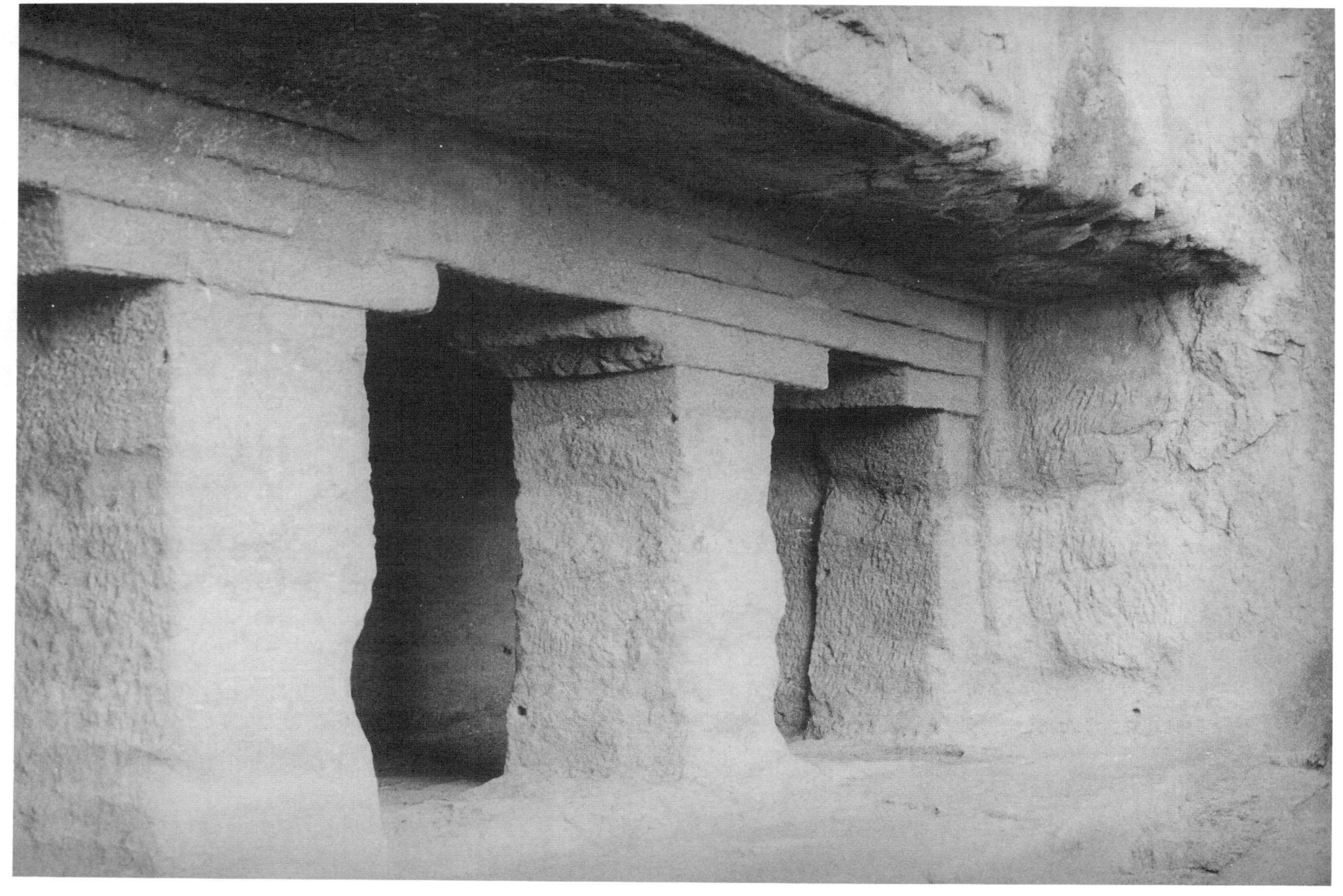

Fig. 149   Cave 11 verandah pillars

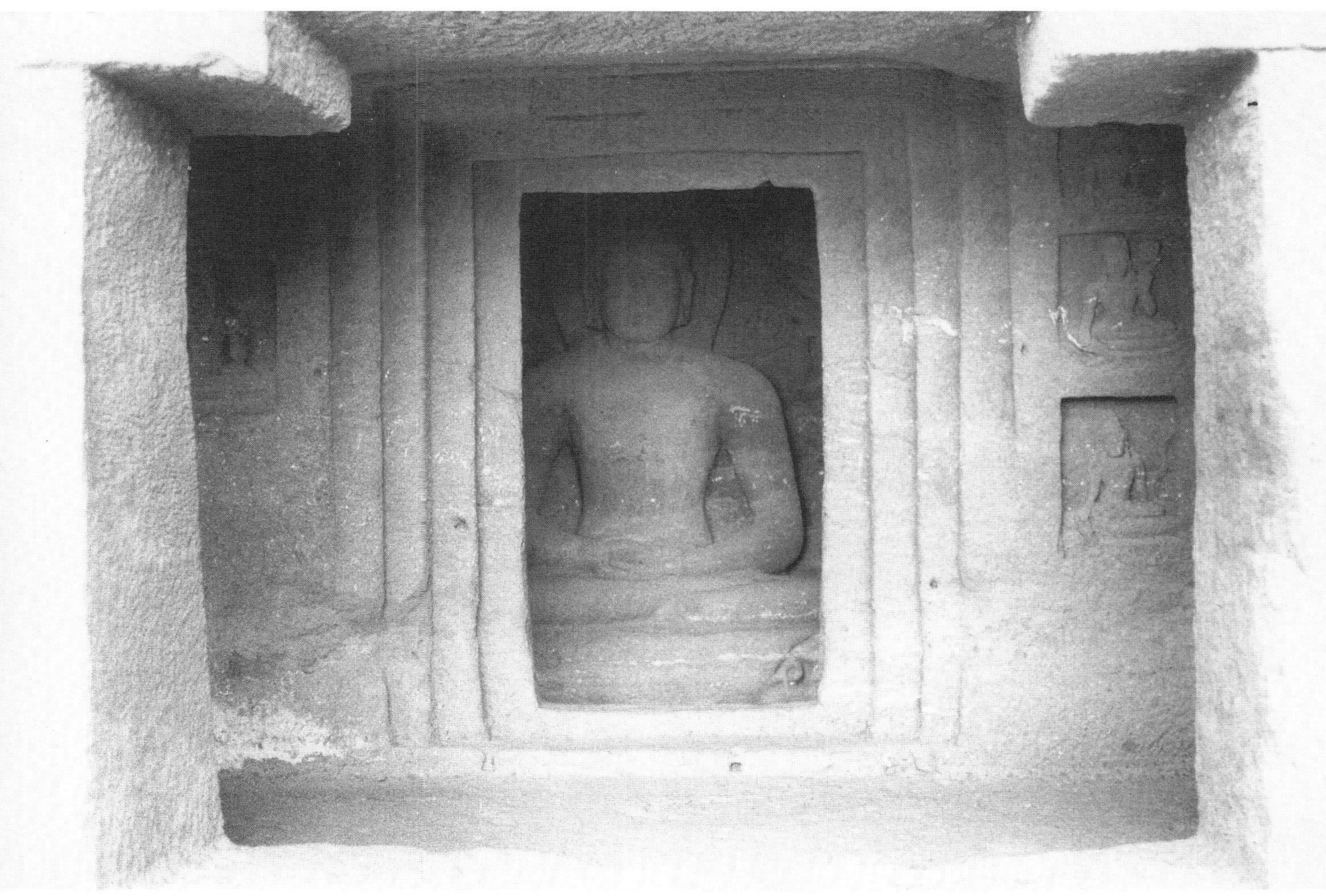

Fig. 150   Cave 11.1 shrine view

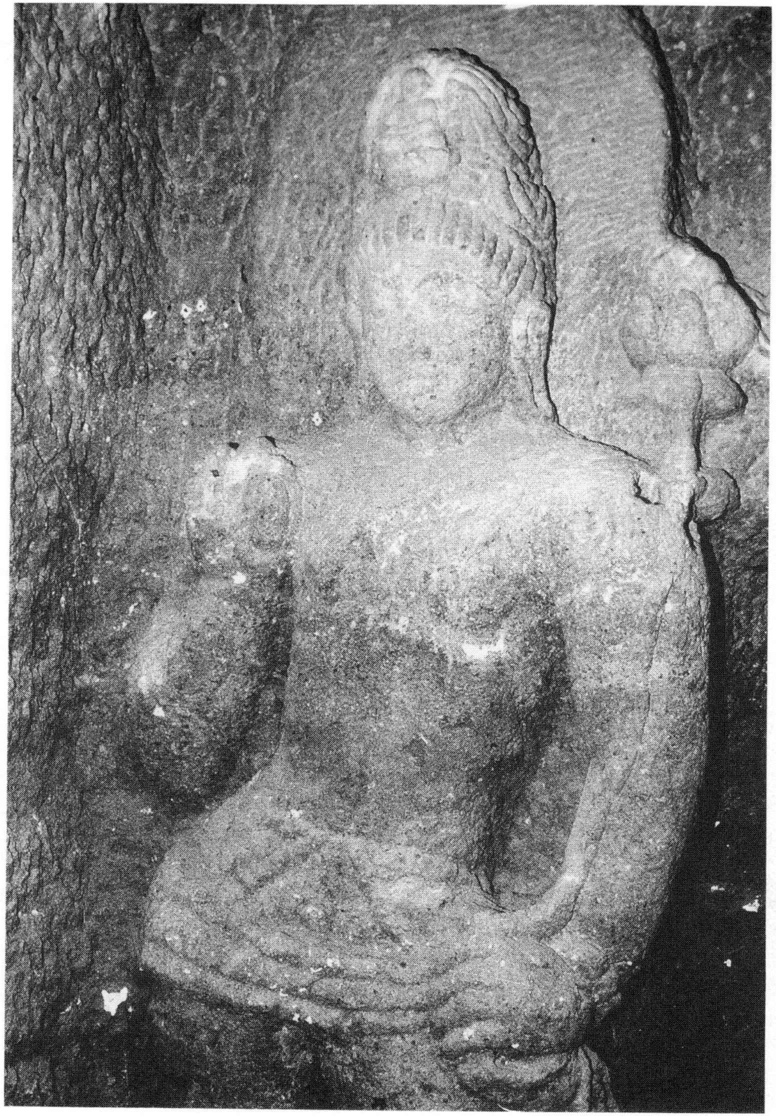

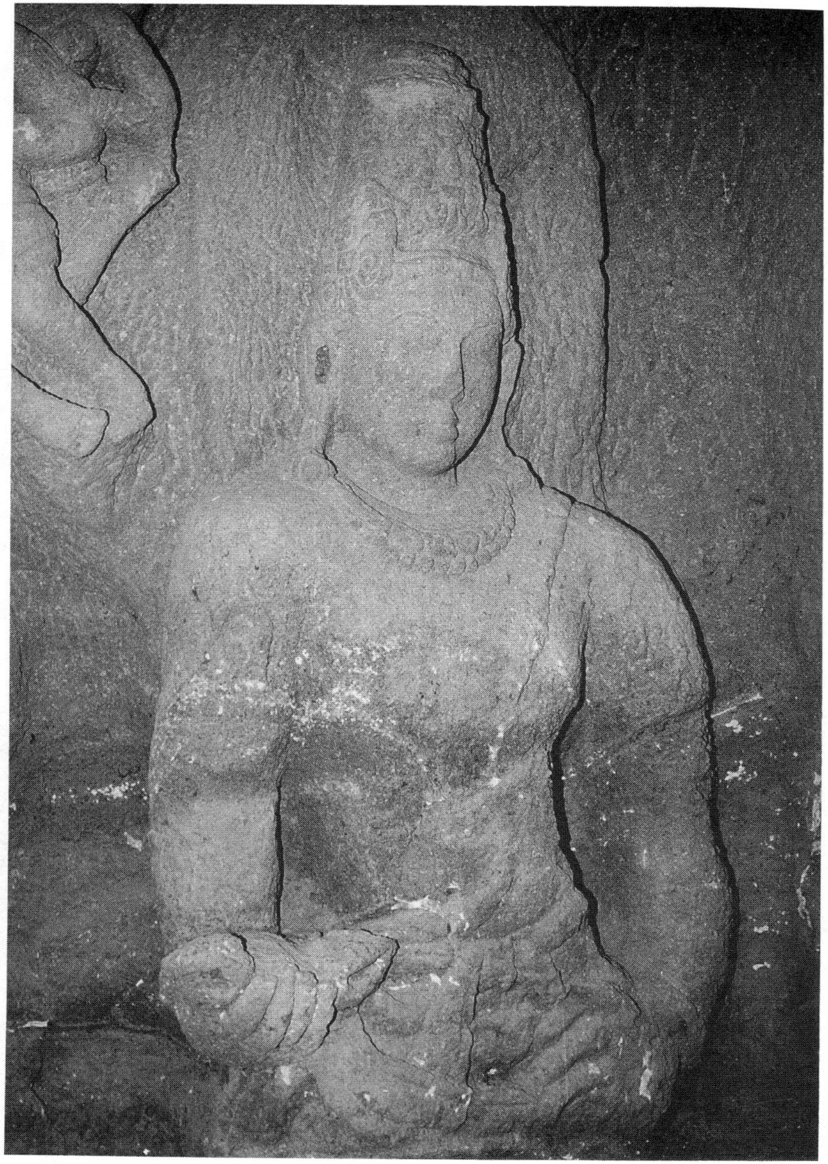

Fig. 152 Cave 11.1 shrine, Vajrapāṇi

Fig. 151 Cave 11.1 shrine, Avalokiteśvara

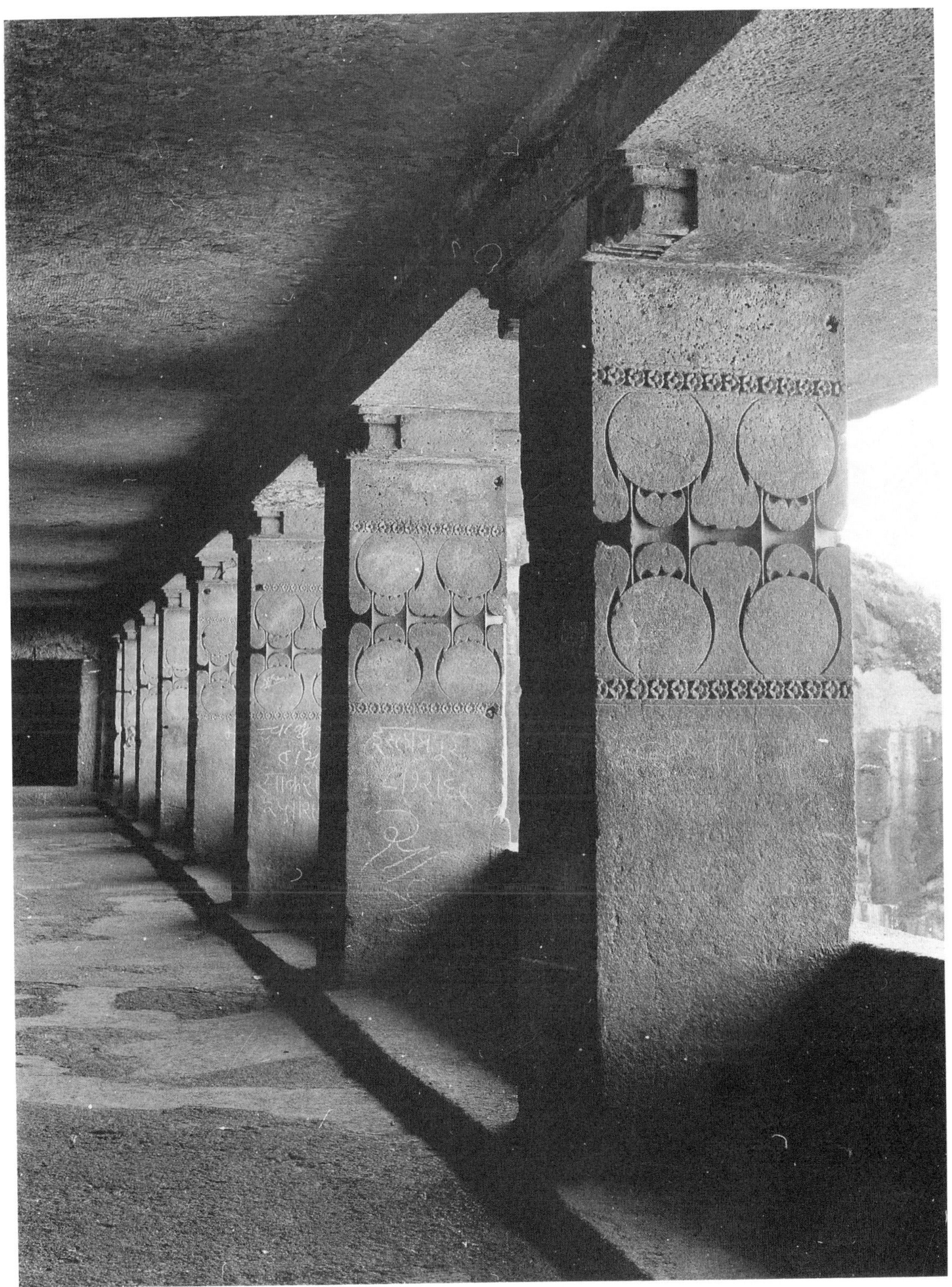

Fig. 153   Cave 11.3 verandah, pillars (AIIS)

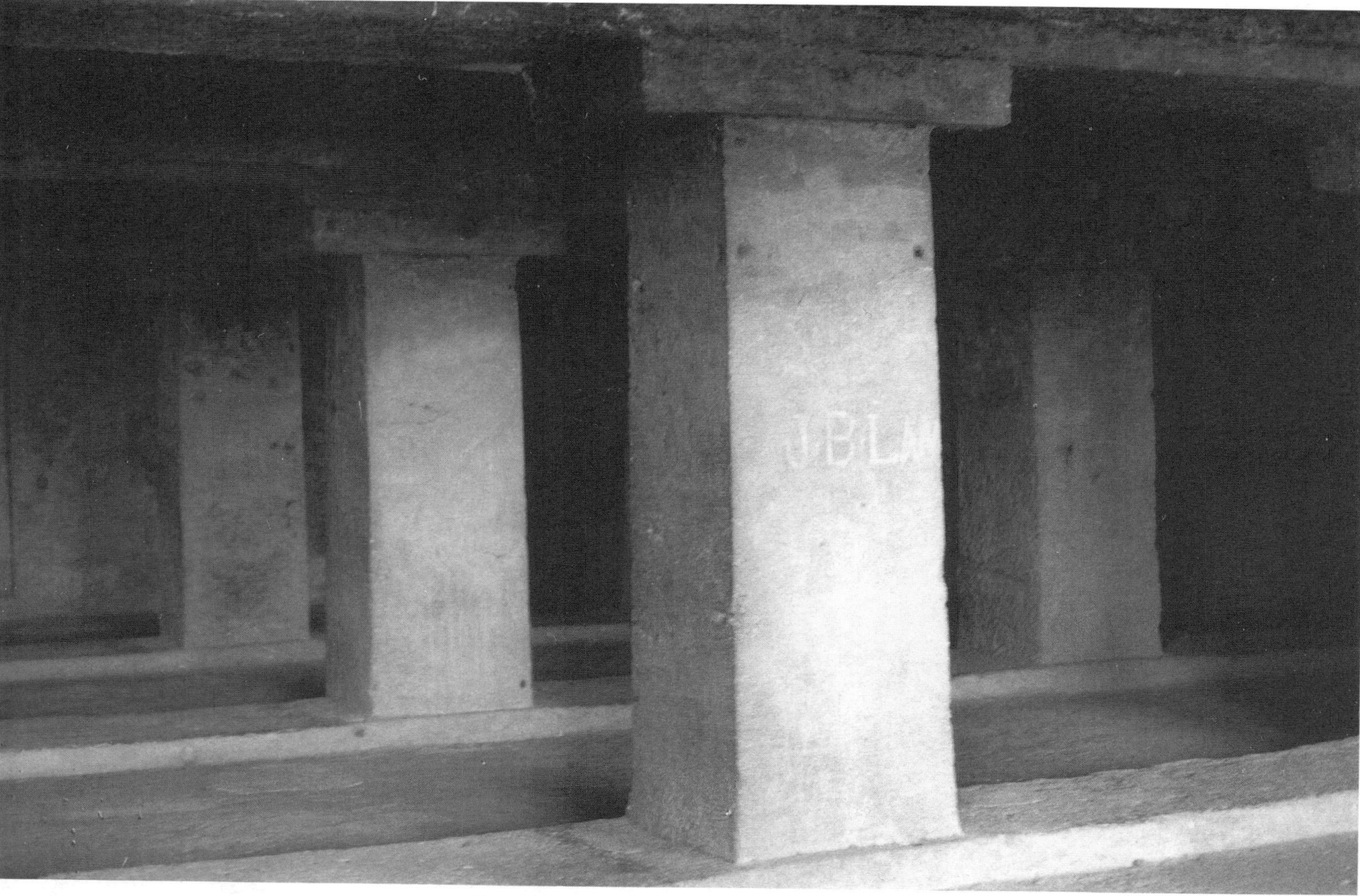

Fig. 154 Cave 11.3 hall, pillars

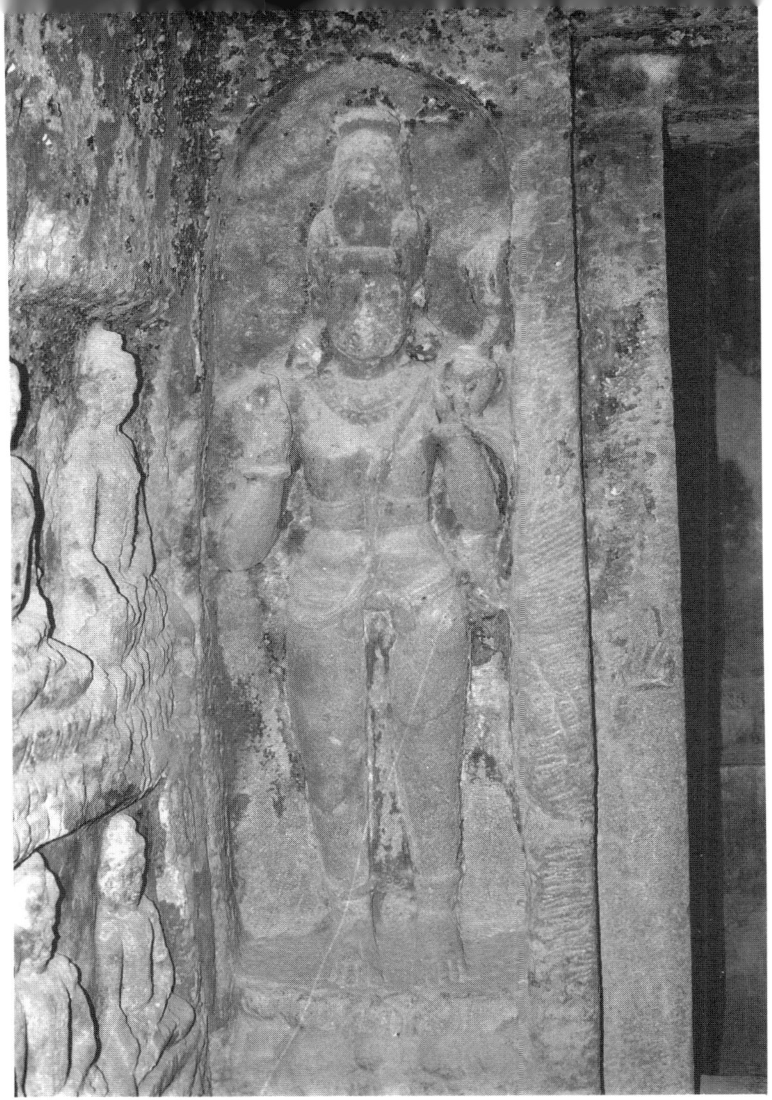

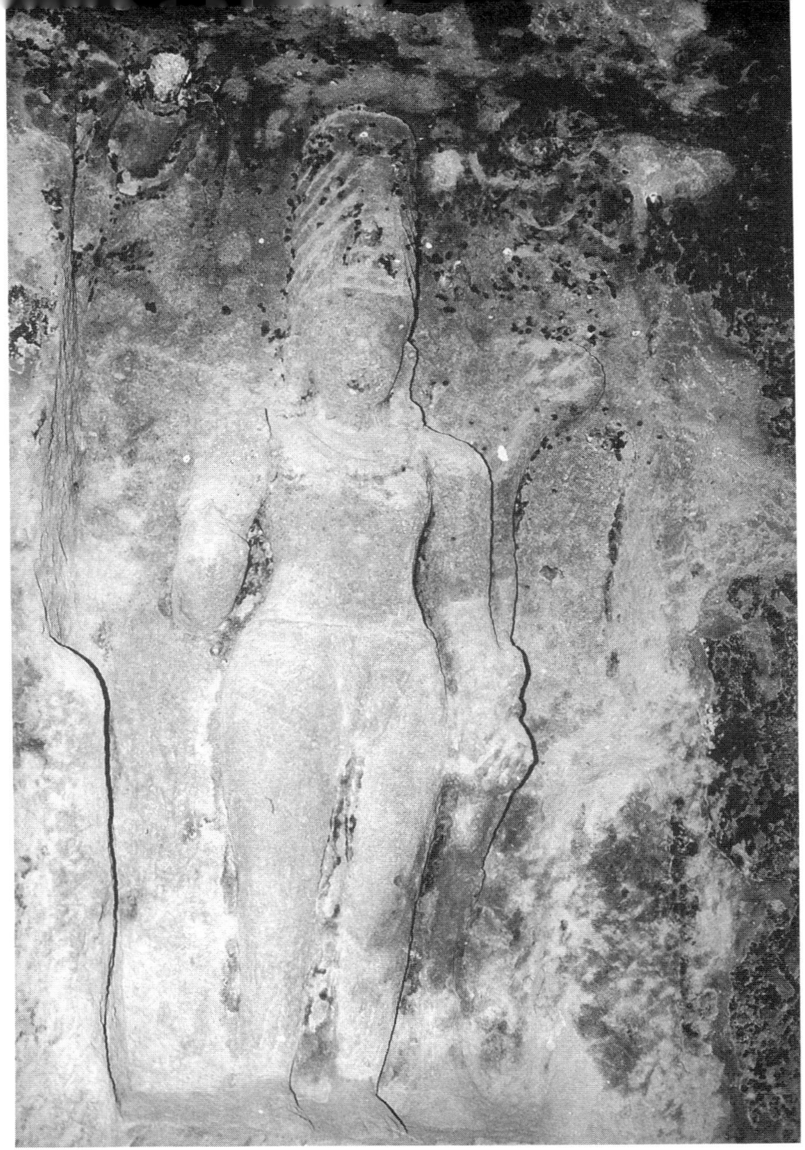

Fig. 156   Cave 11.3 Shrine 1 door, Avalokiteśvara

Fig. 155   Cave 11.3 Shrine 1 door, Maitreya

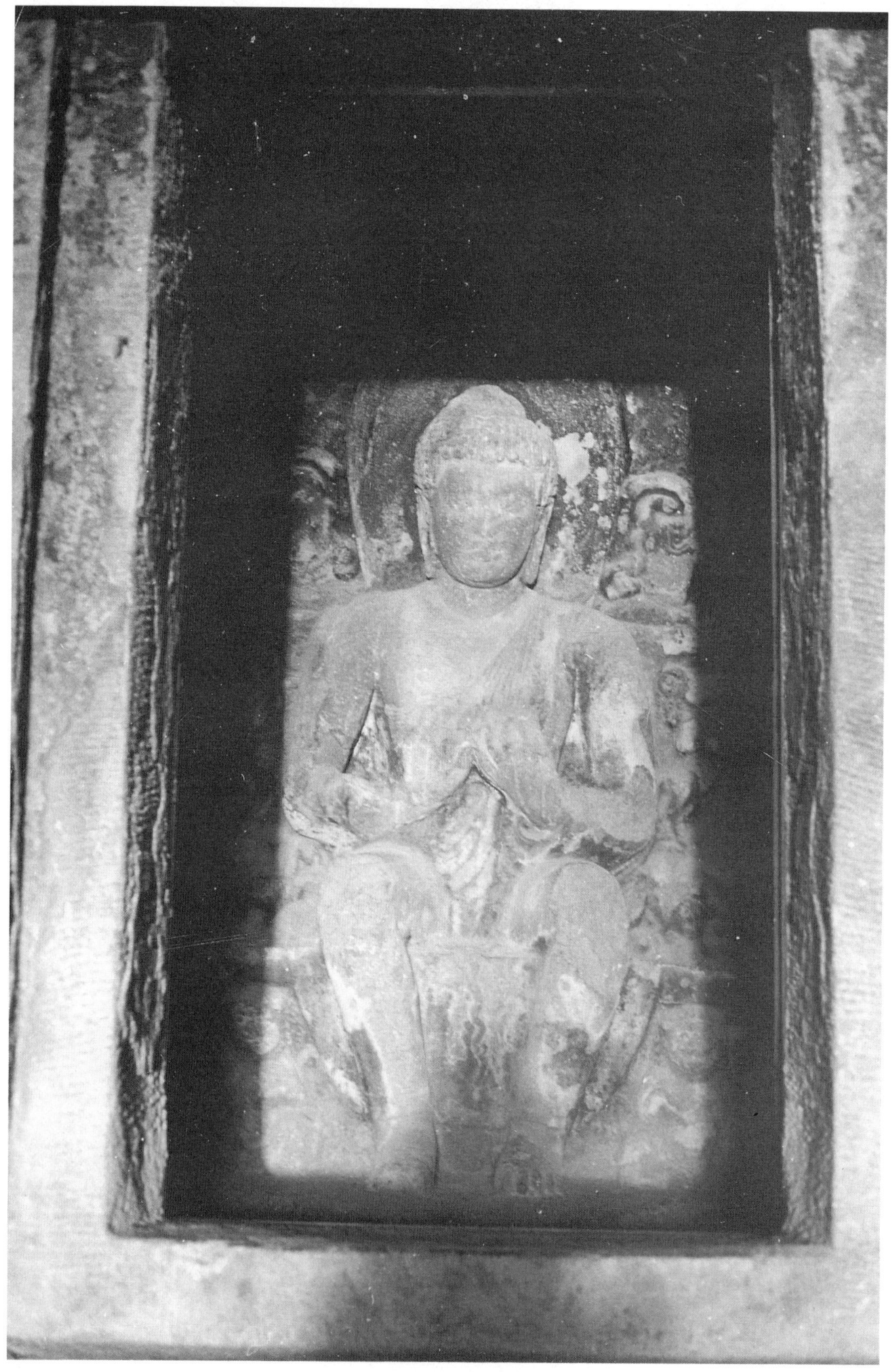

Fig. 157   Cave 11.3 Shrine 2, Buddha

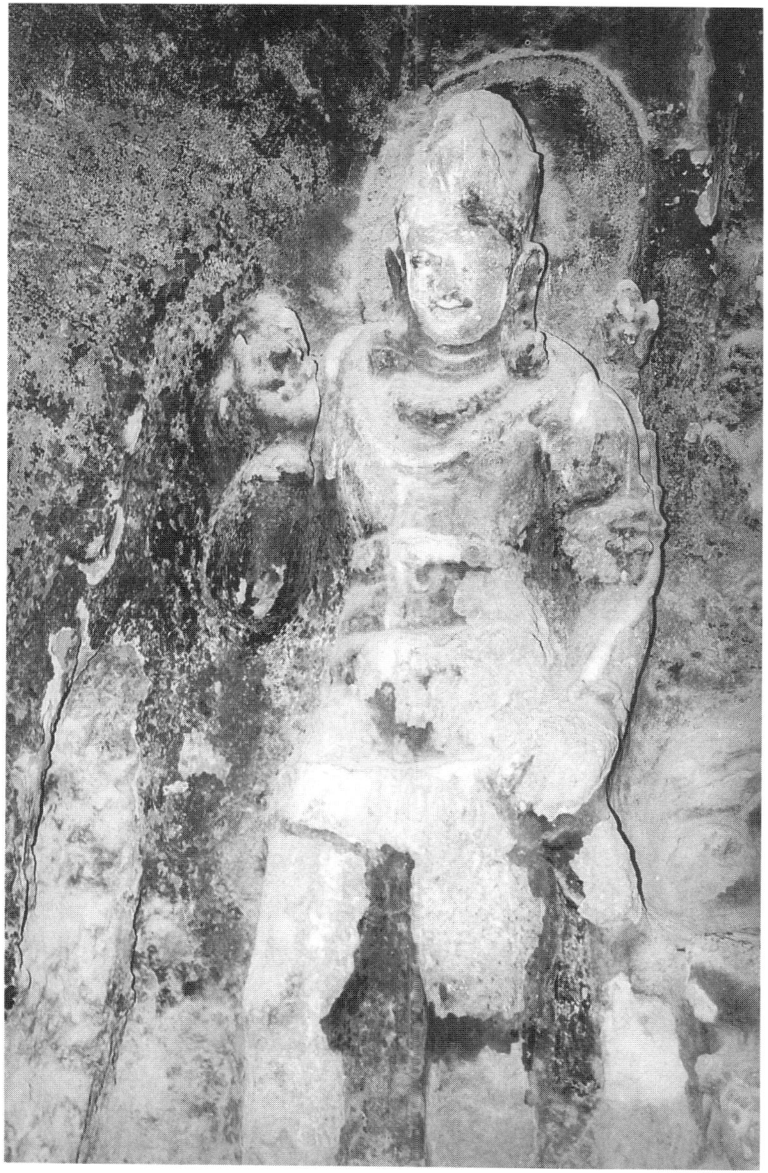

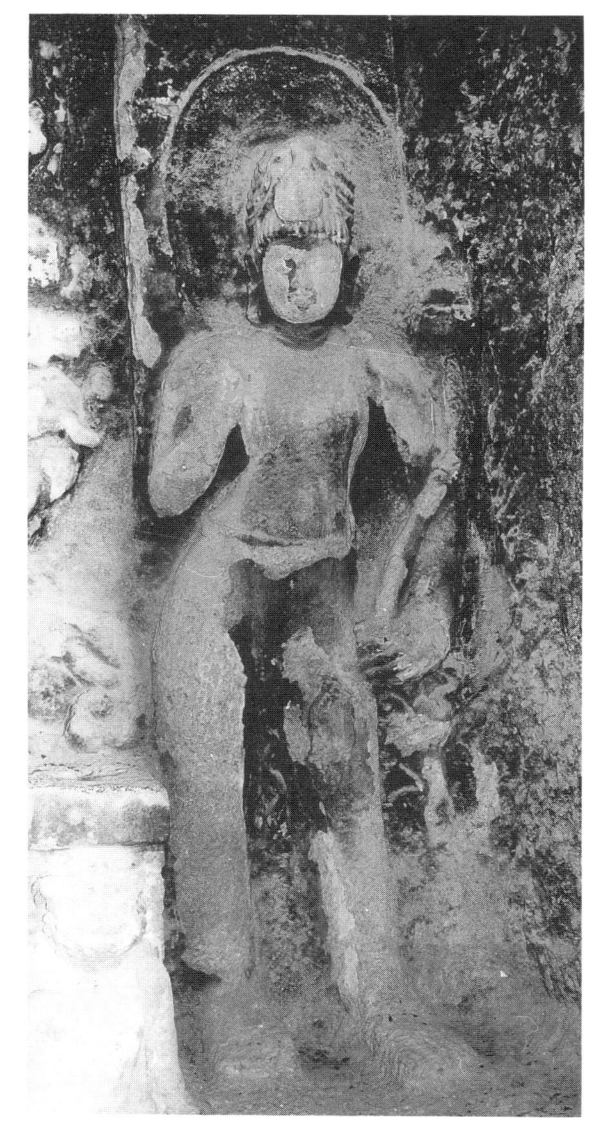

Fig. 158   Cave 11.3 Shrine 2, Maitreya

Fig. 159   Cave 11.3 Shrine 2, Avalokiteśvara (AIIS)

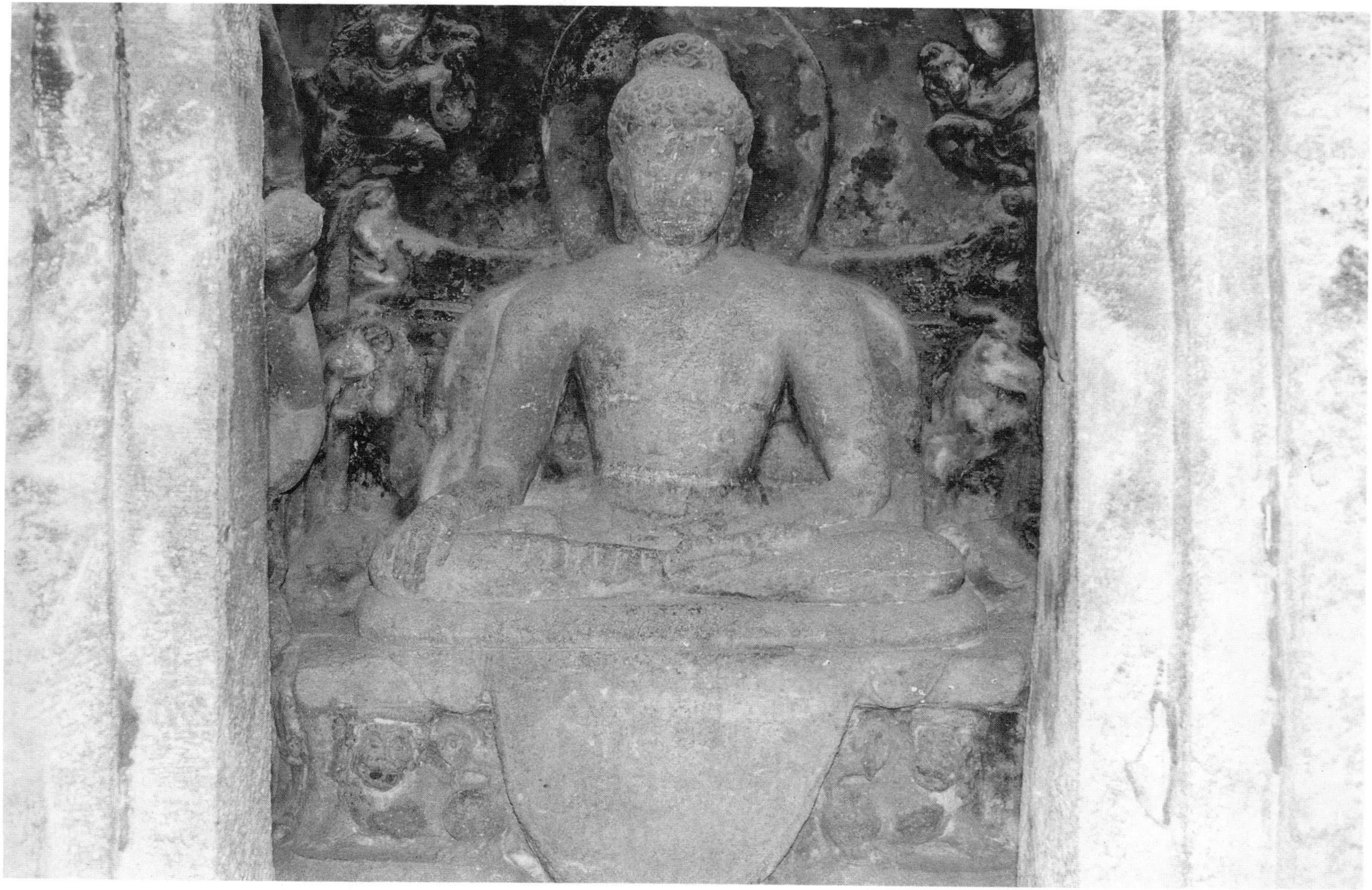

Fig. 160   Cave 11.2 Shrine 2, Buddha

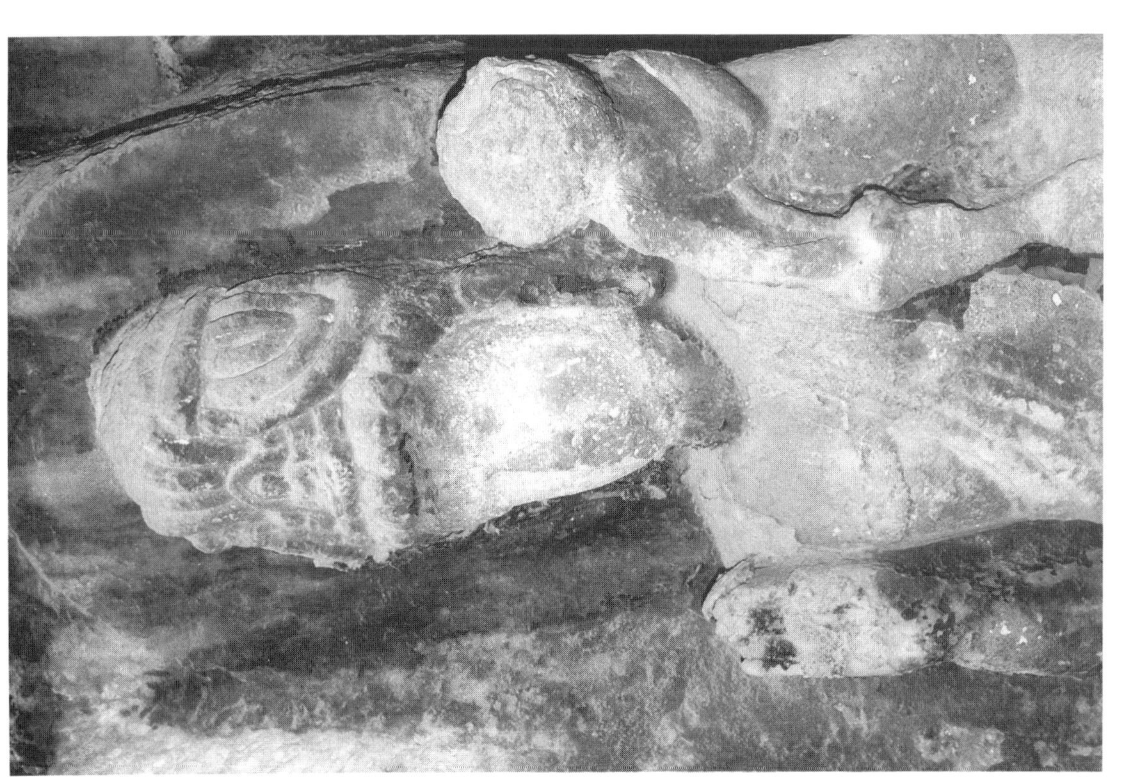

Fig. 162   Cave 11.2 Shrine 2, Vajrapāṇi

Fig. 161   Cave 11.2 Shrine 2, Avalok.teśvara

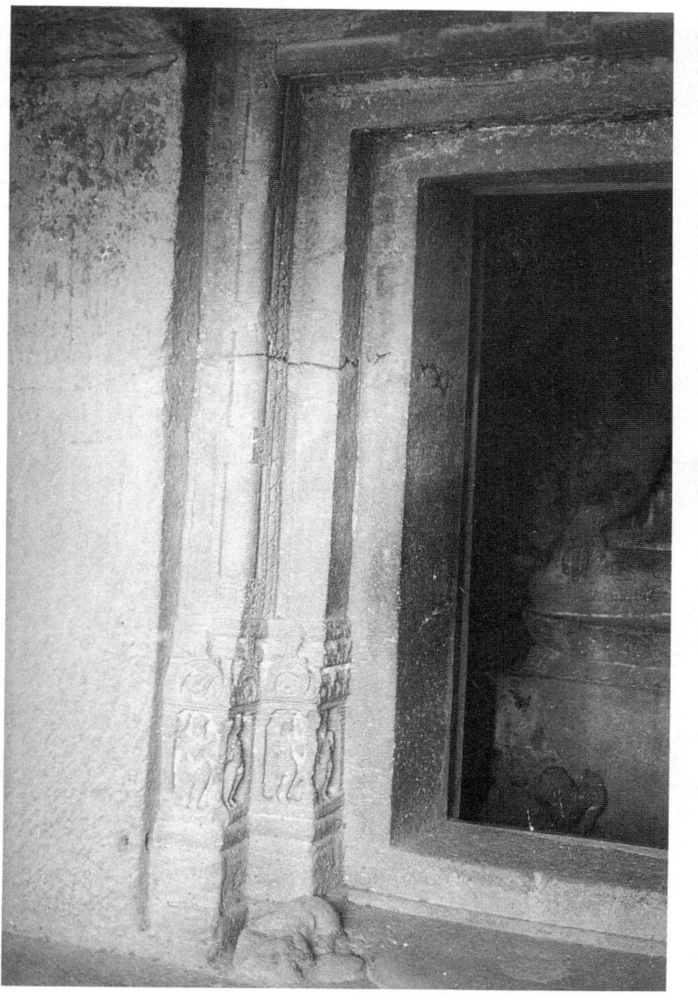

Fig. 163   Cave 11.2 Shrine 1, doorframe

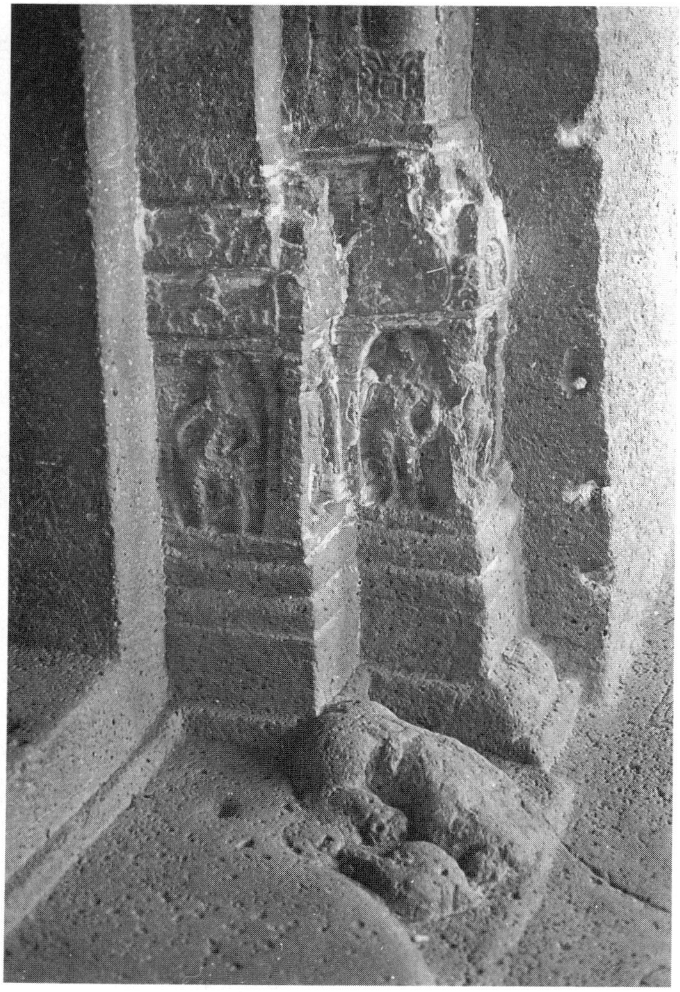

Fig. 164   Cave 11.2 Shrine 1, doorframe

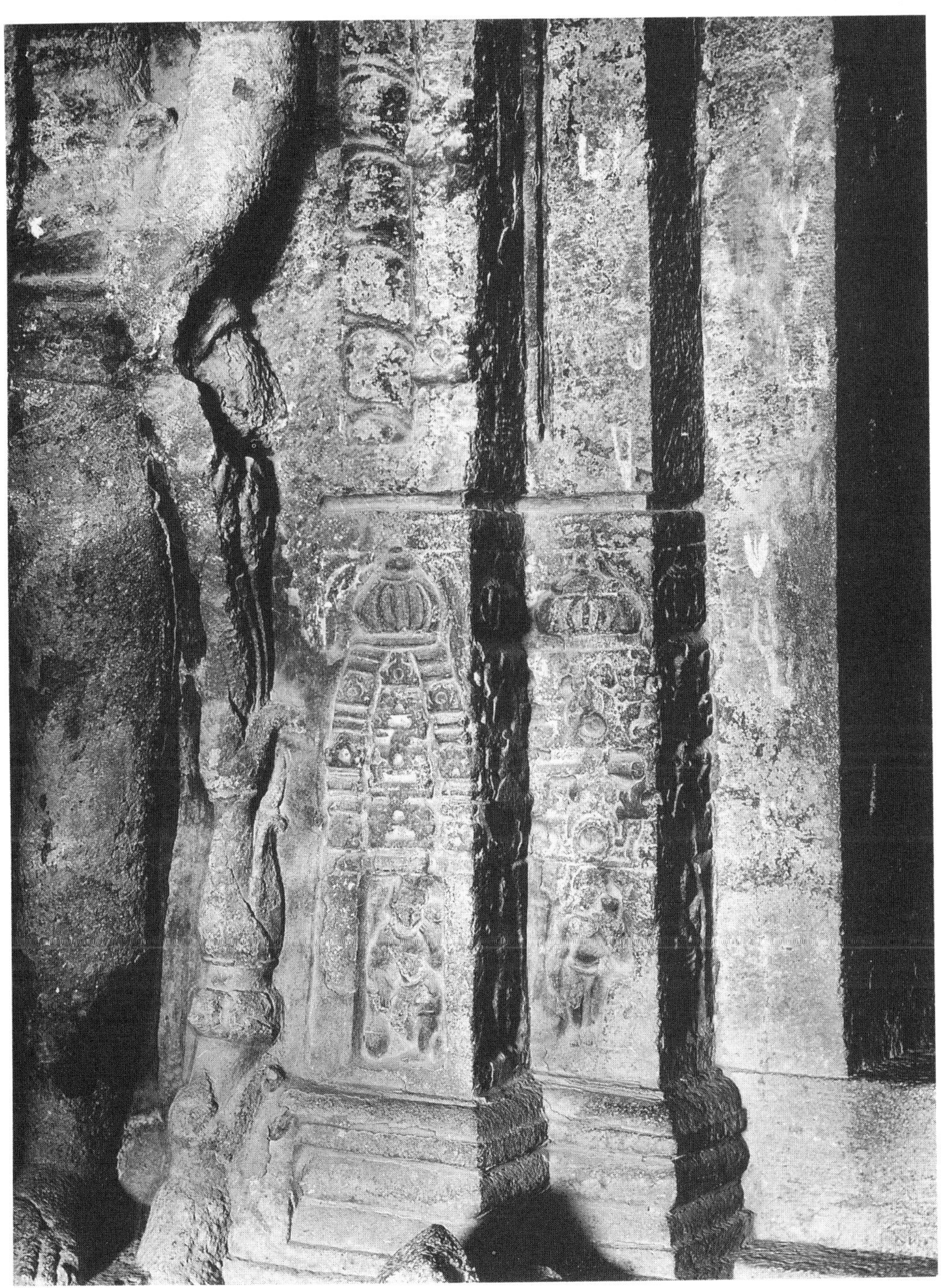

Fig. 165   Cave 12.2 shrine doorframe (AIIS)

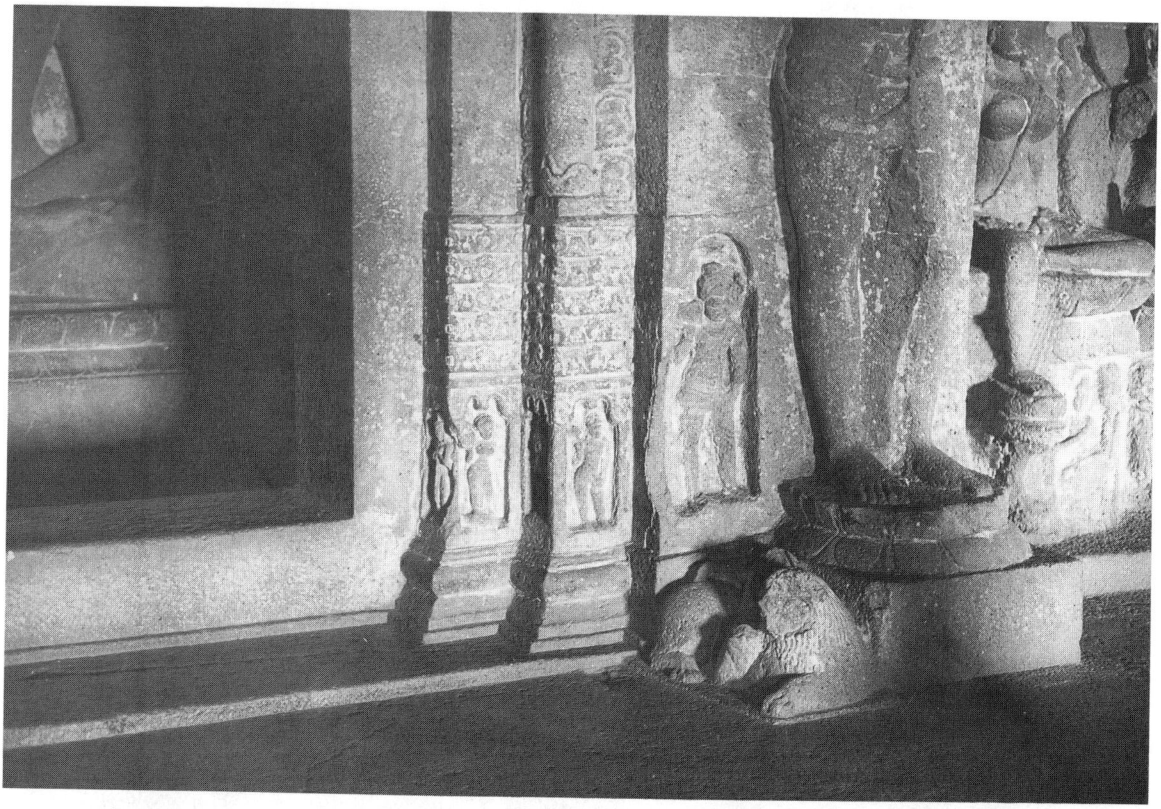

Fig. 166   Cave 12.3 shrine doorframe

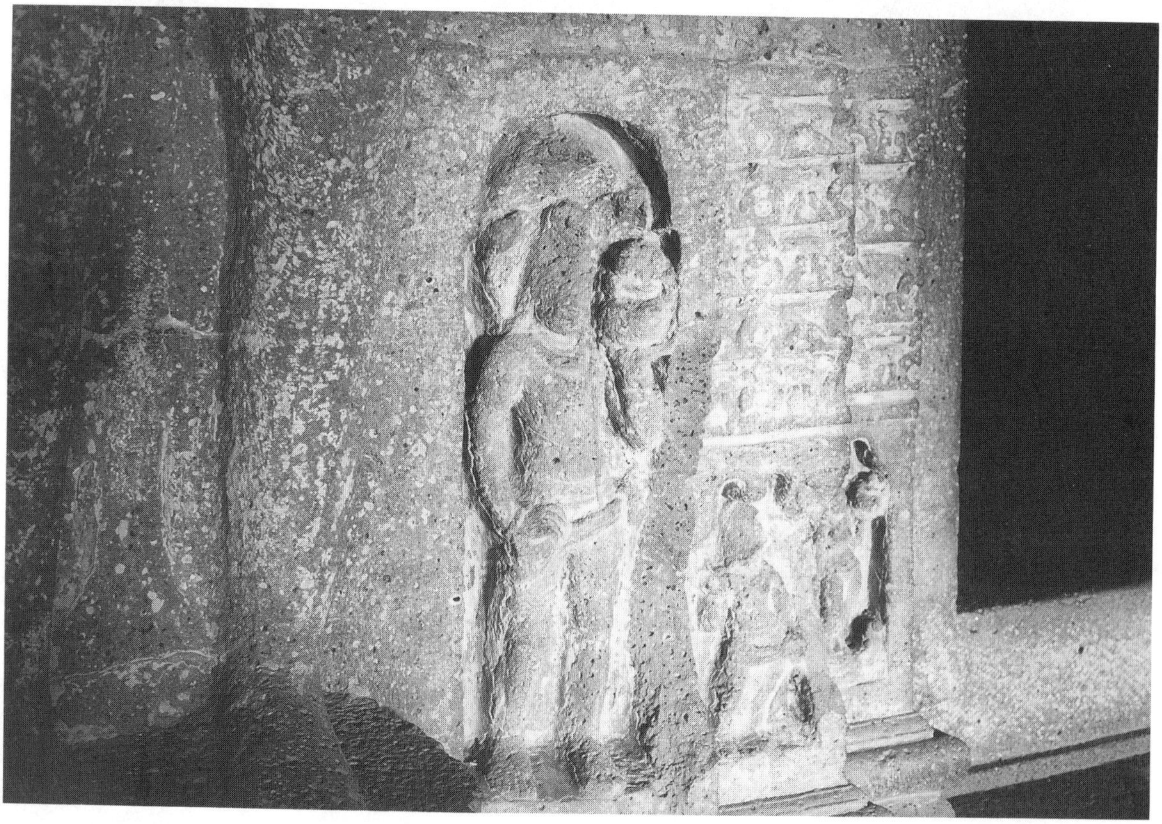

Fig. 167   Cave 12.3 shrine doorframe, closeup

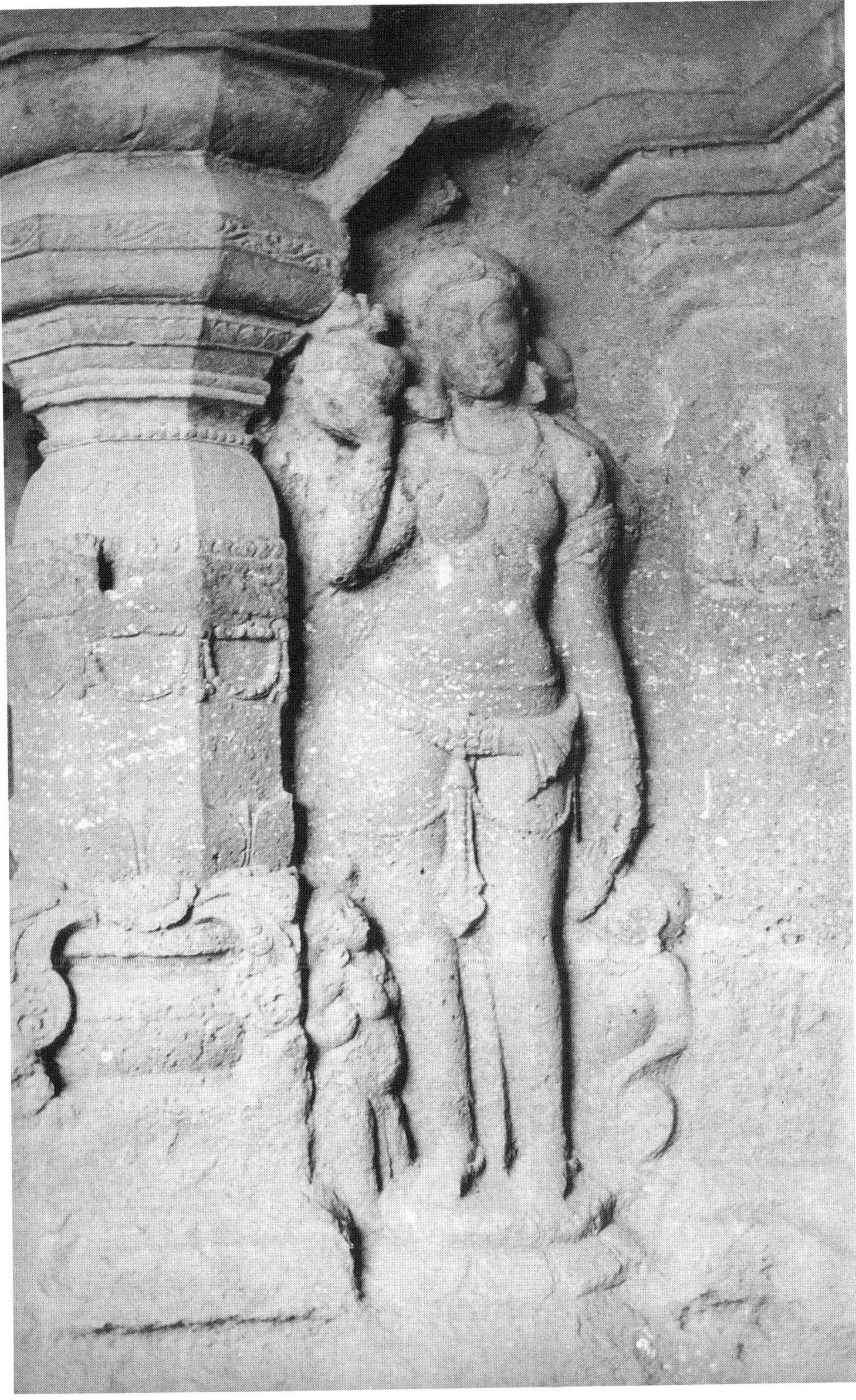

Fig. 168   Cave 16, female door attendant

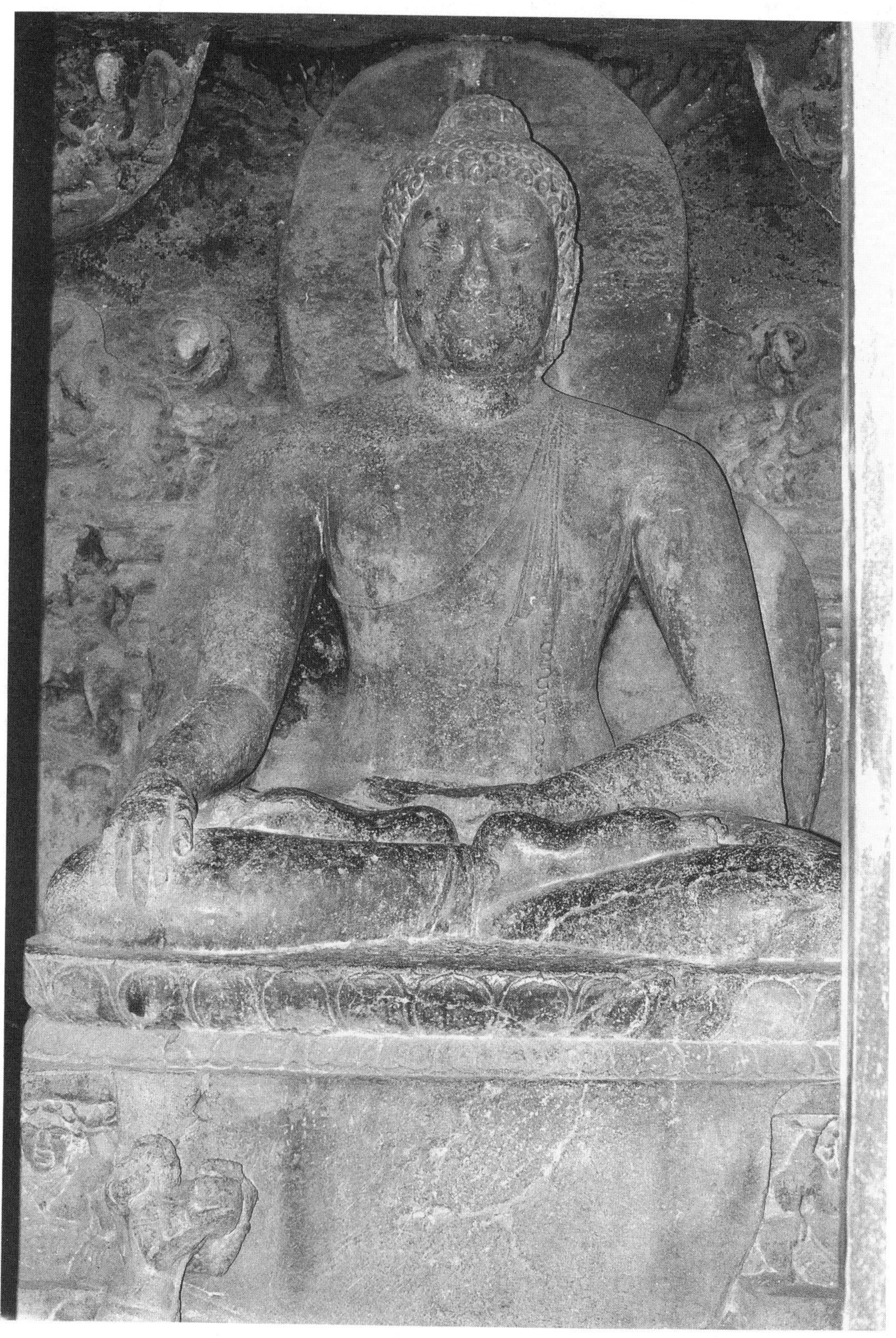

Fig. 169   Cave 11.2 Shrine 3, Buddha

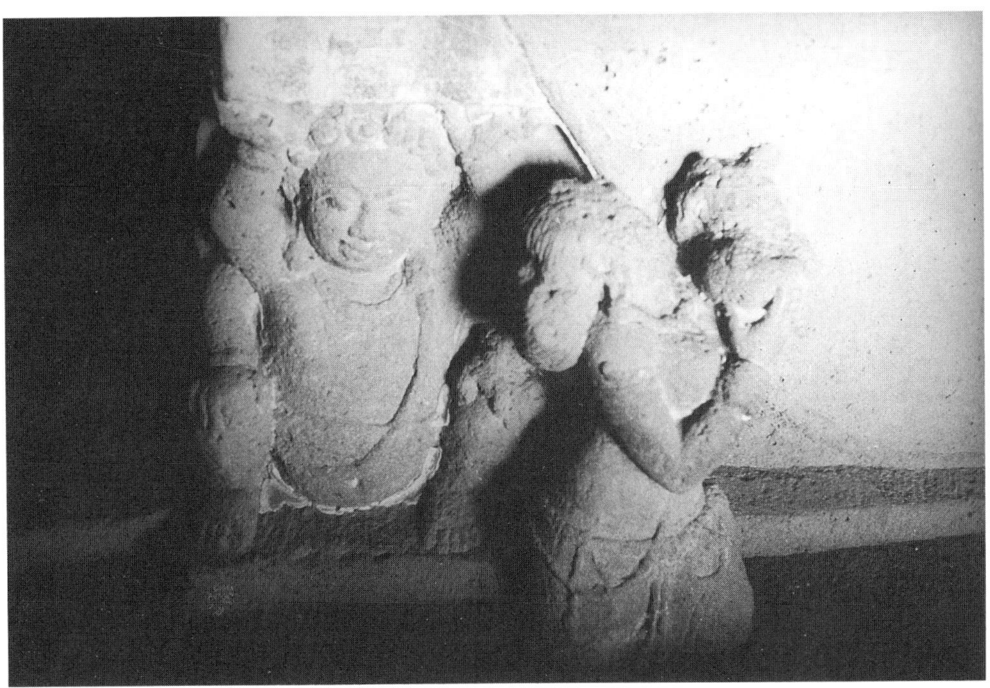

Fig. 170   Cave 11.2 Shrine 1, throne base, Bhūdevī

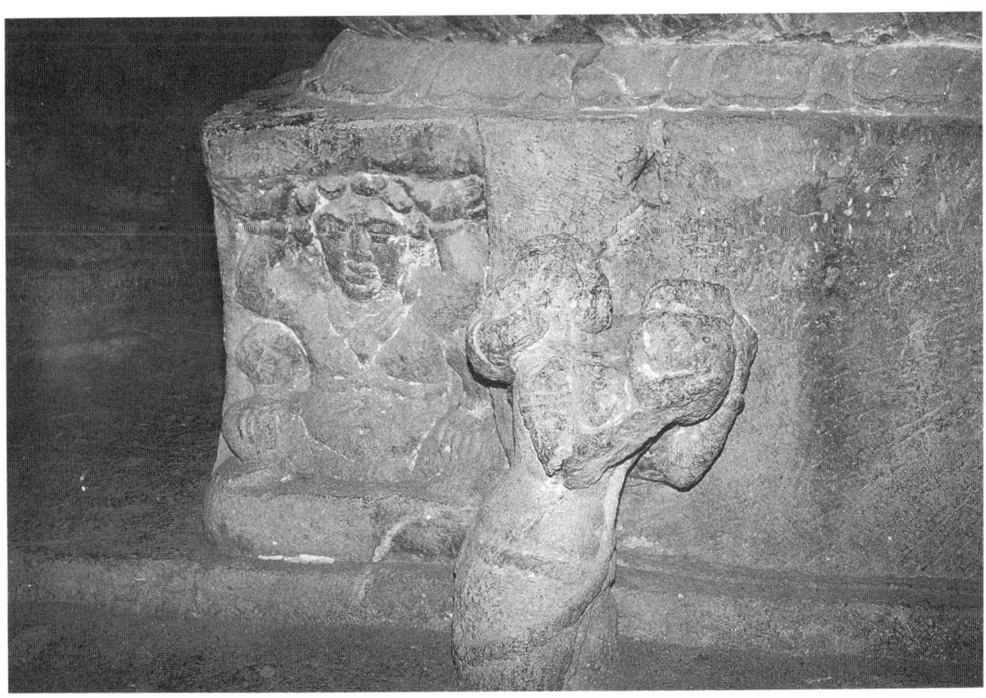

Fig. 171   Cave 11.2 Shrine 3, throne base, Bhūdevī

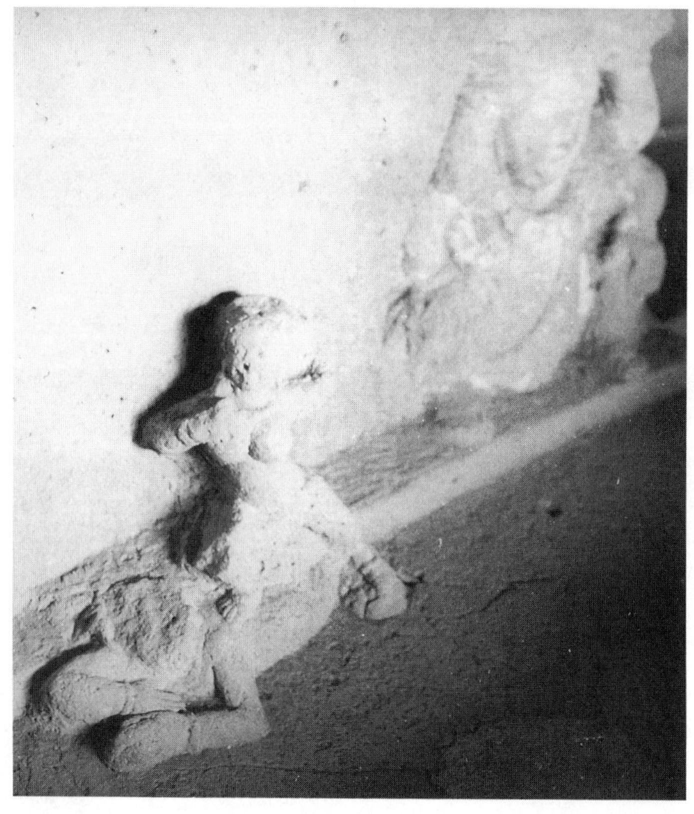

Fig. 172   Cave 11.2 Shrine 1, throne base, Aparājitā

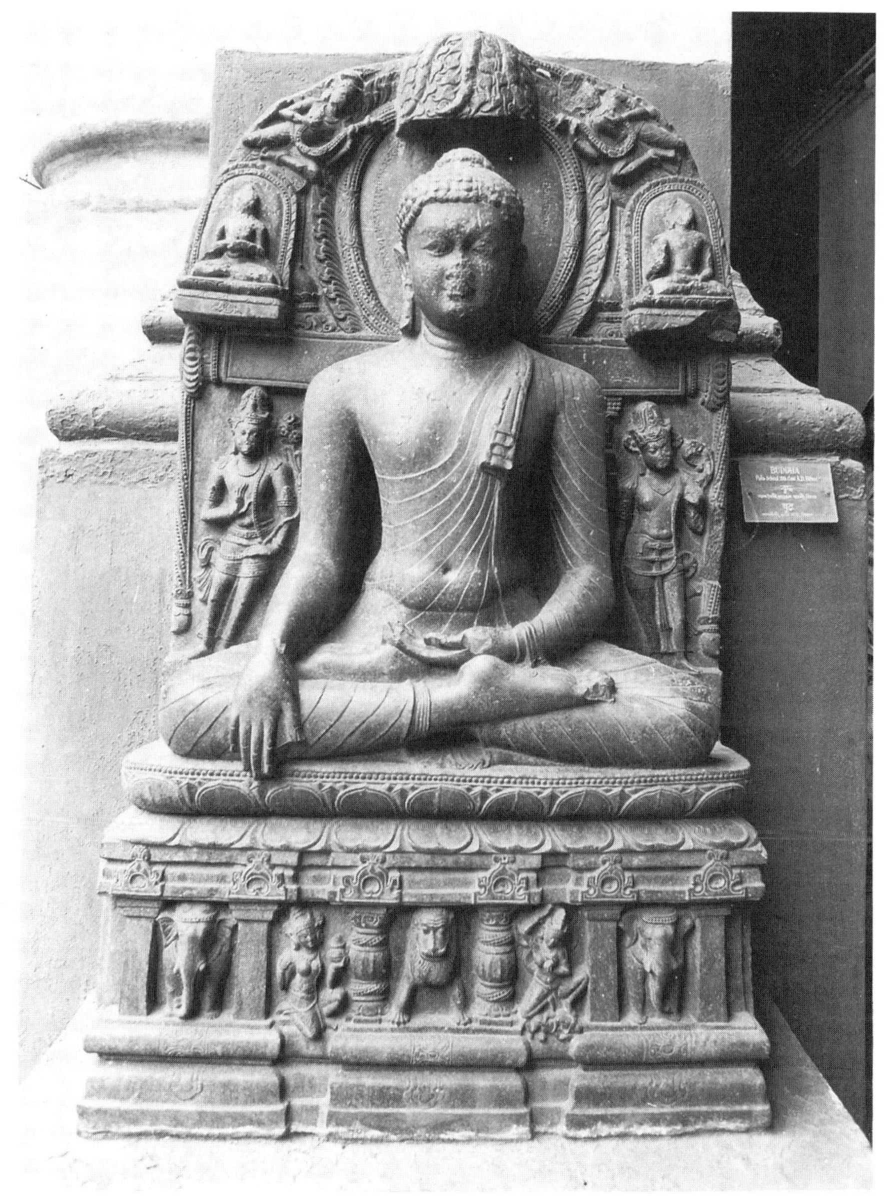

Fig. 173   Kurkihar, Buddha (with permission of the Indian Museum, Calcutta)

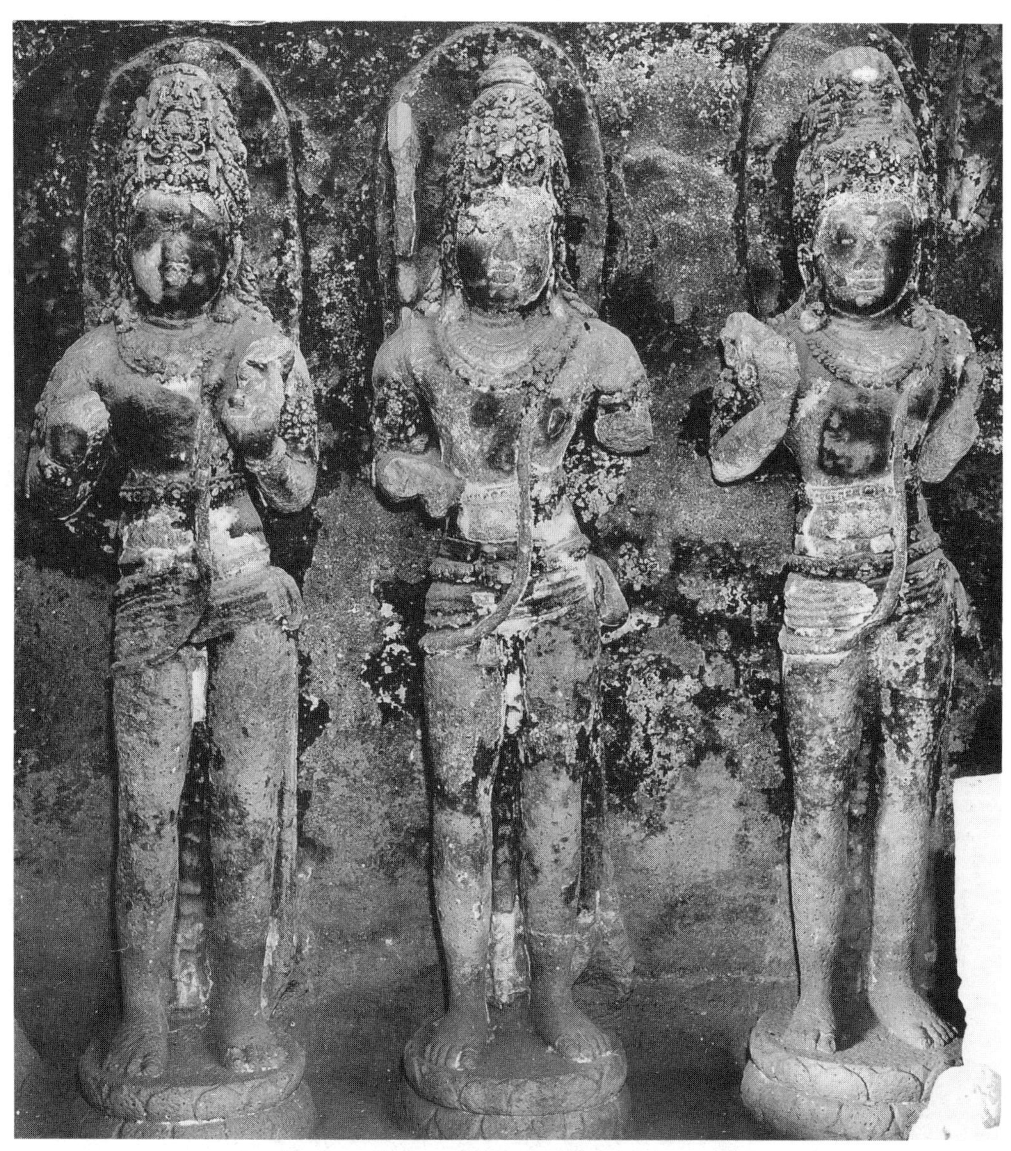

Fig. 174   Cave 11.2 Shrine 1, left wall Bodhisattvas (AIIS)

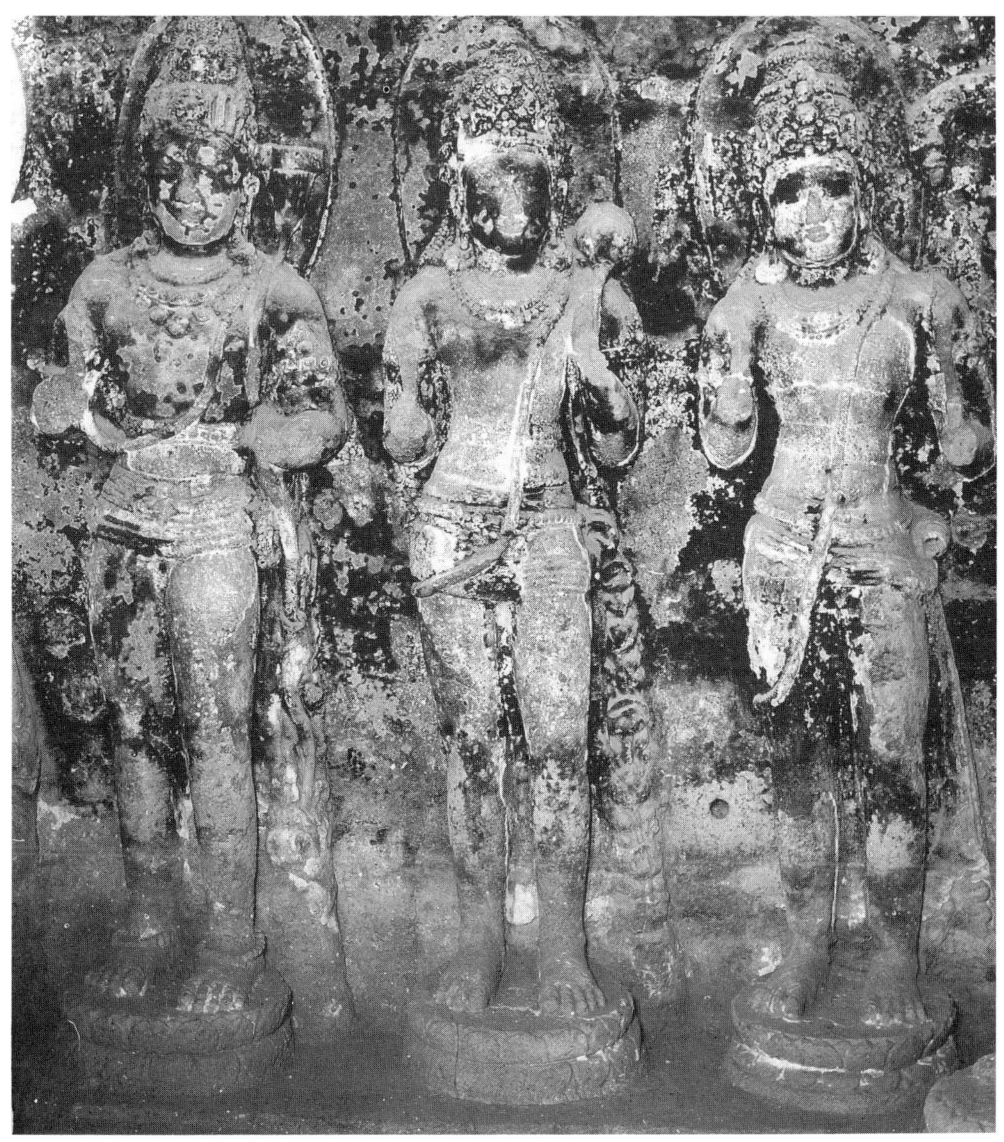

Fig. 175   Cave 11.2 Shrine 1, right wall Bodhisattvas (AIIS)

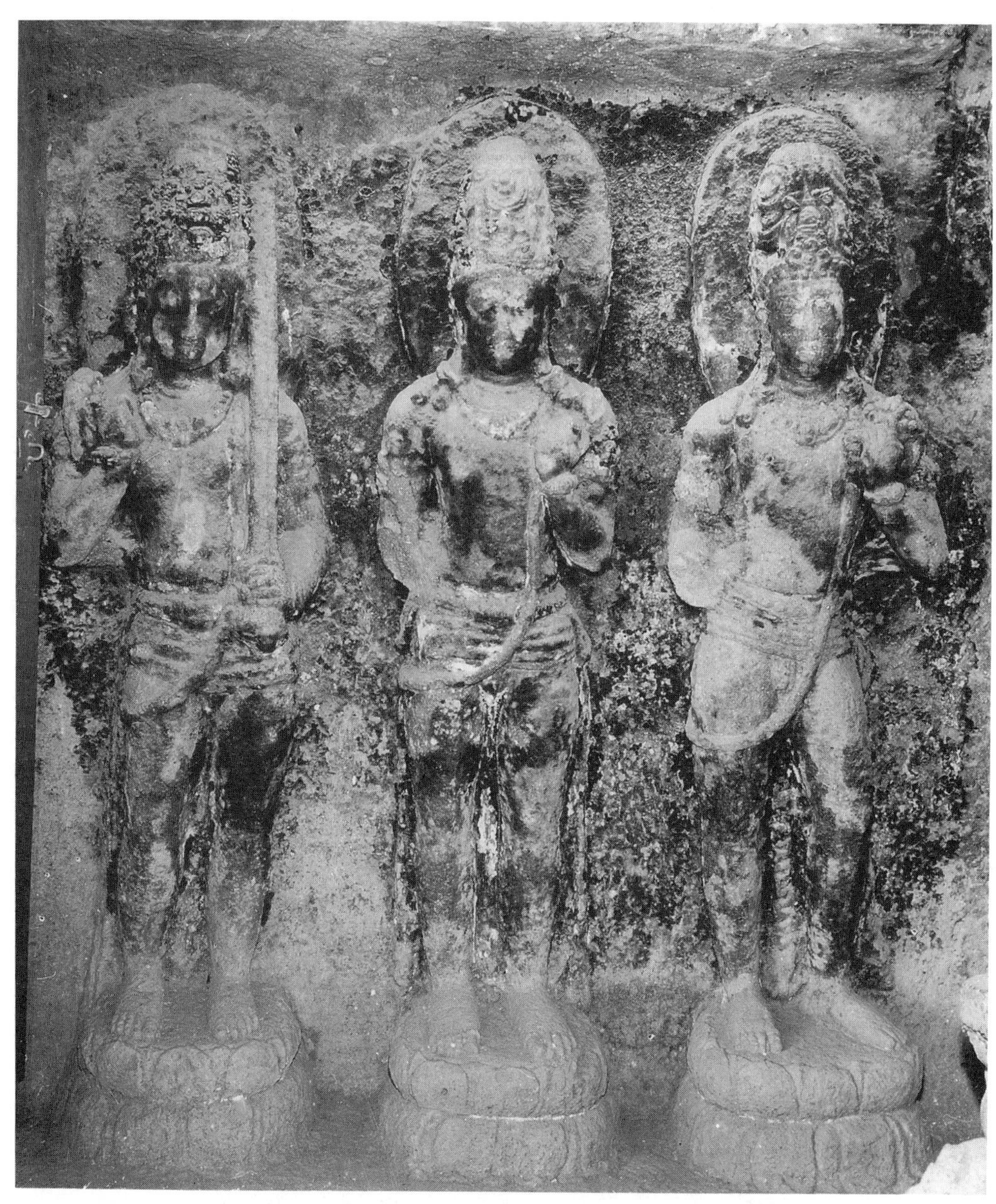

Fig. 176   Cave 11.2 Shrine 3, left wall Bodhisattvas (AIIS)

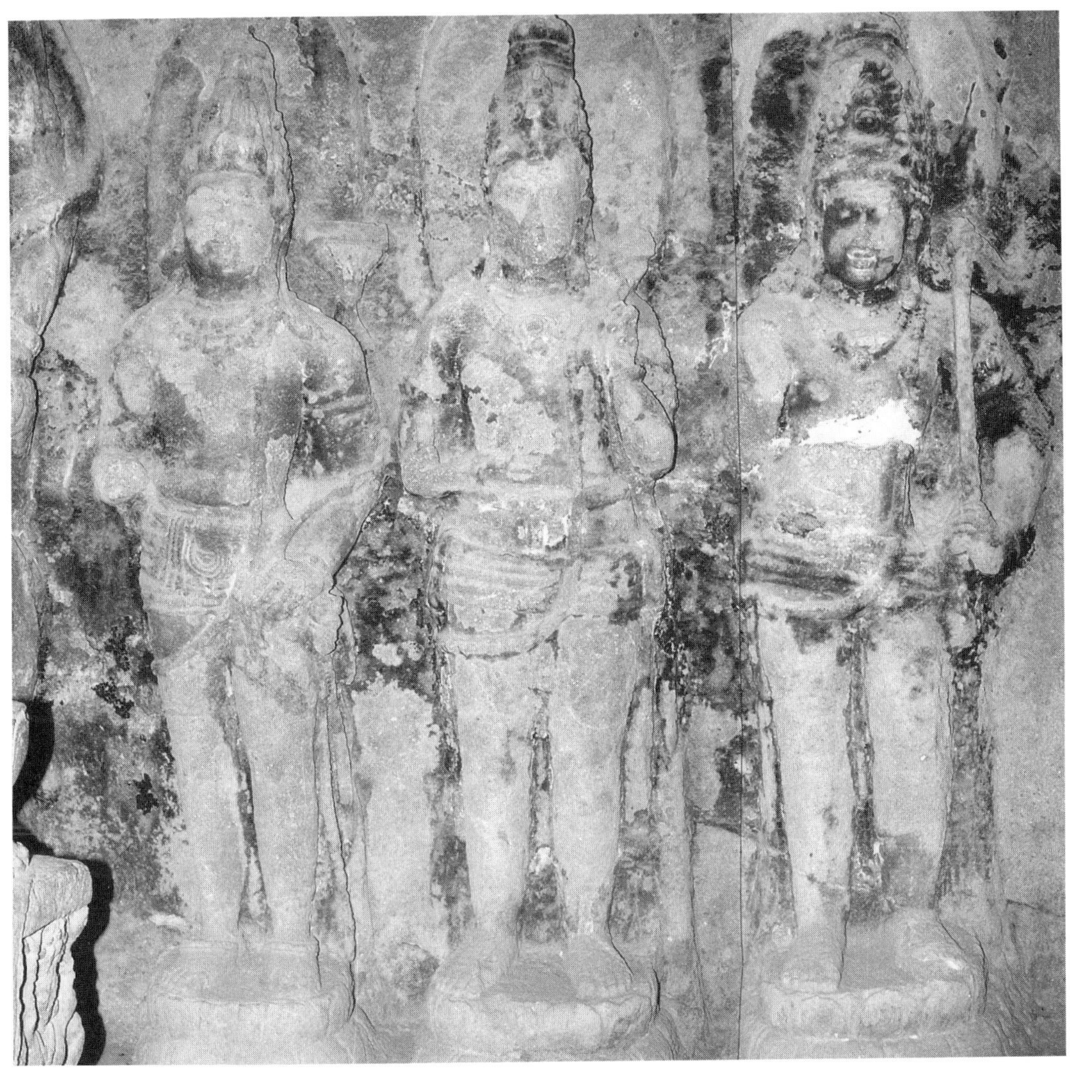

Fig. 177   Cave 11.2 Shrine 3, right wall Bodhisattvas

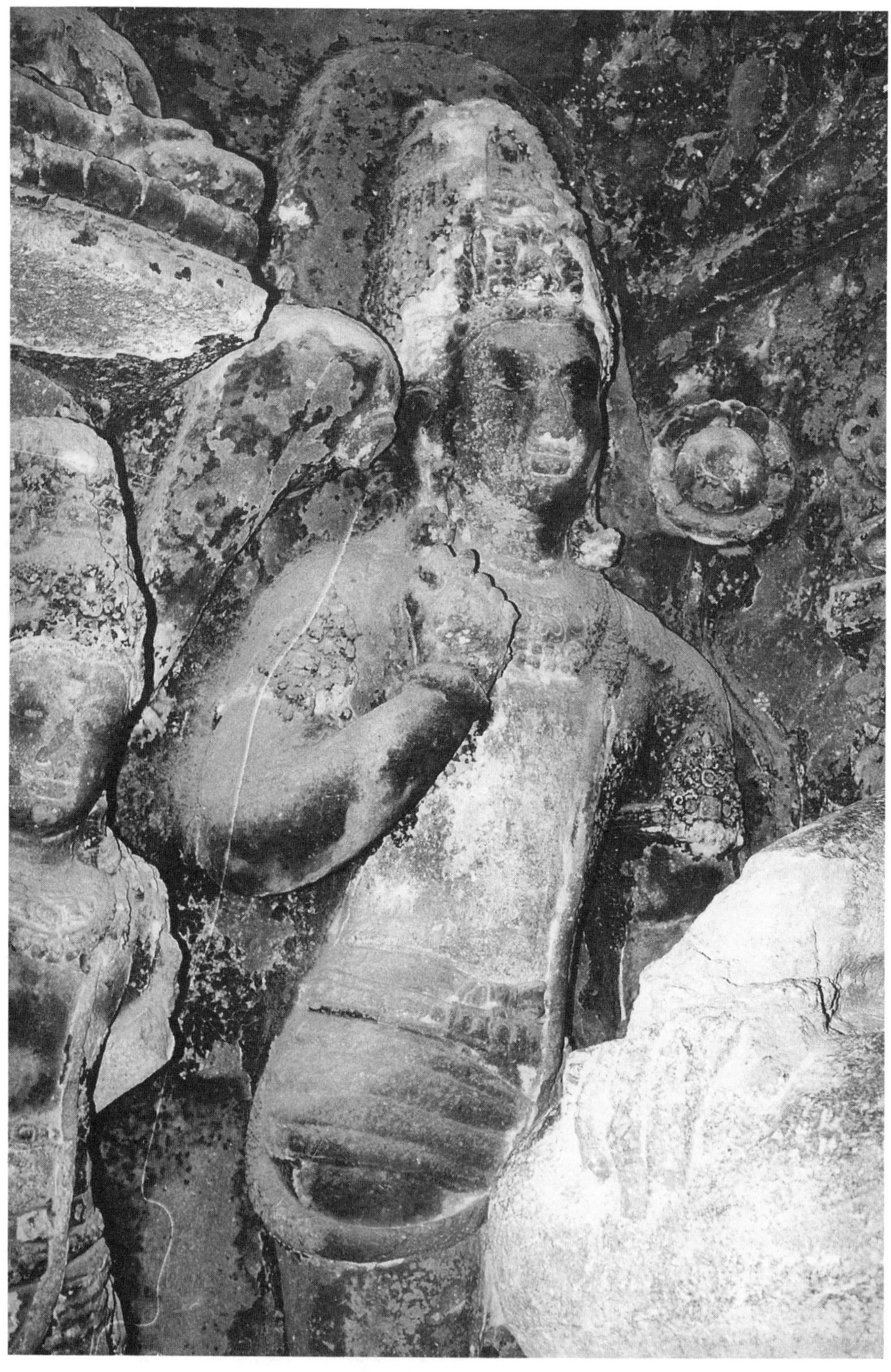

Fig. 178   Cave 11.2 Shrine 1, Avalokiteśvara

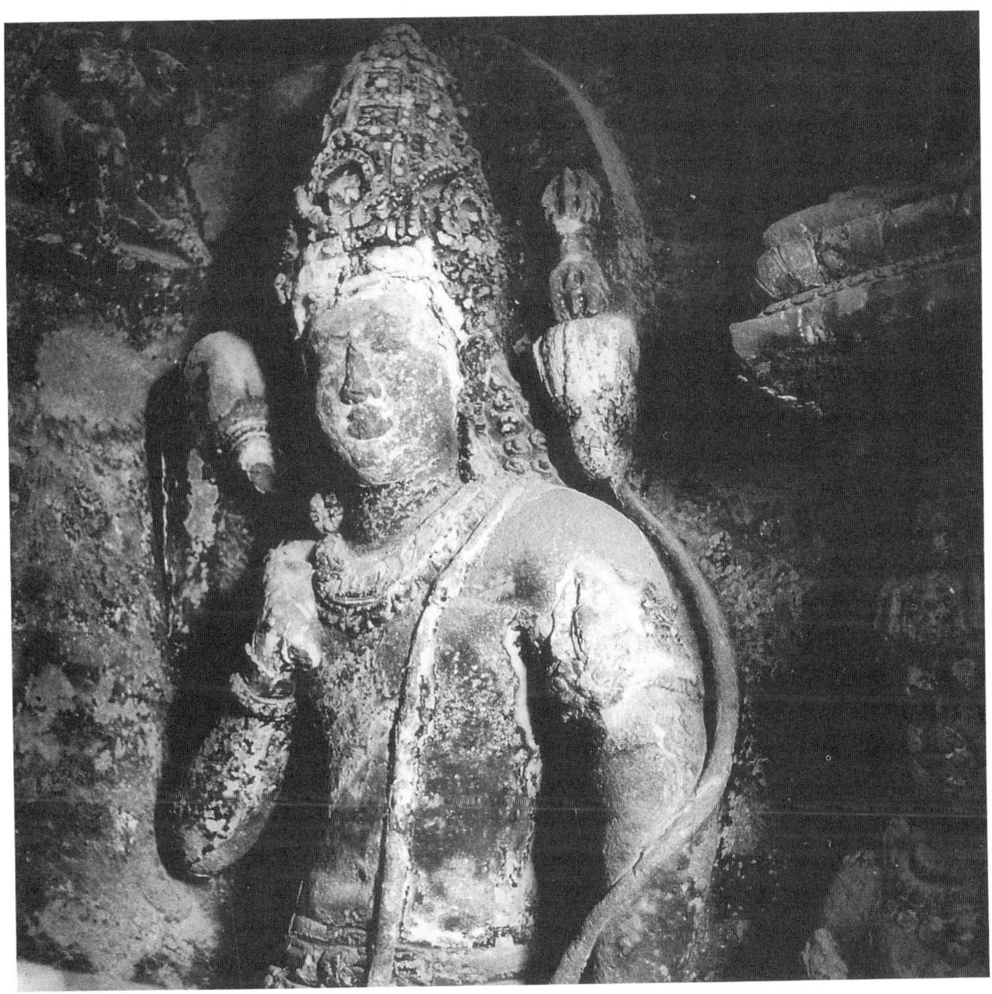

Fig. 179   Cave 11.2 Shrine 1, Vajrapāṇi

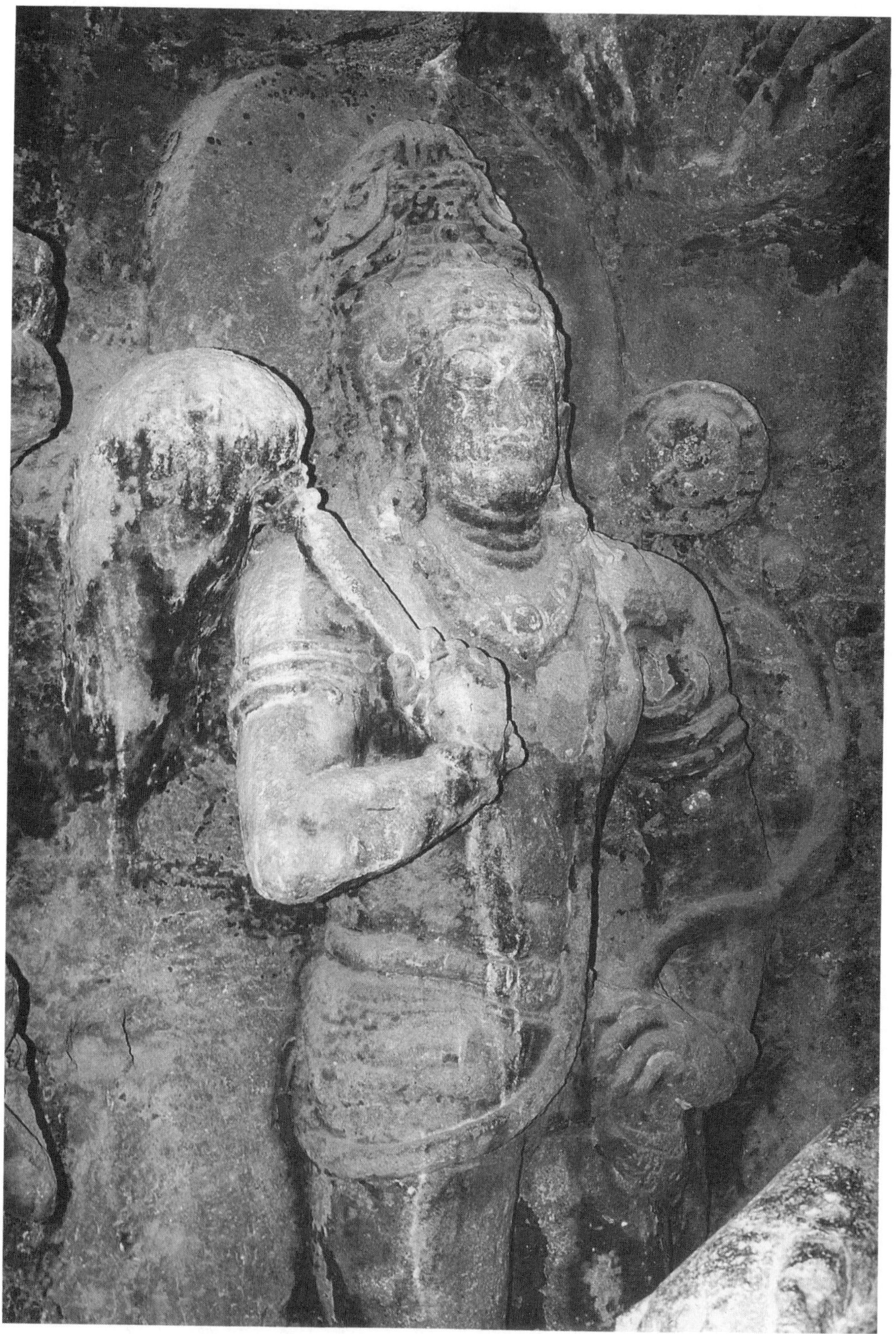

Fig. 180   Cave 11.2 Shrine 3, Avalokiteśvara

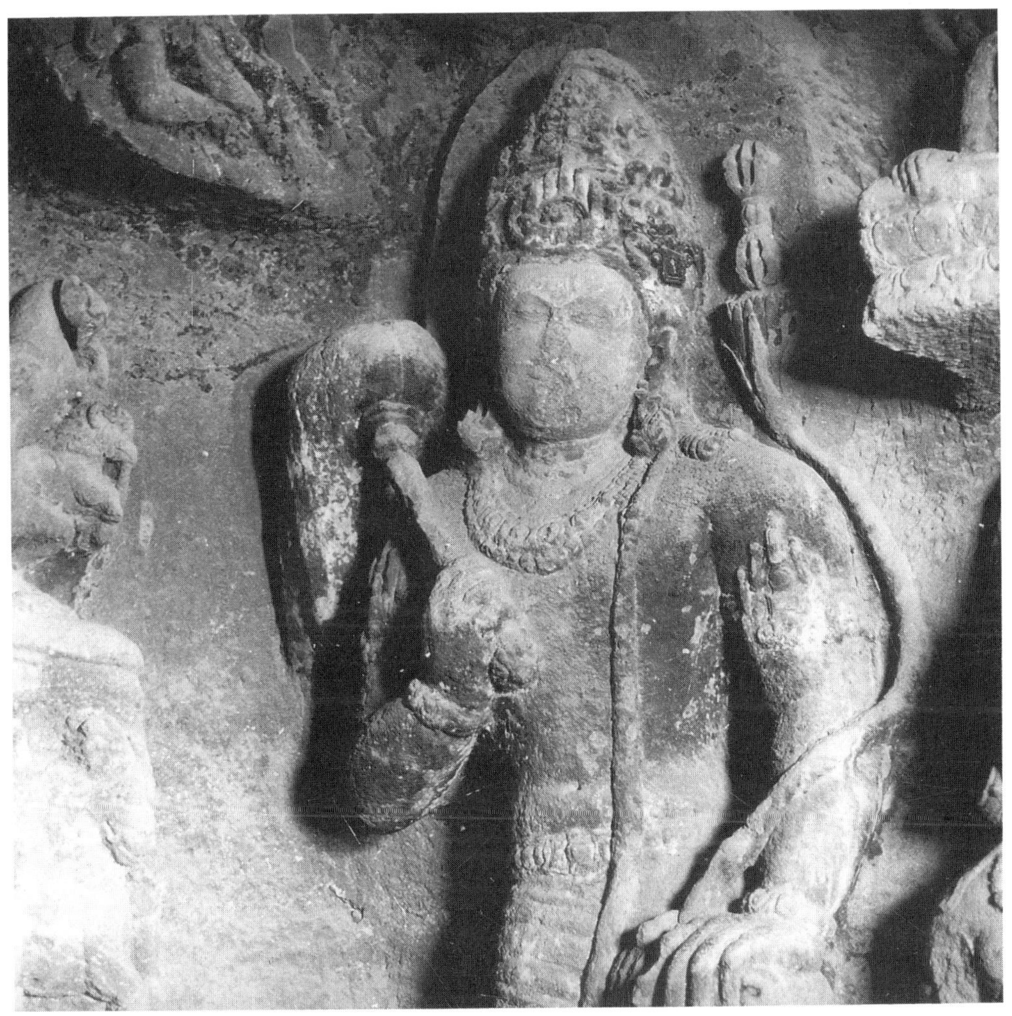

Fig. 181　Cave 11.2 Shrine 3, Vajrapāṇi

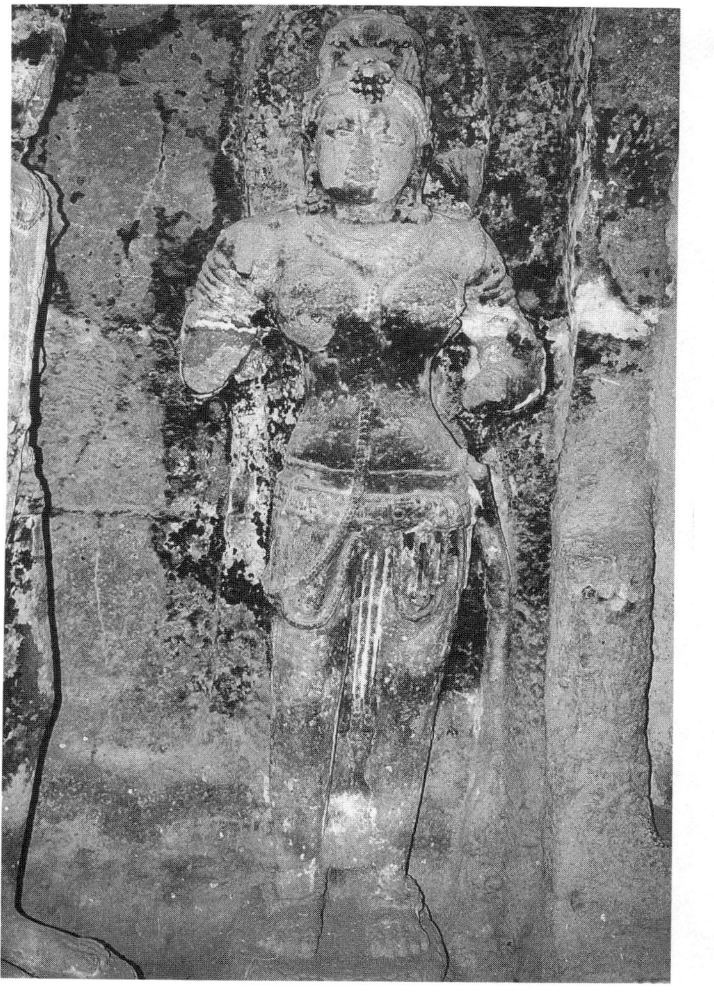

Fig. 182   Cave 11.2 Shrine 1, Tārā

Fig. 183   Cave 11.2 Shrine 1, Jambhala

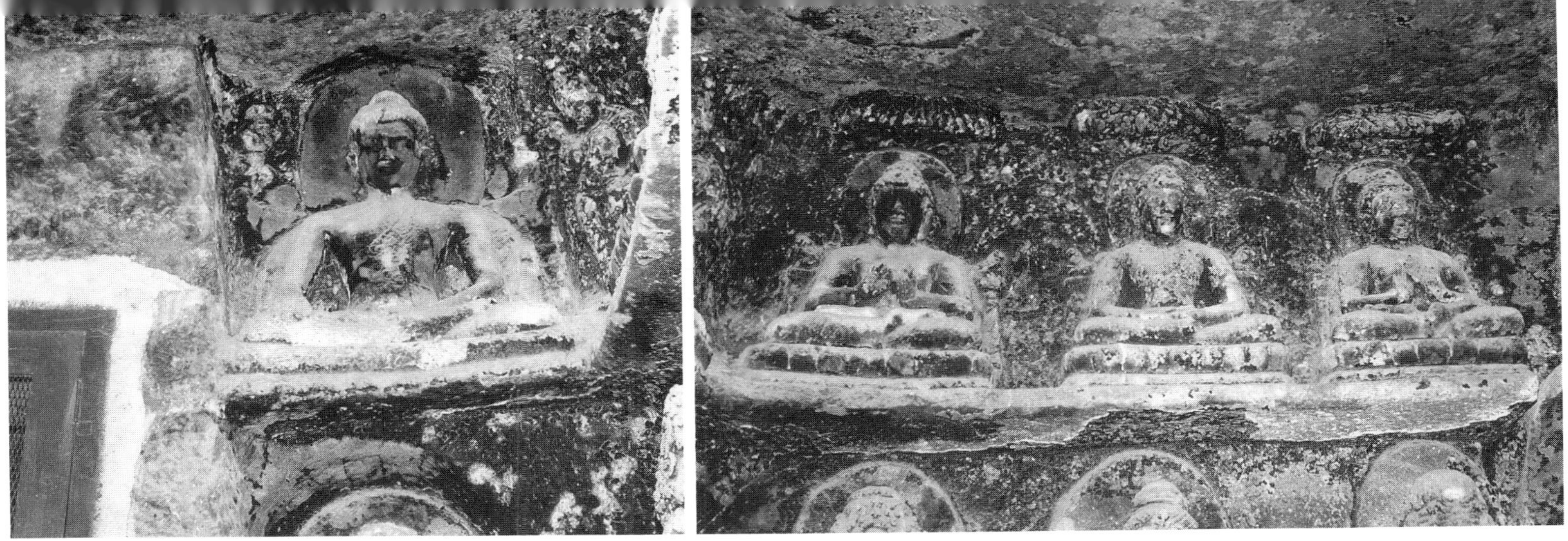

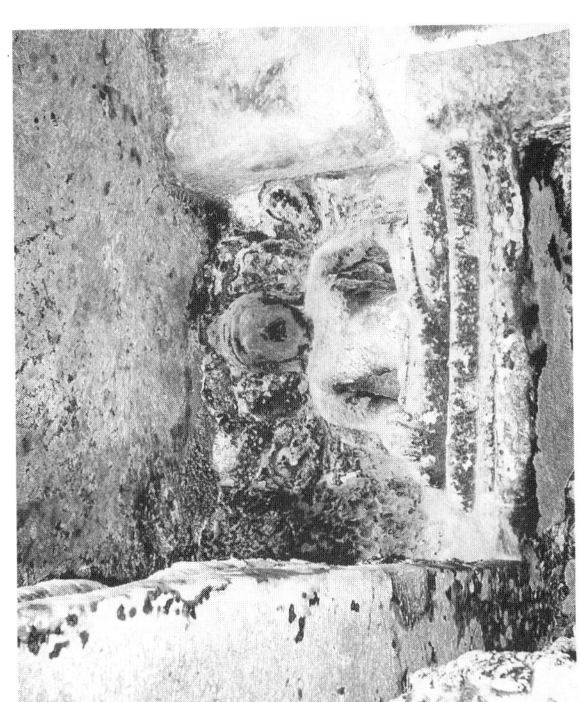

Fig. 184a   Cave 11.2 Shrine 1, Mānuṣi Buddhas, left side

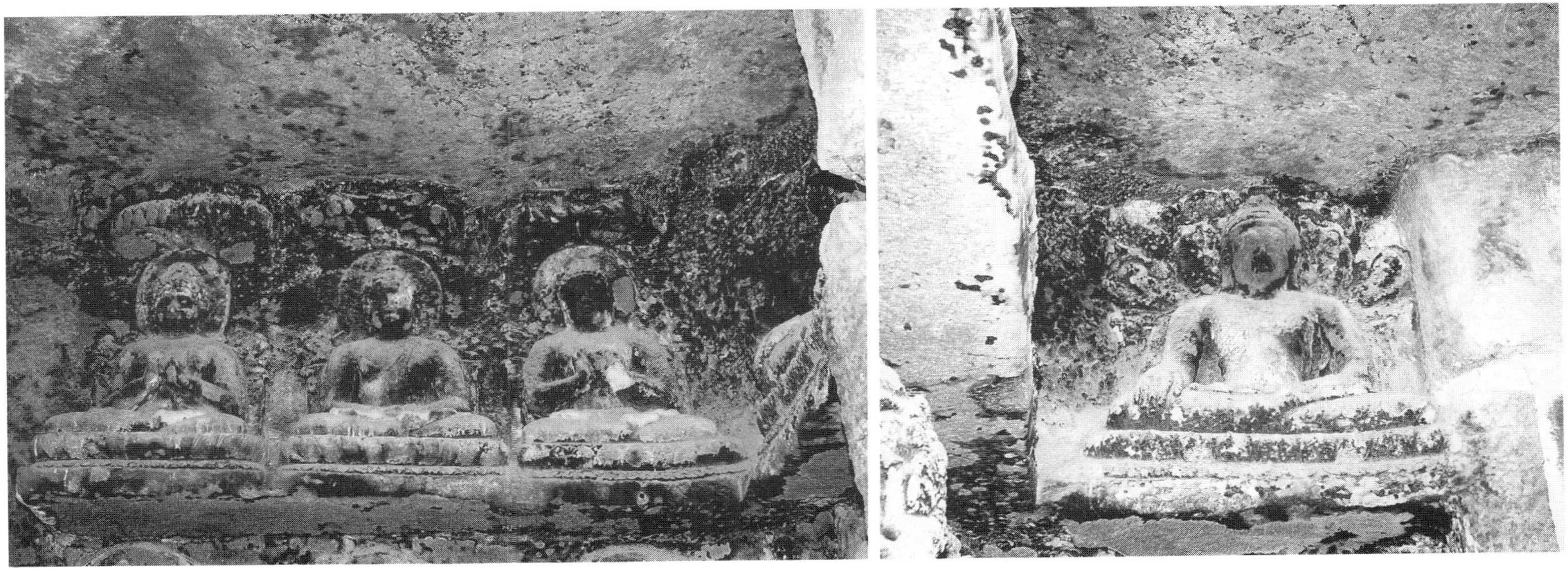

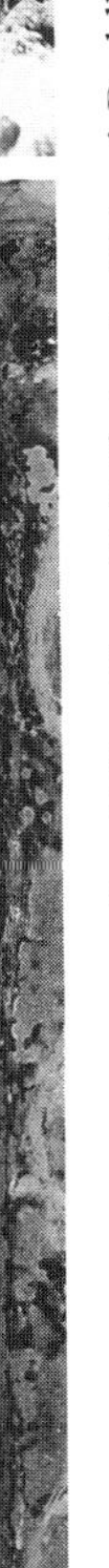

Fig. 184b   Cave 11.2 Shrine 1, Mānuṣi Buddhas, right side

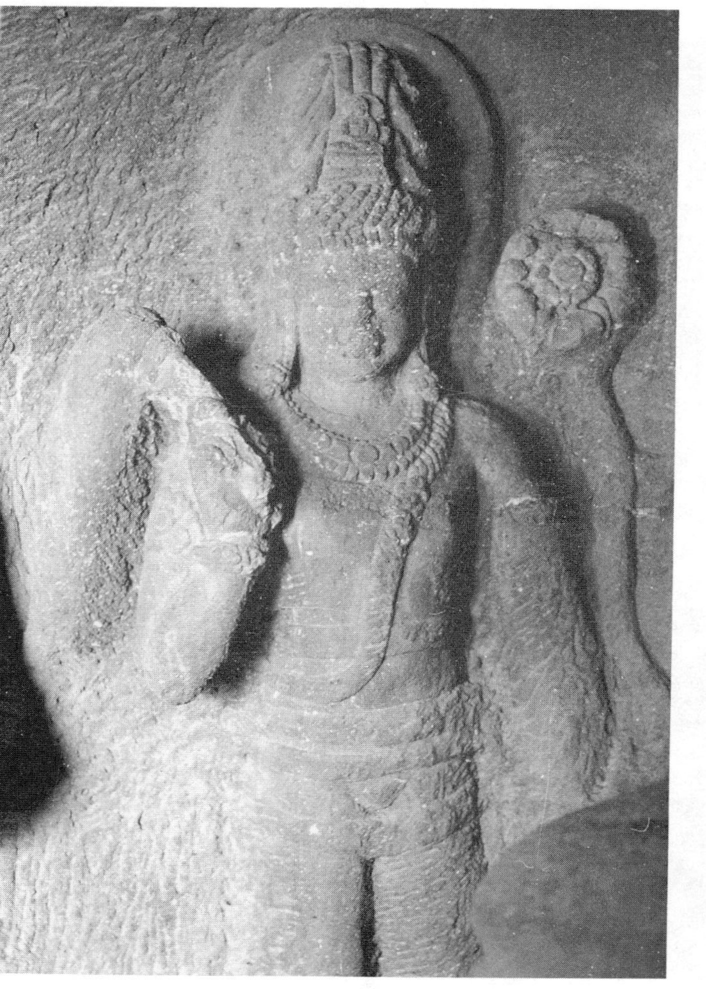

Fig. 185   Cave 11.2 Shrine 5, Avalokiteśvara

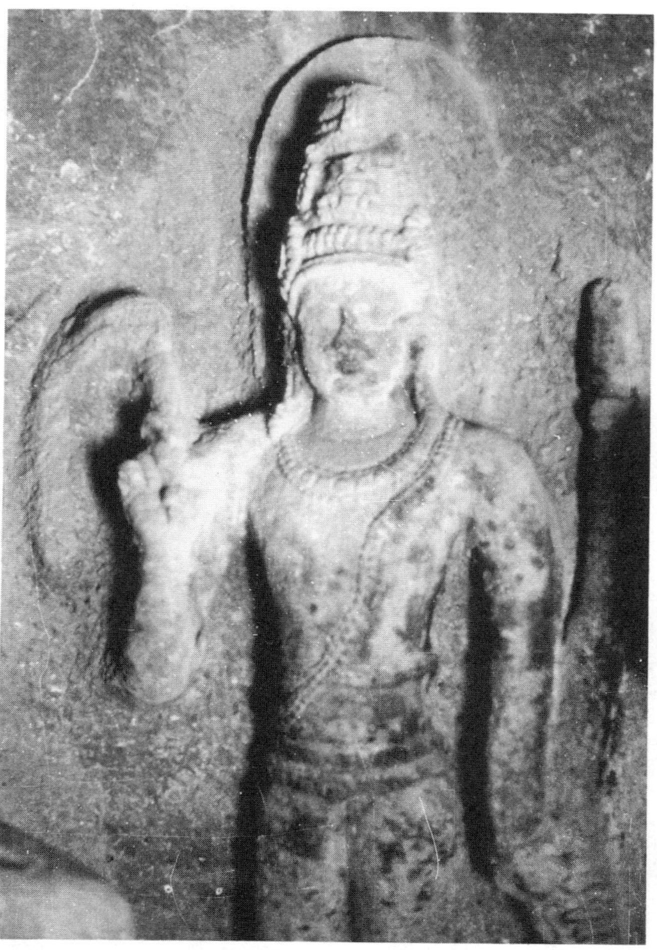

Fig. 186   Cave 11.2 Shrine 5, Vajrapāṇi

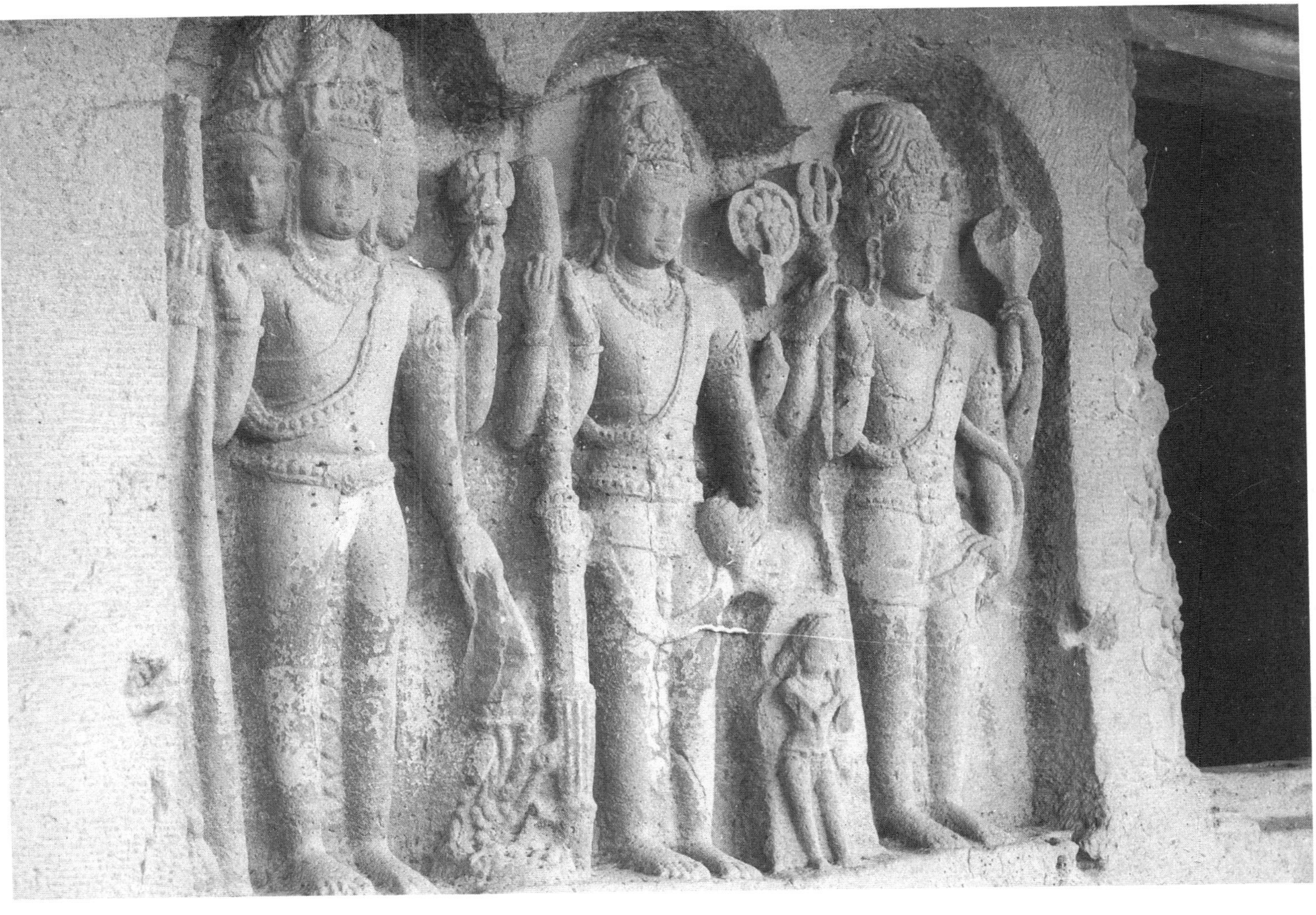

Fig. 187   Cave 27 verandah, Brahmanical triad

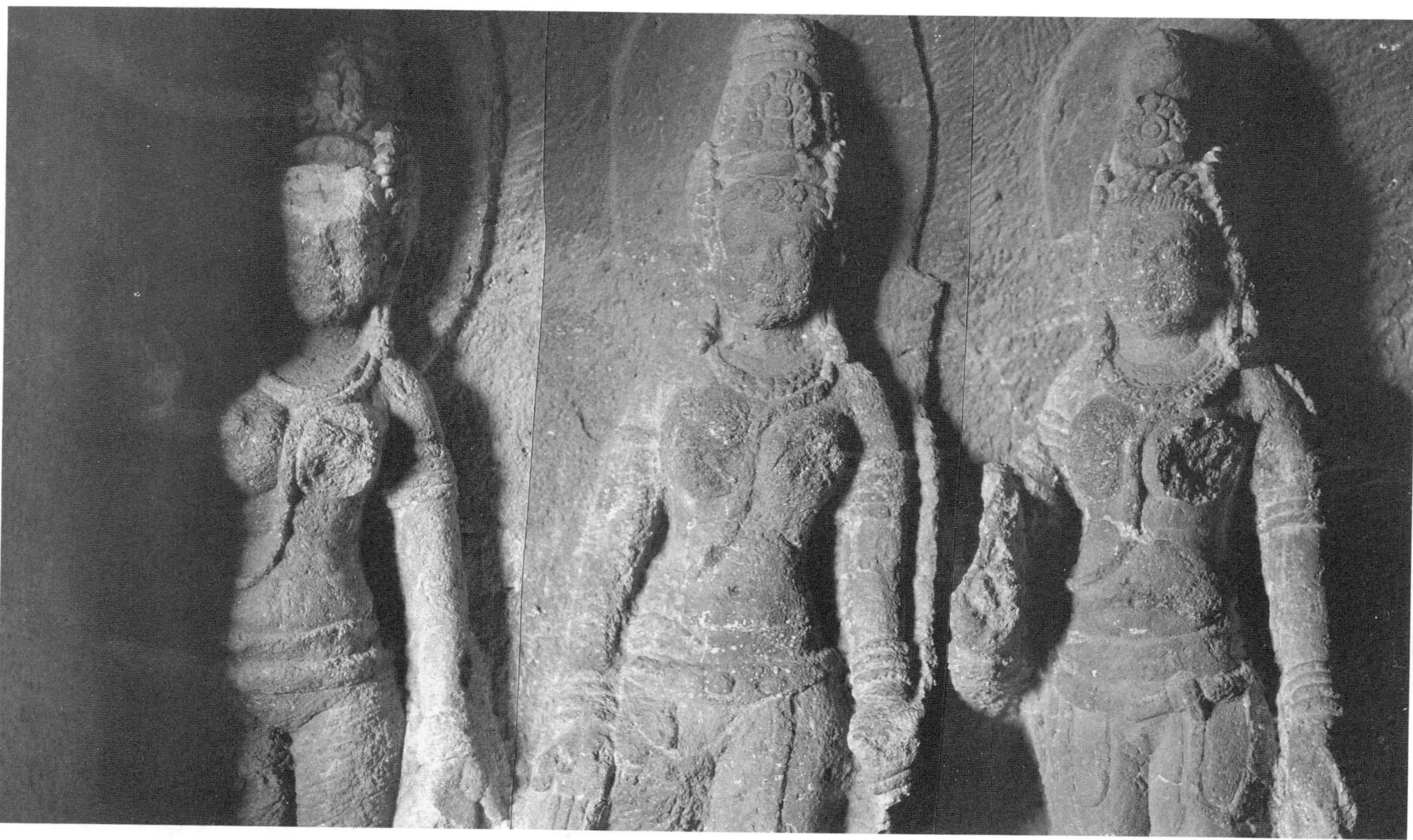

Fig. 188   Cave 11.2 Shrine 5, left wall female deities

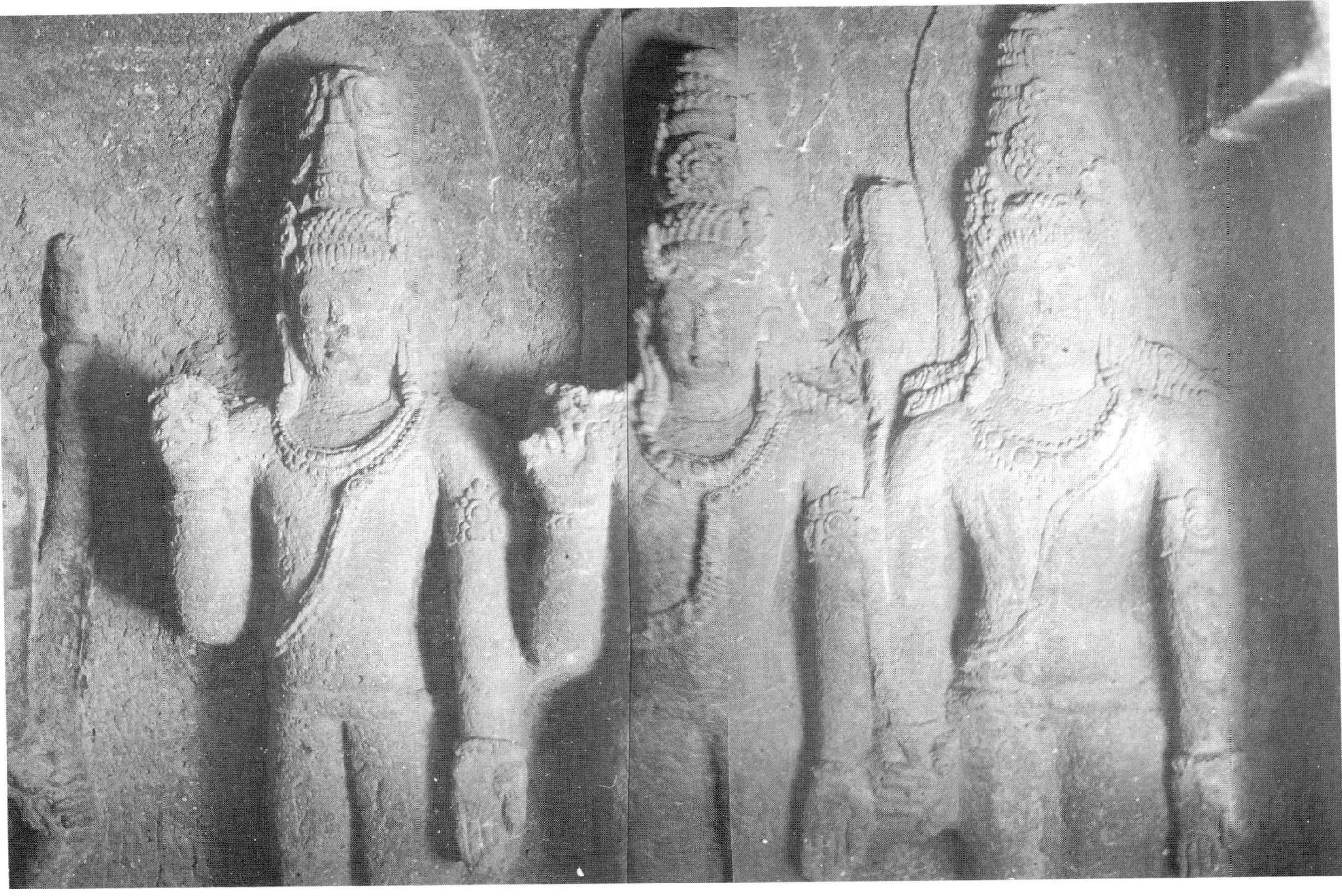

Fig. 189   Cave 11.2 Shrine 5, right wall Bodhisattvas

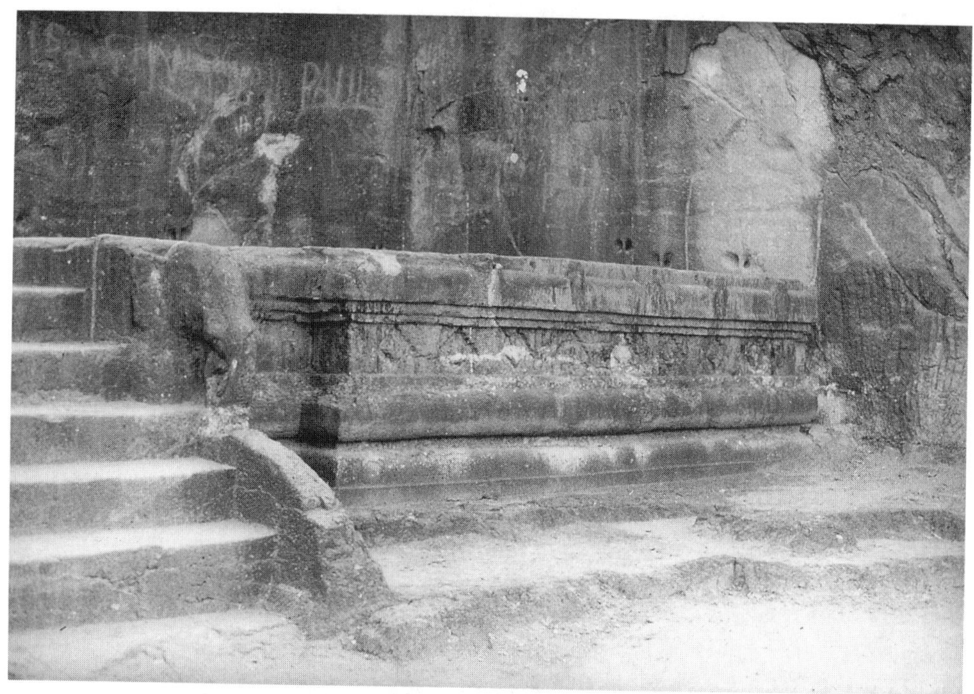

Fig. 190   Cave 12 screen wall

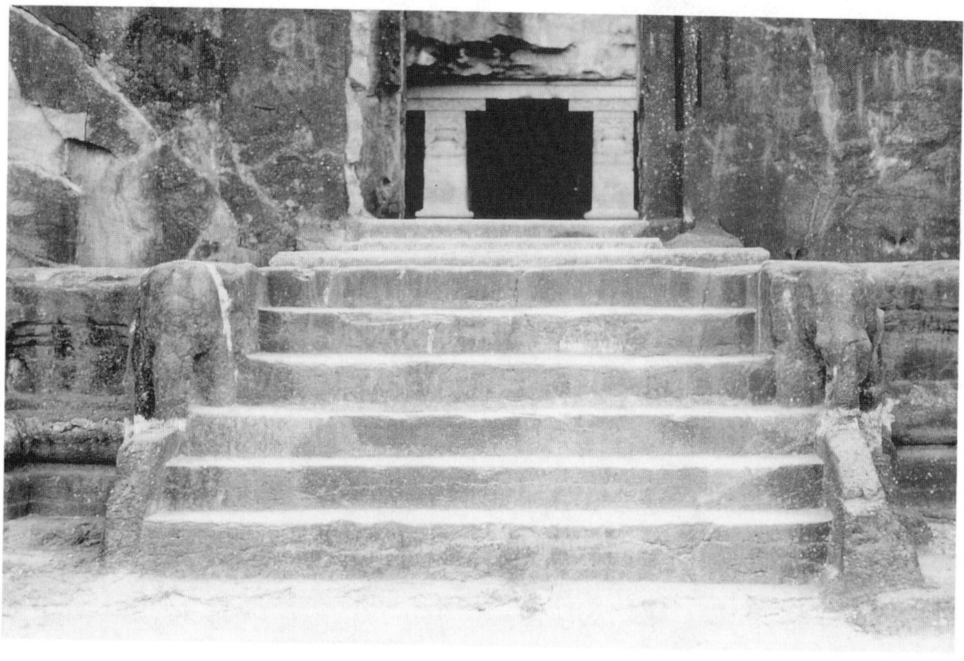

Fig. 191   Cave 12 entrance

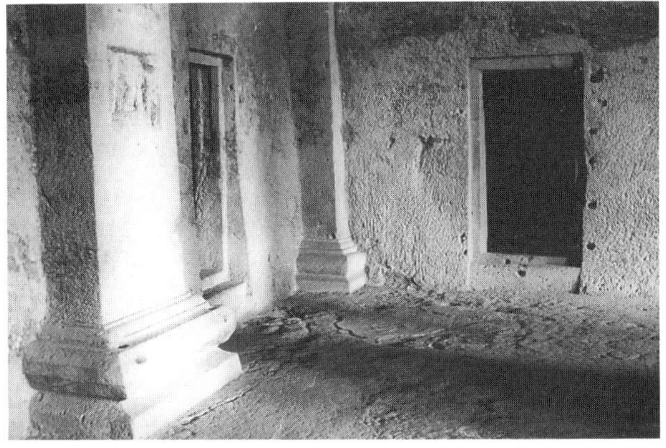

Fig. 192   Cave 12.1 pilasters

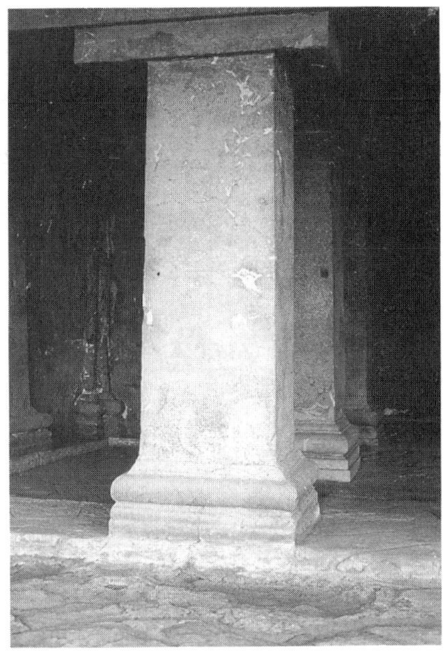

Fig. 193   Cave 25 pillar

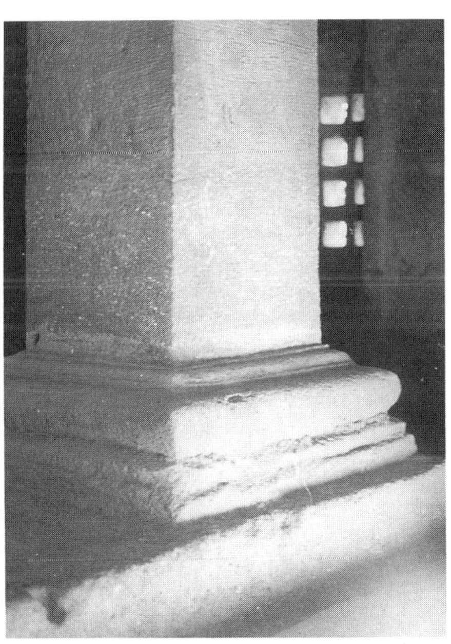

Fig. 194   Cave 15 *maṇḍapa* pillar

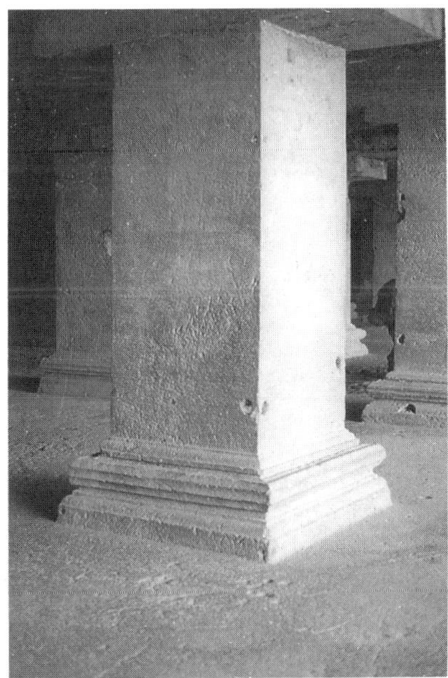

Fig. 195   Cave 15.2 pillar

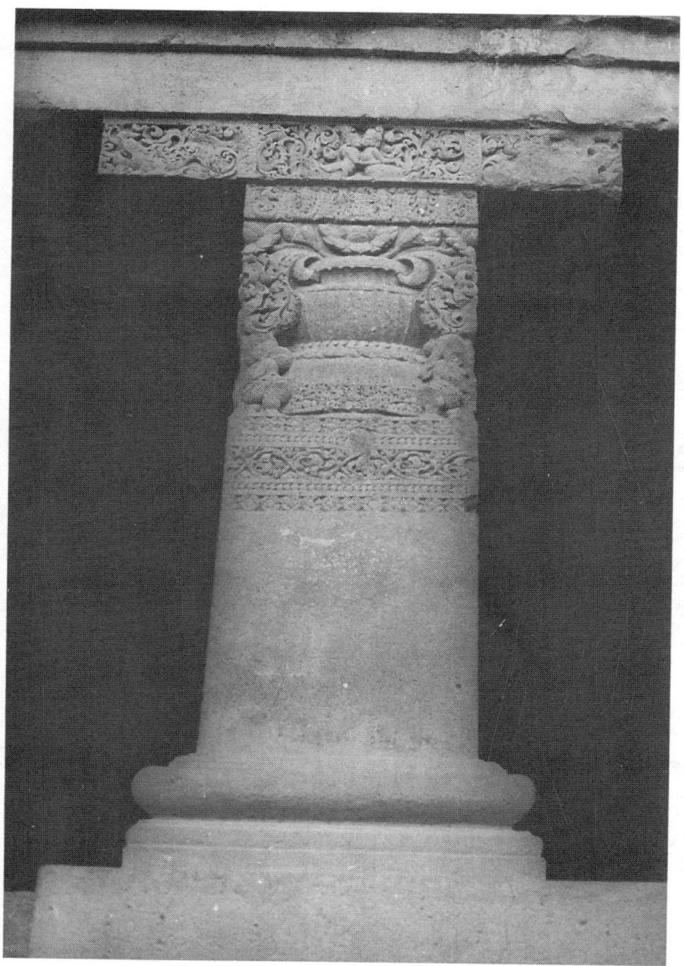
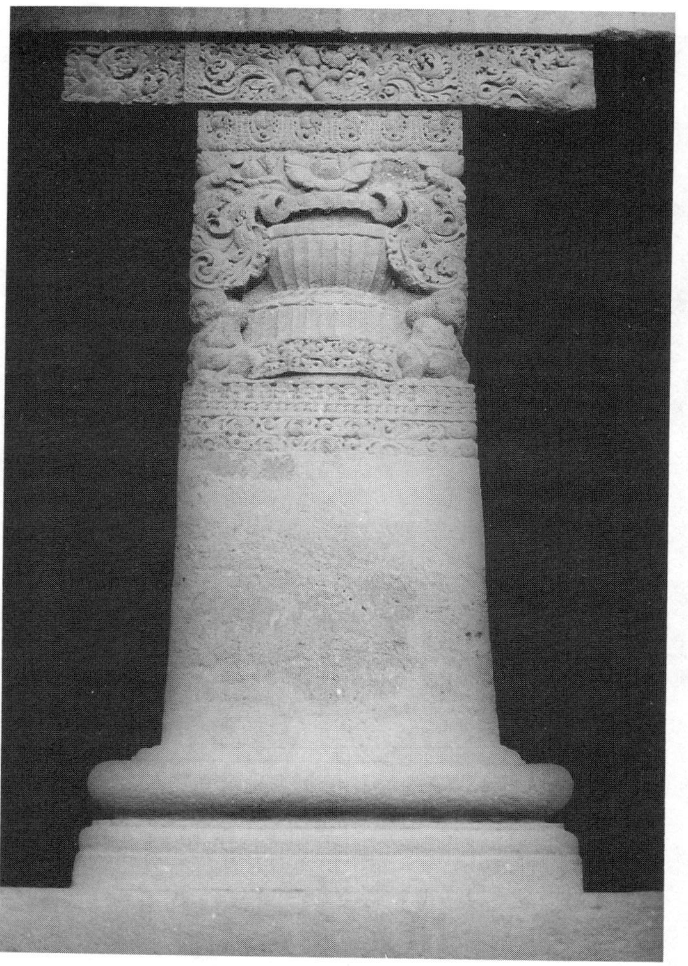

Fig. 196a,b Cave 12.1 pillars

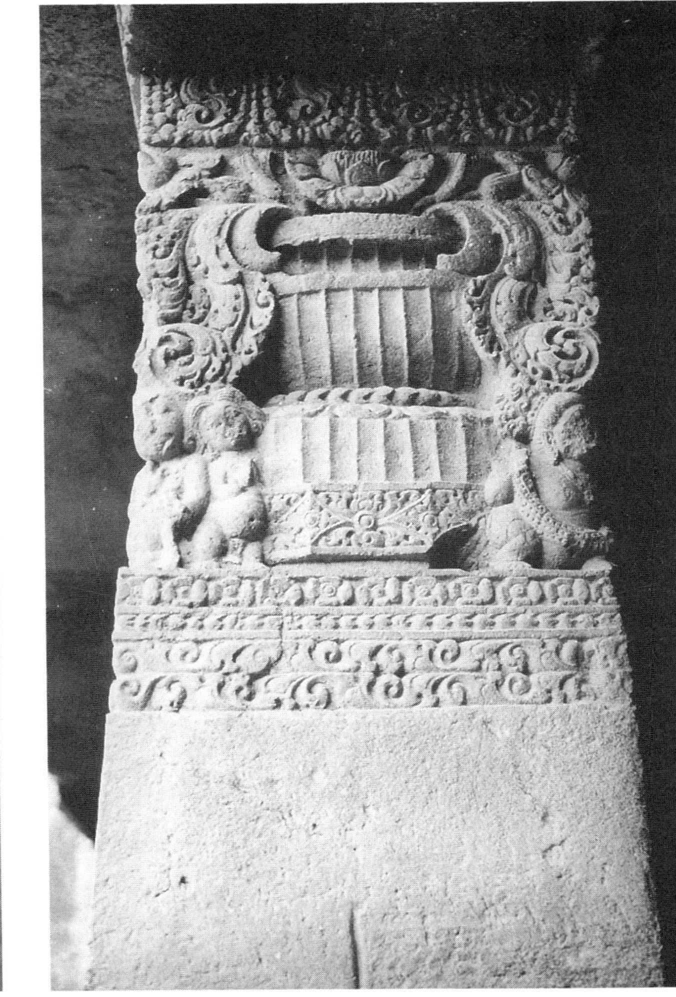

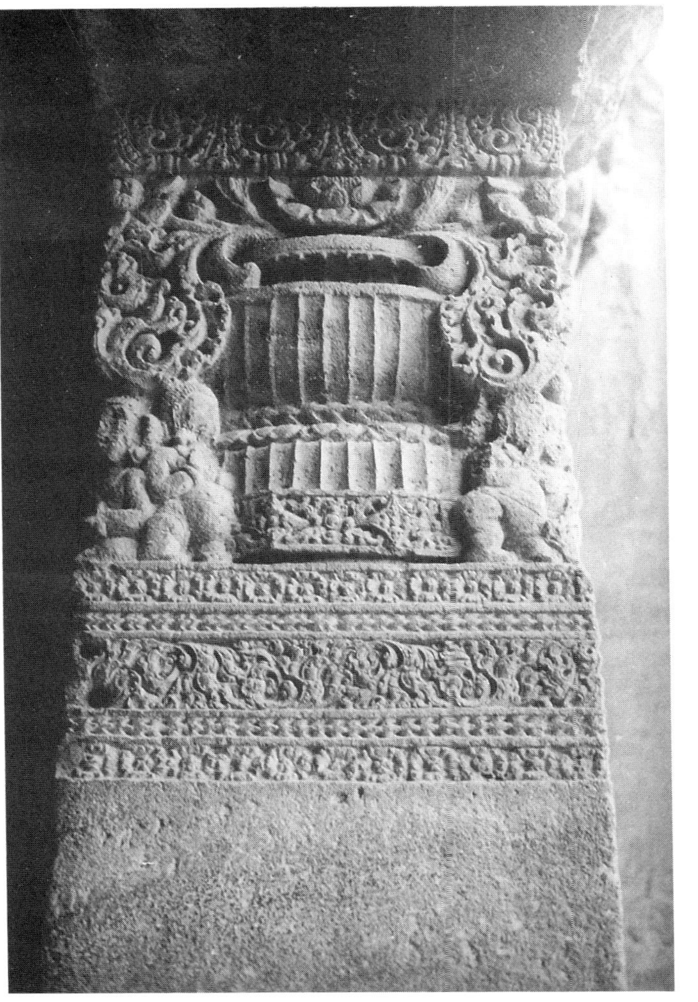

Fig. 197a,b   Cave 12.1 pillars, inner faces

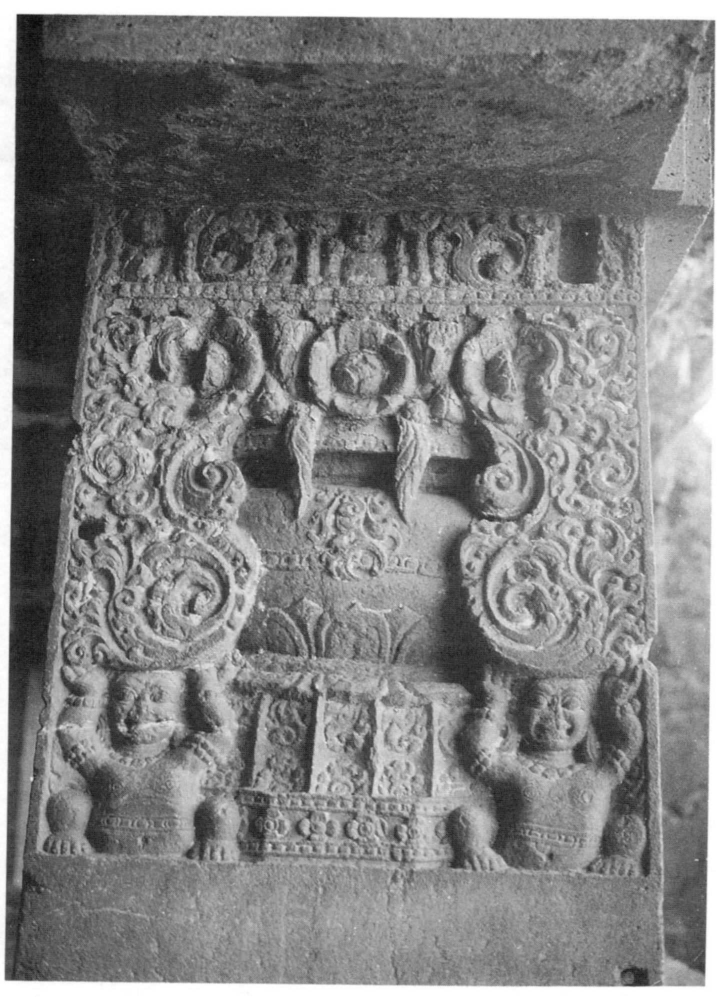

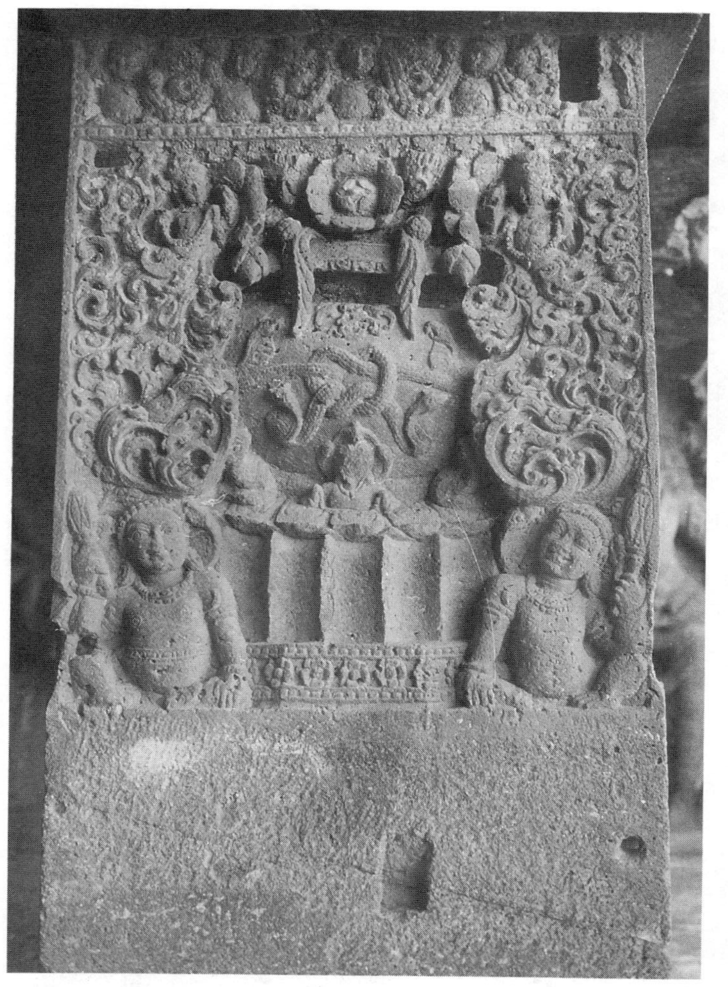

Fig. 198a,b   Cave 15.2 verandah pillars

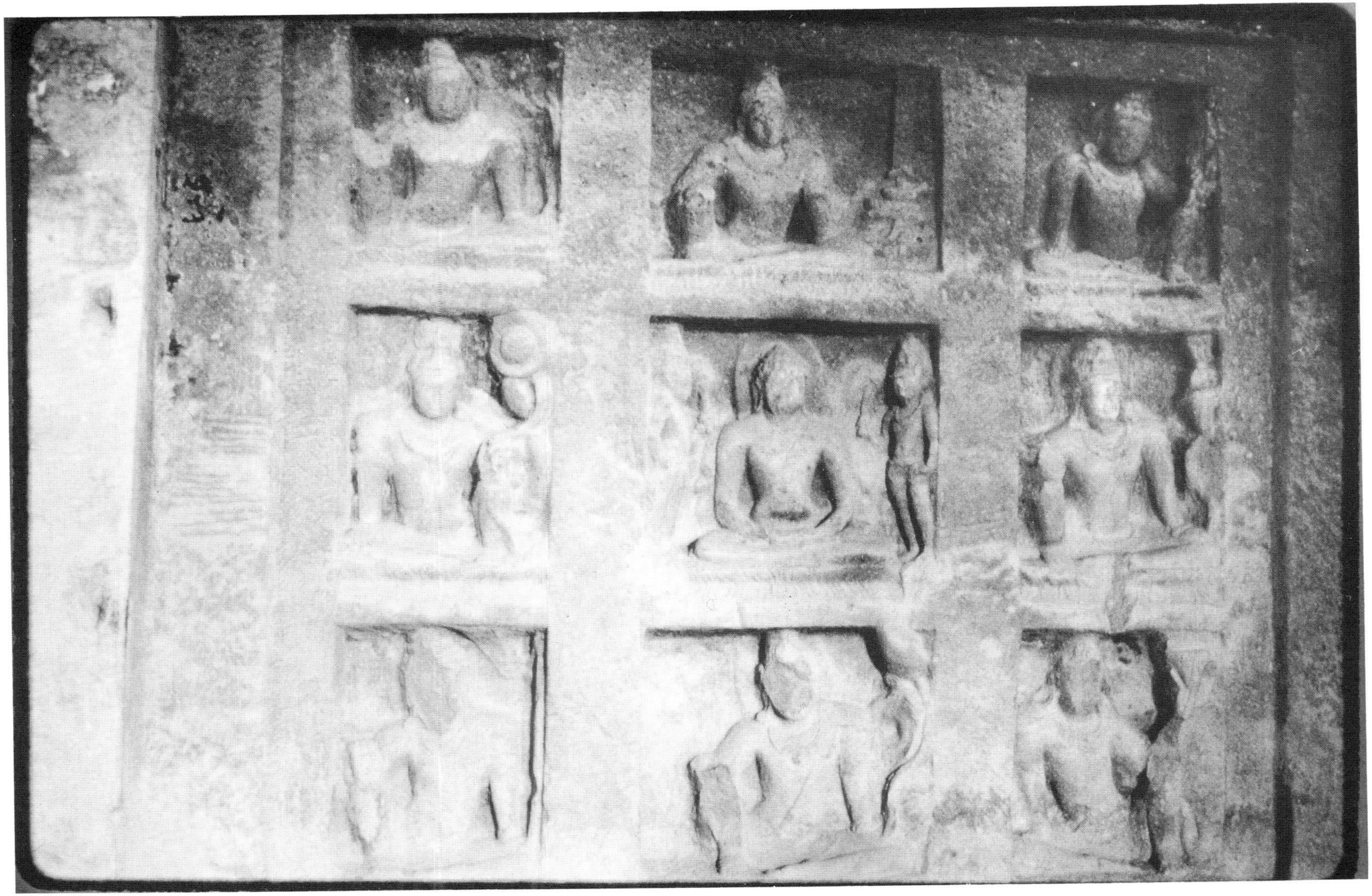

Fig. 199   Cave 12.1 *maṇḍala*

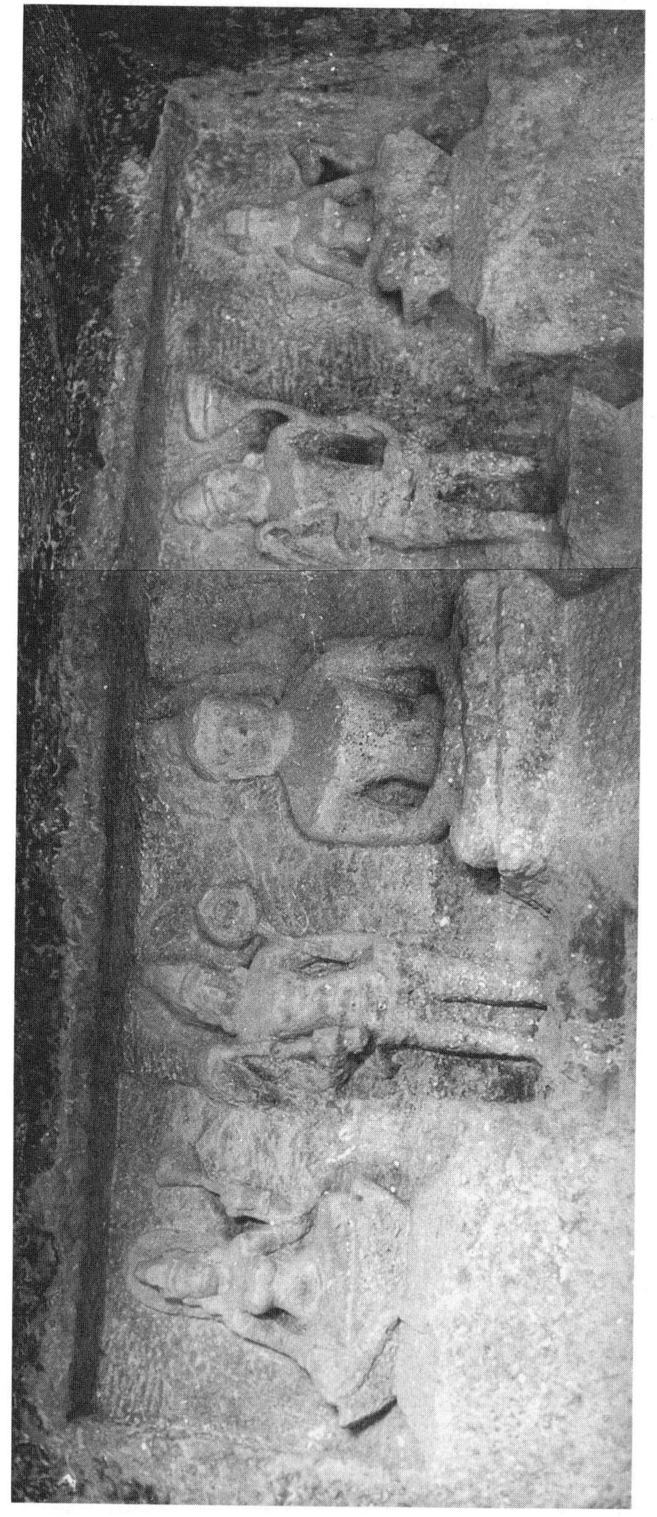

Fig. 200 Cave 12.1 *maṇḍala*, top panel

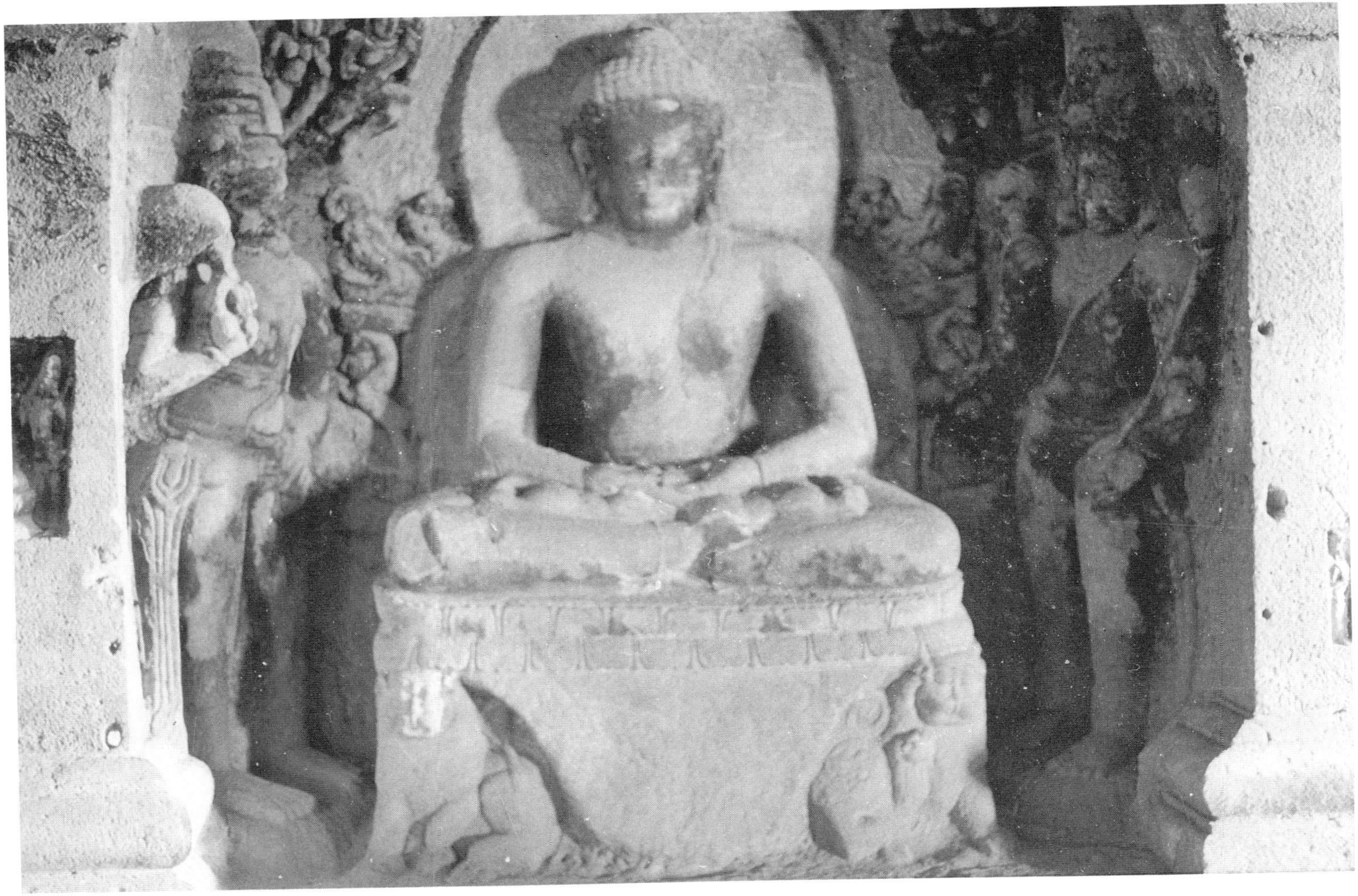

Fig. 201   Cave 12.1, hall Buddha

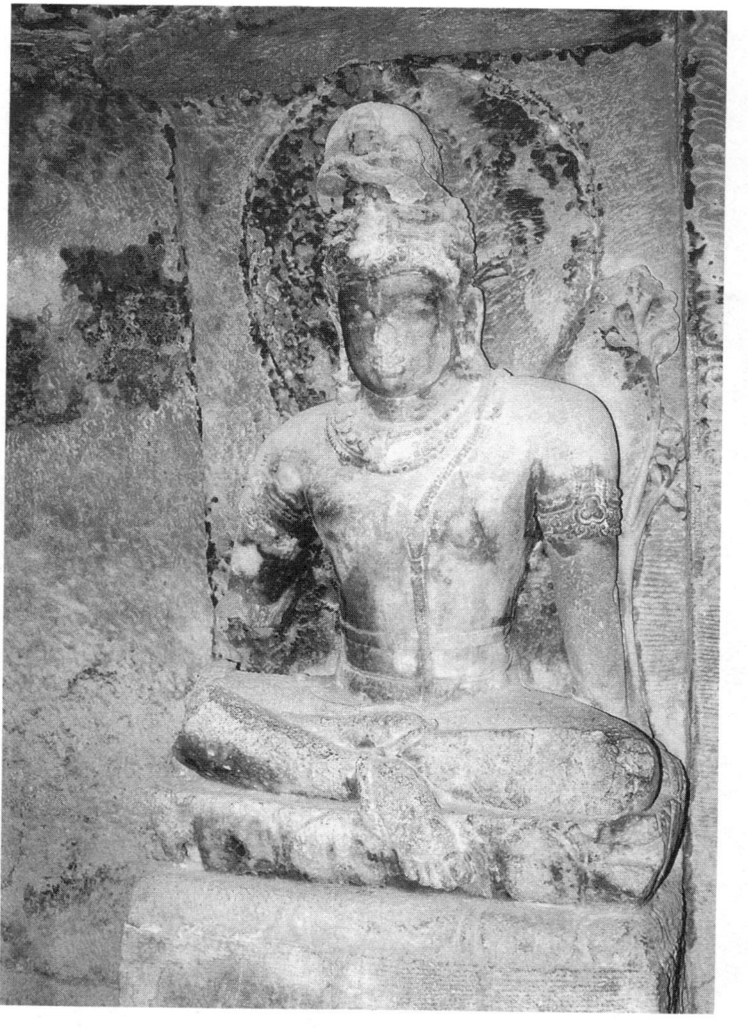

Fig. 202   Cave 12.1 shrine door, Maitreya

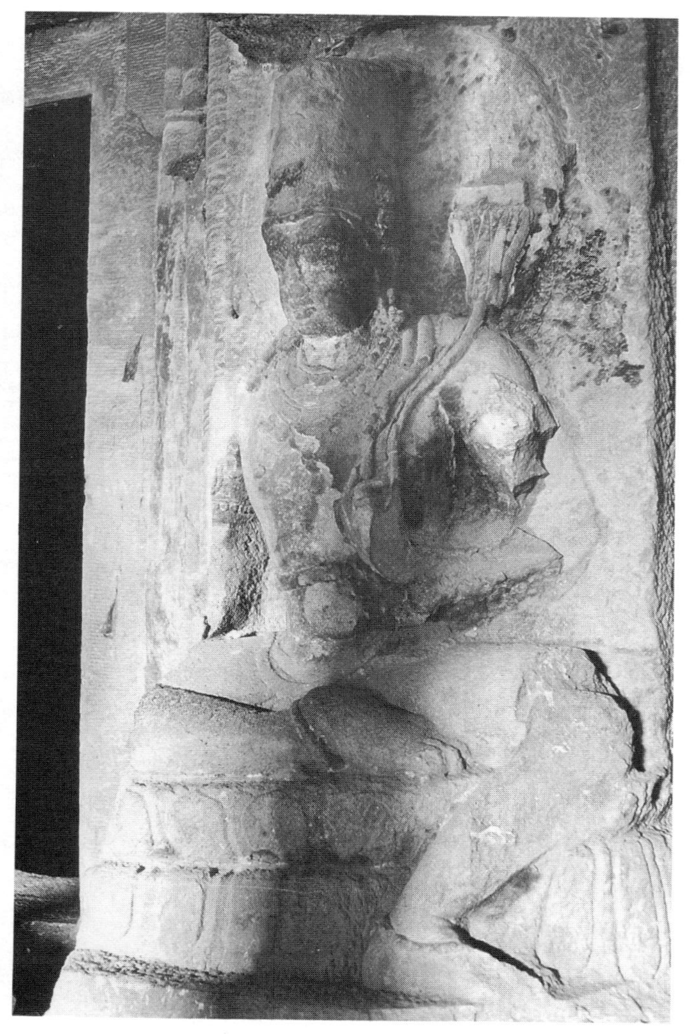

Fig. 203   Cave 12.1 shrine door, Mañjuśrī

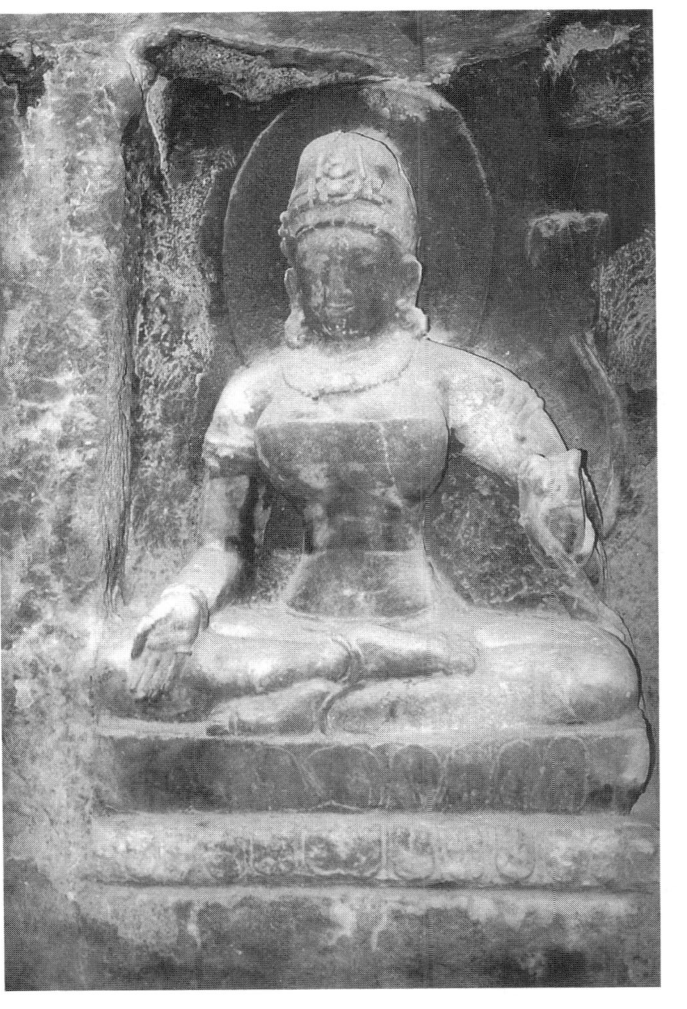

Fig. 204   Cave 12.1 shrine, Tārā

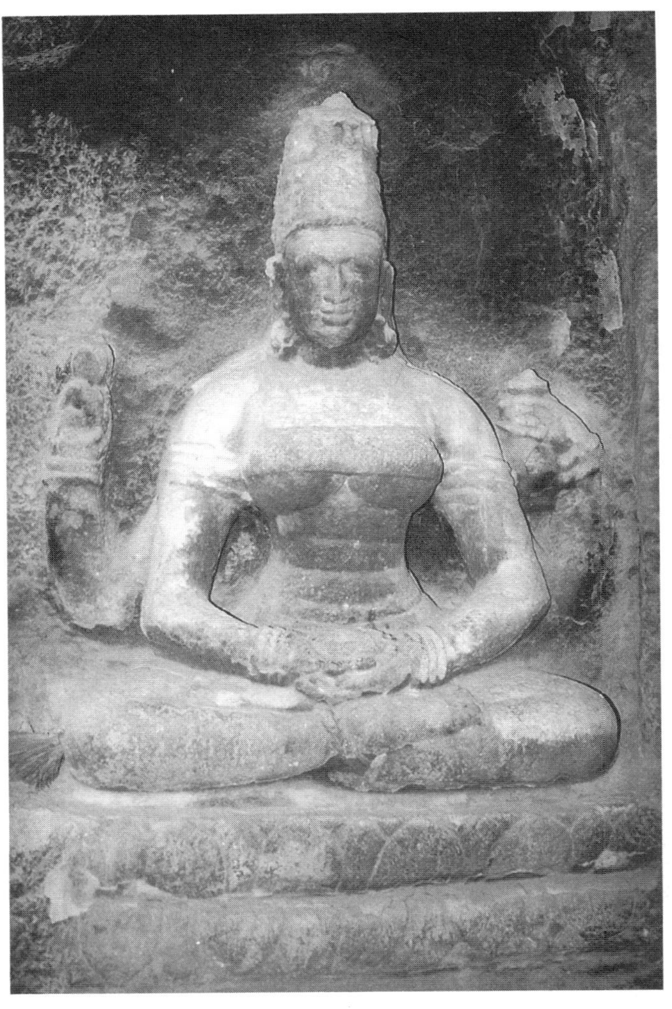

Fig. 205   Cave 12.1 shrine, Cundā

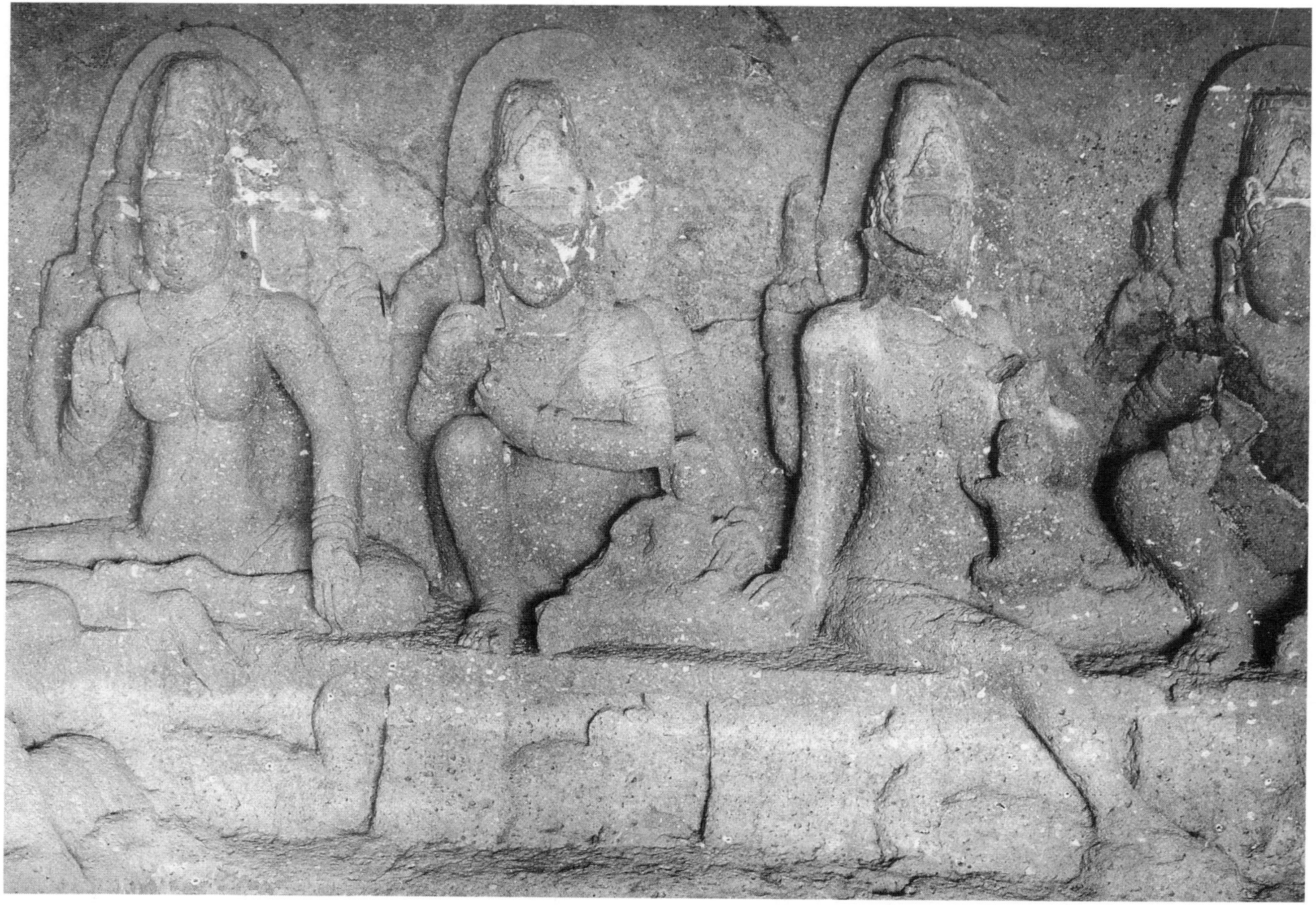

Fig. 206 Cave 22 Mātṛkas

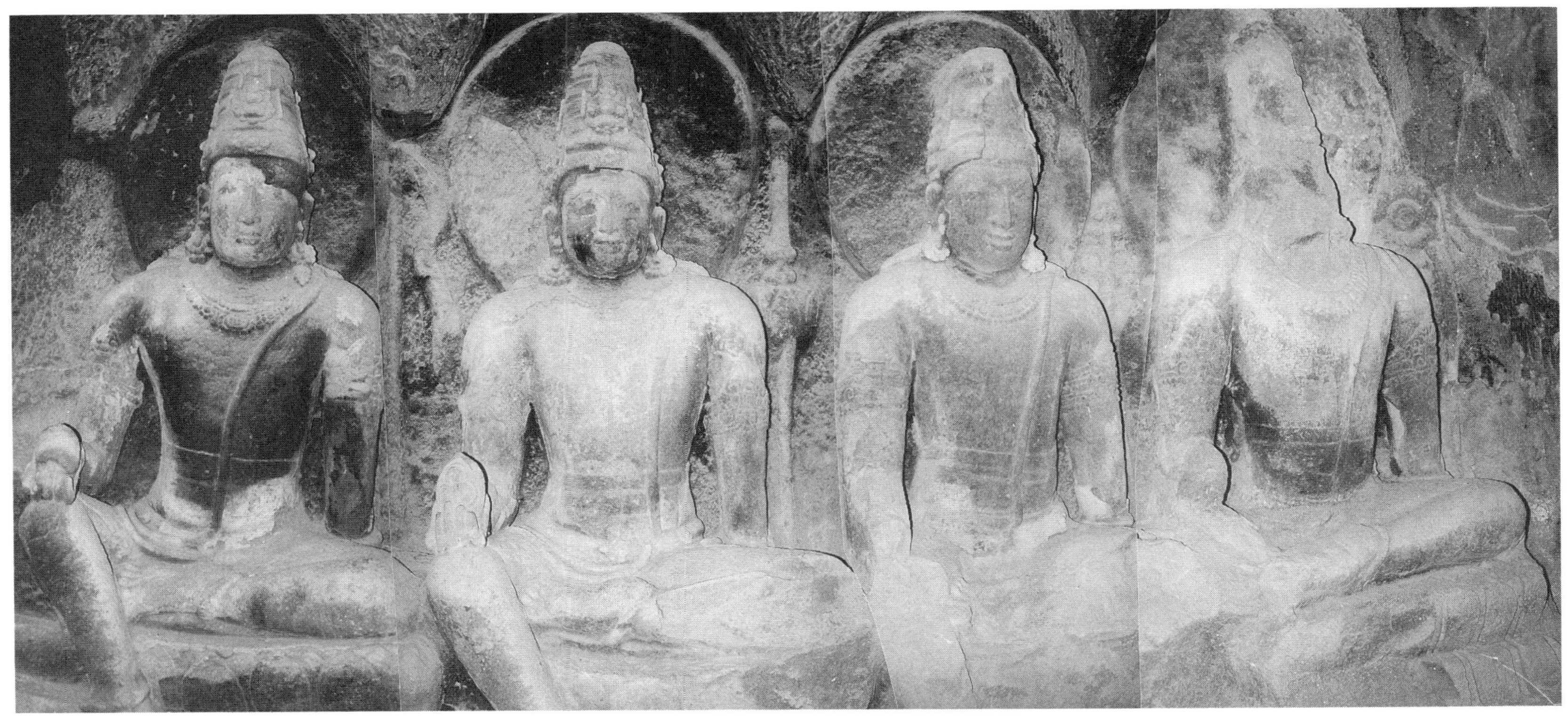

Fig. 207   Cave 12.1 shrine, left wall Bodhisattvas

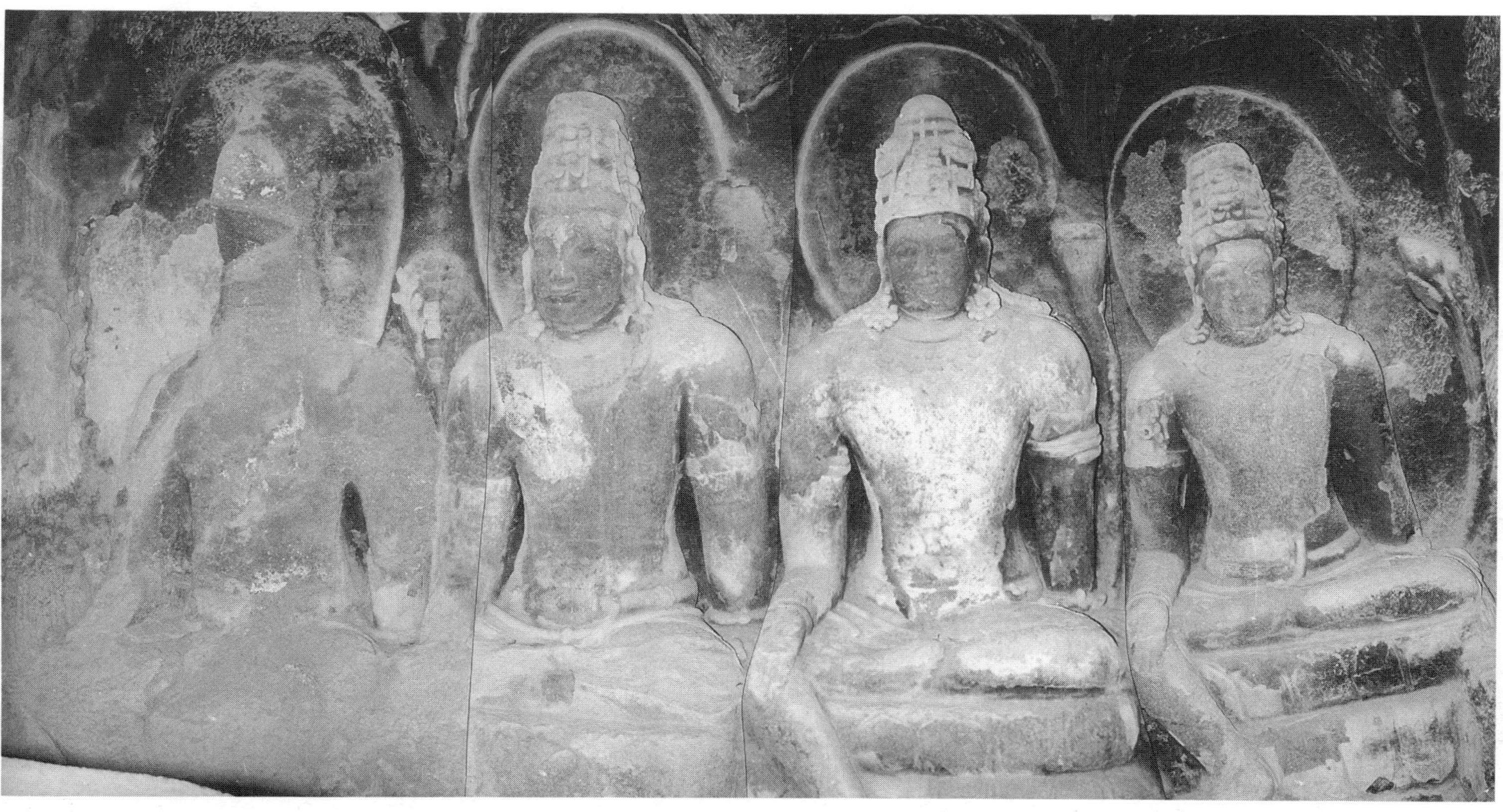

Fig. 208 Cave 12.1 shrine, right wall Bodhisattvas

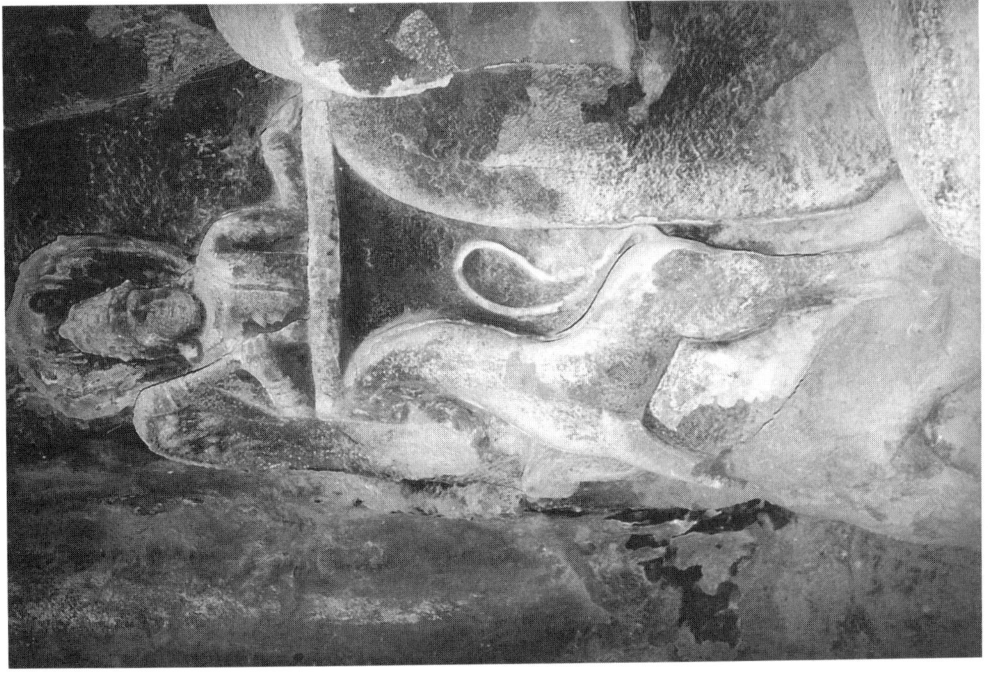

Fig. 210 Cave 12.1 shrine, throne detail

Fig. 209 Cave 12.1 shrine, Buddha

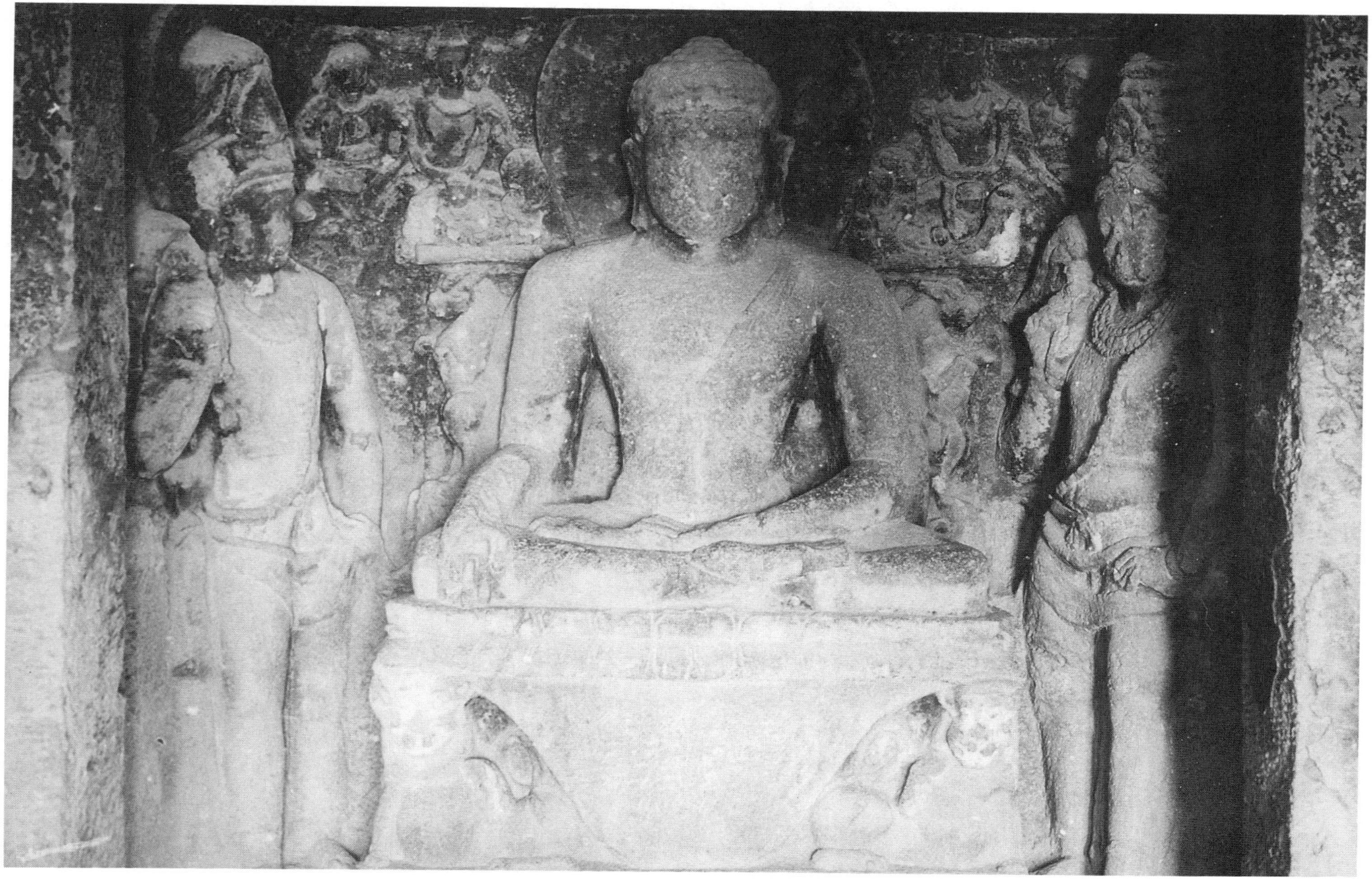

Fig. 211   Cave 12.1-2 Buddha

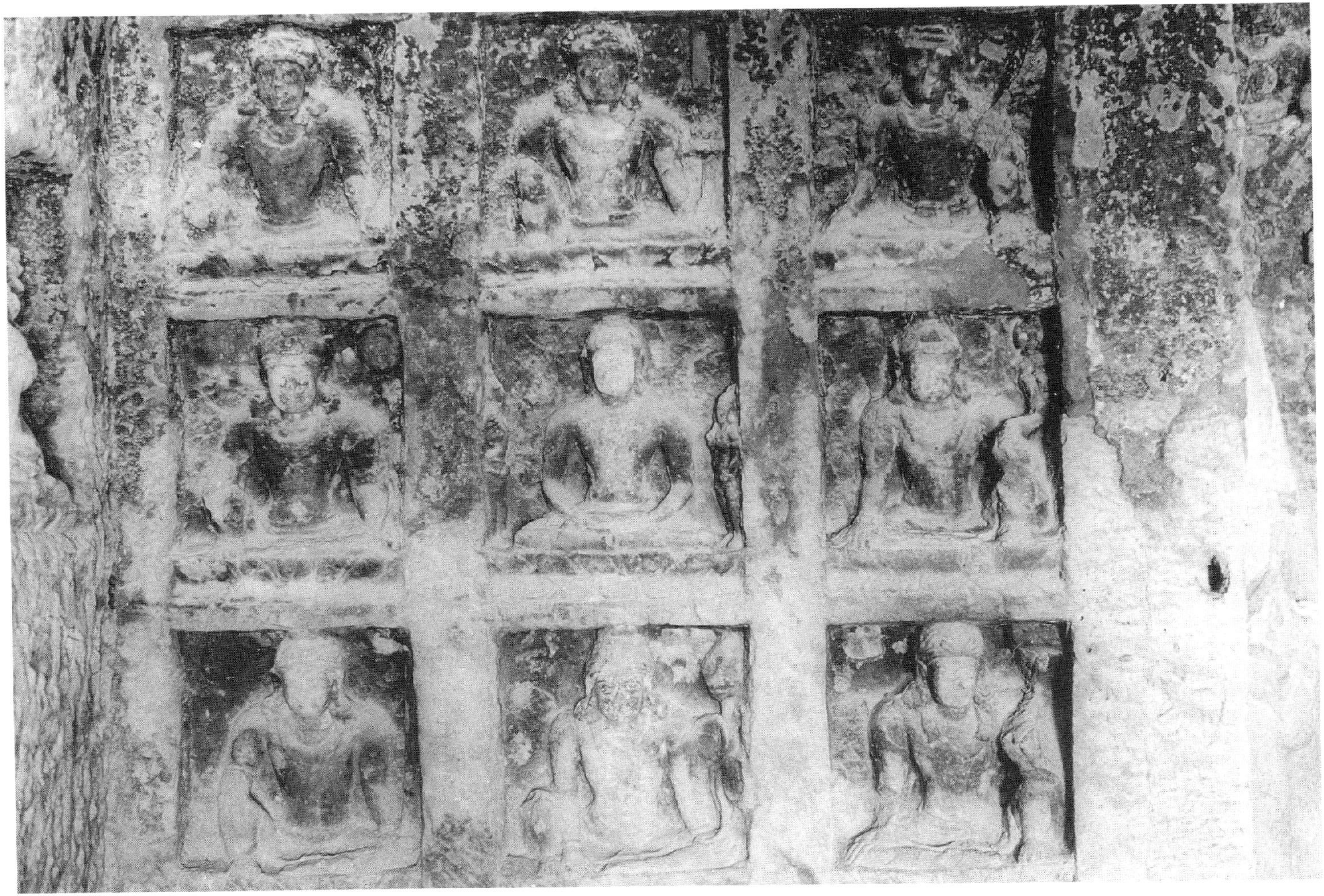

Fig. 212   Cave 12.1-2 left *maṇḍala*

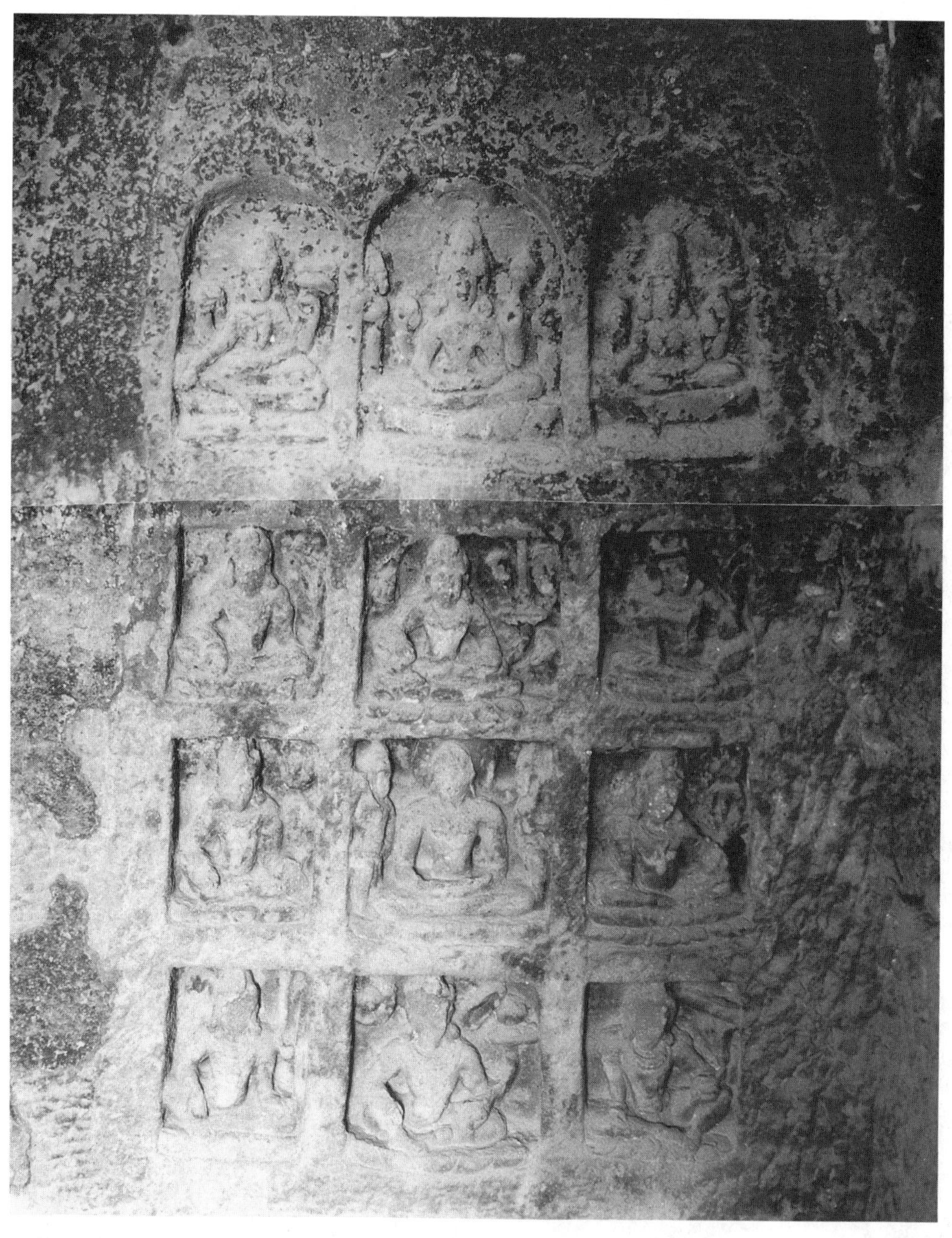

Fig. 213   Cave 12.1–2 right *maṇḍala*

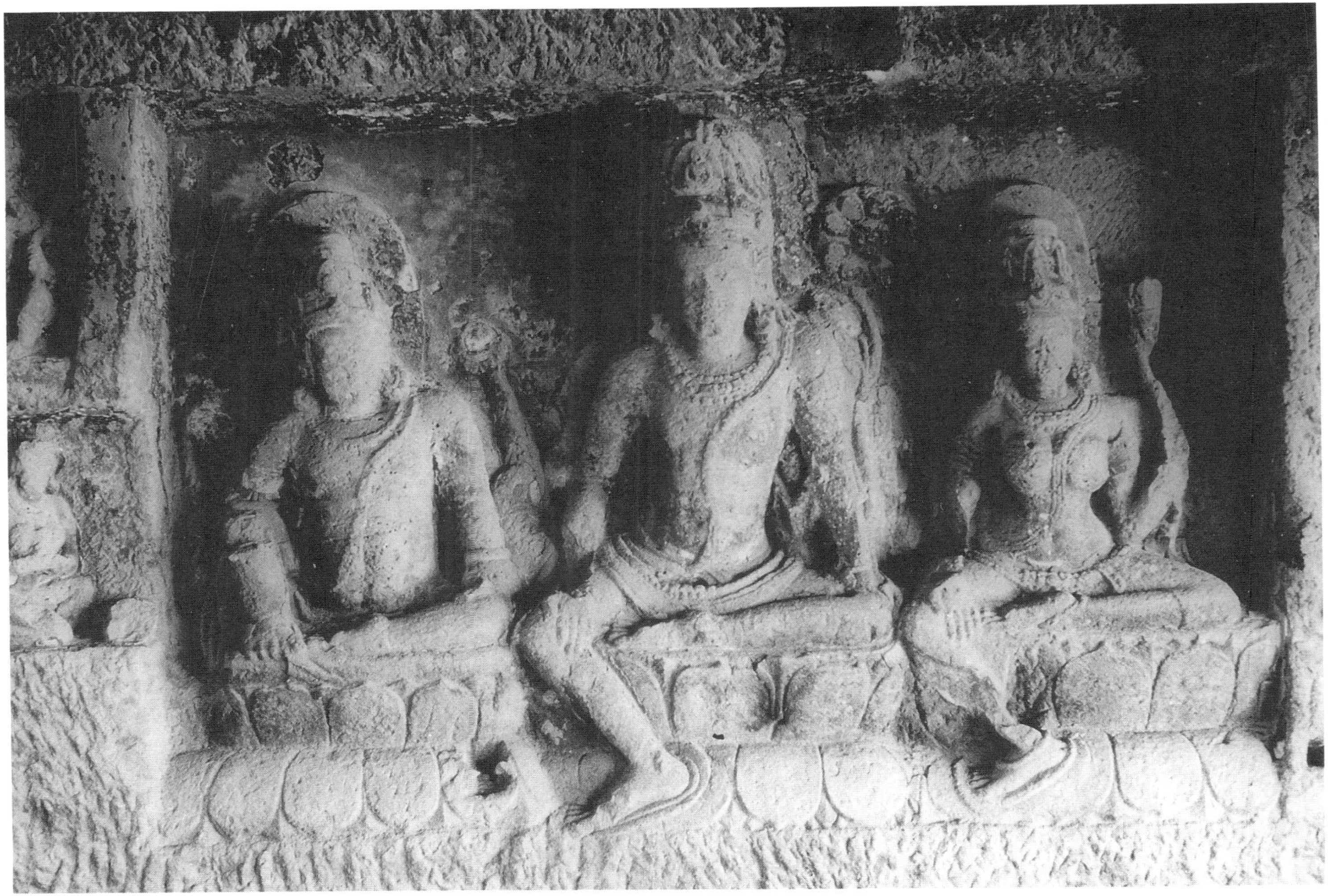

Fig. 214   Cave 12.1–2 triad

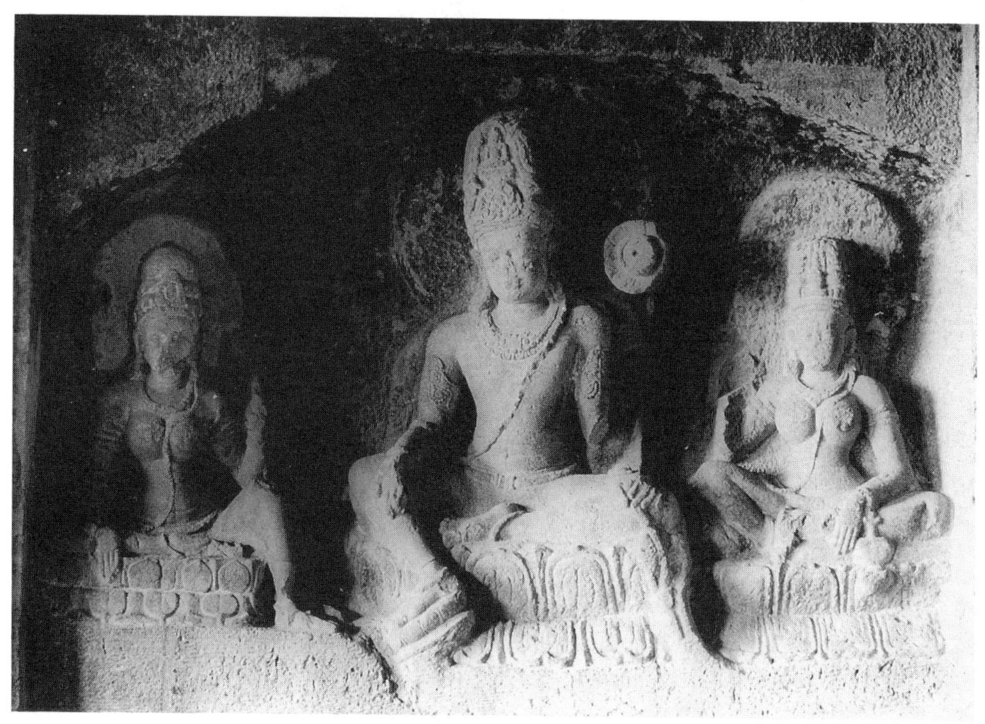

Fig. 215   Cave 12.2 Rakta-Lokeśvara

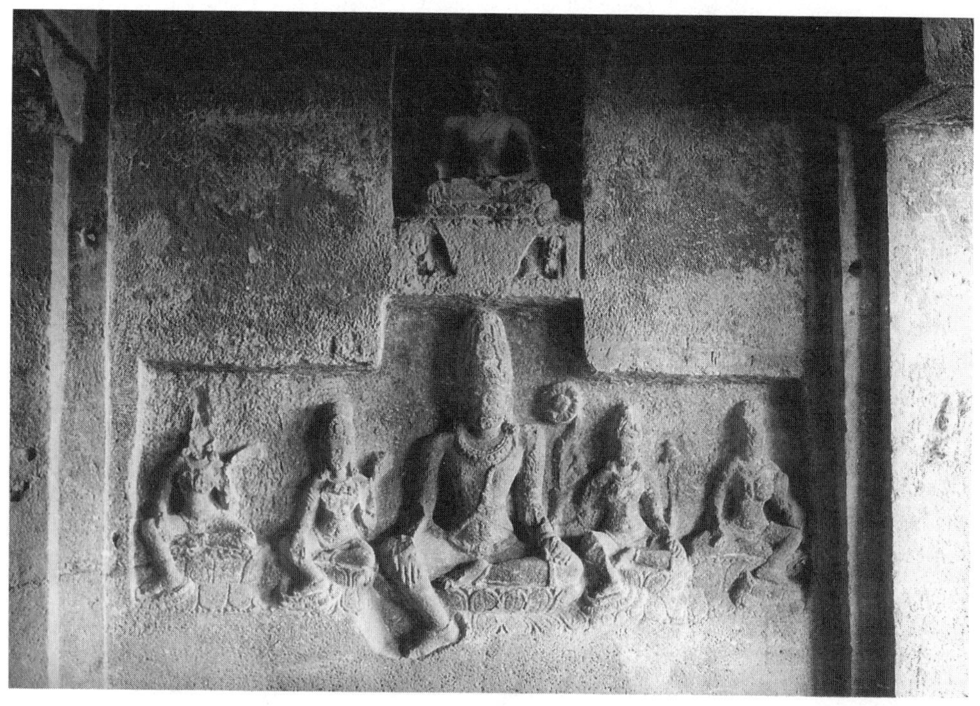

Fig. 216   Cave 12.2 Siddhaikavīra (?)

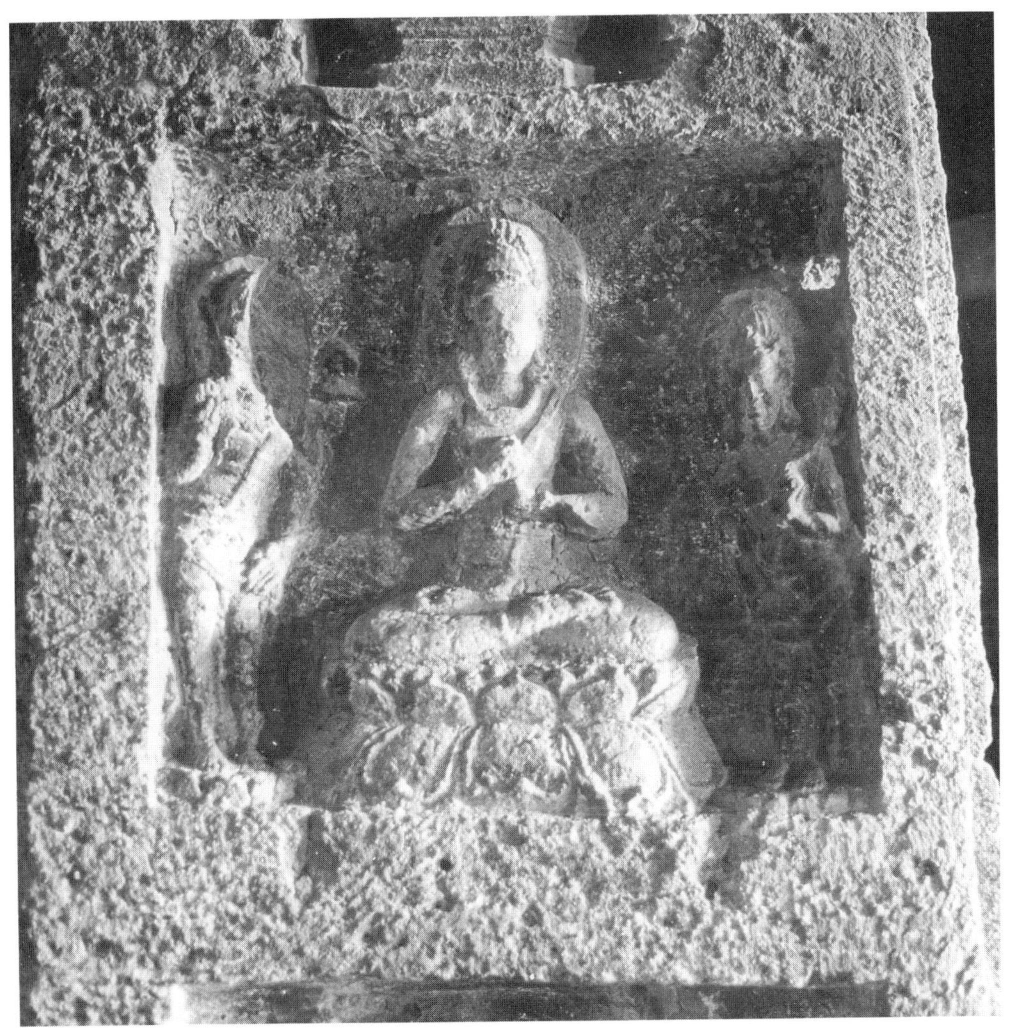

Fig. 217　Cave 12.2 Vajradhāra

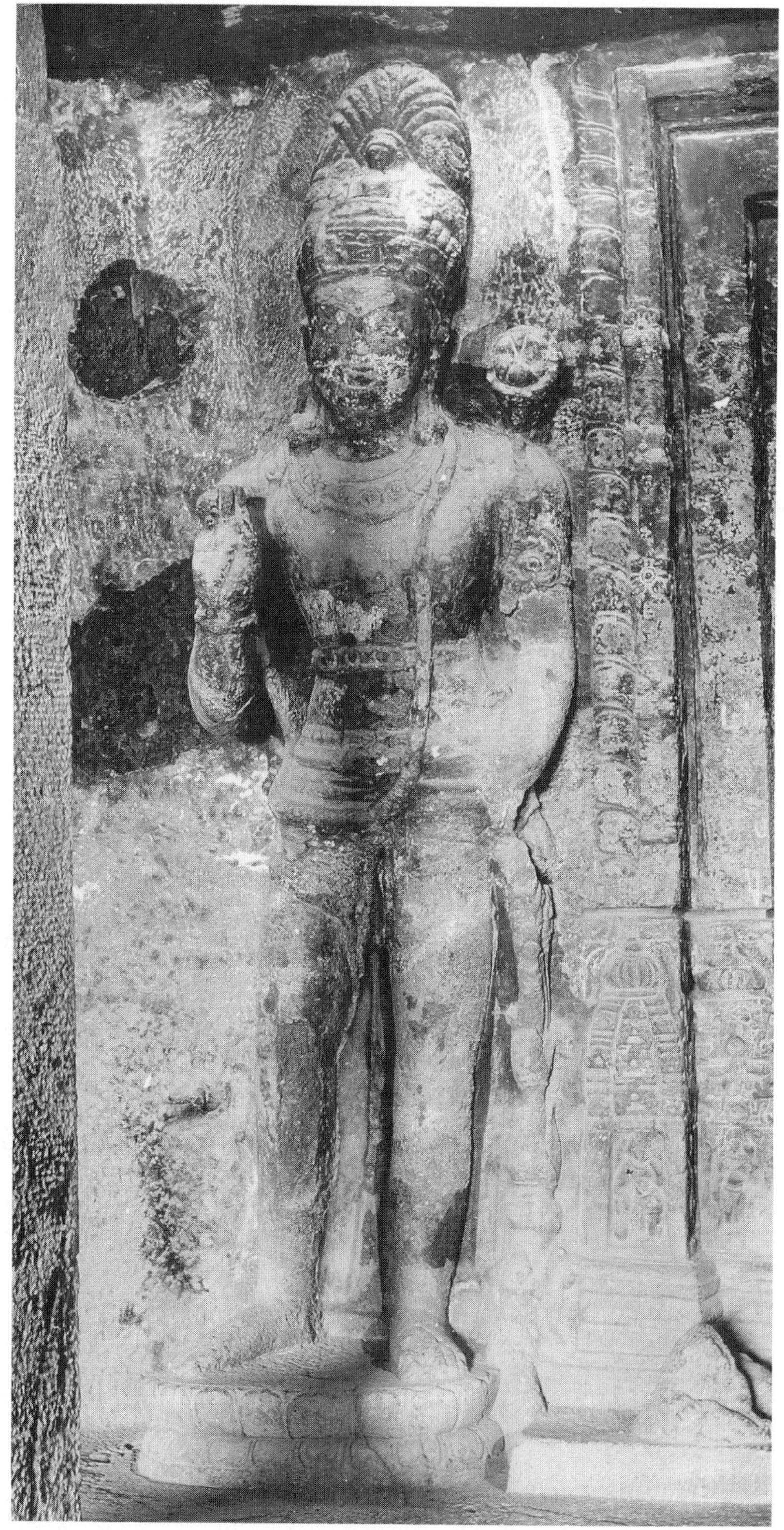

Fig. 218 Cave 12.2 shrine door, Avalokiteśvara (AIIS)

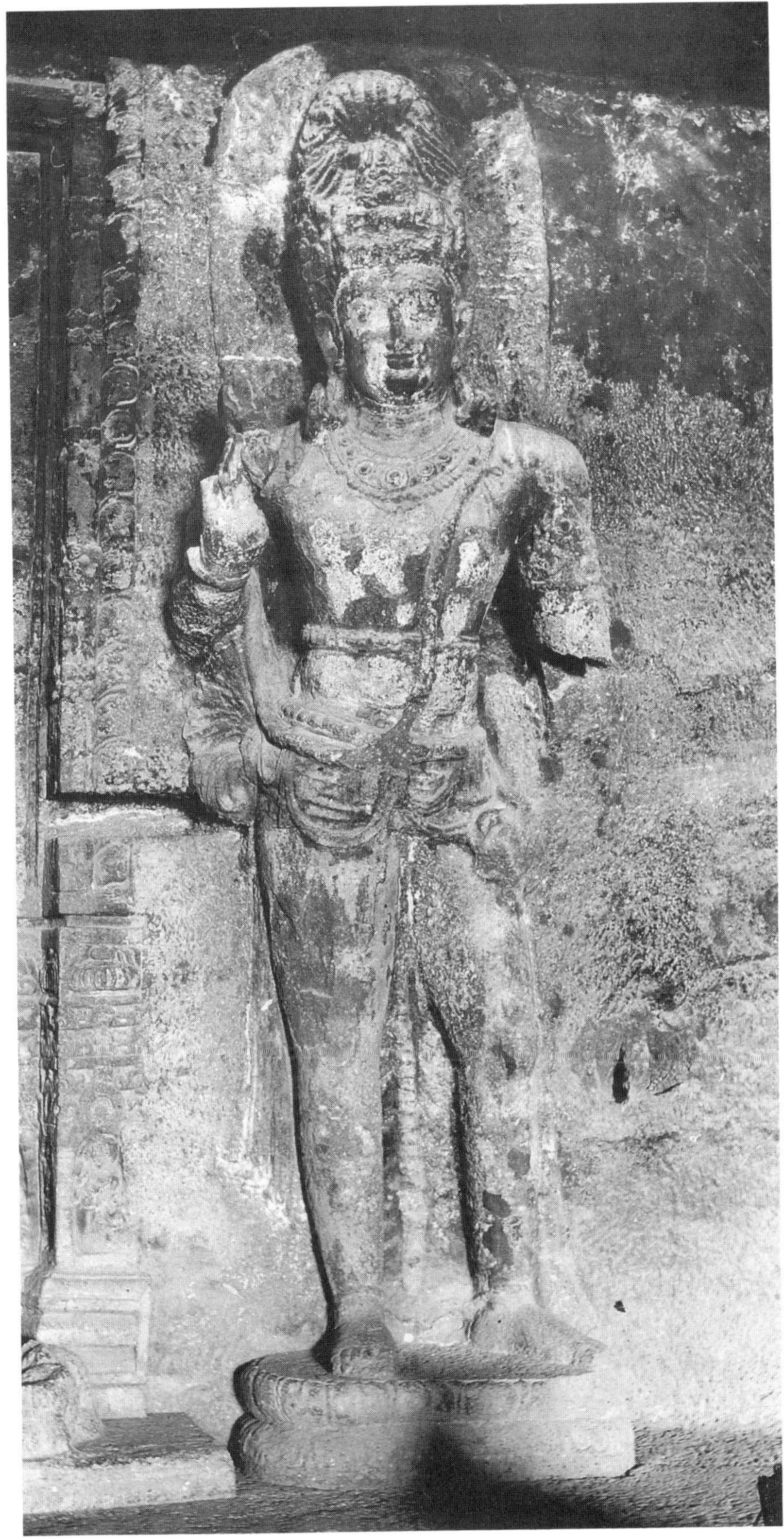

Fig. 219   Cave 12.2 shrine door, Vajrapāṇi (AIIS)

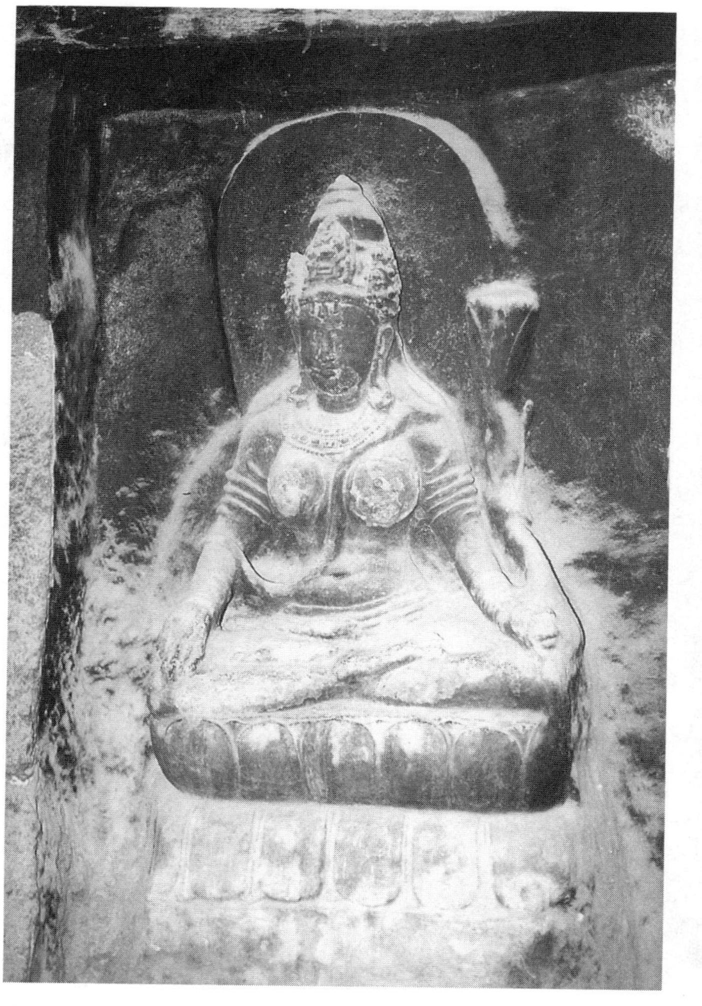

Fig. 220   Cave 12.2 shrine, Tārā

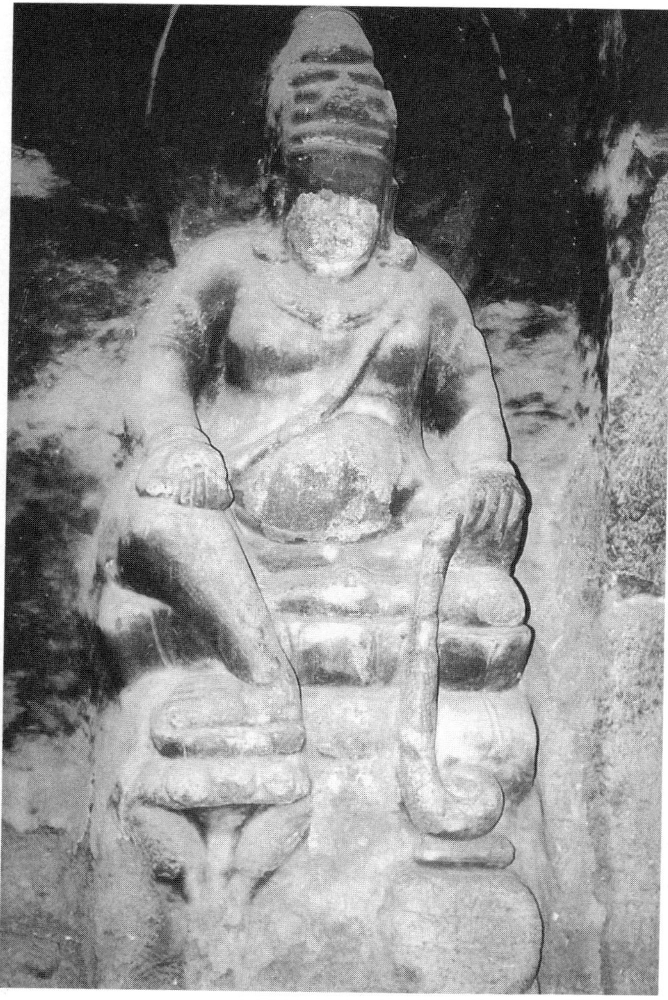
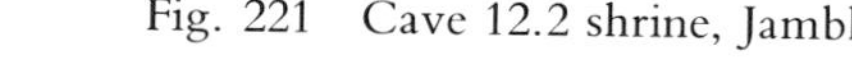

Fig. 221   Cave 12.2 shrine, Jambhala

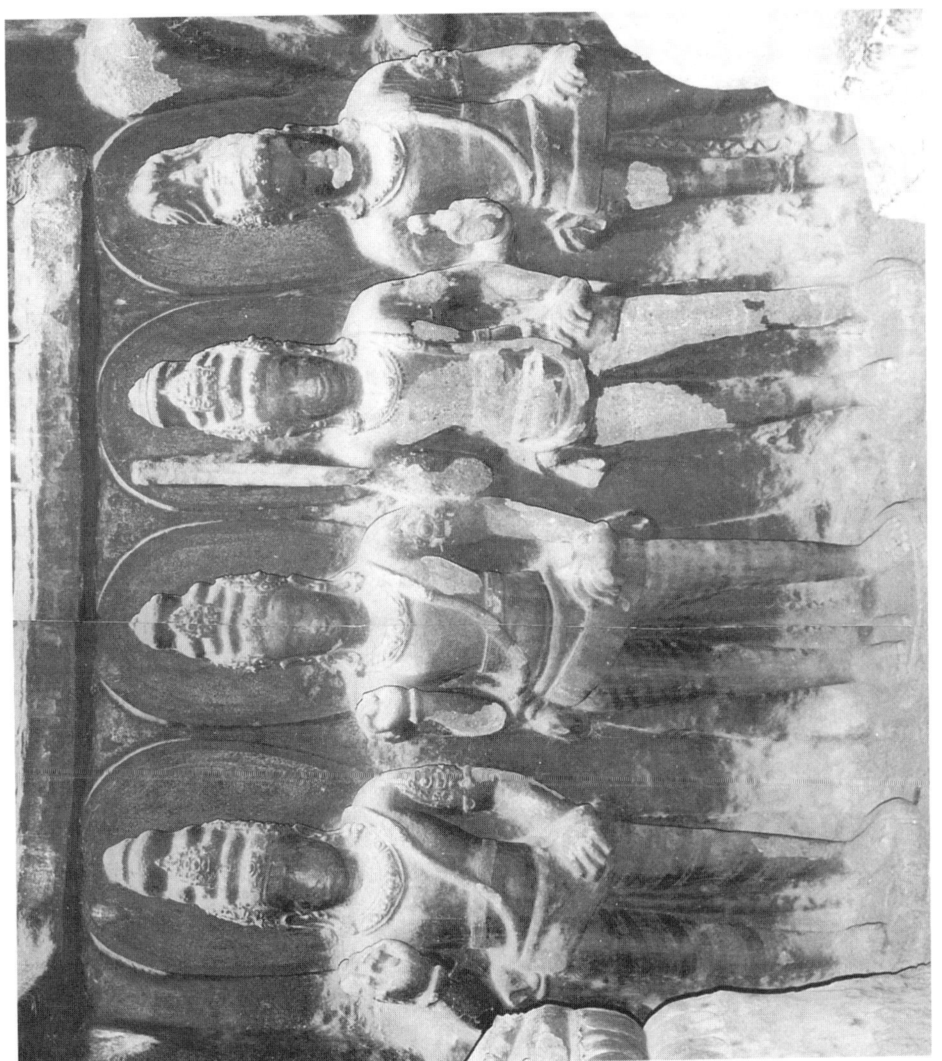

Fig. 222 Cave 12.2 shrine, left wall Bodhisattvas

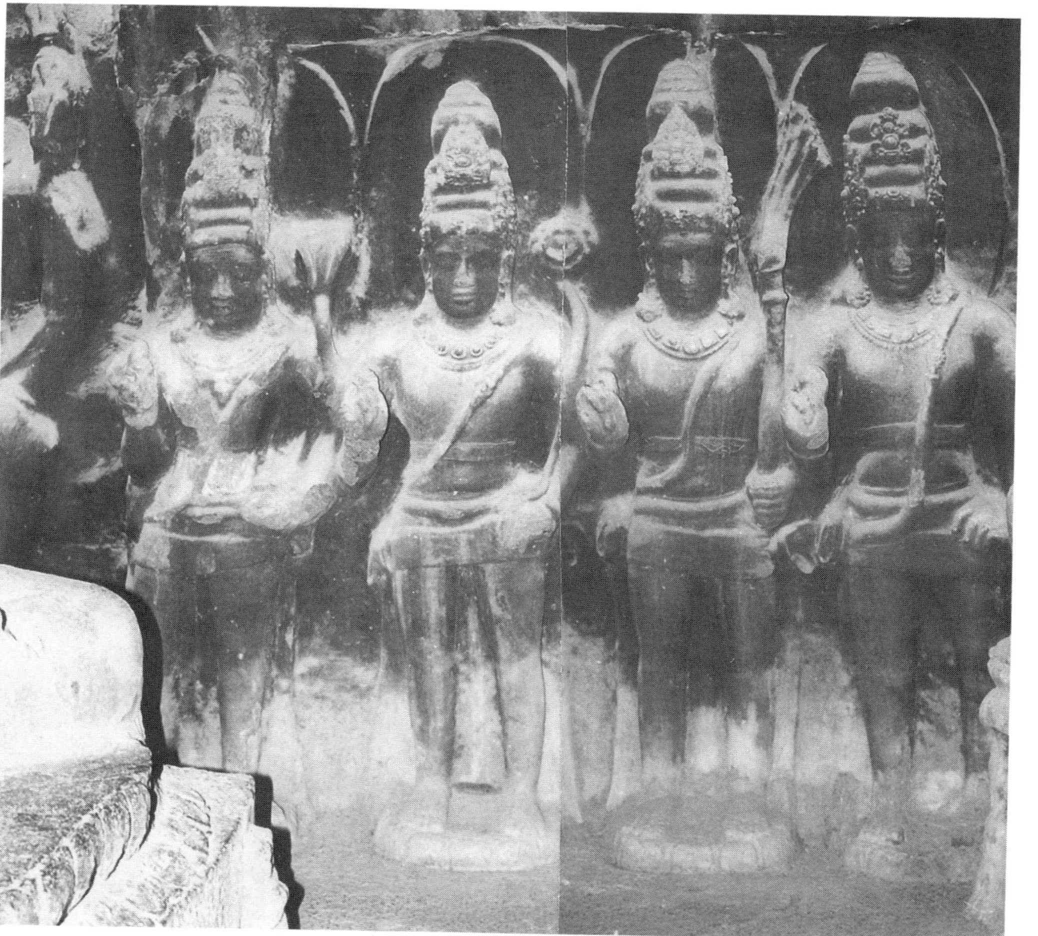

Fig. 223   Cave 12.2 shrine, right wall Bodhisattvas

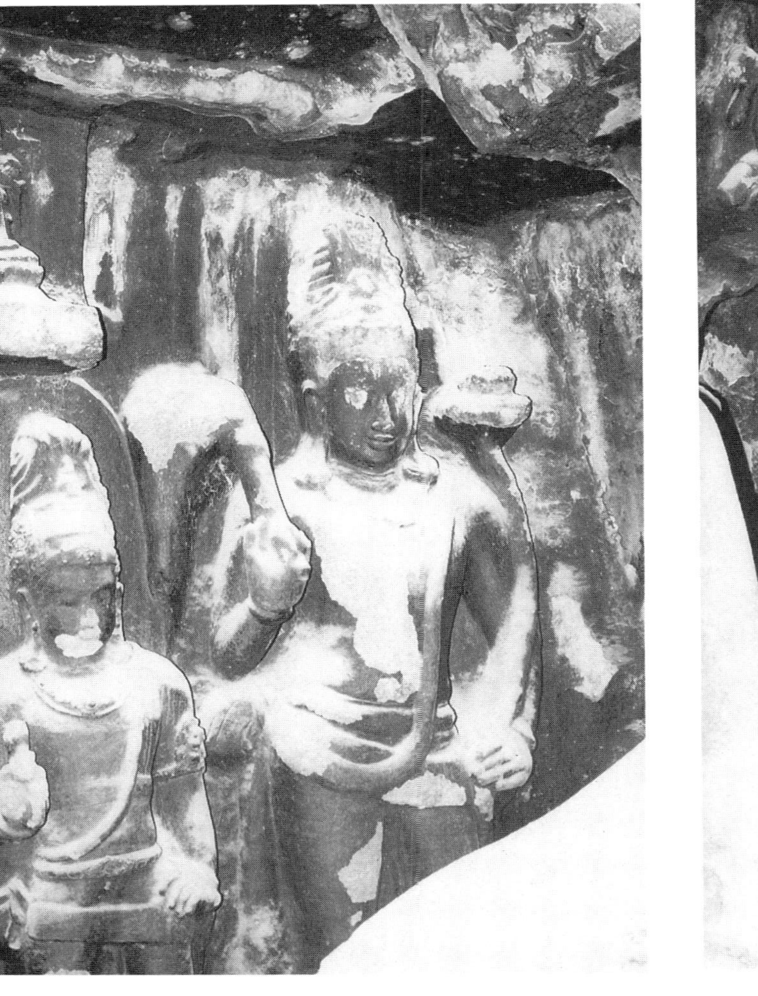

Fig. 224   Cave 12.2 shrine, Avalokiteśvara

Fig. 225   Cave 12.2 shrine, Vajrapāṇi

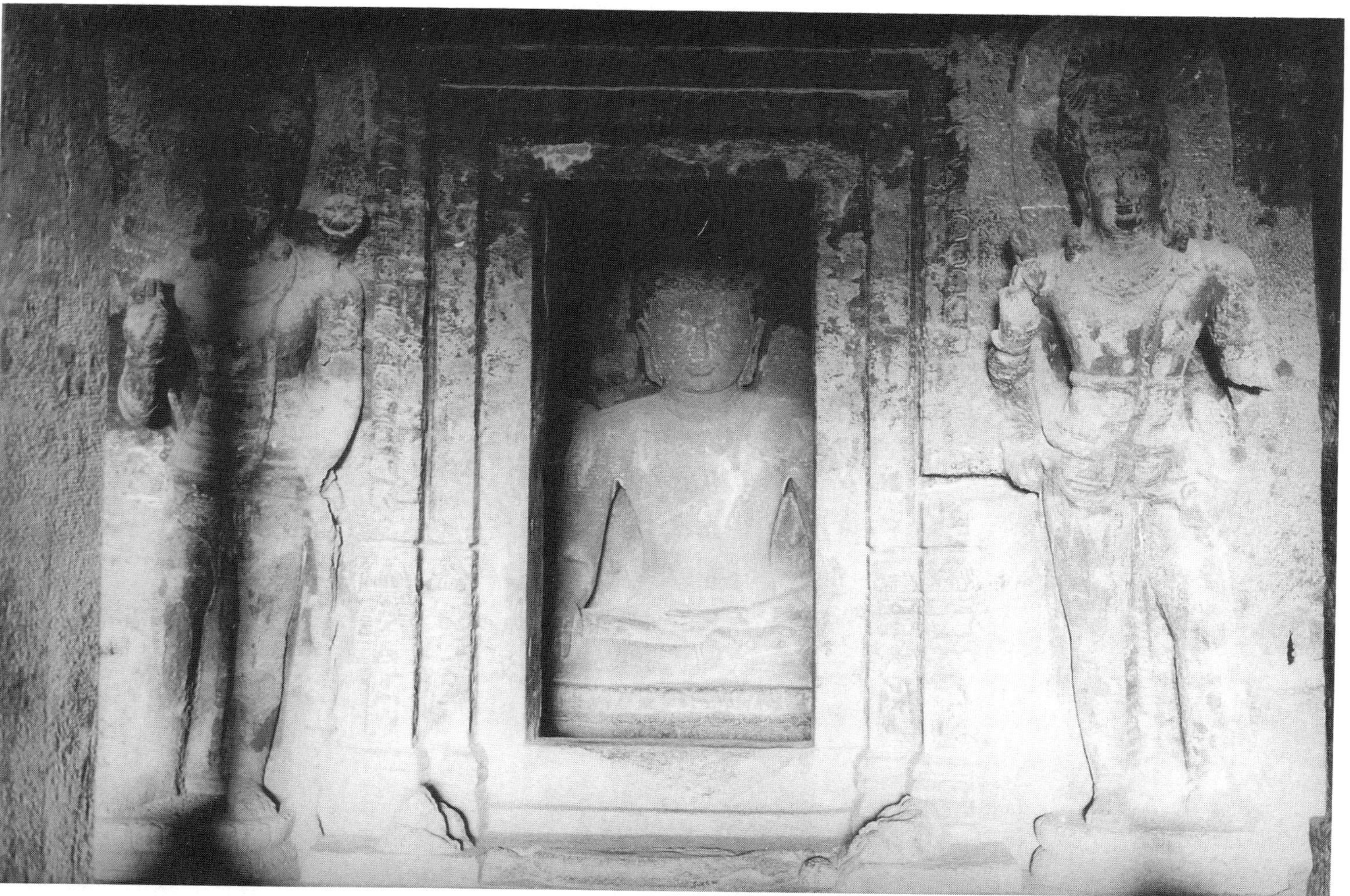

Fig. 226　Cave 12.2 shrine, Buddha

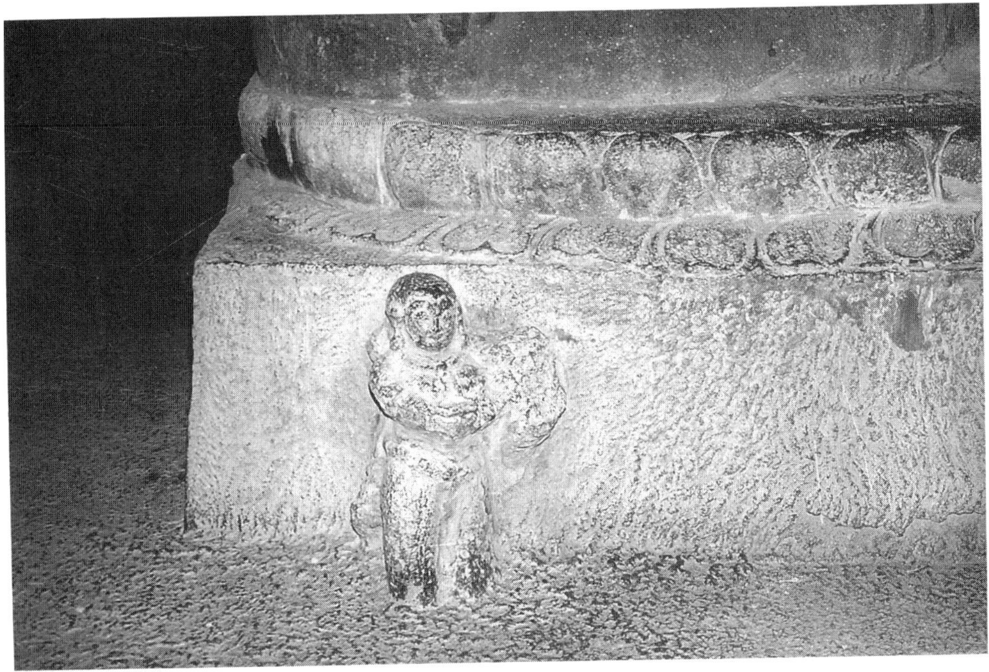

Fig. 227 Cave 12.2 shrine, Bhūdevī

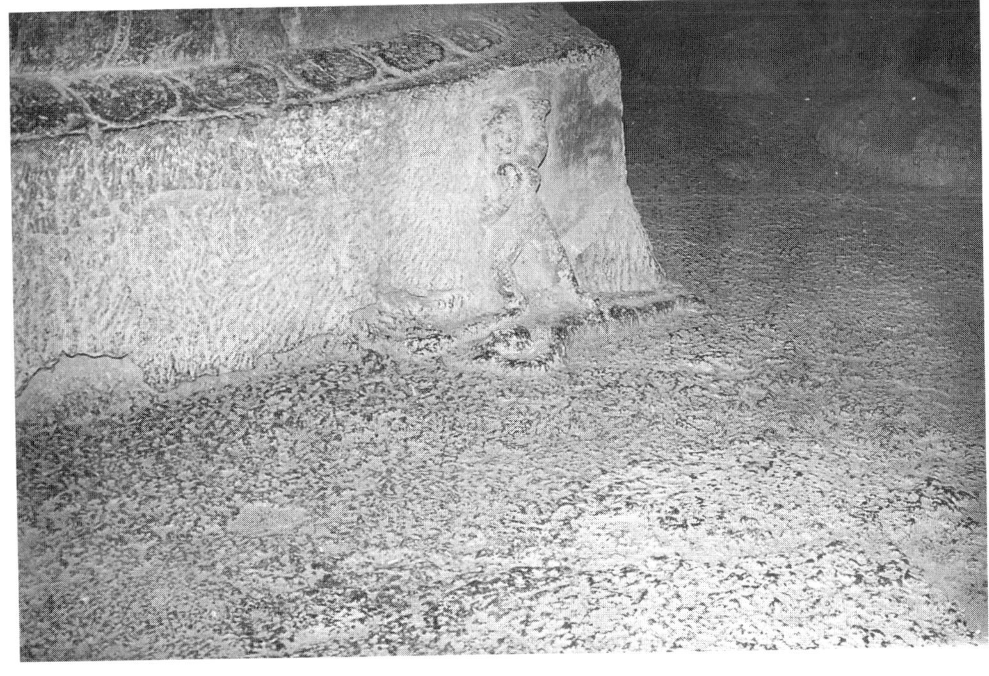

Fig. 228 Cave 12.2 shrine, Aparājitā

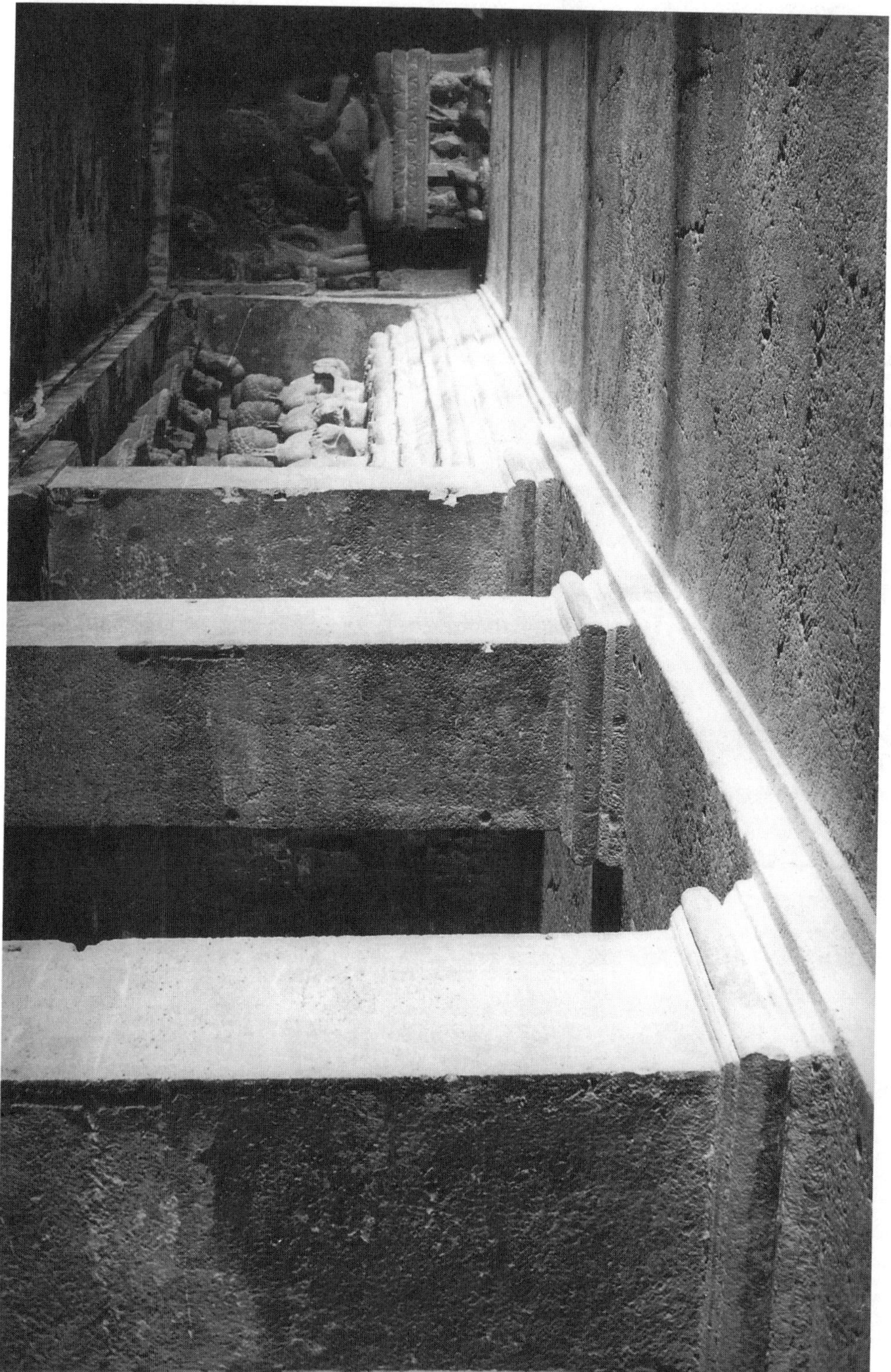

Fig. 229 Cave 12.3 hall, right corner

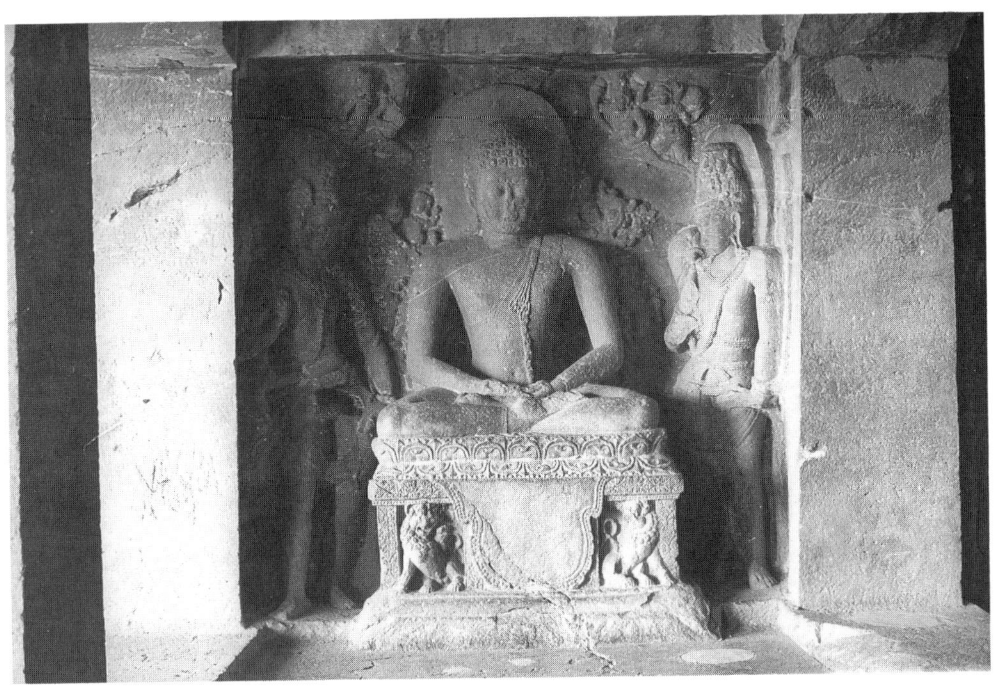

Fig. 230   Cave 12.3 hall, Buddha #1

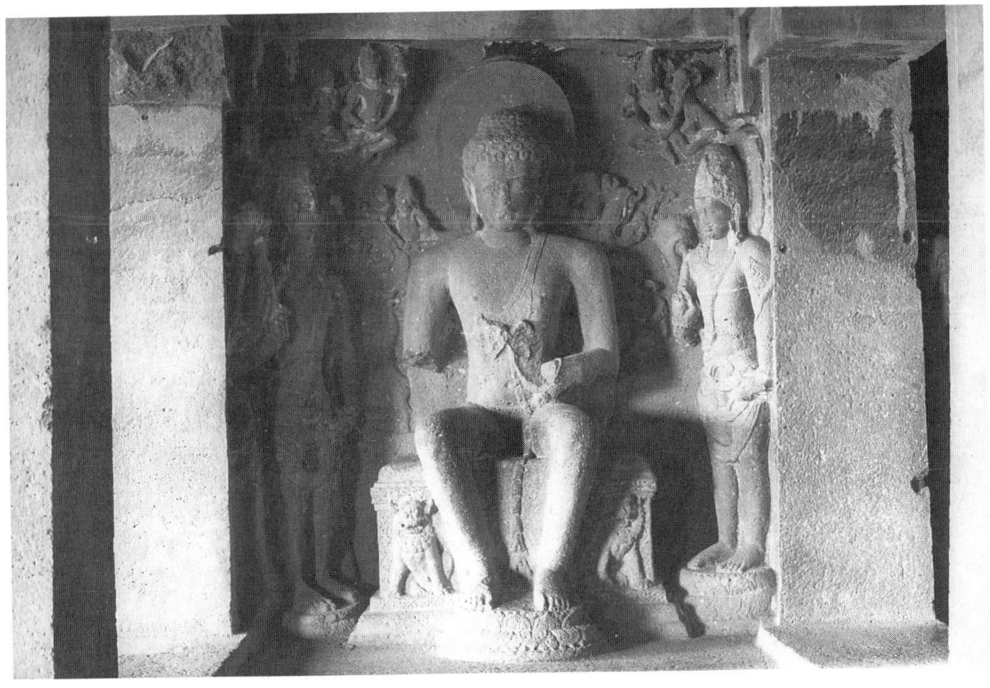

Fig. 231   Cave 12.3 hall, Buddha #2

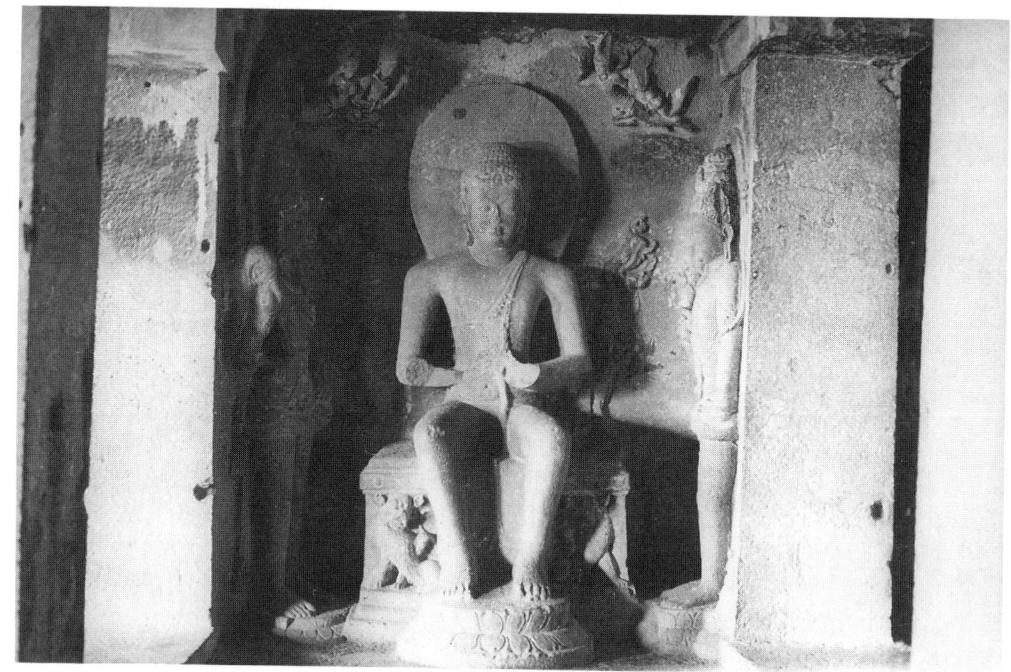

Fig. 232   Cave 12.3 hall, Buddha #3

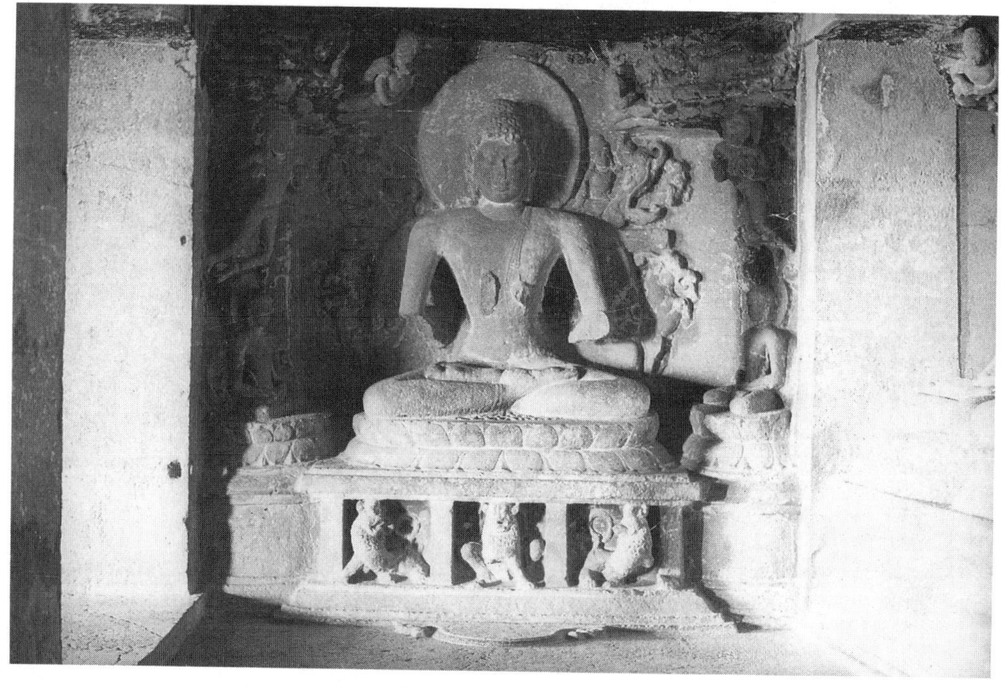

Fig. 233   Cave 12.3 hall, Buddha #4

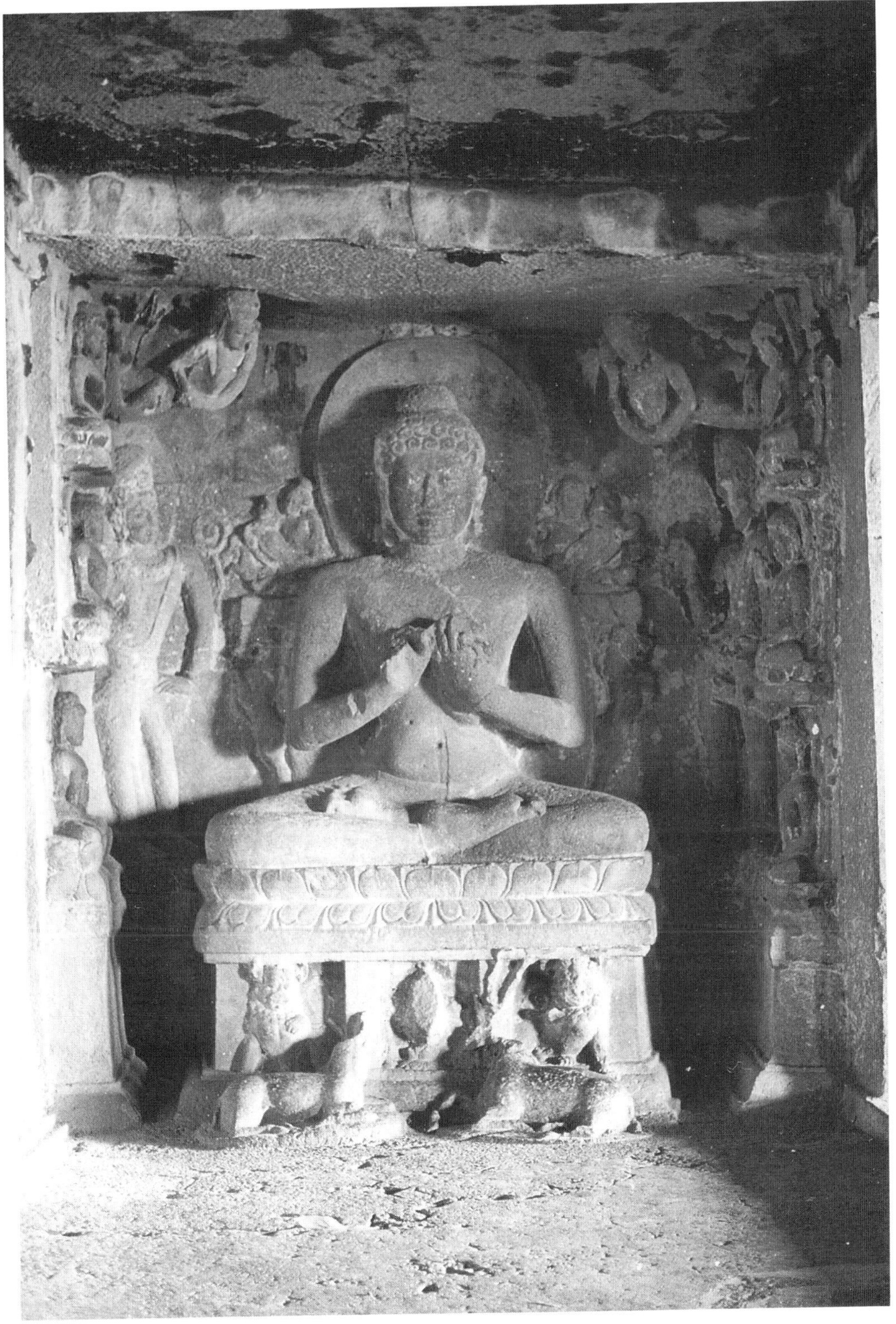

Fig. 234   Cave 12.3 hall, Buddha #5

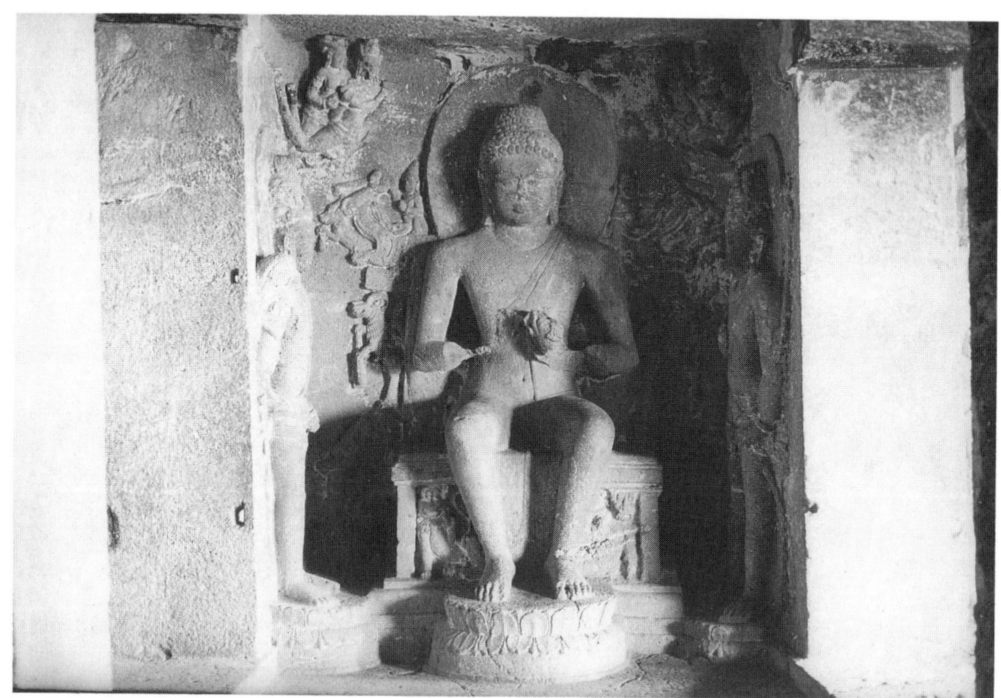

Fig. 235   Cave 12.3 hall, Buddha #6

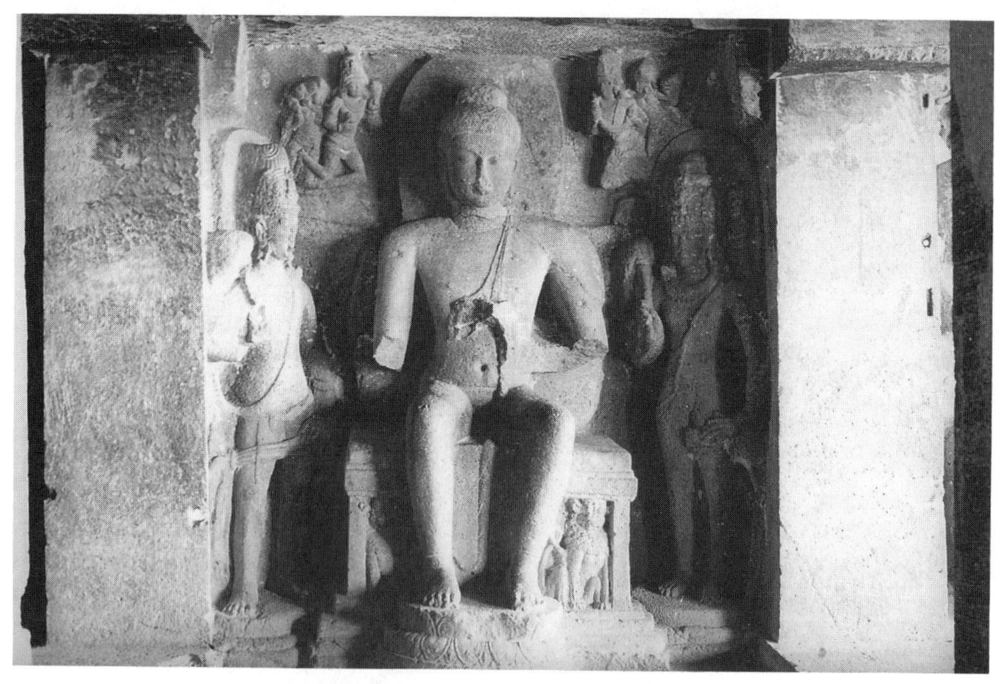

Fig. 236   Cave 12.3 hall, Buddha #7

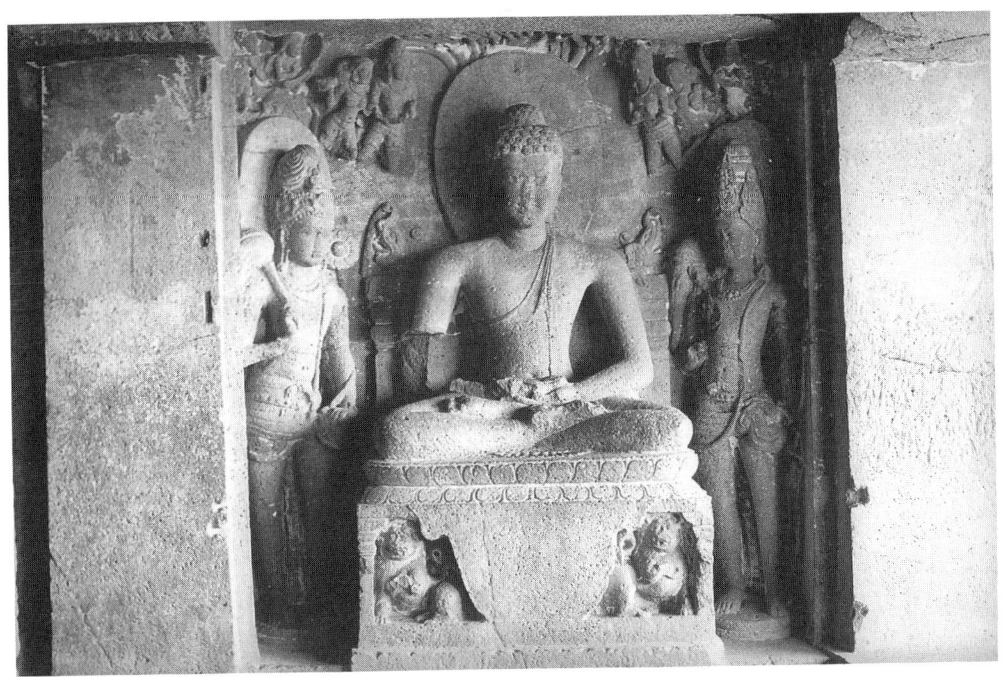

Fig. 237   Cave 12.3 hall, Buddha #8

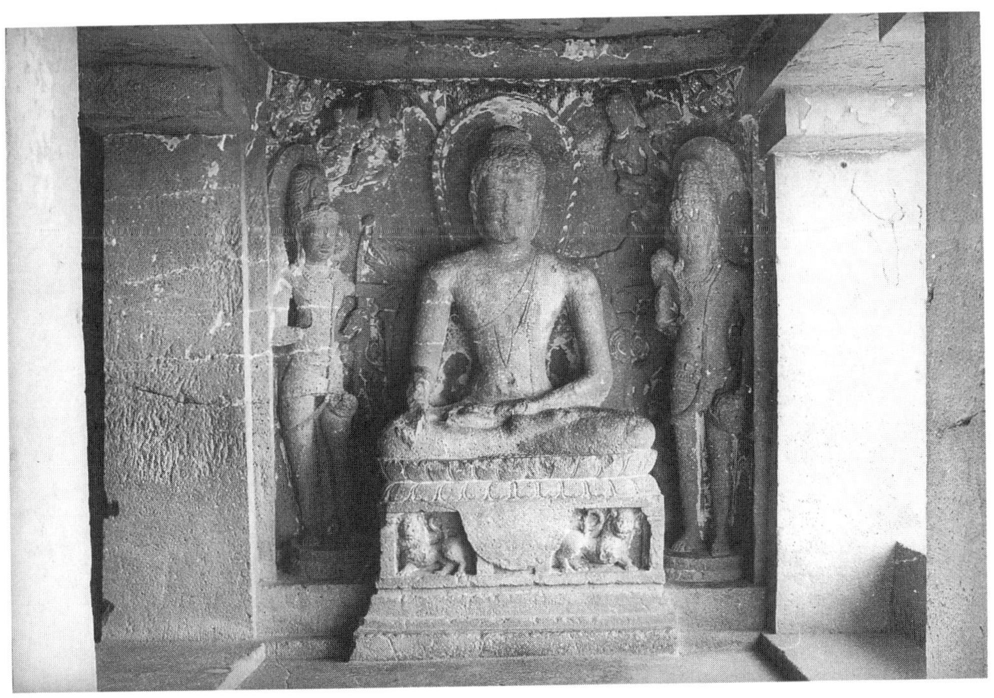

Fig. 238   Cave 12.3 hall, Buddha #9

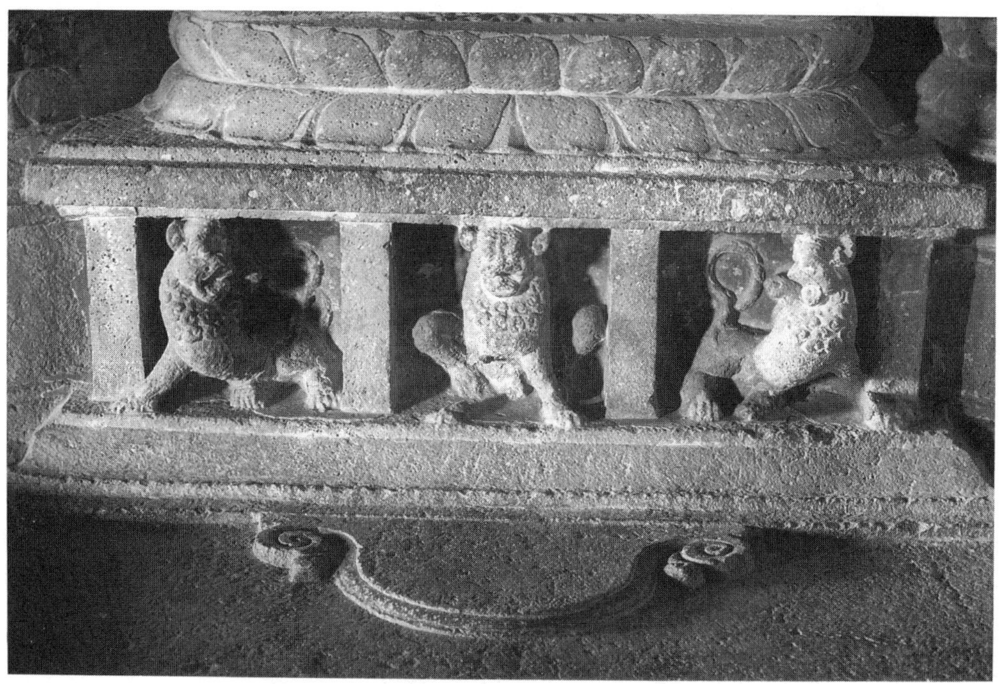

Fig. 239 Cave 12.3 hall, Buddha #4 throne, lions

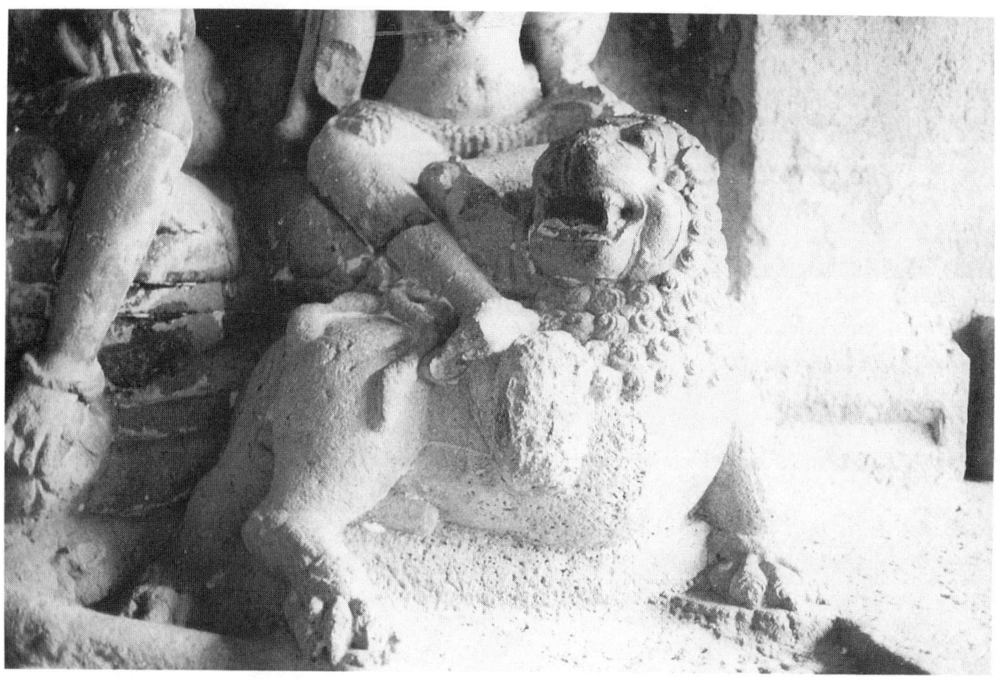

Fig. 240 Cave 16, lion

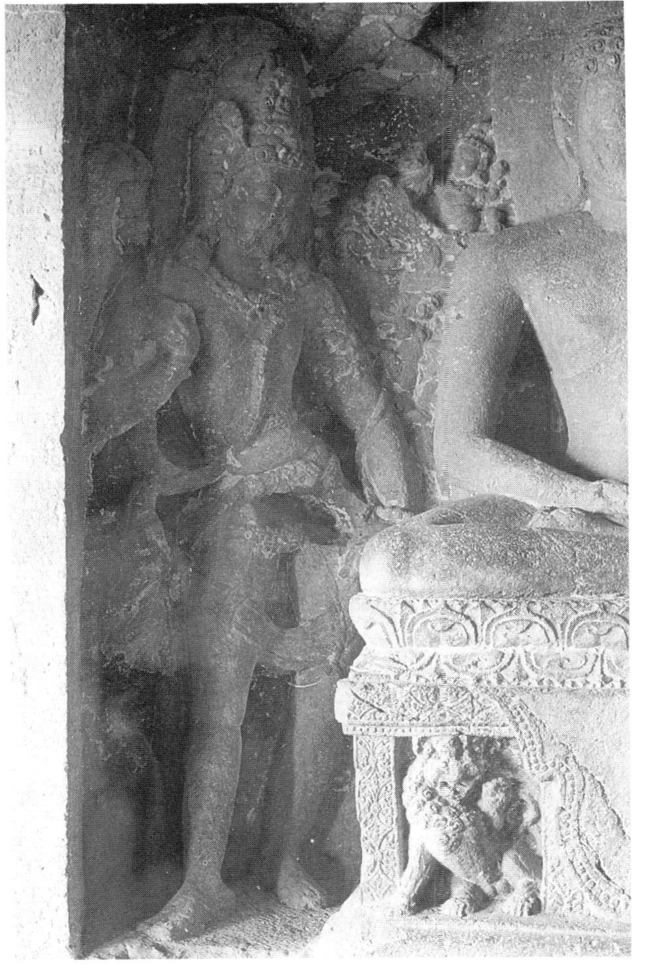

Fig. 241   Cave 12.3 hall, Buddha #1, Avalokiteśvara closeup

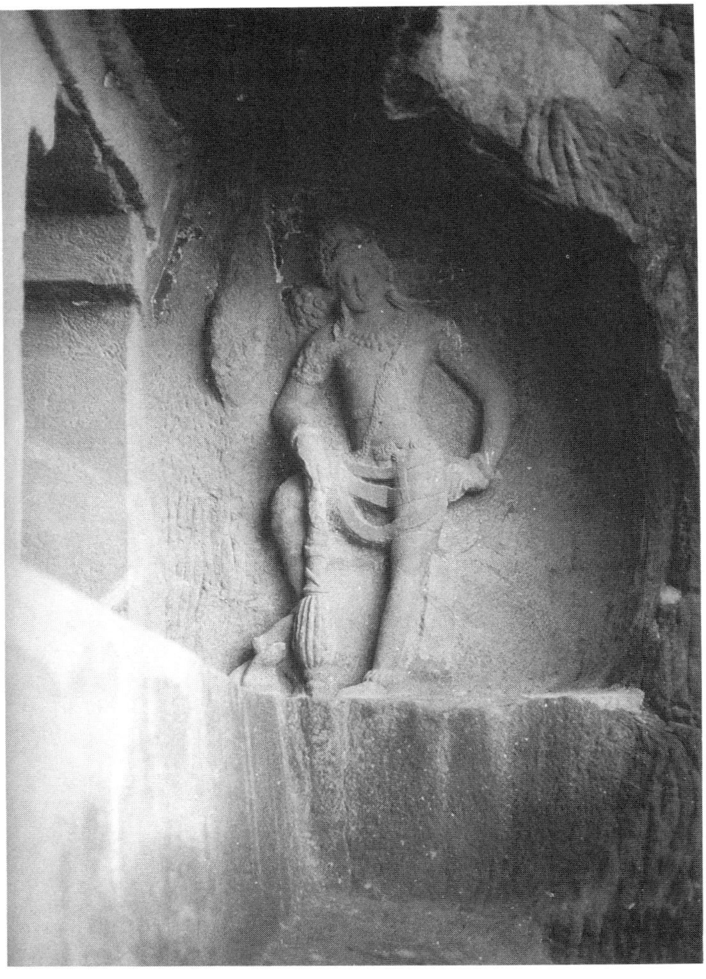

Fig. 241a   Cave 15.2 Guardian

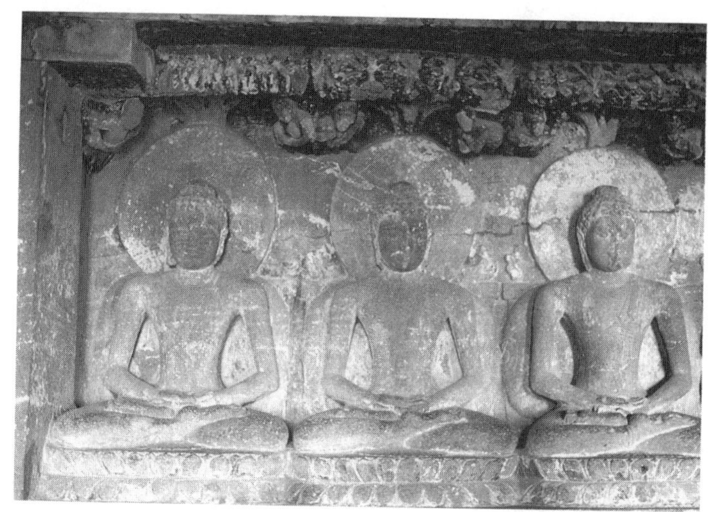

Fig. 242a   Cave 12.3 hall, Mānuṣi Buddha group, #1–3

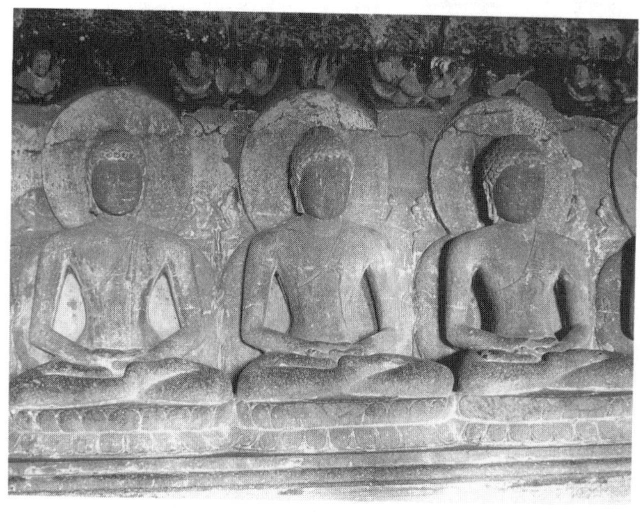

Fig. 242b   Cave 12.3 hall, Mānuṣi Buddha group, #4–6

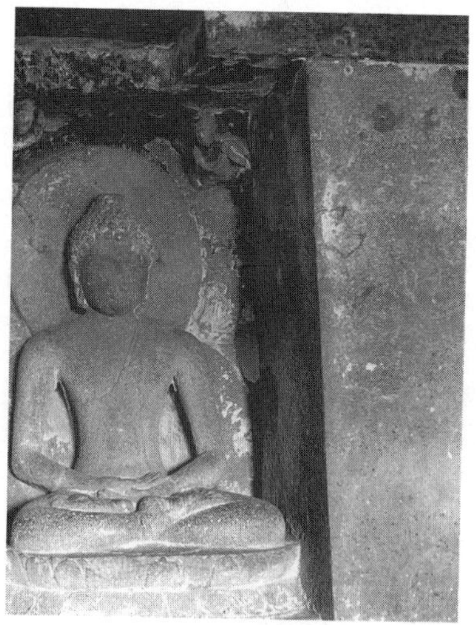

Fig. 242c   Cave 12.3 hall, Mānuṣi Buddha group, #7

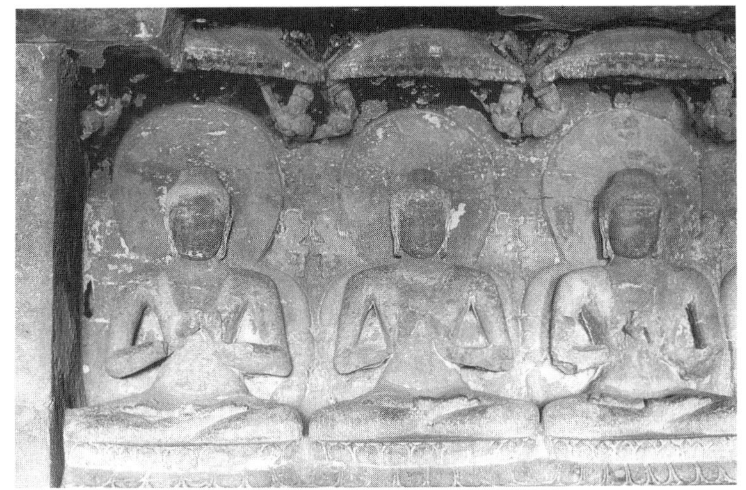

Fig. 243a   Cave 12.3 hall, Buddha group, #1-3

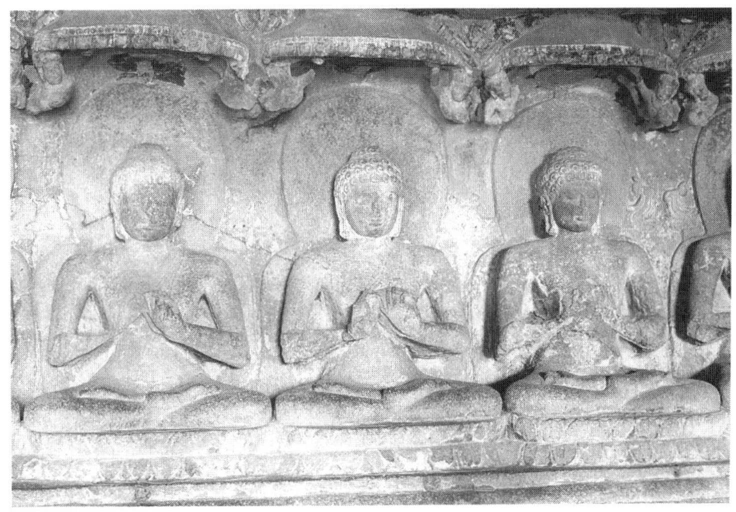

Fig. 243b   Cave 12.3 hall, Buddha group, #4-6

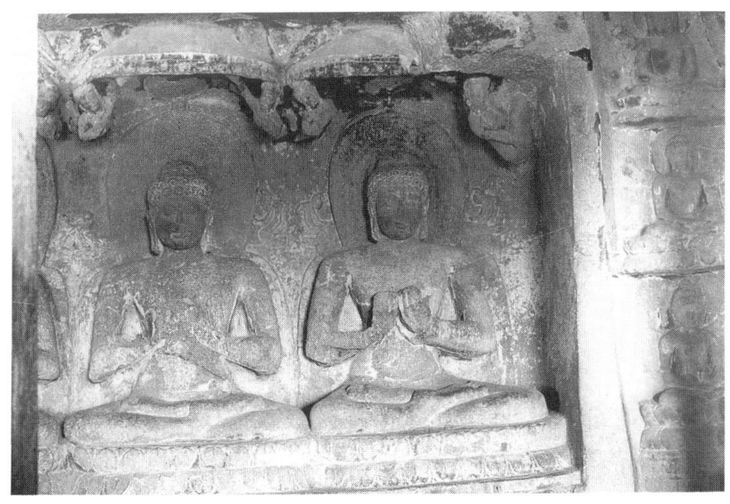

Fig. 243c   Cave 12.3 hall, Buddha group, #6-7

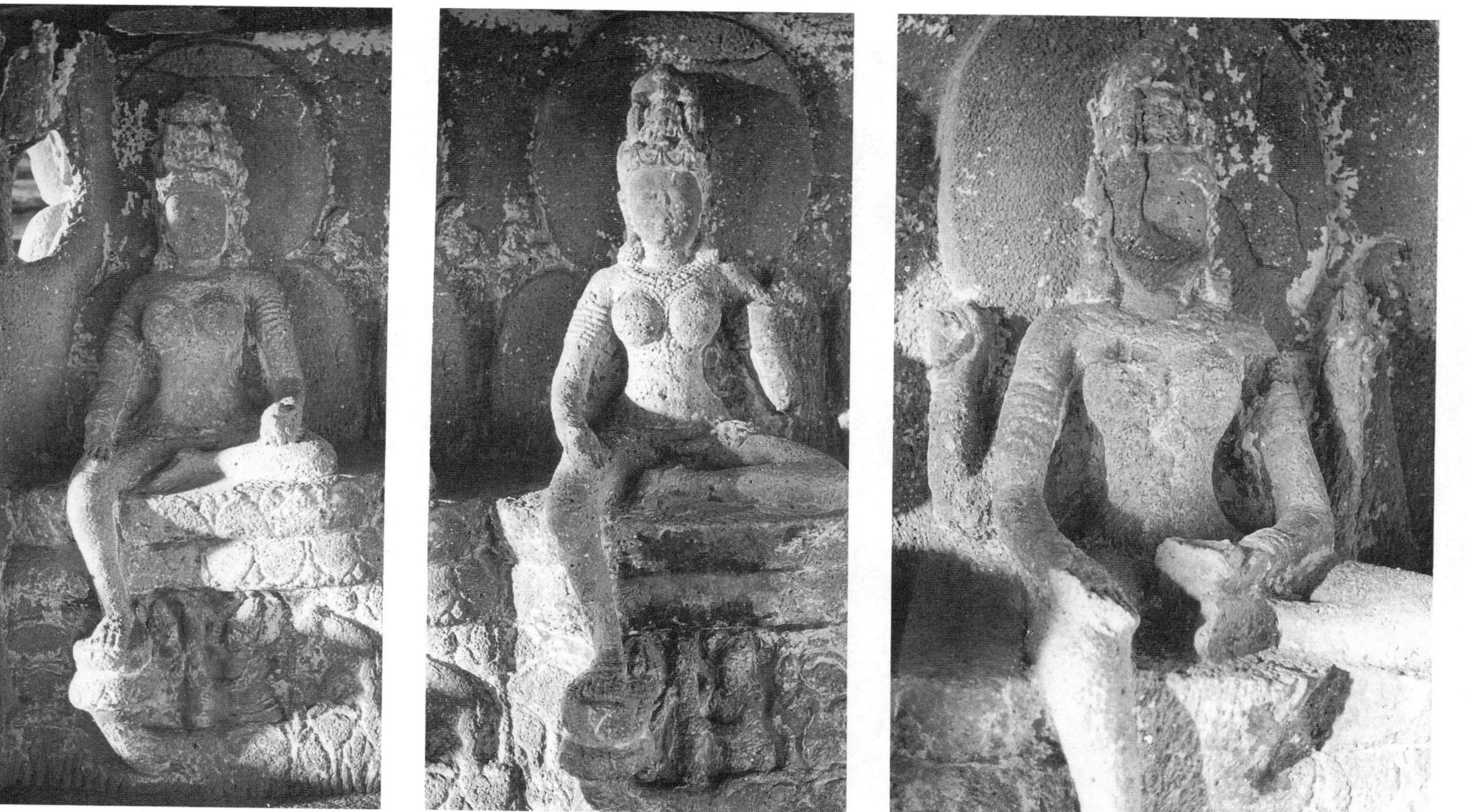

Fig. 244a   Cave 12.3 antechamber, Dhāraṇī #1   Fig. 244b   Cave 12.3 antechamber, Dhāraṇī #2   Fig. 244c   Cave 12.3 antechamber, #3-Cundā

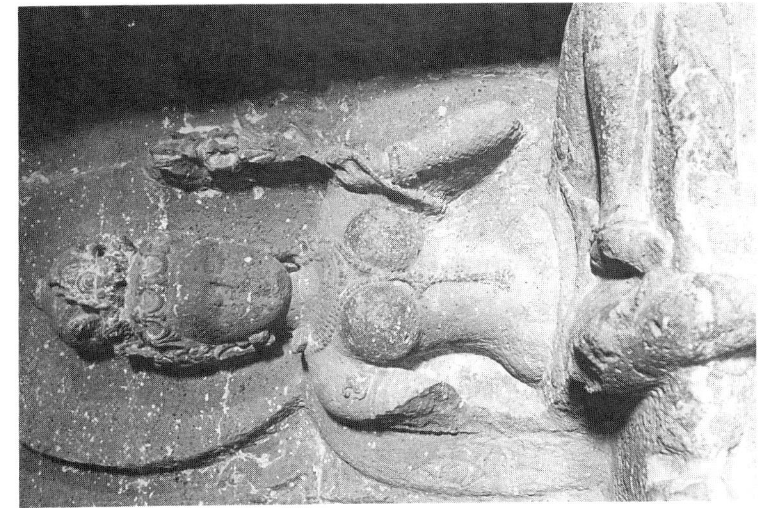

Fig. 245c   Cave 12.3 antechamber, Dhāraṇī #6 (Sarvakarmāvaraṇaviśodhanī)

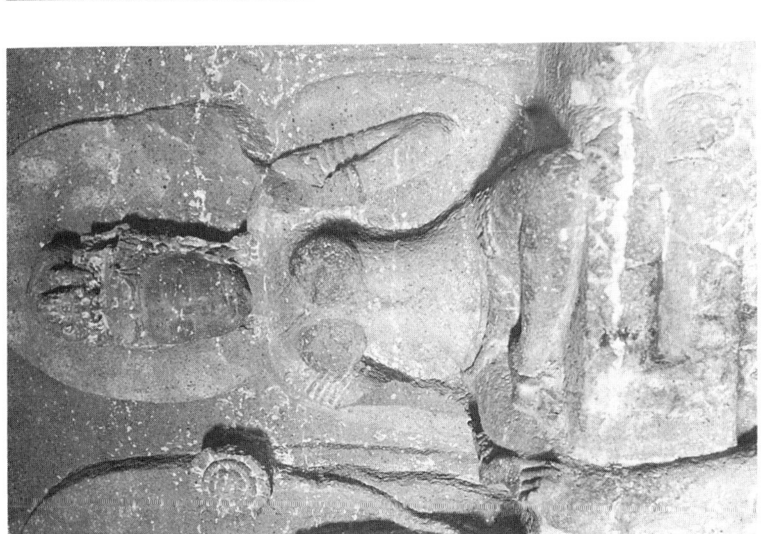

Fig. 245b   Cave 12.3 antechamber, Dhāraṇī #5

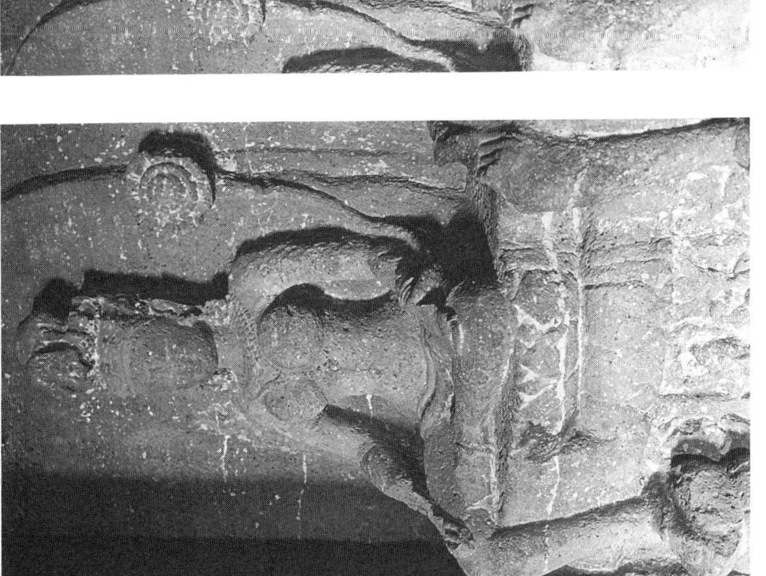

Fig. 245a   Cave 12.3 antechamber, Dhāraṇī #4

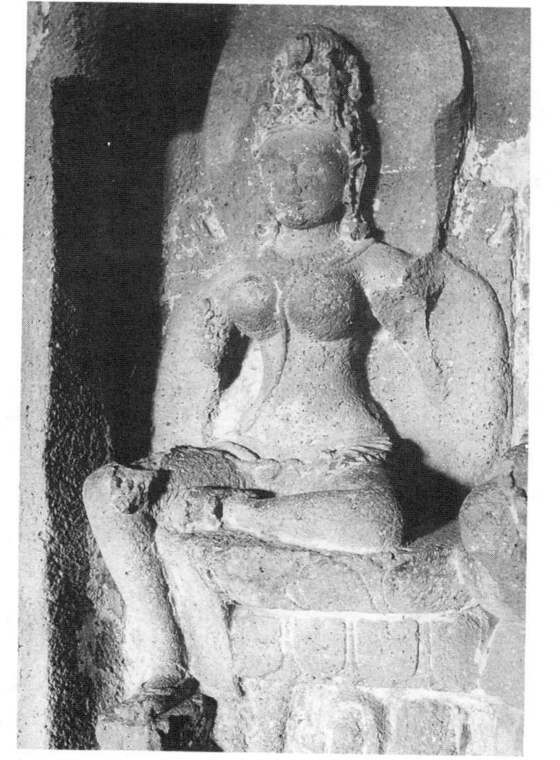

Fig. 246a   Cave 12.3 antechamber,
Dhāraṇī #7 Jaṅgulī

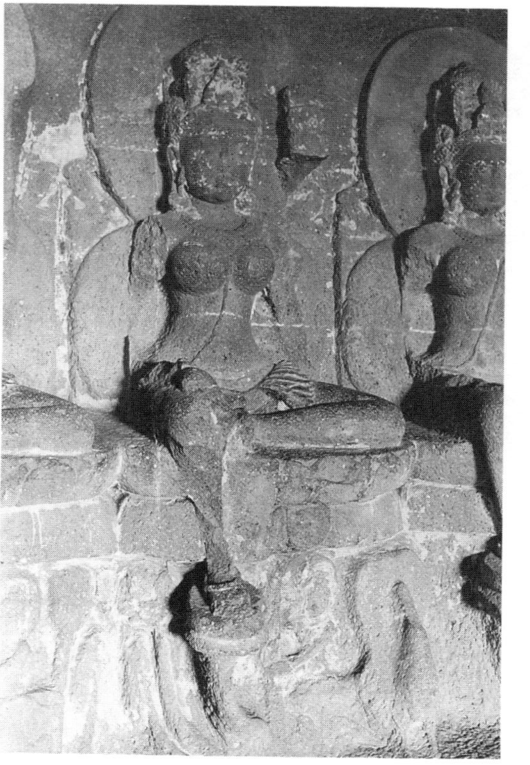

Fig. 246b   Cave 12.3 antechamber,
Dhāraṇī #8–Mahāmāyūrī

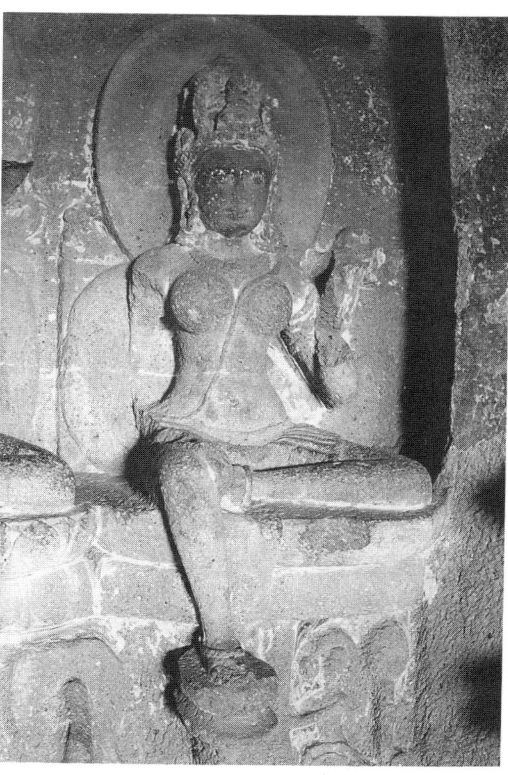

Fig. 246c   Cave 12.3 antechamber, Dhāraṇī #9

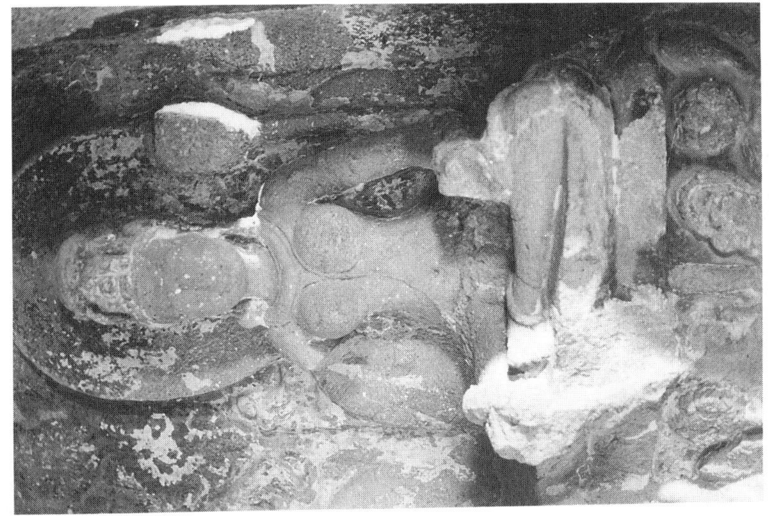

Fig. 247c   Cave 12.3 antechamber, Dhāraṇī #12

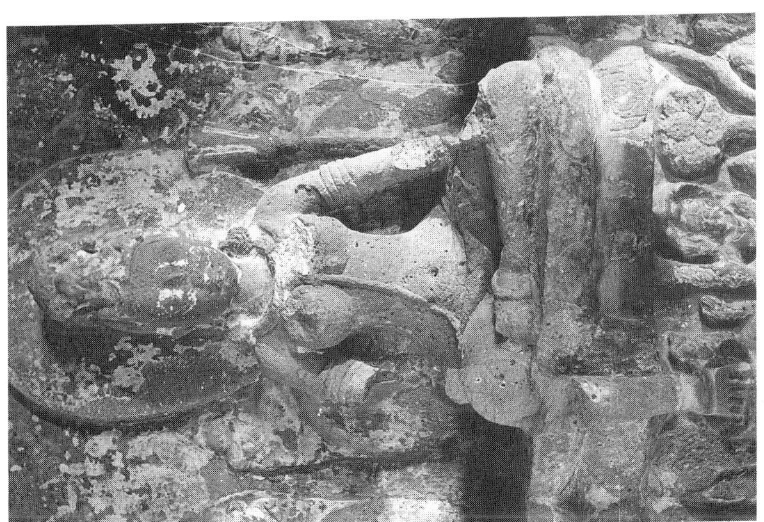

Fig. 247b   Cave 12.3 antechamber,
Dhāraṇī #11-Tārā

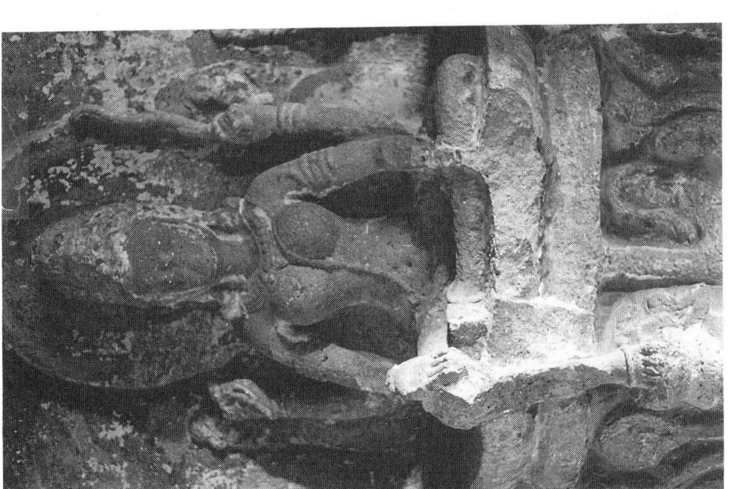

Fig. 247a   Cave 12.3 antechamber,
Dhāraṇī #10-Bhṛkuṭī

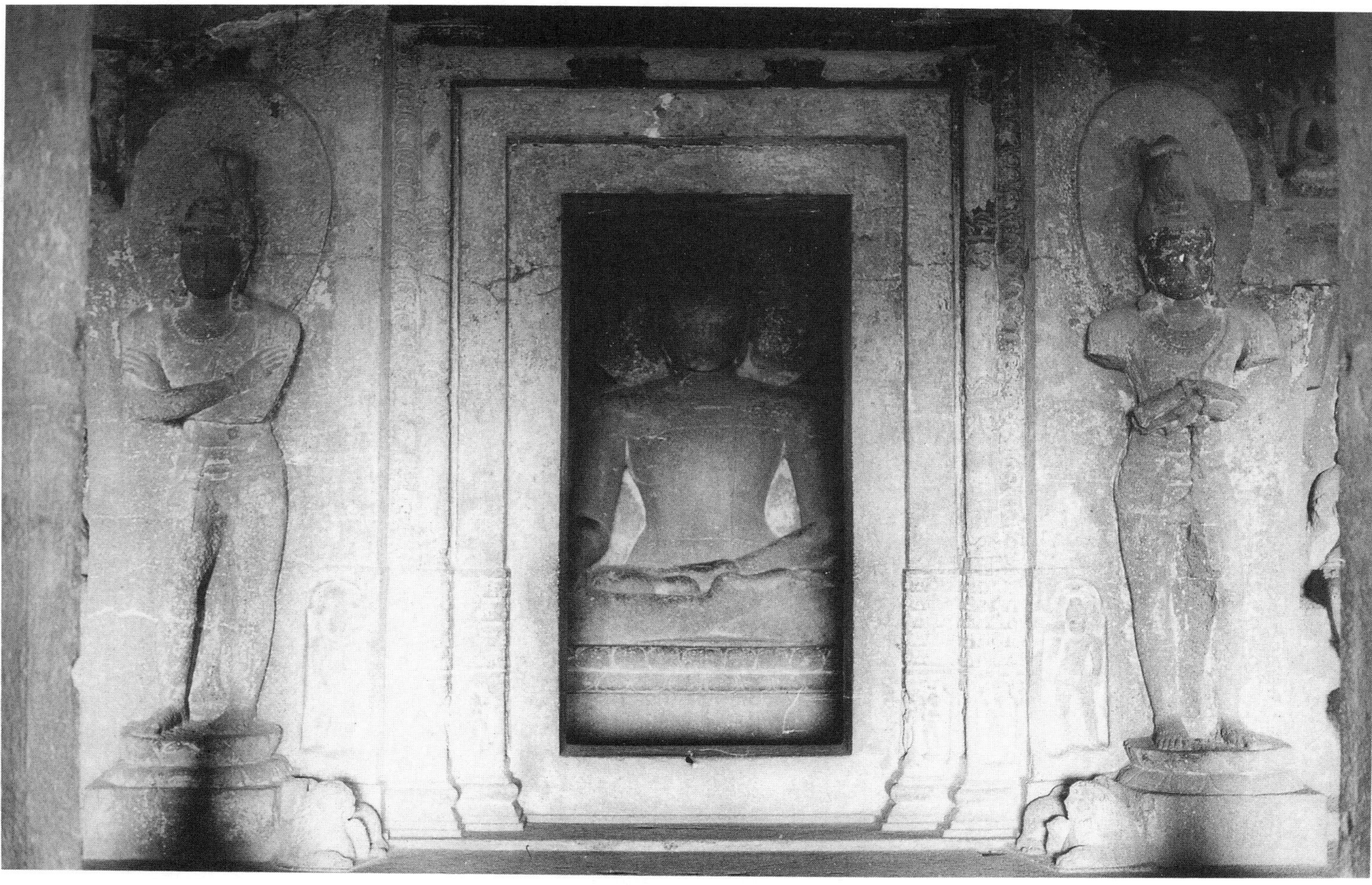

Fig. 248   Cave 12.3 shrine door and Buddha

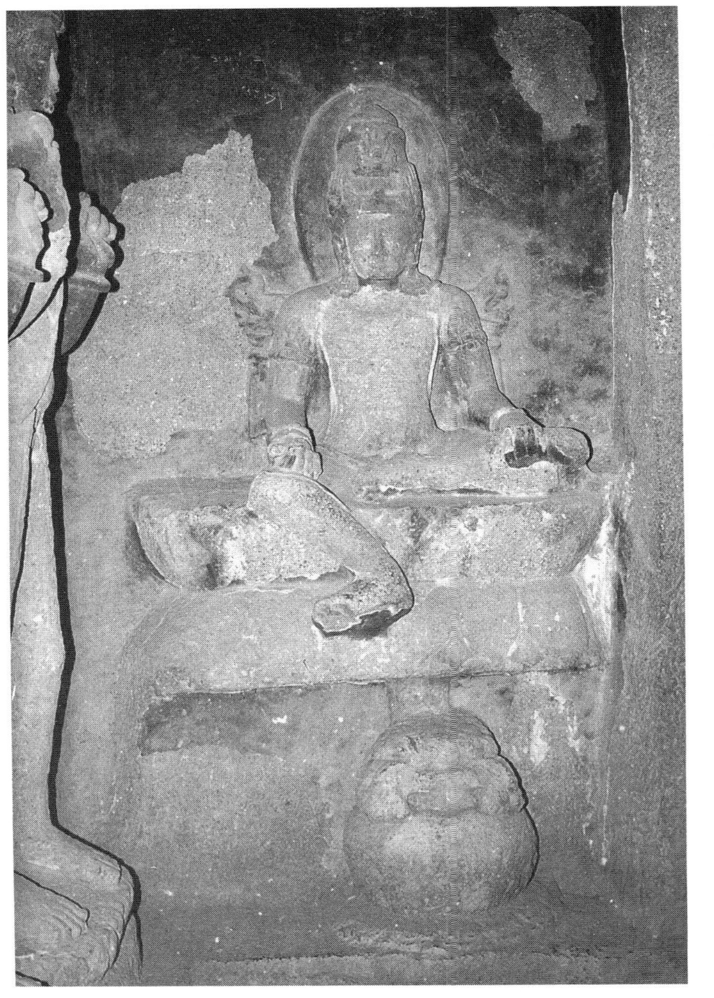

Fig. 249   Cave 12.3 shrine, Jambhala

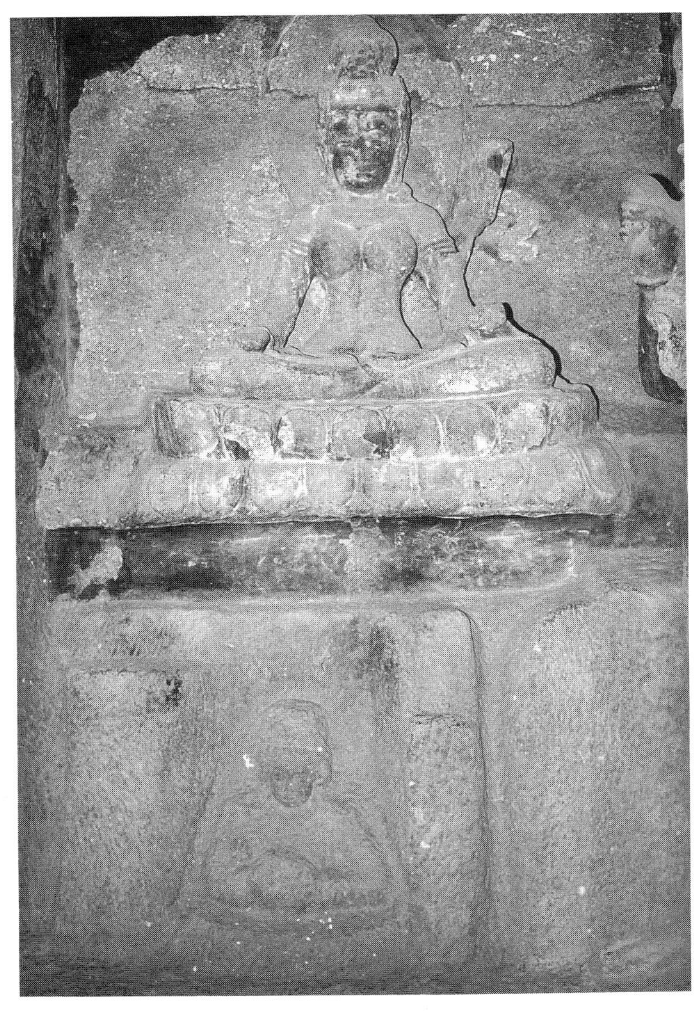

Fig. 250   Cave 12.3 shrine, Tārā

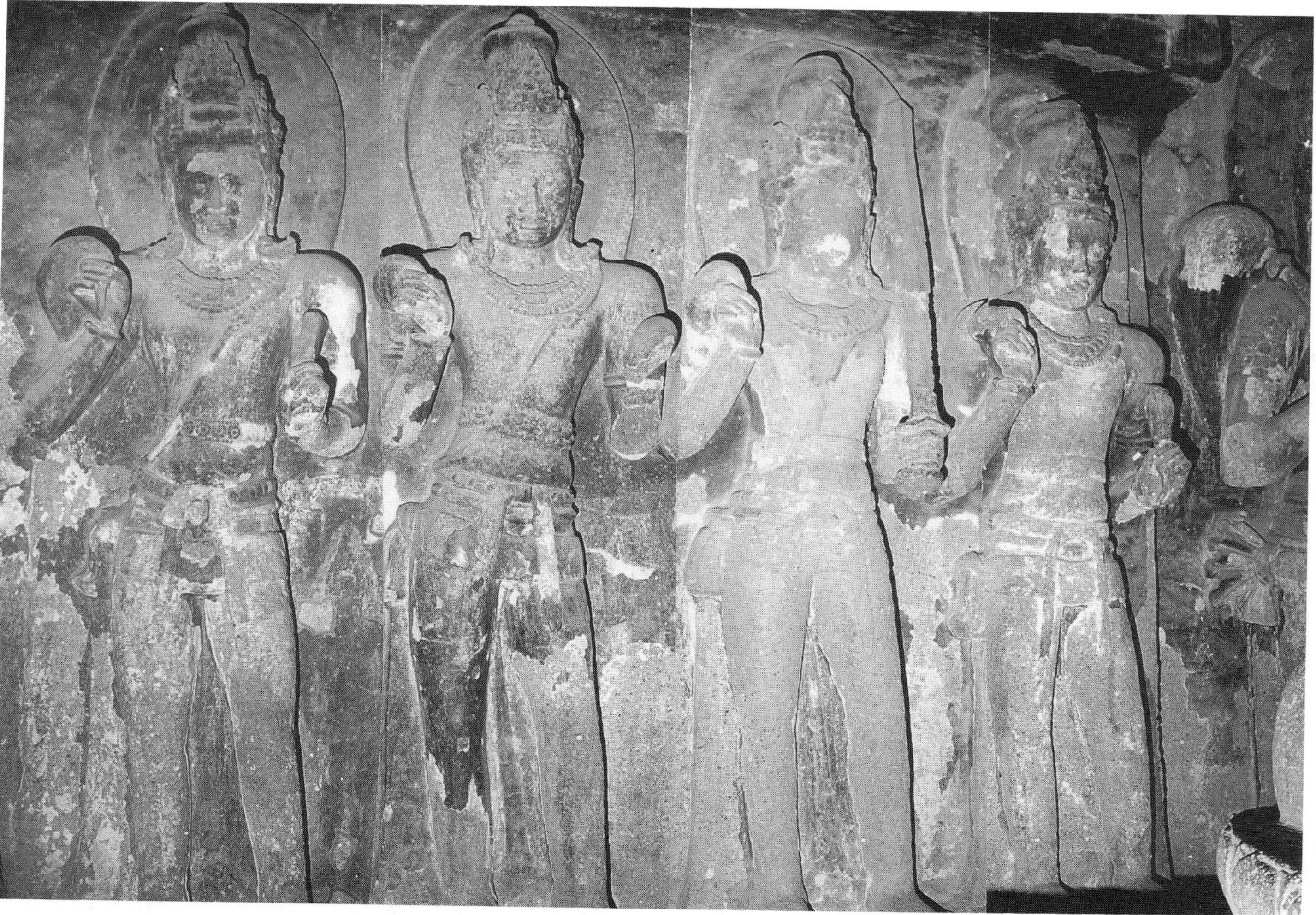

Fig. 251   Cave 12.3 shrine, left wall Bodhisattvas

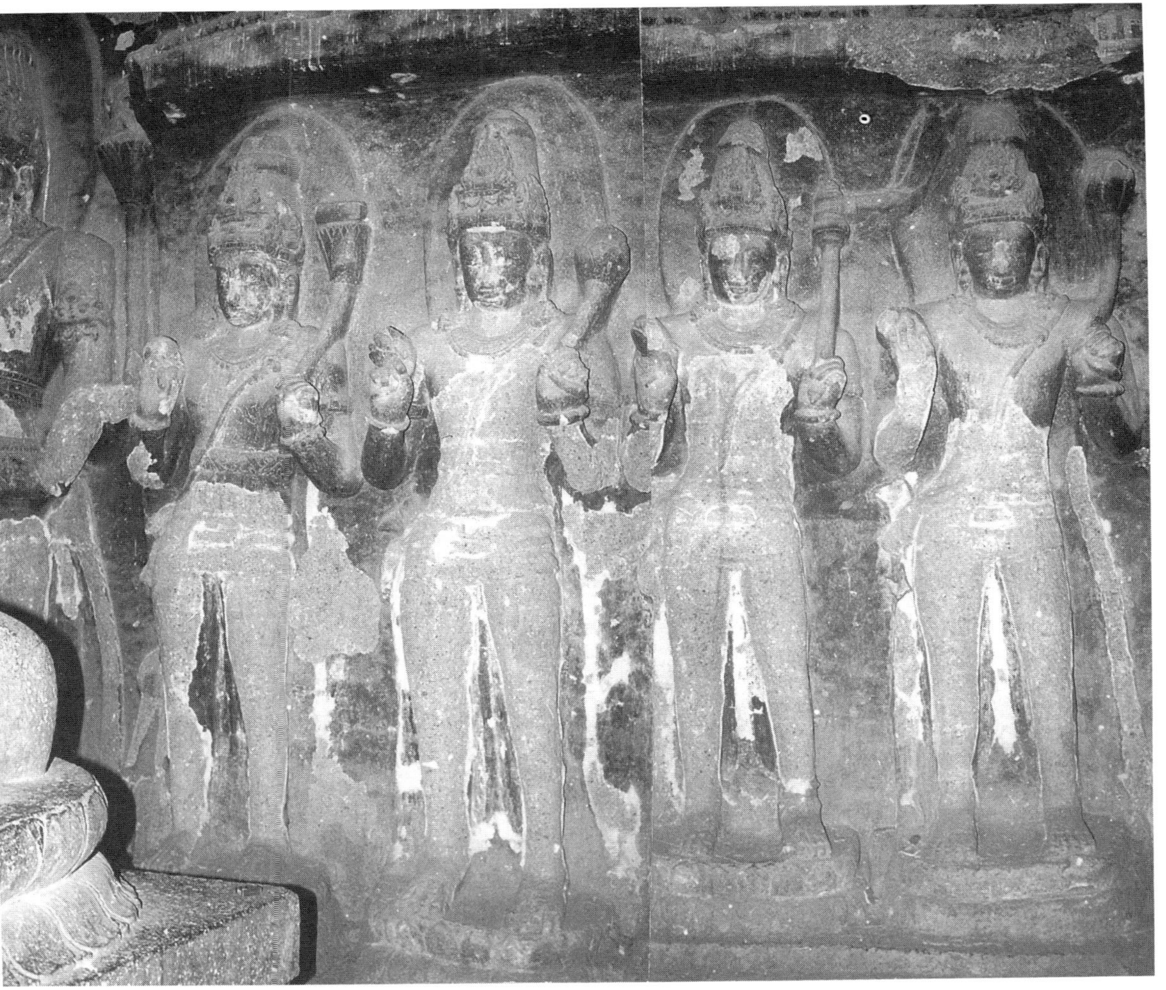

Fig. 252   Cave 12.3 shrine, right wall Bodhisattvas

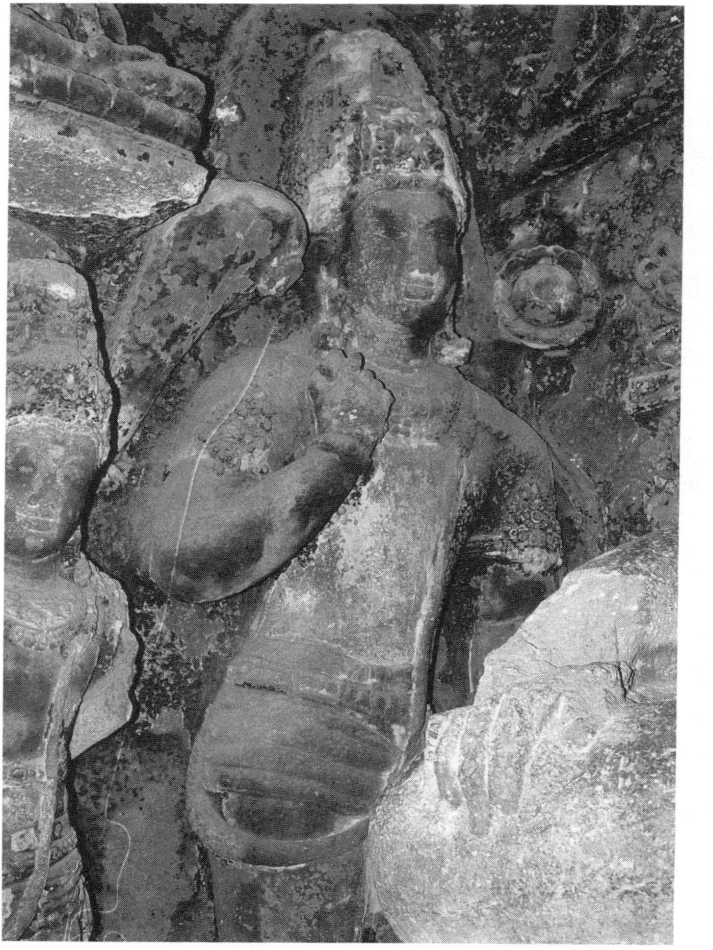

Fig. 253   Cave 12.3 shrine, Avalokiteśvara

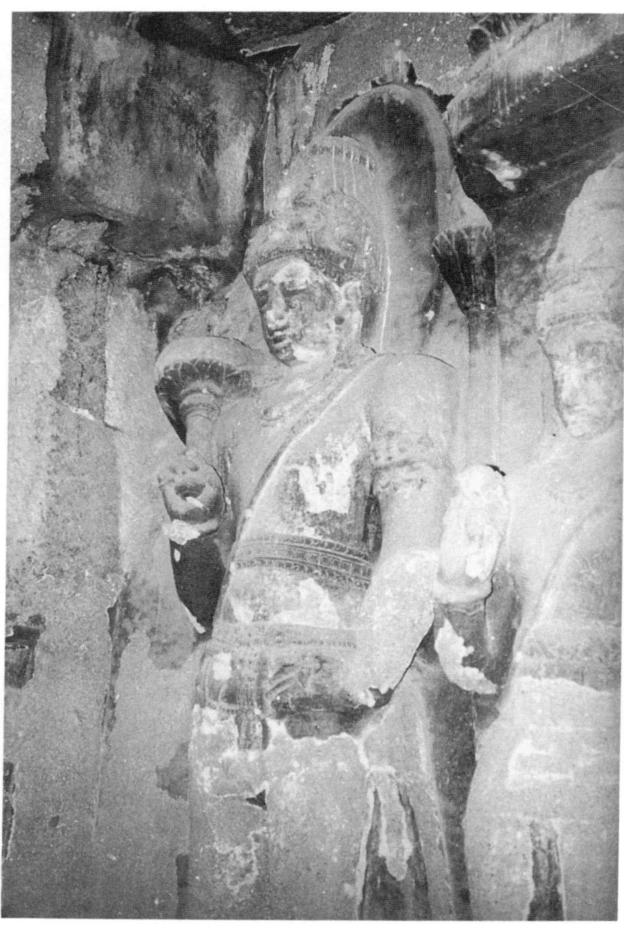

Fig. 254   Cave 12.3 shrine, Vajrapāṇi

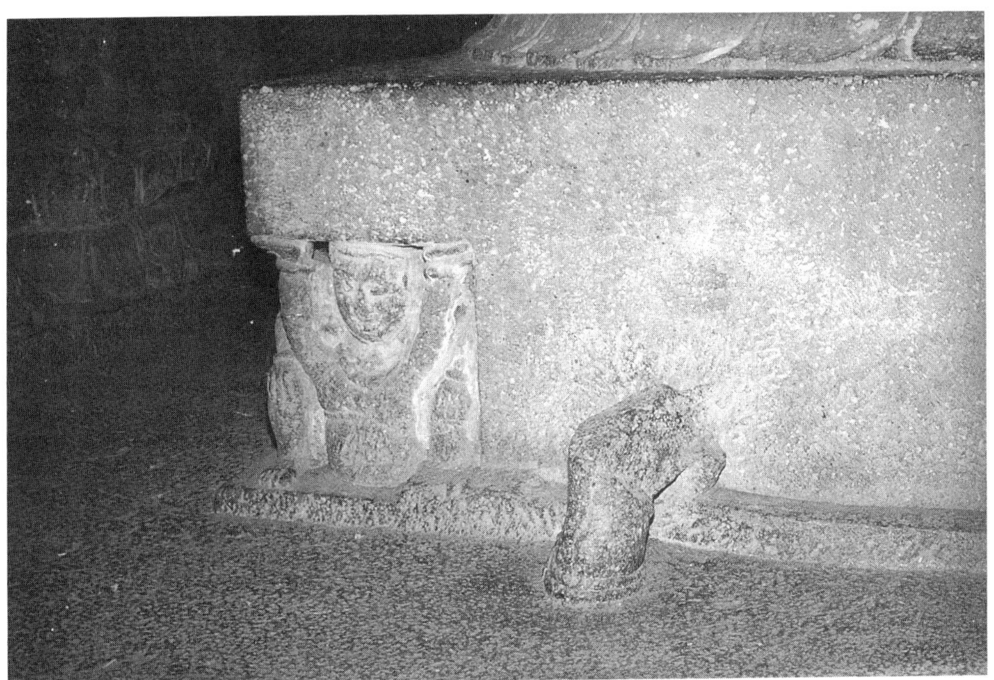

Fig. 255   Cave 12.3, Bhūdevī

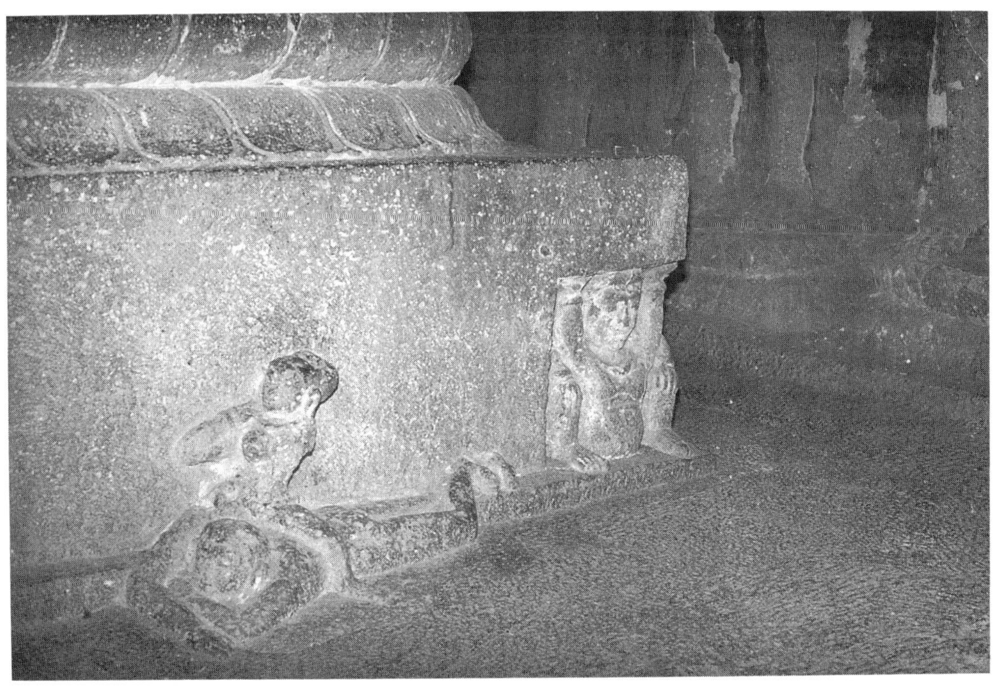

Fig. 256   Cave 12.3 shrine, Aparājitā

—— Development, architectural features in, 56–57; Buddhist phase, 6–7, 9, 14; cave location and chronology, 5, 23–25, 123–126; earliest excavations, 12, 123; early Hindu phase, 5–6, 123; intrusive features in, 24; Jain period, 13; pace of cave completion, 32, 36–37, 43, 66, 75; plaster, evidence for cave completion, 36, 42, 58; proximity to water in, 123

Female figures: at Bodhgaya, 114; at Candi Mendut, 76; at Ratnagiri, 114; in Aurangabad Cave 7, 87, 108–109; in Aurangabad Cave 9, 108; in Kanheri Cave 90, 110; in groups, in Cave 12.3, 87–88; in groups, in Nasik Cave 23, 109; offering deities, in Cave 12.2, 82–84, 103; paired at shrine entrances in Caves 6 and 21, 28, 93; prominence, in Cave 8, 49–50; prominence in Cave 9 façade, 51, 53; triad in Cave 12.1–2, 82
Firishtah, description of Ellora, 3

Gaṇeśa (Gaṇapati), in Kurkihar and Ratnagiri images, 70
Gaṅgā, in Cave 21, 93
Garbhadhātumaṇḍala, at Candi Mendut, 76
Govindarāja, Rāṣṭrakūṭa king, 8
Ghṛṣṇeśvara: *tīrtha* as a *jyotirliṅga*, 11; *tīrtha* equated with Gautameśvara or Ghuṣmeśvara, 131n.54; *tīrtha* in Ellora plates of Dantidurga, 9; *tīrtha*, meaning and development of, 11–12; *tīrtha* near water source, 12, 123; worshipped by Queen Maṇikāvatī, 10
Guhyasamājatantra, 15
Gunda, Sūtradhāri, artisan from Pattadakal, 10

Hārītī: at Candi Mendut, 116; at Ratnagiri, 76, 115–116; with Jambhala, at Ratnagiri, 106; with Pāñcika, 104
Hock, Nancy, on Ratnagiri, 21, 116
Holkar, Ahalyabai: as patron of religious sites, 131n.55; patron of Ghṛṣṇeśvara temple, 13
Hsüan-tsang: description of Buddhism in Maharashtra, 16; in south India, 7, 117
Huntington, John, on Aurangabad as early tantric site, 16, 20

Iconography, Hindu, adapted to Buddhist context, in Bhṛkuṭī images, 96; in Mañjuśrī images, 101; in Pancika images, 103–104
Initiation, in Shingon tradition, 18–19
Inscriptions: absence, at Aurangabad, 108; at Ajanta, 5; at Kanheri, 110; donative, at Buddhist sites, 5; sectarian, in Ajanta Cave 10, 133n.89
Interchange, regional, role in development at Ajanta, 5
I-tsing, description of north Indian monastery, 28, 104, 105, 136n.1

Jainism, caves at Ellora, 13
Jambhala: at Bodhgaya, *toraṇa* image, 106; at Candi Mendut, 116; at Ratnagiri, 76, 106, 107, 115–116; at Sanci, 106, 112; at Sirpur, 106, 112; iconography, 103–107; in Cave 2, 34, 105; in Cave 6, 29; in Cave 11.2.1, 71; in Cave 12.2, 84; in Cave 12.3, 88; in Caves 11 and 12, as guardian of *maṇḍala*, 35, 106–17; with Avalokiteśvara and Mañjuśrī in Cave 6, 101, 103, 107; with Hārītī at Ratnagiri, 106, 107; with Tārā and Avalokiteśvara in Cave 12.1–2, 82, 107
Jaṅgulī, in Cave 12.3, 87
Jaṭāmukuṭa, attribute of ascetic, 28

Jayasiṁha, Cālukya king, in Nasik plates, 9
Jyotirliṅgas: Ghṛṣṇeśvara as, 11; system of, 13, 131n.54

Kailāsa temple. *See* Ellora, Cave 16
Kalacuri dynasty, 5–6, 128n.17
Kalpadruma, emblem of Kṣitigarbha, 81, 115
Kancipuram: Hsüan-tsang at, 117; Kailāsanātha temple, sculptural style, 72
Kanheri, 109–110; Aṣṭamahābhaya Avalokiteśvara, 39; Cave 32 Buddha image, throne design, 48, 50; Cave 32, similarity to Ellora Cave 5, 29–30; Traikūṭaka inscription, 6; wooden Tārā image, 148n.119
Karkarāja, Rāṣṭrakūṭa king, 8, 10
Kāśī. *See* Banaras
Khadipada, inscription, 16–17
Knots: as attributes of Bodhisattva, 40; Buddhist symbolism of, 56, 138–139n.38
Kobo-daishi (Kukai), 14; teachings of, at To-ji, 26; use of *maṇḍalas*, 19
Kokasa, artisan from Paithan, 10
Kongobu-ji temple (Mount Koya), 19
Kṛṣṇarāja, Kalacuri king, silver coins of, 6
Kṛṣṇarāja, Rāṣṭrakūṭa king, 10
Kṛṣṇarāja-*rūpakas*, circulation of, 7
Kṣitigarbha: at Lalitagiri, 115; in Cave 11.2.1, 71; in Cave 12.3, 88; in relief *maṇḍalas*, 79; in Orissan images, 81
Kubera: iconography, 104–106; in Cave 19–20, 104; in Cave 25, 46, 105–106
Kukai. *See* Kobo-daishi
Kurkihar, Buddha image, 70
Kūṭāgāra: as palace housing *maṇḍala*, 18; in Cave 12, 20; theory applied to Barabudur, 134n.101

Ladakh, Buddist temples, *maṇḍalas* in, 19–20
Lakulīśa, at Elephanta, 6
Lalitagiri, 115; Bodhisattva groups from, 76, 102; Kṣitigarbha images from, 81; Mañjuśrī images from, 102
Lecture halls: in Japanese Buddhist temples, 31; in Kanheri Cave 32 and Ellora Cave 5, 29–30
Līlācaritra, description of Ellora, 3
Lohaner (ancient Lohanagara), plates of Pulakeśin II, 7
Lokeśvara: in Cave 12.1, 81; in Cave 12.2, 84; in Cave 12.3, 88

Mahābodhi temple. *See* Bodhgaya
Mahācaṇḍaroṣaṇa, at Panhale-Kaji and Ratnagiri, 111
Maharashtra: Cālukyas in 7, 9; pilgrimage in, 11
Mahākaruṇagarbhodbhavamaṇḍala, 76
Mahāmāyūrī: iconography, 96–97; in Cave 6, 28, 96; in Cave 8, 49, 50, 96; in Cave 10, 87, 88, 97; in Cave 12.3, 88, 97; in Tendai tradition, 97; with Bhṛkuṭī, 93, 94
Mahāvairocanābhisambodhisūtra, 76
Mahāvairocanasūtra: describes *maṇḍala*, 18; *tantric* teachings in, 14–15; teaching at Aurangabad, 108
Maheshwar (Māhiṣmatī), 2
Mahua, Śiva temple, 68
Maitreya: iconography, 29, 99–101; in Cave 2, 37; in Cave 3, 39; in Cave 4, 42; in Cave 5, 32, 100; in Cave 6, 28, 29, 100; in Cave 8 and 8A, 48–49; in Cave 10, 56, 59; in Cave 11.2.1, 71; in Cave 11.2.5, 72; in Cave 11.3, 65; in Cave 12.1, 81; in Cave 12.2, 84; in Cave 12.3, 88; in Kurkihar Buddha image, 70; in relief *maṇ-*